Intentions in Communication

System Development Foundation Benchmark Series

Michael Brady, editor
Robotics Science, 1989

Max V. Mathews and John R. Pierce, editors
Current Directions in Computer Music Research, 1989

Philip R. Cohen, Jerry Morgan, and Martha E. Pollack, editors
Intentions in Communication, 1990

Eric L. Schwartz, editor
Computational Neuroscience, 1990

Intentions in Communication

edited by Philip R. Cohen, Jerry Morgan, and
Martha E. Pollack

System Development Foundation Benchmark Series

A Bradford Book
The MIT Press
Cambridge, Massachusetts
London, England

Second printing, 1992

©1990 Massachusetts Institute of Technology

This book was set in Palatino by Asco Trade Typesetting Ltd, Hong Kong and printed and bound in the United States of America

Library of Congress Cataloging-in-Publication Data

Intentions in communication / edited by Philip R. Cohen, Jerry Morgan, and Martha E. Pollack.

  p.   cm.—(Systems Development Foundation benchmark series)
"A Bradford book."
ISBN 0-262-03150-7
  1. Communication. 2. Intention. 3. Speech arts (Linguistics). 4. Pragmatics.
5. Discourse analysis. I. Cohen, Philip R. II. Morgan, Jerry L. III. Pollack, Martha E.
IV. Series.
P91.I56 1990
302.2—dc20   89-12759
                                          CIP

Contents

List of Contributors

James F. Allen
Department of Computer Science
University of Rochester
Rochester, NY

Kent Bach
Department of Philosophy
San Francisco State University
San Francisco, CA

Michael E. Bratman
Department of Philosophy and
    Center for the Study of Language
    and Information
Stanford University
Stanford, CA

Herbert H. Clark
Department of Psychology
Stanford University
Stanford, CA

Philip R. Cohen
Artificial Intelligence Center and
    Center for the Study of Language
    and Information
SRI International
Menlo Park, CA

Barbara J. Grosz
Division of Applied Sciences
Harvard University
Cambridge, MA

Julia Hirschberg
AT&T Bell Laboratories
Murray Hill, NJ

Jerry R. Hobbs
Artificial Intelligence Center and
    Center for the Study of Language
    and Information
SRI International
Menlo Park, CA

Andrew J. I. Jones
Department of Philosophy
University of Oslo
Oslo, Norway

Henry Kautz
AT&T Bell Laboratories
Murray Hill, NJ

Hector J. Levesque
Department of Computer Science
University of Toronto
Toronto, Ontario
Canada

Diane J. Litman
AT&T Bell Laboratories
Murray Hill, NJ

Jerry Morgan
Department of Linguistics
University of Illinois
Urbana, IL

C. Raymond Perrault
Artificial Intelligence Center
   and Center for the Study of
   Language and Information
SRI International
Menlo Park, CA

Janet Pierrehumbert
AT&T Bell Laboratories
Murray Hill, NJ

Martha E. Pollack
Artificial Intelligence Center
   and Center for the Study of
   Language and Information
SRI International
Menlo Park, CA

Jerrold M. Sadock
Department of Linguistics
University of Chicago
Chicago, IL

John R. Searle
Department of Philosophy
University of California at Berkeley
Berkeley, CA

Candace L. Sidner
Cambridge Research Laboratory
Digital Equipment Corporation
Cambridge, MA

Richmond H. Thomason
Linguistics Department
University of Pittsburgh
Pittsburgh, PA

Daniel Vanderveken
Département de Philosophie
Université du Québec
Trois Rivieres, Québec
Canada

Deanna Wilkes-Gibbs
Department of Psychology
Wesleyan University
Middletown, CT

W. A. Woods
On Technology
Cambridge, MA

Preface

In March 1987 an interdisciplinary workshop on "Intentions and Plans in Communication and Discourse" was held in Monterey, California. The workshop brought together researchers in computer science, artificial intelligence, linguistics, philosophy, and psychology, whose theories of communication take as paramount the role of the communicating agents' intentions and plans. Thirteen papers were presented at the workshop, along with commentaries that had been prepared in advance by other researchers attending. This volume comprises edited versions of those papers and commentaries, plus an additional paper (by Clark and Wilkes-Gibbs) that was included because of its relevance to one of the themes of the workshop. The introduction presents some of the historical background for the papers and points out some of the links between them.

The workshop would not have been possible without the sponsorship of the System Development Foundation. Additional funding was provided by the American Association for Artificial Intelligence. Our thanks to both these organizations. The paper by Clark and Wilkes-Gibbs first appeared in *Cognition*, Vol. 22, No. 1, 1986 and is reprinted with the permission of Elsevier Science Publishers B.V.

Chapter 1

Introduction

Philip R. Cohen, Jerry Morgan, and Martha E. Pollack

Let us begin with an example. With the Wednesday advertising supplement in hand, a supermarket patron approaches the butcher and asks, "Where are the chuck steaks you advertised for 88 cents per pound?" to which the butcher replies, "How many do you want?" Despite all the theorizing about language that has been done by linguists, philosophers, computer scientists, and psychologists over the past thirty years, this simple interchange is magical. What makes the butcher's response a perfectly natural one?

Intuitively speaking, the answer to this question should be straightforward. The shopper wants to know where the steaks are because he wants to go to that location, put them into his cart, take them (along with other items) to the cashier, pay, and leave. The butcher realizes that is what he wants to do but knows that the steaks are behind the counter, where shoppers are not allowed. He decides to help the shopper achieve his goal, by getting the steaks for him. But the butcher is lacking a crucial piece of information: how many steaks should be get for the shopper? Hence his question.

This account seems plausible, but the basic question remains: Precisely what in this account of the butcher's reasoning *explains* the dialogue? What about the dialogue needs explaining anyway?

Students of communication have attempted to explain dialogues such as this one along a number of dimensions. The main currents in contemporary work arise from the tradition of research in philosophy and linguistics on meaning, especially the school of "formal semantics"; work in philosophy, linguistics, and, more recently, artificial intelligence, on theories of speech acts and of pragmatics; and relatively recent work, primarily in artificial intelligence and psychology, on discourse understanding. The central questions being considered include the following:

1. *The question of meaning*: What is meaning? Is there a single notion of meaning that is appropriate for the analysis of all kinds of expressions, from words to sentences, and for characterizing information and communication as they are realized in natural-language discourse?

2. *The question of compositionality*: How is it that meanings of complex expressions are a function of the meanings of their parts, and of the syntactic arrangement of those parts? What are the principles by which the meaning of a complex expression can be projected from the meanings of its parts?

3. *The question of action*: How is it that in uttering a sentence one can thereby perform any number of actions beyond the mere act of saying?

4. *The question of indirectness*: How is it that the utterance of a sentence can convey far more than the literal meaning of the sentence uttered?

5. *The question of discourse compositionality*: How is it that the interpretation of a connected discourse can amount to more than the sum of the meanings of its constituent sentences?

Finally, there is an overarching question, the answer to which seems to depend upon answers to the previous questions:

6. *The question of communication*: What is communication? How is communication in natural language related to nonlinguistic communication? How is linguistic communication related to the meanings of the expressions uttered?

Different lines of research have focused on different subsets of these questions. Many linguistic theories, for example, have been primarily concerned with the first two questions, describing syntactic structures, anaphoric constraints, and the ways in which these can be used to derive, or at least constrain, the "literal" meaning of an individual utterance. Though such theories can provide at least a partial explanation of the sample discourse, they are far from complete; for instance, they fail to shed any light on how it is that the shopper has managed to convey to the butcher that he wants to buy the steaks. Certain species of speech act theory—those that rely on so-called dialogue grammars—can be seen as focusing on the second and fifth questions, trying to characterize the kinds of speech acts one can perform in various circumstances with utterances that have given features, and to use such characterizations in defining legal sequences of speech acts. But again, these accounts do not suffice to fully explain the example dialogue, for it is not enough to note that sometimes one question can legitimately follow another; rather, one should be able to say why the particular question asked by the butcher is an appropriate response to the shopper's question, and why other questions he might ask would not be.

Any theory that purports to explain communication and discourse will have to come to grips with all of the questions listed above. Moreover, it appears that to do this, it will have to place a strong emphasis on issues of *intention*. Consider again the intuitive explanation of the dialogue between the butcher and the shopper. What is crucial is the butcher's reasoning about what the shopper intends and about what intentions he should form in response. An appreciation of the significance of intentions in communication dates back to Grice's important theories of *nonnatural meaning* (1957, 1968) and of *implicature* (1975, 1978). But there is not yet available a complete theory of the role of intentions in communication: one that explains how intentions contribute to linguistic (as well as nonlinguistic) meaning, how smaller intentions combine to form composite ones, how in making an utterance a speaker can satisfy certain intentions, and so on.

There are, however, beginning to be signs that cooperation among the disciplines concerned with communication and discourse can lead to such a theory. For example, computer scientists designing natural-language interfaces have begun to draw heavily on the philosophical insights about intention; linguists developing accounts of indirect meaning are making use of models of plans developed in artificial intelligence; philosophers attempting to relate theories of sentence meaning and theories of utterance meaning are making reference to psychological facts about speakers.

One of the primary motivations behind this book is a belief that the development of a comprehensive theory of communication and discourse, which will necessarily rest on an explanation of the role of intentions in communication, will only arise from an integration of approaches from several disciplines. This book is an attempt to bring together major theorists in the area of communication to develop foundations, to present issues, and to point the way to future theoretical developments. The interdisciplinary nature of the book will be immediately apparent, with contributors and commentators coming from the fields of artificial intelligence, computer science, linguistics, philosophy, and psychology. However, unlike the contributions in many interdisciplinary volumes, groups of papers and commentaries in this volume often address the same problems, though using different methods. Methodologies found in the papers include foundational, logical, computational, and empirical approaches; indeed, a number of papers include more than one of these approaches.

The first group of papers in this volume is concerned with fundamental questions about the nature of intention, as it is to be understood in theories of communication. As we have noted, all of the papers in the volume rest on the premise that much of communication depends upon agents' ability to recognize one another's intentions and plans. But what are intentions and plans? What characterizes the process by which one agent recognizes the intentions and plans of another agent who is attempting to communicate with him?

Analyses of the nature of intention are plentiful in the philosophy of action. (see, for example, Anscombe 1958; Audi 1973; Bratman 1987; Castañeda 1975; Davidson 1980a, b; Goldman 1970; Meiland 1970. Davis 1979, chap. 4, provides an overview of many of the issues that concern philosophers studying intention.) In the first paper in this volume the philosopher Michael E. Bratman provides his analysis. Bratman's approach is to begin with an examination of *future-directed intentions:* Intentions to do something—to act—in the future. In making this move, he breaks with a tradition in philosophy that he has elsewhere called *the methodological priority of intention in action* (1987, 5), which views the central problem for intention theorists as being the explanation of intentional action, as opposed to intentions to act. Indeed, as Bratman suggests, many philosophers have been skeptical of the claim that intentions to act play a distinct role in the mental life of rational agents and have thought that, at best, intentions to act are reducible to certain desires and beliefs.

Bratman argues against this reductionist move, claiming that intentions to act in fact are crucial elements in the psychology of rational agents like human beings who have limited resources for reasoning. Once formed, intentions can focus and constrain the further reasoning of an agent, enabling him to deal with his limitations; so argues Bratman. This line of argument leads him to consideration of the relationship between intention and belief, a complex issue that has concerned many other researchers. (See, for example, Davidson 1980b and Grice 1971.) It also leads him to a discussion of certain of the functional characteristics of intentions; he enumerates a trio of psychological roles that intentions play. This latter discussion in turn hinges on his making a crucial distinction between intended actions and the unintended consequences of actions, or side effects.

In the second paper Philip R. Cohen and Hector J. Levesque, computer scientists, present another model of intention. Their model is meant to capture many of the same intuitions as Bratman's—indeed, Cohen and Levesque have been directly influenced by Bratman's work, and they take great care that their model provides analyses of the trio of functional roles he specifies. They are also concerned with an analysis of the distinction between intended actions and side effects. To develop these analyses, they first focus on the conditions under which an agent can drop his intentions. In other words, they specify what it means for an agent to be *committed* to his intentions, and they take the view that commitment of the appropriate sort is what in fact characterizes an intention. The model of intention developed by Cohen and Levesque is formalized as a modal, temporal, first-order logic. They have used their model of intention in a model of communication that they present in their second paper of this volume.

The focus shifts from intentions to plans in the next paper, by Martha E. Pollack. Pollack, a computer scientist, is concerned with specifying the internal structure of plans. She argues that plans should be analyzed as particular configurations of beliefs and intentions. In providing a fine-grained account of the relations between these beliefs and intentions, Pollack, like Cohen and Levesque, draws heavily on philosophical work, in particular marking use of the *generation* relation introduced by Alvin Goldman (1970).

Pollack uses her analysis in a theory of plan recognition for communication that she describes in her paper. Starting in the late 1970s, a number of researchers in artificial intelligence have provided models of plan recognition that have been used to explain various facets of communicative behavior and that have been implemented in computer systems that communicate with their users. (This includes Allen 1983; Bruce 1981; Carberry 1988; Cohen and Perrault 1979; Genesereth 1979; Litman and Allen 1987; Perrault and Allen 1980; Sidner 1985.) Pollack argues that although these researchers made a great deal of progress in accounting for many facets of communication, one major problem with their models is that they cannot properly handle situations in which there are discrepancies between the beliefs of the various agents involved in the communication situation. She further argues that such discrepancies are perceived by one agent as invalidities in the plans of the other agent and shows how her model of plans permits an account of plan recognition in which such invalidities can be properly treated. In particular, she describes the relationship between inferred invalidities in the plans underlying questions and cooperative responses to those questions.

Like Pollack, Henry Kautz, whose paper is the final one in the first section, is concerned with the process of plan recognition. Also a computer scientist, Kautz is concerned with providing a precise, formal theory of plan recognition. He develops both a model theory and a proof theory for the process of relating observations of actions to conclusions about the likely plans of an actor. The key idea is to analyze plan recognition as an instance of McCarthy's (1986) circumscription problem, thereby relating the work on plan recognition to the large body of recent foundational work on nonmonotonic logics in artificial intelligence.

Plan recognition problems have often been grouped into two classes, depending upon whether or not the agent whose plan is being recognized intends that recognition. When an agent does intend for another agent to recognize his plans, as is the case in communication, the former will structure his behavior so as to make the recognition problem easier for the latter. Kautz's analysis is directed primarily toward unintended recognition, illustrated by the first of his examples, which involves an agent determining the plans of another agent engaged in cooking something. However, he argues that his theory can also be applied to intended recognition, and he provides an example of its use in the understanding of indirect speech acts.

The next seven papers in this volume illustrate strongly the growing convergence of ideas about communication: convergence both across disciplines and across the range of questions addressed. In particular, these papers aim toward a unification of truth-conditional analyses of sentence meaning and speech act analyses of utterance meaning. They also show a recognition of the crucial importance of principles of rational interaction and of the mental states of the speaker and hearer in the analysis of discourse, in every area from intonation to discourse structure.

The approach to meaning commonly referred to as *formal semantics* has its origin in the Frege-Tarski view of meaning as a relation between expressions in a language and the objects in the world to which they correspond. The approach deserves the adjective *formal* in two senses: first, in that analyses are usually stated in a highly developed mathematical formalism; second, and more fundamentally, in that language is viewed as pure form rather than as a means of communication. In this view, language and meaning are characterized in the abstract, independently of the use of language by humans for communicative purposes. The main problems in this approach are to establish the exact nature of the correspondence relation—is it direct, or via some abstract kind of object like "intensions" —and of the principles of compositionality by which the meanings of complex expressions are projected from their parts.

The major contributions of the formal approach are in the standards of rigor that it has established through its insistence on formalization; in an enormous number of insights into details of natural-language semantics that have been been achieved through the kind of close and rigorous analysis that formalization encourages; and especially in contributing toward an answer to the question of compositionality. But formal semantics has had relatively little to say about the other questions listed earlier, not as a matter of omission but as a matter of principle. In formal semantics, language use is taken to be logically separate from semantics, requiring the addition of a theory of use that could be linked in some way to a theory of formal semantics. This linking problem is addressed by Andrew J. I. Jones in the first paper of this section. Taking as his point of departure work by Dretske (1981) on information transmission, Jones, a philosopher, attacks the question of how linguistic devices can be instrumental in the flow of information, with the goal of characterizing the information-carrying capacity of both linguistic and nonverbal devices in communicative acts. He assumes the distinction between formal semantic systems and rules for the use of such systems in communication and, following Lewis (1972), sees the problem of linking them as one of describing "the psychological and sociological facts whereby a particular one of these abstract semantic systems is the one used by a person or population." He provides the beginnings of such a description in terms of a rule schema that makes crucial use of a deontic operator whose interpretation involves "the hearer's interest in being reliably informed," noting that a consequence of the use of this operator is that his approach conflicts with the view of Dretske and others that information is "an objective commodity."

Work in speech act theory and pragmatics has been addressed mainly to the questions of the nature of meaning, of action, and of indirectness. This work concerns itself directly with the use of language for communication, and in some theories—most notably the work of Grice (1957, 1975)—the attempt is to base the definition of meaning itself on a notion of communication that is in turn based on mentalist constructs like action, intention, and recognition of intention. There are two related currents in this line of research: work on the theory of speech acts inspired by J. L. Austin's *How to Do Things with Words* (Austin 1975), and work in pragmatics following Grice's (1975) seminal observations on the logic of conversation and "conversational implicature."

In constrast to the correspondence view of meaning in formal semantics, speech act theorists generally start from the position that the basic unit in the analysis of meaning is the illocutionary act and that the ability to recognize and identify what speech act has been performed in a given utterance is a crucial part of understanding. Fundamental work in this area has included the close analysis and classification of speech act types and the identification of various kinds of conditions that must hold for an act to be successfully performed. Such conditions also have the role of constituting definitions of speech act types, and underlie the taxonomy of acts.

C. Raymond Perrault approaches questions of speech act theory from the perspective of artificial intelligence research on discourse understanding. He takes as a point of departure some earlier work on speech acts by Cohen and Levesque (1985) framed in a logic of attitudes and action. He argues that this work (and much other work like it) fails to take into account the fact that the postutterance mental states of speaker and hearer depend on their mental states before the utterance. This flaw in such theories, he maintains, leads to predictions that are wrong in certain cases like irony, and too weak in others. He argues for a discourse model that incorporates a model of belief revision framed in nonmonotonic default logic, with some of the consequences of speech acts on mental states treated as defaults. For example, there are default rules for the persistence of belief over time and for the transfer of belief between agents. The assumption that actions are intentional is a default rule, as is the assumption that the speaker believes what she asserts. Perrault sketches a definition of speech acts in his system of defaults, based on the initial mental states of the participants, the facts of the event of utterance, and the conditions of observation of the participants. He ends with a discussion of the proper treatment of irony, which he takes to constitute a strong argument for basing the analysis of illocutionary acts on changes in mental state.

The speech acts tradition has made major contributions to the analysis of communication but has been rather vague on two important points: how speech act properties of sentences relate to their truth-conditional properties, and how speech act properties of sentences can be projected compositionally from their parts. Philosopher Daniel Vanderveken's paper addresses the first of these problems, and indirectly the second, attempting to lay the groundwork for a unification of speech act theory and formal semantics, aiming at a unified account of both truth-conditional and speech act properties of sentences and utterances. His theory is based on the hypothesis that illocutionary forces, senses, and denotations are the three main components of sentence meaning and that linguistic competence is the language user's ability to recognize which illocutionary acts can be performed by the utterance of sentences. He distinguishes "conditions of success" from "conditions of satisfaction"; the former relate to the success of the speech acts, the latter to how propositional content (of an assertion or promise, say) "fit" the world. Thus, there are two irreducible sets of semantic values: those relating to success, and those relating to truth-conditions of the propositional content of the sentence.

Vanderveken sets out six components of illocutionary force that determine the success conditions of illocutionary acts, and a set of five primitive illocutionary forces from which all illocutionary forces can be derived by recursive application operations that "enrich" their illocutionary components. He then sketches some of the consequences of his theory for the theory of meaning, including a proliferation of new semantic notions.

Cohen and Levesque, in their second paper of the volume, approach the theory of speech acts from the perspective of artificial intelligence, with the goal of applying speech act analysis to discourse comprehension. They argue that from this perspective there is no need for illocutionary acts as primitives, and no need for recognition and labeling of illocutionary acts as part of the comprehension process. Rather, they argue, the necessary consequences can be derived from a theory of rational interaction, including a treatment of events that change the state of the world. Utterance events are then just a special case in which what is changed is the mental states of speakers and hearers; what is conveyed by an utterance is "a complex propositional attitude expressing the speaker's mental state." They argue that Searle's (1969) and Searle and Vanderveken's (1985) conditions on various illocutionary acts can be derived using the theory of action and interaction from their first paper.

Janet Pierrehumbert, a linguist, and Julia Hirschberg, a computer scientist, extend the study of compositionality to a new direction: the contribution of intonation contour to discourse interpretation. In contrast with proponents of earlier holistic analyses, they argue that intonation contours can be decomposed into pitch accents, phrase accents, and boundary tones and that the meanings of intonation contours can be derived compositionally from the meanings of their parts. The meanings they associate with intonational elements have to do with neither truth-conditional nor speech act properties but with attitudes and beliefs of speaker and hearer; in particular, they analyze intonation contours as conveying the speaker's attitude about the relations between the propositional content of her utterance and earlier and later utterances in the discourse, and between the current utterance and mutual beliefs.

Work in Gricean pragmatics is addressed primarily to the question of indirectness, though it has important implications for the other questions as well. Grice's important work points out that a good deal of what is conveyed by acts of utterance cannot be derived from the literal meanings of the expressions uttered but must be attributed to the participants' knowledge of principles of conversational interaction, based on general principles of rationality and cooperation. Knowledge of such principles, together with the ability to reason, gives rise to the ability to recognize the intentions behind utterances, including the important case of intentions that the speaker intends the hearer to recognize. The Gricean picture of "conversational implicature" has been very influential in all fields that study indirectness, with a large literature of insightful observations and analyses. But theoretical work has remained mostly in an informal state, without much in the way of formalization, and some of the central concepts have remained vague and problematic.

Richmond H. Thomason approaches this problem from the point of view of the formal semanticist, attempting to develop conceptual foundations for pragmatics. He points out that a proper understanding of pragmatics is crucial to the development of formal semantics for natural language, since "truth conditions are not transparent to observation" but are bound up with pragmatic matters of appropriateness and indirectness. Thomason accepts the spirit of Grice's approach to pragmatics but wants to develop "a much finer texture of explanation" by combining some developments in computer science, linguistics, and philosophy. He proposes three classes of "implicature enablers": speaker meaning, accommodation, and the conversational record. Speaker meaning involves intended recognition by the hearer of the speaker's intentions and plans. Accommodation is, roughly, "to swap the initial context for one that would have made the utterance appropriate," a special case of obstacle elimination. The conversational record is a constantly updated representation of the state of a conversation, which Thomason argues contains, not the beliefs of the participants, but "conversational presumptions that are taken to be mutual." He then discusses how implicature can be based on accommodation, by revision either of background assumptions (the usual case of implicature) or of the propositional content, as in the case of irony.

Probably the largest body of research in any field on discourse understanding has grown up in artificial intelligence in the past few years. This work builds to some extent on previous work in philosophy and linguistics on meaning, speech acts, and pragmatics but goes beyond it in an important way. Researchers in artificial intelligence were the first to bring out clearly the necessity to treat discourse as planned activity, requiring theoretical and empirical treatment of plan structure and plan recognition. Diane J. Litman and James F. Allen are computer scientists whose paper is an elaboration on these themes. They generally accept the distinction Grosz and Sidner (1986) make between attentional and intentional components in discourse structure, but they claim that the Grosz-Sidner framework cannot deal adequately with generated subdialogues like clarifications and corrections. On this basis they argue for a further distinction in task-oriented dialogues between "discourse intentions" and "commonsense task knowledge," basically a distinction between the plan structure of the non-linguistic task and that of the dialogue that accompanies execution of the task. They present a plan recognition model for the understanding of task-oriented dialogues that makes this distinction, and a plan recognition technique for relating discourse and task plans.

The last three papers in the book return to the issue of the nature of intention. An emerging theme of the volume is the need to reconceptualize the intentional basis for communication and discourse. The papers by John R. Searle, by Barbara J. Grosz and Candace L. Sidner, and by Herbert H. Clark and Deanna Wilkes-Gibbs represent three different research traditions: philosophy, computer science and artificial intelligence, and psychology, respectively. All three, though, argue that discourse is *collective behavior*; that is, it is a joint accomplishment. Examples of collective action are familiar, for example, jointly pushing a car, checking out of a supermarket, executing a hit-and-run play in baseball, and so on. Although perhaps agreeing with the general research direction of the volume that much can be gained in studying communication from an analysis of intentions and plans, the papers by Searle and by Grosz and Sidner argue that individual intentionality is not by itself sufficient to account for collective action and hence discourse. They argue that what is needed is a characterization of "joint plans" (for Grosz and Sidner) or "collective intentions" (Searle).

Searle first elaborates on the pretheoretic intuition that collective behavior exists and is pervasive. Team sports, orchestral performances, and engaging in conversation are all common examples. Moreover, collective behavior is not just helpful behavior. Engaging in a prizefight is an example of collective behavior in which the pugilists have agreed to compete. Contrast this with the situation of being accosted in a dark alley.

The main thesis of Searle's paper is that collective behavior is not the same as a summation of individual actions, and the difference between them resides in the intentions of the actors. When engaged in collective activity, individuals are guided by collective intentions, termed "we-intentions." On the other hand, even when engaged in collective activity, only individuals act, and those acts are caused by individual intentions. The key problem that Searle poses is how collective intentions relate to the individual intentions that cause the individual actions constitutive of the collective behavior. Searle argues that collective intentions are primitive and cannot be reduced to individual intentions supplemented with mutual beliefs. Instead, Searle proposes that each agent "we-intends" to achieve the collective goal *by means of* having an individual intention to do his part. Finally, he argues that collective intentionality presupposes the existence of a sense of other agents as candidates for collaboration. This raises the interesting question of whether other species (and, dare we say it, future robots) can play this role. Is hunting with a dog a form of collective action?

Grosz and Sidner survey the formalisms in the artificial intelligence literature for modeling plans and intentions that have been used in analyzing communication, and find them lacking—for example, in their assumption of a "master-slave" relationship among the discourse participants, in their use of formal expressions to the effect that one agent can intend that another intends to do some action, and in their failure to distinguish between models of the process by which plan recognition occurs and descriptions of the state in which it occurs. To avoid such problems, the authors extend to the notion of a "joint plan" the analysis that Pollack gives in her paper of single-agent plans as collections of beliefs and intentions. Grosz and Sidner develop a formal analysis for joint plans, in which two agents mutually believe (1) that each agent intends to do his part in achieving a jointly done action and (2) that each agent will do his part if and only if the other agent does likewise. In analyzing joint plans as consisting of mutual beliefs about individuals' intentions (even intentions to contribute to a joint activity), the authors disagree with Searle.

When communicating, agents agree (sometimes implicitly) to construct a shared plan, and they work together to develop it. Technically, Grosz and Sidner model this via "conversational default rules," akin to those found in Perrault's paper. Thus, shared plans are viewed as emerging from dialogue and are not constructed a priori, merely to be revealed during the course of a dialogue. To demonstrate the utility of the approach, Grosz and Sidner deploy it to explain various linguistic and discourse phenomena, including imperative utterances and reference.

Clark and Wilkes-Gibbs argue that even such a seemingly single-agent activity as referring is a collaboration action. To support this claim, they provide numerous examples derived from a "referential communication" task, in which the intended audience contributes to the successful securing of reference. For example, the audience can be seen to suggest referring expressions to the speaker and to complete the speaker's utterance. The authors raise the question of how very general collective intentions underlying dialogue become realized in fine-grained collective intentions underlying reference. In response, they propose a principle of mutual responsibility for dialogue in which the participants are jointly responsible for achieving the mutual belief that listeners have understood what the speaker meant prior to the next conversational contribution.

The data presented in this paper provide a challenge to theories of joint action and to other theories of action, interaction, and communication. If, as implied by a number of the other papers in the volume, special consideration of collective action is not needed, how can the data be explained? To the extent that a principle of mutual responsibility is at work, how would any of the theories proposed in this volume embody it? Searle and Grosz and Sidner provide important first steps in considering the foundations of collective action and in attempting to explain dialogue phenomena as collective action. In so doing, a needed connection is being made with traditions of analyzing dialogue that are unrepresented in this volume, namely, those of conversation analysis and sociolinguistics. A clarification of the relationships among the various disciplines concerned with communication and discourse would surely be welcomed.

References

Allen, James F. (1983). Recognizing intentions from natural language utterances. In Michael Brady and Robert C. Berwick, eds., *Computational models of discourse*. Cambridge, MA: MIT Press.

Anscombe, G. E. M. (1958). *Intention*. Ithaca, NY: Cornell University Press.

Audi, R. (1973). Intending. *Journal of Philosophy* 70, 387–403.

Austin, J. L. (1975). *How to do things with words*. 2nd ed. Cambridge, MA: Harvard University Press.

Bratman, Michael E. (1987). *Intention, plans, and practical reason*. Cambridge, MA: Harvard University Press.

Bruce, Bertram (1981). Plans and social action. In R. Spiro, B. Bruce, and W. Brewer, eds., *Theoretical issues in reading comprehension*. Hillsdale, NJ: L. Erlbaum Associates.

Carberry, M. Sandra (1988). Pragmatic modeling: Toward a robust natural language interface. *Computational Intelligence* 3, 117–136.

Castañeda, Hector-Neri (1975). *Thinking and doing*. Dordrecht, Holland: D. Reidel.

Cohen, Philip R., and Hector J. Levesque (1985). Speech acts and rationality. In *Proceedings of the Twenty-third Annual Meeting*, Association for Computational Linguistics, Chicago, IL.

Cohen, Philip R., and C. Raymond Perrault (1979). Elements of a plan-based theory of speech acts. *Cognitive Science* 3, 177–212. Reprinted in B. Webber and N. Nilsson, eds., (1981). *Readings in artificial intelligence*. Los Altos, CA: Morgan Kaufmann. Also in B. G. Grosz, K. Sparck Jones, and B. Webber, eds. (1986). *Readings in natural language processing*. Los Altos, CA: Morgan Kaufmann.

Davidson, Donald (1980a). Actions, reasons, and causes. In *Essays on actions and events*. New York: Oxford University Press.

Davidson, Donald (1980b). Intending. In *Essays on actions and events*. New York: Oxford University Press.

Davis, Lawrence H. (1979). *Theory of action*. Englewood Cliffs, NJ: Prentice-Hall.

Dretske, Fred I. (1981). *Knowledge and the flow of information*. Cambridge, MA: MIT Press.

Genesereth, Michael R. (1979). The role of plans in automated consultation. In *Proceedings of the Sixth International Joint Conference on Artificial Intelligence*, Tokyo.

Goldman, Alvin I. (1970). *A theory of human action*. Princeton, NJ: Princeton University Press.

Grice, H. P. (1957). Meaning. *The Philosophical Review* 66, 377–388. Reprinted in D. D. Steinberg and L. A. Jakobovits, eds. (1971). *Semantics*. New York: Cambridge University Press.

Grice, H. P. (1968). Utterer's meaning, sentence-meaning, and word-meaning. *Foundations of Language* 4, 1–18.

Grice, H. P. (1971). Intention and uncertainty. *Proceedings of the British Academy* 57, 263–279.

Grice, H. P. (1975). Logic and conversation. In P. Cole and J. L. Morgan, eds., *Syntax and semantics 3: Speech acts*. New York: Academic Press. Also in D. Davidson and G. Harman, eds., (1975). *The logic of grammar*. Encino, CA: Dickenson.

Grice, H. P. (1978). Further notes on logic and conversation. In P. Cole, ed., *Syntax and semantics 9: Pragmatics*. New York: Academic Press.

Grosz, Barbara J., and Candace L. Sidner (1986). Attention, intentions, and the structure of discourse. *Computational Linguistics* 12, 175–204.

Lewis, David K. (1972). General semantics. In D. Davidson and G. Harman, eds., *Semantics of natural language*. Dordrecht, Holland: D. Reidel.

Litman, Diane J., and James F. Allen (1987). A plan recognition model for subdialogues in conversation. *Cognitive Science* 11, 163–200.

McCarthy, John (1986). Applications of circumscription to formalizing commonsense knowledge. *Artificial Intelligence* 28, 89–116.

Meiland, Jack W. (1970). *The nature of intention*. London: Methuen.

Perrault, C. Raymond, and James F. Allen (1980). A plan-based analysis of indirect speech acts. *American Journal of Computational Linguistics* 6, 167–182.

Searle, John R. (1969). *Speech acts: An essay in the philosophy of language*. Cambridge: Cambridge University Press.

Searle, John R., and Daniel Vanderveken (1985). *Foundations of illocutionary logic*. New York: Cambridge University Press.

Sidner, Candace L. (1985). Plan parsing for intended response recognition in discourse. *Computational Intelligence* 1, 1–10.

Chapter 2

What Is Intention?

Michael E. Bratman

1 Introduction

In a symposium on "Intentions and Plans in Communication and Discourse" it is only fitting for a philosopher to ask, What is intention? This is a question I have discussed at some length in a recent book (Bratman 1987). Here my aim is to sketch in condensed form some of the main ideas in that book, focusing on those that seem to me to be particularly relevant to interdisciplinary research on the nature of intelligent agency.

Begin by making a distinction (see Anscombe 1963). We use the concept of intention to characterize both our actions and our minds. You believe (correctly) that I have *intentionally* written this sentence and that I have written it *with the intention* of illustrating a certain distinction. Perhaps you also believe that when I wrote this sentence in January I *intended* to discuss it at the symposium in March. In the former case you use the concept of intention to characterize my action; in the latter case you use the concept of intention to characterize my mind.

In approaching the question "What is intention?" I propose beginning with intending to do something. It is part of our commonsense conception of mind and action that we sometimes intend to do things and that such intentions typically are intentions to act in certain ways in the future. As a first step toward answering our general question about the nature of intention, I want to know what it is to have such a future-direct intention.

How do we go about answering such a question? My approach will be broadly speaking within the functionalist tradition in the philosophy of mind and action. We say what it is to intend to do something by specifying the "functional roles" characteristic of intention. To do this, we need to articulate the systematic relations between such intentions, other psycho-

I am indebted to many people for their help. Among them let me especially mention the members of the Rational Agency Project at CSLI, in particular: Martha Pollack, Charles Dresser, David Israel, Philip Cohen, Mark Crimmins, Todd Davies, Mike Georgeff, Pat Hayes, Kurt Konolige, and Amy Lansky. This research benefited from support from the Center for the Study of Language and Information, made possible in part through an award from the System Development Foundation.

logical states (such as belief and desire), relevant psychological processes and activities (such as practical reasoning), and crucial inputs and outputs: perception and action. Our commonsense understanding of intention, belief, desire, perception, and action depends on the supposition of appropriate underlying regularities within which these phenomena are embedded. These regularities will doubtless be what Grice (1974–75) calls "ceteris paribus laws" and in articulating them we will surely need to abstract away from many complexities. But reliance on ceteris paribus regularities and appropriate abstraction comes with the territory.

When we try in this way to specify the functional roles characteristic of intention, we are quickly faced with a trilemma. Suppose I intend today to drive over the Golden Gate bridge tomorrow. My intention today does not reach its ghostly hand over time and control my action tomorrow; that would be action at a distance. But my intention must *somehow* influence my later action; otherwise, why bother today to form an intention about tomorrow? It will be suggested that, once formed, my intention today will persist until tomorrow and then guide what will then be present action. But presumably such an intention is not irrevocable between today and tomorrow. Such irrevocability would clearly be irrational; after all, things change and we do not always correctly anticipate the future. But this suggests that tomorrow I should continue to intend to drive over the Golden Gate then only if it would be rational of me then to form such an intention from scratch. But then why should I bother deciding today what to do tomorrow? Why not just cross my bridges when I come to them? So it may seem that future-directed intentions will be either (1) metaphysically objectionable (since they involve action at a distance), or (2) rationally objectionable (since they are irrevocable), or (3) just a waste of time.

Such a trilemma might lead some to be suspicious of the very idea of future-directed intention and to suppose that a coherent model of intelligent agency should to without this idea. Indeed, I suspect that worries of the sort captured by this trilemma may go some way toward explaining the tendency in mid–twentieth century philosophy of action to ignore future-directed intention and to focus primarily on intentional action and action done with an intention. But I believe that future-directed intentions play a central role in our psychology, both individual and social, and that it is a serious error to ignore them in a theory of intelligent activity. My proposal, then, is to look for a functionalist treatment of future-directed intention, one that makes it clear how to avoid being impaled on one of the horns of our trilemma.

My procedure will be as follows. I will turn first to the role of future-directed intentions as inputs to ongoing practical reasoning and planning. This will lead me to certain questions about belief and about its relation to intention. In particular, I will focus on the distinction between what one intends and what one merely expects to result from what one intends. This discussion will lead us to a more complex view than we might otherwise have had of the relation between practical reasoning and the intentions in which it issues. At the end I will return to our trilemma to check to see that we have escaped its horns. Throughout I have the hope (dare I say the intention?) that the conception that emerges of intention and its role in our lives will not only seem plausible as a partial conception of human agency but also prove useful in developing a general but realistic model of intelligent agency.

2 Intention and Practical Reasoning

We frequently settle on an intention concerning the future and then proceed to reason about how to do what we intend. Today I decided to go to Monterey tomorrow. Now I must figure out how to get there. In such reasoning my future-directed intention to go to Monterey functions as an important input; and its role as such an input is, I believe, central to our understanding of intention. I want to say what this role is.

Now the philosophical literature about practical reasoning has tended to be somewhat schizophrenic. The dominant literature sees practical reasoning as beginning with certain of the agent's desires and beliefs and issuing in a decision, choice, or action. Practical reasoning is a matter of weighing conflicting considerations for and against conflicting options, where the relevant considerations are provided by what the agent desires/values/ cares about and what the agent believes. Practical reasoning consists in weighing desire-belief reasons for and against conflicting courses of action. This is the picture of practical reasoning sketched by Donald Davidson in his influential series of essays (Davidson 1980; Bratman 1985), and it is the picture that seems to lie behind most work in so-called decision theory (see, for example, Jeffrey 1983). What it is important to notice about this model of practical reasoning is that it provides no distinctive role for an agent's future-directed intentions as inputs to such reasoning. All practical reasoning is a matter of weighing desire-belief reasons for action.

A contrasting literature—best represented by Hector-Neri Castañeda's book *Thinking and Doing* (Castañeda 1975; Bratman 1983)—has emphasized the role of prior intentions as inputs into practical reasoning. The paradigm here, broadly speaking, is reasoning from a prior intention and relevant beliefs to derivative intentions concerning means, preliminary steps, or more specific courses of action. My close advisors on matters of artificial intelligence—David Israel and Martha Pollack—have taught me that this is also the paradigm that dominates there as well, in the guise of the "planning problem."

I think it is clear that these two traditions are each focusing on a real and important phenomenon: we do engage in the weighing of reasons both for and against conflicting options, and we do reason from prior, future-directed intentions to further intentions concerning means and the like. But how are these two kinds of reasoning related? This is a question that needs to be answered by an account of the role of intentions as inputs to further reasoning.

As a first step, return to our question: Why bother with future-directed intentions anyway? Why not just cross our bridges when we come to them? I think there are two main answers. The first is that we are not frictionless deliberators. Deliberation is a process that takes time and uses other resources; this means that there are obvious limits to the extent of deliberation at the time of action. By settling on future-directed intentions, we allow present deliberation to shape later conduct, thereby extending the influence of deliberation and Reason on our lives. Second, and relatedly, we have pressing needs for corrdination. To achieve complex goals, I must coordinate my present and future activities. And I need also to coordinate my activities with yours. Furture-directed intentions help facilitate both intra- and interpersonal coordination.

How? Part of the answer comes from noting that future-directed intentions are typically elements of larger plans. My intention today to go to Monterey tomorrow helps coordinate my activities for this week, and my activities with yours, by entering into a larger plan of action—one that will eventually include specifications of how to get there and what to bring, and one that will be coordinated with, for example, my child-care plans and your plans for meeting me in Monterey. And it will do this in ways compatible with my resource limitations and in a way that extends the influence of today's deliberation to tomorrow's action.

Since talk of plans is rampant in work in artificial intelligence, I had better stop right away and make it clear how I am using this term. A first distinction that needs to be made is between plans as abstract structures and plans as mental states. When I speak here of plans, I have in mind a certain kind of mental state, not merely an abstract structure of a sort that can be represented, say, by some game-theoretical notation. A more colloquial usage for what I intend might be "having a plan." But even after saying this, there remains room for misunderstanding; for there seem to be two importantly different cases of having a plan. On the one hand, I might have only a kind of recipe: that is, I might know a procedure for achieving a certain end. In this sense I can have a plan for roasting lamb whether or not I actually intend to roast lamb. On the other hand, to have a plan to roast lamb is to be planning to roast it: it involves intending to roast it. It is the second kind of case that I intend when I speak of plans. Plans, as I shall understand them, are mental states involving an appropriate sort of commitment to action: I have a plan to A only if it is true of me that I plan to A.

The plans characteristic of a limited agent like me typically have two important features. First, my plans are typically *partial*. When I decide today to go to Monterey tomorrow, I do not settle all at once on a complete plan for tomorrow. Rather, I decide now to go to Monterey, and I leave till later deliberation about how to get there in ways consistent with my other plans. Second, my plans typically have a *hierarchical structure*. Plans concerning ends embed plans concerning means and preliminary steps; and more general intentions embed more specific ones. As a result, I may deliberate about parts of my plan while holding other parts fixed. I may hold fixed certain intended ends, while deliberating about means or preliminary steps.

The strategy of settling in advance on such partial, hierarchically structured plans, leaving more specific decisions till later, has a pragmatic rationale. On the one hand, we need to coordinate our activities both within our own lives and, socially, between lives. And we need to do this in ways compatible with out limited capacities to deliberate and process information. This argues for being planning creatures. On the other hand, the world changes in ways we are not in a position to anticipate; so highly detailed plans about the far future will often be of little use and not worth bothering with. Partial, hierarchically structured plans for the future provide our compromise solution. And with the partiality of plans go patterns of reasoning in which my prior intentions play an important role as inputs: reasoning from a prior intention to further intentions concerning means or preliminary steps. In such reasoning we fill in partial plans in ways required for them successfully to guide our conduct.

To understand such reasoning, we need to reflect on demands that, other things being equal, plans need to satisfy to serve well their roles in coordination and in extending the influence of deliberation. First, there are *consistency constraints*. Plans need to be both internally consistent and consistent with the agent's beliefs. Roughly, it should be possible for my plans taken together to be successfully executed in a world in which my beliefs are true. Second, though partial, my plans need to be filled in to a certain extent as time goes by. My plans should be filled in with subplans concerning means, preliminary steps, and relatively specific courses of action, subplans at least as extensive as I believe is now required to do what I plan. Otherwise, they will suffer from *means-end incoherence*.

Associated with these two demands are two direct roles intentions and plans play as inputs in practical reasoning. First, given the demand for means-end coherence, prior intentions frequently *pose problems* for further deliberation. Given my intention to go to Monterey tomorrow, I need soon to fill in my plan with a specification of some means to getting there.

Second, given the need for consistency, prior intentions *constrain* further intentions. If I am already planning to leave my only car at home for Susan to use, then I cannot consistently solve my problem of how to get to Monterey by deciding to take my car.

Prior intentions, then, pose problems for deliberation, thereby establishing standards of *relevance* for options considered in deliberation. And they constrain solutions to these problems, providing a *filter of admissibility* for options. In these ways prior intentions and plans help make deliberation tractable for agents like us, agents with substantial resource limitations.

This gives us a natural model of the relation between two kinds of practical reasoning: the weighing of desire-belief reasons for and against conflicting options, and reasoning from a prior intention to derivative intentions concerning means and the like. Our model sees prior intentions as elements of partial plans, plans that provide a *background framework* within which the weighing of desire-belief reasons is to occur. It is this framework that poses problems for such further reasoning and constrains solutions to these problems. So practical reasoning has two levels: prior, partial plans pose problems and provide a filter on options that are potential solutions to these problems; desire-belief reasons enter as considerations to be weighed in deliberating between relevant and admissible options.

All this requires that prior intentions and plans have a certain *stability*: prior intentions and plans resist being reconsidered or abandoned. If we were constantly to be reconsidering the merits of our prior plans, they would be of little use in coordination and in helping us cope with our resource limitations. However, as noted earlier, it would also be irrational to treat one's prior plans as irrevocable, for the unexpected does happen. This suggests that rational agents like us need general policies and habits that govern the reconsideration of prior intentions and plans. Roughly speaking, their nonreconsideration should be treated as the "default," but a default that is overridable by certain special kinds of problems. An important area of research is to say more about what sorts of policies and habits concerning the reconsideration of prior plans it would be reasonable for limited agents like us to have. I believe that the consideration of such matters will lead us into general issues about aspects of rational agency that go beyond reasoning and calculation; but I cannot go into this matter further here.

So we now have a sketch of one of the major roles of future-directed intentions in the psychology of limited rational agents like us. As elements of partial, hierarchical plans, prior intentions pose problems and filter out options for deliberation. And throughout they need to exhibit an appropriate kind of stability, resisting reconsideration except when faced with certain unanticipated problems.

This account of the role of prior intention in further reasoning assumes that there is such a thing as flat-out belief. That is, it assumes that we sometimes just believe certain things—for example, that I have a meeting in Monterey tomorrow and that my home is not walking distance from Monterey—and do not just have degrees of confidence or "subjective probabilities" ranging from 0 to 1. Such flat-out beliefs combine with my plans to make certain options inadmissible. If I just assigned a high probability (but a probability less than 1) to my having only one car, the plan of driving a car of mine to Monterey while leaving a car of mine at home for Susan would not run into problems of inconsistency, strictly speaking. So the option of driving a car of mine to Monterey would not be inadmissible. It is my flat-out belief that I have only one car that combines with my prior plans to make inadmissible the option of driving a car of mine to Monterey.

The background framework against which practical reasoning proceeds includes, then, flat-out beliefs as well as prior intentions and plans. Of course, just as I can always stop and reconsider some prior intention, I can also stop and reconsider some background flat-out belief. Still, in a normal case in which there is no such reconsideration my planning will be framed in part by my relevant flat-out beliefs.

None of this denies the importance to practical reasoning of subjective probabilities less than 1. The idea, rather, is to see such subjective probabilities as entering into deliberation, but deliberation that is already framed by the agent's prior plans and flat-out beliefs.

3 Intention and Belief

I need now to discuss how intention is related to belief. This is a complex issue, and I can only discuss some elements of it here.

Our model of the role of future-directed intentions as inputs to further reasoning clearly depends on one main idea about the relation between intention and belief. This is the idea that there is a defeasible demand that one's intentions be consistent with one's beliefs. It is this demand that drives the operation of what I have called the filter of admissibility on options. But there is also a second idea implicit in the model. To see what this is, we need to return to the point—central to this discussion—that prior intentions and plans play a crucial coordinating role. And we need to say more about how that works. How does my prior intention to go to Monterey tomorrow help support coordination within my own life and, socially, between my life and yours?

I think the answer is that it does this normally by providing support for the expectation that I will in fact go there then. That is, my intention normally helps support your expectation that I will go there, thereby enabling you to plan on the assumption that I'll be there. And it normally helps support my expectation that I will go, thereby enabling me to plan on a similar assumption. But how is it that my intention can provide such support?

Part of the answer has already been suggested. My intention will normally lead me to reason about how to get there and to settle on appropriate means. And my intention has a certain stability, so one can expect that it will not be easily changed, Still, there is a gap in the explanation. For all that we have said so far, my intention might stay around and lead to reasoning about means and yet still not control my conduct when the time comes.

What is needed here is a distinction between two kinds of pro-attitudes. Intentions, desires, and valuations are, and ordinary beliefs are not, *pro-attitudes*. Pro-attitudes in this very general sense play a motivational role: in concert with belief they can move us to act. But most pro-attitudes are merely potential influencers of conduct. For example, my desire to play basketball this afternoon is merely a potential influencer of my conduct this afternoon. It must vie with my other relevant desires—say, my desire to finish writing this paper—before it is settled what I will do. In contrast, once I intend to play basketball this afternoon, the matter is settled: I normally need not continue to weigh the relevant pros and cons. When the afternoon arrives, I will normally just proceed to execute my intention. My intention is a *conduct-controlling* pro-attitude, not merely a *potential influencer* of conduct.

It is because intentions are conduct controllers that the agent can normally be relied on try to execute them when the time comes, if the intention is still around and if the agent then knows what to do. It is because intentions are normally stable that they can normally be relied on to persist until the time of action. And it is because intentions drive relevant means-end reasoning and the like that the agent can normally be relied on to put herself in a position to execute the intention and to know what to do when the time comes. Taken together, these features of intention help explain how future-directed intentions normally support coordination by supporting associated expectations of their successful execution.

None of this entails, by the way, that *every* time you intend to A in the future you must believe that you will A. That thesis seems to me a bit too strong, though I will not try to argue the point here. All that is required is that your intention will normally support such a belief, thereby supporting coordination.

So, future-directed intentions will normally be both consistent with the agent's beliefs and support beliefs in their successful execution. In the normal case, then, when I intend to A, I will also believe that I will A. Nevertheless, there remains an important distinction between intention and belief. I now want to focus on one aspect of this distinction: the distinction between what one intends and what one merely expects as an upshot of what one intends. This will shed further light on the way in which intentions can be an output of practical reasoning.

4 Intention and the Problem of the Package Deal

4.1 The Problem

Consider a much discussed example (see, for example, Bennett 1980). Terror Bomber and Strategic Bomber both have as their goal promoting the war effort against Enemy. Both intend to pursue their goal by dropping bombs. Terror Bomber's plan is to bomb the school in Enemy's territory, thereby killing children of Enemy, terrorizing Enemy's population, and forcing Enemy to surrender. Strategic Bomber's plan is to bomb Enemy's munitions plant, thereby undermining Enemy's war effort. However, Strategic Bomber also knows that next to the munitions plant is a school and that when he bombs the plant, he will also kill the children inside the school. Strategic Bomber has worried a lot about this bad effect. But he has concluded that this cost is outweighed by the contribution that would be made to the war effort by the destruction of the munitions plant.

Terror Bomber intends to drop the bombs, kill the children, terrorize the population, and thereby promote victory. In contrast, Strategic Bomber only intends to drop the bombs, destroy the munitions plant, and promote the war effort. While he knows that by bombing the plant he will be killing the children, he does not *intend* to kill them. Whereas killing the children is, for Terror Bomber, and intended means to his end of victory, for Strategic Bomber it is only something he knows he will do by bombing the munitions plant. Though Strategic Bomber has taken the children's deaths quite seriously in his deliberation, these deaths are for him only an expected side effect. Or so, anyway, it would seem.

But now consider a challenge to this distinction between intended and merely expected effects. We may address this challenge directly to Strategic Bomber: "In choosing to bomb the munitions plant, you knew you would thereby kill the children. Indeed, you worried about this fact and took it seriously into account in your deliberation. In choosing to bomb, then, you have opted for a *package*, one that includes not only destroying the plant and contributing to military victory but also killing the children. The bombing is a *package deal*. So how can it be rational of you to intend only a proper part of this package?"

I call this *the problem of the package deal*.[1] This problem raises the following general question: Suppose an agent believes her A-ing would result in a bad effect E, seriously considers E in her deliberation, and yet still goes on to make a choice in favor of her A-ing. How could it be rational of such an agent not to intend to bring about *E*? We have supposed that a rational agent's intentions may fail to include expected effects she seriously considered in the deliberation that led to her choice. But how could this be, given that in deliberation and choice one is faced with a package deal?

To spell out the problem more explicitly, I will borrow from a plausible model of practical reasoning sketched by Wilfred Sellars in his essay "Thought and Action" (Sellars 1966). Sellars would see Strategic Bomber's reasoning as having three main stages. First, there is the stage in which he lays out the larger "scenarios" between which he must chose. These scenarios are to include those features of competing courses of action that are to be given serious consideration in his deliberation. In our example let us suppose that these scenarios will be

(S1)   bomb munitions plant, destroy the plant, kill the children, and weaken Enemy

(S2)   bomb the rural airport, destroy the airport, and weaken Enemy.

Second, Strategic Bomber will evaluate these scenarios "as wholes" and thereby arrive at a "complex intention." In our example this will be the complex intention to bomb and destroy the munitions plant, kill the children, and weaken Enemy. Finally, he will be led from this complex intention to the simpler intention to bomb the plant. And, though Sellars does not emphasize the point, it seems that Strategic Bomber will also be led to the simpler intention to kill the children.

This is a natural model. But so long as this is our model of Strategic Bomber's practical reasoning, we will have great difficulty explaining how he can rationally refrain from intending to kill the children. On the model, Strategic Bomber's initial conclusion of his practical reasoning will be a complex intention which includes his killing the children, and from which he seems to be as justified in reaching an intention to kill them as he is in reaching an intention to drop the bombs.

We can develop the point further by noting a quartet of principles to which this model of practical reasoning seems committed. These principles all concern the situation in which the practical reasoning of a rational agent has been successfully completed and has issued in an intention. There is, first, the idea that such practical reasoning should issue in a conclusion in favor of a scenario *taken as a whole*, where such scenarios include *all* factors given serious consideration in the reasoning. Strategic Bomber, for example, should draw a conclusion in favor of one of the total packages under consideration: (S1)-and-not-(S2), or (S2)-and-not-(S1). Second, there is the idea that this conclusion is a *practical* conclusion, one tied tightly to action. We may express this idea by saying that this practical conclusion is a *choice* of a total scenario. Strategic Bomber, then, should choose one of the total packages under consideration; he cannot simply choose to drop the bombs. The third principle goes on to associate such a choice in favor of an overall scenario with the formation of a complex *intention* in favor of that overall scenario: Strategic Bomber must *intend* a total package. Finally, the fourth principle connects such an intention in favor of an overall scenario with intentions to perform each of the actions included within that scenario that the agent supposes to be within his control.

Here are slightly more precise statements of these principles:

> *Principle of the holistic conclusion of practical reasoning*: If I know that my *A*-ing will result in *E*, and I seriously consider this fact in my deliberation about whether to *A* and still go on to conclude in favor of *A*, then if I am rational, my reasoning will have issued in a conclusion in favor of an overall scenario that includes *both* my *A*-ing *and* my bringing about *E*. (For short, I will call this the *principle of holistic conclusion*.)
>
> *Principle of holistic choice*: The holistic conclusion (of practical reasoning) in favor of an overall senario is a *choice* of that scenario.
>
> *The choice-intention principle*: If on the basis of practical reasoning I choose to *A* and to *B* and to . . . , then I *intend* to *A* and to *B* and to . . . .
>
> *Principle of intention division*: If I intend to *A* and to *B* and to . . . , and I know that *A* and *B* are each within my control, then if I am rational, I will both intend to *A* and intend to *B*.[2]

Once we accept this quarter of principles, we are faced with the problem of the package deal. Strategic Bomber seriously considers the fact that by bombing, he will be killing the children. So the principles of holistic conclusion and holistic choice together require that (if rational) Strategic Bomber choose to bomb and to bring about the deaths of the children and to . . . . But then, by the choice-intention principle he must intend to bomb and to bring about the deaths of the children and to . . . . But Strategic Bomber knows that it is up to him whether to bomb and also that it is up to him whether to kill the children.[3] So by the principle of intention division Strategic Bomber, if rational, will intend to kill the children. So, contrary to our initial impression, there is no room here for a distinction between intended and merely expected upshots.

4.2 Three Roles of Intention

The problem of the package deal argues that, if rational, Strategic Bomber will intend to kill the children. The next step is to see why this conclusion should be rejected.

What is it to intend to kill the children? The problem of the package deal focuses on the prior reasoning on the basis of which intentions are *formed*. But to understand what intentions are, we need also to look at the roles they play, once formed, in *further* reasoning and action. And here we can draw on our earlier discussion of these matters in sections 1–3.

Return to Terror Bomber. He really does intend to kill the children as a means to promoting military victory. As we have seen, this intention to kill the children will play two important roles in his further practical reasoning: it will pose problems for further means-end reasoning, and it will constrain his other intentions. To explore this second role, let us develop the example further. Suppose that after settling on his plan (but before his bombing run), Terror Bomber (who also commands a small battalion) considers ordering a certain troop movement. He sees that this troop movement would achieve certain military advantages. But then he notices that if the troops do move in this way, Enemy will become alarmed and evacuate the children, thereby undermining the terror-bombing mission. The option of moving his troops has an expected upshot (evacuation of the children) that is incompatible with an intended upshot of the bombing mission he already intends to engage in. But Terror Bomber's prior intention to terror-bomb, together with his beliefs, creates a screen of admissibility through which options must pass in later deliberation. And the option of moving the troops does not pass through this screen of admissibility, for it is incompatible with what Terror Bomber intends and believes. So Terror Bomber's prior intention to kill the children stands in the way of his forming a new intention to order the troop movement.

Now consider what happens when Terror Bomber executes his intention. Intentions are conduct *controllers*. This means that an intention to bring about some upshot will normally give rise to one's *endeavoring* to bring about that upshot. To endeavor to bring about some upshot is, in part, to guide one's conduct accordingly. Roughly, one is prepared to make adjustments in what one is doing in response to indications of one's success or failure in promoting that upshot. So Terror Bomber can be expected to guide his conduct in the direction of causing the deaths of the children. If in midair he learns they have moved to a different school, he will try to track them and take his bombs there. If he learns the building they are in is heavily reinforced, he may for that reason decide on a special kind of bomb. And so on.[4]

So, Terror Bomber's intention to kill the children will play a pair of characteristic roles as an input to his further practical reasoning and, when the time comes, it will lead to his endeavoring to kill them and so guiding his conduct in a way that aims at their death. What about Strategic Bomber's attitude toward his killing the children? It seems clear that his attitude toward killing them will *not* play such a trio of roles. Strategic Bomber will not see himself as being presented with a problem of how to kill the children. Nor will he be disposed to constrain his further intentions to fit with his killing them. If he were later to consider the troop movement just described, and if he were to note the resulting likelihood of evacuation, this would *not* block for him the option of moving those troops. And finally, even once he is engaged in the bombing mission, he will not endeavor to kill the children. In the normal case this means he will not guide his activity by keeping track of the children and their deaths.[5] Rather, he will just keep track of the munitions plant and its destruction.

Further, there is good reason for Strategic Bomber to resist having an attitude toward killing the children that would play these three roles. Having such an attitude would not normally help him achieve those goals he wants to achieve, and it might well prevent him from achieving some goals he wants to achieve. For example, it might prevent him from considering the advantageous troop movement, given that option's expected incompatibility with his killing the children.

Since Strategic Bomber does not have an attitude toward killing the children that plays a trio of roles characteristic of intention, he does not intend to kill the children. And this may well be rational of him. So we should resist the pressure from the problem of the package deal to say that Strategic Bomber, if rational, will intend to kill the children.

So we are in the following situation. We have noted four principle that underlie the problem of the package deal. The inference from this quartet of principles to the conclusion that Strategic Bomber should intend to kill the children seems clearly valid. But our account of the functional roles characteristic of intention just as clearly indicates that this conclusion is to be rejected. This means we must reject at least one of these four principles. Our problem is, Which one?

4.3 Intention and Choice

One might try rejecting intention division.[6] There is much to be said here, but for present purposes I just note that even without this principle a serious problem will remain. The remaining trio of principles still tells us that, if rational, Strategic Bomber will intend to kill the children *as a part of a larger intention* to bomb, and so on. But Strategic Bomber need not even have this larger, complex intention. Such a complex intention would play the trio of roles we have been focusing on. But it is clear, for example, that Strategic Bomber can be expected *not* to treat as inadmissible other options whose expected upshots are incompatible with his killing the children. Strategic Bomber may well later go ahead and seriously consider ordering the troop movement.

A second strategy would be to reject the principle of holistic conclusion. But, again, this does not seem promising to me. Granted, it would be too strong to require that a rational agent's practical conclusion include all expected effects of his action. Strategic Bomber expects that in going on his bombing run, he will be slightly heating up the wings of his aircraft. Yet this might well not get into the conclusion of his practical reasoning. Since this effect does not matter to him in the least, Strategic Bomber may well not stop to notice it in his practical reasoning. But all that our principle of holistic conclusion requires is that the agent's conclusion include all expected upshots *that he has seriously considered in his deliberation.* What the principle requires is only a certain clearheadedness and intellectual honesty—an absence of "bad faith," if you will. Once I seriously consider A's anticipated effect, E, in my deliberation about whether to A, I should see that the issue for my deliberation concerns a *complex* scenario, one that includes A *together with E.* If I am clearheaded and intellectually honest about this, my conclusion should concern this complex scenario, and not merely my A-ing simpliciter. My conclusion should concern the total package.

So we cannot solve our problem by rejecting either the principle of holistic conclusion or the principle of intention division. What then should we do?

Our problem arises from the apparent conflict between backward-looking and forward-looking pressures on what we intend. On the one hand, intentions are typically grounded in prior deliberation. Once deliberation enters the picture, however, plausible standards of clearheadedness and intellectual honesty—standards expressed in the principle of holistic conclusion—are engaged. This leads to pressure *for* practical conclusions to be holistic and so, it seems, for intentions to be holistic. This pressure is backward-looking, for it is grounded in the connection between intention and prior deliberation. On the other hand, intentions, once formed, play a trio of characteristic roles in further reasoning and action. This is true not only of a relatively simple intention to drop bombs but also of a more complex intention to drop bombs and (thereby) kill the children. Since Strategic Bomber, for example, can rationally refrain from having an attitude toward killing the children that plays such roles, there is pressure *against* forcing intentions to be holistic. This pressure is forward-looking, for it depends on the roles of intentions in guiding further reasoning and action. The problem of the package deal is the problem of how to reconcile these conflicting pressures. The solution is to deny that these pressures apply to the same thing. I proceed to explain.

The problem of the package deal depends on identifying (or, anyway, linking very tightly) (1) the conclusion of practical reasoning that is subject to pressures for holism (pressures based on standards of clearheadedness and intellectual honesty in reasoning) and (2) the intention in which practical reasoning issues. This identification derives from the combination of the principle of holistic choice and the choice-intention principle. The former identifies (1) with a holistic choice; the latter connects such a choice with (2). The rejection of either of these principles would undermine the identification of (1) with (2). This would allow us to say that the pressure for holism, though it applies to certain conclusions of practical reasoning (that is, (1)), does not apply to the intentions in which the practical reasoning issues (that is, (2)). And in this way we could block the problem of the package deal.

I propose, then, that we challenge either the principle of holistic choice or the choice-intention principle. But which one? Though I cannot argue the point here, it seems clear to me that we should reject the choice-intention principle. We should distinguish what is chosen on the basis of practical reasoning from what is intended. Choice and intention are differently affected by standards of good reasoning, on the one hand, and concerns with further reasoning and action, on the other.

Return to Strategic Bomber. He is obliged by a plausible principle of good reasoning to include the children's deaths in the total package that he chooses on the basis of his *prior* reasoning. But it does not follow that his attitude toward these deaths must, if he is rational, play the roles in *further* reasoning and action that are characteristic of intention. The demand to include the children's deaths in what is chosen comes from a demand for clearheadedness in one's reasoning and choice—a demand to confront clearly and honestly the important features of what one will be doing in plumping as one does. It is this demand that leads to pressure for choice to be holistic. But this demand does not force one's *intentions* to be holistic; for one's intentions are tied not only to prior deliberation but also to a trio of roles concerning further reasoning and action. Nothing in the ideal of clearheaded reasoning forces one to have the dispositions concerning *further* reasoning and action that would be characteristic of holistic intention. Though clearheadedness obliges Strategic Bomber to choose (among other things) to kill the children, it does not oblige him later to screen out options incompatible with his killing them, or to endeavor to kill them. So choice and intention can diverge.

It is natural to assume that whatever one choose one thereby intends (see, for example, Aune 1977, 115). But reflection on the problem of the package deal argues otherwise. What one chooses is constrained by holistic pressures—pressures grounded in standards of clearheadedness in reasoning—in a way in which what one intends is not. And what one intends is tied to further reasoning and action in a way in which what one chooses need not be.

Our model of the roles of intention in practical reasoning sees intentions as both characteristic inputs and outputs of such reasoning. What we have seen here is that what intentions are an output of present practical reasoning is constrained in part by the roles of such intentions as inputs to further practical reasoning.

Of course, having rejected the choice-intention principle, we will need to put something in its place. One's choice in favor of an overall scenario will involve one's coming to have some intentions or others—intentions that will guide further reasoning and action. This is what distinguishes a choice of a scenario from a mere preference or positive evaluation in its favor. A full theory will need to say more about *which* intentions a rational agent will thereby come to have; but I cannot pursue this matter further here. Suffice it to say that an acceptable treatment of the relation between intention, choice, and practical reasoning cannot just assume that one intends all of what one chooses on the basis of practical reasoning.

5 Concluding Remarks

This concludes my brief sketch of aspects of my approach to saying what intention is and to identifying some of the major roles of intention in the intelligent activity of limited agents like us. Intentions are relatively stable attitudes that function as inputs to further practical reasoning in accordance with the two-level model of practical reasoning I have outlined. Intentions will be outputs of practical reasoning, but in a way that comports with the complexity of the relation between choice and intention. As a conduct-controlling pro-attitude, intention is intimately related to endeavoring and action.[7]

What about our original trilemma? Future-directed intentions influence later conduct by way of their influence on intervening practical reasoning and the formation of derivative intentions, by way of their stability, and by way of their tendency to control conduct when the time come. This is not action at a distance; but it is also not irrevocability. These systematic ways in which future-directed intentions shape later deliberation and action are central to the functioning of limited but intelligent agents like us, especially in the pursuit of coordination. So there is little reason to worry that the formation of such intentions is a waste of time. Our model of the role of intention in limited rational agency seems clearly to avoid the horns of our trilemma and so to pass at least this test of adequacy for an account of the nature of intention.

Notes

1. In the discussion to follow I benefited from Gilbert Harman's examination of a related but different problem in Harman 1983. I explain how my problem differs from Harman's, and why I reject important features of his solution, in Bratman 1987, chapter 10, from which the present discussion is taken.
2. Note that this last principle is rather limited. For example, it does *not* say that if I intend to X and I know that it is necessary that if I do X I do Y, then I intend to Y. For the principle of intention division to apply, I must know that X and Y are, each of them, within my control. So, on the present principle, I might intend to belch softly and yet (rationally) not intend to belch, even though I know that it is necessary for me to belch if I am to belch softly. This might happen if I thought that it was not up to me whether I

belched, but only up to me whether, given that I was going to belch, I belched softly or loudly. (The example is due to Gilbert Harman, in correspondence.)

3. Granted, he also knows that it is *not* in his power to bomb *without* killing the children. But that does not affect the present point.

4. Of course, this all depends on his retaining his beliefs about the connection between his killing the children and his promoting military victory. If he finds out, in midair, that the war is over, or that the children in the school are prisoners Enemy would like to see killed, he will not continue to guide his conduct by the children's death.

5. I say "in the normal case," for there are cases in which Strategic Bomber might guide his activity by keeping track of the children and their deaths and yet still not endeavor to kill them. Suppose he wasn't dropping a single bunch of bombs but was launching missiles one at a time, aimed at the munitions plant. However, the only way he has of knowing whether he has hit the plant is to listen to Enemy radio for an announcement of the deaths of the children. After each missile is launched, he waits for a radio announcement. In its absence he launches yet another missile, and so on until he hears of the children's deaths or somehow comes to change his opinion of the link between the destruction of the munitions plant and the deaths of the children. Still, he does not launch his missiles *in order to* kill the children. Nor does he engage in means-end reasoning concerned with how to kill the children, or screen his other options for their compatibility with his killing them. So he still does not intend to kill them.

6. This is, in effect, what Chisholm (1976) suggests; see especially chapter 2, pages 74–75.

7. Once we see intention in this way, how should we understand the relation between intending to act and our classification of actions as done intentionally or with a certain intention? I discuss these matters in Bratman 1987, chapters 8 and 9.

References

Anscombe, G. E. M. (1963). *Intention.* 2nd ed. Ithaca, NY: Cornell University Press.

Aune, Bruce (1977). *Reason and action.* Dordrecht, Holland: D. Reidel.

Bennett, Jonathan (1980). Morality and consequences. In Sterling M. McMurrin, ed., *The Tanner lectures on human values.* Cambridge: Cambridge University Press.

Bratman, Michael (1983). Castañeda's theory of thought and action. In James E. Tomberlin, ed., *Agent, language, and the structure of the world: Essays presented to Hector-Neri Castañeda with his replies.* Indianapolis, IN: Hackett.

Bratman, Michael (1985). Davidson's theory of intention. In Bruce Vermazen and Merrill B. Hintikka, eds., *Essays on Davidson: Actions and events.* New York: Oxford University Press. Reprinted with an added appendix in Ernest LePore and Brian McLaughlin, eds. (1985). *Actions and events: Perspectives on the philosophy of Donald Davidson.* Oxford: Basil Blackwell.

Bratman, Michael E. (1987). *Intention, plans, and practical reason.* Cambridge, MA: Harvard University Press.

Castañeda, Hector-Neri (1975). *Thinking and doing.* Dordrecht, Holland: D. Riedel.

Chisholm, Roderick M. (1976). *Person and object.* La Salle, IL: Open Court.

Davidson, Donald (1980). *Essays on actions and events.* New York: Oxford University Press.

Grice, H. P. (1974–75). Method in philosophical psychology: From the banal to the bizarre. *Proceedings and Addresses of the American Philosophical Association* 48, 23–53.

Harman, Gilbert (1983). Rational action and the extent of intentions. *Social Theory and Practice* 9, 123–41. Revised version published as chapter 9 in Gilbert Harman (1986). *Change in view.* Cambridge, MA: MIT Press.

Jeffrey, Richard (1983). *The logic of decision.* Chicago: University of Chicago Press.

Sellars, Wilfrid (1966). Thought and action. In Keith Lehrer, ed., *Freedom and determinism.* New York: Random House.

Chapter 3

Persistence, Intention, and Commitment

Philip R. Cohen and Hector J. Levesque

1 Introduction

This paper is concerned with specifying the "rational balance"[1] needed among the beliefs, goals, plans, intentions, commitments, and actions of autonomous agents. For example, it would be reasonable to specify that agents should act to achieve their intentions and that agents should adopt only intentions that they believe to be achievable. Another constraint might be that once an agent has an intention, it believes it will do the intended act. Furthermore, we might wish that agents keep (or commit to) their intentions over time and not drop them precipitously. However, if an agent's beliefs change, it may well need to alter its intentions. Intention revision may also be called for when an agent tries and fails to fulfill an intention, or even when it succeeds. Thus, it is not enough to characterize what it means for an agent to have an intention; one also needs to describe how that intention affect the agent's beliefs, commitments to future actions, and ability to adopt still other intentions during plan formation.

Because autonomous agents will have to exist in *our* world, making commitments to us and obeying our orders, a good place to begin a normative study of rational balance is to examine various commonsense relationships among people's beliefs, intentions and commitments that seem to justify our attribution of the term "rational." However, rather than

This research was made possible in part by a gift from the System Development Foundation, in part by support from the Natural Sciences and Engineering Research Council of Canada, and in part by support from the Defense Advanced Research Projects Agency under contract N00039-84-K-0078 with the Naval Electronic Systems Command. The views and conclusions contained in this document are those of the authors and should not be interpreted as representative of the official policies, either expressed or implied, of the Defense Advanced Research Projects Agency or the United States government (or the Canadian one, for that matter).

James Allen, Michael Bratman, Joe Halpern, David Israel, Ray Perrault, and Martha Pollack provided many valuable suggestions. Discussions with Doug Appelt, Jim des Rivières, Michael Georgeff, Kurt Konolige, Amy Lansky, Joe Nunes, Calvin Ostrum, Fernando Pereira, Stan Rosenschein, and Moshe Vardi have also been quite helpful, Thanks to you all.

just characterizing agents in isolation, we propose a logic suitable for describing and reasoning about these mental states in a world in which agents will have to interact with others. Not only will a theorist have to reason about the kinds of interactions agents can have, agents may themselves need to reason about the beliefs, intentions, and commitments of other agents. The need for agents to reason about others is particularly acute in circumstances requiring communication. In this vein, the formalism serves as a foundation for a theory of speech acts (Cohen and Levesque 1985 and chapter 12 of this volume) and applies more generally to situations of rational interaction in which communication may take place in a formal language.

In its emphasis on formally specifying constraints on the design of autonomous agents, this paper is intended to contribute to artificial intelligence research. To the extent that our analysis captures the ordinary concept of intention, this paper may contribute to the philosophy of mind. We discuss both areas below.

1.1 Artificial Intelligence Research on Planning Systems

Artificial intelligence research has concentrated on algorithms for finding plans to achieve given goals, on monitoring plan execution (Fikes and Nilsson 1971), and on replanning. Recently, planning in dynamic, multi-agent domains has become a topic of interest, especially the planning of communication acts needed for one agent to affect the mental state and behavior of another (Allen 1979; Allen and Perrault 1980; Appelt 1981; Cohen and Levesque 1980, 1985; Cohen and Perrault 1979; Georgeff 1983; Georgeff and Lansky, in preparation; Konolige and Nilsson 1980; Rosenschein 1986; Rosenschein and Genesereth 1984). Typically, this research has ignored the issues of rational balance—of precisely how an agent's beliefs, goals, and intentions should be related to its actions.[2] In such systems, the theory of intentional action embodied by the agent is expressed only as code, with the relationships among the agent's beliefs, goals, plans, and actions left implicit in the agent's architecture. If asked, the designer of a planning system may say that the notion of intention is defined operationally: a planning system's intentions are no more than the contents of its plans. As such, intentions are representations of possible actions the system may take to achieve its goal(s). This much is reasonable; there surely is a strong relationship between plans and intentions (Pollack, this volume). However, what constitutes a plan for most planning systems is itself often a murky topic.[3] Thus, saying that the system's intentions are the contents of its plans lacks needed precision. Moreover, operational definitions are usually quite difficult to reason with and about. If the program changes, then so may the definitions, in which case there would not be a fixed set of specifications that the program implements. This paper can be seen as providing both a logic in which to write specifications for autonomous agents and an initial theory cast in that logic.

1.2 Philosophical Theories of Intention

Philosophers have long been concerned with the concept of intention, often trying to reduce it to some combination of belief and desire. We will explore their territory here, but we cannot possibly do justice to the immense body of literature on the subject. Our strategy is to make connection with some of the more recent work and hope our efforts are not yet another failed attempt, amply documented in The Big Book of Classical Mistakes.

Philosophers have drawn a distinction between future-directed intentions and present-directed ones (Bratman 1984, 1987; Searle 1983). The former guide agents' planning and constrain their adoption of other intentions (Bratman 1987), whereas the latter function *causally* in producing behavior (Searle 1983). For example, one's future-directed intentions may include cooking dinner tomorrow, and one's present-directed intentions may include moving an arm now. Most philosophical analyses have examined the relationship between an agent's doing something intentionally and that agent's having a present-directed intention. Bratman (1984) has argued that intending to do something (or having an intention) and doing something intentionally are not the same phenomenon and that the former is more concerned with the coordination of an agent's plans. We agree, and in this paper we concentrate primarily on future-directed intentions. Hereafter, the term "intention" will be used in that sense only.

Intention has often been analyzed differently from other mental states such as belief and knowledge. First, whereas the content of beliefs and knowledge is usually considered to be in the form of propositions, the content of an intention is typically regarded as an action. For example, Castañeda (1975) treats the content of an intention as a "practition," akin (in computer science terms) to an action description. It is claimed that by doing so, and by strictly separating the logic of propositions from the logic of practitions, one avoids undesirable properties in the logic of intention, such as the fact that if one intends to do an action a, one must also intend to do a or b. However, it has also been argued that needed connections between propositions and practitions may not be derivable (Bratman 1983).

Searle (1983) claims that the content of an intention is a causally self-referential representation of its conditions of satisfaction (and see also Harman 1986). That is, for an agent to intend to go to the store, the conditions of satisfaction would be that the intention should cause the agent to go to the store. Our analysis is incomplete in that it does not deal with this causal self-reference. Nevertheless, the present analysis will characterize many important properties of intention discussed in the philosophical literature.

A second difference among kinds of propositional attitudes is that some, such as belief, can be analyzed in isolation—one axiomatizes the properties of belief apart from those of other attitudes. However, intention is intimately connected with other attitudes, especially belief, as well as with time and action. Thus, any formal analysis of intention must explicate these relationships. In the next section we explore what it is that theories of intention should handle.

1.3 Desiderata for a Theory of Intention

Bratman (1987) argues that rational behavior cannot just be analyzed in terms of beliefs and desires (as many philosophers have held). A third mental state, intention, which is related in many interesting ways to beliefs and desires but is not reducible to them, is necessary. There are two justifications for this claim. First, noting that agents are resource-bounded, Bratman suggests that no agent can continually weigh his[4] competing desires, and concomitant beliefs, in deciding what to do next. At some point the agent must just *settle on* one state of affairs for which to aim. Deciding what to do establishes a limited form of *commitment*. We will explore the consequences of such commitments.

A second reason is the need to coordinate one's future actions. Once a future act is settled on—that is, intended—one typically decides on other future actions to take with that action as given. This ability to plan to do some act A in the future, and to base decisions on what to do subsequent to A, requires that a rational agent *not* simultaneously believe he will *not* do A. If he did, the rational agent would not be able to plan past A since he believes it will not be done. Without some notion of commitment, deciding what else to do would be a hopeless task.

Bratman argues that unlike mere desires, intentions play the following three functional roles:

> 1. *Intentions normally pose problems for the agent; the agent needs to determine a way to achieve them.* For example, if an agent intends to fly to New York on a certain date and takes on actions to enable himself to do so, then the intention affected the agent in the right way.
> 2. *Intentions provide a "screen of admissibility" for adopting other intentions.* Whereas desires can be inconsistent, agents do not normally adopt intentions that they believe conflict with their present- and future-directed intentions. For example, if an agent intends to hardboil an egg and knows he has only one egg (and cannot get any more in time), he should not simultaneously intend to make an omelette.
> 3. *Agents "track" the success of their attempts to achieve their intentions.*

Not only do agents care whether their attempts succeed, but they are disposed to replan to achieve the intended effects if earlier attempts fail.

In addition to the above functional roles, it has been argued that intending should satisfy the following properties. If an agent intends to achieve p, then:

4. *The agent believes* p *is possible.*
5. *The agent does not believe he will not bring about* p.[5]
6. *Under certain conditions, the agent believes he will bring about* p.
7. *Agents need not intend all the expected side effects of their intentions*[6].

For example, imagine a situation not too long ago in which an agent has a toothache. Although dreading the process, the agent decides that he needs desperately to get his tooth filled. Being uninformed about anaesthetics, the agent believes that the process of having his tooth filled will necessarily cause him much pain. Although the agent intends to ask the dentist to fill his tooth, and, believing what he does, he is willing to put up with pain, the agent could surely deny that he thereby intends to be in pain.

Bratman argues that what one intends is, loosely speaking, a subset of what one chooses. Consider an agent as choosing one desire to pursue from among his competing desires and, in so doing, choosing to achieve some state of affairs. If the agent believes his action(s) will have certain effects, the agent has chosen those effects as well. That is, one chooses a "scenario" or a possible world. However, one does not intend everything in that scenario; for example, one need not intend harmful expected side effects of one's actions (though if one knowingly brings them about as a consequence of one's intended action, they have been brought about *intentionally*). Bratman argues that side effects do not play the same roles in the agent's planning as true intentions do. In particular, they are not goals whose achievement the agent will track; if the agent does not achieve them, he will not go back and try again.

We will develop a theory in which expected side effects are *chosen* but not intended.

1.4 *Intentions as a Composite Concept*

Intention will be modeled as a composite concept specifying what the agent has chosen and how the agent is committed to that choice. First, consider the desire that the agent has chosen to pursue as put into a new category. Call this chosen desire, loosely, a goal.[7] By construction, chosen desires are consistent. We will give them a possible-worlds semantics, and hence the agent will have chosen a set of worlds in which the goal/desire holds.

Next, consider an agent to have a *persistent goal* if he has a goal (that is, a chosen set of possible worlds) that will be kept at least as long as certain conditions hold. For example, for a fanatic these conditions might be that his goal has not been achieved but is still achievable. If either of those circumstances fails, even the fanatical agent must drop his commitment to achieving the goal. Persistence involves an agent's *internal* commitment to a course of events over time.[8] Although a persistent goal is a composite concept, it models a distinctive state of mind in which agents have both chosen and committed to a state of affairs.

We will model intention as a kind of persistent goal. This concept, and especially its variations allowing for subgoals, interpersonal subgoals, and commitments relative to certain other conditions, is interesting for its ability to model much of Bratman's analysis. For example, the analysis shows that agents need not intend the expected side effects of their intentions because agents need not be committed to the expected consequences of those intentions. To preview the analysis, persistence need not hold for expected side effects because the agent's *beliefs* about the linkage of the act and those effects could change.

Strictly speaking, the formalism predicts that agents only intend the logical equivalences of their intentions, and in some cases intend their logical consequences. Thus, even using a possible-worlds approach, one can get a fine-grained modal operator that satisfies many desirable properties of a model of intention.

2 Methodology

2.1 Strategy: A Tiered Formalism

The formalism will be developed in two layers: atomic and molecular. The foundational atomic layer provides the primitives for the rational action. At this level can be found the analysis of beliefs, goals, and actions. Most of the work here is to sort out the relationships among the basic modal operators. Although the primitives chosen are motivated by the phenomena to be explained, few commitments are made at this level to details of theories of rational action. In fact, many theories could be developed with the same set of primitive concepts. Thus, at the foundational level we provide a framework in which to express such theories.

The second layer provides new concepts defined out of the primitives. Upon these concepts, we develop a partial theory of rational action. Defined concepts provide economy of expression and may themselves be of theoretical significance because the theorist has chosen to form some definitions and not others. The use of defined concepts elucidates the origin of their important properties. For example, in modeling intention with persistent goals, one can see how various properties depend on particular primitive concepts.

Finally, although we do not do so in this paper (but see chapter 12), one can erect theories of rational interaction and communication on this foundation. By doing so, properties of communicative acts can be derived from the embedding logic of rational interaction, whose properties are themselves grounded in rational action.

2.2 Successive Approximations

The approach to be followed in this paper is to approximate the needed concepts with sufficient precision to enable us to explore their interactions. We do not take as our goal the development of an exceptionless theory but rather will be content to give plausible accounts that cover the important and frequent cases. Marginal cases (and arguments based on them) will be ignored when developing the first version of the theory.

2.3 Idealizations

The research presented here is founded on various idealizations of rational behavior. Just as initial progress in the study of mechanics was made by assuming frictionless planes, so too can progress be made in the study of rational action with the right idealizations. Such assumptions should approximate reality—for example, beliefs can be wrong and revised, goals not achieved and dropped—but not so closely as to overwhelm. Ultimately, choosing the right initial idealizations is a matter of research strategy and taste.

A key idealization we make is that no agent will attempt to achieve something forever—everyone has limited persistence. Similarly, agents will be assumed not to procrastinate forever. Although agents may adopt commitments that can only be given up when certain conditions (C) hold, the assumption of limited persistence requires that the agent eventually drop each commitment. Hence, it can be concluded that eventually conditions C hold. Only because of this assumption are we able to draw conclusions from an agent's adopting a persistent goal. Our strategy will be first to explore the consequences of fanatical persistence—commitment to a goal until it is believed to be achieved or unachievable. Then, we will weaken the persistence conditions to something more reasonable.

2.4 Map of the Paper

In the next sections of the paper we develop elements of a formal theory of rational action, leading up to a discussion of persistent goals and the consequences that can be drawn from them with the assumption of limited persistence. Then, we demonstrate the extent to which the analysis satisfies the above-mentioned desiderata for intention and show how the analysis of intention solves various classical problems. Finally, we extend the underlying concept of a persistent goal to a more general one and briefly illustrate the utility of that more general concept for rational interaction and communication. In particular, we show how agents can have interlocking commitments.

3 Elements of a Formal Theory of Rational Action

The basis of our approach is a theory of rational action. The theory is expressed in a logic whose model theory is based on a possible-worlds semantics. We propose a logic with four primary modal operators: BELief, GOAL, HAPPENS (what event happens next), and DONE (which event has just occurred). With these operators, we will characterize what agents need to know to perform actions that are intended to achieve their goals. The world will be modeled as a linear sequence of events (similar to linear time temporal models; see Lamport 1980, Lansky 1985).[9] By adding GOAL, we can model an agent's intentions.

As a general strategy, the formalism will be too strong. First, we have the usual consequential closure problems that plague possible world models for belief. These, however, will be accepted for the time being, and we welcome attempts to develop finer-grained semantics (for instance, Barwise and Perry 1983; Fagin and Halpern 1985). Second, the formalism will describe agents as satisfying certain properties that might generally be true, but for which there might be exceptions. Perhaps a process of nonmonotonic reasoning could smooth over the exceptions, but we will not attempt to specify such reasoning here (but see Perrault, this volume). Instead, we assemble a set of basic principles and examine their consequences for rational interaction. Finally, the formalism should be regarded as a description or specification *of* an agent, rather than one that any agent could or should use.

Most of the advantage of the formalism stems from the assumption that agents have a limited tolerance for frustration; they will not work forever to achieve their goals. Yet, because agents are (often) persistent in achieving their goals, they will work to achieve them. Hence, although all goals will be dropped, they will not be droped too soon.

3.1 Syntax
The language we will use has the usual connectives of a first-order language with equality, as well as operators for the propositional attitudes and for talking about sequences of events:

- (BEL x p) and (GOAL x p), which say that x has p as a belief or goal, respectively;
- (AGT x e), which that x is the only agent of the sequence of events e;
- $(e_1 \leq e_2)$, which says that e_1 is an initial subsequence of e_2;
- time propositions, which say that it is a certain time, as described below; and
- (HAPPENS a) and (DONE a), which say that a sequence of events describable by an *action expression* a will happen next or just happened, respectively.

An action expression here is built from variables ranging over sequences of events using the constructs of dynamic logic (see, for example, Harel 1979; Moore 1980; Pratt 1978):

- a;b is action composition;
- a|b is nondeterministic choice;
- p? is a test action;
- a* is repetition.

The usual programming constructs like IF/THEN actions and WHILE loops will be formed from these (see section 3.2.1). We will use e as a variable ranging over sequences of events, and a and b for action expressions.

Note that there are no syntactic constructs for (what we are calling) persistent goals or intentions. These will be defined out of the above formulas. For simplicity, we adopt a logic with no singular terms, using instead predicates and existential quantifiers. However, for readability, we will sometimes use constants. The interested reader can expand these into the full predicative form if desired.

3.2 Semantics

We will adapt the usual possible-worlds model for belief to goals and events. Informally, a possible world is a string of events that temporally extends infinitely in the past and future and characterizes a possible way the world could have been and could be. Because things will naturally change over a course of events, the truth of a proposition in our language depends not only on world in question but also on an index into that course of events (roughly, a time point).

For the sake of simplicity, these indices are modeled as integers, and possible worlds are modeled by elements of a set, T, of functions from the integers into a set, E, of primitive event types. If $\sigma \in T$, then $\sigma(n)$ is understood as the (unique) event that is happening at point n. We also assume that each event type has a single agent (taken from a set, P, of people) as given by a function Agt. For this paper, the only events that will be considered are those performed by an agent. Although there are no simultaneous primitive events in this model, an agent is not guaranteed to execute a sequence of events without events performed by other agents intervening.

To handle the part of the language that derives from standard first-order logic, we need a domain of quantification D that includes all people and finite sequences of events, and a relation I, which at every world and index point assigns to each k-place predicate symbol a k-ary relation over D. The truth of atomic sentences, conjunctions, quantifications, and so forth, is determined in the usual way. A formula (AGT x e) is true when the person designated by x is the agent of every event in the sequence designated by e. A formula $e_1 \leq e_2$ is true when the event sequence designated by e_1 is an initial subsequence of that designated by e_2.

Time propositions are currently just numerals that can be used to name index points on a course of events. However, for ease of exposition, we will write them as if they were time-date expressions such as 2:30PM/3/6/85. These will be true or false in a world at a given index iff the index is the same as that denoted by the time proposition (that is, numeral). Depending on the problem at hand, we may use timeless propositions, such as (At Robot NY). Other problems are more accurately modeled by conjoining a time proposition, such as (At Robot NY) $\land$ 2:30PM/3/6/85. Thus, if the above conjunction were a goal, both conjuncts would have to be true simultaneously.

Turning now to the attitudes, we imagine that at any given point agents have a collection of possibly conflicting or even contradictory opinions and desires about the world. We assume, however, that when it comes time to act, each agent chooses (if only momentarily) a consistent set of each to work with.[10] We call these the beliefs and goals, respectively, of the agent. As the world evolves—that is, agents perform actions—their beliefs and goals can and will normally change.

Although each world has a fixed, predetermined future, agents usually do not know which world they are in. Instead, some of these worlds are compatible with the agent's beliefs and goals. This is specified by means of two accessibility relations B and G. For a given agent x, $B(\varphi, x, n, \sigma^*)$ holds if the world σ^* could be the actual one as far as x is concerned at point n (that is, x has no beliefs at that point that could rule it out). Similarly, $G(\sigma, x, n, \sigma^*)$ holds if the world σ^* is satisfactory as far as x is concerned at point n (that is, x has no goals at that point that could rule it out). Stated differently, the B relation holds if σ^* is compatible with what x believes in world φ at point n (and similarly for G and goals). Thus, a formula (BEL x p) is true when p is true at every B-related world, and (GOAL x p) is true when p is true at every G-related world.

Turning now to actions, we must first be clear about what it means for an action to occur between two index points: e occurs through an interval if it designates the event sequence in that interval; a;b occurs if a occurs from the start up to some intermediate point and then b occurs from that point to the final one; a|b occurs if either a or b does; the test action, p?, occurs between two index points if they are the same point (that is, no events are involved) and if at that point p is true; finally, a* occurs through an interval if the interval can be broken into some number of subintervals and a occurs through each of them (in other words, a* means the repetition of a some number of times).

Given this, a formula (HAPPENS a) is true at some index point on a world when there is a subsequent (future) index point on that world such that a describes the sequence of events between the two index points. Similarly, (DONE a) is true at some index point when there is a previous (past) index point such that a describes the sequence of events between the two index points. So the former says that something describable by a will happen next, whereas the latter says that it just happened.

This completes our informal description of truth for our language. A semantic structure M has as components D, P, E, Agt, T, B, G, I, as described above. However, we will impose various additional constraints and assumptions on these components as we progress. A formula p is *satisfiable* if there is at least one structure M (satisfying these constraints and assumptions), world $\sigma \in T$, and integer index n, such that p is true at σ and n for this M. A well-formed formula p is *valid*, written $\models$ p, if its negation is not satisfiable.

3.2.1 Abbreviations   It will be convenient to adopt the following abbreviations:

Empty sequence: nil $\overset{def}{=}$ $(\forall x\ (x{=}x))$?.   a=NIL $\overset{def}{=}$ $\forall b\ (a{\leq}b)$.

As a test action, NIL always succeeds; as an event sequence, it is a subsequence of every other one.

Conditional action: [IF p THEN a ELSE b] $\overset{def}{=}$ p?;a | ~p?;b.

That is, as in dynamic logic, an if-then-else action is a disjunctive action of doing action a at a time at which p is true or doing action b at a time at which p is false. Note that the semantics of a conditional action does not require that the condition be believed by someone to be true. However, when agents execute conditionals with disjoint branches, they will have to believe the condition is true (or believe it is false).

While-loops: [WHILE p DO a] $\overset{def}{=}$ (p?;a)*; ~p?

While-loops are a sequence of doing action a zero or more times, prior to each of which p is true. After the iterated action stops, p is false.

Eventually: $\Diamond p \stackrel{def}{=} \exists x \text{ (HAPPENS } x;p?)$.
In other words, $\Diamond p$ is true (in a given possible world) if there is something that happens after which p holds, that is, if p is true at some point in the future.

Always: $\Box p \stackrel{def}{=} \sim \Diamond \sim p$.
$\Box p$ means that p is true throughout the course of events.
A useful application of $\Box$ is $\Box(p \supset q)$, in which no matter what happens, p still implies q. We can now distinguish between $p \supset q$'s being logically valid, its being true in all courses of events, and its merely being true after some event happens.

3.2.2 Constraints on the Model
We impose the following constraints on the model:

> *Consistency*: B is Euclidean, transitive, and serial; G is serial. B's being Euclidean essentially means that the worlds the agent thinks are possible (given what is believed) form an equivalence relation but do not necessarily include the real world (Halpern and Moses 1985). Seriality implies that beliefs and goals are (separately) consistent. This is enforced by there always being a world that is either B- or G-related to a given world.
>
> *Realism*: $\forall \sigma, \sigma^*$, if $\langle \sigma, n \rangle G[p]\sigma^*$, then $\langle \sigma, n \rangle B[p]\sigma^*$. In other words, $G \subseteq B$. That is, the worlds that are consistent with what the agent has chosen are not ruled out by his beliefs. Without this constraint, the agent could choose worlds involving (for example) future events that he believes will never happen. We believe this condition to be so strong, and its model-theoretical statement so simple, that it deserves to be imposed as a constraint. It ensures that an agent does not want the opposite of what he believes to be unchangeable. For example, assume an agent knows that he will die in two months (and he does not believe in life after death). One would not expect that agent, if still rational, to buy a plane ticket to Miami in order to play golf three months hence. Simply, an agent cannot choose such worlds since they are not compatible with what he believes.

3.3 Properties of the Model
We begin by exploring the temporal and action-related aspects of the model, describing properties of our modal operators HAPPENS, DONE, and $\Diamond$. Next, we discuss belief and relate it to the temporal modalities. Then, we explore the relationships among all these and GOAL. Finally, we characterize an agent's persistence in achieving a goal.

Valid properties of the model are termed "Propositions." Properties that constitute our theory of the interrelationships among agent's beliefs, goals, and actions will be stated as "Assumptions." These are essentially non-logical axioms that constrain the models that we consider.[11] The term "Theorem" is reserved for major results.

3.3.1 Events and Action Expressions   The framework proposed here separates primitive events from action expressions. Examples of primitive events might include moving an arm, grasping, exerting force, and uttering a word or sentence. Action expressions denote sequences of primitive events that satisfy certain properties. For example, a movement of a finger may result in a circuit being closed, which may result in a light coming on. We will say that one primitive event happened, but one that can be characterized by various complex action expressions. This distinction between primitive events and complex action descriptions must be kept in mind when characterizing real-world phenomena or natural-language expressions.

For example, to say that an action a occurs, we use (HAPPENS a). To characterize world states that are brought about, we use (HAPPENS $\sim$ p?;a;p?), saying that event a brings about p. To be a bit more concrete, one would not typically have a primitive event type for closing a circuit. So, to say that John closed the circuit, one would say that John did something (perhaps a sequence of primitive events) causing the circuit to be closed—∃e (DONE $\sim$ (Closed c)?;e;(Closed c)?.

Another way to characterize actions and events is to have predicates be true of them. For example, one could have (Walk e) to mean that a given event (type) is a walking event. This way of describing events has the advantage of allowing complex properties (such as running a race) to hold for an undetermined (and unnamed) sequence of events. However, because the predications are made about the events, not the attendant circumstances, this method does not allow us to describe events performed only in certain circumstances. We will need to use both methods for describing actions.

3.3.2 Properties of Acts/Events under HAPPENS   We adopt the usual axioms characterizing how complex action expressions behave under HAPPENS, as treated in a dynamic logic (for example, Harel 1979; Moore 1980; Pratt 1978), including the following:

Proposition 1   Properties of complex acts

$\models$ (HAPPENS a;b) $\equiv$ (HAPPENS a;(HAPPENS b)?).

$\models$ (HAPPENS a|b) $\equiv$ (HAPPENS a) V (HAPPENS b).

$\models$ (HAPPENS p?;q?) $\equiv$ p $\wedge$ q.

$\models$ (HAPPENS a*;b) $\equiv$ (HAPPENS b | a;a*;b).

That is, action a;b happens next iff a happens next, producing a world state in which b then happens next. The "nondeterministic choice" action a|b (read "|" as "or") happens next iff a happens next or b does. The text action action p? happens next iff p is currently true. Finally, the iterative action a*;b happens next iff b happens or one step of the iteration has been taken, followed by a*;b again.

Among many additional properties, note that after doing action a, a would have just been done:

Proposition 2
$\models$ (HAPPENS a) $\equiv$ (HAPPENS a;(DONE a)?).

Also, if a has just been done, then just prior to its occurence, it was going to happen next:

Proposition 3
$\models$ (DONE a) $\equiv$ (DONE (HAPPENS a)?;a).

Although this may seem to say that the unfolding of the world is determined only by what has just happened, and is not random, this determinacy is entirely moot for our purposes. Agents need never know what possible world they are in and hence what will happen next. More serious would be a claim that agents have no "free will"—what happens next is determined without regard to their intentions. However, as we will see, this is not a property of agents; their intentions constrain their future actions. Next, observe that a test action is done whenever the condition holds:

Proposition 4
$\models$ p $\equiv$ (DONE p?).

That is, the test action filters out courses of events in which the proposition tested is false. The truth of Proposition 4 follows immediately from the definition of "?".

For convenience, let us define versions of DONE and HAPPENS that specify the agent of the act:

Definition 1
(DONE x a) $\stackrel{def}{=}$ (DONE a) $\wedge$ (AGT x a).

Definition 2
(HAPPENS x a) $\stackrel{def}{=}$ (HAPPENS a) $\wedge$ (AGT x a).

Finally, one distinction is worth pointing out. When action variables are bound by quantifiers, they range over sequences of events (more precisely, event types). When they are left free in a formula, they are intended as schematic and can be instantiated with complex action expressions.

3.3.3 Temporal Modalities: DONE, $\Diamond$, and $\Box$ Temporal concepts are introduced with DONE (for past happenings) and $\Diamond$ (read "eventually"). To say that p was true at some point in the past, we use $\exists e$ (DONE p?;e). $\Diamond$ is to be regarded in the "linear time" sense and is defined above. Essentially, $\Diamond$p is true iff somewhere in the future p becomes true. $\Diamond$p and $\Diamond \sim$p are jointly satisfiable. Since $\Diamond$p starts "now," the following property is also true:

Proposition 5
$\models$ p $\supset$ $\Diamond$p.

The following are trivial consequences:

Proposition 6
$\models \Diamond$(p $\lor$ q) $\land \Box \sim$q $\supset \Diamond$p.

Proposition 7
$\models \Box$(p $\supset$ q) $\land \Diamond$p $\supset \Diamond$q.

To talk about propositions that are not true now but will become true, we define:

Definition 3
(LATER p) $\stackrel{def}{=} \sim$p $\land \Diamond$p.

A property of this definition that follows from the equivalence of $\Diamond$p and $\Diamond \Diamond$p is:

Proposition 8
$\models \sim$(LATER $\Diamond$p).

3.3.4 Constraining Courses of Events   We will have occasion to state constraints on courses of events. To do so, we define the following:

Definition 4
(BEFORE p q) $\stackrel{def}{=} \forall$c (HAPPENS c;q?) $\supset \exists$a (a $\leq$ c) $\land$ (HAPPENS a;p?).

This definition states that p comes before q (starting at index *n* in the course of events) if, whenever q is true in a course of events, p has been true (after the index *n*). Obviously,

Proposition 9
$\models \Diamond$q $\land$ (BEFORE p q) $\supset \Diamond$p.

That is, if q is eventually true, and q's being true requires that p has been true, then eventually p holds. Furthermore, we have:

Proposition 10
$\models \sim$p $\supset$ (BEFORE ($\exists$e (DONE $\sim$p?;e;p?)) p).

This basically says that worlds are consistent—no proposition changes truth-value without some event happening. In particular, there is no notion in this model for the simple passage of time (without any intervening events) affecting anyone's beliefs or goals. One would like to adopt the view that some event must *cause* that change, but as yet there is no primitive relation of causality.

3.4 The Attitudes

BEL and GOAL characterize what is *implicit* in an agent's beliefs and goals (chosen desires), rather than what an agent actively or explicitly believes, or has as a goal.[12] That is, these operators characterize what *the world would be like* if the agent's beliefs and goals were true. Importantly, we do not include an operator for wanting, since desires need not consistent. Although desires certainly play an important role in determining goals and intentions, we assume that once an agent has sorted out his possibly inconsistent desires in deciding what he wishes to achieve, the worlds he will be striving for are consistent.

3.4.1 Belief   For simplicity, we assume the usual Hintikka-style axiom schemata for BEL (Halpern and Moses 1985) (corresponding to a "Weak S5" modal logic):

Proposition 11   Belief axioms

a. $\models \forall x \, (BEL \, x \, p) \wedge (BEL \, x \, (p \supset q)) \supset (BEL \, x \, q)$

b. $\models \forall x \, (BEL \, x \, p) \supset (BEL \, x \, (BEL \, x \, p))$

c. $\models \forall x \sim (BEL \, x \, p) \supset (BEL \, x \sim (BEL \, x \, p))$

d. $\models \forall x \, (BEL \, x \, p) \supset \sim (BEL \, x \sim p)$.

And we have the usual "necessitation" rule:

Proposition 12
If $\models$ p then $\models$ (BEL x p).

If p is a theorem (in other words, is valid), then it follows from the agent's beliefs at all times. For example, all tautologies follow from the agent's beliefs. Clearly, we also have:

Proposition 13
If $\models$ p then $\models$ (BEL x $\square$p).

That is, theorems are believed to be always true. Also, we introduce KNOW by definition:

Definition 5
(KNOW x p) $\overset{def}{=}$ p $\wedge$ (BEL x p).

Of course, this characterization of knowledge has many known difficulties, but it will suffice for present purposes. Next, we will say an agent is COMPETENT with respect to p if he is correct whenever he thinks p is true:

Definition 6
(COMPETENT x p) $\overset{def}{=}$ (BEL x p) ⊃ (KNOW x p).

Agents competent with respect to some proposition p adopt only beliefs about that proposition for which they have good evidence. For the purposes of this paper, we assume that agents are competent with respect to the primitive actions they have done:

Assumption 1
⊨ ∀x,e (AGT x e) ⊃ [(DONE e) ≡ (BEL x (DONE e))].

Note that this assumption does *not* hold when e is replaced by an arbitrary action expression, even if x is the agent. For example, if the agent does not know the truth-value of p after just doing a, the agent may have done the action a;p? without realizing it was done. But the assumption rules out unknowing execution of *primitive actions by an agent*.

We also assume that an agent cannot believe he is the agent of what is to happen next without his knowing what the next primitive event will be. That is, if an agent thinks he is about to do *something*, then there must be some initial sequence that he believes he is going to do next:

Assumption 2
⊨ (BEL x ∃e ≠ NIL (HAPPENS x e)) ⊃ ∃e ≠ NIL (BEL x (HAPPENS x e)).

The antecedent would be true if the agent believes he is about to do a complex action (for instance, one containing a disjunction, or an iteration until a condition is satisfied). So, there may be uncertainty in his mind about what he is about to do. But for anything to happen at all, we assume that there must be some nonempty initial sequence that he has settled on and thinks he is going to do next.

3.5 Goals
At a given point in a course of events, agents choose worlds they would like (most) to be in—ones in which their *goals* are true. (GOAL x p) is meant to be read as p is true in all worlds, accessible from the current world, that are compatible with the agent's goals. Roughly, p follows from the agent's goals. Since agents choose entire worlds, they choose the (logically and physically) necessary consequences of their goals. At first glance, this appears troublesome if we interpret the facts that are true in all worlds compatible with an agent's goals as intended. However, intention will involve a form of commitment that will rule out such consequences as being intended, although they are chosen.

GOAL has the following properties:

Proposition 14   Consistency
$\models \forall x \, (\text{GOAL } x \, p) \supset \sim(\text{GOAL } x \sim p)$.

What is implicit in someone's goals is closed under consequence:

Proposition 15
$\models (\text{GOAL } x \, p) \wedge (\text{GOAL } x \, p \supset q) \supset (\text{GOAL } x \, q)$.

Again, we have a necessitation property:

Proposition 16
If $\models p$ *then* $\models (\text{GOAL } x \, p)$.

That is, if p is a theorem, it is true in all chosen worlds. However, agents can distinguish such "trivial" goals from others, as explained below.

3.5.1 Achievement Goals   Agents can distinguish between achievement goals and maintenance goals. Achievement goals are those the agent believes to be currently false; maintenance goals are those the agent already believes to be true. We will not be concerned in this paper with maintenance goals. However, to characterize achievement goals, we use:

Definition 7
$(\text{A-GOAL } x \, p) \stackrel{def}{=} (\text{GOAL } x \, (\text{LATER } p)) \wedge (\text{BEL } x \sim p)$.

That is, x believes (and therefore accepts) that p is currently false, but in his chosen worlds p is eventually true. In other words, this is the more standard notion of goals, where what is desired for the future is something that is believed to be currently false.

3.5.2 No Persistence/Deferral Forever   Agents are limited in both their persistence and their procrastination. They cannot try forever to achieve their goals; eventually they give up. On the other hand, agents do not forever defer working on their goals. The assumption below captures both of these desiderata:

Assumption 3
$\models \Diamond \sim(\text{GOAL } x \, (\text{LATER } p))$.

Thus, agents eventually drop all achievement goals. Because one cannot conclude that agents always act on their goals, one needs to guard against infinite procrastination. However, one could have an agent who forever fails to achieve his goals but believes success is still achievable. The limiting case here is an agent who executes an infinite loop. Another case is that of a compulsive gambler who continually thinks success is just around the corner. Our assumption rules out these pathological cases from consideration but still allows agents to try hard. Finally, since no one ever said the world is fair (in the computer science sense), an agent who is ready to act in what he believes to be the correct circumstance may never get a chance to execute his action because the world keeps changing. We only require that if faced with such monumental unfairness, the agent reach the conclusion that the act is impossible.

One might object that there are still achievement goals that agents could keep forever. For example, one might argue that the goal expressed by "I always want more money than I have" is kept forever (or at least as long as the agent is alive);[13] but consider a plausible logical representation of that sentence in our formal language:

$$\Box[\text{GOAL I } \exists x,y \text{ (HAVE I } x) \land y > x \land (\text{LATER (HAVE I } y))].$$

This sentence may be true, but it does not express an achievement goal since at some points the existential part may be believed to be true (and the goal is merely to maintain that truth). To express the achievement aspect, it is necessary to quantify into the GOAL clause as in

$$\Box[\forall x \text{ (KNOW I (HAVE I } x)) \supset (\text{A-GOAL I } \exists y \text{ (} y > x \land (\text{HAVE I } y)))].$$

But here, there is no single sentence that the agent always has as a goal; the goal changes because of the quantified variables. Hence, one cannot argue he keeps anything as an achievement goal forever. Instead, the agent forever gets new achievement goals.

Important consequences will follow from Assumption 3 when combined with an agent's commitments. First, we need to examine what, in general, are the consequences of having goals.

3.5.3 Goals and Their Consequences

Unlike BEL, GOAL needs to be characterized in terms of all the other modalities. In particular, we need to specify how goals interact with an agent's beliefs about the future.

The semantics of GOAL specifies that worlds compatible with an agent's goals must be included in those compatible with his beliefs. This is reflected in the following property:

Proposition 17
$\models (\text{BEL } x \text{ } p) \supset (\text{GOAL } x \text{ } p).$

From the semantics of BEL and GOAL, one sees that p will be evaluated at the same point in the B- and G-accessible worlds. So, if an agent believes p is true now, he cannot now want it to be currently false; agents do not choose what they cannot change. Conversely, if p is now true in all the agent's chosen worlds, then the agent does not believe it is currently false. For example, if an agent believes he has not just done event e, then he cannot have (DONE x e) as a goal. Of course, he *can* have (LATER (DONE x e)) as a goal.

This relationship between BEL and GOAL makes more sense when one considers the future. Let p be of the form $\Diamond$q. From Proposition 17, we derive that if the agent wants q to be true sometime in the future, he does not believe it will be forever false. Conversely, let p be a proposition of the form $\Box$q. So, if an agent believes q is forever true (an example would be a tautology), Proposition 17 says that any worlds that the agent chooses must have q's being true as well.

Notice that although an agent may have to put up with what he believes is inevitable, he may do so reluctantly, knowing that if he should change his mind about the inevitability of that state of affairs, his choices would change. For example, the following is satisfiable:

$$(\text{BEL } x \ \Diamond p \ \wedge \ \Box[\sim(\text{BEL } x \ \Diamond p) \supset (\text{GOAL } x \ \Box \sim p)]),$$

That is, the agent can believe p is inevitable (and hence in all the agent's chosen worlds p will eventually be true) but at the same time believe that if he ever stops believing it is inevitable, he will choose worlds in which it is never true.

Notice also that, as a corollary of Proposition 17, an agent's beliefs and goals "line up" with respect to his own primitive actions that happen next:

Proposition 18
$\models \forall x, e \ (\text{BEL } x \ (\text{HAPPENS } x \ e)) \supset (\text{GOAL } x \ (\text{HAPPENS } x \ e)).$

That is, if an agent believes he is about to do something next, then its happening next is true in all his chosen worlds. Of course, "successful" agents are ones who choose what they are going to do before believing they are going to do it; they come to believe they are going to do something because they have made certain choices. We discuss this further in our treatment of intention.

Next, as another simple subcase, consider the *consequences* of facts the agent believes hold in all of that agent's chosen worlds:

Proposition 19   Expected consequences
$\models (\text{GOAL } x \ p) \ \wedge \ (\text{BEL } x \ p \supset q) \supset (\text{GOAL } x \ q).$

By Proposition 17, if an agent believes $p \supset q$ is true, $p \supset q$ is true in all his chosen worlds. Hence, by Proposition 15, q follows from his goals as well.

At this point we are finished with the foundational level, having described agents' beliefs and goals, events, and time. In so doing, we have characterized agents as not striving for the unachievable and as eventually foregoing the contingent. What is missing is *commitment*, to ensure that none of these goals are given up too easily.

4 Persistent Goals

To capture *one* grade of commitment (fanatical) that an agent might have toward his goals, we define a persistent goal, P-GOAL, to be one that the agent will not give up until he thinks it has been satisfied, or until he thinks it will never be true. The latter case could arise easily if the proposition p is one that specifically mentions a time. Once the agent believes that time is past, he believes the proposition is impossible to achieve. Specifically, we have

Definition 8
$$(\text{P-GOAL x p}) \stackrel{def}{=} (\text{GOAL x (LATER p)}) \wedge (\text{BEL x} \sim\text{p}) \wedge$$
$$[\text{BEFORE ((BEL x p)} \vee (\text{BEL x } \square \sim\text{p}))$$
$$\sim (\text{GOAL x (LATER p))].$$

Notice the use of LATER, and hence $\Diamond$, above. Clearly, P-GOALs are achievement goals; the agent's goal is that p be true in the future, and he believes it is not currently true. As soon as the agent believes it will never be true, we know the agent must drop his goal (by Proposition 17), and hence his persistent goal. Moreover, as soon as an agent believes p is true, the belief conjunct of P-GOAL requires that he drop the persistent goal of achieving p. Thus, these conditions are necessary and sufficient for dropping a persistent goal. However, the BEFORE conjunct does *not* say that an agent *must* give up his *simple* goal when he thinks it is satisfied, since agents may have goals of maintenance. Thus, achieving one's persistent goals may convert them into maintenance goals.

4.1 The Logic of P-GOAL
The logic of P-GOAL is weaker than one might expect. Unlike GOAL, P-GOAL does not distribute over conjunction or disjunction, and it is closed only under logical equivalence. First, we examine conjunction and disjunction Then, we turn to implication.

4.1.1 Conjunction, Disjunction, and Negation   P-GOAL behaves as follows under conjunction, disjunction, and negation:

Proposition 20   The logic of P-GOAL

a. $\not\models (\text{P-GOAL x p}\wedge\text{q}) \supsetneq (\text{P-GOAL x p}) \wedge (\text{P-GOAL x q}).$

b. $\not\models (\text{P-GOAL x p}\vee\text{q}) \supsetneq (\text{P-GOAL x p}) \vee (\text{P-GOAL x q}).$

c. $\models (\text{P-GOAL x} \sim\text{p}) \supset \sim(\text{P-GOAL x p}).$

First, (P-GOAL x p∧q) does not imply (P-GOAL x p) ∧ (P-GOAL x q) because, although the antecedent is true, the agent might believe q is already true and thus cannot have q as a P-GOAL.[14] Conversely, (P-GOAL x p) $\wedge$ (P-GOAL x q) does not imply (P-GOAL x p$\wedge$q), because (GOAL x (LATER p)) $\wedge$ (GOAL x (LATER q)) does not imply (GOAL x (LATER p$\wedge$q)); p and q could be true at different times.

Similarly, (P-GOAL x p$\vee$q) does not imply (P-GOAL x p) $\vee$ (P-GOAL x q) because (GOAL x (LATER p$\vee$q)) does not imply (GOAL x (LATER p)) $\vee$ (GOAL x (LATER q)); p could come to hold in some possible worlds compatible with the agent's goals, and q in others. However, neither p nor q is forced to hold in all G-accessible worlds. Moreover, the implication does not hold in the other direction either, because of the belief conjunct of P-GOAL; although the agent may believe $\sim$p or he may believe $\sim$q, that does not guarantee he believes $\sim$(p$\vee$q) (that is, $\sim$p$\wedge$q).

With respect to the last property, note that although it is impossible to be committed to achieving both p and $\sim$p (since one of them is not believed to be false), it is quite possible to be committed to achieving (p$\wedge \Diamond \sim$p). However, because of Proposition 8, which says that (LATER $\Diamond$p) is always false, (GOAL x (LATER $\Diamond$p)) is always false, and so (P-GOAL x $\Diamond$p) is always false.

4.1.2 No Consequential Closure of P-GOAL   We demonstrate that P-GOAL is closed only under logical equivalence. Below are listed the possible relationships between a proposition p and a consequence q, which we term a *side effect*. Assume in all cases that (P-GOAL x p). Then, depending on the relationship of p to q, we have the cases shown in table 3.1. We will say a "case" fails, indicated by an "N" in the third column, if (P-GOAL x q) does not hold.

Case 1 fails for a number of reasons, most importantly because the agent's persistent goals depend on his beliefs, not on the facts. However, consider Case 2. Even though the agent may believe p $\supset$ q holds, Case 2 fails because that implication cannot affect the agent's persistent goals, which refer to p's being true *later*. That is, the agent believes p is false and does not have the goal of its currently being true.

Table 3.1
P-GOAL and progressively stronger relationships between p and q.

Case	Relationship of p to q	(P-GOAL x q)?
1	p $\supset$ q	N
2	(BEL x (p $\supset$ q))	N
3	(BEL x $\square$(p $\supset$ q))	N
4	$\square$(BEL x $\square$(p $\supset$ q))	Y/N
5	$\models$ p $\supset$ q	Y/N
6	$\models$ p $\equiv$ q	Y

Consider Case 3, where the agent believes the implication *always* holds. Although Proposition 17 tells us that the agent has q as a goal, we show that the agent does not have q as a *persistent* goal. Recall that P-GOAL was defined so that the only reason an agent could give up a persistent goal was if it were believed to be satisfied or believed to be forever false. However, side effects are goals only because of a belief. If the belief changes, the agent need no longer choose worlds in which p ⊃ q holds and thus need no longer have q has a goal. However, the agent would have dropped the goal for reasons other than those stipulated by the definition of persistent goal and so does not have it as a persistent goal.

Now consider Case 4, in which the agent *always* believes the implication. Again, q need not be a persistent goal but for a different reason. Here, an agent could believe the side effect already held. Hence, by the second clause in the definition of P-GOAL, the agent would not have a persistent goal. This reason also blocks Case 5, closure under logical consequence. However, instances of Case 4 and Case 5 in which the agent does not believe the side effect already holds *would* require the agent to have the side effect as a persistent goal. Thus, we do not get closure in these cases, but because of what we believe to be the wrong reasons. A finer-grained semantic model than possible worlds might block closure in a more satisfying way by allowing agents to direct their goals toward situations that do not include side effects. Finally, in Case 6, where q is logically equivalent to p, the agent has q as a persistent goal. Having shown what cannot be deduced from P-GOAL, we now turn to its major consequences.

4.2 Persistent Goals Constrain Future Beliefs and Actions

An important property of agents is that they eventually give up their achievement goals (Assumption 3). Hence, if an agent takes on a P-GOAL, he must give it up subject to the constraints imposed by P-GOAL:

Proposition 21
$\models$ (P-GOAL x q) ⊃ $\Diamond$[(BEL x q) ∨ (BEL x $\square \sim$ q)].

This proposition is a direct consequence of Assumption 3, the definition of P-GOAL, and Proposition 6. In other words, because agents eventually give up their achievement goals, and because the agent has adopted a persistent goal to bring about such a proposition q, eventually the agent must believe q or believe q will never come true. We now give a crucial theorem:

Theorem 1   From persistence to eventualities
If someone has a persistent goal of bringing about p, p *is within his area of competence, and, before dropping his goal, the agent will not believe* p *will never occur, then eventually* p *becomes true:*

$$\models (\text{P-GOAL } y \text{ } p) \land \Box(\text{COMPETENT } y \text{ } p)$$
$$\land \sim(\text{BEFORE (BEL } y \Box \sim p) \sim(\text{GOAL } y \text{ (LATER } p))) \supset \Diamond p.$$

Proof

By Proposition 21, the agent eventually believes either that p is true or that p is unachievable. If he eventually thinks p is true, since he is always competent with respect to p, he is correct. The other alternative sanctioned by Proposition 21, that the agent believes p is unachievable, is ruled out by the assumption that (it so happens to be the case that) any belief of the agent that the goal is unachievable can come only *after* the agent drops his goal. Hence, by Proposition 6, the goal comes about. ∎

If an agent who is not competent with respect to p adopts p as a persistent goal, we cannot conclude that eventually p will be true, since the agent could incorrectly come to believe that p holds. If the goal is not persistent, we also cannot conclude $\Diamond p$, since the agent could give up the goal without achieving it. If the goal actually is unachievable, but the agent does not know this and commits to achieving it, then we know that eventually, perhaps after trying hard to achieve it, the agent will come to believe it is forever false and give up.

4.2.1 Acting on Persistent Goals   As mentioned earlier, one cannot conclude that, merely by committing to a chosen proposition (set of possible worlds), the agent will act; someone else could bring about the desired state of affairs. However, if the agent knows that he is the only one who could bring it about, then, under certain circumstances, we can conclude the agent will act. For example, propositions of the form (DONE x a) can only be brought about by the agent x. So, if an agent always believes the act a can be done (or at least believes it for as long as he keeps the persistent goal), the agent will act.

A simple instance of Proposition 21 is one where q is (HAPPENS x a). Such a goal is one where the next thing that happens is his doing action a. Eventually, either the agent believes the next action is his, or the agent eventually comes to believe he will never get the chance to perform it. We cannot guarantee that the agent will actually do the action next, for someone else could act before him. If the agent never believes his act will never be done, then by Proposition 21, the agent will eventually believe (HAPPENS x a). By Proposition 18, we know that (GOAL x (HAPPENS x a)). *If* the agent acts just when he believes the next act is his, we know that he did so believing it would happen next and having its happening next as his goal. One could say, loosely, that the agent acted "intentionally."

Bratman (1984) argues that one applies the term "intentionally" to foreseen consequences as well as to truly intended ones. That is, one intends a subset of what is done intentionally. Proposition 18 requires only that agents have expected effects as goals, not that they have them as persistent goals. Hence, the agent would in fact bring about intentionally all those foreseen consequences of his goal that actually obtain from his doing the act. However, he would not be committed to bringing about the side effects, and thus he did not intend to do so.

If agents adopt *time-limited* goals, such as (BEFORE (DONE x e) 2:30PM/ 6/24/86), one *cannot* conclude the agent definitely will act *in time*, even if he believes it is possible to act. Simply, the agent might wait too long. However, one *can* conclude (see below) that the agent will not adopt another persistent goal to do a non-NIL act he believes would make the persistent goal unachievable. Still, the agent could unknowingly (and hence, by Proposition 18, accidentally) make his persistent goal forever false. If one makes the further assumption that agents always know what they are going to do just before doing it, then one can conclude that agents will not in fact do anything to make their persistent goals unachievable.

All these conclusions are, we believe, reasonable. However, they do not indicate what the "normal" case is. Instead, we have characterized the possibilities, and we await a theory of default reasoning to further describe the situation.

One final complication worth noting is that even if we assume that agents are perfectly competent about beliefs and goals, it is unreasonable to assume that they are competent about their persistent goals. They may have incorrect beliefs about the BEFORE clause and misjudge the conditions under which they give up their achievement goals. A simple case is an agent who makes a promise (perhaps hastily), thinks he is committed, and then, finding out more about the situation, changes his mind and drops his goal without believing that it is satisfied or unachievable. Given that P-GOAL is based on whether an agent really is committed, the question remains as to the role of beliefs in one's commitments in a theory of this type.

5   Intention as a Kind of Persistent Goal

With our foundation laid, we are now in a position to define the concept of intention. There will be two defining forms for INTEND, depending on whether the argument is an action or a proposition.

5.1   INTEND$_1$

Typically, one intends to do actions. Accordingly, we define INTEND$_1$ to take an action expression as its argument.

Definition 9
(INTEND$_1$ x a) $\stackrel{def}{=}$ (P-GOAL x [DONE x (BEL x (HAPPENS a))?;a]),
where a is any action expression.

Let us examine what this says. First of all, (fanatically) intending to do an action a is a special kind of commitment (that is, persistent goal) to have done a. However, it is not a commitment just to doing a, for that would allow the agent to be committed to doing something accidentally or unknowingly. It seems reasonable to require that the agent be committed to believing he is about to do the intended action, and then doing it. Thus, intentions are future-directed, but here directed toward something happening *next*. This is as close as we can come to present-directed intention.

Second, it is a commitment to success—to having done the action. As a contrast, consider the following inadequate definition of INTEND$_1$:

(INTEND$_1$ x a) $\stackrel{def?}{=}$ (P-GOAL x ∃e (HAPPENS x e; [DONE x a]?)).

This would say that an intention is a commitment to being *on the verge of* doing some event e, after which x would have just done a.[15] Of course, being on the verge of doing something is not the same as doing it; any unforeseen obstacle could permanently derail the agent from ever performing the intended act. This would not be much of a commitment.

5.1.1 Intending Actions   Let us apply INTEND$_1$ to each kind of action expression. First, consider intentions to "test" p. (INTEND$_1$ x p?) expands into

(P-GOAL x (DONE x [BEL x (HAPPENS x p?)]?;p?)).

By Proposition 1, this is equivalent to (P-GOAL x (DONE x (KNOW x p)?)), which reduces to (P-GOAL x (KNOW x p)). That is, the agent is committed to coming to know p (and he does not know it now). However, the agent is not committed to bringing about p himself.

Second, consider action expressions of the form e;p?. An example would be felling a tree:

∃e (Chopping e T) ∧ (Tree T) ∧ (INTEND$_1$ x e;(Down T)?).

That is, there is a chopping event (type) e, such that the agent is committed to felling the tree by doing e, and he believes just prior to doing it that it that it will indeed fell the tree. Notice that e is quantified outside of the INTEND$_1$. This type of intention is appropriate when there is a fixed event (or event sequence) that an agent is willing to commit to. For example, with a small tree and a large axe, an agent may be very confident that the chopping event will do the trick.

However, not all trees are like this. Fortunately, chopping events can be repeated, although it need not be obvious how many times. Thus, certain intentions cannot be characterized in terms of a fixed sequence of events—an agent may never come to believe of any given event sequence that it will achieve the intention. In this case the intention might be expressed by

$$\exists e \ (\text{Chopping } e \ T) \wedge (\text{Tree } T) \wedge$$
$$(\text{INTEND}_1 \ x \ [\text{WHILE} \sim (\text{Down } T) \ \text{DO } e]).$$

That is, the agent intends to do e repeatedly until the tree is down. It is important to notice that at no time does the agent need to know precisely which chopping event will finally knock down the tree. Instead, the agent is committed solely to executing the chopping event until the tree is down. To give up the commitment (that is, the persistent goal) constituting the intention, the agent must eventually come to believe he has done the iterative action believing it was about to happen. Also, in virtue of the definition of iterative actions, we know that when the agent believes he has done the iterative action, he will believe the condition is false (here, he will believe that the tree is down).

Finally, consider intending a conditional action. $(\text{INTEND}_1 \ x \ [\text{IF } p \ \text{THEN } a$ ELSE b]) expands into

$$(\text{P-GOAL } x \ (\text{DONE } x \ [\text{BEL } x \ (\text{HAPPENS } x \ [\text{IF } p \ \text{THEN } a \ \text{ELSE } b])]?;$$
$$[\text{IF } p \ \text{THEN } a \ \text{ELSE } b])).$$

So, we know that eventually (unless, of course, he comes to believe the conditional is forever false), he will believe he has done the conditional in a state in which he believed he was just about to do it. By Assumption 2, an agent cannot believe he is about to do something without at least having some specific first step in mind. Thus, an agent cannot believe he is about to do a conditional involving two distinct primitive events without either believing the condition is true or believing the condition is false. So, if one intends to do a conditional action, one expects (with the usual caveats) not to be forever ignorant about the condition. This seems just right.

In summary, we have defined intending to do an action in a way that captures many reasonable properties, some of which are inherited from the commitments involved in adopting a persistent goal. However, it is often thought that one can intend to achieve states of affairs in addition to just actions. Some cases of this are discussed above. But INTEND_1 cannot express an agent's intending to do *something* himself to achieve a state of affairs, since the event variables are quantified outside INTEND_1. To allow for this case, we define another kind of intention, INTEND_2.

5.2 INTEND_2

One might intend to become rich, to become happy, or (perhaps controversially) to kill one's uncle,[16] without having any idea how to achieve that state of affairs, not even having an enormous disjunction of possible options. In these cases we will say the agent x is committed merely to doing something himself to bring about a world state in which (RICH x) or (HAPPY x) or (DEAD u) hold. Notice that because of the constraints that come along with adopting such a commitment, this is stronger than having only a desire or a simple goal:

Definition 10
(INTEND$_2$ x p) $\overset{def}{=}$ (P-GOAL x
$\exists$e (DONE x [(BEL x $\exists$e' (HAPPENS x e';p?)) $\wedge$
$\sim$(GOAL x $\sim$(HAPPENS x e;p?))]?;e;p?)).

We will explain this definition in a number of steps. First, notice that to INTEND$_2$ to bring about p, an agent is committed to doing some sequence of events e himself, after which p holds. However, as earlier, to avoid allowing an agent to intend to make p true by committing himself to doing something accidentally or unknowingly, we require the agent to think he is about to do *something* (event sequence e') bringing about p.[17] From Assumption 2 we know that even though the agent believes only that he will do *some* sequence of events achieving p, the agent will know which initial step he is about to take.

Now, it seems to us that the only way, short of truly wishful thinking, that an agent can believe he is about to do something to bring about p is if the agent in fact has a *plan* (good, bad, or ugly) for bringing it about. In general, it is quite difficult to define what a plan is, or to define what it means for an agent to have a plan.[18] The best we can do, and that is not too far off, is to say that agent must believe be is about to do something (called e' here) that will bring about p. What is left for us to specify is under what conditions this belief is *justified*, ensuring, for instance, that the agent never has such a belief when he has absolutely no idea of how to proceed.[19]

Finally, we require that prior to doing e to bring about p, the agent not have as a goal e's not bringing about p. In other words, though there may be uncertainty in the agent's mind as to which action will ultimately bring about p (for example, he may have a conditional plan), what does in fact happen had better be compatible with the agent's goals. This condition is required to handle the following example, due to Chisholm (1966) and discussed by Searle (1983). An agent intends to kill his uncle. On the way to his uncle's house, this intention causes him to become so agitated that he loses control of his car and runs over a pedestrain, who happens to be his uncle. Although the uncle is dead, we would surely say that the action that the agent did was not what was intended.

Let us cast this problem in terms of INTEND$_2$, but without the condition stating that the agent should not want e not to bring about p. Call this INTEND$_{2'}$. So, assume the following is true: (INTEND$_{2'}$ x (DEAD u)). The agent thus has a commitment to doing some sequence of events resulting in his uncle's death, and immediately prior to doing it he has to believe there would be some sequence (e') that he was about to do that would result in the uncle's death. However, the example satisfies these conditions, but the event he in fact does that kills his uncle may not be the one foreseen to do so. A jury requiring only the weakened INTEND$_2$ to convict for first-degree murder would find the agent to be guilty. Yet, we clearly have the intuition that the death was accidental.

Searle argues that a prior intention should cause an "intention-in-action" that presents the killing of the uncle as an "intentional object," and this causation is self-referential. To explain Searle's analysis would take us too far afield. However, we can handle this case by adding the second condition to the agent's mental state that just prior to doing the action that achieves p, he also does not want what he in fact does, e, *not* to bring about p. In the case in question (intuitively), the agent's plan is to get to his uncle's house and take it from there. Driving onto the sidewalk (and killing someone) is not one of the possible outcomes of this plan and so is ruled out by the agent's beliefs and goals. So, in swerving off the road, the agent may still have believed he was about to do something e' that would kill his uncle (and, by Proposition 17, he wanted e' to kill his uncle), but even allowing for indeterminacy in his plan, in none of his chosen worlds is his swerving off the road what kills his uncle.

Hence, our analysis predicts that the agent did not do what he intended, even though the end state was achieved, and resulted from his adopting an intention. Let us now see how this analysis stacks up against the problems and related desiderata.

5.3 Meeting the Desiderata
In this section we show how various properties of the commonsense concept of intention are captured by our analysis based on P-GOAL. In what follows we will use INTEND$_1$ or INTEND$_2$ as best fits the example. Similar results hold for analogous problems posed with the other form of intention.

We reiterate Bratman's (1983, 1987) analysis of the roles that intentions typically play in the mental life of agents:

> 1. *Intentions normally pose problems for the agent; the agent needs to determine a way to achieve them.* If the agent intends an action as described by an action expression, then the agent knows in general terms what to do. However, the action expression may have disjunctions and conditionals in it. Hence, the agent would not know at the time of forming the intention just what will be done. However, we have argued in section 5.1.1 that eventually the agent will know what actions should be taken next. In the case of nonspecific intentions,

such as (INTEND$_2$ x p), we can derive via Proposition 21 that, under the normal circumstances where the agent does not learn that p is unachievable, the agent eventually believes there is some sequence of events that he has done prior to which he believed he was about to achieve p. Hence, our analysis shows the problem that is posed by adopting a nonspecific intention, but it does not encode the solution —that the agent will form a plan specifying just what that sequence of events would be.

2. *Intentions provide a "screen of admissibility" for adopting other intentions.* If an agent has an intention to do b, and the agent (always) believes that doing a prevents the achievement of b, then the agent cannot have the intention to do a;b, or even the intention to do a before doing b. Thus, the following holds:

Theorem 2   Screen of admissibility
$\models \forall$x (INTEND$_1$ x b) $\wedge$ $\square$(BEL x [(DONE x a) $\supset$
$\square \sim$(DONE x b)]) $\supset$ $\sim$(INTEND$_1$ x a;b),
*where a and b are arbitrary action expressions, and their free variables
have been bound outside.*

The proof is simply that there are no possible worlds in which the two intentions and the belief could all hold; in the agent's chosen worlds, if a has just been done, b will never be done. Hence, the agent cannot intend to do a before doing b. Similarly, if the agent first intends to do a and believes the above relationship between a and b, then the agent cannot also adopt the intention to do b.[20]

Notice that our agents cannot knowingly (and hence, by Proposition 18, deliberately) act against their own best interests. That is, they cannot intentionally act in a way that would make their persistent goals unachievable. Moreover, if they have adopted a time-limited intention, they cannot intend to do some other act knowing it would make achieving that time-limited intention forever false.

3. *Agents "track" the success of their attempts to achieve intentions.* In other words, agents keep their intentions after failure. Assume an agent has an intention to do a, then does something, e, thinking it will bring about the doing of a, but then comes to believe it did not. If the agent does not think that a can never be done, does the agent still have the intention to do a? Yes.

Theorem 3
$\models$ (DONE x [((INTEND$_1$ x a) $\wedge$ (BEL x (HAPPENS x a)))]?;e) $\wedge$
(BEL x $\sim$(DONE x a)) $\wedge$ $\sim$(BEL x $\square \sim$(DONE x a)) $\supset$
(INTEND$_1$ x a).

The proof of this follows immediately from the definition of INTEND$_1$, which is based on P-GOAL, which states that the intention cannot be given up until it is believed to have been achieved or to be unachievable. Here, the agent believes it has not been achieved and does not believe it to be unachievable. Hence, the agent keeps the intention.

Other writers have proposed that if an agent intends to do a, then

4. *The agent believes that* a *can be done.* We do not have a modal operator for possibility. But we can state, via Proposition 17, that the agent does not believe a will never be done. This is not precisely the same as the desired property but surely is close enough for current purposes.

5. *Sometimes the agent believes he will in fact do* a. This is a consequence of Theorem 1, which states the conditions (call them C) under which $\Diamond$(DONE x a) holds, given the intention to do a. So, if the agent believes he has the intention and believes C holds, $\Diamond$(DONE x a) follows from his beliefs as well.

6. *The agent does not believe he will never do* a. This principle is embodied directly in Proposition 17, which is validated by the simple model-theoretical constraint that worlds that are consistent with one's choices are included in worlds that are consistent with one's beliefs (worlds one thinks one might be in).

7. *Agents need not intend all the expected side effects of their intentions.* Recall that in an earlier problem an agent intended to have his teeth filled. Not knowing about anaesthetics (one could assume this took place just as they were being first used in dentistry), he believed that it was always the case that if one's teeth are filled, one will feel pain. One could even say that surely the agent *chose* to undergo pain. Nonetheless, one would not like to say that he intended to undergo pain.

This problem is easily handled in our scheme: Let x be the patient. Assume p is (Filled-teeth x), and q is (In-pain x). Now, we know that the agent has surely chosen pain (by Proposition 19). Given all this, the following holds (see section 4.1.2, Case 3):

$$\not\models (\text{INTEND}_2 \ x \ p) \wedge (\text{BEL} \ x \ \Box(p \supset q)) \supset (\text{INTEND}_2 \ x \ q).$$

Thus, agents need not intend the expected side effects of their intentions. Contrast this, however, with a situation where the belief in the inevitability of pain is unshakeable (section 4.1.2, Case 4):

$$\models (\text{INTEND}_2 \ x \ p) \wedge \Box(\text{BEL} \ x \ \Box(p \supset q)) \supset (\text{INTEND}_2 \ x \ q).$$

In this case, if the patient does not experience pain, he will believe that he has not had his tooth filled and so will persist, as with any intention.

At this point we have met the desiderata. Thus, the analysis so far has merit; but we are not finished. The definition of P-GOAL can be extended to make explicit what is only implicit in the commonsense concept of intention—the background of other justifying beliefs and intentions. Doing so will make our agents more reasonable.

6   An End of Fanaticism

As the formalism stands now, once an agent has adopted a persistent goal, he will not be deterred. For example, if agent A receives a request from agent B and decides to cooperate by adopting a persistent goal to do the requested act, B cannot "turn A off." This is clearly a defect that needs to be remedied. The remedy depends on the following definition:

Definition 11   Persistent, relativized goal
(P-R-GOAL x p q) $\overset{def}{=}$ (GOAL x (LATER p)) $\wedge$ (BEL x $\sim$p) $\wedge$
(BEFORE [(BEL x p) $\vee$ (BEL x $\square$ $\sim$p) $\vee$
(BEL x $\sim$q)] $\sim$(GOAL x (LATER p))).

That is, a necessary condition for giving up a P-R-GOAL is that the agent x believes it is satisfied, or believes it is unachievable, or believes $\sim$q. Such propositions q form a background that justifies the agent's intentions. In many cases such propositions constitute the agent's *reasons* for adopting the intention. For example, x could adopt the persistent goal to buy an umbrella relative to his belief that it will rain. He could then consider dropping his persistent goal should he come to believe that the forecast has changed.

Our analysis supports the observation that intentions can (loosely speaking) be viewed as the contents of plans (for example, Bratman 1987; Cohen and Perrault 1979; Pollack 1986). Although we have not given a formal analysis of plans here, the commitments one undertakes with respect to an action in a plan depend on the other planned actions, as well as the pre- and postconditions brought about by those actions. If x adopts a persistent goal p relative to (GOAL x q), then necessary conditions for x's dropping his goal include his believing that he no longer has q as a goal. Thus, (P-R-GOAL x p (GOAL x q)) characterizes an agent's having a persistent *subgoal* p relative to the *supergoal* q. An agent's dropping a supergoal is now a necessary (but not sufficient) prerequisite for his dropping a subgoal.[21] Thus, with the change to relativized persistent goals, we open up the possibility of having a complex web of interdependencies among the agent's goals, intentions, and beliefs. We always had the possibility of conditional P-GOALs. Now we have added background conditions that could lead to a revision of one's persistent goals. The definitions of intention given earlier can now be recast in terms of P-R-GOAL:

Definition 12
$(\text{INTEND}_1 \ x \ a \ q) \stackrel{def}{=} (\text{P-R-GOAL} \ x$
$\qquad\qquad [(\text{DONE} \ x \ (\text{BEL} \ x \ (\text{HAPPENS} \ x \ a))?;a)]$
$\qquad\qquad q).$

Definition 13
$(\text{INTEND}_2 \ x \ p \ q) \stackrel{def}{=} (\text{P-R-GOAL} \ x$
$\qquad\qquad \exists e \ (\text{DONE} \ x \ [(\text{BEL} \ x \ \exists e' \ (\text{HAPPENS} \ x \ e';p?)) \ \wedge$
$\qquad\qquad \sim (\text{GOAL} \ x \ \sim (\text{HAPPENS} \ x \ e;p?))]?;e;p?)$
$\qquad\qquad q).$

With these changes, the dependencies of an agent's intentions on his beliefs, other goals, intentions, and so on, become explicit. For example, we can express an agent's intending to take an umbrella relative to believing it will rain on March 5, 1986 as

$\exists e,u \ (\text{Take} \ u \ e) \ \wedge \ (\text{INTEND}_1 \ x \ e;3/5/86? \ \Diamond(\text{Raining} \ \wedge \ 3/5/86)).$

One can now describe agents whose primary concern is with the end result of their intentions, not so much with achieving those results themselves. An agent may first adopt a persistent goal to achieve p and then (perhaps because he does not know any other agent who will, or can, do so) subsequently decide to achieve p himself, relative to that persistent goal. So, the following is true of the agent: $(\text{P-GOAL} \ x \ p) \ \wedge \ (\text{INTEND}_2 \ x \ p \ (\text{P-GOAL} \ x \ p))$. If someone else achieves p (and the agent comes to believe it is true), the agent must drop $(\text{P-GOAL} \ x \ p)$ and is therefore free to drop the commitment to achieving p himself. Notice, however, that for goals that can be reachieved, the agent is *not forced* to drop the intention, as the agent may truly be committed to achieving p himself.

Matters get more interesting still when we allow the relativization conditions q to include propositions about other agents. For example, if q is $(\text{GOAL} \ y \ s)$, then y's goal is an *interpersonal supergoal* for x. The kind of intention that is engendered by a request seems to be P-R-GOAL. Namely, the speaker tries to bring it about that

$\qquad (\text{P-R-GOAL} \ \text{addressee} \ (\text{DONE} \ \text{addressee} \ a)$
$\qquad\qquad [\text{GOAL} \ \text{speaker} \ (\text{DONE} \ \text{addressee} \ a)]).$

The addressee can get "off the hook" if he learns the speaker does not want him to do the act after all.

Notice also that given this partial analysis of requesting, a hearer who merely says "OK" and thereby accedes to a request has (made it mutually believed that he has) adopted a commitment relative to the speaker's desires. In other words, he is committed *to* the speaker to do the requested action. This helps to explain how social commitments can arise out of communication. However, this is not the place to analyze speech acts (but see chapter 12 in this volume).

Finally, interlocking commitments are obtained when two agents are in the following states: (P-R-GOAL x p (GOAL y p)), and (P-R-GOAL y p (GOAL x p)). Each agent will keep his intention at least as long as the other keeps it. For example, each might have the intention to lift a table. But each would not bother to try unless the other also had the same intention.[22]

In summary, persistent relativized goals provide a useful analysis of intention and extend the commonsense concept by making explicit the conditions under which an agent will revise his intentions.

7 Conclusion

This paper establishes basic principles governing the rational balance among an agent's beliefs, actions, and intentions. Such principles provides specifications for artificial agents and approximate a theory of human action (as philosophers use the term). By making explicit the conditions under which an agent can drop his goals—that is, by specifying how the agent is *committed* to his goals—the formalism captures a number of important properties of intention. Specifically, the formalism provides analyses for Bratman's (1983, 1987) three characteristic functional roles played by intentions and shows how agents can avoid intending all the foreseen side effects of what they actually intend. Finally, the analysis shows how intentions can be adopted relative to a background of relevant beliefs and other intentions or goals. By relativizing one agent's intentions in terms of beliefs about another agent's intentions (or beliefs), we derive a preliminary account of interpersonal commitments.

The utility of the theory for describing people or artificial agents will depend on the fidelity of the assumptions. It does not seen unreasonable to require that a robot not procrastinate forever. Moreover, we surely would want a robot to be persistent in pursuing its goals, but not fanatically so. Furthermore, we would want a robot to drop goals given to it by other agents when it determines the goals need not be achieved. So, as a coarse description of an artificial agent, the theory seems workable.

The theory is not only useful for describing single agents in dynamic multiagent worlds, it is also useful for describing their interactions, especially via the use of communicative acts. In a companion paper (see chapter 12 in this volume) we present a theory of speech acts that builds on the foundations laid here.

Much work remains. The action theory only allows for possible worlds consisting of single courses of events. Further developments should include basing the analysis on partial worlds/situations (Barwise and Perry 1983) and on temporal logics that allow for simultaneous action (Allen 1984; Georgeff 1987; Lansky 1987). Finally, the theory would be strengthened by the use of default and nonmonotonic reasoning.

Notes

1. We thank Nils Nilsson for this apt phrase.
2. Exceptions include the work of Moore (1980), who analyzed the relationship of knowledge to action, and that of Appelt (1981) and Konolige (1980, 1985). However, none of these works addressed the issue of goals and intention.
3. Rosenschein (1981) discusses some of the difficulties of hierarchical planners and presents a formal theory of plans in terms of dynamic logic.
4. Or her. We use the masculine version here throughout.
5. The rationale for this property was discussed above.
6. Many theories of intention are committed to the undesirable view that expected side effects to one's intentions are intended as well.
7. Such desires are ones that speech act theorists claim to be conveyed by illocutionary acts such as requests.
8. This is not a *social* commitment. It remains to be seen whether the latter can be built out of the former.
9. This is unlike the integration of similar operators by Moore (1980), who analyzes how an agent's knowledge affects and is affected by his actions. That research meshed a possible-worlds model of knowledge with a situation-calculus-style, branching-time model of action (McCarthy and Hayes 1969). Our earlier work (Cohen and Levesque 1985) used a similar branching-time/dynamic logic model. However, the model's inability to express beliefs about what was in fact about to happen in the future led to many difficulties.
10. Without this choice, it is far from clear that any kind of coherent action would be possible.
11. One also needs to show that there is at least one model that satisfies these assumptions. This is straightforward.
12. For an exploration of the issues involved in explicit versus implicit belief, see Levesque 1984.
13. However, we have assumed immortal agents.
14. For example, someone may be committed to your knowing q but not to achieving q itself.
15. Notice that e could be the last step of a.
16. We are not trying to be morbid here, just setting up a classic example.
17. The definition does not use e instead of e' because that would quantify e into the agent's beliefs, requiring that he (eventually) have picked out a precise sequence of events that he thinks will bring about p. If we wanted to do that, we could use INTEND_1.
18. See Pollack 1986 for a discussion of these issues.
19. One possibility is to make sure this belief *only* arises by existential generalization from a belief involving a particular action description (that is, the plan) achieving p. However, one cannot express this constraint in our logic since one cannot quantify over action expressions.

20. Notice that the theorem does not require quantification over primitive acts but allows a and b to be arbitrary action expressions.
21. Also, notice that (P-GOAL x p) is now subsumed by (P-R-GOAL x p ~p).
22. Ultimately, one can envision circular interlinkages in which one agent adopts a persistent goal provided another agent has adopted it relative to the first agent's having adopted it relative to the second agent's having adopted it, and so on. For an analysis of circular propositions that might make such concepts expressible, see Barwise and Etchemendy 1987.

References

Allen, J. F. (1979). A plan-based approach to speech act recognition. Technical Report 121, Department of Computer Science, University of Toronto, Toronto, Ont.

Allen, J. F. (1984). Towards a general theory of action and time. *Artificial Intelligence* 23, 123–154.

Allen, J. F., and C. R. Perrault (1980). Analyzing intention in utterances. *Artificial Intelligence* 15, 143–178.

Appelt, D. (1981). Planning natural language utterances to satisfy multiple goals. Doctoral dissertation, Stanford University, Stanford, CA.

Barwise, J., and J. Etchemendy (1987). *The liar: An essay on truth and circularity.* New York: Oxford University Press.

Barwise, J., and J. Perry (1983). *Situations and attitudes.* Cambridge, MA: MIT Press.

Bratman, M. (1983). Castañeda's theory of thought and action. In J. Tomberlin, ed., *Agent, language, and the structure of the world: Essays presented to Hector-Neri Castañeda with his replies.* Indianapolis, IN: Hackett.

Bratman, M. (1984). Two faces of intention. *The Philosophical Review* 93, 375–405.

Bratman, M. (1987). *Intentions, plans, and practical reason.* Cambridge, MA: Harvard University Press.

Castañeda, H.-N. (1975). *Thinking and doing.* Dordrecht, Holland: D. Reidel.

Chisholm, R. M. (1966). Freedom and action. In K. Lehrer, ed., *Freedom and determinism.* New York: Random House.

Cohen, P. R., and H. J. Levesque (1980). Speech acts and the recognition of shared plans. In *Proceedings of the Third Biennial Conference,* Canadian Society for Computational Studies of Intelligence, Victoria, B.C.

Cohen, P. R., and H. J. Levesque (1985). Speech acts and rationality. In *Proceedings of the Twenty-third Annual Meeting,* Association for Computational Linguistics, Chicago, IL.

Cohen, P. R., and C. R. Perrault (1979). Elements of a plan-based theory of speech acts. *Cognitive Science* 3, 177–212. Reprinted in B. Webber and N. Nilsson, eds. (1981). *Readings in artificial intelligence.* Los Altos, CA: Morgan Kaufmann. Also in B. G. Grosz, K. Sparck Jones, and B. Webber, eds. (1986). *Readings in natural language processing.* Los Altos, CA: Morgan Kaufmann.

Fagin, R., and J. Y. Halpern (1985). Belief, awareness, and limited reasoning: Preliminary report. In *Proceedings of the Ninth International Joint Conference on Artificial Intelligence,* Los Angeles, CA.

Fikes, R., and N. J. Nilsson (1971). STRIPS: A new approach to the application of theorem proving to problem solving. *Artificial Intelligence* 2, 189–208.

Georgeff, M. P. (1983). Communication and interaction in multi-agent planning. In *Proceedings of the National Conference,* American Association for Artificial Intelligence, Washington, DC.

Georgeff, M. P. (1987). Actions, processes, and causality. In *Reasoning about actions and plans: Proceedings of the 1986 workshop.* Los Altos, CA: Morgan Kaufmann.

Georgeff, M. P., and A. L. Lansky (in preparation). A BDI semantics for the procedural reasoning system. Technical Note, Artificial Intelligence Center, SRI International, Menlo Park, CA.

Halpern, J. Y., and Y. O. Moses (1985). A guide to the modal logics of knowledge and belief. In *Proceedings of the Ninth International Joint Conference on Artificial Intelligence*, Los Angeles, CA.

Harel, D. (1979). *First-order dynamic logic*. New York: Springer-Verlag.

Harman, G. (1986). *Change in view*. Cambridge, MA: MIT Press.

Konolige, K. (1980). A first-order formalization of knowledge and action for a multiagent planning system. Technical Note 232, Artificial Intelligence Center, SRI International, Menlo Park, CA. (Appears in *Machine Intelligence 10*.)

Konolige, K. (1985). Experimental robot psychology. Technical Note 363, Artificial Intelligence Center, SRI International, Menlo Park, CA.

Konolige, K., and N. J. Nilsson (1980). Multiple-agent planning systems. In *Proceedings of the National Conference*, American Association for Artificial Intelligence, Stanford, CA.

Lamport, L. (1980). "Sometimes" is sometimes better than "not never." In *Proceedings of the Seventh Annual ACM Symposium on Principles of Programming Languages*, Association for Computing Machinery.

Lansky, A. L. (1985). Behavioral specification and planning for multiagent domains. Technical Note 360. Artificial Intelligence Center, SRI International, Menlo Park, CA.

Lansky, A. L. (1987). A representation of parallel activity based on events, structure, and causality. In *Reasoning about actions and plans: Proceedings of the 1986 workshop*. Los Altos, CA: Morgan Kaufmann.

Levesque, H. J. (1984). A logic of implicit and explicit belief. In *Proceedings of the National Conference*, American Association for Artificial Intelligence, Austin, TX.

McCarthy, J., and P. J. Hayes (1969). Some philosophical problems from the standpoint of artificial intelligence. In *Machine intelligence 4*. New York: American Elsevier.

Moore, R. C. (1980). Reasoning about knowledge and action. Technical Note 191, Artificial Intelligence Center, SRI International, Menlo Park, CA.

Pollack, M. E. (1986). Inferring domain plans in question-answering. Doctoral dissertation, Department of Computer Science, University of Pennsylvania, Philadelphia, PA.

Pratt, V. R. (1978). Six lectures on dynamic logic. Technical Report MIT/LCS/TM-117, Laboratory for Computer Science, MIT, Cambridge, MA.

Rosenschein, S. J. (1981). Plan synthesis: A logical perspective. In *Proceedings of the Seventh International Joint Conference on Artificial Intelligence*, Vancouver, B.C.

Rosenschein, J. S. (1986). Rational interaction: Cooperation among intelligent agents. Doctoral dissertation, Department of Computer Science, Stanford University, Stanford, CA.

Rosenschein, J. S., and M. R. Genesereth (1984). Communication and cooperation. Technical Report 84–5, Heuristic Programming Project, Department of Computer Science, Stanford University, Stanford, CA.

Searle, J. R. (1983). *Intentionality: An essay in the philosophy of mind*. New York: Cambridge University Press.

Chapter 4

Two Views of Intention: Comments on Bratman and on Cohen and Levesque

James F. Allen

The premise of this volume is that the fields of philosophy and artificial intelligence study many of the same problems and should be able to benefit greatly from each other's experience. I don't think that one could find a better demonstration of this than the papers by Michael Bratman and by Philip Cohen and Hector Levesque. Here are two papers studying the same topic, intention, from quite different starting points. It is satisfying to see evidence in both papers of influence from the other discipline.

Bratman, working from the tradition of the philosophy of mind and action, addresses the problem of defining the nature of intentions. Crucial to his argument is the subtle distinction between doing something intentionally and intending to do something. The former case might be paraphrased as deliberately doing an action. In particular, if one deliberately performs an act with the knowledge that it will have a certain effect, then one deliberately caused the effect as well. On the other hand, one may not be performing the action in order to achieve the effect—it might be a side effect that is unavoidable if the action is to be performed for other purposes. Thus, the agent may deliberately cause the effect yet not intend to cause it. Bratman expands on these ideas by invoking a notion of planning as studied in artificial intelligence. In essence, he develops the model sufficiently to show significant differences between intended and unintended consequences of plans (which I will call *goals* and *side effects*). One example involves the influence of goals and side effects on future behavior. In particular, if a situation changes such that a particular plan no longer achieves one of its goals, the agent will modify the plan. On the other hand, if the situation changes such that a side effect is no longer achieved, the agent does not need to revise the plan.

Cohen and Levesque, on the other hand, develop a logic in which intention is defined. In particular, they take several important properties that seem to hold intuitively for intention and develop a modal operator with these properties. Most important for them are that (1) an intention should not be abandoned without good reason (in the simplest version this means it should not abandoned unless the goal becomes true or the agent believes it is impossible to achieve) and (2) if an agent intends to achieve p, and q is a consequence of p, then it is not necessary that the agent intends q.

These properties, of course, are crucial to Bratman's development as well and account for the close overlap between the two papers.

With this close overlap of topics, it would be ideal if the papers formed a continuum, with Bratman providing the motivation for the distinctions and laying the overall framework for a theory of intention, and Cohen and Levesque developing a logic that could then be used as the basis of the mechanizable model of rational behavior. Though there are encouraging signs in this direction, the papers do fall short of meeting at some common ground. In the remainder of this commentary I will consider some of the issues that still need to be addressed. As can be expected, I will be asking Bratman for more detail and mechanism, and asking Cohen and Levesque for more generality and coverage.

The issues I would like to address in Bratman's paper are the nature of plans and the filter of inadmissibility. I think that his notion of plans may be closer to the traditional AI notion than he thinks, and I think that the notion of flat-out beliefs, though important, does not help much in defining the filter of admissibility. Let us consider these in turn.

Bratman is very careful to distinguish between plans as structures, which are essentially "abstract recipes"—say, instructions for how to cook a meal, or a detailed plan of how to rob a bank—and plans as mental states, most commonly described as "having a plan in mind." It is obviously the second that is relevant for intention, and Bratman defines his plans as "mental states involving an appropriate sort of commitment to action." The problem is that he tries to develop a theory of plans using only the latter sense. This, I think, leads to confusion and does not allow him to take advantage of the structural theories developed in artificial intelligence.

For example, he discusses the properties of plans: plans are typically partial, and they have a hierarchical structure. Though I agree with this, I am thinking of structural plans, not mental states. What does it mean for a mental state to be partial? Does it mean that an agent only partially enters the state, or does it mean that the agent is fully in the state but that the state itself is lacking in some way? I think not. Instead, it means that the plan does not fully specify the actions of the agent. But this is partial with respect to the structural definition of plans—in other words, it is a partial recipe. I think it would be much clearer for Bratman to adopt the structural definition of plans and talk about the mental state of having a plan. I have the same problem with Bratman's assertions that one "may deliberate about parts of [a] plan while holding others parts fixed." Surely this is not the type of thing one can do to a mental state.

This change in definition would not affect any of the points that are discussed later in the paper. It would simply allow the theory to be more precise and would open avenues for further elaboration and development.

The filter of admissibility—according to which an agent's prior intentions and background knowledge of the current situation are used to constrain the set of possible plans the agent may find acceptable—is a crucial part of the theory. Bratman points out that in order for the theory to be viable, we must accept that agents have flat-out beliefs. His example involves evaluating a plan that depends on owning two cars given the belief that he owns only one. If it is just very likely that he owns only one car, rather than certain, then the plan will not be inadmissible as desired. Though this is true, I think it is not a viable solution. In particular, we cannot have many flat-out beliefs about the future. For instance, if it is possible that he could buy a new car tomorrow, then he cannot have a flat-out belief that he will own only one car tomorrow. Thus, any belief that could be changed by future actions cannot be a flat-out belief. Having the flat-out belief that he will own only one car makes any plan involving obtaining a car inadmissible. I feel this is operating in the wrong direction. It is the feasibility of different plans that allows us to hold certain beliefs about the future, rather than our beliefs about the future constraining our possible plans. I think a more promising approach is to restrict the range of actions that the agent finds reasonable in any situation. Then, given flat-out beliefs about the present, one could use the restrictions on the allowable actions to eliminate plans. For example, if Bratman wants to eliminate the possibility of acquiring a new car and has the present flat-out belief that he has only one car, then the plan to drive to Monterey that requires him to own two cars will be inadmissible. The key point, however, is that it is inadmissible because the act of buying a car is considered undesirable or unreasonable. Of course, fully elaborating this requires a full theory of practical reasoning, and Bratman can make the points he wants to make in his paper without developing this. To go further, however, these issues must be faced.

Cohen and Levesque define a modal operator INTEND in a logic and use the distinctions that Bratman identifies for intending as the "acid test" for their theory. In particular, they want to formally show that they can represent the difference between the intended and unintended effects of an action. Crucial to their development is the operator GOAL, which has caused so much confusion every time I've seen it discussed that I think it deserves further clarification. In essence, the formula (GOAL x p) does not assert that the agent x has p as a goal in the intuitive sense of the word. Rather, it says that p will be true in any world where the agent's goals are achieved. In some ways, the term "consequence-of-goals" might be a better name for the operator. Cohen and Levesque use this as the basic building block for defining intention mainly for technical reasons. The GOAL operator, like the BEL operator, is closed under logical consequence and can be given a straightforward possible-worlds semantics. In fact, given a set of worlds that are possible given what an agent believes, a subset of these are the worlds in which the agent's goals are achieved. As a result, (BEL x p) implies (GOAL x p). Using this definition, Cohen and Levesque then introduce the notion of having a persistent goal—and this is the construct on which their theory of intention rests. An agent x has a persistent goal p if three conditions hold:

1. The agent does not currently believe p; that is, ∼(BEL x p).

2. A consequence of the agent's goal is that p is true later; that is, (GOAL x (LATER p)).

3. p (being true later) will remain a consequence of the agent's goals until the agent either believes it to be true or believes it to be impossible.

With this definition Cohen and Levesque achieve the distinction between goals and side effects; namely, goals must be achieved (or believed impossible) before they are abandoned, whereas side effects may be abandoned for any reason. In fact, this means that a side effect is never a persistent goal.

Cohen and Levesque show this explicitly in section 4.1 describing the logic of P-GOAL. They show, given (P-GOAL x p), under what conditions one could derive (P-GOAL x q). In fact, the only condition is when p and q are logically equivalent. When we look at their arguments closely, however, many of the cases appear to fall through only because of what seem to be the wrong reasons. In particular, cases 4 and 5 fall through only because the agent might believe that the side effect already holds, violating part 1 of the definition of persistent goal. In other words, given case 4, if the agent always believes that it is always the case that p implies q, then (P-GOAL x p) does not imply (P-GOAL x q) only in the case where (BEL x q) is already true. Presumably, when Cohen and Levesque develop a theory of maintenance goals, the three cases 4, 5, and 6 will always imply that the side effect q is a persistent goal.

The question then arises whether some example can be constructed that fits cases 4, 5, or 6, where intuitively the side effect q is not a persistent goal. My best attempt is as follows: Let p be "drinking a full bottle of wine in five minutes" and q be "getting drunk." Now I think it is clear that we all will be believe that p will always imply q, and so the formula in case 4 will hold. Furthermore, if agent x is not presently drunk, then if x has the P-GOAL of p (for whatever reason), then x must have the P-GOAL of q. This means that even though x adopts the persistent goal of drinking the wine in order to win a bet, x must also adopt the persistent goal to get drunk.

I believe this then carries over to the definition INTEND. If x intends to drink the wine, then x must intend to get drunk. This seems counterintuitive given Bratman's discussion. I think that Cohen and Levesque's defense against this might involve some sort of counterfactual reasoning as follows.

Even though we always believe that drinking the wine implies getting drunk, if this were not the case then we could abandon the goal of getting drunk without its becoming true or impossible. I'm not sure that this could be formalized without significant extensions to the formalism. Even so, I think Cohen and Levesque's formulation does cover a wide range of examples adequately, including the Strategic Bomber example that Bratman describes.

Though the above discussion appears to show that the axiomatization may be too strong in some cases, I also initially feared that it was too weak in other areas. This led me to a better understanding of the temporal aspects of the theory, so my train of thought may be worth repeating here. I was troubled by the fact that one could have a P-GOAL of p, and a P-GOAL of q, yet not have P-GOAL of p ∧ q. This is because the p and q may be needed at different times and never be true simultaneously. If we add specific temporal information into goals, I believe we do get the desired results. In particular, if t is a temporal predicate—say, t is only true at noon on June 25, 1988—then I believe the following is a theorem:

$$(\text{P-GOAL } x \; p \wedge t) \; \wedge \; (\text{P-GOAL } x \; q \wedge t) \Rightarrow (\text{P-GOAL } x \; p \wedge q \wedge t).$$

I think the largest IOU left in Cohen and Levesque's paper has to do with the temporal aspects. In particular, the present theory says nothing about worlds in which more than one action can occur at a time, and nothing about how one's beliefs may change over time. It is perfectly consistent to change one's beliefs at random at each time step (except where an explicit assertion that one must always believe something is involved). There are no axioms relating how one's present beliefs affect one's future beliefs. Though I recognize this as an extemely difficult problem, it is the crucial one to address if this work is to lead to a formal theory of rational behavior.

Conclusion

I have dwelt mostly on what these papers do not give us, as I believe is the tradition in commentaries. I want to close by restating that I am greatly encouraged by these two papers and the level of interaction between them. There may be a large gulf between the two, but these papers demonstrate how that gulf may be diminished. I look forward to seeing the results of the next iteration of this interaction.

Chapter 5

Plans as Complex Mental Attitudes

Martha E. Pollack

1 Introduction

There are plans and there are plans. There are the plans that an agent "knows": essentially recipes for performing particular actions or for achieving particular goal states. And there are the plans that an agent adopts and that subsequently guide his action. The distinction is between knowing that a plan for assassinating the president is shooting him, and actually planning to assassinate the president by shooting him.

To keep matters straight, we can refer to what one knows when he knows a way to do something as a *recipe-for-action*. Schematically, if we let r denote some recipe-for-action, A denote an agent, and PLANS be a binary relation between agents and the recipes-for-action they adopt, PLANS(A, r) will denote that A has a plan to do r. (I am temporarily suppressing issues of time.) A potential ambiguity remains, however. For there is A's plan r, the particular recipe-for-action he has adopted, and there is the state of mind that A is in when PLANS(A, r) is true. It is this latter distinction that Bratman is addressing when he notes that in speaking of an agent's plan we might "mean an appropriate abstract structure—some sort of partial function from circumstances to actions, perhaps. On the other hand, [we might] mean an appropriate state of mind, one naturally describable in terms of such structures" (1987, 271). We thus need more terminology: if PLANS(A, r) is true, we can say that the recipe-for-action r is the *object* of A's plan, which is itself what Bratman calls a "state of mind." Indeed, I will argue that the plan itself is usefully seen as a complex mental attitude, one comprising a structured collection of beliefs and intentions.

Artificial intelligence (AI) research in plan generation has always been primarily concerned with the recipes-for-action that are the object of an

Preparation of this paper was supported by a gift from the System Development Foundation. The research was done as part of my Doctoral thesis (Pollack 1986), which was supported by a gift from the System Development Foundation, by an IBM Graduate Fellowship, by the Defense Advanced Research Projects Agency under contract N000039-84-K-0078, and by the Office of Naval Research under contract N00014-855-C-0013. My sincere thanks to Barbara Grosz and to all the others, too numerous to list here, who contributed to my thesis effort.

agent's plans. The focus of such research has been on automating the process by which an agent can compute a recipe-for-action. Thus, Nilsson describes plan generation as "the problem of synthesizing a sequence of robot actions that will (if properly executed) achieve some stated goal, given some initial situation" (1980, 275). Although the assumption has always been that the computed recipe-for-action would be adopted as the object of a plan, and some robots have been designed that did actually adopt and execute the recipe-for-action, the plan generation literature has paid very little attention to plans qua mental attitudes.[1] The same is true of much of the plan inference literature in AI, which began later than the work on plan generation and which inherited many of its techniques.

In this paper I claim that a model of plan inference adequate to support a theory of cooperative communication must concern itself with the structure of the complex mental attitude of having a plan, as well as with the structure of the objects of that attitude. In section 2 I recount the traditional AI approach to performing plan inference in communication and describe some limitations of that approach. In section 3 I present an alternative analysis of plans, one that emphasizes their nature as action-guiding, complex mental phenomena. In section 4 I describes the role of this analysis of plans in a theory of cooperative communication that is not subject to the limitations discussed in section 2. In section 5 I return to the traditional AI model of plans and show how it is subsumed by the model presented here.

The theory of cooperative communication discussed in section 4 has been developed in some detail and has been implemented in SPIRIT, a system that reasons about the plans underlying the queries that it is asked and that generates appropriate responses. SPIRIT is able to infer plans even when they are invalid, that is, when their objects are not recipes-for-action that SPIRIT would itself construct. This ability distinguishes SPIRIT from earlier plan inference systems, which do not rely on a careful analysis of plans as complex mental attitudes. Details of SPIRIT and of the plan inference framework it embodies can be found in Pollack 1986.

2 The Traditional Approach

If you overheard the following conversation, you would probably find it quite unremarkable:

> A: "I want to talk to Kathy, so I need to find out the phone number of St. Eligius."
>
> S: "St. Eligius closed last month. Kathy was at Boston General, but she's already been discharged. You can call her at home. Her number is 555-1238."

Intuitively, it is quite clear what is occurring in this discourse. Agent A believes that Kathy is at St. Eligius and plans to call her there. Agent S believes that A's intended act of calling St. Eligius cannot be performed, since St. Eligius is closed. Moreover, S believes that even if A could call St. Eligius, it would not contribute to his goal of talking to Kathy, because she is actually at home. Consequently, S, being cooperative, provides A with information she believes will contribute to his goal: she tells him the correct phone number for reaching Kathy. She also tells him why she believes the information he requested was not appropriate to his goal.

Conversations such as this one, in which the beliefs of the inferring agent differ significantly from the beliefs of the actor whose plan she is inferring, provide a serious challenge to most existing AI systems for plan inference in communication (see, for instance, Allen 1979; Carberry 1985; Litman 1985; Sidner 1985). To see why, it is instructive to consider briefly how these systems work. Each of them has an *operator library*, which encodes a set of recipes-for-action. These operators are a direct outgrowth of the representations first developed in the STRIPS system (Fikes and Nilsson 1971) and later expanded in the NOAH system (Sacerdoti 1977). Each operator may contain some or all of the following parts:

- a *header*, which names the action α for which the operator is a recipe;
- a *precondition list*, which describes what must be true for α to be performed;
- an *effect list*, which describes what will be true after α is performed;
- a *list of constraints*, which describes restrictions on legal instantiations of the operator;[2]
- a *body*, which may be a set of subactions whose performance constitutes performance of α, or a set of subgoals whose achievement constitutes performance of α.

The operators in the library represent relatively simple recipes-for-action. More-complex recipes can be constructed out of the simpler ones. Both in plan generation and in plan inference, the more-complex recipes-for-action are represented as directed acyclic graphs, whose nodes are labeled with operator headers and propositions; when a node is labeled with a proposition P, it should be interpreted as denoting any action that would achieve P. Graphs, rather than linear orderings, are necessary because the recipes are seen as having both a hierarchical and a temporal dimension. Recipe graphs are sometimes referred to as macro-operators.

All the plan inference systems include a set of rules for constructing recipe graphs out of the simpler recipes in the operator library. Each rule states the conditions under which a piece of a recipe graph can be constructed. The conditions for constructing a subgraph always refer both to the subgraphs that have already been constructed and to operators in the operator library. A typical rule, for example, allows a subgraph that

A plan subgraph with nodes α and β and an arc from α to β,

$$\beta \atop \uparrow \atop \alpha$$

can be constructed provided either α or β is already in the subgraph and $\alpha R \beta$ holds, where R is one of the following relations:

1. R = *causes*; that is, β is on the effect list of α, so there is an operator in the operator library of the form

> Header: α
> Effects: ... β ...

2. R = *is-a-precondition-of*; that is, α is on the precondition list of β, so there is an operator in the operator library of the form

> Header: β
> Preconditions: ... α ...

3. R = *is-a-way-to*; that is, α is part of the body of β, so there is an operator in the operator library of the form

> Header: β
> Body: ... α ...

Figure 5.1
Rules for constructing plan graphs.

includes a node labeled α to be expanded by adding an arc from α to a new node labeled β, if there is an operator whose header is β and which includes α in its body. In all, there are only three basic conditions under which the various plan inference systems will construct a recipe subgraph. These are shown in figure 5.1. Note that each condition corresponds to one of the ways that actions and propositions can be related in an operator.[3]

Plan inference systems begin with some action α believed to be part of the recipe-for-action that is the object of the actor's plan. They then attempt to construct larger recipes-for-action by repeatedly applying inference rules, until one of the computed recipes satisfies some termination condition. (Typically, the termination condition is that the recipe constructed is for an action that an agent in the domain is likely to want to perform.) The computed recipe is taken to be the object of the actor's plan.

In fact, the inference rules are often written in such a way as to acknowledge the importance of plans as mental attitudes; after all, inferring another agent's plan means figuring out what actions he "has in mind." Consider Allen's model, which was one of the earliest accounts of plan inference in conversation and inspired much of the subsequent work in the field (Allen 1979, 1983). Allen writes AW(P), where P is some proposition, to express the fact that A has a plan to achieve P; AW(ACT), where ACT names some action, expresses the fact that A has a plan to perform ACT. A typical plan inference rule, then, is expressed as

SBAW(P) → SBAW(ACT), if P is a precondition of ACT.[4]

This rule corresponds to one direction of application of Condition 1 of figure 5.1.[5] It can be glossed as follows: if the system (inferring agent) believes that the actor wants some proposition P to be true, then the system may draw the inference that the actor wants to perform some action ACT of which P is a precondition. Notice that it is left unstated precisely who it is—the system or the actor—that believes that P is a precondition of ACT. If we take this to be a belief of the system, it is not clear that the system will infer the actor's plan; but, on the other hand, if we take it to be a belief of the actor, it is unclear how the system comes to have direct access to it. In practice, there is only a single set of operators relating preconditions and actions in Allen's system: these represent recipes-for-action that are assumed to be mutually known to the system and the actor.

In effect, the "SBAW" context is transparent to the reasoning process that is performed by Allen's system: its reasoning is all performed directly on its object, and the B and W operators are carried directly from antecedent to consequent in each inference rule. Without any repercussions, the B and W operators can be omitted, resulting in rules that are completely equivalent to those in figure 5.1. In fact, in his example plan graphs Allen often omits the B and W operators entirely, and this practice has been continued in more recent work in plan inference (Carberry 1985; Litman 1985). For Allen, as well as for most of those whose work he inspired, "the properties of the W operator [are] specified only by the ... plan inference rules." Allen's W operator is equivalent to the PLAN relation introduced here in section 1: it is the relationship that holds between an agent and a recipe-for-action he adopts.[6] His plan inference rules apply essentially directly to the object of the plan under construction. Thus Allen, and his followers, analyze the state of having a plan only in terms of the structure of its object.

In sum, the traditional approach to plan inference has been to reason directly about the object of a actor's plan, constructing a recipe-for-action using a library of simpler recipes that are assumed to be mutually known to the actor and the inferring agent. Though this approach has proved to be successful for modeling a number of conversational phenomena, it has at least three shortcomings that preclude it from handling in a principled way dialogues like the one presented at the beginning of this section—

dialogues in which one of the participants has a plan that the other deems to be invalid.

First, such a system will infer a plan subgraph linking nodes labeled X and Y, where X and Y are either operator headers or propositions, only if X and Y are both encoded in the system's operator library in one of the configurations shown in figure 5.1. This fact, combined with the fact that the operator library includes only valid domain information, may at first seem to suggest that traditional systems cannot infer *any* invalid plans. It turns out, however, that there are certain types of invalid plans that can, in principle, be inferred by a traditional system. For example, such a system could use a rule based on Condition 3 of figure 5.1 to infer a subgraph joining some actions α and β, even if the system also believes that one of the preconditions in the operator relating α and β is false.[7] However, without understanding why such a subgraph might be part of the object of the actor's plan, the system will not able to determine whether or not it is reasonable to include such a subgraph in the inferred plan. In fact, existing systems have not focused on the inference of such invalid plans and indeed have included various control heuristics that bias the inference process against finding them (see, for example, Allen's Heuristic H1 (1983, 127)). The first shortcoming of the traditional approach is an inability to state within it general heuristics for rule application.

Second, there are other types of invalid plans that cannot be inferred at all under the traditional approach. For instance, an actor A may be relying upon a simple recipe-for-action that is not in the system's operator library. In the case mentioned in the previous paragraph, S and A mutually know a recipe-for-action linking α and β: A's plan is invalid because the necessary preconditions for doing β by doing α do not hold. However, there are other cases in which A plans to do some action β by doing some α, where S does not at all believe that α will, under any set of preconditions, lead to β. (Indeed, S may even believe that α—or β, or both—cannot be done at all.)

One way to enable a system to reason about plans with such invalidities is to encode directly sets of erroneous beliefs that handle such cases by encoding directly sets of erroneous recipes that their users are likely to have; this is the approach taken by many computer-aided instruction (CAI) systems (Brown and Burton 1978; Collins, Stevens, and Goldin 1979; Genesereth 1979; Woolf and McDonald 1983). Although this seems to be a useful strategy, it is necessarily incomplete. It is impossible for any person to have complete knowledge of the potential beliefs of other people, since the range of beliefs is, in principle, infinite. This means that system designers cannot anticipate a priori all of the potential misconceptions the users of their system may have. It also means that the intelligent agent that such systems emulate—the human being—cannot know a priori all of the potential misconceptions that people asking her questions might have.

Sometimes she will have to deal with a novel (to her) belief. A more general approach is to try to understand the structure of the beliefs that an agent has when she has some plan, thereby making it possible to apply various belief-attribution techniques to the problem of plan inference.

A third weakness of the traditional approach concerns the generation of appropriate responses in conversation. To explain why S's response in the example dialogue is a cooperative one, it is necessary to understand what beliefs S is attributing to A by virtue of attributing to her some plan.

To handle these issues—to make room in the theory of plan inference for discrepancies between the beliefs of the actor and the inferring agent, thereby allowing for the proper treatment of "invalid" plans—it is necessary to undertake an analysis of what the context "SBAW" means: to analyze plans as mental phenomena. We now turn to that task.

3 An Alternative Model of Plans

To develop an account of plans as mental phenomena, we could begin with the traditional AI models, which, as we have seen, have focused on the objects of plans: we could attempt to determine what sort of mental states would reasonably have such objects. However, it will prove to be more fruitful to begin with our commonsense conceptions of what it means to have a plan. The resulting model can be shown to subsume and make more precise the model implicit in the traditional AI accounts.

3.1 The Belief Component of Plans

Let us begin with the plan (referred to earlier) to ask Kathy how she is feeling. I plan to do this, believing that Kathy is at St. Eligius, by finding out the phone number of St. Eligius, calling there, and then saying to Kathy "How are you doing?"[8] The performance of these acts is meant to "entail" —in a sense of *entail* yet to be further specified—the performance of my goal act.

One's plans, however, may fail. If, unbeknownst to me, Kathy has already gone home, then my plan will not lead to my goal of asking her how she is feeling. For me to have a plan to do β, which consists in the doing of some collection of acts Π, it is not necessary that the performance of Π actually lead to the performance of β. What is necessary is that I *believe* that its performance will do so.[9] This insight is at the core of a view of plans as mental phenomena; on this view, plans "exist"—that is, gain their status as plans—by virtue of the beliefs of the person whose plans they are.

So far, then, I have associated the state of having a plan to do β with a belief that executing some collection of acts Π will lead to doing β. Note that the temporal ordering of the acts is an essential part of the plan: I may well have a plan to prepare onions for a sauce by chopping them and then sautéing them—believing that by so doing I will perform my goal—and not have a plan that involves sautéing and then chopping the onions. However, the ordering need not be total: as Sacerdoti (1977) demonstrated, there are many plans with objects that include acts whose temporal order with respect to one another is irrelevant. For example, I may have a plan to set the table that includes the following acts: carrying the flatware, plates, and glasses to the table; setting out the flatware; setting out the plates; and setting out the glasses. I may believe that is essential that the first act in the list be performed prior to the others, but I may also believe that the other three acts can be performed in any order with respect to one another and can even be interleaved. Of course, when I actually execute my plan, the acts I perform will be totally ordered with respect to one another. So there is a sense in which the beliefs that are part of my plan are partial.

There is also another sense in which my beliefs may be partial: they may concern acts only to an arbitrary level of abstraction. The set of acts that I believe will entail my asking Kathy how she is feeling includes the act of finding out the phone number of St. Eligius. It includes this despite the fact that I may not yet have considered how I will do this—for example, whether I will call the information operator or look in a phone book.[10]

An agent A's belief that performing the acts in Π will entail performing β is not by itself sufficient to guarantee that A has a plan, consisting of doing Π, to do β. To see why not, consider the following scenario. Suppose that I decide that while I am finding out the phone number of St. Eligius (say, by looking in the phone book), I might as well at the same time find out the phone number of my bank (perhaps because I know I have to call there later to check on a wire transfer). As before, I believe that finding out and dialing the phone number of St. Eligius, and then saying certain words, will entail my asking Kathy how she is feeling. I do not believe that this will cease to be true if I also find out my bank's phone number. Thus, there is a temporally ordered collection of acts Π, which equals finding out the phone number of St. Eligius, finding out the phone number of my bank, calling St. Eligius, and saying to Kathy "How are you doing?", such that I believe that executing Π will lead to my goal of asking Kathy how she is feeling.[11] However, it seems incorrect to say that my plan to ask Kathy how she is feeling includes my act of finding out the phone number of my bank; instead, this act is part of another plan (to check on my wire transfer) that I intend to interleave with my original plan. For an act to be included in my plan, I must believe that it plays a role in that plan; for the case at hand I do not believe that finding out the phone number of the bank plays any role in my plan to ask Kathy how she is feeling.

3.2 Playing a Role in a Plan
What does it mean for an act to play a role in a plan? Consider once more my plan to ask Kathy how she is feeling. Part of this plan, I claimed,

involves my calling St. Eligius. What would we say about my beliefs about these two acts: my asking Kathy how she is feeling and my calling St. Eligius? We might say that I believe that the latter will enable the former— that is, that by calling St. Eligius, I will establish a communication channel (a phone link) to Kathy, which will enable my saying something to her. Similarly, we might say that I believe that finding out the phone number of St. Eligius plays a role in my plan because I believe that doing the former will enable my calling St. Eligius, which itself plays a role in my plan. In general, then, if an agent believes that doing one act α will enable either his goal or some other act γ that plays a role in his plan, then α may play a role in his plan. In order to strengthen the "may" to "will," we need to consider the agent's intentions. I will discuss this presently.

Next consider the relationship between my acts of saying to Kathy "How are you doing?" and asking her how she is feeling. We would not say that I believe that the first act will enable the second. Instead, we could describe my beliefs using the "by-locution" in English: we could say that I believe that by saying "How are you doing?", I will be asking Kathy how she is feeling. Similarly, consider a slightly more detailed analysis of my plan to ask Kathy how she is feeling, which makes explicit the way in which I go about finding out the phone number of St. Eligius. One way in which I might plan to do this is by looking the number up in the phone book. We would not say that I believe that my looking up St. Eligius's phone number will *enable* my finding it out; rather, we would say that I believe that by looking it up, I will find it out. Or I might, instead of looking up the phone number, plan to discover it by getting my office mate to tell it to me, as a result of my asking her to tell it to me, which consists in my uttering the question "Do you know the phone number of St. Eligius?" Once again, we would not say that I believe that my uttering the question "Do you know the phone number of St. Eligius?" will *enable* my asking my office mate to tell me the phone number of St. Eligius, nor would we say that my asking her to tell me the phone number will *enable* my getting her to tell it to me. What we would say is that I believe that by uttering the question, I will be asking my office mate to tell me the phone number; that by asking her, I will be getting her to tell it to me; and that by getting her to tell it to me, I will be finding it out. Notice that the by-locution does *not* completely correlate with causation: although it is true that asking to be told the phone number seems to relate causally to getting a listener to tell you the phone number, there is no such causal flavor to the relation between uttering the question and asking to be told the phone number.

The claim is that if an agent believes that by doing α, he will be doing either his goal act β or some other act γ that plays a role in his plan, then α may play a role in his plan. Of course, to some extent this just begs the question, since I have left vague the conditions under which one act can be said to be done *by* doing another. Goldman's (1970) concept of *generation* can be used to make these conditions more precise (Pollack 1986, 52–67). I will adopt the term *generation* to describe the relation between two acts that we commonly express with the *by*-locution. What is important to notice here is that there does seem to be an intuitive difference between the relation between acts that we describe as enablement and the one I am now calling generation. Just as we would not describe the relations between the acts discussed in the previous paragraph as enablement, so we would not, in general, use *by* to describe the relations earlier discussed as examples of enablement. We would not, for example, say that I believe that I can call St. Eligius by finding out the phone number there.[12]

What does the difference between enablement and generation consist in? Most importantly, it is the case that when one action α generates another action β, then the agent need only do α and β will automatically be done also. However, when α enables β, then the agent needs to do something more than α to guarantee that β will be done. I cannot simply find out the phone number of St. Eligius and then rationally expect that I will have called St. Eligius. But if I utter the words "Do you know the phone number of St. Eligius?" in the appropriate circumstances, then I need do nothing more to have asked my office mate the phone number of St. Eligius. And having done that, if the circumstances are right (say, my office mate knows the phone number of St. Eligius and is willing to tell it to me), then I need do nothing more to have caused my office mate to tell me St. Eligius's phone number.

Of course, if the circumstances are not right, then by asking my office mate for the phone number, I will not have caused her to tell it to me. For instance, she might not hear me ask her. In that case I may repeat my question. It is important not to confuse things here. It is true that in this case I *do* "do something more" than my original act of asking for the phone number in order to perform the act of causing my office mate to tell it to me. But here my first act—of asking for the phone number—does *not* generate my act of causing my office mate to tell it to me. My second act—repeating my request—might do so, if my office mate hears me this time and responds, but then I have not "done anything more" than this second act, of repeating my question, to cause my office mate to tell it to me.

Analogously, I might dial the phone number and get a busy signal. I then need to do something more to establish a communication channel to Kathy. I might dial the number again, or I might drive to St. Eligius. In either case, if I succeed in establishing a communication channel, I succeed in doing so by dialing the second time, or by going to St. Eligius: it is my act of redialing or my act of going to St. Eligius, and not my original act of dialing, that generates my act of establishing the communication channel.

3.3 The Intention Component of Plans

So far we have seen that for an agent A to have a plan to do β that consists of doing Π, he must have a certain set of beliefs about the acts that Π comprises. Specifically,

1. A must believe that executing the acts in Π, in their (possibly partial) temporal order, will entail his performance of β

and

2. A must believe that each act α in Π plays a role in his plan; that is, either he believes that by doing α he will do β or some other γ that plays a role in his plan (in other words, that α generates β or γ), or he believes that doing α will enable doing β or some other γ that plays a role in his plan.

Condition 1 can be thought of as a sufficiency condition: it guarantees that if A believes that α is part of what he will do to achieve his goal, then α is in the plan. Condition 2 can be thought of as a necessity condition: it guarantees that if α is part of A's plan, he believes it will play a role in achieving his goal.

Although these beliefs are necessary, they are not sufficient to guarantee that doing Π is A's plan to do β. It is also necessary that A have a certain set of intentions with respect to Π. In particular, for my plan to do β to consist in my doing Π, I must intend to execute each of the acts in Π. Let Π once more be finding out the phone number of St. Eligius, calling St. Eligius, and saying "How are you doing?" I may believe that executing Π would entail my asking Kathy how she is feeling, but if I intend instead to wait until next Thursday and then talk to her face to face, Π is not a plan I have to ask Kathy how she is feeling.

Further, in order for doing Π to count as my plan to β, not only must I intend to execute Π, but I must also intend it *as a way* of doing β; that is, I must intend to do the acts in Π in order to do β. Imagine that I am a teenager whose parents have forbidden me to stay out past midnight. Imagine further that there is some club, "The May Day Late-Night Club," whose membership is limited to those who show up at the movies at 1 a.m. on May 1. Now let Π be the singleton set going to the movies at 1 a.m. on May 1. I may intend to execute Π, and I may believe that doing so will entail both becoming a member of the May Day Late-Night Club and aggravating my parents. But if I intend my execution of Π as a way to do the former—and *not the latter*—then doing Π will count as a plan I have to join the Late-Night Club, but not as a plan I have to aggravate my parents.

Notice the this is true even if I intend to aggravate my parents in some other way—say, by getting a Mohawk haircut.

An argument similar to that made in the belief case also applies here. Thus, not only must I intend to execute Π in order to do β, I must also intend each act α in Π to play a role in my doing β; that is, I must intend each α either to generate or to enable β or some other γ that itself plays a role in my plan. Thus, we can state three more conditions on A's having a plan to do β that consists in doing Π, namely:

3. A must intend to execute each act α in Π, in the (possibly partial) temporal order;

4. A must intend to execute Π as a way of doing β;

and

5. A must intend each act α in Π to play a role in his plan. In other words, either he must intend by doing α to do β or some other γ that plays a role in his plan, or he must intend by doing α to enable doing β or some other γ that plays a role in his plan.

The close parallel between Conditions 2 and 5 should lead us to ask whether one subsumes the other. The discussion so far has shown that having the beliefs defined in Condition 2 does not entail having the intentions in Condition 5. But does having the intentions in Condition 5 entail the beliefs in Condition 2?

The question of whether an agent's intention to do α entails a belief that the agent will do α has been debated in the philosophical literature, and no consensus seems to have been reached. Whereas Grice (1971), for one, answers in the affirmative, Davidson (1980) goes to great lengths to provide a counterargument.[13] A telling comment on the controversy is provided by Bratman (1983), who notes that "plans normally support expectations of their successful execution..., [although] there may still be cases in which I plan to A but do not believe I will" (p. 286, fn. 4). Within this paper it will prove to be sufficient to assume this "normal" state of affairs and accept the view that if one intends to X, one must believe that one will.

Given this, we can see that Condition 5 directly entails Condition 2. For if, for each α in Π, A intends α to play a role in his plan, then A also believes that α will play a role in his plan. If A intends to do β or some other γ by doing α, he also believes that he will do β or this other γ by doing α; if he intends to enable β or some other γ by doing α, he also believes that he will enable β or this other γ by doing α.

Similarly, Condition 4 entails Condition 1. For if A intends to do Π as a way of doing β, then A must believe he will do β by doing Π, and this is exactly Condition 1.

To state the commonsense requirements on A's having a plan, it is thus sufficient to state the conditions on intending—Conditions 3 through 5. However, although the conditions on belief—Conditions 1 and 2—are entailed by Conditions 4 and 5, respectively, and are thus redundant, it is worth keeping them in mind, for it will turn out that when an inferring agent deems an actor's plan invalid, it is because she believes it includes invalid beliefs. In fact, it is even worthwhile to make explicit yet another belief that is requisite to having a plan. Condition 3 asserts that A intends to execute each act α in Π, this then entails that A believes he will do each act α in Π. And this belief, in turn, entails a belief that A can do each act α in Π. Adding this condition to the definition, we can summarize the analysis of "having a plan" as follows:

> *Definition P0* An agent A has a plan to do β that consists in doing some set of acts Π, provided that
> 1. A believes that he can execute each act in Π.
> 2. A believes that executing the acts in Π will entail the performance of β.
> 3. A believes that each act in Π plays a role in his plan. (See discussion below.)
> 4. A intends to execute each act in Π.
> 5. A intends to execute Π as a way of doing β.
> 6. A intends each act in Π to play a role in his plan.

4 Plans in Cooperative Communication

We can now consider how the model of plans just developed can be incorporated in a theory of communication that does not suffer from the shortcomings described in section 2—that is, one in which even invalid plans can be reasoned about properly. To begin, it is useful to develop a more formal representation of the analysis given in Definition P0.

4.1 A Representation for Simple Plans

I will restrict my attention to a subset of plans, which I call *simple plans*. An agent has a simple plan if and only if he believes that all the acts in that plan play a role in it by generating another act—in other words, if it includes no acts that the agent believes are related to one another by enablement. The representation language I will use builds upon Allen's (1984) interval-based temporal logic, a typed first-order predicate calculus. In particular, I will make use of the predicates HOLDS and OCCURS. HOLDS is a binary relation over propositions and time intervals: HOLDS(P, t) is taken to be true if and only if proposition P holds throughout time interval t. OCCURS, as I will use it, is a ternary relation: OCCURS(α, A, t) is true if and only if agent A performs an act of type α during time interval t.

Note that the first argument to OCCURS is an act-type. The distinction between act-types and actions is crucial. Actions or acts—I will use the two terms interchangeably—can be thought of as triples of act-type, agent, and time. Thus, typing **DEL** . is an example of an act-type, whereas my typing **DEL** . right now is an example of an action. Generation is a relation over actions, not over act-types. Sometimes an act of typing **DEL** . will generate an act of deleting the current mail message (say, when the former act is performed while the agent is using a particular electronic mail system). But not every case of an agent's typing **DEL** . will result in the agent's deleting the current message; for example, my typing it just now did not, because I was not typing it to a computer mail system. However, when an act of A's doing α at time t generates an act of his doing β at time t, there are certain conditions C such that any time there occurs an act of α while C holds, there will also occur a simultaneous act of β. The regularity of the generation-enabling conditions C is what enables us to reason about whether by doing some action we will do another action, and consequently what enables us to construct and reason about (simple) plans.

To encode these regularities, I will introduce the following abbreviatory device: I will say that act-type α *conditionally generates* act-type β under conditions C, and I will write $CGEN(\alpha, \beta, C)$, where C denotes the generation-enabling conditions relating α and β. Thus, the CGEN predicate is defined as follows:

Definition C1
$CGEN(\alpha, \beta, C) \leftrightarrow$

1. $\forall A \forall t_1 [[HOLDS(C, t_1) \wedge OCCURS(\alpha, A, t_1)]$
$\rightarrow OCCURS(\beta, A, t_1)] \wedge$
2. $\exists A \exists t_2 [OCCURS(\alpha, A, t_2) \wedge \neg OCCURS(\beta, A, t_2)] \wedge$
3. $\exists t_3 \exists A [HOLDS(C, t_3) \wedge \neg OCCURS(\beta, A, t_3)].$

It is then straightforward to define the generates relation, GEN, in terms of CGEN:[14]

Definition G1
$GEN(\alpha, \beta, A, t) \leftrightarrow \exists C [CGEN(\alpha, \beta, C) \wedge HOLDS(C, t)].$

That is, agent A's doing α at time t will generate his doing β if and only if there are some generation-enabling conditions relating α and β and, further, those conditions hold at time t.

In translating Definition P0 into the representation language, I will also make use of several other relations, which I will treat as primitive in this paper. (See, however, Pollack 1986, 67–72.) The relation $EXEC(\alpha, A, t)$ will be taken to be true if and only if the act of A's doing α during time interval t is *executable*. The relation $BEL(A, P, t)$ is true if and only if agent A believes proposition P throughout time interval t; $INT(A, \alpha, t_2, t_1)$ is true if and only if throughout time t_1, A intends to do α at time t_2. I also make use of one function: *by* maps two act-types into a third, composite act-type—$by(\alpha, \beta)$ denotes the act of doing β by doing α.

These various components of the representation language then can be combined in Definition P1, which encodes in the representation language the definition of having a simple plan:

Definition P1
$SIMPLE\text{-}PLAN(A, \alpha_n, [\alpha_1, \ldots, \alpha_{n-1}], t_2, t_1) \leftrightarrow$

    1. $BEL(A, EXEC(\alpha_i, A, t_2), t_1)$, for i $= 1, \ldots, n \wedge$
    2. $BEL(A, GEN(\alpha_i, \alpha_{i+1}, A, t_2), t_1)$, for i $= 1, \ldots, n - 1 \wedge$
    3. $INT(A, \alpha_i, t_2, t_1)$, for i $= 1, \ldots, n \wedge$
    4. $INT(A, by(\alpha_i, \alpha_{i+1}), t_2, t_1)$, for i $= 1, \ldots, n - 1.$

The left-hand side of Definition P1 denotes that the agent A has, at time t_1, a simple plan to do α_n, consisting of doing the set of acts $\{\alpha_1, \ldots, \alpha_{n-1}\}$ at t_2. Note that all these are simultaneous acts; this is a consequence of the restriction to simple plans. The right-hand side of Definition P1 corresponds directly to Definition P0, except that, in keeping with the restriction to simple plans, specific assertions about each act generating another replace the more general statement regarding the fact that each act plays a role in the plan. Clause 1 of Definition P1 captures Clause 1 of Definition P0.[15] Clause 2 of Definition P1 captures both Clauses 2 and 3 of Definition P0: when i takes the value $n - 1$, Clause 2 of Definition P1 captures the requirement, stated in Clause 2 of Definition P0, that A believes his acts will entail his goal; when i takes values between 1 and $n - 2$, it captures the requirement of Clause 3 of Definition P0, that A believes each of his acts plays a role in his plan. Similarly, Clause 3 of Definition P1 captures Clause 4 of Definition P0, and Clause 4 of Definition P1 captures Clauses 5 and 6 of Definition P0.

4.2 Invalid Plans and Cooperative Responses

Given Definition P1, it is straightforward to state what it means for an agent to have an invalid simple plan: A has an invalid simple plan if and only if he has the set of beliefs and intentions listed in Definition P1, where one or more of those beliefs is incorrect, and, consequently, one or more of the intentions is unrealizable. We can also see what it means for one agent to believe that another has a simple plan: I will say that S believes that A has some (simple) plan to do the action β by doing the actions $\alpha_1, \ldots, \alpha_n$ if S believes that A has the configuration of beliefs and intentions represented in Definition P1. And these two statements can be combined, so that S will be said to believe that A has a simple plan that is invalid if S believes to be false some belief she attributes to A virtue of attributing to him some simple plan (and consequently, S also believes to be unrealizable some intention she attributes to A in virtue of attributing to him that same simple plan).

The structure of Definition P1 suggests that there are two types of plan invalidities, corresponding to the two types of beliefs that are part of the mental attitude of having a simple plan. An incorrect belief corresponding to Clause 1 of Definition P1 will indicate a plan that includes an intention to do an *unexecutable act*, and an incorrect belief corresponding to Clause 2 will indicate what I will call an *ill-formed plan*: one in which the intended acts will not lead to the goal. Of course, in accounting for cooperative conversation, what is at issue is not the absolute correctness of the actor's beliefs but, as explained above, the inferring agent's beliefs about the beliefs she attributes to the actor. So, I will say that S judges A's plan to contain an unexecutable act if S believes to be false one of the beliefs she attributes to A in satisfaction of Clause 1 of Definition P1. Likewise, I will say that S judges A's plan to be ill formed if she believes to be false one of the beliefs she attributes to A in satisfaction of Clause 2 of Definition P1. Of course, this is not to say that any agent S would assent to a description of A's plan as "ill formed": to say that an agent believes a plan is ill formed is to describe a configuration of beliefs that agent has.

Consider again the dialogue presented in section 2:

A: "I want to talk to Kathy, so I need to find out the phone number of St. Eligius."

S: "St. Eligius closed last month. Kathy was at Boston General, but she's already been discharged. You can call her at home. Her number is 555-1238."

We can accout for S's response there by assuming that she believes that A has a certain set of beliefs and intentions satisfying Definition P1. A portion of those beliefs is shown in figure 5.2. S believes that A believes that calling St. Eligius at time t_2 is executable, though S believes it is not executable, and she informs A of this in her response. Also, S believes that A believes that the act of calling St. Eligius will generate the act of

$BEL(S, BEL(A, EXEC(call(St.\ Eligius), A, t_2), t_1), t_1)$
$BEL(S, BEL(A, EXEC(establish\text{-}channel(Kathy), A, t_2), t_1), t_1)$
$BEL(S, BEL(A, GEN(call(St.\ Eligius), establish\text{-}channel(Kathy), A, t_2), t_1), t_1)$
$BEL(S, INT(A, call(St.\ Eligius), t_2, t_1), t_1)$
$BEL(S, INT(A, establish\text{-}channel(Kathy), t_2, t_1), t_1)$
$BEL(S, INT(A, by(St.\ Eligius), establish\text{-}channel(Kathy), t_2, t_1), t_1)$

Figure 5.2
The plan S infers for A.

establishing a communication channel to Kathy. S believes that it will not—that even if A could call St. Eligius, that act would not have the desired effect. This belief also affects S's response.

Strategies for producing cooperative responses to questions must incorporate decisions about what information to include. The view of plans developed here—in which plans are seen as complex mental attitudes, and plan inference is seen as the process of attributing such attitudes to an actor—provides the basis for determining a class of information that may need to be included in a cooperative response to a question. Specifically, to be cooperative, a response may need to include information about the particular discrepancies S finds between her own beliefs and those she attributes to A as part of her belief that he has some particular plan. Note, however, that a cooperative response may not necessarily include all such information, for S may deem some or all of it to be irrelevant. The plan inferred to underlie a query and any invalidities it is judged to have are but two factors affecting the response generation process, the most significant others being relevance and salience.

4.3 Explanatory Plans

When S judges A's plan to be invalid in one of the ways discussed above, she has intuitively "made sense" of the plan and understands the source of the invalidities. However, there are also cases in which an inferring agent simply cannot make sense of an actor's query. As a somewhat whimsical example, imagine A saying,

> A: "I want to talk to Kathy, so I need to find out how to stand on my head."

In many contexts a perfectly reasonable response to this query is "Huh?" A's query is *incoherent*: a listener S may be unable to understand why A believes that finding out how to stand on his head (or standing on his head) will lead to talking with Kathy. One can, of course, construct scenarios in which A's query makes perfect sense: Kathy might, for example, be currently hanging by her feet in gravity boots. The point here is not to imagine such circumstances in which A's query would would be coherent but instead to realize that there are many circumstances in which it would not.

The model of plans as I have so far presented it does not distinguish between a query of this type and one in which the inferred underlying plan is ill formed. The reason is that, given a reasonable account of semantic interpretation, it is transparent from the query just given above that A intends to talk to Kathy, intends to find out how to stand on his head, and intends his doing the latter to play a role in his doing the former. Further, as consequences of these intentions A believes that he can talk to Kathy, believes that he can find out how to stand on his head, and believes that his doing the latter will play a role in his doing the former.[16] But these beliefs and intentions are precisely what are required by Definition P0 to have a plan; and if S could determine that the intended role of the supporting act of standing on his head was generation, then these beliefs and intentions would also be exactly what is required by Definition P1. Consequently, after hearing the query, S can in fact infer a plan underlying A's query, namely, the obvious one: to find out how to stand on his head in order to talk to Kathy. Then, since S does not herself believe that the former act will lead to the latter, on the analysis so far given, we would regard S as judging A's plan to be ill formed. Unfortunately, this is not the desired analysis: the model should instead capture the fact that S cannot make sense of A's query here—that it is *incoherent*.

To capture the difference between ill-formedness and incoherence, I will claim that, when an agent S is asked a question by an actor A, S needs to attempt to ascribe to A more than just a set of beliefs and intentions satisfying Definition P1. Specifically, for each belief satisfying Clause 2 of Definition P1, S must also ascribe to A another belief that explains the former in a certain specifiable way. The beliefs that satisfy Clause 2 are beliefs about the relation between two particular actions. For instance, the plan underlying the example query includes A's belief that his action of calling St. Eligius at t_2 will generate his action of establishing a communication channel to Kathy at t_2. This belief can be explained by a belief A has about the relation between the act-types "calling a location" and "establishing a communication channel to an agent." A may believe that acts of the former type generate acts of the latter type, provided that the agent to whom the communication channel is to be established is at the location to be called. Such a belief can be encoded using the CGEN relation introduced earlier. So, for instance, S may attribute to A a belief that we can express as follows:

$$BEL(A, CGEN(call(X), establish\text{-}channel(Y), at(X, Y)), t_1).$$

This belief, combined with a belief that Kathy will be at St. Eligius at time t_2, expains A's belief that, by calling St. Eligius at t_2, he will establish a communication channel to Kathy. In contrast, S may have no basis for ascribing to A beliefs that will explain why he thinks that standing on his head will lead to talking with Kathy. Consequently, she will deem the second example query to be incoherent.

Explanatory beliefs are incorporated in the plan inference model by the introduction of *explanatory plans*, or *eplans*. Saying that an agent S believes that another agent A has some eplan is shorthand for describing a set of beliefs possessed by S, specifically:

Definition P2
$BEL(S, EPLAN(A, \alpha_n, [\alpha_1, \ldots, \alpha_{n-1}], [\rho_1, \ldots, \rho_{n-1}], t_2, t_1), t_1) \leftrightarrow$

1. $BEL(S, BEL(A, EXEC(\alpha_i, A, t_2), t_1), t_1)$, for i = 1, ..., n ∧
2. $BEL(S, BEL(A, GEN(\alpha_i, \alpha_{i+1}, A, t_2), t_1), t_1)$,
   for i = 1, ..., n − 1 ∧
3. $BEL(S, INT(A, \alpha_i, t_2, t_1), t_1)$, for i = 1, ..., n ∧
4. $BEL(S, INT(A, by(\alpha_i, \alpha_{i+1}), t_2, t_1), t_1)$, for i = 1, ..., n − 1 ∧
5. $BEL(S, BEL(A, \rho_i, t_1), t_1)$,
   where each ρ_i is $CGEN(\alpha_i, \alpha_{i+1}, C_i) \wedge HOLDS(C_i, t_2)$.

Clauses 1–4 of Definition P2 are similar to Clauses 1–4 of Definition P1. The key clause in the definition of eplans is Clause 5: for S to believe that A has some eplan, she must attribute to A beliefs that explain the other beliefs that are constituents in his plan. I will call the beliefs that S attributes to A in satisfaction of Clause 5 *explanatory beliefs*.

It is now possible to sketch the process of inferring the eplan that underlies a query. To begin, S will believe that A intends to do some act α, possibly because A tells her this in the query. S thus may believe that A has a trivial eplan, that is,

$BEL(S, EPLAN(A, \alpha, [\quad], \rho, t_2, t_1), t_1)$,
where ρ is nil (logically true).

Let us suppose then that S has reason to believe—on the basis of something other than A's query itself—that it is plausible that A believes that act-type α conditionally generates some other act-type γ, under some specific condition C, and that she has no reason to suppose that A believes that C will not hold at the intended performance time of his plan. Then S can decide that it is plausible for A to believe that by his act of α, he will do γ and, further, that it is plausible for him to intend to do α in order to do γ, and to intend to do γ. The plausibility of A's having these intentions depends upon the plausibility of his having the aforementioned beliefs, so S will attribute to A as a bundle the plausible intentions and supporting beliefs. That is, S will reason from the trivial eplan to a larger one. The process of belief and intention ascription can be iterated: believing that it is plausible that A intends to do γ, S can then reason about what A might believe he can do by this act. S can also reason about what A might plausibly intend to do in order to do his goal act β and can then iterate as well in the "backward" direction. Again, the reasoning is from one plausible eplan to another.

What is crucial in this picture is the way in which S attributes to A particular explanatory beliefs. As noted, when S decides that it is plausible for A to believe that by doing α he will be doing some γ, the plausibility of that belief must be established on the basis of something other than A's query itself; otherwise, the very distinction that eplans were set up to support—the distinction between incoherent and ill-formed plans—will collapse. Though it is true that if A says "I want to talk to Kathy, so I need to find out how to stand on my head," S can figure out that A believes that by standing on his head he can talk to Kathy (or at least enable his talking to Kathy), this belief can only be attributed to A on the basis of his query. The types of evidence that can be used to attribute explanatory beliefs to an agent are encoded in a set of *plan inference rules* that describe the reasoning that is permitted in going from one plausible eplan to another. If the plan inference process proceeds only through the use of plan inference rules, the distinction between ill-formed plans and incoherent queries is maintained.

In the simplest plan inference rule, S attributes to A a belief that she herself has:[17]

Rule PI1
$BEL(S, EPLAN(A, \alpha_n, [\alpha_1, \ldots, \alpha_{n-1}], [\rho_1, \ldots, \rho_{n-1}], t_2, t_1), t_1) \wedge$
    $BEL(S, CGEN(\alpha_n, \gamma, C), t_1)$
$\rightarrow$
$BEL(S, EPLAN(A, \gamma, [\alpha_1, \ldots, \alpha_n], [\rho_1, \ldots, \rho_n], t_2, t_1), t_1),$
where $\rho_n = CGEN(\alpha_n, \gamma, C) \wedge HOLDS(C, t_2)$.

This rule says that, if S's belief that A has some eplan includes a belief that A intends to do an act α_n, and S also believes that act-type α_n conditionally generates some γ under condition C, then S may infer that A has the additional intention of doing α_n in order to do γ—that is, that he intends to do $by(\alpha_n, \gamma)$. A's having this intention depends upon his also having the supporting belief that α_n conditionally generates γ under some condition C, and the further belief that this C will hold at performance time.[18]

One way to view Rule PI1 is as an explication of condition 3 of figure 5.1 in the language of plans as mental phenomena. If a system made use only of Rule PI1 (and its symmetric partner), it would be implicitly committing to the assumption that A has the same beliefs about conditional generation as it does. Additional plan inference rules are needed to move beyond this assumption. In one obvious form of reasoning, S may attribute to A beliefs that are slight variations of her own, for example as encoded in Rule PI2:

Rule PI2
$BEL(S, EPLAN(A, \alpha_n, [\alpha_1, \ldots, \alpha_{n-1}], [\rho_1, \ldots, \rho_{n-1}], t_2, t_1), t_1) \wedge$
    $BEL(S, CGEN(\alpha_n, \gamma, C_1 \wedge \ldots \wedge C_m), t_1)$
$\rightarrow$
$BEL(S, EPLAN(A, \gamma, [\alpha_1, \ldots, \alpha_n], [\rho_1, \ldots, \rho_n], t_2, t_1), t_1),$
where $\rho_n = CGEN(\alpha_n, \gamma, C_1 \wedge \ldots \wedge C_{i-1} \wedge C_{i+1} \wedge \ldots \wedge C_m) \wedge$
    $HOLDS(C_1 \wedge \ldots \wedge C_{i-1} \wedge C_{i+1} \wedge \ldots \wedge C_m, t_2)$.

What Rule PI2 expresses is that S may ascribe to A a belief about a relation between act-types that is a slight variation of one she herself has. It asserts that, if there is some CGEN relation that S believes true, she may attribute to A a belief in a similar CGEN relation that is weaker, in that it is missing one of the required conditions. As another example, if S believes that two act-types α and β are quite similar, she thereby has reason to believe that it is plausible that A has confused them or has made a bad analogy from one to the other. Such reasoning is encoded in Rule PI3:

Rule PI3
$$BEL(S, EPLAN(A, \alpha_n, [\alpha_1, \ldots, \alpha_{n-1}], [\rho_1, \ldots, \rho_{n-1}], t_2, t_1), t_1) \wedge$$
$$\quad BEL(S, SIMILAR(\alpha_n, \delta), t_1) \wedge$$
$$\quad BEL(S, CGEN(\delta, \gamma, C), t_1)$$
$$\rightarrow$$
$$BEL(S, EPLAN(A, \gamma, [\alpha_1, \ldots, \alpha_n], [\rho_1, \ldots, \rho_n], t_2, t_1), t_1),$$
where $\rho_n = CGEN(\alpha_n, \gamma, C) \wedge HOLDS(C, t_2)$.

Rules PI1, PI2, and PI3 are merely meant to be suggestive of the sort of plan inference rules that can be stated within the analysis of plans as complex mental attitudes; a number of other such rules, along with examples of their use, can be found in chapter 6 of Pollack 1986. Such rules can enable a system to infer a wide range of plans, including plans that are constructed out of recipes-for-action that are not stored in the system's operator library. Adopting a view of plans as mental phenomena also makes it possible to reason about whether a particular set of actions is likely actually to be the object of an agent's plan. Consider once more the sample dialogue presented at the beginning of section 2. Imagine, however, that when the query is posed, S has reason to believe that A believes that Kathy is at home. In these circumstances S cannot use Rule PI1 to reason to the set of beliefs shown in figure 5.2; indeed, in this case A's query may be deemed to be incoherent. To distinguish between these two cases, it is necessary to have both a concern with the beliefs and intentions that are entailed by having a particular plan and a framework that distinguishes between the beliefs of the inferring agent and those that she attributes to the actor.

5 Reconsidering the Traditional Model

As I have emphasized throughout this paper, the traditional models in AI are models of the object of a plan, whereas my concern has been with the mental state of having a plan. But of course, when an agent has a plan, that plan does have an object—to wit, the set of acts he intends. What is the correspondence between the structure imputed to the actions that constitute a plan under the traditional approach and the structure imputed to the actions that are intended by an agent that has a plan under my approach? More specifically, what correspondences, if any, are there between the relations between acts used in the traditional models—*causes, is-a-precondition-of*, and *is-a-way-to*—and those used in the account of plans I have developed here—*generation* and *enablement*?

The relations used in the traditional view involve some redundancy, as illustrated by the following two operators:

Header: flip switch   Header: turn on light
Effect: light on   Body: flip switch

These operators encode the same information, provided we equate the act of turning on the light with the act of achieving that the light is on. In general, whenever some act α *causes* some proposition P, it is also true that α *is-a-way-to* achieve(P). It will thus be sufficient to restrict our attention to the two relations *is-a-precondition-of* and *is-a-way-to*.

Consider then the following generic operator, in which α *is-a-way-to* β, and P *is-a-precondition-of* β:

Header: β
Preconditions: P
Body: α

Is there a way to map the relations expressed in it into the two relations *generation* and *enablement*? In fact, there are a number of plausible mappings. Figure 5.3 shows some of these.

Sentence 1 of figure 5.3 encodes the interpretation, apparently implicit in certain operators, that the preconditions P are sufficient for the performance of the header β by performance of the body α, but without necessarily being sufficient for the performance of α itself (and consequently, without necessarily being sufficient for the performance of β itself). This is the interpretation that most straightforwardly translates into the relations between act-types used in this paper: under this interpretation, the entire generic operator is associated with the sentence CGEN(α, β, C). However, it is not always the interpretation implicit in existing planning work. Sentences 2a and 2b encode the interpretation of the preconditions P as necessary for the occurrence of β: these two sentences differ from one another in the time interval during which P is meant to hold. Consider a typical planning operator in which a proposition representing that the power is on is included as a precondition for an operator with a header representing the act of turning on the light. It is not always obvious whether the former is intended to be a necessary, or merely a sufficient, condition for performance of the latter. (It might be merely sufficient, if, say, the light is attached to an emergency generator.) The preconditions in an action operator are sometimes also meant to be related to the perfor-

Given

> Header: β
> Precondition: P
> Body: α

Does this mean

1. $CGEN(\alpha,\beta,P)$, that is,
   $OCCURS(\alpha,G,t) \wedge HOLDS(P,t) \rightarrow OCCURS(\beta,G,t) \wedge \ldots$

2a. $OCCURS(\beta,G,t) \rightarrow HOLDS(P,t)$
2b. $OCCURS(\beta,G,t) \rightarrow \exists t_0[MEETS(t_0,t) \wedge HOLDS(P,t_0)]$

3a. $OCCURS(\alpha,G,t) \rightarrow HOLDS(P,t)$
3b. $OCCURS(\alpha,G,t) \rightarrow \exists t_0[MEETS(t_0,t) \wedge HOLDS(P,t_0)]$

4a. $HOLDS(P,t) \rightarrow \forall G[EXEC(\alpha,G,t)]$
4b. $HOLDS(P,t) \rightarrow \forall t_1[MEETS(t,t_1) \rightarrow EXEC(\alpha,G,t_1)]$
   where some further restriction on the length of t_1 is also given

5a. $HOLDS(P,t) \rightarrow \forall G[EXEC(\beta,G,t)]$
5b. $HOLDS(P,t) \rightarrow \forall t_1[MEETS(t,t_1) \rightarrow EXEC(\beta,G,t_1)]$
   where, again, some further restriction on the length of t_1 is also
   given

or some combination of these—say, Sentences 4a and 1?

Figure 5.3
Interpretation of the standard relations.

mance of the act-type in the body of the operator—either to be necessary
for it, as encoded in sentences 3a and 3b, or to be sufficient for it, as
encoded in sentences 4a and 4b. One illustration of the preconditions
being related to the body act-type α instead of the header act-type β would
be an operator with a header representing turning on the light, body
representing flipping the switch, and precondition representing both the
power being on and the agent standing near the switch. The agent may
well be able to turn on the light without standing near the switch—say, by
throwing something at it. Standing near the switch is meant, in an example
like this, to be necessary for the body action to occur. Combinations of the
sentences shown in the figure are also possible: the interpretation underlying Sacerdoti's (1977) work seems to be a combination of sentences 1 and
4a.

Unfortunately, much of the existing planning literature has been vague
about the intended interpretation of action operators and has used them at
different times to mean different things. It is because of the resulting

ambiguity of interpretation that I have avoided using the relations *causes*, *is-a-precondition-of*, and *effects* in this work and have instead made use of *generates* and *enables*. Any particular operator that makes use of the former set of relations can be expressed in terms of the primitive relations OCCURS and HOLDS—the two relations that were themselves used to define *generates* and *enables*. The translation must proceed on an operator-by-operator basis, however; because of the variety of ways in which the traditional relations have been used, there is no one translation that will apply uniformly to all the operators that have been proposed in the literature.

6 Conclusion

For nearly two decades, research on cooperative conversation has entailed a concern with the notion of plans and with the process by which one agent can infer the plans of the other agents with whom she is conversing. In this paper I have argued that in understanding plan inference, it is important to go beyond studying the structure of the object of an agent's plan: it is necessary to analyze the nature of the mental state of the plan itself. I presented such an analysis, in which having a plan amounts to having a particular configuration of beliefs and intentions. I then showed how this analysis can be put to use in a model of conversation that avoids certain limitations of any approach that does not consider the nature of plans as complex mental attitudes. In particular, I showed how an analysis of plans as complex mental attitudes makes it possible to reason about the plans of an actor even when those plans are invalid: how to reason about whether it is likely that the actor has an invalid plan, how to reason about the ways in which the plan may be invalid, and how to reason about what information to consider including in a cooperative response to a query that arises from an invalid plan.

When plans are viewed as complex mental attitudes, the process of plan inference can be seen as that of attributing a collection of beliefs and intentions to an actor. Under this analysis there can be discrepancies between an agent's own beliefs and the beliefs that she ascribes to an actor when she thinks he has some plan. I associated such discrepancies with a judgment that the actor's plan is invalid. Then I showed that the types of any invalidities judged to be present in a plan inferred to underlie a query affect the content of a cooperative response. I further suggested that, to guarantee a cooperative response, an inferring agent must attempt to ascribe to a questioner more than just a set of beliefs and intentions sufficient to believe that he has some plan; she must also attempt to ascribe to him beliefs that explain those beliefs and intentions. The *eplan* construct was introduced to capture this requirement. I described the process of inferring eplans—that is, of ascribing to another agent beliefs and intentions that explain his query and can influence a response to it. Finally, I compared the representation used in traditional AI models of plans with the representation used here for the objects of an agent's plans, showing that the latter can be used to express and make more precise the intended meaning of uses of the former.

Notes

1. Recent work by Georgeff and Lansky (1986) is an exception.
2. For example, restrictions on the types of parameters, on the relations between parameters, and on the ordering of the subactions into which an action is decomposed. Constraints can be thought of as preconditions that the planning agent never attempts to achieve.
3. Several of the plan inference systems have additional rules that apply only to nodes that encode information-seeking actions. For example, many systems will construct a link from a node encoding "finding out whether P" to one encoding "achieving P." This construction is meant to capture the intuition that if an agent wants to know whether P is true, he may want P to be true. Kautz (1985) has shown how these rules, along with rules for handling nested plan inference, can be viewed as special cases of the three relations shown in figure 5.1.
4. This rule should be seen not as a sound rule of logical inference but as a rule that suggests an inference that is likely to be true. See Kautz and Allen 1986.
5. Condition 1, as well as Conditions 2 and 3, can be applied in "either direction": they can be used to add β when α is already in the subgraph, and they can be used to add α when β is already in the subgraph. Allen's Precondition-Action Rule, given above, corresponds to the former case for Condition 1. His system also includes the converse rule:

    SBAW(ACT) → SBAW(P), if P is a precondition of ACT.

6. Actually, there seems to be some tension regarding what is really meant by the W operator. Allen states that AW(P) means "A has a goal to achieve P," which seems to imply that P is a single action or property, not a whole plan. Consistent with this, he says that "SBAW(X) → SBAW(Y)" should be taken to mean that "if S believes A has a goal of X, then S may infer that A has a goal of Y" (1983, 120). But he uses these rules to infer not just that A has a goal of Y (that is, that his plan contains Y) but also that it contains X and Y related to one another in some particular way specified by the rule. So the rule relation preconditions and actions mentioned above should probably be written "SBAW(P) → SBAW(P → (is-a-precondition-of) ACT), if P is a precondition of ACT." Writing the rule this way would clarify Allen's model, but it would not affect the claim that the B and W operators are transparent to the inference rules.
7. Strictly speaking, the truth or falsity of the precondition at the time of the inference should not be what is at issue, but rather its truth or falsity at the time that the agent executes the action. Since the traditional systems have no explicit representation of time, however, this distinction collapses for them.
8. Throughout the rest of this paper I will make the simplifying assumption that when one dials a hospital, one reaches directly the person with whom one wants to speak. If the reader is uncomfortable with this simplification, the action of asking for Kathy can be inserted before the action of saying to Kathy "How are you doing?"
9. In fact, this condition may be slightly too strong: the agent need not be sure that performing his plan will entail performing his goal. In the normal state of affairs,

though, he will at least think this likely and will act as if he believed it. See the further discussion in section 3.3.

10. Bratman (1987) discusses the significance of partiality of plans in resource-bounded agents like humans and robots.

11. Notice that Π in this example need only be partially ordered: I may consider it irrelevant whether I first find out the phone number of St. Eligius and then the phone number of bank, or vice versa.

12. This claim may be less clear for the acts of asking Kathy how she is feeling and calling St. Eligius: it seems possible to say that I plan to ask Kathy how she is feeling by calling St. Eligius. The ordinary-language test is a rough one and occasionally fails to correlate with the phenomenal distinctions I want to draw.

13. Davidson's case rests upon examples such as the following: I might intend to make ten legible copies of what I am writing by pressing hard on carbon paper, without believing with any confidence that I will succeed. Grice maintains that many such examples are actually elliptical versions of conditional intentions. Contra Grice, Davidson argues that such an intention is *not* an elliptical version of a conditional intention to make the ten copies if I can, for since one cannot intend to do what is impossible, intending to do X if one can is equivalent to intending to do X simpliciter; nor is it an elliptical version of some more detailed conditional intention to do X if, for example, the carbon paper is particularly good, my hand muscles are more powerful than I thought, and so on. His argument against this is that "there can be no finite list of things we think might prevent us from doing what we intend, or of circumstances that might cause us to stay our hand" (1971, 94). This is obviously a description of the notorious "frame problem" that plagues AI.

14. Throughout, all variables should be taken to be universally quantified with widest possible scope, unless otherwise noted.

15. In fact, it captures more: to encode Clause 1 of Definition P0, the parameter i in Clause 1 of Defintion P1 need only vary between 1 and $n - 1$. However, given the following relationship between EXEC and GEN,

$$EXEC(\alpha, A, t) \wedge GEN(\alpha, \beta, A, t) \rightarrow EXEC(\beta, A, t),$$

the instance of Clause 1 of Definition P1 with $i = n$ is a consequence of the instance of Clause 1 with $i = n - 1$ and the instance of Clause 2 with $i = n - 1$. A similar argument can be made about Clause 3.

16. Recall the discussion in section 3.3 about assuming that an intention to α entails a belief that the agent will do α.

17. The plan inference rules should really be stated in terms of plausible eplans, that is, collections of beliefs and intentions that S thinks A plausibly has. When S has found some set of these that is large enough to account for A's query, their epistemic status can be upgraded to beliefs and intentions that S will, for the purposes of forming her response, consider A actually to have. See Pollack 1986, 126–130.

18. A rule symmetric to Rule PI1 is also needed since S can reason not only about what acts might be generated by an act that she already believes A plausibly intends but also about what acts might generate such an act.

References

Allen, James F. (1979) A plan-based approach to speech act recognition. Technical Report 121, Department of Computer Science, University of Toronto, Toronto, Ont.

Allen, James F. (1983). Recognizing intentions from natural language utterances. In Michael Brady and Robert C. Berwick, eds., *Computational models of discourse.* Cambridge, MA: MIT Press.

Allen, James F. (1984). Towards a general theory of action and time. *Artificial Intelligence* 23, 123–154.

Bratman, Michael E. (1983). Taking plans seriously. *Social Theory and Practice* 9, 271–287.

Bratman, Michael E. (1987). *Intention, plans, and practical reason.* Cambridge, MA: Harvard University Press.

Brown, John Seely, and Richard R. Burton (1978). Diagnostic models for procedural bugs in basic mathematical skills. *Cognitive Science* 2, 155–192.

Carberry, M. Sandra (1985). Pragmatic modeling in information system interfaces. Doctoral dissertation and Technical Report 86-07(1986), University of Delaware, Newark, DE.

Collins, Allan, Albert Stevens, and Sarah E. Goldin (1979). Misconceptions in student's understanding. *International Journal of Man-Machine Studies* 11, 145–146.

Davidson, Donald (1980). Intending. In *Essays on actions and events.* New York: Oxford University Press.

Fikes, R. E., and Nils J. Nilsson (1971). STRIPS: A new approach to the application of theorem proving to problem solving. *Artificial Intelligence* 2, 189–208.

Genesereth, Michael R. (1979). The role of plans in automated consultation. In *Proceedings of the Sixth International Joint Conference on Artificial Intelligence,* Tokyo.

Georgeff, Michael P., and Amy L. Lansky (1986). Procedural knowledge. *Proceedings of the IEEE, special issue on knowledge representation,* 1383–1398.

Goldman, Alvin I. (1970). *A theory of human action.* Princeton, NJ: Princeton University Press.

Grice, H. P. (1971). Intention and uncertainty. *Proceedings of the British Academy* 57, 263–279.

Kautz, Henry A. (1985). Toward a theory of plan recognition. Technical Report 162, University of Rochester, Rochester, NY.

Kautz, Henry A., and James F. Allen (1986). Generalized plan recognition. In *Proceedings of the National Conference,* American Association for Artificial Intelligence, Philadelphia, PA.

Litman, Diane (1985). Plan recognition and discourse analysis: An integrated approach for understanding dialogues. Doctoral dissertation and Technical Report 170, University of Rochester, Rochester, NY.

Nilsson, Nils J. (1980). *Principles of artificial intelligence.* Palo Alto, CA: Tioga Publishing Co.

Pollack, Martha E. (1986). *Inferring domain plans in question-answering.* Technical Report 403, SRI International, Menlo Park, CA. Also Doctoral dissertation, University of Pennsylvania, Philadelphia, PA.

Sacerdoti, Earl D. (1977). *A structure for plans and behavior.* New York: American Elsevier.

Sidner, Candace L. (1985). Plan parsing for intended response recognition in discourse. *Computational Intelligence* 1, 1–10.

Woolf, Beverly, and David McDonald (1983). Human-computer discourse in the design of a Pascal tutor. In *Proceedings of the Conference on Human Factors in Computing Systems,* Association for Computing Machinery's Special Interest Group on Computer and Human Interaction, Boston.

Chapter 6
A Circumscriptive Theory of Plan Recognition
Henry Kautz

1 Introduction

1.1 Motivation

Perhaps the central concern of artificial intelligence is to devise methods for representing and reasoning about actions and plans. Whereas plan synthesis has received careful formal analyses (McCarthy and Hayes 1969), the inverse problem of plan recognition (or action interpretation) has appeared in mainly empirical and domain-specific programs of research. These include work on story understanding (Bruce 1981; Wilensky 1983), psychological modeling (Schmidt, Sridharan, and Goodson 1978), natural-language pragmatics (Allen 1983a; Litman and Allen 1984), intelligent computer system interfaces (Huff and Lesser 1982), and strategic planning. In each case one is given a fragmented, impoverished description of the actions performed by one or more agents and is expected to infer a rich, highly interrelated description. The new description fills out details of the setting and relates the actions of the agents in the scenario to their goals and future actions. The result of the plan recognition process can be used to generate summaries of the situation, to help (or hinder) the agent(s), and to build up a context for use in disambiguating further observations. This paper develops a formal analysis of plan recognition. The analysis provides a firm foundation for much of what is loosely called "frame-based inference" (Minsky 1975) and directly accounts for problems of ambiguity, abstraction, and complex temporal interactions, which were ignored by previous approaches.

Plan recognition problems can be classified as cases of *intended* or *keyhole recognition* (Cohen, Perrault, and Allen 1982). In the first case, but not the second, the observer can assume that the agent is deliberately structuring his activities in order to make his intentions clear. Recognition problems can also be classified according to whether the observer has complete knowledge of the domain and whether the agent may try to perform

This work was supported in part by the National Science Foundation under grant DCR-8502481.

erroneous plans (Pollack 1986). This paper concentrates on keyhole recognition of correct plans, where the observer has complete knowledge. However, I will also consider some examples from discourse, which are cases of intended recognition.

An important preliminary step is to define the scope of inferences that must be treated by a theory of plan recognition. Plan synthesis can often be viewed as purely hypothetical reasoning (that is, if I did A, then P would be true). Some attempts have been made (Charniak and McDermott 1985) to formalize plan recognition as a similar kind of hypothetical reasoning: infer a plan P, such that if the agent did P, then he would do the observed action A. Only a space of *possible* inferences is outlined, and little or nothing is said about why one should infer one conclusion over another or what one should conclude if the situation is truly ambiguous. (Such criticism also applies to work based on "likely" inference (Allen 1983a; Cohen 1984; Pollack 1986).) A satisfactory theory of plan recognition must specify what conclusions are absolutely *justified* on the basis of the observations, our knowledge of actions, and other explicit assumptions. In fact, the framework presented in this paper allows one to draw conclusions based on the *class* of *simplest* plans that contain the observed actions.

What form should a theory of plan recognition take? Recognition is not a kind of deductive inference, and so the theory cannot be represented solely by a set of axioms (unless a metalanguage is used; see Genesereth 1983). I begin with a model theory, which relates the models of the observation statements to the models of the conclusions. Next I present a proof theory, which describes how the observation statements are mechanically (but nondeductively) transformed so that the conclusions logically follow. Finally I describe an algorithmic (or process) theory, as a practical means of automatically generating "interesting" conclusions.

The vocabulary that has been used to describe plan recognition varies considerably. I will speak uniformly of observations as *descriptions of events*. The observer's knowledge is represented by a set of first-order statements called an *event hierarchy*. The result of the recognition process is a description of the *End events*, those that are self-contained and self-justifying, which make up the situation. The wide applicability of the event vocabulary suggests that this work is relevant to areas of artificial intelligence not normally associated with planning or plan recognition, such as diagnostic reasoning.

1.2 Overview

An event hierarchy is a collection of restricted-form first-order axioms, used to define the abstraction, specialization, and functional relationships between various kinds of events. The functional, or "role/value," relationships include the relation of an event to its *component* subevents. There is a

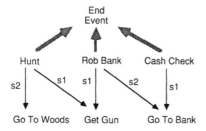

Figure 6.1
A simple event hierarchy.

distinguished type-predicate, End, which holds of events that are not components of any other events. Recognition is the problem of classifying the End events that generate a set of observed events.

An event hierarchy does not, however, by itself justify inferences from observations to End events. Consider the example shown in figure 6.1. (The thick grey arrows denote abstraction or "isa," and the thin black arrows denote component or "has part.") Suppose GetGun(c) is observed. This statement, together with the hierarchy, H, does not entail $\exists x . Hunt(x)$, or $\exists x . Hunt(x) \lor RobBank(x)$, or even $\exists x . End(x)$. There are models of $\{GetGun(c)\} \cup H$ in which none of these statements hold. For instance (where we describe a model by listing its positive atoms), none hold in $\{GetGun(c)\}$, and only the last holds in $\{GetGun(c), End(d), CashCheck(d), GoToBank(s1(d))\}$.

Yet it does seem reasonable to conclude that someone is either hunting or robbing a bank, on the basis of the given hierarchy. This conclusion is justified by assuming that the event hierarchy is *complete*: that is, whenever a non-End event occurs, it must be part of some other event, and the relationship from event to component must appear in the hierarchy. This completeness assumption can be expressed by defining a special subclass of models of H, called *covering models*. For the example, $\{GetGun(c), c = s1(d), Hunt(d), GoToWoods(s2(d)), End(d)\}$ and $\{GetGun(c), c = s1(d), RobBank(d), GoToBank(s2(d)), End(d)\}$ are covering models of H, but none of the other models described above are.

The notion of a covering model is used to define a new semantic relation, called *c-entailment*. In this example GetGun(c) c-entails $\exists x . Hunt(x) \lor RobBank(x)$. We relate c-entailment to ordinary entailment and deduction by defining a *closure* function such that a statement is c-entailed by an observation if and only if that statement deductively follows from the observation and the closure of the event hierarchy.

When several events are observed, still stronger assumptions are commonly employed. Suppose that $\{GetGun(c), GoToBank(d)\}$ is observed.

This set does not c-entail an instance of robbery; the model containing an instance of hunting *and* an instance of check cashing provides a counter-example. By Occam's razor (do not multiply entities unnecessarily) we *would* be justified in concluding $\exists x . \text{RobBank}(x)$; this principle can be realized by distinguishing the *minimum covering models* of the observations. These models define a final semantic relation between observations and conclusions, *mc-entailment*.

This formal framework shows how one can infer "up" an event hierarchy and unify the alternative explanations of several observations in order to reach to a strong conclusion. Very few restrictions are placed on the kinds of events that can be encoded: disjunctions may appear in plans or in observations; observations may be incomplete; and, as explained below, arbitrary temporal constraints may appear between events. We will consider examples from a "cooking" microworld, speech act theory, and an intelligent operating-system interface.

Has the framework's power and generality been bought at the cost of computational intractability? I believe not. Though it is easy to show that the *worst-case* cost of solving a plan recognition problem matches that of general deduction (namely, exponential on the size of the knowledge base), careful use of event *abstraction* can significantly collapse the search space. Furthermore, many examples can be quickly solved in practice by *graph-matching* algorithms. I will briefly sketch a graph-based recognition algorithm that implements the formal theory. The algorithm is also useful and interesting in that it suggests what (forward-chaining) conclusions *should* be drawn, whereas the formal framework only specifies what conclusions *can* be drawn. The algorithm has been implemented (Kautz 1987) and used to solve all the examples discussed here.

2   Representation

2.1   Language

The representation language is first-order predicate calculus with equality. A model provides an interpretation of the language, mapping terms into individuals, functions into mappings from tuples of individuals to individuals, and predicates into sets of (tuples of) individuals. If M is a model, then this mapping can be made explicit by applying M to a term, function, or predicate. For example, for any model M,

Loves(Sister(Joe),Bill) is true in M if and only if
⟨M[Sister](M[Joe]), M[Bill]⟩ ∈ M[Loves].

Metavariables (not part of the language) that stand for domain individuals begin with a colon. Thus, one may write

Let :C be an event token in Domain(M).

Models map free varibles in sentences to individuals. We write $M\{x/:C\}$ to mean the model that is just like M, except that variable x is mapped to individaul :C. Quantification is defined as follows:

$\exists x . p$ is true in M if and only if
    there exists $:C \in Domain(M)$ such that p is true in $M\{x/:C\}$.

The universal quantifier and the propositional connectives are defined in the ususal way.

2.2 Time, Properties, and Events

Most formal work on representing action has relied on the situation calculus or dynamic logic (Harel 1979). Though these formalisms are convenient for planning, they prove awkward for plan recognition: it is impossible (without extreme convolutions; see Cohen 1984) to state that some particular action *actually occurred* at a particular time. We therefore adopt a "reified" representation of time and events.

Time is linear, and time *intervals* are individuals, each pair related by one of Allen's interval logic relations: Before, Meets, Overlaps, and so on (Allen 1983b). Event *tokens* are also individuals, and event *types* are represented by unary predicates. Various "role" functions on event tokens yield the parameters of the event, including its *time*.

The predicate Holds relates a time-dependent *property* and a time interval over which the property holds. For example, the fact that John is unhappy at time T1 might be represented by the formula

Holds(unhappy(John),T1).

All properties are dense: if one holds over an interval, then it holds over all subintervals of that interval. The prediacte Never holds of property and a time when the property holds over no subinterval of the time.

2.3 Event Hierarchy

An event hierarchy is a collection of restricted-form axioms and may be viewed as a logical encoding of a *semantic network*, as in Allen and Frisch 1982. An event hierarchy H contains the following parts, H_E, H_A, H_{EB}, H_D, and H_G:

• H_E is the set of unary event type predicates, including the distinguished predicates AnyEvent and End.

• H_A is the set of abstraction axioms, each of the form

$\forall x . E_1(x) \supset E_2(x)$,

for some $E_1, E_2 \in H_E$. In this case we say that E_2 *directly abstracts* E_1.

The transitive closure of direct abstraction is abstraction; and the fact that E_2 is the same as or abstracts E_1 is written E_2 abstracts* E_1. AnyEvent abstracts* all event types.

• H_{EB} is the set of basic type predicates, those members of H_E that do not abstract any other event type.
• H_D is the set of decomposition axioms, each of the form

$$\forall x . E_0(x) \supset E_1(f_1(x)) \wedge E_2(f_2(x)) \wedge \ldots \wedge E_n(f_n(x)) \wedge \kappa,$$

where $E_0, \ldots, E_n \in H_E$; $f_1, \ldots, f_n$ are role functions; and κ is a subformula containing no member of H_E. The formula κ describes the *constraints* on E_0. E_1 through E_n are called *direct components* of E_0. The type End never appears as a direct component of another type; nor does any type that End abstracts.
• H_G is the set of general axioms, those that do not contain any member of H_E. H_G includes the axioms for the temporal interval relations, the density axioms for Holds and Never, and any other facts not specifically relating to events.

2.4 Components of Event Tokens

The component relation may be applied to event tokens in model M as follows. Suppose :C_i and :C_0 are event tokens. Then :C_i is a direct component of :C_0 in M if and only if

1. There are event types E_i and E_0, such that :$C_i \in M[E_i]$ and :$C_0 \in M[E_0]$.
2. H_D contains an axiom of the form

$$\forall x . E_0(x) \supset E_1(f_1(x)) \wedge \ldots \wedge E_i(f_i(x)) \wedge \ldots \wedge$$
$$E_n(f_n(x)) \wedge \kappa.$$

3. :$C_i = M[f_i](:C_0)$.

The component relation is the transitive closure of the direct component relation, and the fact that :C_n is either the same as or a component of :C_0 is written :C_n is a component* of :C_0.

2.5 Acyclic Hierarchies

An *acyclic* hierarchy is one that can be exhaustively searched in finite time. It is formally defined as follows. Two event predicates E_1 and E_2 are *compatible* if there is an event type E_3 such that both E_1 and E_2 abstract* E_3. A hierarchy is acyclic if it contains no series of event predicates $E_1, E_2, \ldots, E_n$ such that

1. E_i is a direct component of E_{i+1} for odd i, $1 \leq i \leq n - 1$.
2. E_j is compatible with E_{j+1} for even j, $2 \leq j \leq n - 2$.
3. E_n is compatible with E_1.

We will consider only acyclic hierarchies in this paper, although most results extend to cyclic hierarchies as well.

2.6 Example: The Cooking Microworld

The actions involved in cooking form an interesting yet tractable domain for plan recognition. The specialization relations between various kinds of foods are mirrored by specialization relations between the actions that create those foods. Decompositions are associated with the act of preparing a type of food, in the manner in which a recipe spells out the steps in the food's preparation. Good cooks store information at various levels in their abstraction hierarchies. For example, one knows certain actions that are needed to create any cream-based sauce, as well as conditions (constraints) that must hold during the preparation. The sauce must be stirred constantly, the heat must be moderate, and so on. A specialization of the type cream-sauce, such an Alfredo sauce, adds steps and constraints: for example, one should slowly stir in grated cheese at a certain point in the recipe. Different End events may share steps. For example, the cook may prepare a large batch of tomato sauce and then use the sauce in two different dishes. Figure 6.2 illustrates part of a cooking hierarchy. The figure illustrates some of the elements that make up the event hierarchy:

- The set of event types, H_E, includes PrepareMeal, MakeNoodles, MakeFettucini, and so on.

Figure 6.2
Part of the cooking microworld hierarchy.

- The abstraction axioms, H_A, include

  $\forall x . \text{MakeSpaghetti}(x) \supset \text{MakeNoodles}(x)$
  $\forall x . \text{MakeFettucini}(x) \supset \text{MakeNoodles}(x)$
  $\forall x . \text{MakePastaDish}(x) \supset \text{PrepareMeal}(x)$.

- The basic event types, H_{EB}, at the bottom of the abstraction (gray) hierarchy, include Boil, MakeSpaghettiMarinara, MakeChicken Marinara, and MakeFettucini. Note that basic event types may have components (but no specializations).
- The decomposition axioms, H_D, include much information that does not appear in the diagram.

Following is (an abbreviated version of) the decomposition axiom for the MakePastaDish event. This act includes at least three steps: making noodles, making sauce, and boiling the noodles. The equality constraints assert, among other things, that the agent of each step is the same as the agent of the overall act and that the noodles the agent makes (specified by the **result** role function applied to the MakeNoodles step) is the thing boiled (specified by the **input** role function applied to the Boil step). Temporal constraints explicitly state the temporal relations between the steps and MakePastaDish. For example, the time of each step is during the time of the MakePastaDish, and the Boil must follow the MakeNoodles. The constraints include the *preconditions* and *effects* of the event. A precondition for MakePastaDish is the fact that the agent is dexterous (making pasta by hand is no mean feat!). An effect of the event is that the **result** of the event is ready to eat during a time period **postTime**, which immediately follows the time of the cooking event.

$\forall x . \text{MakePastaDish}(x) \supset$

Components	$\text{MakeNoodles}(s1(x)) \land$
	$\text{MakeSauce}(s2(x)) \land$
	$\text{Boil}(s3(x)) \land$
Equality	$\text{agent}(s1(x)) = \text{agent}(x) \land$
constraints	$\text{result}(s1(x)) = \text{input}(s3(x)) \land$
Temporal	$\text{During}(\text{time}(s1(x)), \text{time}(x)) \land$
constraints	$\text{Before}(\text{time}(s1(x)), \text{time}(s3(x))) \land$
	$\text{Meets}(\text{time}(x), \text{postTime}(x)) \land$
Preconditions	$\text{Dexterous}(\text{agent}(x)) \land$
Effects	$\text{Holds}(\text{readyToEat}(\text{result}(x)), \text{postTime}(x))$.

The event types that specialize MakePastaDish add additional constraints and steps to its decomposition; for example, the event type MakeSpaghetti Marinara further constrains its decomposition to include MakeSpaghetti (rather than the more generic MakeNoodles) and MakeMarinaraSauce (rather than simply MakeSauce).

Using this axiomatization, the English statement "Joe made the noodles on the table yesterday" might be recorded as follows:

MakeNoodles(Make33) ∧
agent(Make33) = Joe ∧
result(Make33) = Noodles72 ∧
Holds(onTable(Noodles72), Tnow) ∧
During(time(Make33), Tyesterday).

3 Covering Models

We have seen that there are too many models of an event hierarchy to construct a semantic basis for recognition. A technique known as *model minimization* can be used to select a suitable subset, called *covering models*. In a covering model, any non-End event is a component of some End event. Each covering model for an observation serves as an *explanation*, in terms of End events, of the observation. Though it would be unwise to arbitrarily adopt a *particular* covering model, it is reasonable to conclude whatever propositions hold in *all* covering models. These propositions are *c-entailed* by the observation. The sequence of model minimizations used to construct the covering models corresponds to a complex (yet easily computed!) application of McCarthy's *predicate circumscription* schema.

3.1 Model Minimization

Let M_1 be a member of a class of models μ, and let π be a set of predicates. M_1 is *minimal in π among μ* if and only if there does not exist any other model M_2 such that

1. M_2 is a member of μ.
2. M_1 and M_2 have the same domain.
3. M_1 and M_2 agree on the interpretation of all constants, functions, and predicates not in π.
4. The extension of every member of π in M_2 is a subset of the extension of that predicate in M_1.
5. The extension of some member of π in M_2 is a proper subset of the extension of that predicate in M_1.

If M_1 fails to be minimal because of such an M_2, we say that M_2 *defeats the candidacy* of M_1.

3.2 Completing the Abstraction Hierarchy

Construction of the covering models involves two steps: first, the abstraction hierarchy is completed; second, the decomposition hierarchy is completed. (The order is important; the reverse order eliminates all models. See

Kautz 1987 for details.) This section defines the *A-closed* models. For example, if End does not abstract* E_1, then any model containing an event that is both an E_1 and an End is not A-closed. Let M be a model of H_A. Then

- M is *closed under specialization* if M is minimal in $H_E - H_{EB}$ among models of H_A. That is, all nonbasic event predicates are minimized.
- M is *closed under abstraction* if M is minimal in $H_E - \{AnyEvent\}$ among models of H_A that are closed under specialization.
- Finally, we define M to be an *A-closed* model of H just in case M is a model of H, and M is also a model of H_A that is closed under abstraction.

The following theorems describe the A-closed models in proof-theoretic terms. Proofs appear in Kautz 1987. Theorem 3 shows that we have assumed that all event types are disjoint, unless H explicitly states otherwise. (Disjointedness assumptions are used heavily in recognition, as demonstrated below. We do not assert that different event types cannot occur simultaneously; only that a particular token cannot be of two noncompatible types.) Theorem 4 says that every event is of exactly one basic type. Theorem 5 presents a complete axiomatization of the A-closed models.

Theorem 1   Exhaustion
Suppose $\{E_1, E_2, \ldots, E_n\}$ are all the predicates directly abstracted by E_0 in H_A. Then the statement

$$\forall x . E_0(x) \supset (E_1(x) \lor E_2(x) \lor \ldots \lor E_n(x))$$

is true in all models of H_A that are closed under specialization.

Theorem 2   Exhaustion Completeness
Let EXA be the set of all statements that instantiate Theorem 1 for a particular H. M_1 is a model of H_A closed under specialization if and only if M_1 is a model of $H_A \cup EXA$.

Theorem 3   Disjointedness
If event predicates E_1 and E_2 are not compatible, then the statement

$$\forall x . \neg E_1(x) \lor \neg E_2(x)$$

is true in all models of H_A that are closed under abstraction.

Theorem 4   Unique Basic Types
If :C is an event token in M_1, a model of H_A closed under abstraction, then there is a unique basic event type E_b such that :C $\in M_1[E_b]$. Any event type that holds of :C abstracts* E_b.

Theorem 5   Abstraction Completeness
Let DJA be the set of all statements that instantiate Theorem 3 for a particular H. M_1 is an A-closed model of H if and only if M_1 is a model of $H \cup EXA \cup DJA$.

3.3 Completing the Decomposition Hierarchy

Once the abstraction hierarchy has been closed, it is a simple matter to close the decomposition hierarchy, by minimizing the set of non-End event types. C-entailment is then defined in terms of the covering models. Theorem 6 says that every non-End event must be a component of some other event, and Theorem 7 allows one to infer the disjunction of possible uses of the observed event token. One must consider all the possible abstractions and specializations of an event in order to account for all of these uses— and therefore predicate completion in the style of Clark (1978) does not correctly implement this step. By Theorem 8, every event is part of an End event, and by Theorem 9, the upward-inference assumptions exactly axiomatize the covering models. Theorem 10 states the obvious corollary that c-entailment is computable.

Definition of Covering Model and C-Entailment
M is a *covering model* of H if M is minimal in $H_E-\{End\}$ among A-closed models of H. Then Γ *c-entails* Ω, written

$$\Gamma \ _H\!\models_c \Omega,$$

when Ω holds in all covering models of H in which Γ holds. If Ω holds for any Γ, Ω is *c-valid*.

Theorem 6   No Useless Events
Let M_1 be a covering model of H containing event token $:C_1$. Then either $:C_1 \in M_1[End]$ is true, or there exists some event token $:C_3$ such that $:C_1$ is a direct component of $:C_3$.

Theorem 7   Upward Inference
Let $E \in H_E$, and Com(E) be the set of event predicates with which E is compatible. Consider all the decomposition axioms in which any element of Com(E) appears on the right-hand side. The j-th such decomposition axiom has the following form, where E_{ji} is the element of Com(E):

$$\forall x . E_{j0}(x) \supset E_{j1}(f_{j1}(x)) \wedge \ldots \wedge E_{ji}(f_{ji}(x)) \wedge \ldots \wedge E_{jn}(f_{jn}(x)) \wedge \kappa.$$

Suppose that the series of these axioms, where an axiom is repeated as many times as there are members of Com(E) in its right-hand side, is of length m > 0. Then the following statement is c-valid:

$$\forall x \,.\, E(x) \supset End(x) \,\lor$$
$$(\exists y \,.\, E_{1,0}(y) \,\land\, f_{1i}(y) = x) \,\lor$$
$$(\exists y \,.\, E_{2,0}(y) \,\land\, f_{2i}(y) = x) \,\lor$$
$$\dots \,\lor$$
$$(\exists y \,.\, E_{m,0}(y) \,\land\, f_{mi}(y) = x).$$

Theorem 8   No Infinite Chains
If M_1 is a covering model of H containing event token :C, then there is a $:C_n$ such that $:C_n \in M_1[End]$ and :C is a component* of $:C_n$.

Theorem 9   Decomposition Completeness
Let CUA be the set of all formulas that instantiate Theorem 7 for a particular H. M_1 is a covering model of H if and only if M_1 is a model of $H \cup EXA \cup DJA \cup CUA$.

Theorem 10   Computability of C-Entailment
There is a computable function **cl** that maps a hierarchy H into a set of axioms with the property that

$$\Gamma \,_{H}\!\models_c \Omega$$

if and only if

$$cl(H) \cup \Gamma \vdash \Omega.$$

Cl simply generates $H \cup EXA \cup DJA \cup CUA$.

3.4 Circumscription
Predicate circumscription (McCarthy 1984) provides a proof-theoretic realization of the model-theoretic minimalization operation used above. Direct use of the circumscription schema is difficult, however. Its most general form is a second-order, rather than a first-order, statement. Techniques are known for automatically computing first-order circumscriptions for certain kinds of axiom sets—for example, for horn-clauses, or "separable" data-bases (Lifschitz 1985) None of these previously known techniques apply in the case under consideration here. However, the restricted form of event hierarchies has allowed us to directly compute a set of first-order statements that characterize all models resulting from a certain sequence of minimizations. This work thus describes a special but useful case in which circumscription can be efficiently computed.

The circumscription of the set of predicates π over a formula S, written $Circum(S[\pi], \pi)$, stands for the second-order formula

$$S[\pi] \,\land\, \forall\sigma \,.\, (S[\sigma] \,\land\, \sigma \leq \pi) \supset \pi \leq \sigma,$$

where the expression $\sigma \leq \pi$ abbreviates the formula stating that the extension of each predicate in σ is a subset of the extension of the corresponding predicate in π; that is,

$$(\forall x . \sigma_1(x) \supset \pi_1(x)) \wedge \ldots \wedge (\forall x . \sigma_n(x) \supset \pi_n(x)).$$

Theorem 11   C-entailment and Circumscription
For a given hierarchy H, a statement Ω is c-entailed by Γ if and only if Ω follows from the following schema:

$$\Gamma \wedge \text{Circum}(H \wedge \text{Circum}(\text{Circum}(H_A, H_E - H_{EB}),$$
$$\{\text{AnyEvent}\}),$$
$$H_E - \{\text{End}\}).$$

The two inner circumscriptions correspond to completing the abstraction hierarchy, and the final circumscription completes the decomposition hierarchy.

3.5 Example: The Cooking World, Continued

Let us return to the domain of cooking and consider some of the statements that appear in the closure of the event hierarchy. We will then use these statements to solve a simple plan recognition problem.

Exhaustion Assumptions (EXA)   In the cooking world, EXA includes the assertion that all End events are instances of either preparing meals or washing dishes:

$\forall x . \text{End}(x) \supset$
$\quad \text{PrepareMeal}(x) \vee$
$\quad \text{WashDishes}(x).$

Similarly, all instances of preparing meals are instances of either making a pasta dish or making a meat dish:

$\forall x . \text{PrepareMeal}(x) \supset$
$\quad \text{MakePastaDish}(x) \vee$
$\quad \text{MakeMeatDish}(x).$

One such axiom appears for every event type not in H_{EB}.

Disjointedness Assumptions (DJA)   DJA includes the assumptions that preparing a meal and washing dishes are disjoint, making a pasta dish and making a meat dish are disjoint, and so on:

$\forall x . \neg \text{PrepareMeal}(x) \vee \neg \text{WashDishes}(x)$
$\forall x . \neg \text{MakePastaDish}(x) \vee \neg \text{MakeMeatDish}(x).$

Component/Use Assumptions (CUA)   These axioms take us from an event to an event that has a compatible type as a component. It is frequently possible to simplify the statements in CUA, by taking advantage of the abstraction axioms. For example, according to the rule for construction of CUA, the component/use axiom for MakeNoodles is

$\forall x$. MakeNoodles(x) $\supset$
    ($\exists y$. MakePastaDish(y) $\wedge$ x = s1(y)) $\vee$
    ($\exists y$. MakeSpaghettiMarinara(y) $\wedge$ x = s1(y)) $\vee$
    ($\exists y$. MakeSpaghettiPesto(y) $\wedge$ x = s1(y)) $\vee$
    ($\exists y$. MakeFettuciniAlfredo(y) $\wedge$ x = s1(y)).

The following axiom is equivalent, because MakePastaDish abstracts the other types:

$\forall x$. MakeNooldes(x) $\supset$ $\exists y$. MakePastaDish(y) $\wedge$ x = s1(y).

We will use without further comment simplified versions of the assumptions in CUA.

The CUA for MakeSauce demonstrates the importance of considering compatible types. The only *direct* use of MakeSauce is MakePastaDish; however, MakeSauce abstracts MakeMarinara, and *that* event type appears in the decomposition of MakeChickenMarinara. Therefore, the axiom is

$\forall x$. MakeSauce(x) $\supset$
    ($\exists y$. MakePastaDish(y) $\wedge$ x = s1(y)) $\vee$
    ($\exists y$. MakeChickenMarinara(y) $\wedge$ x = s5(y)).

A Simple Recognition Problem   Let us suppose that the observer learns that the cook is preparing Marinara sauce. This is not enough information to conclude that a particular basic dish is being created: we cannot (as appears to be the case in most "script"-based story-understanding systems) imagine that a *single* plan is evoked. Instead, we are justified in concluding that the cook is making Spaghetti Marinara *or* Chicken Marinara. This disjunction collapses, via the abstraction axioms, to the fact that an event of type PrepareMeal is occurring. This final piece of information, nonspecific as it is, may still be of great interest—for instance, if we are hungry! Following is a sketch of the deductions one can make from the observation together with the closure of the hierarchy. (The proofs employ natural deduction, where new constants introduced by the rule of existential instantiation are prefixed by a *. These *-constants should be replaced by existentially quantified varibales for the conclusions to follow properly from the assumptions.)

    Observation
        MakeMarinara(Obs1)
    Component/Use, Existential Instantiation
        MakeSpaghettiMarinara(*I1) $\vee$ MakeChickenMarinara(*I1)

Abstraction
MakePastaDish(*I1) ∨ MakeMeatDish(*I1)
PrepareMeal(*I1)
End(*I1)

4 Minimum Covering Models

C-entailment does not combine information from several observations. We would like to intersect possible explanations for each event. This is done by selecting covering models that minimize the *number* of events. The previous section, and the theory of cicumscription, rely on *setwise* (not numeric) minimization. We can show that certain cases of *circumscription with variables* correspond to numeric minimization.

4.1 Minimum Covering Models

Let M_1 be a number of a class of models μ, and let π be a predicate. M_1 *has minimum cardinality in* μ if and only if there does not exist any other model M_2 such that

1. M_2 is a member of μ.
2. The size of the extension of π in M_2 is smaller than the size of the extension of π in M_1. That is, $|M_2[\pi]| < |M_1[\pi]|$.

For a given H, M_1 is a *minimum cover* of Γ just in case M_1 is a covering model of Γ, and M_1 has minimum cardinality in End among covering models of Γ. Ω is *mc-entailed* by Γ, written

$$\Gamma \mathrel{_H\!\models_{mc}} \Omega,$$

if Ω holds in all minimum covers of Γ.

The proof-theoretic counterpart of cardinality minimization is to adopt the strongest statement that limits the number of distinct End events. Unfortunately, this step is not always effectively computable (the usual problem with default reasoning). In practice, one makes the strongest assumption possible; forward chains a limited amount; if a contradiction is detected, then makes the next weaker assumption; and repeats.

Theorem 12 Minimum Cardinality Defaults
Consider the following sequences of statements.

$MA_0. \forall x. \neg End(x)$
$MA_1. \forall x,y. End(x) \wedge End(y) \supset x = y$
$MA_2. \forall x,y,z. End(x) \wedge End(y) \wedge End(z) \supset (x = y) \vee (x = z)$
    $\vee (y = z)$

Suppose there is a minimum covering model in which the extension of End is finite. Then

$$\Gamma_{H} \models_{mc} \Omega$$

if and only if

$$\Gamma \cup H \cup DNA \cup DJA \cup UPA \cup MA_i \vdash \Omega,$$

where i is the smallest integer such that the left-hand side of the provability relations is consistent.

4.2 Cardinality Minimization and Circumscription

At first glance it would seem that the theory of circumscription cannot handle the problem of minimizing the cardinality of the extension of a predicate. The circumscription schema states that there is no predicate that satisfies the axioms for the minimized predicate that has an extension that is a proper subset of that of the predicate. The extension must be minimal, not a minimum. But the more general theory of circumscription (McCarthy 1986) allows one to specify that certain predicates, functions, and/or constants *vary* during the minimization: models may be comparable even if they do not agree on those symbols. We can prove that (under easily met conditions) circumscribing a predicate where *all* other symbols are allowed to vary is equivalent to minimizing the cardinality of the extension of the predicate.

Theorem 13   Cardinality Circumscription

Let α include all the predicate, function, and constant symbols in our langauge other than End. Suppose that all models of H are infinite, and in some model of $\Gamma \cup cl(H)$, End has a finite extension. Then

$$\Gamma_{H} \models_{mc} \Omega$$

if and only if

$$Circum(\Gamma \cup cl(H), \{End\}, \alpha) \vdash \Omega,$$

where $Circum(\Gamma \cup cl(H), \{End\}, \alpha)$ means to circumscribe with α varying.

4.3 Example: The Cooking World, Continued

Let us continue with the example of plan recognition in the cooking world. The first observation leads to a disjunctive conclusion. Suppose the next observation is itself disjunctive: the cook is either making fettucini *or* making spaghetti. This disjunction can be collapsed to an instance of MakeNoodles, from which we can infer that an instance of MakePastaDish occurs. By itself, this conclusion leads to predictions about future acts, such as that the cook will boil water. But we can arrive at stronger conclusions by assuming the End event inferred from the first observation is the same as the End event inferred from the second. We conclude that the plan is MakeSpaghettiMarinara and that the second observed event must have been one of making spaghetti.

Second Observation
MakeFettucini(Obs2) ∨ MakeSpaghetti(Obs2)

Abstraction
MakeNoodles(Obs2)

Component/Use, Existential Instantiation
MakePastaDish(*I2)

Abstraction
PrepareMeal(*I2)
End(*I2)

Strongest Minimality Assumption
$\forall x,y . End(x) \land End(y) \supset x = y$

Universal Instantiation & Modus Ponens
*I1 = *I2

Substitution of Equals
MakePastaDish(*I1)

Disjointedness
$\forall x . \neg MakePastaDish(x) \lor \neg MakeMeatDish(x)$

Disjunction Elimination
¬MakeMeatDish(*I1)

Abstraction
MakeChickenMarinara(*I1) ⊃ MakeMeatDish(*I1)

Modus Tolens
¬MakeChickenMarinara(*I1)

Disjunction Elimination
MakeSpaghettiMarinara(*I1)

Decomposition & Substitution of Equals
MakeSpaghetti(Obs2)

5 Other Examples

The closure and minimality assumptions form a "bare-bones" theory of plan recognition. In many domains, additional information exists that further constrains the interpretation of the data (for example, shifts between different plans or End events may be explicitly signaled.) Nonetheless, the theory as described can be applied to more realistic domains. We will briefly consider an application to computer system interfaces and then a more detailed example in discourse analysis.

5.1 System Interfaces: Multiple Events

Several research groups have examined the use of plan recognition in "smart" computer interfaces, which could answer user questions and/or watch what the user was doing, and make suggestions about potential pitfalls and more efficient ways of accomplishing the same tasks (Huff and Lesser 1982; Wilensky 1982). A user often works on several different tasks during a single session at the terminal and frequently jumps back and forth between uncompleted tasks. Therefore, a plan recognition system for this domain must be able to handle multiple concurrent unrelated plans. Our framework directly handles these cases.

Kautz (1987) presents a detailed analysis of the following situation. The event hierarchy includes several plans for renaming a file: one employs the *move* command, whereas the other (less efficient) plans involve copying a file and then deleting the original version. Suppose the user types the following sequence of commands:

(1)   % copy foo bar

(2)   % copy jack sprat

(3)   % delete foo

Any minimum cover for these events contains two end events: the first is a "rename by copy," which has events (1) and (3) as components; the second is any plan (perhaps a different "rename by copy") that has (2) as a component. Though some uncertainty exists, the system can respond

  *** You can rename a file by typing
  *** % move oldname newname

This example again stresses the fact that a recognition system need not develop a *single* interpretation of all its observations in order to respond intelligently. It also demonstrates the importance of a reified language of events, since we may need to reason explicitly about multiple event tokens of the same type.

5.2 Indirect Speech Acts

One of the most important application areas for plan recognition is in discourse analysis. The following example shows how one could recognize an indirect request. It deomonstrates the use of the constraints that appear in the decomposition of an event to reduce the number of alternative interpretations.

We will use a very simple representation of belief. Recall that properties are represented by terms. The property that an agent A knows P is simply represented by applying the function **know** to terms for the agent and property P. The function **can** relates an agent and a property the agent can bring about. We assume that for every act (event) type, there is a property that holds just after an instance of the event occurs. Thus, the fact that John knows at time T_1 that Mary can give John the salt might be written

Holds(know(John,can(Mary,gave(Mary,John,salt))), T_1).

Finally, we need the function **knowif**, which relates an agent and a property whose truth-value the agent knows. Many objections can be raised to this notation (such as the omission of time indexes on the objects of beliefs), but it suffices for the example.

Figure 6.3 shows part of the event hierarchy. The types SurfaceQuestion and SurfaceImperative are utterances types. Role functions of the event type, such as **speaker**, **hearer**, and **content**, appear in a smaller font. Request and InformIf are speech act event types. A request can be special-

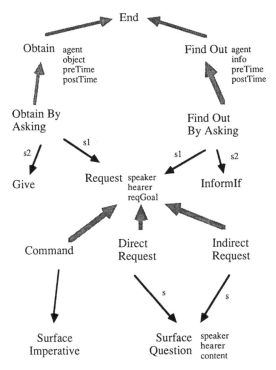

Figure 6.3
A simplified language use hierarchy.

ized as a Command, a DirectRequest, or an IndirectRequest. Each of these specializations corresponds to a different decomposition of the Request speech act, such as appears in Litman and Allen 1984. Some of the discourse plans that employ speech acts are ObtainByAsking and FindOutBy-Asking. These discourse plans specialize more general methods for obtaining objects and finding out whether a piece of information is true or false.

Following is an abbreviated list of the axioms for this hierarchy. All the actions have roles of **agent** and **time**, and other roles as specified.

- *Nonlinguistic Acts:* Obtain has the role of the **object** to be obtained. During **preTime** the **agent** does not have the **object**; during **post-Time** the **agent** does. FindOut has the role **info**, a property, whose truth-value is to be determined. During **preTime** the **agent** does not **knowif** the **info** is true or false; during **postTime** the **agent** does.

$\forall x \,.\, \mathrm{Obtain}(x) \supset$
$\quad \mathrm{Never}(\mathrm{have}(\mathrm{agent}(x),\mathrm{obj}(x)), \mathrm{preTime}(x)) \wedge$
$\quad \mathrm{meets}(\mathrm{preTime}(x), \mathrm{time}(x)) \wedge \ldots$
$\quad \mathrm{Holds}(\mathrm{have}(\mathrm{agent}(x),\mathrm{obj}(x)), \mathrm{postTime}(x)) \wedge$
$\quad \mathrm{meets}(\mathrm{time}(x), \mathrm{postTime}(x)) \wedge \ldots$
$\forall x \,.\, \mathrm{FindOut}(x) \supset$
$\quad \mathrm{Never}(\mathrm{knowif}(\mathrm{agent}(x), \mathrm{info}(x)), \mathrm{preTime}(x)) \wedge$
$\quad \mathrm{meets}(\mathrm{preTime}(x), \mathrm{time}(x)) \wedge$
$\quad \mathrm{Holds}(\mathrm{knowif}(\mathrm{agent}(x), \mathrm{info}(x)), \mathrm{postTime}(x)) \wedge$
$\quad \mathrm{meets}(\mathrm{time}(x), \mathrm{postTime}(x)) \wedge \ldots$

- *Discourse Acts:* The decomposition of ObtainByAsking states that the **agent** performs a Request, whose **reqGoal** is that the **hearer** gave the **agent** the **object**. This step, **s1**, is followed by step **s2**, in which the **hearer** gives the **agent** the **object**.

$\forall x \,.\, \mathrm{ObtainByAsking}(x) \supset$
$\quad \mathrm{Requests}(s1(x)) \wedge$
$\quad \mathrm{reqGoal}(s1(x)) = \mathrm{gave}(\mathrm{hearer}(s1(x)), \mathrm{agent}(x), \mathrm{obj}(x)) \wedge$
$\quad \mathrm{Give}(s2(x)) \wedge \ldots$

FindOutByAsking is very similar; the decomposition states that the **agent** of the truth-value of the **info**. In **s2** the **affected** performs an InformIf to the **agent**.

$\forall x \,.\, \mathrm{FindOutByAsking}(x) \supset$
$\quad \mathrm{Request}(s1(x)) \wedge$
$\quad \mathrm{reqGoal}(s1(x)) = \mathrm{informedIf}(\mathrm{hearer}(s1(x)), \mathrm{agent}(x),$
$\quad \mathrm{info}(x)) \wedge$
$\quad \mathrm{InformIf}(s2(x)) \wedge \ldots$

• *Speech Acts:* Each of the specializations of a Request contains a single *utterance act* in its decomposition. The single step in a Direct-Request is a surface yes-no question. The **reqGoal** of the Direct-Request must be that the **affected** has informed the **agent** of the truth-value of the (propositional) **content** of the SurfaceQuestion.

$\forall x$. DirectRequest$(x) \supset$
    SurfaceQuestion$(s(x)) \land$
    reqGoal$(x) =$ informedIf(hearer(x), speaker(x),
      content$(s(x))) \land \ldots$

The single step of an IndirectRequest is also a SurfaceQuestion; however, there is a different relation between the **content** of the question and the **reqGoal** of the request. The question must be a "can" question, of the form "Can the affected bring about the goal of the request?"

$\forall x$. IndirectRequest$(x) \supset$
    SurfaceQuestion$(s(x)) \land$
    content$(s(x)) =$ can(hearer(x), reqGoal$(x)) \land \ldots$

• *Completeness Assumptions:* The following axioms are generated by assuming that the hierarchy is complete. Whenever a SurfaceQuestion occurs, it must be part of a DirectRequest or an IndirectRequest; and whenever a Request occurs, it must be part of an ObtainByAsking or a FindOutByAsking.

$\forall x$. SurfaceQuestion$(x) \supset$
    $(\exists y$. DirectRequest$(y) \land x = s(y)) \lor$
    $(\exists y$. IndirectRequest$(y) \land x = s(y))$.
$\forall x$. Request$(x) \supset$
    $(\exists y$. ObtainByAsking$(y) \land x = s1(y)) \lor$
    $(\exists y$. FindOutByAsking$(y) \land x = s1(y))$.

The problem   Suppose S says to H, "Can you give me the salt?" Real-world knowledge (part of H_G) includes the statement that at all times S knows whether or not H can give S the salt:

$\forall t$. Hold(knowIf(S, can(H, gave(H,S,salt))), t).

An instance of a SurfaceQuestion, Q1, occurs, with the content "H can give S the salt."

SurfaceQuestion(Q1) $\land$ speaker(Q1) $=$ S $\land$ hearer(Q1) $=$ H $\land$
    content(Q1) $=$ can(H, gave(H,S, salt)).

Now apply the component/use assumption for SurfaceQuestion. It must be the case that Q1 is either a step of some DirectRequest(call it *R1) or a step of some IndirectRequest. In either case the constraints can be used to determine the possible reqGoals. In the direct case the goal must be for H to tell S whether or not H can give S the salt. In the indirect case the goal must be for H to give S the salt:

DirectRequest(*R1) $\land$ Q1 = s(*R1) $\land$
    reqGoal(*R1) = informedIf(H,S, can(H, gave(H,S,salt)))

$\lor$

IndirectRequest(*R1) $\land$ Q1 = s(*R1) $\land$
    reqGoal(*R1) = gave(H,S,salt).

Neither alternative can (yet) be eliminated on the basis of inconsistent constraints. So we apply the second component/use assumption to this statement, yielding a four-way disjunction describing the act *R2 that has step *R1. Constraint information can now be used to eliminate all but one alternative.

> *FindOut Action*
>> *Direct Request : Precondition Fails*
>>> *R1 is a direct request, and the goal of *R1 is to be informed if H can pass the salt. *R1 is the first step of the FindOut action. However, the constraint that S does not know if H can pass the salt before the action occurs is provably false.
>>
>> *Indirect Request : Ill Formed*
>>> *R1 is an indirect request, and the goal of *R1 is for H to pass the salt. *R1 is the first step of the FindOut action. However, to be part of FindOut, the goal of *R1 must be of the form informedIf(—), instead of gave(—). Therefore, this alternative is ill formed.
>
> *Obtain Action*
>> *Direct Request : Ill Formed*
>>> *R1 is a direct request, and the goal of *R1 to be informed if H can pass the salt. *R1 is the first step of the Obtain action. However, to be part of Obtain, the goal of *R1 must be of the form gave(—), instead of informedIf(—). Therefore, this alternative is ill formed.
>>
>> *Indirect Request : Accepted*
>>> *R1 is an indirect request, and the goal of *R1 is for H to pass the salt. *R1 is the first step of the Obtain action. This alternative is well formed, and no violated constraints can be found.

The following statement encodes this analysis. An x appears at the point in each alternative where an inconsistency is detected.

> FindOutByAsking(*R2) ∧ *R1 = s1(*R2) ∧
> DirectRequest(*R1) ∧ Q1 = s(*R1) ∧
> reqGoal(*R1) = informedIf(H,S, can(H, gave(H,S,salt))) ∧
> reqGoal(s1(*R2) = informedIf(H,S, info(*R2)) ∧
> info(*R2) = can(H, gave(H,S,salt)) ∧
> x   Never(knowif(S, can(H, gave(H,S,salt))), preTime(*R4))

> ∨

> FindOutByAsking(*R2) ∧ *R1 = s1(*R2) ∧
> IndirectRequest(*R1) ∧ Q1 = s(*R1) ∧
> reqGoal(*R1) = gave(H,S,salt)
> x   reqGoal(s1(*R2)) = informedIf(H,S, info(*R2)) ∧

> ∨

> ObtainByAsking(*R2) ∧ *R1 = s1(*R2) ∧
> DirectRequest(*R1) ∧ Q1 = s(*R1) ∧
> reqGoal(*R1) = informedIf(H,S, can(H, gave(H,S,salt))) ∧
> x   reqGoal(s1(*R2)) = gave(H,S, obj(*R2)) ∧

> ∨

> ObtainByAsking(*R2) ∧ *R1 = s1(*R2) ∧
> IndirectRequest(*R1) ∧ Q1 = s(*R1) ∧
> reqGoal(*R1) = gave(H,S, salt) ∧
> reqGoal(s1(*R2)) = gave(H,S,object(*R2)) ∧
> √   object(*R2) = salt.

The final disjunct must be true: the recognizer is justified in concluding that S is performing the plan to obtain the salt by asking for it.

6 Algorithms for Plan Recognition

Two related problems arise in implementing our theory of plan recognition: inference must be *directed* toward some particular goal and must be *limited* in some manner to ensure that our programs don't run forever. The pattern of inference apparent in the previous examples suggests some answers: from each observation, apply upward-inference assumptions until an instance of type End is reached. Reduce the number of alternatives by checking constraints *locally* at each disjunction. In order to combine information from two observations, equate the instances of End inferred from each and propagate the equality, further reducing disjunctions. If all alterna-

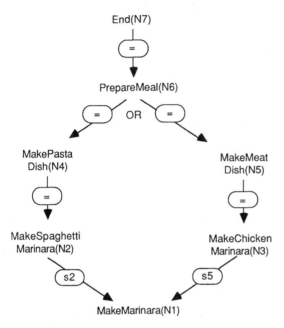

Figure 6.4
The explanation graph created to explain MakeMarinara.

tives are eliminated, then conclude that the observations belong to distinct
End events.

These operations suggest a *graph-based* implementation, rather than one
that stores sentences in clausal form. The result can be considered a "constraint propagation network," as well as a notational variation of FOPC. A
graph is built bottom-up, from a node that represents an observed event, to
a node that represents an End event. When we need to infer up the
abstraction hierarchy, we create a new node of the more abstract kind and
record the more specialized node as an "alternative for" the abstract node.
If this is done properly, the result can be viewed as an and/or graph, *rooted
at the End node.* The "alternative" arcs are "or" arcs, and the arcs that
represent component (step) relations are "and" arcs. Figure 6.4 shows the
graph that is generated by the first cooking example above.

Figure 6.5 provides sketches of the algorithms that search upward from
each observation and match two graphs. The **match** algorithm is called
with the End nodes of two graphs and returns the End node of the
combined graph. The algorithms have been abbreviated for presentation;
see Kautz 1987 for the full, correct versions.

Restricting ourselves to local constraint checking limits computation
considerably. Yet a great concern remains the possibility of generating an

infer-upward($n1$)

    if have already visited a node na that has the same type and role/values as $n1$
    then

        equate $n1$ and na
        return

    endif

    check temporal and fact constraints on $n1$

    forall types tu with a direct component fr of type($n1$)

        if have not already created a node nu which has a node na as its fr role
            such that na is a more abstract or more specialized version of $n1$
            then

                create a new node nu of type tu with $n1$ as its fr role
                infer-upward(nu)

        endif

    endfor

    forall $ta \in$ direct-abstractions(type($n1$))

            create a new node na of type ta
            add $n1$ as an alternative for na
            copy appropriate roles of $n1$ to na
            infer-upward(na)

    endfor

    if $n1$ is not a more abstract version of some other node **then**

        forall $ts \in$ direct-specializations(type($n1$))

                create a new node ns of type ts
                copy roles of $n1$ to ns
                infer-upward(ns)

        endfor

    endif

end infer-upward

match($n1, n2$)

    if $n1$ and $n2$ have already been matched **then**

        return that result

    endif

    check that type($n1$) and type($n2$) are compatible

    create a new node $n3$ of the greatest lower bound type of type($n1$) and
        type($n2$)

    add all known role/values of $n1$ and $n2$ to $n3$, matching identical roles

    check temporal and fact constraints on $n3$

    for every alternative $a1$ for $n1$

        for every alternative $a2$ for $n2$

            add match($a1, a2$) as an alternative to $n3$, if match is successful

        endfor

    endfor

    fail if there were alternatives of $n1$ or $n2$, but none matched

    return $n3$

end match

Figure 6.5
Algorithms for creating and combining explanation graphs.

unmanageably large number of alternatives; indeed, some have suggested that a plan recognition system should never infer past a disjunction (Sidner 1985). Careful design of the abstraction hierarchy, however, greatly reduces search. If the only roles defined in the hierarchy H are components, then we can guarantee that the upward search will never create more than $O(size(H))$ nodes. If other roles (such as agent, time, and so on) appear, the search space will be larger. During the upward-inference process, however, very few of these roles will have known values. Thus, the first step in **infer-upward** will very frequently find a similar node and cut off search.

The algorithms have been implemented in Common LISP, and appear practical in small domains. (Recognition problems in a more elaborate cooking microworld run in a few seconds.)

7 Conclusions and Extensions

In this paper I have presented a formal theory of plan recognition, in terms of model, proof, and process theories. This work does not make claims of psychological validity but does attempt to clear up some of the mystery surrounding nondeductive inference in high-level artifical intelligence. The framework reveals the assumptions that underlie previous work in plan recognition, while providing a more general basis for future development. The theory does not assume that there is a single plan underway, which can be uniquely identified from the first input. It also does not assume that the sequence of observations is complete. Finally, it does not assume that all the steps in a plan are linearly ordered.

7.1 Learning and Errors

Every day new kinds of events occur, and yet they do not baffle us. An intelligent agent cannot rely only on a recognition system; it must contain a learning component as well. An appropriate strategy is to invoke a "learning module" when recognition fails. The ability of the framework to handle levels of abstraction provides a crucial feature needed for learning. For example, one might be able to conclude that the agent is cooking some kind of pasta dish, even if one can rule out any of the particular pasta dishes in our library. It may be possible to modify the minimal model construction so that the exhaustiveness assumption is weakened and thus allow the recognition and learning modules to be integrated.

Nonetheless, much of what a plan recognition system must handle is routine. A more serious problem is that of recognizing erroneous plans. Our framework assumes all plans are internally consistent and that all acts are purposeful. Yet real people make frequently make planning errors and change their minds in midcourse.

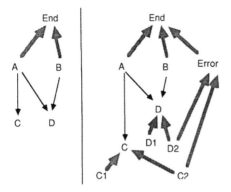

Figure 6.6
Extending an event hierarchy with the Error event.

A large class of errors can be handled without significant change. Suppose every basic event type is given two new specializations, one of which also specializes a new type called Error. Figure 6.6 illustrates how a hierarchy would be transformed. Then each observed event could be either an End event on its own by being an Error or part of an End event in a correct plan from the original hierarchy. Minimizing the number of End events prefers interpretations in which Errors do not occur; but observations sequences that must be part of erroneous plans can still be recognized.

7.2 Quantitative Measures

Some plan recognition problems require principles other than Occam's razor for determining the class of preferred interpretations. Rather than ordering models during the minimization process by the number of End events, one may wish to include other factors, such as qualitative likelihoods of various event types. It reamins to be seen how far the general framework can be pushed, or whether other, more quantitative measures belong in a separate theory, which applies to the conclusions of our system.

7.3 Open Problems: Scale-Up and Primitives

Several important unresolved issues remain. One is the question of scale-up. As discussed above, the worst-case behavior of our recognition algorithms can be bad, although proper structuring of the hierarchy greatly reduces search. How much of a problem will this be in more realistically sized knowledge bases? Experience in creating and examining the structure of larger domains is necessary.

A more philosophical problem is the whole issue of what serves as primitive input to the recognition system. Throughout this paper I have assumed that arbitrary high-level descriptions of events are simply presented to the recognizer. This assumption is reasonable in many domains, such as understanding written stories or observing the words typed by a computer operator at a terminal. But real plan recognizers—human beings—do not always get their input in this way. How do visual impressions of simple bodily motions—John is moving his hands in such and such a manner—translate into the impression that John is rolling out dough to make pasta? The semantic gap between the output of the low-level processes and the high-level inference engines remains wide, and few have ventured to cross it.

References

Allen, James (1983a). Recognizing intentions from natural language utterances. In Michael Brady and Robert C. Berwick, eds., *Computational models of discourse*. Cambridge, MA: MIT Press.

Allen, James (1983b). Maintaining knowledge about temporal intervals. *Communications of the ACM* 26, 832–843.

Allen, James, and Alan Frisch (1982). What's in a semantic network? In *Proceedings of the Twentieth Annual Meeting*, Association for Computational Linguistics, Toronto, Ont.

Bruec, B. C. (1981). Plans and social action. In R. Spiro, B. Bruce, and W. Brewer, eds., *Theoretical issues in reading comprehension*. Hillsdale, NJ: L. Erlbaum Associates.

Charniak, Eugene, and Drew McDermott (1985). *Introduction to artificial intelligence*. Reading, MA: Addison-Wesley.

Clark, K. L. (1978). Negation as failure. In J. Minker, ed., *Logic and databases*. New York: Plenum Press.

Cohen, Philip (1984). Referring as requesting. In *Proceedings of the Tenth International Conference on Computational Linguistics*, Stanford, CA.

Cohen, Philip, Raymond Perrault, and James Allen (1982). Beyond question-anwering. In W. Lehnert and M. Ringle, eds., *Strategies for natural language processing*. Hillsdale, NJ: L. Erlbaum Associates.

Genesereth, Michael (1979). The role of plans in automated consultation. In *Proceedings of the Sixth International Joint Conference on Artificial Intelligence*, Tokyo.

Genesereth, Michael (1983). An overview of meta-level architecture. In *Proceedings of the National Conference*, American Association for Artificial Intelligence, Washington, DC.

Harel, David (1979). *First-order dynamic logic*. New York: Springer-Verlag.

Huff, Karen, and Victor Lesser (1982). Knowledge-based command understanding: An example for the software development enviroment. Technical Report 82–6, Computer and Information Sciences, University of Massachusetts, Amherst, MA.

Kautz, Henry (1987). A formal theory of plan recognition. Technical Report 215, Department of Computer Science, University of Rochester, Rochester, NY.

Lifschitz, Vladimir (1985). Computing circumscription. In *Proceedings of the Ninth International Joint Conference on Artificial Intelligence*, Los Angeles, CA.

Litman, Diane, and James Allen (1984). A plan recognition model for clarification sub-dialogues. Technical Report 141, Department of Computer Science, University of Rochester Rochester, NY.

McCarthy, John (1986). Applications of circumscription to formalizing commonsense knowledge. *Artificial Intelligence* 28, 89–116.

McCarthy, J., and P. Hayes (1969). Some philosophical problems from the standpoint of artificial intelligence. In *Machine intelligence 4*. Edinburgh: Edinburgh University Press.

Minsky, Marvin (1975). A framework for representing knowledge. In P. H. Winston, ed., *The psychology of computer vision*. New York: McGraw-Hill.

Pollack, Martha (1986). A model of plan inference that distinguishes between the beliefs of actors and observers. In *Proceedings of the Twenty-fourth Annual Meeting*. Association for Computational Linguistics, New York, NY. Reprinted in M. Georgeff and A. Lansky, eds., *Reasoning about actions and plans: Proceedings of the 1986 workshop*. Los Altos, CA: Morgan Kaufmann.

Schmidt, C. F., N. S. Sridharan, and J. L. Goodson (1978). The plan recognition problem: An intersection of psychology and artificial intelligence. *Artificial Intelligence* 11, 45–83.

Sidner, Candace (1985). Plan parsing for intended response recognition in discourse. *Computational Intelligence* 1, 1–10.

Wilensky, Robert (1982). Talking to UNIX in English: An overview of U.C. In *Proceedings of the National Conference*, American Association for Artificial Intelligence, Pittsburgh, PA.

Wilensky, Robert (1983). *Planning and understanding*. Reading, MA: Addison-Wesley.

Chapter 7

On Plans and Plan Recognition: Comments on Pollack and on Kautz

W. A. Woods

First, I would like to say that I liked both papers. Both are well done and provide contributions to our understanding of intentional communication. Pollack's focus on digging out more of the structure of plans (as mental entities) and the degree to which a hearer must understand a speaker's plan is definitely progress in the research direction set by her predecessors: Schmidt, Bruce, Perrault, Cohen, and Allen. Kautz's tour de force in formalizing a model-theoretic semantics for the notion of a minimum independent assumption criterion for plan recognition and his characterization of the problem as an instance of McCarthy's circumscription operation gives us a perspective on how plan recognition (at least this version of it) ties in to foundational work on theories of nonmonotonic reasoning.

Neither paper is the final word in the endeavor, but both are making progress in a beneficial direction. In these comments, I want to endorse and support the direction and the progress, at the same time pointing out where further progress is required.

It is important to recognize that in understanding the problems of intentional communication, and the role of plan recognition in it, we are still at the earliest stages. For example, though Kautz's paper appeals to the notion of circumscription, the theory of circumscription is still an infant theory of nonmonotonic reasoning, and in the end he gets no effective deduction system from his characterization of plan recognition as circumscription. Instead, he has to develop his own algorithm for the kind of circumscription that he is doing (which is not itself formally characterized). Moreover, one must recognize that the model of planning that is being formalized is itself but a crude approximation as a model of plans (as Pollack's paper begins to demonstrate).

On the positive side, Kautz's characterization of a hierarchy of actions with a fairly rich model of temporal relationships is definite progress in the scope of problems to which the plan recognition approach has been applied. On the other hand, his version of plan recognition, which explicitly formalizes only keyhole recognition of correct plans, omits the key insight of Allen's previous work that in *intended* plan recognition there are additional (essentially computational) constraints that one can exploit to recognize that one's hypotheses are on the wrong track if they begin to explode with local ambiguity.

My verdict on Kautz's paper is that it is an impressive technical achievement, but primarily a technical exercise, illustrating a perspective on a very special class of plan recognition (unintended recognition of complete plans). It is unwarranted to conclude, "... I have presented a formal theory of plan recognition ...".

For perspective, we might liken the situation to that of the early days of transformational grammar theory when people were constructing transformational grammars of just the predicate complement construction, without any effective computational algorithms that could parse nontrivial grammars, or any idea of the size and nature of a full grammar of English. At the time, that constituted a significant achievement, but it was recognized as only a beginning. Twenty years later, linguists are still making progress in grammar theory, but today's grammatical theories look very different from those of the early 1960s.

In a similar way, it is premature to think that we have yet found anything close to a theory of Plan Recognition. McCarthy and Hayes were careful to characterize their endeavor (which Kautz characterizes as "careful formal analysis") as just a beginning.

I would like to caution Kautz and others that it takes more to make a theory of something than just formalizing it in a Tarskian model theory and proving some theorems. As cleverly and elegantly as Kautz's formalization has been done, I can't help but feel that the result tends to mask the essence of plan recognition rather than illuminate it. For example, throughout the paper, the embedding of the ideas within the notations of the predicate calculus seems consistently to make them less clear and less intuitive than the corresponding English statements of the principles.

Moreover, the effort to cast them into this language has almost the feel of programming in assembly language or Turing machine quintuples when one would like a higher-level language. There is nothing native in the predicate calculus that lets me declaratively talk about searching for a minimum number of end events—rather, it is an impressive feat to find a way to express that intuitive insight within the formalism. Moreover, nothing seems to be bought as a result of the effort other than a certain aesthetic appreciation and the respect of one's colleagues.

The insight that one is looking for a plan that makes the minimum number of independent assumptions ("end events") does not come as a result of this encoding but is rather a source insight that has to be rather laboriously fitted into the predicate calculus framework. Similarly, the appeal to circumscription does not result in a computational algorithm. Instead, a tractable algorithm has to be developed for this special case. Moreover, the question of whether the real criterion for plan recognition should in fact be minimum independent assumptions, which is not seriously addressed in Kautz's paper, is encoded into the basic representation of the problem in such a way that the entire formalization needs to be scrapped if one wants to consider any other criterion—for instance, something about the degree of coherence of the plan, or the likelihood that the speaker has the plan.

Finally, there is no provision for modeling a hearer's ability to detect when the plan recognition process has gone astray and to rediscover a more correct plan (in "garden path" discourses)—in fact, there is no notion of tracking a plan through a discourse as the discourse develops. Rather, one would seem to need the entire discourse to be present and then begin the search for a minimum covering plan.

My major disappointment with Kautz's paper is that he doesn't give the same care and rigor to presenting and proving the capabilities of his algorithm that he gives to the formal model theory. For all his effort devoted to formalizing a model-theoretic semantics for plan recognition and his identification of the problem as one that can be expressed as circumscription, he gets as a result only a general appreciation of how the problem relates to formal nonmonotonic reasoning. Comparable care and rigor applied to the *computational* questions of how to tractably find the plan from the evidence would have more payoff, both in utility and (I suspect) in understanding the essence of plan recognition. If we are to make progress in this area, we need that kind of rigor and discipline applied to the computational problems of plan recognition.

In summary, Kautz's feat is impressive, but one questions whether more effort spent in the direction of a computational formalization wouldn't have been more productive.

Turning to Pollack's paper, I would like to emphasize the importance of the kind of activity that she has undertaken—pushing against the limitations of the notion of speech act understanding as plan recognition and then extending the capabilities of the model to deal more completely with the phenomenon being modeled. The realization that understanding a discourse in terms of a speaker's plan does not require that plan to be objectively well formed is clearly on target, and the identification of the need to keep track of who believes that the steps of the plan will succeed is a major advance. Likewise, her focus on the structure of a plan as a mental attitude is on target. However, once again, we are far from done.

A speaker can have a plan with very little structure ("I plan to go to college"/"I plan to become a millionaire somehow"). Just as it is too strong to require a recognized plan to be factually correct or correct in the belief space of the hearer, it is also too strong to require it to be complete and correct in the belief space of the speaker (Pollack acknowledges this in a footnote). One can have a plan that is incomplete. For example, one might plan to teach at a university after finishing one's doctorate, and then to achieve tenure. One can have this plan without having worked out any of the steps in any detail. Pollack's work does not deal with such partially specified plans.

Can such vague plans play the role of relating the utterances in a discourse in the same way that a complete plan does in Pollack's paper? It's quite easy to find examples where they do. For example, consider this discourse: "I have a tenure track position. I've written 12 papers this semester and I'm organizing a conference for next spring. I'm also on the admissions committee because the dean asked me to." Clearly the tenure plan is a likely organizing principle here, and yet no step of this plan has any definite goal to achieve nor does the speaker believe that these acts will necessarily achieve the overall goal. It is conventional wisdom that such actions will contribute toward the desired goal and increase its likelihood, and that is sufficient to make the actions predictable as part of a plan.

Hence, we must be aware that this paper addresses only one aspect of the oversimplification of plan recognition as a search for plans that are factually correct (that is, that will provably achieve their goals). It improves on this model by relaxing the constraints to allow plans that are only believed to be correct by the speaker, but it still fails to handle plans that may not be complete or whose individual steps may only justify some expectation that they will possibly achieve their goals—far short of believing that they will.

Moreover, the insight that speech act understanding involves *intentional* communication means that the issue for the hearer is not just to find some plan that could relate the utterances in the discourse but in fact to find a plan that the hearer believes he or she was intended to recognize. This requires additional constraints that the plan hypothesized must be in some sense obvious or salient—there must be reason to believe that the speaker could have expected the hearer to arrive at it.

In addition, it will probably be necessary, in general, not only to take into account the speaker's beliefs about the effectiveness of plan steps but also to keep track of when the speaker might have had such beliefs. For example, consider the sentence "When I was little I wanted my brother to be quiet, so I called the telephone operator." (This sentence was actually uttered by the child of a friend of mine). Although it's not clear what plan the child (when he was younger) had had in mind when he called the telephone operator, the dialogue is comprehensible, in part because my friend and I recognized that the child could have had some kind of plan in mind.

Finally, we will need to deal with conditional plans and plans that involve information seeking and replanning or plan elaboration as part of the plan.

The above considerations deal with further extensions of the notion of intentional communication as plan recognition that will be necessary in order to use the discovery of a plan as a criterion for the coherence of connected discourse. However, there are other problems that indicate that this is not the only criterion for discourse coherence.

On the one hand, there are situations in which one can deduce the possibility of a plan, but the discourse still seems ill formed—for example, "I wanted to become a millionaire, so I bought a newspaper."

Moreover, there are purely configurational characteristics of a discourse that can signal that two utterances are to be related in terms of a plan, even when it is not possible to infer anything at all about the plan—for example, "I want to get tenure, so I've rented a car." This clearly demands the response "How will renting a car help you to get tenure?", but the question of whether renting the car is part of the plan doesn't seem to be in doubt. The conjunction "so" unambiguously signals the intended goal-achieving relationship without the necessity of determining the plan in order to infer it. How do we integrate situations in which surface clues tell us that a step is part of a plan with situations in which no surface clues are present, but the evidence comes from being able to infer a probable plan?

This obviously requires different principles to be exploited in understanding a speaker's plans than a search through a space of known plan recipes and perhaps even more than a search through a productive space of possible plans generated from first principles. One cannot simply rely on discovery of a plan as the primary (certainly not the only) leverage point in understanding discourse.

Now let us consider further the issue of the structure of a plan. Though the characterization of plans as complex mental attitudes rather than merely sequences of actions is progress in the characterization of the problem, the examples that Pollack considers are still essentially sequences of actions. To be faithful to the insight, one should strive to encompass a more general range of plans. At the very least, plans should be thought of as networks of intended actions, with conditional choices and perhaps with iteration and looping within them—something like augmented transition networks or augmented Petri nets.

I believe that the essence of what makes such a structure a plan is not so much the actions making up the steps as the expectations of what the actions are to achieve. Moreover, an adequate model of a plan seems to demand a breakdown of those expectations into those that are desired, those that one is expecting as necessary or potential consequences, not necessarily desired, and those whose absence would lead us to abandon or modify the plan. In my view, a plan is more a network of sequential goals and expectations than it is a sequence of actions. A typical plan step (one of the edges in a plan net) involves not only an action but also an expectation of what that action will achieve. To execute a plan, it is not sufficient to merely do the planned action—that action must also achieve the planned result. Moreover, one can have a plan involving a sequence of goals with only a sketchy understanding of how those goals will be realized. A plan for which one has worked out all the details is a rather special case, and one that is almost never achieved in reality.

In summary, a plan is more than a sequence of actions, and even viewed as a mental attitude, its structure is more than a sequence or a partial order. For less restricted notions of plan and for nontrivial situations in which there are more than a few possible plans to choose from, the plan recognition process will not be so easy (and it is difficult enough already). What mechanisms and approaches can we see that might bring computational tractability to this problem? We come back again to the problem we were left with after Kautz's paper—we need more work on algorithms for performing plan recognition before we can exploit the benefits of these insights.

Chapter 8

Toward a Formal Theory of Communication and Speech Acts

Andrew J. I. Jones

1 The Flow of Information

According to Dretske (1981, 1983), a flow of information between a source s and a receiver r is possible only if what occurs at r depends nomically on what occurs at s. That is, we are correct in describing one event as carrying information about another event only if the occurrence of these events instantiates a lawlike regularity between them:

> The ring [of the telephone] *tells* me (informs me) that someone is calling my number, just as fingerprints carry information about the identity of the person who handled the gun, tracks in the snow about the animals in the woods, the honeybee's dance about the location of the nectar, and light from a distant star about the chemical constitution of that body. Such events are pregnant with information, because they depend, in some lawfully regular way, on the conditions about which they are said to carry information. (Dretske 1983, 56)

On the basis of these examples, one might be led to think that Dretske's analysis applies merely to cases of what Grice (1957) would have classified as instances of natural meaning; perhaps, therefore, it is of limited interest to one whose concern is information, and the flow of information, in genuine acts of communication, verbal or nonverbal.

However, Dretske clearly does not intend that a conclusion of this sort should be drawn; one of his earliest examples (1981, chap. 1), which he uses in describing the key features of Shannon and Weaver's account of "amount of information," concerns a manager in a firm who receives a written note indicating which one of a group of eight employees has been assigned to a particular task. Here again, according to Dretske, the event at r's end (the manager receives a piece of paper with the name HERMAN written on it) carries information about the event at s's end (the group's selection of one of its members) just to the extent that the occurrence of the former event depends, in some regular, lawful way, on the occurrence of the latter event. (So if, for instance, the messenger had lost the piece of paper on the way from the employees to the manager and then—not in fact knowing which name the employees had written—had made a blind guess, writing HER-MAN on a new slip of paper and then handing it to the boss, *that* event at *r* would have carried no information about the event at *s*, even though the employees did in fact select Herman). The main point here is that, as Dretske sees it, the fact that a linguistic device is employed is inessential in regard to what it is that makes the flow of information possible:

> The manner in which this theory applies to the transmission of information by linguistic means is the same as the way it applies to the transmission of information by any other means. This generality is one of its strengths. (Dretske 1981, 22)

Dretske does not want his concept of information to be confused with the concept of meaning. In a significant footnote (1981, 242, fn. 10), Dretske indicates that he takes Grice's account of nonnatural meaning to provide an analysis "of the sense of meaning that is relevant to language and semantic studies." He insists that nonnatural meaning is to be distinguished from information but allows that where the word "meaning" is used in Grice's *natural* sense, its sense is more or less indistinguishable from that of "information." For example, the spots on the child's face may mean (naturally mean) that the child has measles; the occurrence of the one event (the appearance of the spots) is nomically connected with the occurrence of the other event (the child's becoming infected with measles), and the former event carries information about the latter. *In this case* we have an instance of a causal dependency making possible a flow of information. However, it is important to note that Dretske goes to some lengths to argue that a flow of information between events *may* occur *in the absence of* a causal dependency between them:

> *If* one views the cause of an event as an essential part of some nomically sufficient condition for that event, then a causal relationship between A and B is *not* necessary for the transmission of information from A to B .... Questions about the flow of information are, for the most part, left unanswered by meticulous descriptions of the causal processes at work in the transmission of a signal. One can have full information without causality, and one can have no information with causality. And there is every shade of gray between these two extremes. (Dretske 1981, 33)

Now this point, it would seem, has an important bearing on the question of how it is that linguistic devices may be instrumental in conducting the flow of information. For intance—to use another of Dretske's examples (1981, 185)—it is not at all clear that the event of *r*'s reading the sentence "Elmer died" in the newspaper carries the information that Elmer died in virtue of some causal connection between these two events. But then what is the nature of the dependency that, in a case of this very familiar kind, makes the flow of information possible? As I understand it, Dretske's insistence on a distinction between information and nonnatural meaning indicates that he would not want to accept a Gricean line of answer to this question, which would presumably turn the focus of attention onto the intentions of language-users, in this case the intention of the newspaper reporter to produce in a reader a particular belief (by means of the recognition of that intention, and so on). Rather, Dretske wants to maintain that language-users may *mean something by* what they say or write—that is, mean something in more-or-less Grice's nonnatural sense—in virtue of the fact that the devices they employ in speaking or writing have an information-carrying capacity. I am convinced that this is the right strategy to adopt and have argued in support of it elsewhere, along lines different from Dretske's (Jones 1983). But its adoption leaves us, of course, with the task of supplying an adequate characterization of the information-carrying capacity of both the linguistic and the nonverbal devices used in genuine acts of communication.

It was a central point in Barwise's (1983) comments on Dretske 1981 that Dretske has simply not told us enough about what is "specific to the way *linguistic* situations carry information." Further, "we must understand the various types of nomic relations that allow information flow, and how one comes to be attuned to such relations" (p. 65). Within situation semantics, what are called "constraints" play a role very similar to that of Dretske's nomic dependencies, at least as regards explaining how one situation may contain information about another. Given what Barwise says about the shortcomings of Dretske's account, it is perhaps surprising that we do not find so very much in Barwise and Perry 1983 by way of characterization of the particular features of *conventional* constraints, since these are central to an understanding of how "linguistic situations" may contain information. Ironically, this is a point that Dretske himself took up in his own comments on *Situations and Attitudes*; indeed, he is not prepared to accept that conventional constraints are genuine constraints at all. After emphasizing what he takes to be the fundamental difference between natural and conventional signs, he goes on to say,

> In order to find something that can mean it is 4 [o'clock] when it isn't 4, and this is the sort of meaning we need for language, one must (in the Barwise-Perry program) have constraints (since all meaning is identified with constraints) but constraints that don't *really* constrain (since otherwise misinformation—something meaning that P when P isn't the case—would be impossible).... In Chapter 5 (on Constraints) Barwise and Perry concentrate on natural (necessary and nomic) con-

straints to the neglect of conventional constraints. Constraints, in general, are represented in terms of one event type *involving* another in the way kissing involves touching and smoke involves fire. But unless one lives in a community of truth-telling automata, "smoke" doesn't involve smoke in *this* way. It can't. If it did, it could never carry misinformation about the existence of smoke.... Their one example of a conventional constraint ("Here's a cookie" meaning there is a cookie present) may be respected by well-intentioned parents, but unless the relation "involves" permits probabilistic realizations (something they never suggest) it is not a constraint at all according to their definition of a constraint. (Dretske 1985, 11)

This is a curious dispute, with both parties accusing each other of the same failing. My present interest in it lies in the problem around which it revolves: how is the information-carrying capacity of conventional communicative devices to be characterized? My view is that Dretske has in fact given a more detailed answer to this question than Barwise would have us believe. There is a revealing passage (Dretske 1981, 191, first paragraph) where Dretske explains how the lines, marks, and symbols on a map are able to carry information about—to represent—the layout of a town; these marks on paper do not carry information about the town unless they are "*underwritten* by the intentions, integrity and executive fidelity of the people who make the maps" (Dretske's emphasis). It is thus only under "optimal conditions"—that is, in the absence of "ignorance, carelessness, or deceit" (Dretske's expressions, same paragraph)—that the map functions as a means of showing how things stand regarding the town's layout. But now, it seems to me, something quite essential has emerged: specification of those dependencies in virtue of which the flow of information along conventional channels becomes possible, calls for reference to be made to *optimal* or *ideal* conditions; it calls for reference to how things *ought* to be if the interests of the audience/receiver are to be met—how things *ought* to be if their interest in being reliably informed is to be satisfied. So it appears that a conventional information-carrying device functions as such if it is used in conformity to a rule, for the characterization of which a *deontic* modality will be required.

Expressed in the terms of situation semantics—that is, in terms of the constraints that allow one situation to contain information about another —it would seem that my point is, essentially, that conventional constraints will have to be construed as conditional constraints (Barwise and Perry 1983, 99–100; Barwise 1985, sec. 3.3), for which the background conditions will include the requirement that optimal conditions obtain: that the communicator can be relied upon not to mislead, that he is behaving as he ought to, relative to the receiver's interest in being reliably informed.

Expressed in terms borrowed from Wertheimer (1972), my position is that the lawlike dependencies that make possible the flow of information along conventional channels are the laws not of a System of Actuality but of a System of Ideality. There are good reasons for supposing that this is a conclusion that neither Dretske nor Barwise and Perry would welcome, for—depending on one's position regarding the ontological status of rules and norms—it may be impossible to square a deontic characterization of conventional constraints/dependencies with the view, shared by Dretske, Barwise, and Perry, that information "is an objective commodity" (Dretske 1983, 57). Dretske goes on to say, "It [information] is something that was in this world before we got here. It was...the raw material out of which minds were manufactured." Compare Barwise, who takes information to be something that is "out there in the world, not in the head,...it is not dependent on there being a representation of it—linguistic or otherwise. It is out there because lawlike constraints obtaining between situations enable one situation to carry information about another" (1983, 65).

To discuss this last issue further would be to digress from the main point I want to make in this opening section. But it is nevertheless relevant for me to mention that one way of replying to my comments is to argue that the conventions that make verbal and nonverbal signaling possible, as a means for transmitting information, are themselves properly viewed as *regularities in behavior*. This, of course, is the position taken by Lewis (1969, 1975). It is largely via a criticism of Lewis's theory that I have attempted to motivate my own approach, in previously published work (Jones 1981, 1983). What I have tried to do here is to indicate how essentially the same conclusions might be drawn on the basis of some difficulties apparently facing Dretske's theory, and situation semantics.

However, although my earlier work represents a critical reaction to Lewis's theory, it also trades heavily on certain fundamental features of Lewis's general approach to the study of semantics, pragmatics, and their interrelation. (And, in turn, it trades on the theory presented in Stenius 1967; see Lewis 1969, 177, fn. 8. Regrettably, Stenius's paper has received far less attention from speech act theorists than it deserves.) It is appropriate, then, that I try to indicate some of the main ways in which my view derives from Lewis's.

I accept, as a working hypothesis, the following distinction:

> I distinguish two topics: first, the description of possible languages or grammars as abstract semantic systems whereby symbols are associated with aspects of the world; and second, the description of the psychological and sociological facts whereby a particular one of these abstract semantic systems is the one used by a person or population. Only confusion comes of mixing these two topics. (Lewis 1972, 170).

My chief concern in Jones 1983, and in the next section of this paper, is with the second half of Lewis's distinction, which poses a fundamental characterization problem: that of specifying the conditions under which a possible language L (an abstract semantic system) may be said to be the (or a) language used by, or adopted by, a group of agents. As I see it, the task here is essentially one of specifying the kinds of mutual beliefs agents have in virtue of which it is possible for them to use an abstract semantic system as a device for communicating with each other, that is, as a device for transmitting information, asking questions, issuing orders, and so forth. The mutual beliefs are beliefs about acts of delivering (uttering or writing) sentences of L.

It is the account given under the first of the two distinguished topics that tells what the sentences of L mean: it is the model of L provided by the abstract semantic system that gives an account of sentence meanings and word meanings and of the ways in which the meanings of sentences are composed out of the meanings of their constituents. To my knowledge, the most comprehensive account Lewis offered of an abstract semantic system for a (fragment of a) natural language is found in Lewis 1972. There we are given a variant of Montague-style semantics, constructed upon a categorial syntax, together with an account of the way in which certain types of contextual coordinates play a role in the determination of the truth-conditions of sentences.

As indicated in Jones 1983, 32–33, I follow Lewis in accepting this mode of approach to the characterization problems raised in the first half of his distinction. It may well be, however, that alternative versions of truth-conditional semantics would be equally compatible with both Lewis's and my own analysis of what constitutes language use.

Note, further, that Lewis's account of language use is based upon his treatment of rather simple cases of nonverbal signaling (Lewis 1969, chap. 4). As he "progresses" from nonverbal signaling to language use, it is the structure of the underlying abstract semantic system that becomes more complex, rather than the account of what constitutes *use* of an abstract semantic system, which remains essentially the same. This is another point at which I have followed Lewis's lead.

Not too much has been written about how formal-semantical models of natural languages are to be incorporated within an account of language use. Very few of those who are sympathetic to the aims and methods of, for instance, Montague semantics, have addressed the issues raised in the second part of Lewis's distinction; a fair amount has been written, of course, about the treatment of various types of context-dependence, within formal models of natural language. But the general problem of specifying what constitutes language use—and thereby characterizing the overall framework within which the study of linguistic pragmatics is to be conducted—

has been by and large avoided. Lewis was a most interesting exception, and his work provided a natural point of departure.

2 Toward a Formal Theory

I have suggested that a deontic component must figure in any adequate account of what makes conventional signaling possible. But what are the properties of this deontic concept, and how does it fit into the family of concepts we need for describing the essential features of communicative interaction? These questions dominate the remainder of this paper, which outlines a somewhat modified version of the formal model set forth in Jones 1983.

Suppose that there exists a signaling system according to which an agent s may, in certain circumstances, indicate to agent a that the state of affairs described by "q" obtains, by bringing it about that the state of affairs described by "p" obtains. In other words, s may make use of a signaling rule, the content of which can be represented as follows: if, in certain circumstances, s brings it about that p, and his bringing it about that p is not misleading for a, then it is the case that q. In section 1 the suggestion was made that a signaling act fails to mislead if it may be said to be ideal, or optimal relative to the receiver's interest in being reliably informed. This, in turn, suggests the following form for the content of the signaling rule:

(1) $(E_sp \ \& \ Z \ \& \ O_aE_sp) \rightarrow q,$

where "E_sp" is read "s brings it about that p," "Z" describes some features of the context, and "O_aE_sp" is a relativized deontic expression to be read "s's bringing about p is optimal/ideal relative to a's interest in being reliably informed." ("$\&$" stands for truth-functional conjunction, "$\rightarrow$" for the truth-functional conditional.) For instance, it may be that s's hoisting a particular sequence of flags, the context being that he is on board a ship that is sailing in sight of land, is a way of signaling that the ship is carrying a cargo of explosives. I interpret this as meaning that any performance by s of this act (in these circumstances) that is optimal relative to a's interest in being formed does indeed indicate that the ship is carrying a cargo of explosives.

Given one further qualification, I want to maintain that the existence of rules of type (1) plays a central role in explaining how many, ordinary cases of signaling (nonverbal and verbal) are successfully accomplished. The qualification is that these rules "exist" as the objects of the agents' beliefs; usually, the rule describes the content of a shared, mutual belief of s and a, that is,

(2) $B_{sa}^*((E_sp \ \& \ Z \ \& \ O_aE_sp) \rightarrow q),$

where a formula of type "B_{sa}^*p" is read "s and a mutually believe that p." In the next section I shall make some brief comments on the semantics of the various modalities I use; for the moment I want to focus on how I use them in describing aspects of communicative interaction.

Suppose that (2) is true and that, on a particular occasion, s brings it about that p in circumstances of the type described by "Z," that is,

(3) $E_s p$ & Z.

Assume further that, on this occasion, a believes (3), that is,

(4) $B_a(E_s p$ & Z).

If it is now also the case that

(5) $B_a O_a E_s p$,

then I shall say that a trusts the reliability of s's signaling act. In virtue of elementary properties of the logic of mutual belief and the logic of (individual) belief, the truth of (2), (4), and (5) jointly implies the truth of

(6) $B_a q$.

Note that nothing has so far been said about s's intentions. The semantics of the operator "E_s" is defined in such a way that it may be true that s brings it about that p even though this was not an intentional action on his part. Furthermore, in (1) and (2) I do not assume that the specification of context ("Z") contains reference to the effects s may have intended to produce in a by bringing it about that p. In particular, there is no implicit reference here to Gricean intentions on the part of s. However, it will ordinarily be the case that—even though he has belief (4)—a will not also form a belief of type (5) unless he is prepared to attribute a certain sort of intention to s's bringing it about that p. What kind of intention might this be? Well, I think that, ordinarily, it will be a necessary condition of a's forming belief (5) that he believes that s's bringing about p was intended by s to be seen by a as an instance of implementation of the signaling rule whose content is expressed in (1). In other words, a must believe that s intends him to view his bringing it about that p as an act falling under—to be interpreted in the light of—this signaling rule. (Note that this necessary condition for a's forming belief (5) will not also be sufficient, unless a is extremely gullible). The question now arises how an intention of this kind on the part of s (and thus a's belief that s has this intention) is to be characterized.

Before I follow up this question, let me say that there are circumstances, which are not so ordinary, where the above-mentioned condition (for a's forming belief (5)) appears not to be necessary: for instance, it is possible that words s utters in his sleep, or that just slip out, unintended, under the stress of an interrogation, might be taken (perhaps correctly) by a to be a reliable indicator of the truth.

But putting these relatively unusual cases to one side, let me return to the issue of how to represent s's intention to implement a signaling rule. First, regarding the general question of how agents' intentions are to the represented, I adopt the proposal made by Pörn (1977, chap. 2). A sentence of the form

(7) $p \rightarrow \text{ShallE}_s q$

is understood as expressing a *norm* to the effect that, if p obtains, s is to bring it about that q. The core of Pörn's proposal was that the content of an agent's intention may be represented as a norm pertaining to that agent's action. What then would be the relationship between, say, the norm expressed by (7) and the agent , if it is the case that s intends to bring it about that q on the condition that p? Pörn chose the belief modality to capture this relationship and thus offered (8) by way of answer:

(8) $B_s(p \rightarrow \text{ShallE}_s q)$.

So, having an intention to do q on the condition that p amounts to having a belief to the effect that, if p obtains, q is to be done.

Now, if s intends that a is to view his bringing about p in circumstances Z as an instance of implementation of (1), then surely the least that has to be required of s is that he intends a to be aware of his bringing about p in Z. According to the proposal just outlined, (9) would represent this intention of s:

(9) $B_s((E_s p \text{ \& } Z) \rightarrow \text{ShallE}_s B_a(E_s p \text{ \& } Z))$.

Supposing that (2) is true and that, on a particular occasion, s brings about p in Z with the intention expressed by (9), but that s has no further intentions directed at producing changes in a's belief-state, should we then be prepared to say that s has implemented the signaling rule expressed by (1)? Suppose, in particular that s is totally indifferent in regard to the question of whether a is prepared to trust the reliability of his signaling act. Would we then have a genuine case of implementation of the signaling rule?

Intuitions may well vary on this issue. Although not much hinges on it as regards the rest of what I want to say, I am inclined to think that there are cases of informing that fit the above description—cases, for instance, where a messenger functions simply as a middleman in the process of transmitting information from one agent to another; he just relays the information, just repeats what he has been asked to say. Such cases are not typical acts of informing, but what is interesting about them is what they lack. What seems odd about them, and what marks off the key difference from typical communicative acts of the informing type, is the lack of commitment on the part of the messenger: apart from intending to get the audience to be aware of the communicative act he is performing, his attitude toward the effects of his action on the belief-state of the audience may be one of indifference.

What happens in the more typical cases, I suggest, is that s intends not merely to get a to form belief (4) but also to get a to form belief (5). That is, he has both the intention expressed by (9) and that expressed by (10):

(10) $B_s((E_s p \ \& \ Z) \rightarrow \text{ShallE}_s B_a O_a E_s p)$.

So I am now suggesting that, for the typical cases of informing, s intends his communicative act to be seen by a as an instance of implementation of the rule (1) provided that s intends to get a to believe that, on the occasion in question, the conditions specified in the antecedent of the rule have been satisfied. If an additional premise is now assumed, to the effect that, if an agent intends to bring about p, then he also intends to bring about whatever he believes will be a further consequence of p, then it will be possible to derive the result that s also has the intention of getting a to believe that q.[1]

Commitment, on the part of the communicator, is a notion that has figured rather prominently in presentations of speech act theory. It has also been assigned a leading role in Winograd and Flores's arguments to the effect that a computer could never truly be said to engage in genuine communicative interaction (because it could never enter into a commitment; see, for instance, Winograd and Flores 1986, 123). I do not find their account of commitment particularly clear, nor do I claim to be able to clarify *their* notion. What I do want to suggest is that my model of what I take to be typical acts of informing does provide a way of characterizing a notion of committed participation by a communicator, s: *for* s intends to get the audience a to believe that his (a's) interest in being reliably informed is being met. Committed participation links the communicator's intentions with the audience's interest in reliability; s has acted in a committed way *because* he has carried out his communicative act with the intention of getting his audience to believe that their interest in being reliably informed was satisfied.

The core of my proposal is, then, that acts of informing are essentially acts of intentionally implementing rules of information. In summary, for typical cases (2), (3), and (4) are true, and s has carried out the act described in (3) with the intentions described in (9) and (10). But informing can of course occur without a's being convinced of the truth of the information transmitted. a may be said to be convinced by s's act if he also forms belief (5); as noted earlier, he will then also have belief (6).[2]

Suppose now that, in the senses just described, s has informed and a has been convinced. I shall say that s is *sincere* only if

(11) $B_s q$

is also true. In terms of the model as so far outlined, a treatment of Moore's puzzle about saying and disbelieving, along lines similar to those proposed by Searle (1969, 65, fn. 1), is readily forthcoming. Suppose that s's act of bringing it about that p is his act of uttering the sentence "It is raining and I do not believe that it is raining." Where "r" stands for the sentence "It is raining," we may now represent "q" in (2) as "r & $\sim B_s r$," where "$\sim$" is standard truth-functional negation. Assume now that a trusts the reliability of s's speech act, in the sense defined earlier. Then he forms the belief

(12) $B_a (r \text{ & } \sim B_s r)$.

If it were now also to be assumed that a believes that s is sincere in his performance of the speech act, then—according to elementary principles in the logic of belief—a contradiction could be derived. For,

(13) $B_a B_s (r \text{ & } \sim B_s r)$

implies

(14) $B_a B_s r$,

and (12) implies

(15) $B_a \sim B_s r$,

and the conjunction of (14) and (15) is contradictory. So s's speech act can be assumed to be sincere only if it is not taken to be reliable; and it can be taken to be reliable only if it is assumed to be insincere. (For a comparison with Hintikka's (1962) treatment, see Jones 1983, sec. III.2.)

Accounts of communicative interaction inspired by Grice (1957) put a great deal of emphasis on the audience's *recognition* of the communicator's intention, in their explanation of the mechanism by means of which the communicator expects to be able to secure his intended effects on the audience. What then is the role of recognition of intention in my account of (typical cases of) informing? Assuming that s intended to produce in a the belief that q, and that the effect of the communicative act was that a came to believe that q, would it have been the case, according to my model, that a's recognition of s's intention to produce in him the belief that q was instrumental in producing that effect? Well, a's recognition of s's intention plays *some* role in the production of the final effect, but I think it is a considerably more modest role than that which the Gricean approach assigns to it. Basically, on my account, recognition of s's intentions enters the picture inasmuch as a must recognize that s intends to implement the signaling rule (1)—in particular, a must recognize that s intends to produce in him the belief that his communicative act can be trusted. But unless a is peculiarly gullible, *recognizing* that s intends to produce in him the belief that his (s's) act can be trusted will not *itself* persuade him that it *is* trustworthy (and hence, in virtue of (2), that q is true). Recognition of s's intention, on my account, is no more than a *preliminary* step in the communicative process, in the sense that the process (leading, perhaps, to a's becoming convinced that q) will not get off the ground unless a sees that s intends his act to be viewed as falling under the governing signaling rule. (I have tried to argue for the same conclusion in my criticism of Bennett's (1976) reformulation and defense of the Gricean theory; see Jones 1983, sec. V.1).

However, it might be supposed that the Gricean recognition-of-intention mechanism does play a more significant role in cases where communicative acts are performed *in the absence of* established, mutually accepted signaling rules. Consider, for instance, Bennett's example (1976, §43) of two members of a primitive tribe (primitive in the sense that it lacks a semantically structured communication system), who are observed a few meters apart in the forest, in full view of one another. One of them is moving his arm up and down, in a way clearly visible by the other, and in a manner that might be thought to resemble the movements of a snake; at the same time he is making a hissing sound, loudly enough for the other to hear him. Given that s here intends to produce in a the belief that there is a snake in the grass nearby, is he relying on the Gricean mechanism to produce his effect? Does a's recognition of s's intention play a more decisive role in a case like this? I feel very unsure about the answer to this; but one aspect of the situation that should not be overlooked (and Bennett too is clear about this) is that, even though there is no established signaling rule to implement, s is attempting to exploit an *iconic* connection between his actions and snakes —a connection that he must assume, at least hope, a will be aware of. (It obviously was not accidental, given what he wanted to get a to believe, that s chose to perform just *these* actions.)

I suggested above that s's intention to implement a signaling rule of form (1) may be characterized, given (2), as an intention to produce in a the belief (4) and, more importantly, the belief (5). (This was what I proposed for what I called "typical" cases of informing.) In cases in which s performs the communicative act with *these* intentions, I shall say that s intends a *literal* implementation of the signaling rule. However, I do not believe that the literal mode of implementation is the only possible mode; I shall define a sort of *nonliteral* implementation of signaling rules and show how this might figure in explaining the possibility of one type of *indirect* communicative act—one way of saying one thing and meaning another.

Suppose, for instance, that s is giving a lecture in a crowded room and that he is finding the atmosphere uncomfortably hot and stuffy. If he wants to make his audience a aware of how he feels, there are of course various options open to him. Various communicative strategies are available; the most straightforward one—the one that is perhaps most likely to come off—is a literal utterance of the sentence "It is uncomfortably hot and stuffy in here." But an alternative strategy he could try would be to utter—in an appropriate tone of voice, and perhaps with appropriate accompanying gestures—the sentence "They certainly keep it nice and cool in here." It seems clear that in a case of this sort, it is the function of the tone of voice, the gestures, and perhaps some other factors s may be relying on, to indicate to a that the speech act itself is *not* to be taken literally. I want to suggest that in both the literal and the nonliteral cases of utterance of a sentence, the same signaling rule is being implemented; but, for *nonliteral* implementation, s must intend to produce in a, not the belief (5), but rather the belief

(16) $B_a \sim O_a E_s p$

together with the further belief (17) that it was s's *intention* to produce belief (16):

(17) $B_a B_s ((E_s p \ \& \ Z) \rightarrow \text{ShallE}_s B_a \sim O_a E_s p)$.

One of the expectations that is built into s's plan is that, if he can produce belief-state (17) in a, then a will attempt to figure out why it was that s performed the speech act in the first place. His hope that a will arrive at the correct explanation will be based on a number of factors; for instance, he may be assuming that a too is finding the atmosphere uncomfortable. But note, in particular, that he will expect a significant role to be played by a's understanding of the *literal* meaning of the sentence he uttered (that is, by a's awareness of what would have been true had the utterance satisifed his (a's) interest in being reliably informed). For it was clearly no accident that s chose a sentence whose literal interpretation pertains to the temperature in the room (he could hardly expect to achieve his intended effect if he said, instead, for instance, "There are three lights on in the room"). So although this case, and other types of indirect speech act, clearly indicate the need for analyzing communicative behavior within the context of the participants' plans, and of their beliefs about one another's plans (see for example, Cohen and Perrault 1979; Allen and Perrault 1980; Appelt 1985), it is nevertheless clear, in my opinion, that much of the planning (and reasoning about planning) in both literal and nonliteral communicative acts centers around the use or exploitation of established, mutually recognized signaling rules. An adequate formal analysis of the reasoning involved in communicative interaction must attempt to make fully explicit the role played by these rules. Thus, I hesitate to accept that "indirect speech acts ... are the touchstone of any theory of speech acts" (Cohen and Perrault 1979, 187). To repeat: one may use the phenomenon of indirect speech acts to demonstrate to anyone who may doubt it that the theory of communicative interaction needs to be placed within the theory of planning; but one should not then lose sight of the fact that, to a considerable extent, the successful execution of communication plans relies on the exploitation of mutually accepted signaling rules. Questions about the form of these rules, and about the role they play, are of central importance.

I have so far considered only one type of indirect speech act. What, for example, is the proper analysis of the following, different kind of case? A mother says to her child, "Your dinner is on the table," meaning by this to tell the child to come to the table to eat. In terms of my model, the obvious approach would seem to be to suggest that the mother intends a literal implementation of the governing signaling rule and intends that this will result in the child's coming to believe that dinner is on the table. Achieving this result is a crucial step in reaching the assumed end-goal of getting the child to the table, for, presumably, the mother expects the child to reason in the following kind of way: since my dinner *is* on the table, it is ready to be eaten; but if I am to eat it, then I must come to the table; so I shall come to the table.

Many of the other best-known cases of indirect speech acts (such as "Can you pass the mustard?") involve the utterance of nonindicative sentences. So far I have confined my attention to communicative acts of the informing kind, so let me next say a little about how I propose to treat some other types.

For *requesting* I propose to use the same general form for the signaling rules as is given in (1), except that the consequent of the conditional will now take the form

(18) $E_s \text{Shall} E_a q$,

where a's bringing it about that q is the requested act. (18) is true if and only if s has brought about—created—a *normative relation* between himself and a, according to which a is expected to bring it about that q. I thus view acts of requesting as a special kind of act of informing, in which the information transmitted pertains to the establishing of a normative relation between communicator and recipient. Suppose that s performs a communicative act of the requesting type; then I shall say, as before, that he does this with the intention of literally implementing the governing signaling rule only if he intends to produce in a beliefs (4) and (5). Suppose, for instance, that s utters the sentence "Open the door, please," intending a literal utterance, and that a is now aware that the act has been performed (he has belief (4)). If a now recognizes that s also intends to produce in him the belief (5)—that s's act satisfies a's interest in being reliably informed—then it would seem that a does indeed have good grounds for forming belief (5) and thus for accepting that the normative relation has been established. The creation of the relation requires no more than the literal implementation of the signaling rule. "Saying makes it so"; that is, the request is made—the normative relation is established—by the mere literal utterance of the sentence.

Those familiar with Lewis's treatment of nonindicatives (Lewis 1972), and with the attempt to analyze performatives as sentences "verifiable by their use" (see, for example, Lemmon 1962), will know the direction I am moving in here. There is not space for details in this paper, so I refer the reader to sections IV.1 and IV.2 of Jones 1983 for a more thorough account of my approach. Let it be mentioned, however, that there are types of imperative communicative acts where the mere literal performance of the act is not sufficient to guarantee the creation of the normative relation. For instance, if the imperative is intended to be of the *commanding* type, then certain contextual factors—specified in the "Z-component" in the signaling rule—will have to be satisfied. So if s is to establish a normative relation of the commanding type with respect to a, he must be in a position of authority with respect to a. a would not be justified in trusting the reliability of s's communicative act, in a case of this sort, if he did not believe that s had the necessary authority.

The immediate consequence of the successful performance of a communicative act of the requesting type will be that a forms the belief

(19) $B_a E_s \text{ShallE}_a q$;

that is, a becomes aware of the normative relation that has been established. It is a further issue whether or not a now decides to satisfy s's expectation. This is just as it should be: the communicative act *itself* merely transmits information about what a is required to do.

As regards questioning (asking questions), I propose to follow the rather standard line of treating questions as requests for information. So a signaling rule for yes-no questioning might take the form

(20) $(E_s p \,\&\, Z \,\&\, O_a E_s p) \rightarrow E_s \text{ShallE}_a(K_s q \,\vee\, K_s \sim q)$,

where "$K_s q$" stands for "s knows that q." The formal treatment of *wh*-questions will presumably call for the use of quantification into contexts governed by epistemic operators (see Cohen and Perrault 1979). The details lie beyond the scope of this paper.

Since the treatment of requesting and questioning is subsumed under the analysis of informing, indirect communicative acts involving requests and questions can perhaps be handled in the same kind of way as those involving indicatives. Thus, when s asks a the question "Can you pass the mustard?", his utterance is to be interpreted literally, as a question, that is, as a request for information. But his intention is also that a will see that his (s's) asking the question is one step in a plan, the goal of which is to get the mustard. If *a does* see this, it may still be appropriate for *a* to respond by saying "Yes" (if he can indeed pass the mustard), but it will certainly not be very helpful if *a limits* his response to the *utterance* and does not also *pass* the mustard. If, on the other hand, *a* as a matter of fact *cannot* pass the mustard, it would be perfectly appropriate for him to convey that information to *s*, which again supports the contention that a request for information (that is, a literal utterance of the interrogative speech act) is a part of *s*'s plan. But how does *a* find out what *s*'s overall plan is? By the context, presumably; *a* sees *s* sitting there at the dinner table with slices of ham and no mustard left. Or perhaps it may also be the case that the particular turn of phrase "Can you pass ...?" has become established in ordinary conversation as a way of indicating that one's overall plan is to get hold of the goods themselves, and not just the information.

There is a problem raised by Winograd (Winograd and Flores 1986, 55) that, I think, can also be solved as soon as one accepts that an agent ordinarily chooses the form of his response to a question in the light of what he takes to be the questioner's overall plan. The situation is, briefly, that *s* asks "Is there any water in the refrigerator?", *a* replies "Yes," *s* then says "Where? I don't see it," and *a* then responds by saying "In the cells of the eggplant." It seems that Winograd wishes to draw from this example the conclusion that "It is impossible to establish a context-independent basis for circumscribing the literal use of a term even as seemingly simple as 'water'" (Winograd and Flores 1986, 55). But that is surely an unnecessarily drastic diagnosis. In my opinion it is reasonable to suppose that *s* can expect his initial question to be interpreted by *a* in the same literal fashion, regardless of whether he (*s*) is looking for something to drink, or for a place to store his photographic plates, or for an argument about the physics of condensation. But he also expects that, when *a* has first interpreted the question literally, he will choose his response in the light of what he assumes (rightly or wrongly) *s*'s overall plan is. So if *a* is aware that the question was put as a step in *s*'s plan for getting hold of something to drink, he will only reply "Yes" if he believes there is some *drinking* water available in the refrigerator. If, on the other hand, he thinks *s* is looking for an argument about the nature of condensation, he will plan his response accordingly. The issue has nothing to do with definitional problems about "water."

3 Comments on the Modalities

In closing, I shall make some brief remarks about the modalities used here in the description of communicative interaction. Very few details are given: the full account is to be found in Jones 1983, chap. II. With the exception of one of the modalities, a standard possible-worlds semantics was used. The exception was the belief modality, one of three modalities whose analysis I took from Pörn 1977. Pörn's semantics for belief has not, I feel, been given the attention it deserves; appearing some years before the situation semanticists began to emphasize the need to pay attention to the *partial* structures required for representing situations, this semantics for belief showed one way of capturing—within a modified possible-worlds frame, in which truth-value gaps are permitted—"the sort of selective attention that is an obvious feature of belief" (Pörn 1977, 18). A solution is forthcoming to the notorious consequential closure problem; that is, it is not a valid principle of this system that an agent believes all of the logical consequences of what he believes. (There are, nevertheless, some questions to be raised about the precise way in which Pörn chooses to characterize the selectivity of attention of a believer, but formulation of these questions would call for a detailed exposition of Pörn's semantics.)

Despite the fact that this logic of belief is a clear improvement on the standard possible-worlds treatment (for example, that of Hintikka), the point remains that what we are really going to need in this field, and in all other branches of the theory of practical reasoning, is a logic of belief that is "dynamic," in the sense that it can cope adequately with belief revision.

The second logic taken from Pörn 1977 is that for action; despite its obvious advantages over earlier versions of the logic of action, the fact that it lacks a built-in temporal dimension will perhaps make it less attractive than alternative approaches based on dynamic and process logic. The reconstruction of my analysis of communicative interaction on the basis of a dynamic logic of action is a task for further work. Some interesting observations on Pörn's system are to be found in Segerberg 1985.

The semantics for "Shall" (the third modality taken from Pörn 1977) takes the form of a serial standard model in the sense of Chellas (1980, 80). Pörn's interesting use of "Shall" in the characterization of intentions and expectations is a matter requiring much further discussion, beyond the scope of this paper, where I have been mainly concerned to try to assess the role of communicator's intentions in communicative interaction. I take it that my proposals on the latter topic may be compatible with various ways of analyzing the notion of intentional action itself. Let me, however, just mention one of the more conspicuous holes in the account as I have offered it: I have talked of agents acting on, or on the basis of, their intentions, where these intentions are represented as beliefs of a particular kind; but I have not shown how to represent formally this very idea of the *grounding* of an action on an intention, and this is a serious omission. To what extent this problem can be solved within the present framework for analyzing actions and intentions remains to be seen. For some suggestions, see Pörn 1977, chap. 2.

Considered in isolation from the other modalities, the relativized "O" modality gets the same kind of semantic analysis as would be given in standard deontic logic to (a relativized) "ought." Thus, the basic *form* of the model is like that for "Shall" (the two modalities, "Shall" and (relativized) "O," of course each have their own associated accessibility relation).

It will be recalled that sentences of the type "O_ap" pertain to a particular kind of "ought," a particular kind of ideality: that which is ideal relative to a's interest in being reliably informed. It is thus natural that the characteristic features of this modality are those that show how it stands in relation to the modalities for belief and knowledge. There follows a brief summary of some of these features (the positive results are achieved by specifying the appropriate relations between the accessibility relations for the belief and deontic modalities). (21) and (22) are valid sentence forms:

(21) $O_a(B_ap \rightarrow p)$

(22) $O_aB_ap \rightarrow p$.

However, (23) will not be valid, since it may well be the case that, relative to his interest in being reliably informed, a ought to believe that p, even though he does not in fact believe that p:

(23) $O_aB_ap \rightarrow B_ap$.

Furthermore, neither (24) nor (25) will be in the class of valid sentence forms, since it is hardly reasonable to insist that it is ideal that an agent's information is *complete*, in the sense that he accept as true every truth. Such an "ideal" would be totally unrealistic, given the fact that the human's information storage capacity is not unlimited:

(24) $O_a(p \rightarrow B_ap)$

(25) $p \rightarrow O_aB_ap$.

Finally, a further characteristic of the intended interpretation of the deontic operator is brought out by the role it is assigned in the definition of "a knows that p":

(26) $K_ap =_{df} (B_ap \,\&\, O_aB_ap)$.

(In virtue of the validity of (22), knowledge implies truth.)

Three short notes, in conclusion:

1. There are well-known puzzles (for example, Ross's, Chisholm's) associated with the standard deontic logic interpretation of "ought." Jones and Pörn (1985, 1986) provide, we think, novel solutions to these problems. Work is in progress on grafting our new semantics for the moral/legal "ought" onto the special notion of ideality proposed here.

2. The logic of mutual belief is defined in a simple, straightforward way on the basis of the logic of (individual-agent) belief.

3. The reader who does venture to consult Jones 1983 should ignore completely the modality "V_a" found there! I have omitted it from the present version because I am no longer satisfied with its semantic characterization, and because not *much* seems thereby to have been lost as regards the description of what goes on when people try to communicate with one another.

Notes

1. Although this additional premise may perhaps not be assumed to hold in general (see Bratman's contribution to this volume), I think that it can be assumed to hold in regard to what the agent (s) believes will be the immediate consequence of a's accepting the truth of the antecedent of the governing signaling rule.

2. To repeat: the basic idea is that standard cases of informing essentially involve the intentional implementation of signaling rules. The rules say what must be the case when the performance of a signaling act is trustworthy. The relativized deontic modality is used to capture this notion of trustworthiness: to be trustworthy, the act must be optimal, or ideal, relative to an interest I assume the audience has, namely, an interest in being reliably informed.

   The modality "Shall," on the other hand, is used to capture the notion of the intention behind an act, the goal or end toward which the performance of the act is *directed*. Perhaps it may help to give a better understanding of the intuition formula (8) expresses, if (8) is contrasted with

   (8*) $B_c(p \rightarrow \text{Shall}E_s q)$,

   where $c \neq s$. (8*) expresses a normative expectation c has vis-à-vis s, under circumstances described by "p." c expects s to bring it about that q; this is a normative—not a predictive—expectation c has of s. At the battle of Trafalgar, Nelson (or whoever) may have expected every man to do his duty, while at the same time fearing that none of them actually would.

References

Allen, J. F., and C. R. Perrault (1980). Analyzing intention in utterances. *Artificial Intelligence* 15, 143–178.

Appelt, D. E. (1985). *Planning English sentences.* Cambridge: Cambridge University Press.

Barwise, J. (1983). Information and semantics. *The Behavioral and Brain Sciences* 6, 65.

Barwise, J. (1985). The situation in logic–II: Conditionals and conditional information. CSLI Reports 21, Center for the Study of Language and Information, Stanford, CA.

Barwise, J., and J. Perry (1983). *Situations and attitudes.* Cambridge, MA: MIT Press.

Bennett, J. (1976). *Linguistic behaviour.* Cambridge: Cambridge University Press.

Chellas, B. F. (1980). *Modal logic: An introduction.* Cambridge: Cambridge University Press.

Cohen, P. R., and C. R. Perrault (1979). Elements of a plan-based theory of speech acts. *Cognitive Science* 3, 177–212. Reprinted in B. Webber and N. Nilsson, eds. (1981). *Readings in artificial intelligence.* Los Altos, CA: Morgan Kaufmann. Also in B. G. Grosz, K. Sparck Jones, and B. L. Webber, eds. (1986). *Readings in natural language processing.* Los Altos, CA: Morgan Kaufmann.

Dretske, F. I. (1981). *Knowledge and the flow of information.* Oxford: Basil Blackwell.

Dretske, F. I. (1983). Précis of *Knowledge and the flow of information. The Behavioral and Brain Sciences* 55–63.

Dretske, F. I. (1985). Constraints and meaning. *Linguistics and Philosophy* 9–12.

Grice, H. P. (1957). Meaning. *The Philosophical Review* 66, 377–388.

Hintikka, J. (1962). *Knowledge and belief.* Ithaca, NY: Cornell University Press.

Jones, A. J. I. (1981). On describing interpersonal communication. In I. Pörn, ed., *Essays in philosophical analysis. Acta Phil. Fenn.,* vol. 32.

Jones, A. J. I. (1983). *Communication and meaning: An essay in applied modal logic.* Dordrecht, Holland: D. Reidel.

Jones, A. J. I., and I. Pörn (1985). Ideality, sub-ideality and deontic logic. *Synthese* 65, 275–290.

Jones, A. J. I., and I Pörn (1986). "Ought" and "Must." *Synthese* 66, 89–93.

Lemmon, E. J. (1962). On sentences verifiable by their use. *Analysis* 22, 86–89.

Lewis, D. K. (1969). *Convention: A Philosophical study.* Cambridge, MA: Harvard University Press.

Lewis, D. K. (1972). General semantics. In D. Davidson and G. Harman, eds., *Semantics of natural language.* Dordrecht, Holland: D. Reidel.

Lewis, D. K. (1975). Language and languages. In K. Gunderson, ed., *Language, mind and knowledge.* Minneapolis, MN: University of Minnesota Press.

Pörn, I. (1977). *Action theory and social science: Some formal models.* Dordrecht, Holland: D. Reidel.

Searle, J. R. (1969). *Speech acts: An essay in the philosophy of language.* Cambridge: Cambridge University Press.

Segerberg, K. (1985). On the question of semantics in the logic of action: Some remarks on Pörn's logic of action. In G. Holmström and A. J. I. Jones, eds., *Action, logic and social theory. Acta Phil. Fenn.,* vol. 38.

Stenius, E. (1967). Mood and language-game. *Synthese* 17, 254–274.

Wertheimer, R. (1972). *The significance of sense: Meaning, modality and morality.* Ithaca, NY: Cornell University Press.

Winograd, T., and F. Flores (1986). *Understanding computers and cognition: A new foundation for design.* Norwood, NJ: Ablex.

Chapter 9

An Application of Default Logic to Speech Act Theory

C. Raymond Perrault

Speech act theory aims to relate three aspects of utterances:

- the types of actions they are being used to perform, such as asserting and convincing,
- the syntactic and semantic features of the utterances, such as their sentence type (declarative, interrogative, imperative), propositional content, and intonational pattern, and
- The state of the world before and after the utterance, particularly the mental state of participants and observers.

After arguing that all utterances should be viewed as actions of the speaker, Austin (1962) proposes three levels of speech act description. In saying "It's cold here," I utter a well-formed sentence of English, with definite sense and reference. Austin calls this act *of* saying something the *locutionary* act. In so saying, I may also be asserting that it is cold, or even asking you indirectly to turn the heat up. These actions performed *in* saying something Austin labels *illocutionary* acts. Finally, I may convince you that it is cold, or even that you should turn up the heat. These actions performed *by* saying something Austin calls *perlocutionary* acts. A speaker can perform an illocutionary act successfully while failing to carry out a related perlocutionary act. Thus, I can assert successfully that it is cold here without convincing you of that fact. One important feature of illocutionary verbs is that they can be used in so-called explicit performative sentences such as "I hereby *assert* that it is cold here," whereas perlocutionary verbs cannot.

In some of the most widely read literature on the subject (for example, Searle 1969), speech act theory seems, at first glance, reducible to the problem of characterizing the successful performance of illocutionary acts, that is, of specifying conditions under which the performance of an action, and, in particular, the utterance of one or more sentences, can be interpreted

The research reported here was made possible in part by a gift from the System Development Foundation. Alex Borgida, Phil Cohen, Robin Cohen, David Etherington, Hector Levesque, Jerry Morgan, Martha Pollack, and Ray Reiter kindly read and commented on earlier drafts, but any remaining errors are mine alone.

as the successful performance of a given speech act. Finding a solution to this problem is a useful contribution to the lexical semantics of the language, but it is interesting mostly as a route to a general understanding of the difference between actions that are inherently communicative (illocutionary acts) and those that can be achieved by noncommunicative means (perlocutionary acts). Iago, for example, convinces Othello of Desdemona's infidelity by leaving her handkerchief on his path. Clearly, he does not thereby *communicate* anything to the Moor.

Illocutionary acts can be performed *mistakenly* (as in assertions whose content happens to be false), *insincerely* (as with lies), *indirectly* (as in using "It's cold here" as a request to turn on the heat), and *nonseriously* (as in using "This was a terrific meal" to mean that it was terrible). Largely because of this range of uses, it is difficult to give direct definitions relating the form of utterances to the illocutionary acts they are used to perform. Searle's account says little on the subject, save his claim that the hearer's recognition of the speaker's intentions is to be "in virtue of (by means of) [the hearer's] knowledge of the meaning of [the utterance]." He discusses indirect speech acts further in Searle 1975.

Searle views illocutionary acts primarily as moves made as part of a larger social activity, and he regards their felicitous performance as being governed by what he calls constitutive rules. Though this approach may be necessary for a full account of "institutional speech acts," such as betting, convicting, and marrying (see Strawson 1964), it has not been very useful in explicating the relation between the form and function of utterances. To address that issue, Allen, Cohen and Levesque, and I have been developing versions of speech act theory that place the burden on a direct account of the effects of utterances on the mental state of the participants. Illocutionary acts are relegated to a secondary role.

Cohen and Levesque (1985) (hereafter C&L) propose a theory of speech acts in four parts:

- an account of some propositional attitudes (such as belief, knowledge, intention),
- a theory of action and its relation to the attitudes, describing those necessary to engage in action and those resulting from it,
- a description of the effects of locutionary acts on the mental state of the participants, that is, of sentences with particular syntactic and semantic features, and
- definitions of the performance of illocutionary acts as the performance of *any* action, linguistic or otherwise, under appropriate circumstances, by a speaker holding certain intentions.

C&L's account, couched in a logic of attitudes and action, is by far the most detailed and precise proposal yet. They provide a formal language in which to axiomatically state properties of some propositional attitudes, actions, and time, and they give the language a formal semantics. However, it still fails in two crucial respects: it makes arguably wrong predictions in some circumstances and predictions that are too weak in others. Although I focus on C&L because of its detail, earlier proposals, such as those of Cohen and Perrault (1979) and Perrault and Allen (1980), suffer from the same flaws. The heart of the problem is that the mental state of the speaker and hearer after an utterance is strongly dependent on their mental state before. Several examples are given in the next section.

These problems, I claim, can be overcome by defining many of the consequences of speech acts as *defaults* that are assumed to hold as long as there is no evidence to the contrary. I will show that a more perspicuous account of speech act consequences can be derived from a default theory describing

- the change in an agent's attitudes over time,
- the transfer of attitudes between agents,
- the consequences of an action on an observer's mental state,
- the assumption that actions are intentional, and
- the assumption that the utterance of sentences with particular features reveals particular aspects of the speaker's mental state.

In the next section I expand upon the problems encountered in specifying speech act consequences. I then postulate a simple theory of the change of beliefs over time, which I use to discuss informally what should be the result of performing declarative sentences in a variety of contexts. These are the facts my theory will explain. I then introduce the requisite notions from Default Logic, present the default theory necessary for speech acts, and explore some of its consequences. Finally I examine a number of methods of defining illocutionary acts in this framework and outline systematic differences among various uses of utterances that, in different ways, do not conform to simple correspondences between form and function.

1 The Importance of Attitude Revision

A theory of speech acts should at least account for the fact that communicative acts must be overt and that moods can be used in nonstandard ways, as suggested in the preceding section.

Before considering C&L's axioms for imperative and declarative sentences, some notation will be helpful. If p is a proposition and x an agent, we take $K_x p$, $B_x p$, and $G_x p$ to mean that x *knows* that p, x *believes* that p, and x has the *goal* that p. We say that x and y mutually know that p, notated $MK_{x,y} p$, if and only if $K_x p$ & $K_y p$ & $K_x K_y p$ & $K_y K_x p$ & .... Mutual belief is defined analogously. A one-sided version of mutual belief is also useful: $BMB_{x,y}p$ if and only if B_xp & B_xB_yp & $B_xB_yB_xp$ & ..., that is, if x believes that p and that x and y mutually believe that p. It will be convenient to think of mutual knowledge and belief formulas as the set of their conjuncts.

In monotonic logics, the consequences of actions are specified by axioms of the form "If p, then, after action α, q." We will refer to p as the *gating condition* and q as the *consequent*. Exceptional conditions are handled by stating axioms with different gating conditions and by specifying the strongest condition that holds after all instances of the action that are performed in states satisfying the gating conditions.

C&L's only axiom for the use of declarative sentences can be glossed as follows: if it is mutually known by speaker S and hearer H that e is an event of utterance of the sentence s to H, that S is the agent of e, and that s is a declarative sentence with propositional content p, then, after the utterance, it becomes the case that the hearer believes that it is mutually believed (BMB) that the speaker intends the hearer to recognize his intention that the hearer believe that the speaker believes that the propositional content of the declarative is true:

$$MK_{S,H}(\text{Utter}(H, s, e) \ \& \ \text{AGT}(S, e) \ \& \ \text{Attend}(H, S) \ \& \ \text{declarative}\,(s, p)$$
$$\supset \text{after}(e, BMB_{H,S}G_SB_HG_SB_HB_Sp)).$$

They give a similar axiom for imperative sentences:

$$MK_{S,H}(\text{Utter}(H, s, e) \ \& \ \text{AGT}(S, e) \ \& \ \text{Attend}(H, S) \ \& \ \text{imperative}\,(s, p)$$
$$\supset \text{after}(e, BMB_{H,S}G_SB_HG_SB_HG_SG_Hp)).$$

In the declarative axiom, $\text{Utter}(H, s, e)$ & $\text{AGT}(S, e)$ & $\text{Attend}(H, S)$ & declarative(s, p) is used as a gating condition. In a full theory of action and attitudes, these axioms must, along with others, allow the inference, under "normal" conditions, that B_Hp is a consequence of a declarative sentence with propositional content p, or that G_Hp is a consequence of an imperative. This second set of axioms must then, under some circumstances, allow for B_Hp to follow from

$$BMB_{H,S}G_SB_HG_SB_HB_Sp.$$

When the speaker is mistaken or lying, B_Hp is still a consequence, as long as the hearer does not recognize the mistake or detect the lie. In the first case he might come to believe that B_Sp, that $G_SB_HB_Sp$, and that G_SB_Hp. In the second he should come to believe that $\neg B_Sp$, that $G_SB_HB_Sp$, and that G_SB_Hp. It is unnecessary to delve here into what the axioms need be.

Unfortunately, the consequent of the declarative axiom is still too strong to hold in all conditions of utterance. Consider, for example, the ironic use of "This is the best meal I ever had." It is easy to verify that none of the following conditions hold after the utterance (where p, of course, is the propositional content of the utterance):

$$B_S p$$
$$B_H B_S p$$
$$G_S B_H B_S p$$
$$B_H G_S B_H B_S p$$
$$G_S B_H G_S B_H B_S p$$
$$BMB_{H,S} G_S B_H G_S B_H B_S p.$$

Thus, in the nonserious cases, the predictions of the declarative axioms are too strong.

This observation might suggest that some modification of the consequents of the axioms might suffice, but such is not the case. The main difficulty arises from the fact that the consequents of the declarative and imperative axioms are unaffected by the mental state of speaker and hearer *before* the utterance: the theory only places constraints on their mental state afterward.

Consider what one might take as the simplest possible context-independent consequence of a declarative sentence, namely, that H believes p. Now, of course, this is unacceptable, as H might not be convinced by the utterance: H might have good reasons, for example, to continue to believe ¬p. In the context-insensitive accounts, this problem might be handled by having the more complex attitude $B_H B_S p$ as the innermost subformula of the consequent. But this move merely defers the problem: H might previously have had reason to not believe that S believes p, as would be the case, for example, if H had just seen S observe a physical situation in which ¬p was true. By a similar argument, no formula of the form $B_H B_S B_H \ldots p$ can be taken to hold after *all* uses of a declarative sentence, since imposing $B_S B_H \ldots p$ as a belief of H after the utterance may conflict with the beliefs he had before.

The next possible way out is to weaken the consequent by having the hearer come to believe that the speaker has certain goals or intentions, not just beliefs. In the simplest case involving declaratives, this would be having H come to believe that S has the goal that H believe p, that is, $B_H G_S B_H p$. Again there is trouble ahead, as one would suspect from the fact that one is still postulating a *belief* of the hearer's. The only way this could work is if it were possible for H, after the utterance, to acquire a belief about S's goals that could never contradict H's mental state before the utterance. However, this hope vanishes once it is recognized that one must assume that an agent cannot hold goals (or intentions) that he believes to be impossible. Thus, if the speaker believes before the utterance that the hearer believes ¬p, and would not change his belief even if the speaker asserted p, then the speaker cannot have the goal that the hearer should come to believe p as a consequence of S's uttering a declarative sentence with content p. Therefore, for H to come to believe, after the utterance of the declarative p, that S's utterance reflected his goal that H believe p is inconsistent with H's believing (both before and after the utterance) that S believes that H believes ⌐p. Thus, H's recognition that S intends H to recognize that S believes p cannot be true after *all* utterances by S of a declarative p. This argument can be extended to show that *no* formula of the form $B_H G_S q$ can be taken as a context-independent consequence of the utterance of a declarative sentence.

One must therefore conclude that the consequences of declarative sentences must depend on the mental state of the participants before the utterance. It is possible that one could formulate context-dependent axioms, as Cohen and Levesque attempt in chapter 12 of this volume. I follow the route of nonmonotonic systems since it is in some ways simpler, cleaner, and more revealing of the relation between utterances and attitude revision. For a brief discussion of some of the differences between the approach presented here and in chapter 12, see section 8.

2   The Persistence Theory of Belief

Speech acts reveal certain aspects of the speaker's mental state and cause changes in the state of the hearer(s) that are based on their perception of the state of the speaker. An agent's beliefs after an utterance, for example, will in general depend on his beliefs before it, as well as on its content. Ideally, one would like to have a theory in which it is possible for one agent's beliefs, say, to change according to how strongly he believed something before the utterance, as well as on how much he believes what the speaker says. I cannot give such an account in detail, so I will rely on something simpler. I assume what might be called a *persistence theory of belief*: that old beliefs persist and that new ones are adopted as a result of observing external facts, provided that they do not conflict with old ones. In particular, I assume that an agent will adopt the beliefs he believes another agent has, as long as those do not contradict his existing beliefs.

Let us examine the consequences of this assumption for speech acts. We will do so from the perspective of an observer who initially has a (partial) theory of the mental states of both speaker S and hearer H. What is to be accounted for is the observer's picture of S's and H's mental state after the utterance. We will limit ourselves at first to a consideration of the participants' beliefs; intentions will be discussed later.

Example 1: Sincere Assertion
Let a speaker S address a declarative sentence with propositional content p to a hearer H in an initial state in which S believes that p, and in which

neither S nor H has other beliefs about p or about the beliefs others hold regarding p. In declaring that p, S "expresses" his belief that p. We would like to claim here that, after the utterance, S still believes p, and that, as a consequence of the utterance, H comes to believe that S believes p; thus, H comes to believe p as well. If we also assume that S believes that H was observing S's utterance, then as long as S has no reason to believe that H does not believe that S believes p, S will also come to believe that H believes that S believes p; thus, S will come to believe that H believes p. Continuing this argument, it should be true after the utterance that S believes p, that S believes that H believes p, that S believes that H believes that S believes p, and so on, and that H believes p, that H believes that S believes p, that H believes that S believes that H believes p, and so on again. Taken together, these progressive more complex formulas describe what has been called *mutual belief* by S and H that p. Mutual belief and its analogue for knowledge are discussed at length by Schiffer (1972) and Smith (1982).

Two points should be noted here. First, mutual belief occurs only by virtue of the assumption that H was observing S's actions, and that S was observing H observing S, and so on—namely, solely because of the overtness of the utterance. Thus, in the simpler situation in which, say, S is lifting a rock and H is observing S without being observed in turn by S, S comes to believe that the rock has been lifted, and H comes to believe that S believes that the rock has been lifted, but S has no further beliefs about H. Second, we are not claiming that the justification we gave for why it was rational for each agent to have certain beliefs had to be computed in the same step-by-step fashion by the agents themselves. One can think of overt actions producing mutual belief directly, in virtue of mutual observation of the situation. We are simply trying to describe the joint mental state of S and H, ignoring for now the structures necessary to implement this mental state and the procedures necessary to change them.

Now let us look at a slightly more complex example.

Example 2: Lie
Suppose now that S utters the same declarative sentence, but this time believing ⌐p; suppose also, as in Example 1, that S and H have no further beliefs about p. From the assumption of persistence, we would expect S to continue to believe ⌐p, as his beliefs about p should not be affected by what he says about it. However, as before, we would expect H to come to believe that S believes p and therefore H to come to believe p. S would have no reason not to believe that H believes that S believes p and thus no reason not be believe that H believes p. Thus, in the state following the utterance, S and H mutually believe that p, except that S believes ⌐p instead of believing p.

Example 2 is just one of many examples of ways in which the context of utterance affects the resulting state. The next is a slightly more complex case.

Example 3: Unsuccessful Lie
Consider the following sequence of events. Felix is a very fat cat who can jump down from chairs but never climbs up anything. Suppose H enters a room behind S, who does not notice him. H sees S put Felix on a chair. S looks away from Felix (still not noticing H), whereupon Felix jumps to the floor, noticed by H but not S. H then leaves the room, still unobserved. S now leaves the room and, meeting H in the hall, tells him, "Felix is on the floor." Let p be the proposition "Felix is on the floor." Prior to the utterance, S believes ¬p, H believes that S believes ¬p, but H believes p. After S's utterance, S continues to believe ¬p, while H continues to believe p and that S believes ¬p. However, S comes to believe that H believes that S believes p, so that S also comes to believe that H comes to believe p. H has no reason not to believe that S believes that H believes that S believes p, and he also comes to believe that S believes H believes p. The final state is that S and H mutually believe p, except that S believes ¬p, and H believes that S believes ¬p.

Example 4: Irony
In our final example, we assume that it is initially mutually believed that ¬p. S's declaring that p, as in saying "This was a wonderful meal" after one that patently was not, has no effect on the beliefs held by the participants about the quality of the meal. Thus, the state after the utterance is that S and H still mutually believe ¬p.

3 Default Logic

The monotonic accounts of speech acts start with axioms that describe complex consequences of utterances—these consequences to hold in all contexts satisfying some condition. The consequences are complex, in the sense that they consist of deeply nested formulas and that the "simple" consequences (say, that the hearer believe the content of the assertion) must be inferred from further conditions (say, that the speaker is (believed to be) sincere). The account I propose turns the formula complexity picture on its head: it assumes that the utterance of, say, a declarative sentence indicates that the speaker believes its content p, but that this consequence occurs *by default*, only if it is not contradicted by the context of the utterance. Similarly, the fact that the hearer comes to believe p may follow his believing that the speaker believes p, as long as the hearer's believing p is consistent with his other beliefs.

The formal account follows Reiter's Default Logic (Reiter 1980). Default Logic was developed to deal with the following kind of reasoning:

(1)   Birds (normally) fly.

(2)   Tweety is a bird.

(3)   Penguins don't fly.

(4)   Penguins are birds.

(5)   Tweety is a penguin.

From (1) and (2), it should be possible to *assume*, by default, that Tweety flies, as no available information prevents the assumption from being made consistently. Adding (3) and (4), it should still be possible to assume that Twenty flies, as there is no evidence that Tweety is a penguin. From (1)–(5), however, it should follow that Tweety doesn't fly. The reasoning demonstrated here is *nonmonotonic*: adding (5) to (1)–(4) cancels the conclusion that Tweety flies. Note also that, if (1) and (3) are jointly represented as

$$\forall x \ \text{bird}(x) \ \& \ \neg \text{penguin}(x) \supset \text{fly}(x),$$

then fly(Tweety) is not a *logical consequence* of (1)–(4), although it is a default consequence.

Reiter's approach to default rules is to take them as rules of inference rather than axioms. Given a base language L (for the moment first-order predicate calculus), a *default rule* is of the form

$$\frac{\alpha : M\beta}{\omega},$$

where α is the *prerequisite* of the rule and ω its *consequent*. The rule is read: if α is believed and β is consistent with what is believed, then ω can be assumed. Of particular importance are rules of the form

$$\frac{\alpha : M\beta}{\beta},$$

which are called *normal defaults*. All the default rules used in this paper are normal; we will abbreviate the rule above as $\alpha \Rightarrow \beta$. A *default theory* $\Delta = (D, W)$ consists of a set D of defaults and a set W of well-formed formulas of L called the *assumptions*.

In part because it is possible to have both $\alpha \Rightarrow \beta$ and $\alpha \Rightarrow \neg\beta$ as default rules of the same default theory, the notion of consequence in Default Logic is different from the notion of theorem in monotonic logical theories. The appropriate notion here is that of an *extension*. Given a default theory Δ, an *extension* of Δ is a set of formulas E that is the closure of W under the defaults D. Reiter suggests that E should have the following properties:

- it contains all the assumptions, namely, $W \subseteq E$;
- it is closed under the logical consequence relation of the base language, which we write $Th(E) = E$; and
- it is closed under the default rules, in the sense that it contains the consequents of defaults whose antecedents it also contains, as long as the extension is consistent with the consequents, where "consistent with" means "does not also contain its negation": If $\alpha \Rightarrow \beta$ is in D, α is in E, and $\neg\beta$ is not in E, then β is in E.

Reiter's definition of an extension is given in terms of a fixed-point operator. However, he gives an alternative characterization that is better suited to our purposes:

Definition
Let $E \subseteq L$ and $\Delta = (D, W)$. Let $E_0 = W$, and for all $i \geq 0$, $E_{i+1} = Th(E_i) \cup \{\beta \| \alpha \Rightarrow \beta \in D, \text{ where } \alpha \in E_i, \text{ and } \neg\beta \notin E\}$.
Then E is an extension for Δ iff $E = \cup E_i$, over all i.

Because of the occurrence of E in the definition of E_{i+1}, the definition of extension is nonconstructive: it gives a rule for *verifying* that a theory E is an extension of a default theory Δ. This limitation is, unfortunately, the price one pays for the sort of nonlocal reasoning that nonmonotonic logics allow. In contrast to the unique set of theorems of monotonic theories, default theories may have several extensions, each of which is a consistent way of applying the defaults to the assumption. Reiter shows that theories containing only normal defaults can be shown to have at least one extension; if they have more than one, these must be mutually inconsistent.

4 Default Rules for Speech Acts

We can now begin develop our account of the role of default reasoning in speech act theory, restricting ourselves here to declarative sentences. I will present a set of default rules D that will be applied as follows. Let W be a theory describing an observer's knowledge of the state of the world before an utterance is performed. W will contain propositions labeled with the time—say, 0—at which the utterance is performed. Let W' be W augmented by the statement that an utterance has been performed at time 0 as well as by statements describing the facts about who is observing whom at that time. I claim that each extension E of the default theory (W', D) describes a consistent view of the observer's knowledge of the world both before and after the utterance. Generally, the extensions will contain additional information about the beliefs of the participants after, and about the intentions of the speaker before, the utterance.

First we define a language L to express facts about agents, actions, and propositional attitudes. L has expressions of type *agent, time, action, untensed proposition,* and *tensed proposition* (which we call simply *proposition*). The constants S and H and the variables x and y are the only expressions of type *agent*. The integer constants, 0, 1, ... and the variables t and u are of type *time*. If p is of type *proposition*, then p. is of type *action* and denotes the action of uttering a declarative sentence with (tensed) propositional content p. If z is of type *agent*, Obs(z) is of type *action* and denotes the action of observing z.

The expressions of type *untensed proposition* consist of propositional variables r, s, .. and their Boolean combinations. The expressions r_t, $DO_{x,t}\alpha$, $B_{x,t}p$, and $I_{x,t}p$ are of type *proposition*, where r is of type *untensed proposition*, p is of type *proposition*, t is of type *time*, x is of type *agent*, and α is of type *action*. They are read as "r is true at time t," "x did α at time t," "x believes at time t that p," and "x intends at time t that p," respectively.

In the rest of this section I offer a simple account of beliefs and declarative sentences in a default theory. Intentions are added to the account in the next section.

Beliefs are constrained by both axioms and default rules. We assume that an agent's beliefs at any one time follow the standard weak S5 axioms:

The beliefs of one agent at one time are taken to be consistent, distributive over conjunctions, closed under logical consequence and positive introspection. Beliefs need not be true but should be believed to be.

Consistency
$\vdash B_{x,t}p \supset \neg B_{x,t}\neg p.$

Closure
$\vdash B_{x,t}p\ \&\ B_{x,t}(p \supset q) \supset B_{x,t}q.$

Positive Introspection
$\vdash B_{x,t}p \supset B_{x,t}B_{x,t}p.$

Negative Introspection
$\vdash \neg B_{x,t}p \supset B_{x,t}\neg B_{x,t}p.$

Accuracy
$\vdash B_{x,t}(B_{x,t}p \supset p).$

We assume that agents remember their previous beliefs.

Memory
$\vdash B_{x,t}p \supset B_{x,t+1}B_{x,t}p.$

More important is what beliefs x has about p at t + 1. Agent x could continue to believe p at t + 1 if he believed it at time t. He could also come to believe p if he believes that some other (reliable) agent y believes it.

Obviously, these two rules could come into conflict, which could be resolved by giving priority to x's previous belief or to x's belief about y's belief, or by allowing different extensions for different possibilities. For the moment we opt for the former.

Persistence
$$\vdash B_{x,t+1}B_{x,t}p \supset B_{x,t+1}p.$$

The belief that an action has been performed is acquired from observation of an action. The observability axiom is oversimplified as we take agents to be observed, rather than actions. Observation of one agent is assumed to imply observation of all actions performed by him.

Observability
$$\vdash DO_{x,t}\alpha \text{ \& } DO_{y,t}Obs(x) \supset B_{y,t+1}DO_{x,t}\alpha.$$

As rules of inference we assume modus ponens and the usual rule of necessitation.

Necessitation
If $\vdash p$ then $\vdash B_{x,t}p.$

Finally, two default rules are necessary. They both address how new beliefs can be added to old ones. The first allows for transfer of beliefs from one agent to another, provided that the new beliefs are consistent with the old ones.

Belief Transfer Rule
$$B_{x,t}B_{y,t}p \Rightarrow B_{x,t}p.$$

The second default associates with the utterance of sentences bearing particular linguistic features an aspect of the speaker's mental state—for declarative sentences, for example, that he believes the propositional content.

Declarative Rule
$$DO_{x,t}(p.) \Rightarrow B_{x,t}p.$$

Because the relation between an utterance and the attitude it expresses is given as a default and is thus defeasible, there is no need to give anything more complicated. As we will see, the inference of mutual belief follows from the interaction of these rules.

Whereas the belief transfer rule allows simple (that is, less deeply nested) belief formulas to be inferred from complex ones, the observation axiom allows complex formulas to be inferred from simple ones. The tension between the application of these two principles is crucial to enabling lies to function much like true assertions, while differing in that liars, for example, are not convinced by their own lies.

One more mechanism is necessary: we need, for example, to allow an agent x, who believes that $DO_{y,t}(p.)$ and that $B_{y,t}p$ is a *default* consequence of $DO_{y,t}(p.)$, to come to believe that $B_{y,t}p$, as long as $B_{y,t}p$ is consistent with x's other beliefs. It is necessary, therefore, that the beliefs of agents be closed under the default rules. One way to view this mechanism is as an analogue for defaults of closure under logical consequence. We need something like the following:

$$B_{x,t}p \ \& \ B_{x,t}(p \Rightarrow q) \Rightarrow B_{x,t}q.$$

One problem here, of course, is that such an expression is ill formed, both as a formula in the base language and as a default rule. More importantly, it does not capture the fact that it is the *totality* of x's beliefs that must be closed under defaults, not just those that follow from some p. We account for this requirement by adding the following metarule, mirroring the closure of the axiom system under beliefs:

For all agents x and times t, if $p \Rightarrow q$ is a default rule, so is $B_{x,t}p \Rightarrow B_{x,t}q$.

Let W_0 be the set of axioms given above, D_0 the set of default rules.

We can now examine the interaction of axioms and rules in various settings. A bit of notation will be useful. Let (D, W) be a default theory. For any two sets E, $E' \subseteq L$, let

$$D(E,E') = \{\beta \| \alpha \Rightarrow \beta \in D, \ \alpha \in E, \ \neg\beta \notin E'\},$$

$$MB_{x,y,t}p = B_{x,t}p \ \& \ B_{y,t}p \ \& \ B_{x,t}B_{y,t}p \ \& \ B_{y,t}B_{x,t}p \ \& \ \ldots,$$

$$^*B_{x,t}p = MB_{x,x,t}p, \text{ and}$$

$$\Phi = DO_{S,0}p. \ \& \ DO_{S,0}Obs(H) \ \& \ DO_{H,0}Obs(S) \ \& \ DO_{S,0}Obs(S) \ \& \ DO_{H,0}Obs(H).$$

It will be convenient at times to treat $MB_{x,y,t}P$, $^*B_{x,t}p$, and Φ as the set of their conjuncts.

We can now examine our key examples more carefully.

Example 1 (Continued): Sincere Assertion
Let S utter a declarative sentence with propositional content p to H at a time 0, where $B_{S,0}p$ and there are no other beliefs about p or believing p. Let it also be the case that S and H are observing each other (and themselves), so that $DO_{u,0}(Obs \ v)$ is true for all substitutions of S and H for u and v. An extension of these assumptions under the rules D_0 contains the mutual belief by S and H that p, as well as the mutual belief that the observation conditions hold.

Slightly more formally, we can show that the following theory E is an extension of the default theory (Φ, D_0):

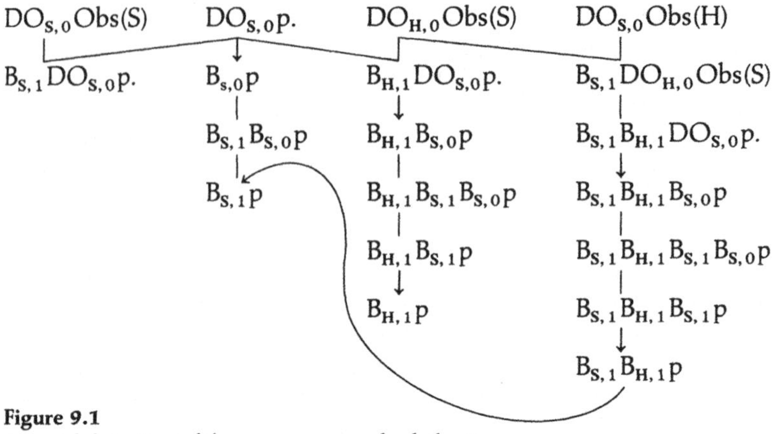

$DO_{S,0}Obs(S)$ $\quad DO_{S,0}p.$ $\quad DO_{H,0}Obs(S)$ $\quad DO_{S,0}Obs(H)$

$B_{S,1}DO_{S,0}p.$ $\quad B_{S,0}p$ $\quad B_{H,1}DO_{S,0}p.$ $\quad B_{S,1}DO_{H,0}Obs(S)$

$\quad\quad\quad B_{S,1}B_{S,0}p$ $\quad B_{H,1}B_{S,0}p$ $\quad B_{S,1}B_{H,1}DO_{S,0}p.$

$\quad\quad\quad B_{S,1}p$ $\quad B_{H,1}B_{S,1}B_{S,0}p$ $\quad B_{S,1}B_{H,1}B_{S,0}p$

$\quad\quad\quad\quad\quad B_{H,1}B_{S,1}p$ $\quad B_{S,1}B_{H,1}B_{S,1}B_{S,0}p$

$\quad\quad\quad\quad\quad B_{H,1}p$ $\quad B_{S,1}B_{H,1}B_{S,1}p$

$\quad\quad\quad\quad\quad\quad\quad B_{S,1}B_{H,1}p$

Figure 9.1
A partial derivation of the consequences of a declarative.

$$E = Th(\Phi) \cup MB_{S,H,1}(\Phi \,\&\, B_{S,0}p \,\&\, p) \cup {}^*B_{S,0}(\Phi \,\&\, p) \cup {}^*B_{S,1}(\Phi \,\&\, p)$$
$$\cup {}^*B_{H,1}(\Phi \,\&\, p).$$

Before doing so, however, let us examine the rules that contribute to the licensing in E of the first few terms of its most important part, $MB_{S,H,1}p$. Figure 9.1 illustrates the derivation of the four shortest terms. The lines ending in arrowheads indicate applications of the default rules; those without arrowheads indicate applications of the axioms.

To show that E is an extension of (Φ, D_0), let $E_0 = \Phi$ and $E_{i+1} = Th(E_i) \cup D(E_i, E)$. $Th(E_0)$ contains the proposition that everyone comes to believe Φ and, by repeated application of the observation axiom and closure axioms, that Φ comes to be mutually believed. The default rule for declaratives lets us add that S initially believes p. Thus,

$$E_1 = Th(\Phi) \cup MB_{S,H,1}\Phi \cup {}^*B_{S,1}\Phi \cup {}^*B_{H,1}\Phi \cup B_{S,0}p.$$

In E_2 we can add that S continues to believe p, by virtue of memory and persistence, that ${}^*B_{S,0}p$, by repeated application of introspection, and that it becomes mutually believed that S believed p at time 0, by repeated application of the declarative rule:

$$E_2 = Th(E_1) \cup {}^*B_{S,0}p \cup \{B_{S,1}p, B_{S,1}B_{S,0}p\} \cup MB_{S,H,1}B_{S,0}p$$
$$\cup {}^*B_{S,1}B_{S,0}p \cup {}^*B_{H,1}B_{S,0}p.$$

In E_3 all S's beliefs can be advanced to time 1 by nested applications of memory and persistence:

$$E_3 = Th(E_2) \cup MB_{S,H,1}B_{S,1}B_{S,0}p \cup MB_{S,H,1}B_{S,1}p$$
$$\cup {}^*B_{S,1}B_{S,1}B_{S,0}p \cup {}^*B_{S,1}B_{S,1}p \cup {}^*B_{H,1}B_{S,1}B_{S,0}p \cup {}^*B_{H,1}B_{S,1}p.$$

Finally, in E_4 we find mutual belief that p, as expected, from repeated

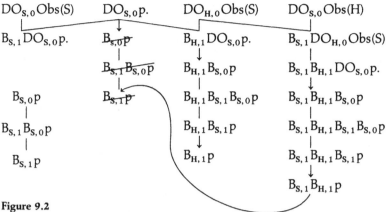

Figure 9.2
A partial derivation of the consequences of a lie.

application of the transfer rule:

$$E_4 = Th(E_3) \cup MB_{S,H,1}p \cup {}^*B_{S,1}p \cup {}^*B_{H,1}p.$$

E is now $Th(E_4)$, as the defaults can contribute nothing further.

We conjecture that E is the only extension of (Φ, D_0) and, to some extent, the division of labor between axioms and default rules is designed to ensure this. We return to this question after the second example, in which some of the rules are blocked.

Example 2 (Continued): Lie
This case is much like the previous one, but we now assume that $B_{S,0} \urcorner p$. The consequences for H should be exactly the same as with a sincere assertion, and so should the consequences for S, except that S continues to believe $\urcorner p$. The following E is an extension of $(\Phi \& B_{S,0} \urcorner p, D_0)$:

$$E = Th(\Phi \cup MB_{S,H,1}(\Phi \& B_{S,0}p \& p) - \{B_{S,1}B_{S,0}p, B_{S,1}p\}$$
$$\cup \{B_{S,1}B_{S,0} \urcorner p, B_{S,1} \urcorner p\} \cup {}^*B_{S,1}(\Phi \& \urcorner p) \cup {}^*B_{H,1}(\Phi \& p)$$
$$\cup {}^*B_{S,0}(\Phi \& \urcorner p)).$$

First, figure 9.2 shows informally the derivation of the first few terms of what is mutually believed about p at time 1. The crossed-out terms are those introduced by default rules in the standard case but blocked here.

This time we take $E_0 = \Phi \& B_{S,0} \urcorner p$. E_1 is as in Example 1, except that it does not contain $B_{S,0}p$ because the declarative rule is blocked by $B_{S,0} \urcorner p$. The last three terms are the result of applying introspection, memory, and persistence to $B_{S,0} \urcorner p$:

$$E_1 = Th(\Phi) \cup MB_{S,H,1}\Phi \cup {}^*B_{S,1}\Phi \cup {}^*B_{H,1}\Phi \cup {}^*B_{S,0} \urcorner p \cup$$
$${}^*B_{S,1}B_{S,0} \urcorner p \cup {}^*B_{S,1} \urcorner p.$$

In E_2 it becomes mutually believed that S believed p at time 0, by repeated application of the declarative rule, with the exception that S does not change his mind about $\neg p$:

$$E_2 = Th(E_1) \cup MB_{S,H,1}B_{S,0}p - \{B_{S,1}B_{S,0}p\} \cup {}^*B_{H,1}B_{S,0}p.$$

In E_3 memory and persistence apply to all S's beliefs at time 0:

$$E_3 = Th(E_2) \cup MB_{S,H,1}B_{S,1}B_{S,0}p - \{B_{S,1}B_{S,1}B_{S,0}p\} \cup MB_{S,H,1}B_{S,1}p - \{B_{S,1}B_{S,1}p\} \cup {}^*B_{H,1}B_{S,1}p.$$

In E_4 we confirm mutual belief that p at time 1, save that S continues to believe $\neg p$:

$$E_4 = Th(E_3) \cup MB_{S,H,1}p - \{B_{S,1}p\} \cup {}^*B_{H,1}p.$$

No further rules apply and $E = E_4$.

Conjecture: E is the only extension of $(\Phi \ \& \ B_{S,0}\neg p, D_0)$.

Other defective cases of the use of declaratives can be handled similarly. Initial assumptions are not overriden by beliefs about the content of the declarative, but mutual belief about the existence of the utterance and the observation facts is achieved, along with as much of mutual belief regarding the propositional content as is consistent with the assumed private facts.

One might ask here whether different belief revision strategies can be described in Default Logic. One obvious step to try is to change some of the axioms into default rules. A belief revision strategy in which old beliefs do not always persist can be obtained by replacing the persistence axiom with the persistence rule $B_{x,t+1}B_{x,t}p \Rightarrow B_{x,t+1}p$. Thus, if S declared that p in a state 0, where $B_{S,0}B_{H,0}\neg p$, the axioms would let us infer $B_{S,1}B_{H,1}B_{H,0}\neg p$ (that H continues to believe that he used to believe $\neg p$) and $B_{S,1}B_{H,1}B_{S,1}p$ (that H comes to believe that S believes p). The question is, what, at time 1, S's beliefs about H's beliefs about p ought to be. Having both persistence and belief transfer rules would ensure two extensions of the set of assumptions: one in which $B_{S,1}B_{H,1}\neg p$ (that is, in which H's beliefs are believed to persist) and an (incompatible) one in which $B_{S,1}B_{H,1}p$ (that is, in which H is believed to have been convinced by the declaration). The theory would then give no precedence to either.

One might wish, intuitively, for a single extension in which $B_{S,1}(B_{H,1}\neg p \lor B_{H,1}p)$, that is, in which S would not be committed to believing one outcome rather than the other. I do not believe this can be done in Default Logic with the current definition of extension.

5 Adding Intentions

The main characteristic of illocutionary acts is that they are performed successfully only when the hearer recognizes some of the speaker's intentions (see Grice 1957). In the case of a sincere assertion, the hearer should recognize (come to believe) that the speaker intended to make the utterance, that he intended that the hearer recognize that the believes the propositional content p, that he intended that the hearer recognize that he intended that the hearer recognize that he believes the propositional content p, and so on. Schiffer (1972) provides a detailed discussion of these conditions. In this section I extend the analysis to include the role of the intentions the speaker has about his utterances and their consequences for the mental state of the participants. As with beliefs, I propose an analysis in which the speaker's intentions, including those that have to do with the hearer's recognizing his intentions, are assumed as the result of the application of default rules and depend both on the form of the actions and on the facts about the joint mental state of the participants. A liar who initially believes $\neg p$ cannot intend to believe p after his declarative. Under this model of belief, if S believes that H believes $\neg p$, then S cannot intend that H will come to believe p, at least not as the result of S's declaring p.

The formal analysis of the full notion of intention and its relation to desires, goals, and beliefs is difficult and still quite controversial (see, for example, Bratman 1984; Cohen and Levesque, chapter 3 of this volume). The version given here focuses on the interaction between intentions and beliefs; it is assumed, moreover, that the objects of intentions are (tensed) propositions. Intentions are taken to be consistent—an agent cannot intend that both p and $\neg p$ will hold simultaneously.

I-consistency
$$\vdash I_{x,t}p_{t'} \supset \neg I_{x,t}\neg p_{t'}.$$

We also assume that intentions are consistent with beliefs, so that believing that p cannot become true is inconsistent with rationally intending that it should become true.

IB-consistency
$$\vdash I_{x,t}p_{t'} \supset \neg B_{x,t}\neg p_{t'}.$$

We add a new default rule and reformulate another slightly. First we assume that actions are taken to be performed intentionally, as long as this is consistent.

Intentionality
$$DO_{x,t}\alpha \Rightarrow I_{x,t}DO_{x,t}\alpha.$$

The declarative rule can now be reformulated so that only intentionally performed declaratives are taken to indicate that the speaker believes the propositional content.

Declarative Rule
$$I_{x,t}DO_{x,t}(p.) \Rightarrow B_{x,t}p.$$

These new axioms and rules are relatively uncontroversial. More difficult is the question of the closure of intentions under logical consequence and the default rules. Cohen and Levesque (chapter 3 of this volume) present two different forward-looking attitudes, GOAL and P-GOAL, and argue that only GOAL is closed logical consequence. A full integration of their analysis (or of something similar) within the framework presented earlier is beyond the scope of this paper. We assume analogues for intentions of the closure rules we used for beliefs. First, an axiom for logical closure:

I-closure
$$\vdash I_{x,t}p \ \& \ B_{x,t}(p \supset q) \supset I_{x,t}q.$$

We also assume that intentions are closed under the default rules, implemented as before through a metarule:

For all agents x and times t, if $B_{x,t}p_{t'} \Rightarrow B_{x,t}q_{t'}$ is a default rule, so is $I_{x,t}p_{t'} \Rightarrow I_{x,t}q_{t'}$.

Let D_1 be the set of default rules obtained by adding the new rules to those given in the previous section and then closing the class under the metarules for belief and intention.

Although as a general analysis, our view of intention is controversial, we need to deal here only with an agent's intentions relative to the speech act he is in the process of performing and its resulting state. The aspect of intention that is especially crucial to the analysis of speech acts is the commitment to—or the willingness to accept—the consequences of an utterance. What needs to be captured is the fact that, if an agent performs an utterance expressing some aspect of his mental state—say, a belief— and if he believes he is being observed, then a default consequence is that he intends to have it recognized that he holds the belief. This must, of course, be a default consequence, since there may be prior reasons for believing that he in fact does not hold the belief.

Example 1 (Revisited)

Let us consider now the extension E' of the set of assumptions of Example 1 under the revised set of defaults D_1. All the consequences E under the old set of defaults D_0 are in E'. The extension E' now also contains $I_{S,0}q$, $B_{S,1}q$, and $B_{H,1}q$ for every formula q in E'. Thus, the default consequences include the fact that the utterance was performed intentionally $(I_{S,0}DO_{S,0}(p.))$, that it was intended to be recognized as such $(I_{S,0}B_{H,1}I_{S,0}DO_{S,0}(p.))$ and that this be recognized $(I_{S,0}B_{H,1}I_{S,0}B_{H,1}I_{S,0}DO_{S,0}(p.))$, and so on. S also intends that the perlocutionary effects take place (say, $I_{S,0}B_{H,1}p$), that this intention be recognized $(I_{S,0}B_{H,1}I_{S,0}B_{H,1}p)$, and so on.

Here too, the case of lies is only slightly different. Initially S believes $\neg p$ and thus does not intend that he should not believe $\neg p$, but, as before, S intended to perform the utterance, intended that the hearer H recognize his intention to utter something, intended that H believe p, and intended that H recognize his intention that H believe p. It must be assumed that it is not the case that S intends that H should believe that S should believe ¬p: the contrary leads to exposure of the liar.

6 What Is a Speech Act?

Speech acts can be defined in the proposed framework by stating conditions that must hold in the extension(s) obtained by closing under the default rules D_1 the theory describing the initial mental state of the participants, the fact of the utterance, and the conditions of observation. I attempt here to define the acts of asserting, informing, lying, and convincing.

Searle points out that illocutionary acts are somewhat different when examined from the perspectives of the speaker and hearer, respectively. An illocutionary act has been performed *successfully* if the speaker did it while in a certain mental state, whereas it has been *fully consummated* if the hearer recognized that the speaker performed it successfully. The fully consummated act is what Austin calls the *securing of uptake*. Both perspectives are available in our analysis; examples are given below. Perlocutionary acts are defined in terms of the change in mental state brought about the utterance.

One of the essential features of a theory of illocutionary acts is its account of the relation between explicit performative and declarative sentences. Some accounts (such as Searle 1969) do not attempt to relate them at all. I believe that the theory should predict that an utterance of "I hereby assert that p" is indeed an assertion if and only if the speaker's mental state when making the utterance satisfies the conditions of the action's being an assertion, by virtue of the utterance of a declarative sentence. Such an account requires a more detailed analysis of the propositional content of the utterance than I can provide (but see Cohen and Levesque, chapter 12 of this volume). Asserting p is doing something that is intended to bring about recognition by the hearer that the speaker believes that p, and doing so sincerely and overtly. S *successfully asserted* p to H in performing an action (utterance) U at time 0 if $B_{S,0}p$ & $I_{S,0}B_{H,1}B_{S,0}p$ & $I_{S,0}B_{H,1}I_{S,0}B_{H,1}$ $B_{S,0}p$ & .... This definition allows S to not intend that H actually come to believe p: the utterance of a declarative sentence in a situation in which it is mutually believed that H believes ¬p is still an assertion according to this definition, and S cannot intend that H believe p in that circumstance. Lies, however, are not assertions, as they are not sincere, nor are any actions by S that are not done overtly. S *fully consummated* an assertion that p if S asserted that p and H recognized that S did so.

Another possible definition of asserting is that S should intend that S and H come to mutually believe that S believes p. This definition would be too weak if we were not already requiring that S be the agent of the action: it would then be satisfied by having a reliable third party declare p to S and H simultaneously. Even if we require S to be the agent, if actions need not be intended, S and H could mutually believe that S believes p if S did something overtly and unintentionally (say, move a block) and perceived its consequences (say, that the block is at location L). We would not want to say that any assertion had been performed under the circumstances. It should be noted that both defining conditions stated here (and many others) are true in the extension of the default theory given in Example 1 but are not true in that of Example 2.

Assuming our definition of assertions, it is quite simple to distinguish them from lies and convincings. Lies are insincere assertions: S *lied about* p to H in performing an action (utterance) U if $B_{S,0} \neg p$ & $I_{S,0}B_{H,1}B_{S,0}p$ & $I_{S,0}B_{H,1}I_{S,0}B_{H,1}B_{S,0}p$ & . . . . Consequently, illocutionary acts are those resulting in a state in which the speaker has a certain attitude and overtly intends that it be recognized. In perlocutionary acts, the overtness is unnecessary, as with convincing: S *convinced* H of p in performing an action (utterance) U if S uttered U, intending that H believe p, and H comes to believe p.

Informing is asserting with the intention that the content be believed. S *informed* H that p in performing an action (utterance) U if $B_{S,0}p$ & $I_{S,0}B_{H,1}(p \& B_{S,0}p)$ & $I_{S,0}B_{H,1}I_{S,0}B_{H,1}(p \& B_{S,0}p)$ & . . . .

7 Irony and Indirection

One of the main reasons for basing an analysis of illocutionary acts on changes in mental state is to circumvent the problems created by accounts that postulate a direct connection between utterance features and illocutionary act type—in particular, the treatment of nonserious and indirect illocutionary acts. So far we have attempted to describe the effect of utterances on mental state, on the basis of their features and the conditions of utterance. Let us now examine the nonserious and indirect uses a bit more carefully.

Propositional attitudes play three quite distinct roles in speech act theory; accordingly, these are clearly distinguished from each other in our treatment. First, sentences (utterances, actually) are conventionally related by their features to attitudes that the speaker could, but need not, have toward, among other things, the world and subsequent actions of both speaker and hearer. Declaratives are related to beliefs of the speaker, requests to intentions or desires with regard to actions of the hearer, commissives to commitments of the speaker to future actions, and so on. Let us call these the *literal attitudes* carried by the utterances. In our framework, the relation between the features of an utterance and the literal attitude it expresses is captured by the declarative default rule (and its analogues for other clusters of utterance features and attitudes).

Second, a speaker makes use of utterances to express attitudes he may or may not have toward the world and subsequent actions of speaker and hearer. Although these attitudes may correspond to the literal attitudes carried by the utterances the speaker makes to express them, they need not, as in indirect and nonserious uses, nor need they be held by the speaker, as in insincere uses. Let us call these attitudes of the speaker the *core attitudes*.

Finally, besides core attitudes, speakers have attitudes toward the utterances themselves and toward the change in the mental states of all participants that is effected by the recognition of the speaker's intentions. Let us call these *Gricean attitudes*. In our framework, expressions describing the Gricean attitudes are of the form $I_{S,0}B_{H,1}q$, $I_{S,0}B_{H,1}I_{S,0}B_{H,1}q$, and so on, where q is a core attitude. They (or rather their descriptions) are generated by application of the various axioms and default rules to the assumptions regarding the initial mental state of the participants and the action performed.

Gricean attitudes characterize the class of illocutionary acts. A speaker performs a communicative act successfully if he has the right Gricean attitudes toward the core attitude he is trying to convey, as discussed in the definitions of asserting and informing presented in the preceding section. The Gricean attitudes are parameterized, if you will, by core attitudes.

As Searle (1975) suggests, communicative conventions can be systematically violated to good effect. The violations take several forms. The most obvious kind occurs when it is incompatible with the initial mental state of the participants that the speaker should have the Gricean attitudes expressed by the given utterance. This is the case with ironic usage. After a terrible meal shared with the hearer, the speaker, in saying "This is the best meal I ever had," does not really believe that the meal was wonderful, nor does he intend that it should be recognized that he does; the initial joint mental state is such that all this is mutually believed. Thus, no illocutionary act with core attitude $B_{S,0}$ (this is the best meal) can be performed by uttering this sentence. However, this need not mean that *no* useful illocutionary act was performed.

What the speaker of an ironic utterance *did* mean can be determined by finding a related core attitude that the speaker could have Gricean intentions about. In ironic uses, the propositional attitude in the core remains the same, but the propositional content changes—in this case, to something like "This is the worst meal I ever had." The speaker's belief in that proposition can now be the core attitude for a successful illocutionary act, as it is now possible for the speaker to believe that this was the worst meal, intend that that intention be recognized, and so on. The "derived" content is new to the hearer and it is consistent with what he knows of the speaker's previous mental state the speaker should hold it. Though it still remains, of course, to establish the details of the process for determining the conveyed core attitude from the literal one, I have nothing new to say about that process here. Note that ironic uses can also be insincere: the speaker may in fact believe privately that he has just had a pretty good meal yet convey ironically that it was terrible. He can also be recognized as lying, and so on.

Indirect uses fall in two categories. The first, exemplified by "It's cold here," said by one person to another upon entering a cold room, has the speaker expressing a true attitude, but his expressing it cannot lead to a change in the beliefs of the hearer, as the fact being expressed is already mutually believed (or can be presumed to be mutually believed by ideal interlocutors). The second kind of indirect use is exemplified by a different use of the same sentence, uttered, say, by a tenant to his landlord over the telephone. Here again the literal core attitude is sincerely held, but this time the literal assertion is a useful illocutionary act: the speaker intends that the hearer recognize his belief, recognize also that he intends that that intention be recognized, and so on. However, the literal core attitude does not exhaust the message the speaker intends to convey.

In the indirect cases, the derived content can be obtained from inferences regarding the speaker's plans. Heuristic methods for plan recognition have been presented by Schmidt, Sridharan, and Goodson (1978) and Allen and Perrault (1980). A formal definition of the problem based on an extension of circumscription is given by Kautz (this volume). Here too, it must be noted that the result of the plan inference—say, that the speaker wants the hearer to turn the heat up—must be appropriate as the core attitude of a successful illocutionary act. In other words, it must be possible for the speaker to have the appropriate Gricean intentions toward the derived attitude. If, for example, it was mutually believed that there was no heat to be turned up in the building, the speaker could not be trying to convey, even indirectly, his desire to have it be turned up. He might, however, be trying to imply that a furnace should be installed. Also, as was the case with irony, the speaker can be insincere about the indirectly conveyed attitudes: he may not really want the heat turned on but merely wish to distract the landlord from watching the Super Bowl. In fact, indirection and irony can be used simultaneously. In saying "It's cold here" with an ironic intonation or in a very warm room, the speaker can be indirectly conveying that he wants the room to be made colder. And, of course, he may be lying about that too.

Finally, a comment about force indicators other than sentence type. Some violations of conventional uses of sentence type can be marked, in particular by gestures and intonation. Nothing in our treatment precludes, at least in principle, the possibility that the rules relating utterance features to literal attitudes could be sensitive to information conveyed by other markers. Oversimplifying, if the derived core attitude in an ironic declarative with propositional content p where $B_{s,t} \neg p$, then a feature rule could be added expressing directly that, if S utters a declarative with propositional content p under ironic intonation, it should be assumed that $B_{s,t} \neg p$. One would probably want this rule to have precedence over the declarative rule, in the sense that, if it could apply, the other should not. Some problems arise in Default Logic if rules with distinct but not mutually exclusive defaults are allowed. These are discussed by Reiter and Criscuolo (1983) and by Etherington (1986).

8 Comparison with Cohen and Levesque

Cohen and Levesque's paper "Rational Interaction as the Basis for Communication" (chapter 12 of this volume) is a major revision and elaboration of C&L, developed largely in parallel with this one. It is a more ambitious enterprise than this one, containing a comprehensive theory of intention and derived explanation of directives, all developed in a monotonic framework. My more modest aims are to explore the relation between action, observation, and belief revision. However, some differences between the two accounts are worth noting.

Cohen and Levesque's account in chapter 12 allows participants to change their mind about asserted propositions (that is, go from believing $\neg p$ to believing p), whereas mine does not. This is obviously desirable in some circumstances, but the question is what price must be paid to allow it. Their version of my declarative default is an axiom postulating that the hearer, observing a declarative, comes to believe the literal attitude—namely, that the speaker believes p—as long as the hearer does not believe that the speaker is insincere about believing p. Simplifying their formulation slightly, and recasting it in the notation of this paper, they assume

$$B_{H,0}(DO_{H,0}(Obs\ S))\ \&\ B_{H,0}(DO_{S,0}(p.))\ \&\ \neg B_{H,0}\ \neg Sincere_{S,H,0}B_{S,0}p$$
$$\supset B_{H,1}B_{S,1}p.$$

More deeply nested forms are also postulated but are not immediately relevant here. This allows an agent to go from believing $\neg p$ to believing p, and to go from not believing p to believing it, neither of which is allowed by the present account.

The price Cohen and Levesque pay for allowing true changes of belief is twofold. First, they need to postulate an extra concept, sincerity, to gate between H's beliefs before and after an utterance. The notion of sincerity itself is quite tricky, and I am still not convinced that it is necessary. The difficulty is to make it nontrivial, so that using the declarative axiom is not simply a matter of postulating, arbitrarily, that insincerity fails. It should be possible, for example, to prove, in some circumstances, that the failure of sincerity follows from interesting features of the utterance context, or that it is possible to infer the speaker's insincerity from what he says. Cohen and Levesque do not show how this can be done. Second, they make no claims about what happens when the gating condition on sincerity is not satisfied. If they did—say, by claiming that H continues to believe whatever he believed before concerning S's beliefs about p—they would make it clear that their solution, like all monotonic theories of actions, would encounter what McCarthy (1980) called the qualification problem: that the only way of being able to prove anything about the state resulting from an action is to be able to prove the truth of all the qualifying preconditions, and that these can be arbitrarily complex.

9 Conclusion

I have argued that a theory of speech acts intended to consider various nonstandard uses of utterances must be based not only on static accounts of the attitudes but on attitude revision as well. I used Default Logic for a restricted analysis of belief revision, showing how it could be used to account for various insincere, nonserious, and indirect utterances of declarative sentences.

Although speech act theory is typically considered a part of natural-language pragmatics, I prefer to think of it as a part of semantics, albeit not a truth-functional one. The restriction of the realm of semantics to truth-conditional aspects of meaning precludes a uniform semantic treatment of declarative, imperative, and interrogative sentences and even leaves out (declarative) explicit performative sentences. Although very useful work has been done on the satisfaction conditions of interrogatives and imperatives, these accounts are unsatisfactory in that they postulate one kind of object as the interpretation of declarative sentences (truth-values or intensions or relations between a discourse situation and a described situation), other kinds for questions and imperatives. Making the object of the interpretation a bit more complex allows a uniform treatment. There are two possibilities. The first is what I called the core attitude; the second is the function from mental state to mental state resulting from the performance of the utterance. If the main argument of this paper is correct, then systematic handling of explicit performatives, irony, and indirection requires the second, more complex route. I also believe it to be the only way leading to a systematic semantics of extended discourses, but that question is best left for another time.

References

Allen, J. F., and C. R. Perrault (1980). Analyzing intention in utterances. *Artificial Intelligence* 15, 143–178. Reprinted in Grosz, Sparck Jones, and Webber 1986.

Austin, J. L. (1962). *How to do things with words.* New York: Oxford University Press.

Bratman, M. (1984). Two faces of intention. *The Philosophical Review* 93, 375–405.

Cohen, P. R., and H. J. Levesque (1985). Speech acts and rationality. In *Proceedings of the Twenty-third Annual Meeting,* Association for Computational Linguistics, Chicago, IL.

Cohen, P. R., and C. R. Perrault (1979). Elements of a plan-based theory of speech acts. *Cognitive Science* 3, 177–212. Reprinted in Webber and Nilsson 1981 and in Grosz, Sparck Jones, and Webber 1986.

Etherington, D. W. (1986). Reasoning with incomplete information: Investigations of non-monotonic reasoning. Doctoral dissertation, Department of Computer Science, University of British Columbia, Vancouver, B.C.

Grice, H. P. (1957). Meaning. *The Philosophical Review* 66, 377–388.

Grosz, B. G., K. Sparck Jones, and B. L. Webber, eds. (1986). *Readings in natural language processing.* Los Altos, CA: Morgan Kaufmann.

McCarthy, J. (1980). Circumscription: A form of non-monotonic reasoning. *Artificial Intelligence* 13, 27–39. Reprinted in Webber and Nilsson 1981.

Perrault, C. R., and J. F. Allen (1980). A plan-based analysis of indirect speech acts. *American Journal of Computational Linguistics* 6, 167–182.

Reiter, R. (1980). A logic for default reasoning. *Artificial Intelligence* 13, 81–132.

Reiter, R., and G. Criscuolo (1983). Some representational issues in default reasoning. *International Journal of Computers and Mathematics* 9, 1–13.

Schiffer, S. R. (1972). *Meaning.* London: Oxford University Press.

Schmidt, C. F., N. S. Sridharan, and J. L. Goodson (1978). The plan recognition problem: An intersection of psychology and artificial intelligence. *Artificial Intelligence* 11, 45–83.

Searle, J. R. (1969). *Speech acts: An essay in the philosophy of language.* New York: Cambridge University Press.

Searle, J. R. (1975). Indirect speech acts. In P. Cole and J. Morgan, eds. *Syntax and semantics 3: Speech acts.* New York: Academic Press.

Smith, N. V. (1982). *Mutual knowledge.* New York: Academic Press.

Strawson, P. F. (1964). Intention and convention in speech acts. *The Philosophical Review* 73, 439–460. Reprinted in J. R. Searle, ed. (1971). *The philosophy of language.* London: Oxford University Press.

Webber, B. L., and N. J. Nilsson, eds. (1981). *Readings in artificial intelligence.* Palo Alto, CA: Tioga Press.

Chapter 10

Comments on Jones and on Perrault

Jerry Morgan

As Andrew Jones tells us, the background to his paper is the general approach to meaning and its relation to communication proposed by David Lewis, among others. In this approach a fundamental distinction is made between matters of the use of expressions for comunication on the one hand, and on the other hand semantic properties of expressions, construed as abstract relations of correspondence between expressions and things/states/situations in the world. For proponents of this approach, the correspondence side of things and the accompanying questions of compositionality have naturally occupied center stage, for the most part, with little said about how it is that a community (or an individual) can *use* such a correspondence system to achieve communicative ends. Jones's paper lays out the beginnings of a theory to fill this gap, with the goal of "specifying the kinds of mutual beliefs agents have in virtue of which it is possible for them to use an abstract semantic system as a device for communicating with each other." He lays out a view of things in which deontic modalities involving the audience's "interest in being reliably informed" form a foundation for communicative use and interpretation of language.

The paper is a little difficult for a data-monger like myself to evaluate. It is primarily a work of conceptual analysis, a task that is an indispensable stage in theory construction, and one at which philosophers excel. As such, the paper is suggestive and thought-provoking. But at this point in its development the theory has little to offer to the empirically inclined researcher in semantics, pragmatics, or their interactions in human communication, in that it is hard to see just what the empirical consequences are. In fact, it may well be that Jones (and Lewis, for that matter) would not accept as a measure of success the kind of empirical considerations that interest the Chomskyan linguist, for whom the central problem is one of discovering the form and substance of the mental systems that underlie linguistic ability in ordinary humans and explaining how such mental systems arise anew in each individual. From this standpoint one need not share Lewis's apparent confidence in the fundamental distinction between "grammars as abstract semantic systems" and "the psychological and sociological facts whereby [such a system] is the one used by a person or population." Lewis may well be right to some extent in saying that "only confusion comes of mixing these two topics," but nature does not guarantee that the human mind is not a confusing object. It is not inconceivable that the best empirically motivated treatment of literal meaning and its relation to use will be one that is not conceptually simple in rigidly compartmentalizing matters of meaning versus matters of use in communication. It would be unwise, of course, to assume at the outset that chaos reigns. But it has become clear over the past couple of decades that matters of "context of use" are crucially involved in the determination not only of interpretation-in-context but also of truth-conditions and other properties one would want to identify with literal meaning, not just in a few "indexicals" like pronouns, but quite pervasively. There are even expressions—a minority, certainly—for which it is hard to see how to construct a plausible meaning analysis in correspondence terms. Words like *goodbye* and *please*, for example, seem to require an analysis that deals directly in communicative acts, rather than indirectly via conditions of correspondence with states-of-the-world. So the clean theoretical distinction between literal semantics and matters of use could turn out to be empirically untenable in the long run.

In fact, given the pervasively context-bound nature of the interpretation of language, it ought to be considered a remarkable empirical discovery if the psychological system underlying language use and interpretation *does* turn out to be so compartmentalized, since as far as I can see there is no a priori reason, other than historical bias or judgments of theoretical simplicity, to expect to find either compartmentalization or lack of it. But here, as often, the interests of the philosopher and of the linguist may be at loggerheads, in spite of the apparent convergence of interest. One can imagine a kind of Neoplatonist philosopher (or linguist, for that matter) for whom the goal is a theory of language that meets certain conditions of organization laid down a priori, for whom the reflection of such systems in human psychology is largely irrelevant. But the convergence of interest—and the possibility of argument—between such a philosopher and a psychologically oriented linguist is for the most part an illusion. They are doing radically different things, pursuing quite different questions.

Jones agrees with Lewis on another point, in assuming that linguistic communication rests on the same conceptual foundation as simpler nonlinguistic communicative acts. Surely this is the most reasonable assumption to make at the outset, but again what is most plausible a priori might not turn out to be empirically the best theory. For all we know, the theory of communication humans tacitly use in linguistic interaction is quite different from what underlies simpler communicative interactions.

But I think Jones's proposals in this paper are not inextricably tied to Lewis's position on the relation of meaning and use. Rather, their potential value lies in the insights they might provide into the fundamental nature of human communication. In this light I have some questions about the role of intention in Jones's theory. As I understand it, the heart of his proposal is this: a theory in which the information conveyed by an act of linguistic communication is simply "out there" for the audience of the act can't work without a certain additional assumption, namely, the assumption that the act of signaling was optimal relative to the audience's interest in being reliably informed. Jones says that in his formulation nothing is said about the signaler's intentions. His model operator E is defined in such a way that "it may be true that s brings it about that p even though this was not an intentional action on his part." By also disallowing statements of intention in specifications of context, he maintains, "there is no implicit reference here to Gricean intentions on the part of s." He then goes on to note that ordinarily the audience will not form a judgment that the signaling act was optimal without also attributing to the signaler the intention that the act be seen by the audience as an implementation of a signaling rule.

Jones's approach seems to differ from some other current approaches, then, in that he bases his theory of communication not directly on recognition-of-intention but on a concept of optimality that may have attribution of intention as a side effect. There are several thing in his discussion of intentions that elude me, but I read him to imply that the intention-free nature of the theory is somehow an advantage. Perhaps I have misread him; but I don't see what advantage derives from beating about the bush on intentions. Intentionality is surely fundamental to the interpretation by ordinary people of the communicative acts they encounter. In fact, to classify some event as an act is to attribute certain intentions to the event, as far as I can see. For example, if I observe an event in which I perceive issuing from another human a series of sounds analyzable as the English expression "Your hair's on fire," nothing whatever follows from my observation unless I assume that the event was an intentional act, rather than a fortuitous consequence of a miraculous belch, or a pharyngeal spasm, or the output of a random number generator driving a speech synthesizer implanted in the person's throat, or the impromptu rehearsal of lines from a play, or the sincere utterance of a sentence of Albanian that by pure coincidence happens to be acoustically indistinguishable from a certain sentence of English. If I have any common sense, of course, I will not consider such outlandish explanations for the events I observe. But there is certainly nothing either in logic or "out there" that prevents me from doing so. Rather, in human practice the strategy is to maximize attribution of intention; everything that could be taken as intentional is taken as intentional, unless there is some good reason to believe otherwise.

Turning to Raymond Perrault's paper, I think the basic idea is very promising, but I have some reservations about some of the details, which I will try to bring out.

First, the basic idea: in another paper (Perrault 1987, a brief, informal talk-piece apparently prepared for a panel discussion), Perrault provides a context for the present work, with some remarks that seem to me to understate the difference between his work and mainstream work in formal semantics:

> I don't feel comfortable trying to build reliable, well-understood NLP systems without providing a semantics for their "mental state," including the data structures they encode. One step in that direction is a semantics of sentences, for example that of Montague. However, to handle extended discourses, the methods of model-theoretic semantics need to be extended in (at least) three directions. First, anaphora and deixis require that the interpretation (of phrases, sentences, and entire discourses) should be made sensitive to context, both linguistic and physical. Second, non-declarative sentences must be treated uniformly with declarative ones. Finally, it should be possible to make room in the semantics for interpretation constraints based on the subject-matter of the discourse and on the communication itself.

Perrault gives the impression in these remarks, and in fact here and there in the present paper, that he is following the agenda of Montague-style formal semantics, merely doing a bit of tinkering to extend the apparatus of formal semantics to matters of discourse interpretation. But in fact it seems to me that what he suggests there, and what he develops in the present paper, is quite a departure from the spirit of formal semantics, and much the better for it.

An important brick in the foundation of modern formal semantics is the view of meaning as a language-world relation that can be described without reference to things like utterances or other features of the use of language, nor to minds, mental representations, intentions and goals of speakers and hearers, and so on. Where such things do rear their ugly heads—like indexical expressions, for example—the attempt has been to try to relativize truth and reference to abstract "indices," as a way of continuing to avoid bringing speakers and acts of utterance per se directly into the picture.

There is no question that a great deal of important and insightful work has been done in this mode. But it is logically possible, of course, to construe the central problem of semantics not as a purely mathematical one but as a scientific question, with the goal of constructing a theory of semantic competence, of the knowledge structures and abilities that allow humans to understand expressions of their language—or at least of constructing a partial theory of such abilities, if one accepts (is there anybody left who doesn't?) that linguistic meaning underdetermines understanding. And it's not inconceivable that the formal semanticists might turn out to be scientifically as well as philosophically on the right track—that when one learns a word meaning, for example, one forms a mental representation of an expression-world correspondence, and that such representations, together with compositional rules that make no mention of speaker, hearer, communicative intentions, or act of utterance, will do all the work required of an empirical theory of literal meaning. But at the moment there is no candidate formal theory that can be straightforwardly interpreted as even a partial theory of semantic competence, a problem that semanticists (those who care, at least) are well aware of.

On the other hand, it is possible that we will eventually discover that the best empirical theory of sentence meaning is one that makes crucial use of notions of the sort one finds in speech act theory, and perhaps some concepts from cognitive psychology as well. This is a question that can only be settled over the course of time, by constructing theories of various kinds and comparing them empirically.

The same question arises in constructing a theory of discourse interpretation: Can the formalist strategy be extended to account for discourse phenomena? Or do matters of human communication—speakers, hearers, actions, plans, goals, participants' models of each other's mental states, maybe other matters of human psychology like salience and attention—play such a central role that it's waste of time to ignore them? Personally, I think it's obvious that they do, and that the formalist strategy, whatever its merits as a theory of sentence semantics, is just the wrong kind of theory to deal with discourse. And it seems to me that Perrault's work in these two papers takes that line as well, in spite of his (laudable) use of some formal devices of semantic theory. He construes the nature of his theory as (grossly) a function from mental states to mental states of speaker and hearer, and he makes heavy use of notions from speech act theory. So I think it would be a mistake to construe this work as a simple extension of formal semantics to discourse. It's something quite different.

Turning to matters of detail: it seems to me that the general approach he proposes—Default Logic as a model of the mental-state to mental-state function—is on the right track. But the details are probably so oversimplified here that it is bound to encounter serious problems. The belief transfer rule in particular is a great oversimplification. According to this default principle, lacking evidence to the contrary I should believe everything I'm told about the beliefs of other people (or can infer about their beliefs, unless Perrault intends x and y in the formalization to be restricted to S and H). This is so clearly wrong (am I pathologically skeptical?) that it is bound to create problems.

The defaults he gives look tantalizingly like they should be derivable from something more general. The declarative rule, for example, ought to be a consequence of four things (defaults) taken together: first, that people are aware of and accept the consequences of their acts; second, that an indirect consequence of assertion (under some circumstances, anyway) is that the hearer may come to believe the propositional content; third, that having false beliefs is usually detrimental to the believer; fourth, that people are ethical, that is, do not knowingly cause harm to others. Likewise, the belief transfer rule should be derivable as a consequence of a more general system, perhaps a system of defaults, that people use in weighing all sorts of perceptual evidence, assessing reliability, expertise, and evidential grounding of other minds, as we all do in everyday life without thinking about it.

In sum, the general approach of Default Logic makes good sense, but the defaults given are, as I suppose is natural at such an early stage in the development of the theory, much too simple.

I also have some disagreements with Perrault's discussion of irony. First of all, the picture he gives is one where ironic utterance of p can only occur when speaker and hearer mutually believe that p is false *prior* to the utterance. This is just wrong. Notice that Perrault's characterization implies that an ironic utterance can never inform, since both S and H must already believe p is false, and that belief is not changed by the utterance. Then it should follow that an ironic utterance of "p" is a total waste of time, since it can only convey not-p, and only when S and H already knew that anyway.

But in my experience people frequently use irony in cases where there is no reason to believe the hearer has any views one way or the other. One can give ironical answers to sincere questions, for example, as long as it is somehow made clear—by intonation, gesture, facial expression, whatever—that the utterance is to be taken as ironic. If I am asked my opinion of our president, I might well answer "I think he's got a terrific mind" while making just the right face to make my point. There are even phrases that come to have mainly ironic use. For example, if I ask my twelve-year-old daughter to be careful not to lose her algebra book, she might well answer "Oh yeah, Dad, I'm sure I'm going to go out and just drop it in the street," with perfectly innocent expression and intonation. But the "Oh yeah, Dad, I'm sure" somehow marks her utterance as ironic.

In fact, I think Perrault's discussion of irony suffers from the usual flaw of appealing to miracles, in a way that obscures what may be a fundamental limitation of his approach to discourse (and all others that I am aware of). The miracle occurs when H decides (or recalls) that S, having uttered "p," nonetheless does not believe that p. H then immediately leaps to the miraculous inference that in uttering "p," S clearly meant not-p. How to derive that the inference is never spelled out, and it defies common sense (to say nothing of the smaller problem of explaining why H doesn't decide S is just lying). And to rely on some ad hoc principle to fill in the miraculous gap would miss the whole point of irony. The picture given is one of perverse obscurity: one just says "p" to convey not-p, which must strike the Spock-like observer of humans as a damned funny way to run a language.

Here is a better stab at irony: irony is transparent pretense. When I say "That was a terrific meal," I am transparently pretending to believe it; I want H to contemplate the thought of my having that belief and to experience just how bizarre that would be, thereby to appreciate even better how awful the meal was. But I have to be careful to make the pretense transparent, either by using some extralinguistic means like gesture, facial expression, or tone of voice or by relying on the very outlandishness of my having such a belief to convey that I am shamming. If irony is transparent pretense, rather than a verbal magic trick, then there should be nonlinguistic irony, as indeed there is. For example, when the small child shakes his fist at the bully, the bully may transparently feign fright (ostentatiously raising his arms to protect himself, for example) to taunt the smaller child. This is a kind of irony, it seems to me.

There are similar things to be said about metaphor. Some treatments of metaphor construe the problem as entirely a matter of unpacking and eliminating the metaphor, to get at what the speaker really meant. As with irony, this strategy misses the whole point: the resulting picture is one of metaphor as intentional obscurity. If you meant p, why on earth didn't you say p outright, instead of making me figure out what you really meant? But with metaphor (some cases, at least), as with irony, getting there is half the fun. It is the *experience* of contemplating (or at least trying to contemplate) what the world would be like if the figurative utterance were literally true that is the heart and soul of such figurative language. And this is a point that Perrault's approach, for all its appeal, is in principle incapable of dealing with, as far as I can see, insofar as it treats interpretation as a function from belief states to belief states. This idealization, sensible on most grounds, has no way of dealing with what goes on "between states," so to speak, in the very process of interpretation. In metaphor and irony, it seems to me, something like aesthetic judgment is a factor in determining the nature of the second belief state, so the account can never be fully explanatory unless it includes an account of such aesthetic judgments, something that is outside the realm of the formal approach to meaning.

It remains to be seen whether the effects of interpretation-as-experience are so pervasive as to be a serious problem for the state-to-state approach. But if Perrault's theory can eventually deal with everything but figurative language, it will turn out to be a very good theory indeed.

References

Perrault, C. Raymond (1987). Toward a semantic theory of discourse. Presented at TINLAP III (Theoretical Issues in Natural Language Processing), New Mexico State University, Las Cruces, NM.

Chapter 11

On the Unification of Speech Act Theory and Formal Semantics

Daniel Vanderveken

The primary units of meaning in the use and comprehension of natural languages are speech acts of the type called by Austin (1956) *illocutionary acts*. Any speaker who uses a sentence with an intention of communication in a context of utterance means to perform an illocutionary act such as an assertion, a request, a promise, or a declaration. When the speaker's meaning is literal, that illocutionary act is the one expressed by the sentence used in the context of the utterance. Thus, for example, interrogative sentences such as "Is it snowing?" are used to ask questions and imperative sentences such as "Please, come here!" are used to make requests. Most elementary acts that are performed by successful utterances are of the form F(P) and consist of an illocutionary force F and of a propositional content P. They are expressed by elementary sentences of the form f(p), where f is an illocutionary force marker and p is a clause.

In Vanderveken 1981 and 1983 and with Searle in Searle and Vanderveken 1985 I have developed the foundations of a general logical theory of speech acts providing recursive definitions of the set of all possible illocutionary forces and of the conditions of success of all types of elementary illocutionary acts. The main purpose of this paper is to use the resources of that illocutionary logic in order to formulate the general principles of a semantic theory of natural languages based on the hypothesis that illocutionary forces, senses, and denotations are the three main components of sentence meaning. In formulating these principles, I will further develop illocutionary and intensional logics so as to characterize more fully the logical forms of illocutionary forces and of propositions. Thus, I will proceed to a partial unification of speech act theory as developed in the tradition of Austin and Searle (1969, 1979) and of classical truth-conditional formal semantics as developed in the tradition of Frege (1984) and Tarski (1956).

I am grateful to the Natural Science and Engineering Research Council of Canada and to the FCAR Foundation for financial help that enabled me to work on this subject and related topics.

Until now, logicians like Montague (1974) and Kaplan (1979), who have constructed extensions of Tarski's formal semantics in order to interpret directly or after translation fragments of natural language, have been confined to the truth-conditional aspects of sentence meaning and have tended to reduce linguistic competence to the speaker's ability to understand the truth-conditions of the sentences of his language. Because they have ignored other illocutionary aspects of meaning, they have been unable to give a satisfactory account of nondeclarative sentence types. They have failed to analyze adequately the meaning differences existing between sentences like "John will be nice," "Please, John, be nice!" and "If only John would be nice!," which express the same propositions in the same possible contexts of utterance but are used to perform illocutionary acts with different forces. They have also failed to explain and predict semantic relations of entailment or of relative inconsistency that exist between declarative sentences like "John orders you to learn French and Russian," "John tells you to learn French," and "John forbids you to learn Russian," which are used to report the performance of illocutionary acts with logically related conditions of success. Thus, until now formal semantics has only been able to construct adequate interpretations of very restricted fragments of declarative sentences of natural languages.

In this paper I will develop a new semantic approach to natural languages aiming at a systematic, unified account of both the truth- and the success-conditional aspects of sentence meaning. In that approach, meaning and use are logically related and linguistic competence is not dissociated from performance. On the contrary, linguistic competence is construed as the speaker's ability to understand which illocutionary acts can be performed by literal utterances of sentences in the various possible contexts of use of his language.

This approach (see Vanderveken 1990) enables formal semantics to interpret sentences of any syntactic type (whether declarative or not) that express elementary speech acts with any possible illocutionary force, and to predict and explain non-truth-conditional types of entailment and of inconsistency that were until now completely ignored by logicians and philosophers.

As I said earlier, my fundamental hypothesis is that complete illocutionary acts and not only truth-conditions are the primary units of sentence meaning in the use of natural languages. On this view, every sentence expresses with respect to each possible context of utterance one or (if it is ambiguous) several illocutionary acts whose conditions of success and of satisfaction are entirely determined by the meaning of that sentence and by the relevant contextual features. Thus, every sentence, whenever its logical form is fully analyzed, contains words or other syntactic features whose meaning determines which types of illocutionary acts can be performed by literal utterances of that sentence. In particular, all elementary sentences contain an illocutionary force marker. By the *illocutionary force marker* of an elementary sentence, I mean here the syntactic features of that sentence whose meaning determines that its literal utterances have one or several possible illocutionary forces. The mood of the verb, word order, intonation, and punctuation signs are the most common illocutionary force markers in actual natural languages.

Unlike logicians, grammarians and linguists have long acknowledged the illocutionary aspects of sentence meaning in their analysis of the classification of the different syntactic types of sentence of natural languages.[1] Using speech act theory, one can reformulate as follows their analysis of the main illocutionarily significant types of sentence that exist in English and other actual natural languages:

1. *Declarative sentences* like "Julius speaks French" are used to make assertions.
2. *Imperative sentences* like "Come here!" are used to give directives to the hearer.
3. *Interrogative sentences* like "Are you ill?" are used to ask questions.
4. *Exclamatory sentences* like "How glad I am!" are used to express the speaker's psychological states.
5. *Optative sentences* like "God bless you!" and "If only it would rain!" are used to express wishes.

As Austin pointed out, English and most actual natural languages also have a large number of *performative verbs* such as "promise," "vow," "remind," "assure," "supplicate," "require," and "apologize" that name possible illocutionary forces of utterances and can be used by speakers in order to make explicit the illocutionary forces of their utterances. Thus, for example, utterances in appropriate contexts of performative sentences like "I ask you if it is raining" and "I hereby promise to come" normally constitute the asking of a question and the making of a promise. As in Searle and Vanderveken 1985, I will analyze such performative sentences as declarative sentences that express with respect to each possible context of utterance a *declaration* by the speaker that he performs the illocutionary act with the force named by the performative verb. In speech act theory, it is the defining feature of a declaration that the speaker in representing himself as performing an action performs that action by the sole fact of his representation. On this account, any successful utterance of a performative sentence has the secondary illocutionary force named by the performative verb by way of having the primary illocutionary force of declaration. Indeed, a successful declaration makes its propositional content true and the propositional content in the case of performative utterances is that the speaker performs an illocutionary act. Thus, for example, by a successful performa-

→ It's a "(ritual)" statement of itself.

tive utterance of the sentence "I request you to come," the speaker derivatively requests the hearer by way of primarily declaring that he makes a
request.[2] Moreover, he also derivatively asserts that he makes that request,
since any declaration contains an assertion of its propositional content.

This semantic analysis of performative sentences is consistent with the
general classification of sentential types stated above. Just like in other
declarative sentences, the indicative mood of the main verb of performative
sentences serves to represent how things are. However, what is peculiar in
the case of performative sentences is that their illocutionary force marker is
more complex than the declarative sentential type. Indeed, it also contains
(at least implicitly) certain words, such as the adverb "hereby," which
express conventionally the characteristic mode of achievement of declara-
tions.

In section 1 of this paper I formulate the basic principles of the analysis
of the logical forms of illocutionary acts and of propositions that I will
develop in the illocutionary and intensional logics of my general success-
and truth-conditional semantics. In section 2 I develop an analysis of
sentence meaning that applies to all types of elementary sentences and
construct the relations that exist between sentences and illocutionary acts
in the use of natural languages. In Vanderveken 1990 I have developed on
the basis of these considerations a logico-philosophical semantics of natural
language (with an ideal object-language, a model-theoretic interpretation,
and a generally complete axiomatic system). One interesting feature of that
formalization is that general semantics is both a conservative extension and
a natural generalization of Montague grammar.

1 Basic Principles of Speech Act Theory concerning Illocutionary Forces and Propositions

1.1 Illocutionary acts of the form F(P) have conditions of success and of satisfaction.

As is the case for human actions in general, attempts to perform illocutionary acts of the form F(P) can succeed or fail. The *conditions of success* of an
illocutionary act are the conditions that must be obtained in a possible
context of utterance in order that the speaker succeed in performing that
act in that context. For example, a condition of success of a promise is that
the speaker commit himself to carrying out a future course of action. If a
speaker does not commit himself to doing something in a context of
utterance, he does not make a promise in that context.

Moreover, illocutionary acts of the form F(P) are directed at states of
affairs and, even when they are successfully performed, they can still fail to
be satisfied in case the world does not fit their propositional content. The

conditions of satisfaction of an illocutionary act are the conditions that
be obtained in a possible context of utterance in order that that act
satisfied in the world of that context. For example, a condition of satisfaction of a promise is that the speaker carry out in the world the future course
of action represented by the propositional content. If the speaker does not
carry out that future action, the promise is not satisfied.

The notion of a condition of satisfaction is an obvious generalization of
the notion of a truth-condition that is necessary to quantify over all illocutionary forces. Just as an assertion is satisfied if and only if it is true, an
order is satisfied if and only if it is obeyed, a promise is satisfied if and only
if it is kept, a request is satisfied if and only if it is granted, and similarly for
all other illocutionary forces. The semantic notion of a condition of satisfaction is based on the traditional correspondence semantic theory of truth for
propositions. Whenever an elementary illocutionary act is satisfied in an
actual context of utterance, there is a *success of fit* or correspondence
between language and the world because to the propositional content of
the illocutionary act corresponds an actual state of affairs in the world.
Thus, an elementary illocutionary act of the form F(P) is satisfied in a context of utterance *only if* its propositional content P is true in the world of
that context. For example, a request is satisfied only if the hearer makes its
propositional content true by carrying out in the world the course of action
that it represents.

Although they are logically related, the conditions of success and of
satisfaction of elementary illocutionary acts are different and cannot be
reduced to each other. Thus, for example, an assertion (considered as a type
of illocutionary act) can be true although no one makes it, and one can
make assertions that are false.

1.2 There are two sets of semantic values: the success- and the truth-values.
Because illocutionary acts have both conditions of success and conditions
of satisfaction, and their conditions of satisfaction are a function of the
truth-conditions of their propositional contents, there are two different sets
of semantic values in general semantics, namely, the *success-values*, which
are success (or successful performance) and insuccess (or nonperformance),
and the *truth-values*, which are truth and falsehood.

The success-value of an illocutionary act is *success* in a possible context
of utterance when the speaker performs that act in that context, and it is
insuccess otherwise. *Failure* to perform an illocutionary act is a special case
of insuccess that occurs only in the contexts where the speaker makes an
unsuccessful attempt to perform that act. For example, an utterance of the
performative sentence "I hereby appoint you chairman of the board" is a
failure in a context of utterance where the speaker does not have the
authority to appoint the hearer by declaration. As in the correspondence

ıth-value of the propositional content of an illocu-
a context of utterance if the state of affairs repre-
ıtional content exists in the world of that context,
wise.

ıntics, I will identify hereafter success- and truth-
ıns from possible contexts of utterance into success-
and truth-values. Thus, the success-conditions of an illocutionary act will be
represented formally by the function that associates with each possible
context of utterance the success-value of that act in that context. Similarly,
the truth-conditions of a proposition will be represented by the function
that associates with each context the truth-value of that proposition in that
context.

*1.3 Each illocutionary force has six types of components that serve to determine
the conditions of success and of satisfaction of the illocutionary acts with that force.*
As Searle and I pointed out in Searle and Vanderveken 1985, each illocutionary force can be divided into an illocutionary point, a mode of achievement of that point, propositional content, preparatory and sincerity conditions, and a degree of strength. Such components are part of the logical
form of each illocutionary force. In illocutionary logic, two illocutionary
forces F_1 and F_2 with the same components are identical because all
illocutionary acts of the form $F_1(P)$ and $F_2(P)$ have the same conditions of
success and of satisfaction and consequently serve the same linguistic
purposes in the use of language. I will now briefly explain the nature of
these components. See my other papers for more explanation.

Illocutionary Point. Illocutionary point is the principal component of an
illocutionary force because it determines the direction of fit of utterances
with that force.

As Searle (1979) pointed out, there are five and only five illocutionary
points of utterances in language: the *assertive point*, which consists in representing as actual a state of affairs; the *commissive point*, which consists in
committing the speaker to a future course of action; the *directive point*,
which consists in making a linguistic attempt to get the hearer to do
something; the *declarative point*, which consists in performing an action that
brings about a state of affairs solely in virtue of the utterance by representing oneself as performing that action; and the *expressive point*, which consists in expressing propositional attitudes of the speaker about a state of
affairs.

One can justify the completeness of this classification of illocutionary
point by noting that these five illocutionary points exhaust the different
possible directions of fit between language and the world. The four directions of fit are as follows:

1. *The words-to-world direction of fit.* In case the illocutionary act is satisfied, its propositional content fits a state of affairs existing (in general independently) in the world. Illocutionary acts with the assertive point have the words-to-world direction of fit. Their point is to represent how things are in the world.

2. *The world-to-words direction of fit.* In case the illocutionary act is satisfied, the world is transformed to fit the propositional content. Illocutionary acts with the commissive or directive point have the world-to-words direction of fit. Their point is to get the world to be transformed by the future course of action of the speaker (commissives) or of the hearer (directives) in order to match the propositional content of the utterance. Speakers and hearers play such important roles in the performance of illocutionary acts that language distinguishes here two different illocutionary points (a speaker- and a hearer-based illocutionary point) with the same world-to-words direction of fit.

3. *The double direction of fit.* In case the illocutionary act is satisfied, the world is transformed by an action of the speaker to fit the propositional content by the fact that the speaker represents it as being so transformed. Illocutionary acts with the declarative illocutionary point have the double direction of fit. Their point is to get the world to match the propositional content by saying that the propositional content matches the world.[3]

4. *The null or empty direction of fit.* For some illocutionary acts, there is no question of success or failure of fit, and their propositional content is in general presupposed to be true. Such are the illocutionary acts with the expressive point that have the null or empty direction of fit. Their point is to express a propositional attitude of the speaker about the state of affairs represented by the propositional content. It is not to represent that state of affairs as actual or to try to get it to be actual in the world.

Illocutionary points are expressed in natural languages by verb mood or syntactic types of elementary sentences. Thus, the indicative and imperative moods express the assertive and directive illocutionary points, respectively. The syntactic type of exclamatory sentences expresses the expressive illocutionary point. There is no need of a sentence type for the declarative point since that point can be achieved in successful utterances of performative sentences. The commissive point is not realized in a sentence type in English and most other natural languages. However, a commissive mood exists in Korean.

Mode of Achievement.   Illocutionary points, like most purposes of our actions, can be achieved in various ways or by different means. The mode of achievement of an illocutionary force determines how its point must be achieved on the propositional content in case of a successful performance of an act with that force. For example, in a command the speaker must invoke a position of authority over the hearer and in a request he must give option of refusal to the hearer. The modes of achievement of illocutionary forces restrict the conditions of achievement of their point. They are expressed in English by adverbs such as "please" and "whether you like it or not," which modify the mood of the verb in sentences such as "Please, do it!" and "Whether you like it or not, come!"

Propositional Content Conditions.   Many illocutionary forces impose conditions on the set of propositions that can be taken as propositional contents of acts with that force in a context of utterance. For example, the propositional content of a prediction must represent a future state of affairs. Such conditions are called *propositional content conditions*. Some propositional content conditions are determined by illocutionary point. For example, all illocutionary forces with the commissive point have the condition that their propositional content must represent a future course of action of the speaker. Other propositional content conditions—for example, those of predictions—are peculiar to certain illocutionary forces with a given point. Propositional content conditions are expressed in English by syntactic constraints on the grammatical form of the clauses of elementary sentences. For example, the tense of the main verb of performative sentences with a commissive verb cannot be past, and sentences such as "I promise to have come yesterday" are linguistically odd.

Preparatory Conditions.   By performing an illocutionary act, the speaker also presupposes that certain propositions are true in the world of the utterance. For example, a speaker who promises to do something presupposes that his future action is good for the hearer. The preparatory conditions of an illocutionary force F determine which propositions the speaker would presuppose if he were performing an act with that force and a propositional content P in a possible context of utterance. Many, but not all, preparatory conditions are determined by illocutionary point. For example, all illocutionary forces with the commissive point have the preparatory condition that the speaker is capable of carrying out the future course of action represented by their propositional content. Preparatory conditions are expressed in English by adverbs like "unfortunately" and expressions used vocatively in sentences such as "Father, unfortunately, he is here."

Sincerity Conditions.   By performing an illocutionary act, the speaker also expresses psychological states of certain modes about the state of affairs represented by the propositional content. For example, a speaker who requests expresses a desire and a speaker who thanks expresses gratitude.

The sincerity conditions of each illocutionary force F determine the modes of the psychological states that the speaker would have if he were sincerely performing an illocutionary act with that force. Thus, a sincerity condition is just a set of modes of propositional attitudes.[4] As is the case for propositional content and preparatory conditions, some sincerity conditions are determined by illocutionary point. For example, all commissive illocutionary forces have the sincerity condition that the speaker intends to carry out the future course of action represented by their propositional content. Sincerity conditions are expressed in English by adverbs like "alas" and "hurrah" in sentences such as "Alas, he is dead" and "Hurrah, they have won."

Degree of Strength.   The psychological states that enter into sincerity conditions are expressed with different degrees of strength depending on the illocutionary force. For example, the degree of strength of the sincerity conditions of a promise is greater than that of an acceptance because a speaker who promises to do something expresses a stronger intention than a speaker who simply accepts to do it. Degree of strength is in general expressed by the strength of intonation contour in English.

1.4 The set of illocutionary forces of possible utterances is recursive.
On the basis of the preceding componential analysis of illocutionary forces, the set of illocutionary forces can be defined recursively as follows in a general semantics for natural languages.

There are five primitive illocutionary forces. These are the simplest possible illocutionary forces: they have an illocutionary point, no special mode of achievement of that point, a neutral degree of strength, and only the propositional content, preparatory, and sincerity conditions that are determined by their point. These primitive forces are (1) the *illocutionary force of assertion*, which is named by the performative verb "assert" and which is realized syntactically in English in the indicative mood, word order, and full stop of declarative sentences, (2) the *primitive commissive illocutionary force*, which is not realized syntactically in a mood in English but is named by the performative verb "commit", (3) the *primitive directive force*, which is realized syntactically in English in the imperative mood and the exclamation mark of imperative sentences, (4) the *illocutionary force of declaration*, which is named by the performative verb "declare" and expressed in performative utterances, and (5) the *primitive expressive illocutionary force*, which is realized syntactically in the type of exclamatory sentences.

All other illocutionary forces are derived from the primitive forces by a finite number of applications of Boolean or Abelian operations that consist in enriching the components of these forces. *These operations consist in restricting the mode of achievement of the illocutionary point by imposing a new mode, in increasing or decreasing the degree of strength, and in adding new propositional content, preparatory, or sincerity conditions.* Thus, for example, the illocutionary force of promise is obtained from the primitive commissive force by imposing a special mode of achievement of the commissive point involving the undertaking of an obligation. The illocutionary force of a report is obtained from the illocutionary force of assertion by adding the propositional content condition that the propositional content represents a past or present state of affairs with respect to the time of the utterance. The illocutionary force of a pledge is obtained from the primitive commissive force by increasing by one the degree of strength of the sincerity conditions. The illocutionary force of a threat is obtained from the primitive commissive force by adding the preparatory condition that the future course of action represented by the propositional content is bad for the hearer. Similarly, the illocutionary force of a complaint is obtained from assertion by adding the sincerity condition that the speaker is dissatisfied (or unhappy) with the state of affairs represented by the propositional content.[5]

As I said earlier, components of illocutionary force are expressed in English by modifiers such as the adverbs "please" and "alas" in the sentences "Please, do it!" and "Alas, he is dead." Such modifiers, when they are combined with simpler illocutionary force markers such as the imperative or indicative mood, compose syntactically complex markers expressing the derived illocutionary forces obtained by adding the component that they express to the simpler illocutionary forces expressed by their arguments. For example, "please" expresses the mode of achievement that consists in giving option of refusal to the hearer and "alas" expresses the sincerity condition that the speaker is unhappy with the state of affairs represented by the propositional content. Thus, an imperative sentence whose main verb is modified by "please" expresses the illocutionary force of request. Similarly, a declarative sentence whose main verb is modified by "alas" expresses the illocutionary force of complaint or lament. An increase in the degree of strength is in general expressed by an increase in the degree of strength of intonation contour or by adverbs like "frankly" in sentences such as "Frankly, he is dead."

1.5 The conditions of success of elementary illocutionary acts are uniquely determined by the components of their illocutionary force and by their propositional content.

As Searle and I pointed out in Searle and Vanderveken 1985, an illocutionary act of the form F(P) is *(successfully) performed* in the context of an utterance if and only if the following conditions hold: In that context, the speaker achieves the illocutionary point of the force F on the proposition P with the mode of achievement of F, and P satisfies the propositional content conditions of F with respect to the context of that utterance; the speaker moreover presupposes the propositions determined by the preparatory conditions of F, and he also expresses with the degree of strength of F the psychological states of the modes determined by the sincerity conditions of F about the state of affairs represented by the propositional content P.

For example, a speaker makes a promise in a context of utterance if and only if the following conditions hold:

1. The point of his utterance is to commit himself to doing an act A (illocutionary point).

2. In his utterance, the speaker puts himself under an obligation to do act A (mode of achievement).

3. The propositional content of the utterance is that the speaker will do act A (propositional content conditions).

4. The speaker presupposes that he is capable of doing act A and that act A is in the interest of the hearer (preparatory conditions).

5. The speaker expresses with a strong degree of strength an intention to do that act (degree of strength).

Because a speaker can presuppose propositions that are false and express psychological states that he does not have, some successful performances of illocutionary acts are defective from a logical point of view. In illocutionary logic, an illocutionary act is said to be *nondefectively performed* in a context of utterance if and only if first, it is successfully performed and second, its preparatory and sincerity conditions are fulfilled in that context.[6] On this account, every nondefective illocutionary act is successful, but the converse is not true in cases of, say, insincerity or failure of presupposition.

1.6   The conditions of satisfaction of elementary illocutionary acts of the form F(P) are a function of the truth-conditions of their propositional content and of the direction of fit of their illocutionary force.

In the successful performance of an illocutionary act of the form F(P), the speaker expresses in general the proposition P with the aim of achieving a success of fit between language and the world from a certain direction. On the basis of the previous considerations on direction of fit, I will adopt the following definition of the conditions of satisfaction of illocutionary acts in general semantics.

First, I will say that an illocutionary act with the words-to-world direction of fit is *satisfied* in a context of utterance if and only if its propositional content is true in that context. Indeed, in such a case the success of fit between language and the world is achieved by the fact that its proposi-

tional content corresponds to a state of affairs existing (in general independently) in the world.

Second, I will say that an illocutionary act with the world-to-words or
the double direction of fit is *satisfied* in a context of utterance if and only if
its propositional content P is true in that context *because of* its performance.
Unlike assertive utterances, commissive, directive, and declarative utterances have conditions of satisfaction that are not independent of these
utterances. An assertion is true if and only if its propositional content
corresponds to an existing state of affairs no matter how it got into
existence. But strictly speaking, a promise is kept or an order is obeyed
only if the speaker or hearer carries out in the world a future course of
action because of the promise or the order. Similarly, a declaration is
satisfied only if the speaker makes its propositional content true by saying
that it is true in the performance of that declaration. Thus, in the case of
satisfaction of an elementary illocutionary act with the double or the
world-to-words direction of fit, the success of fit is achieved by the fact
that the speaker or hearer performs an action in the world in order to
satisfy the performed illocutionary act. This is why the conditions of
success of such illocutionary acts are part of their conditions of satisfaction.
When an order is obeyed, it has been given. Similarly, when a promise is
kept, it has been made.

Illocutionary acts with the empty direction of fit do not have conditions
of satisfaction, properly speaking, since in their performance the speaker
does not aim to achieve a success of fit between language and the world.
However, for the sake of generality, I will continue attributing conditions
of satisfaction to such illocutionary acts. In case an illocutionary act is
expressive, I will say that it is satisfied in a context of utterance if and only
if its propositional content is true in that context.

*1.7 Two elementary illocutionary acts are identical if and only if they have the
same propositional content and the same conditions of success.*
This law of identity for illocutionary acts is based on the very notion of an
illocutionary act. Illocutionary acts are natural kinds of use of language.
They serve linguistic purposes in relating propositions to the world with a
direction of fit. Now different illocutionary acts should have different
linguistic purposes, and different linguistic purposes should be either
achievable under different conditions or directed at states of affairs repre-
sentable or obtainable under different conditions. Hence the requirement of
the identity of the propositional content and of the success-conditions.

On this view, each illocutionary act is an ordered pair consisting of the
proposition that is its propositional content and of the function from
contexts into success-values that determines its success-conditions. Moreover, the logical type of an illocutionary force F is that of a function that

associates with each proposition P the ordered pair corresponding to the elementary illocutionary act F(P).

1.8 Propositions have a content in addition to having truth-conditions.
One cannot identify in the intensional logic of general semantics, as is the case in usual intensional logics, propositions with their truth-conditions. Indeed, elementary speech acts of the form $F(P_1)$ and $F(P_2)$ with the same illocutionary force and strictly equivalent propositions do not necessarily have the same conditions of success. For example, one can ask the question whether Kiev is in Russia without asking eo ipso whether Kiev is in Russia and $2 + 1 = 3$. Clauses that express strictly equivalent propositions are not substitutable *salva felicitate* within the scope of illocutionary force markers and *salva veritate* within the scope of performative verbs.

The reason why this is the case is that all strictly equivalent propositions are not cognitively realized (and understood) by speakers under the same conditions. As I said earlier, a speaker who performs an illocutionary act of the form F(P) must have in mind its propositional content P and relate it to the world with the direction of fit of an illocutionary point. Now it is quite obvious that one can have in mind and express a proposition with an illocutionary force without eo ipso having in mind all other propositions with the same truth-conditions. Thus, it is necessary to take into account cognitive aspects of meaning in the characterization of the logical form of propositions in a general success- and truth-conditional semantics.

From a logical point of view, one can distinguish different features in the apprehension or understanding of the propositional contents of utterances. A speaker who understands the proposition that is expressed in a context of utterance understands altogether (1) the propositional constituents of that proposition, (2) the ways in which these propositional constituents relate in terms of predication in atomic propositions, and (3) how the truth-conditions of that proposition are determined from these atomic propositions. Thus, for example, if a speaker understands the propositional content of an utterance of the sentence (1),

(1)   I dream much and you drink a lot.

then he knows who are the speaker and the hearer of the context of that utterance, he understands the properties expressed by the first and second verb phrases in that context, and he also understands that these properties are respectively predicated to the speaker and hearer. Moreover, he understands that the complete proposition is true if and only if its two constituent atomic propositions are true.

In natural languages, the propositional constituents of the proposition expressed by a clause in a context are in general identical with the senses expressed by the complete categorematic expressions that occur in that clause. For example, the senses of "dream much" and "drink a lot" in a context are propositional constituents of the proposition expressed by the clause of sentence (1) in that context. Moreover, the order of predication and the truth-conditions are determined from the meaning of syncategorematic features such as word order and truth connectives. For example, the meaning of word order in sentence (1) determines that the property expressed by each verb phrase is predicated of the denotation of the preceding noun phrase. Similarly, the meaning of the truth connective "and" determines that the expressed proposition is a truth-functional conjunction.

On the basis of these considerations, I will characterize as follows the logical form of propositions in general semantics. A proposition is a *structured entity* that is composed out of a finite number of atomic propositions (where attributes are predicated of entities under senses), and it has truth-conditions that are determined from these atomic propositions. Thus, in order to identify a proposition, one must identify its atomic propositions as well as its truth-conditions. The atomic propositions into which a proposition can be divided constitute what I will call hereafter the *content* of that proposition (what it is about and which predications are made in that proposition). Each atomic proposition (in the content of a proposition) contains a finite number of propositional constituents including a main attribute and other senses logically related in terms of predication. The main attribute is indeed predicated of the denotations of these senses in a certain fixed order, and that predication determines truth-conditions. Thus, from a logical point of view, an atomic proposition is an ordered pair consisting of a set of senses (its propositional constituents) and of a function that determines truth-conditions in accordance with the internal relation of predication existing between these senses.

Now, once the content of a proposition has been apprehended, it only remains to understand how the truth-conditions of that proposition are determined from the truth-conditions of its atomic propositions in order to identify that proposition. As I argue in Vanderveken 1990, the truth-value of a proposition in a context is always a *function* of the truth-values of its atomic propositions in that context. For example, the proposition expressed in an utterance of sentence (1) is true in a context if and only if its two atomic propositions are true in that context.

This purely truth-functional view of the determination of truth-conditions is not reductionist as in Wittgenstein 1961. On the contrary, it is perfectly compatible with referential opacity and the existence of intensional operators such as modal connectives whose meaning obliges us to quantify over the set of all possible contexts of utterance in order to determine truth-conditions. Indeed, one can argue that modal and other intensional operations on propositions affect both the content and the truth-conditions. They serve to predicate attributes of the propositions to which they are applied. Thus, they introduce new atomic propositions (see Vanderveken 1990).

On that account, two propositions are identical if and only if they have the same content and their truth-conditions are determined in the same truth-functional way. From a logical point of view, a proposition is thus an ordered pair whose first term is a finite nonempty set of atomic propositions and whose second term is a set of truth-value assignments to atomic propositions. By a *truth-value assignment* to atomic propositions, I mean here a function from the set of atomic propositions into the set of truth-values. Since the truth-value of a proposition P is a function of the truth-values of its atomic propositions, there is a unique set of truth-value assignments to atomic propositions under which P is true. For example, the proposition that Paul is in France or in Germany is true under all and only the truth-value assignments to atomic propositions that associates the true to at least one of its atomic propositions. Thus, the second element of a proposition represents set-theoretically the nature of the truth-function by the application of which its truth-conditions are determined.

On this account, a proposition P is *true in a context* if and only if there is at least one truth-value assignment under which P is true that associates to each atomic proposition Q of P the actual truth-value of Q in that context. Moreover, P is a *tautology* if and only if its second element is the total set of truth-value assignments to atomic propositions.

My law of propositional identity is stronger than the one formulated by Carnap (1956), which requires only strict equivalence. Indeed, strictly equivalent propositions like the proposition that John is or is not French and the proposition that $2 + 2 = 4$ are not identified in general semantics since they have different propositional constituents. Moreover, strictly equivalent propositions are different when their truth-conditions are determined by the application of different truth-functions. For example, the tautological proposition that arithmetic is either complete or incomplete is different from the necessary proposition that arithmetic is incomplete.[7] Finally, my criterion of propositional identity is also weaker than intensional isomorphism.[8] Indeed, it is not sensitive to syncategorematic features such as word order and reiteration of truth-connectives when these features do not affect the truth-conditions. For example, the proposition that John is Mary's husband, the proposition that Mary's husband is John, and the proposition that it is not the case that John is not Mary's husband are identical in general semantics.

1.9 The set of propositions is closed under logical operations.
A complete proposition can contain in its content one or more atomic propositions. From a logical point of view, a proposition is *elementary* if it is

composed out of one and only one atomic proposition and it is true under all truth-value assignments to atomic propositions that associate the true to that atomic proposition. *Complex* propositions are obtained from elementary propositions by the application of operations such as the truth-functional and modal operations.

One of the primary aims of intensional logic is to define the various logical operations on propositions and to characterize the logical structure of the set of all propositions. As Wittgenstein (1961) had anticipated, the logical operations on propositions do not transform the content. Thus, the content of a complex proposition that is the result of the application of a logical operation on several propositions is just the union of the contents of these propositions. For example, the truth-functional operations on propositions are logical. They only rearrange the ways in which the truth-conditions agree and disagree with the truth possibilities of the propositions to which they are applied. On this view, the negation of a proposition P is the proposition $\sim P$ that is composed out of the same atomic propositions as P and is true in a context if and only if P is false in that context. Thus, the set of truth-value assignments to atomic propositions under which $\sim P$ is true is just the set-theoretical complement of the set of truth-value assignments under which P is true. And similarly for conjunction & and for material implication.[9]

Now, given the fact that propositions, in addition to having truth-conditions, also have a content, there is in general semantics a finer logical relation of implication between propositions than that of strict implication, which I will call hereafter *strong implication*. By definition, a proposition P_1 *strongly implies* a proposition P_2 if and only if first, all atomic propositions that are in the content of P_2 are also in the content of P_1 and second, all truth-value assignments under which P_1 is true are also truth-value assignments under which P_2 is true.

Unlike strict implication, which is not antisymmetric, the relation of strong implication is a relation of partial order on the set of propositions and can consequently be used to state the law of propositional identity of general semantics. Thus, two propositions are identical if and only if each of them strongly implies the other. As I show in Vanderveken 1990, the relation of strong implication is important for the purposes of illocutionary logic because it is cognitively realized by speakers in the sense that any speaker who understands a proposition P_1 also understands all propositions P_2 that are strongly implied by it and moreover realizes that these propositions are strictly implied by P_1.

All laws of elimination of truth-connectives of natural deduction generate strong implications in the sense that the conjunction of their premises strongly implies their conclusion. For example, the conjunction of two propositions strongly implies each conjunct. On the other hand, some laws of introduction do not generate strong implication, because the content of their conclusion is not necessarily included in the content of their premises. For example, a proposition does not strongly imply its disjunction with another proposition that contains atomic propositions that it does not contain.

1.10 Competent speakers are rational.

Language is the work of reason, and from the point of view of speech act theory, rationality is built up in the very use of language for at least two reasons.

First, *speakers are minimally consistent.* They cannot perform or even mean to perform simultaneously two elementary illocutionary acts of the form $F_1(P)$ and $F_2(\sim P)$ with the aim of achieving success of fit between language and the world from a certain direction. Indeed, competent speakers and hearers mutually know that a proposition P and its truth-functional negation $\sim P$ cannot simultaneously be true in the world, and consequently that no success of fit could be achieved in the simultaneous performance of two illocutionary acts with these propositions as contents. Thus, for example, a speaker cannot simultaneously order and forbid the hearer to carry out the same action. It would indeed not be rational for a speaker to make a linguistic attempt to achieve a success of fit between language and the world that he and the hearer mutually know a priori to be condemned to failure.[10]

Second, *there is a restricted law of compatibility of strong implication with respect to illocutionary points with a nonempty direction of fit.* A speaker who achieves an illocutionary point with a nonempty direction of fit on a proposition expresses that proposition with the aim of achieving a success of fit between language and the world from the direction determined by that illocutionary point. Now, as I have argued elsewhere, strong implication is cognitively realized in the minds of the speakers. Whenever a speaker expresses a proposition, he also expresses all propositions strongly implied by that proposition and realizes that these propositions are strictly implied by it. Indeed, whenever a proposition P_1 strongly implies a proposition P_2, the content of P_2 is included in the content of P_1. One cannot have in mind all atomic propositions of P_1 without also having in mind all atomic propositions of P_2. Moreover, one must understand that P_1 strictly implies P_2 if one understands the logical operations by the application of which P_1 is determined since the proposition $(P_1 \rightarrow P_2)$ is a tautology.

On this account, a rational speaker cannot express and relate a proposition to the world with the aim of achieving a success of fit from the direction of an illocutionary point without also relating to the world with the same direction of fit all weaker propositions that satisfy the propositional content conditions of that illocutionary point. Indeed, he (and the hearer) mutually know that the truth of these weaker propsitions is a necessary condition for the success of fit of his utterance. Thus, for example, a speaker who means to promise to a hearer that he will come tomorrow in the morning or in the afternoon must mean to commit himself to coming tomorrow.

As I show in Vanderveken 1990, strong implication is the finer logical relation that is needed in order to characterize adequately the cases of strong illocutionary commitment between illocutionary acts that are due to an inclusion of the truth-conditions of their propositional contents. Indeed, an illocutionary act $F(P_1)$ with a primitive nonexpressive illocutionary force commits the speaker to the illocutionary act $F(P_2)$ in case P_1 strongly implies P_2 and P_2 satisfies the propositional content conditions of F whenever P_1 satisfies these conditions. For example, an assertion that (P & (P $\rightarrow$ Q)) contains an assertion of Q.

In general semantics, one can explain as follows the cases of failure of the law of compatibility of strict implication with respect to illocutionary point. In case a proposition P_1 strictly implies a proposition P_2, a speaker can achieve an illocutionary point on P_1 without also necessarily achieving that point on P_2, first, when that proposition P_2 has atomic propositions that are not in the content of P_1, second, when the proposition that $(P_1 \rightarrow P_2)$ is not a tautology, or third, when P_2 does not satisfy the propositional content conditions determined by this point. In the first case the speaker can indeed express P_1 without expressing P_2. In the second case the speaker does not necessarily know that P_1 implies P_2. In the third case the proposition P_2 is not necessarily a possible content for that type of illocutionary point.[11]

2 Analysis of Sentence Meaning

As I have said repeatedly, meaning and use are logically related in natural language, and one cannot understand the meaning of a sentence without also understanding that it can be used literally to perform illocutionary acts with certain conditions of success and of satisfaction in actual and possible contexts of utterance. On this account, there are two types of contributions that words and other syntactic features can make to the meanings of the sentences in which they occur. Some words like proper names, predicates, and truth or modal connectives contribute to the meanings of sentences by determining the propositional contents of the possible utterances of these sentences. Other syntactic features like verb mood, punctuation signs, and intonation contribute to the meaning of sentences by determining the illocutionary forces of their possible utterances. Both types of linguistic expressions can be analyzed in my semantic approach where illocutionary acts are the primary units of sentence meaning in the use and comprehension of language. Thus, my theory of meaning permits me to enrich significantly the logico-philosophical lexicon of formal semantics and to analyze illocutionary force markers as well as clauses.

It is necessary to account for certain basic facts in the construction of sentence meaning in a semantic theory of natural language. For example, there is no one-to-one correspondence between illocutionary acts and sentences. I will now explain the principles of my theory of meaning by stating some of these basic facts of language.

2.1 Natural languages are both ambiguous and not perspicuous.
Many sentences, such as "Let's go to the bank with Jane and Kathy or Paul," are ambiguous and express different illocutionary acts in the same possible contexts of use because one of their lexical items or the scope of their connectives is ambiguous. Moreover, the logical forms of illocutionary acts expressed by sentences in contexts are often not apparent on the surface in their grammatical forms. For example, the performative verbs "order" and "forbid" have the same superficial syntactic behavior in English but do not have the same logical form. "Order" names a derived directive illocutionary force obtained from the primitive directive by adding the special mode of achievement that consists in invoking a position of authority or power over the hearer. However, "forbid" does not name a directive illocutionary force at all, since an act of forbidding the hearer to carry out a future course of action is just an order not to carry out that action.

For these reasons I will analyze indirectly in general semantics the meanings of elementary sentences of natural languages after having translated them into an ideal disambiguous and perspicuous object-language in which the logical forms of these sentences can be clearly exhibited. From the point of view of logical syntax, the ideal language of general semantics is a particular extension of that of Church's (1951) intensional logic. It incorporates a simple modal theory of types with two additional primitive type symbols for success-values and atomic propositions and contains a small number of new logical constants and syncategorematic symbols (such as constants for success-values and illocutionary points) expressing the few primitive semantic indispensable notions of the logic of elementary illocutionary acts. These logical constants and syncategorematic expressions constitute the theoretical vocabulary of my philosophical semantics. They express formal or material universals of language use. All other semantic notions that are important for the purposes of the semantics of elementary sentences (for instance, the primitive illocutionary forces, the different operations on forces, the various logical relations between illocutionary acts and propositions) are defined by rules of abbreviation.

Like the language of intensional logic, the ideal language of general semantics will play an intermediate role between natural languages and their semantic interpretation. Sentences of actual natural language must first be translated into formulas of that language describing the illocutionary acts that they express before being evaluated in a semantic interpretation. The translation of an elementary sentence of a natural language will serve the purpose of disambiguating (in case that sentence expresses several illocutionary acts in each context) and of making apparent in the surface structure of the formulas into which it is translated the logical forms of the illocutionary acts that it expresses.

2.2 Sentences can express different illocutionary acts in different contexts (if, for example, they contain indexical expressions).
Many sentences contain words that can express different senses in different contexts. For example, the interrogative sentence "Did it rain yesterday?" is used to ask different questions in contexts where the days of the utterance are different. Thus, the linguistic meaning of (a translation of) a sentence in a semantic interpretation is a function from possible contexts of utterance into illocutionary acts rather than one or several illocutionary acts. In general semantics, linguistic meanings apply to sentence types whereas illocutionary acts apply to sentences-in-contexts or sentence tokens.

2.3 Illocutionary act types and not tokens are the primary units of sentence meaning in the use of natural languages.
It is important to point out that the illocutionary act expressed by a sentence in a context of utterance is a type (and not a token) of speech act in a semantic interpretation. It can be defined counterfactually as the type of illocutionary act that the speaker would mean to perform in that context if he were using that single sentence speaking literally. Such an illocutionary act type exists even if that sentence is not uttered in that context or if the speaker utters it without meaning to perform or succeeding in performing the illocutionary act.

Utterance acts take time and in each context of use of a natural language, only a finite number of sentences are uttered by the speaker. However, all sentences of a language express illocutionary acts in every possible context of use of that language. Thus, the primary aim of general semantics is to characterize the meanings of sentences-in-contexts and not only the meanings of actual or possible utterances.

2.4 Speaker meaning is reduced to sentence meaning.
General semantics is a theory of sentence meaning, and consequently it adopts the convention that speaker meaning is literal and coincides with sentence meaning (whenever this is possible) in every possible context of use of an interpretation.

Thus, the illocutionary acts that the speaker means to perform in a possible context of use of an interpretation are the illocutionary acts expressed by the sentences that he utters in that context, whenever these expressed illocutionary acts are simultaneously performable. For example, if a speaker utters only the two sentences "It is snowing" and "Are you mad?" in a context of use of an interpretation, that speaker means in that context to assert that it is snowing at the time of the utterance and to ask the hearer if he is mad.

2.5 There is a double semantic indexation.
Because the same sentence can express different illocutionary acts in different contexts, sentence meaning is evaluated in two steps in general semantics. In a first step, each sentence is analyzed via each of its translations as expressing in every possible context of utterance one or several literal illocutionary acts whose conditions of success and of satisfaction are entirely determined by its meaning and the relevant contextual features. Thus, one can predict and explain why sentences with indexical expressions can express different illocutionary acts with respect to different possible contexts of utterance, although the linguistic meaning of these sentences is invariant from one context to another. Moreover, one can explain that speakers can understand the meaning of a sentence without understanding the literal illocutionary act that it expresses in a context of utterance (if, for example, they do not have the relevant contextual information). In the second step of analysis, the illocutionary act expressed by a sentence in a context of an interpretation is evaluated as having a success and a satisfaction value in every possible context considered in that interpretation. As in illocutionary logic, these success and satisfaction values are uniquely determined from the existence or nonexistence of relevant facts in these contexts of utterance. Thus, one can explain why the illocutionary act expressed by a sentence can have different success or satisfaction values in contexts where utterances are made in different circumstances although the conditions of success and of satisfaction of that act remain invariant. On this account, the satisfaction- and success-predicates of general semantics are binary predicates that express semantic relations that hold between illocutionary acts expressed by sentences-in-contexts and possible contexts of utterance.

2.6 The definition of sentence meaning in a semantic interpretation is recursive.
Because natural languages can be learned and understood by human speakers with restricted finitary cognitive capacities, it is necessary to formulate a recursive definition of meaning in the logical structure of a semantic interpretation of general semantics.

Following Frege's compositionality principle, I will construct the meaning of a complex linguistic expression as a function of the meanings of its constituent expressions and syncategorematic features. To put the point more precisely, I will formulate the semantic rules of assignments of meanings to linguistic expressions in a recursive definition that will be made by induction on the length of these expressions. Thus, the meaning of (a translation of) an elementary sentence in a semantic interpretation is that function from possible contexts of use into illocutionary acts that gives as value, for each context, the elementary illocutionary act with the illocutionary force and the propositional content respectively expressed in that context by the illocutionary force marker and the clause of that (translation of that) sentence. Moreover, the illocutionary force expressed by a complex illocutionary force marker in a context contains the components expressed in that context by its constituent modifiers. For example, the illocutionary force marker obtained by combining the adverb "unfortunately" with the illocutionary force marker of a simple declarative sentence expresses the illocutionary force that is obtained by adding to the illocutionary force of assertion the preparatory condition that the state of affairs represented by the propositional content is unfortunate. Similarly, the proposition expressed by a clause in a context is composed out of the senses of its categorematic constituent expressions and has the truth-conditions that are determined from these senses in accordance with the meaning of the syncategorematic expressions that it contains. For example, the proposition expressed by the clause of the declarative sentence "The actual queen of Belgium is Spanish" in a context of utterance is composed out of one atomic proposition whose propositional constituents are the sense of the definite description and the property expressed by the complete verb phrase of that sentence in that context. Moreover, in that atomic proposition, the property expressed by the verb phrase is predicated of the denotation of the definite description.

On this recursive account of sentence meaning, the truth- and success-predicates of general semantics must be defined by induction on the length of (the translations of) sentences in the canonical notation of its ideal object-language. Such inductive definitions do not eliminate the defined truth- and success-predicates. However, they have the advantage to fix completely the use of these predicates and to allow for attempts of (generally complete) axiomatizations of semantic laws.

2.7 There are various principles of semantic interchange.
Because there are two types of meaning, two principles of semantic interchange are valid in general semantics.

1. *A principle of substitutivity for sentence types.* If two sentences differ only with respect to constituent features that have the same meaning, then the

linguistic meaning of these sentences is the same. For example, the sentences "Is it raining?" and "Please, tell me if it is raining!" are synonymous since their illocutionary force markers and clauses have the same semantic values in all contexts.

2. *A principle of substitutivity for occurrences of sentences in contexts.* Suppose two sentences, each taken in (possibly different) contexts, differ only with respect to constituent features that, when taken in their respective contexts, have the same semantic values. Then such sentences, each taken in its own context, express the same illocutionary acts in these contexts. For example, the assertion expressed by an utterance today of the sentence "It has rained yesterday in Paris" is the same assertion as that expressed by an utterance tomorrow of the slightly different sentence "It has rained the day before yesterday in Paris."

2.8 There is a proliferation of new semantic notions.

Because of the existence of two sets of semantic values and of a double semantic indexation, there is a general ramification of the fundamental semantic notions of consistency, analyticity, and logical entailment in general semantics. For example, there are two different types of consistent sentences. A sentence is *truth-conditionally* (or *illocutionarily*) *consistent* if and only if, in at least one interpretation, it expresses with respect to some possible context of use an illocutionary act that is satisfiable (or performable) in at least one context considered in that interpretation. For example, the sentence "I order and forbid you to come" is both illocutionarily and truth-conditionally inconsistent. Notice that these different notions of consistency do not coincide in extension. Thus, some illocutionarily inconsistent sentences like "It is raining and I do not believe it" are truth-conditionally consistent. Conversely, some truth-conditionally inconsistent sentences like "Peano's arithmetic is complete" are illocutionarily consistent.

There are also many different types of entailment between sentences with related logical forms in general semantics. First, a sentence A *truth-conditionally* (or *illocutionarily*) *entails* another sentence B if and only if in every semantic interpretation where that sentence expresses in a context an illocutionary act that is satisfied (or successful), the sentence B also expresses in that same context an illocutionary act that is satisfied (or successful). For example, the sentence "I ask you if it is raining" illocutionarily entails the sentence "Is it raining?"

Second, a sentence A *truth-conditionally entails the success* of (the illocutionary act expressed by) another sentence B if and only if in every interpretation where that sentence A expresses in a context a satisfied illocutionary act, the other sentence B expresses in the same context a successful illocutionary act. Conversely, a sentence A *illocutionarily entails the satisfaction* of another sentence B if and only if in every interpretation where that sentence expresses in a context a successful illocutionary act, the sentence B expresses in the same context a satisfied illocutionary act. For example, the sentence "I am making an assertion" illocutionary entails its own satisfaction and a performative sentence such as "I request you to come" truth-conditionally entails the success of the corresponding non-performative sentence "Please, come!"

As is the case for consistency, these different types of entailment do not coincide in extension. For example, the declarative sentence "John is here" truth-conditionally entails the sentence "John is here or John is in Paris" but does not illocutionarily entail that sentence.

The illocutionary acts expressed by two sentences in a context also have success and satisfaction values in other contexts. In general semantics I will quantify over these success and satisfaction values in order to study other stronger relations of entailment between sentences expressing illocutionary acts with logically related conditions. Two especially important types of strong entailment are the following: A sentence *strongly illocutionarily (or strongly truth-conditionally) entails* another sentence if and only if, in every semantic interpretation, that sentence expresses with respect to each context an illocutionary act that has stronger conditions of success (or of satisfaction) than the illocutionary act expressed by the other sentence in the same context. For example, the imperative sentence "Please, come and see me tomorrow at home or in the office" both strongly illocutionarily entails and strongly truth-conditionally entails the sentence "Come and see me tomorrow!"

As can be expected from the results obtained in the logic of demonstratives, the strong and weak notions of entailment do not coincide in extension. Thus, for example, a performative sentence like "I assert that it is raining" illocutionarily entails (but not strongly) the corresponding sentence "I report that it is raining." Similarly, the sentence "I am identical with myself" truth-conditionally entails (but not strongly) the sentence "I exist." See Vanderveken 1990.

One of the most important purposes of general semantics is to use the resources of modern logic in order to characterize adequately these different semantic notions of analyticity, consistency, and entailment and to state and explain in terms of them philosophically and linguistically significant generalizations that express universals of language use.

Notes

1. See, for example, Nuchelmans 1973, Arnauld and Lancelot 1966, Jespersen 1924, Paul 1970 and Zaefferer 1983.
2. On this account, a semantic relation of illocutionary entailment exists between a performative sentence like "I request you to come" and the corresponding sentence "Please

come!" The performative sentence illocutionarily entails the corresponding sentence in the sense that it expresses in every possible context of use an illocutionary act that the speaker could not perform in that context without also performing the illocutionary act expressed by the corresponding sentence in that same context. However, the converse is not true since one can perform an illocutionary act without declaring that one performs that act. As a consequence of this, it is not the case that a sentence and the corresponding performative sentence have the same meaning, and the performative hypothesis is false in my semantic approach.

3. In Searle and Vanderveken 1985, Searle and I failed to notice that the declarative illocutionary forces have the propositional content condition that their propositional content represents a present course of action of the speaker. The admission of that propositional content condition is needed both for philosophical and for logical reasons. First, it is needed to explain logical relations that exist between the declarative illocutionary forces and assertive, commissive, and directive forces that have a simpler direction of fit. For example, all preparatory and sincerity conditions of primitive illocutionary forces with a simple direction of fit are preparatory and sincerity conditions of the primitive illocutionary force with the double direction of fit. Second, it permits me to keep the simple idea that the propositional content of an illocutionary act is the same as the propositional content of the psychological states that are expressed in its performance.

4. This simple definition of the logical type of sincerity conditions is made possible by the admission of a propositional content condition for declaratives.

5. Because the expressive illocutionary point has variable sincerity conditions, there are no exclamatory sentences whose illocutionary force markers express only the primitive expressive illocutionary force. That force is like a theoretic construct. Indeed, it is not possible to achieve the expressive point on a proposition P without expressing a psychological state of a particular mode about the state of affairs that P represents. Consequently, every actual expressive illocutionary act always has an illocutionary force with particular sincerity conditions. Thus, all actual exclamatory sentences express derived expressive illocutionary forces obtained by adding particular sincerity conditions to the primitive expressive. These particular sincerity conditions are in general determined by the meaning of the adjectives occurring in their prefixes.

6. Austin (1956) with his notion of felicity conditions failed to distinguish between successful performances of illocutionary acts that are defective and attempts at performance of illocutionary acts that are not even successful.

7. Indeed, the truth-function that serves to determine the truth-conditions of the second proposition is the identity function that associates with each truth-value the same truth-value, whereas the truth-function of the first proposition is the constant function that associates the true with each truth-value. Thus, every speaker who understands the first proposition knows a priori in virtue of linguistic competence that it is true, whereas he does not necessarily know that the second one is true.

8. See, for example, Lewis 1972.

9. Thus, the content of a conjunction $(P_1 \& P_2)$ is identical with the union of the contents of P_1 and of P_2, whereas the set of truth-value assignments to atomic propositions under which $(P_1 \& P_2)$ is true is just the intersection of the sets of truth-value assignments under which P_1 is true and under which P_2 is true.

10. Speakers of course often perform simultaneously illocutionary acts with the same force and relatively inconsistent propositional contents P and Q. But in these cases they do not know, or at least it is possible for them to be competent and not to know, the relative inconsistency of these propositional contents. Thus, it is not the case that Q is the negation of P and the contents of these propositions are different.

11. My law of a restrictive compatibility of strong implication with respect to illocutionary point validates all and only the principles of inference that are valid for illocutionary commitment. Thus, for example, whenever F is a primitive illocutionary force with a nonempty direction of fit, F(P & Q) strongly commits the speaker to both F(P) and F(Q). F(P$_1$ ∨ P$_2$) strongly commits the speaker to F(Q) whenever both F(P$_1$) and F(P$_2$) strongly commit the speaker to F(Q). F(P) strongly commits the speaker to F(P ∨ Q) if and only if the content of Q is included in the content of P, and Q satisfies the propositional content conditions of F whenever P does. (Similarly for the other truth-functional operations on propositions.)

References

Arnauld, A., and C. Lancelot (1966). *Grammaire générale et raisonnée*, ed. H. Brekle. Stuttgart: F. Fronman.

Austin, J. L. (1956). *How to do things with words*. Oxford: Clarendon Press.

Carnap, R. (1956). *Meaning and necessity*. Chicago: University of Chicago Press.

Church, A. (1951). A formulation of the logic of sense and denotation. In Paul Henle et al., eds., *Structure, method and meaning*. New York: Liberal Arts Press.

Frege, G. (1984). *Collected papers on mathematics, logic and philosophy*. Oxford: Basil Blackwell.

Jesperson, O. (1924). *The philosophy of grammar*. London: Allen and Unwin.

Kaplan, D. (1979). On the logic of deomonstratives. *Journal of Philosophical Logic* 8.1.

Lewis, D. (1972). General semantics. In D. Davidson and G. Harman, eds., *Semantics of natural language*. Dordrecht. Holland: D. Reidel.

Montague, R. (1974). *Formal philosophy*. New Haven, CT: Yale University Press.

Nuchelmans, G. (1973). *Theories of proposition*. Amsterdam: North Holland.

Paul, H. (1970). *Principles of the history of language*. College Park, MD: McGrath Publishing Company.

Searle, J. R. (1969). *Speech acts*. Cambridge: Cambridge University Press.

Searle, J. R. (1979). *Expression and meaning*. Cambridge: Cambridge University Press.

Searle, J. R., and D. Vanderveken (1985). *Foundations of illocutionary logic*. Cambridge: Cambridge University Press.

Tarski, A. (1956). *Logic, semantics and meta-mathematics*. Oxford: Clarendon Press.

Vanderveken, D. (1981). What is an illocutionary force? Invited lecture at the International Encounter in the Philosophy of Language, Campinas, Brazil. The proceedings of this congress are published in M. Dascal, ed. (1985). *Dialogue: An interdisciplinary study*. Amsterdam: Benjamins.

Vanderveken, D. (1983). A model-theoretical semantics for illocutionary forces. *Logique et Analyse* 102–103.

Vanderveken, D. (1990). *Meaning and speech acts*. Volume 1, *Principles of language use*. Volume 2, *Formal semantics of success and satisfaction*. Cambridge: Cambridge University Press.

Wittgenstein, L. (1961). *Tractatus logico-philosophicus*. London: Routledge and Kegan Paul.

Zaefferer, D. (1983). The semantics of sentence mood in typologically differing languages. In Shiro Hattori, ed., *Proceedings of the Thirteenth International Congress of Linguists*. August 29–September 4, 1982, Tokyo.

Chapter 12

Rational Interaction as the Basis for Communication

Philip R. Cohen and Hector J. Levesque

1 Introduction

This paper explores the consequences of viewing language as action. This approach provides us with not just a slogan, but rather a program of research directed at identifying those aspects of language use that follow from general principles of rational, cooperative interaction. Our pursuit of such a program does not mean that we believe all language use is completely and consciously thought out and planned. Far from it. Rather, just as there are grammatical, processing, and sociocultural constraints on language use, so may there be constraints imposed by the rational balance that agents maintain among their beliefs, intentions, commitments, and actions. Our goals are to discover such constraints, to develop a logical theory that incorporates them and predicts dialogue phenomena, and finally to apply them in developing algorithms for human-computer interaction in natural language.

In our pursuit of this research, we treat utterances as instances of other events that change the state of the world; utterance events per se change the mental states of speakers and hearers. Utterance events are typically performed by a speaker to effect such changes. Moreover, they do so because they signal, or convey (at least), the information that the speaker is in a certain mental state, such as intending the hearer to adopt a certain

This research was made possible by a gift from the System Development Foundation, by a grant from the Natural Sciences and Engineering Research Council of Canada, by the Defense Advanced Research Projects Agency under contract N00039-84-K-0078 with the Naval Electronic Systems Command, and by a contract from the Nippon Telegraph and Telephone Corporation. The paper is approved for public release, distribution unlimited. The views and conclusions contained in this document are those of the authors and should not be interpreted as representative of the official policies, either expressed or implied, of the Defense Advanced Research Projects Agency, the United States government, the Canadian government, or NTT Corporation.

We would like to express our appreciation to Ray Perrault, who provided valuable criticism and suggestions. Also quite helpful were discussions with Doug Appelt, Michael Bratman, Herb Clark, Jim des Rivières, Lyn Friedman, Barbara Grosz, Jerry Hobbs, David Israel, Kurt Konolige, Joe Nunes, Calvin Ostrum, John Perry, Martha Pollack, Syun Tutiya, and Dietmar Zaefferer. Many thanks to them all.

mental state. Conversations are initiated and proceed because of an interplay among agents' mental states, their capabilites for purposeful behavior, their cooperativeness, the content and circumstances of their utterances, and other factors that surely remain to be elucidated. A theory of conversation based on this approach would explain dialogue coherence in terms of the participants' mental states, how the latter lead to communicative action, how these acts affect the mental states of the hearers, and so on.

1.1 Thesis: Illocutionary-Force Recognition Is Unnecessary

Speech act theory appears to offer a natural route leading toward some of these goals. After all, it is in this context theorists have promoted, and in some depth examined, many of the implications of treating language as action. Speech act theory was originally conceived as part of action theory. Many of Austin's insights about the nature of speech acts, felicity conditions, and modes of failure were derived from a study of noncommunicative actions. Searle (1969) mentions repeatedly that many of the conditions he attributes to various illocutionary acts (such as requests and questions) apply more generally to noncommunicative action. However, Searle and Vanderveken (1985) formalize communicative acts and propose a logic in which their properties, such as "preparatory conditions" and "modes of achievement," are stipulated primitively, rather than being derived from more basic principles of action. We believe such an approach overlooks significant generalities. Moreover, it leads one to build logics of illocutionary acts independently of theories of action. Our research shows how to derive properties of illocutionary acts from principles of rationality; hence, it suggests that the theory of illocutionary acts is not explanatory but descriptive.

Consider the following seemingly trivial dialogue fragment:

A: "Open the door."

B: "Sure."

From a syntactic standpoint, these utterances are uninteresting. Of course, the semantics and effects of imperatives (which we will explain) are nontrivial, and the meaning of "Sure" is unclear. Yet it seems that the speakers' intentions and the situations in which their utterances are made play the crucial role in determining what has happened during the dialogue and how what has changed can influence agents' subsequent actions. It would be reasonable to describe what has happened by saying that A has performed a directive speech act (say, a request) and that B has performed a commissive (say, a promise). To verify that B did in fact do this, imagine B's saying "Sure" and then doing nothing. A would surely be justified in complaining or asking for an explanation. A competence theory of communication needs to elucidate just how an interpersonal commitment becomes established. The theory presented in this paper does so by explaining what effects are brought about by a speaker's uttering an imperative in a given situation, and how the uttering of "Sure" relates to those effects. These explications will make crucial reference to intention but need not involve the hearer's recognizing which illocutionary acts were performed.

It is tempting to read (or perhaps misread) philosophers of language as saying that illocutionary-force recognition is necessary for successful communication. Austin (1962) and Strawson (1971) require that "uptake" take place. Searle and Vanderveken (Searle 1969; Searle and Vanderveken 1985) contend that illocutionary force is part of the meaning of an utterance and that the latter's intended effect is "understanding." Hence, because hearers are intended to understand the utterance, presumably its meaning, one interpretation of Searle and Vanderveken's claim is that the hearer is intended to recognize the utterance's illocutionary force.[1] Bach and Harnish (1979) also make a similar claim.[2]

It is so tempting to read these writers thus that many researchers, including us, have made this assumption. For example, computational models of dialogue (Allen 1979; Allen and Perrault 1980; Brachman et al. 1979) our colleagues have developed have required the computer program to recognize which illocutionary act the user has performed so that the system can respond as intended. However, we now claim that force recognition is usually unnecessary. For example, in both of the systems mentioned above, all the inferential power of the recognition of illocutionary acts was already available from other inferential sources (Cohen and Levesque 1980). Instead, we argue that many properties of illocutionary acts can be *derived* from the speaker's and hearer's mental states, especially from their beliefs and intentions. What speakers and hearers have to do is only to recognize each other's intentions (based on mutual beliefs). Contrary to other proposed theories, we do not require that those intentions include intentions that the hearer recognize precisely which illocutionary act(s) were being performed.

Although one can *label* parts of a discourse with names of illocutionary acts, illocutionary labeling does not constitute an explanation of a dialogue. Rather, the labeling itself, if reliably obtained, constitutes data to be explained by constraints on mental states and actions. That is, one would show how to derive the labelings, given their definitions, from (for example) the beliefs and intentions the participants are predicted to have by the analysis of the preceding interaction. Although hearers *may* find it heuristically useful to determine just which illocutionary act was performed, our view is that illocutionary labeling is an extra task in which dialogue participants may be able to engage only retrospectively. Among other things, this will allow the participants in a successful conversation to disagree on what constitutes the true definition of some illocutionary act.

The view that illocutionary acts are not primitive and therefore need not be recognized explicitly is a liberating one. Once this position is adopted, it becomes apparent that many of the difficulties in applying speech act theory to discourse or incorporating it into computer systems stem from taking these acts too seriously—namely, as primitives.

1.2 Illocutionary Actions as Complex Event-Types

Despite Austin's concern for speakers' performance of illocutionary acts by means of locutionary acts, most of the interesting speech act theories have dealt primarily with the illocutionary act. In so doing, theorists have treated (perhaps out of convenience) illocutionary acts as unitary and nondecomposable primitives, though subject to many conditions. For example, Searle's (1969) analysis provided necessary and sufficient conditions for the nondefective and successful performance of illocutionary acts. Early linguistic analyses attempted to derive illocutionary classifications via transformations of implicit performative elements (Sadock 1984) or by conversational postulates applied to primitive illocutionary act elements (Gordon and Lakoff 1971).

One sees this view of illocutionary acts as primitives most clearly in examining various treatments of indirect speech acts. In classifying the utterance "Can you reach the hammer?" in terms of illocutionary acts, the speaker's questioning the hearer's ability to reach the hammer and his requesting that the hearer pass the hammer are regarded as different actions he may be performing simultaneously. For Searle (1975) and Bach and Harnish (1979), an analysis of indirect speech acts is concerned with specifying how, for example, such a request can be made by means of the illocutionary act of questioning. That is, the nub of the analysis rests on uncovering relationships among illocutionary acts. Other difficult problems for a theory of speech acts that arise when the primary unit of analysis is the illocutionary act include specifying how multiple illocutionary acts not in a by-means-of relation can occur simultaneously and how multiple utterance acts can somehow constitute the performance of one illocutionary act. To address these problems, one needs a calculus of acts.[3]

Goldman (1970) attempts to provide such a calculus by giving an inductive definition of the "generation" relation that holds among actions, roughly, where one action can be said to be done "by" doing another. Based on a notion of primitive action, Goldman inductively defines actions that are generated by those primitives using four types of generation relationships: causal, conventional, simple, and augmentation generation. It would take us too far afield to provide the definitions (but see Pollack 1986 and chapter 5 of this volume for further discussion). Goldman takes the view that agents perform indefinitely many actions when they do any-thing. Consider Searle's (1983) examples of Gavrilo Princip's pulling a trig-ger, firing a gun, killing Archduke Ferdinand, and starting World War I. According to Goldman, all the actions that Princip does are different. Goldman contrasts this approach with that of Davidson (1968), who argues that agents perform specific events, about which one can have many different descriptions (which can be regarded as terms in a formal language). Thus, Princip does one thing, pull the trigger, and his firing the gun, his killing the archduke, and his starting World War I are all different descrip-tions of that event. Goldman finds problems with this approach since descriptions denoting the same entity (the event) should be intersubstitut-able yet preserve truth. This clearly doesn't hold; pulling a trigger causes a bullet to be emitted, but killing the archduke does not.

Clearly, there is something to be said for both approaches—for Gold-man's use of complex properties to describe actions, and for Davidson's intuition that only one act was performed. We advocate a position incor-porating some of the advantages of each approach, namely, that agents perform single instances of primitive act- or event-types (ignoring simul-taneous events), but each specific act or event can realize many different complex actions. We have chosen to develop a characterization of complex event-types based on operators familiar from the computer science litera-ture, namely temporal and dynamic logics. The chosen operators are not wholly satisfactory (for instance, they do not characterize simultaneous action), but they have a precise semantics and can approximate Goldman's relations adequately for our purposes.

Essentially, we assume a set of primitive event-types, which incorporate the agent and other intrinsic arguments but are abstracted over time. So, an instance of a primitive event-type can occur more than once. Then, we allow the formation of complex event-types, characterized by *action expres-sions* in the formal language we develop, in terms of composition via sequence, disjunction, and circumstance. The latter allows us to describe the situation-specific effects that result when events occur in certain contexts. Moreover, the treatment of action is sufficient to model conditional and iterative actions, an important desideratum for any theory of action. Thus, our complex event-types describe sequences of instances of primitive event-types occurring in various circumstances.

On the basis of such a logic of action, one ought to be able to derive the properties of the complex event-types from the properties of their defining elements. In the domain of illocutionary acts, given an utterance event performed in the context of the speaker's and hearer's specific mental states, the theorist ought to be able to determine which illocutionary actions were performed and what relationships exist among them from an analysis of the situation-specific effects of an utterance event. So, for example, we would explain indirection by showing how the direct and indirect illocutionary act classifications are both derivable from the utterance event, given the circumstances and properties of rational interaction. We would not attempt to derive the indirect illocutionary act classification from the direct one. The purpose of this paper is to show how properties of illocutionary acts can be derived from a sufficiently detailed logic of action.

2 Form of the Argument

We demonstrate the fact that illocutionary actions can be treated as action expressions by deriving Searle's conditions on illocutionary acts from an independently motivated theory of action. The realm of communicative action is entered in accordance with Grice's method (1969): by postulating a correlation between the uttering of a sentence with a certain syntactic feature (say, with its dominant clause an imperative) in a certain context, and a complex propositional attitude expressing the speaker's mental state. As a result of the speaker's uttering a sentence with that feature under those conditions, the hearer comes to have various beliefs (assumptions) that the speaker has the corresponding attitude. Because of general principles governing mental states, other consequences of the speaker's having the expressed state can be derived. Such derivations will be used to form complex action expressions that capture illocutionary acts in terms of the speaker's attempting to bring about some part of the chain of consequences by bringing about an antecedent. For example, the action expression to be called REQUEST will encapsulate a derivation in which a speaker attempts to have (1) the hearer form the intention to act because (2) it is mutually believed the speaker wants him to act. The conditions justifying the inference from (2) to (1) can be shown to subsume those claimed by Searle (1969) to be felicity conditions. However, they have been derived here from first principles and without any need for a primitive action of requesting. Moreover, they satisfy a set of adequacy criteria, which consist of the following: differentiating the form of an utterance from its illocutionary force; handling the major kinds of illocutionary acts; modeling a speaker's insincere performance of illocutionary acts; providing an analysis of performative utterances; showing how illocutionary acts can be performed with multiple utterances and how multiple illocutionary acts can be simultaneously performed with one utterance; and explaining indirect speech acts.

Our approach is similar to that of Bach and Harnish (1979) in its reliance on inference. A theory of rational interaction will provide the formal foundation for drawing the necessary inferences. A notion of sincerity is essential for treating deception and nonserious utterances. Finally, a characterization of utterance features (say, mood) is required in making a transi-

$$C : A \rightarrow E_1 \overset{c_1}{\rightarrow} E_2 \overset{c_2}{\rightarrow} E_3 \rightarrow \cdots \overset{c_{i-1}}{\rightarrow} E_i$$

Figure 12.1
Events producing gated effects.

tion from the domain of utterance syntax and semantics to that of utterance effects (on speakers and hearers). There are three main steps in constructing the theory:

1. *Infer illocutionary point from utterance form.* The theorist derives the chains of inference needed to connect the intentions and beliefs signaled by an utterance's form with typical "illocutionary points" (Searle and Vanderveken 1985), such as getting a hearer to do some action. These derivations are based on principles of rational interaction and are independent of theories of speech acts and communication.

Specifically (referring to figure 12.1), assume that actions (A) are characterized as producing certain effects E_1 when executed in circumstances C. Separately, assume that the theorist has either derived or postulated relationships between effects of type E_{i-1} and other effects—say, of type E_i such that, if E_{i-1} holds in the presence of some gating condition C_{i-1}, then E_i holds as well. One can then prove that, in the right circumstances—specifically, those satisfying the gating conditions—doing action A makes E_i true.

2. *Treat illocutionary acts as attempts.* Searle (1969) points out that many communicative acts are attempts to achieve some effect. For example, requests are attempts to get (in a certain way) the hearer to do some action. Roughly, we will say that an agent *attempts* to achieve some state of affairs E_i if he performs some action or sequence of actions A that, he intends, will bring about effect E_i. The intended effect may not be an immediate consequence of the utterance act but could be related to act A by some chain of causally related effects. Under these conditions, for A to be an attempt to bring about E_i, the agent would have to want the gating conditions C_i to hold after A. Consequently, in intending to do A in circumstances C, he wants E_i to obtain.

3. *Create an action expression to capture the illocutionary-act type.* This expression will involve events performed in the context of a speaker's attempting to achieve various effects. Because illocutionary acts can be performed through utterances of different forms, we abstract from any specific type of utterance event in defining illocutionary acts.

This way of treating communicative acts has many advantages. The framework clarifies the degrees of freedom available to the theorist by showing which properties of communicative acts are consequences of independently motivated elements and which properties are stipulated. Furthermore, it shows the freedom available to linguistic communities in naming patterns of inference as illocutionary verbs. It also lends technical substance to the use of such terms as "counts as," "felicity conditions," and "illocutionary force." However, it makes no commitment to a reasoning strategy. For example, the theorist's derivations from first principles may be encapsulated by speakers and hearers as frequently used lemmas. Speakers and hearers need not in fact believe that the gating conditions hold but may instead assume that they hold and then "jump" to the consequent of the lemma. The key to achieving these goals is to have an adequate analysis of intention, one that relates intending to other mental states as well as to the agent's actions. We sketch our theory of intention below; further information can be found in chapter 3 and in other publications of ours (Cohen and Levesque 1990a).

We model intention as a composite concept specifying what an agent has *chosen* and how he is *committed* to that choice. First, consider the case of an agent's choosing from his possibly inconsistent desires those he wants most to see fulfilled. In a loose sense, let us call these chosen desires *goals*.[4] By assumption, chosen desires are consistent. We will give them a possible-worlds semantics and the agent will thus have selected a set of worlds in which the goals hold.

Next, consider an agent to have a *persistent goal* if he has a goal (a proposition true in all of the agent's chosen worlds) that he believes currently to be false and that he will continue to choose—at least as long as certain facts remain valid. Persistence involves an agent's *internal* commitment over time to his choices.[5] For example, the complete fanatic is persistent until he believes his goal has been achieved or is impossible. The fanatical agent will drop his commitment to achieving the goal only if either of those circumstances holds.

Intention will be modeled as a kind of persistent goal—that is, a persistent goal to do an action, believing one is about to do it, or to achieve some state of affairs, believing one is about to achieve it. When modeled this way, our concept of intention can be shown to (1) satisfy Bratman's (1984, 1987, chapter 2 of this volume) functional characteristics of intention and (2) to lack the undesirable trait of being closed under expected consequence (Cohen and Levesque 1990a).

Generally, intentions are formed against a background consisting, as a minimum, of agents' beliefs, desires, and other intentions. To capture this fact, we extend the concept of persistent goal and, by derivation, intention, so as to expand the conditions under which an agent can give up his goal. When necessary conditions for an agent's discarding of a goal include his having other goals (call them "supergoals"), the agent can generate a chain of goals such that, if the supergoals given up, so may be the subgoals. If the conditions necessary for an agent's giving up a persistent goal include his believing that some *other* agent has a persistent goal, a chain of interperson-

ally linked goals is created. For example, if Mary
and Sam agrees, Sam's goal should be persister
Mary no longer wants him to do the requeste
earlier, he has done the action or has found it i
and promises are analyzed in terms of such "in
persistent goals.

In summary, we provide an analysis of intention
a persistent goal to perform an action. Intention is ...guished from the
more atomic concept of "choice," modeled as chosen possible worlds.
Choice is closed under expected consequence, whereas intention is closed
only under logical equivalence and embodies a precise notion of commitment—if the agent fails to accomplish the intended action, the agent is
committed to trying again (except under certain specified circumstances).

In this paper we characterize the effects of utterance events and, using
persistent goals, define the notion of an attempt. Then, illocutionary acts,
specifically requests, are defined as attempts. To demonstrate the viability
of the analysis, we show that it fulfills a substantive adequacy criterion:
that it can be used to derive Searle's felicity conditions for requesting.
Finally, we describe extensions of the formalism and theory that make it
possible to handle other illocutionary acts.

3 Some Preliminaries

The formal theory of rational action of chapter 3 provides a foundation upon which to erect a theory of communicative acts. But before talking about
utterances and illocutionary acts, we need to consider some auxiliary notions related to communication: first, we present two properties of cooperative agents, sufficient to handle a simple request; next, we describe the
notion of alternating and mutual belief; next, we present a few domain
predicates to give us something to communicate; finally, we describe the
properties of sentences with specific "features" (Grice 1957), such as utterance mood.

3.1 Properties of Cooperative Agents

We describe agents as sincere and helpful. Essentially, these concepts
capture constraints (quite simplisitc ones) on influencing someone else's
beliefs and goals, as well as on adopting someone else's beliefs and goals as
one's own. More refined versions are certainly desirable. Although both
concepts are independent of the use of language, ultimately we expect such
properties of cooperative agents, embedded in a theory of rational interaction, to provide formal descriptions of the kinds of conversational behavior
Grice (1975) describes with his "conversational maxims."

will say that an agent x is SINCERE with respect to some other y and p, if whenever x has chosen to do something next in order to se y to believe p, x has chosen to bring it about that y knows p.

Definition 1

(SINCERE x y p) $\overset{def}{=}$

$\forall$e (GOAL x (HAPPENS x e; (BEL y p)?)) $\supset$
(GOAL x (HAPPENS x e; (KNOW y p)?)).

SINCERE is nothing more than an implication; it can be true at some times and false at others. For example, an agent x would be insincere to y about p if x wants y to believe p, and x wants p to false.[6] Notice that an agent would be insincere if he wants to produce a false belief in another agent, even though he may not believe that he will be successful. That is, as far as we are concerned, insincerity is a matter of agent's chosen desires, not his beliefs.[7] This characterization of insincerity in terms of the agent's wanting to induce false beliefs differentiates our approach from Perrault's (chapter 9 of this volume).

To illustrate the difference between a theory of sincerity based on agents' chosen desires and one based on agents' beliefs, imagine an agent who sabotages a nuclear power plant (or even orders a henchman to do so) by making its primary sensor always give the wrong reading. Being a good saboteur, the agent decides never again to be in the vicinity of the sensor, and so he never again (if he ever did) knows the sensor's value. That is, he has no beliefs that the sensor has a particular value. However, in rigging up the sensor as he does, the saboteur wants whoever reads it to have false beliefs. Now, someone could observe the saboteur preparing to do his deed, infer that he wants to alter the sensor, and come to the conclusion that he wants whoever sees the sensor to have false beliefs. The observer would surely want to say that such a saboteur is insincere, even though he (the saboteur) has no beliefs about the facts (the sensor's current reading); such is the nature of sabotage.

In summary, insincerity involves wanting others to come to believe false things and is a notion independent of language.

Next, consider an agent to be HELPFUL to another agent if for any action, he adopts the other agent's goal that he eventually do that action, whenever such a goal would not conflict with his own.

Definiton 2

(HELPFUL x y) $\overset{def}{=}$

$\forall$e ([(BEL x (GOAL y $\Diamond$(DONE x e))) $\land$
$\sim$(GOAL x $\Box$ $\sim$(DONE x e))] $\supset$
(GOAL x $\Diamond$(DONE x e))).

Notice that helpfulness is a disposition only: not taking on another's goals does not indicate unhelpfulness, since the agent may have reasons for not wanting the goal. To be truly unhelpful, the agent must refuse to take on a goal to do something even if he himself has no objection to doing it.

The notion of helpfulness that we have involves taking on goals that do not conflict with existing goals. We will also assume that in the absence of conflicting goals, an agent is willing to be committed to doing the action. Moreover, the agent adopts this commitment relative to the other's goals. Should the other agent change his mind, the first agent could nullify his persistent goal.

Assumption 1

$(\text{HELPFUL } x \ y) \wedge (\text{BEL } x \ (\text{GOAL } y \ \Diamond(\text{DONE } x \ a))) \wedge$
$\sim(\text{GOAL } x \ \Box \sim (\text{DONE } x \ a))$
$$\supset$$
$[\text{INTEND}_1 \ x \ a \ [(\text{HELPFUL } x \ y) \wedge (\text{GOAL } y \ \Diamond(\text{DONE } x \ a))]].$

This assumption is similar to the definition of HELPFUL, but it refers to an arbitrary action expression and it makes the intention contingent on y's remaining helpfully disposed.

3.2 Alternating Belief and Mutual Belief

Our account of utterance events will characterize them in terms of the dependence and the effects they have on the beliefs and goals of the participants. Typically, someone who thinks he is observing such an event (for example, the person being addressed) will come to believe something about the speaker, unless he has other beliefs to the contrary. However, an utterance may also occur in a very different context. For example, the observer himself may not have such beliefs about the event but only think that the speaker thinks that he has them. In this case, although we do not want to claim as before that the observer comes to believe something about the speaker, we would at least like to claim that the observer thinks that the speaker thinks that the observer would form that belief. This type of reasoning can continue to further levels. In general, if an utterance is produced when there are beliefs at a certain level of nesting, then the result will be effects appropriate for that level. To be able to state such conditions, we need to be able to easily refer to what a person x believes about what y believes about what x believes, and so on, to arbitrary depths. To do so, we use the notion of ABEL.

The following defines the auxiliary concept of alternating belief to some level n between two agents x and y that p holds.

Definition 3

$$(\text{ABEL n x y p}) \overset{def}{=} \underbrace{(\text{BEL x (BEL y (BEL x ... (BEL x p}}_{n} \underbrace{)...)}_{n} .$$

For example,

If n is	(ABEL n x y p) is
1	(BEL x p)
2	(BEL x (BEL y p))
3	(BEL x (BEL y (BEL x p)))
etc.	

That is, ABEL characterizes the nth alternating belief between x and y that p, built up "from outside in," that is, starting with x's belief that p. On this basis, one can define unilateral mutual belief—what one agent believes is mutually believed—as follows:

Definition 4

$$(\text{BMB x y p}) \overset{def}{=} \forall n \,(\text{ABEL n x y p}).$$

In other words, (BMB x y p) is the infinite conjunction[8] (BEL x p) ∧ (BEL x (BEL y p)) ∧ .... Based on the introspective properties we have assumed for beliefs, one can show the following is true:

Proposition 1

(BMB x y p) ⊃ (BMB x y (BEL x p)).

Furthermore, from Proposition 1 and from the fact that (BEL x p) ⊃ (GOAL x p), one easily can show that

Proposition 2

(BMB x y (BEL x p)) ⊃ (BMB x y (GOAL y (BEL x p))).

These properties will be useful for describing the intended effects of imperatives when used as requests.

3.3 Some Domain Predicates

Before turning to the definition of illocutionary acts, we first add some domain predicates to allow us to specify an illocutionary act's propositional content, then develop notation for describing the effects of utterance events compactly.

To have something to communicate, let us introduce a few domain predicates for the logic:

(CLEAN f)—f is clean.

(FLOOR f)—f is a floor.

(DOOR d)—d is a door.

(OPEN d)—d is open.

Next we introduce a few predicates that are true of events:

(FLOORWASHING e)—e is an event of washing a floor.

(DOOROPENING e)—e is an event of opening a door.

3.4 Properties Specifically related to Communication
We add to our language the following nonlogical predicates:

(IMPERATIVE s)	s's dominant clause is an imperative.
(DECLARATIVE s)	s's dominant clause is a declarative.
(INTERROGATIVE s)	s's dominant clause is a yes-no interrogative.
(UTTER y s e)	e is a sequence of events in which s is uttered by the agent of e to addressee y.
(ATTEND x y)	x is attending to y.

Next, we supply predicates that characterize the semantics of declarative and imperative sentences. Since the development of a full semantic theory lies beyond the scope of this paper, we will content ourselves with a simplistic version thereof. To say that a *natural-language* declarative sentence is true, we use

(TRUE s).[9]

Next, we add a predicate that relates imperative sentences to the properties of events they describe:

(FULFILL-CONDS s e)—Event e fulfills the satisfaction conditions imposed by sentence s.

Clearly, FULFILL-CONDS is just a placeholder for a semantic theory that can characterize the meanings of imperatives. The only requirement we make for analyzing imperatives is that such a semantic theory have the capacity to supply predicates (or properties) that are true of events, especially the utterance event itself (in order to handle performative sentences).

We assume a long list of conditions of the following form:

$\forall$e (FULFILL-CONDS "Wash the floor" e) $\equiv$ (FLOORWASHING e)

$\forall$e (FULFILL-CONDS "Open the door" e) $\equiv$ (FLOORWASHING e).[10]

4 Imperatives

All theories of speech acts and natural-language communication need to consider the contribution of utterance mood to the effects of the utterances themselves. We assume that the effects of mood will apply to something like propositional content, which we assume for purposes of this paper to be determinable independently of the theory of rational interaction that we are about to develop. Clearly this latter assumption is simplistic; for example, any account of the interpretation of referring phrases or word sense disambiguation must consider the speaker's intentions (Appelt 1985; Clark and Marshall 1981; Cohen 1984; Grosz and Sidner 1985; Perrault and Cohen 1981). However, our strategy is first to develop the theory of rational interaction, then to apply it to sentence-level phenomena before making the transition to problems of utterance interpretation.

It is well known that the form of an utterance does not determine its illocutionary force uniquely. For example, the same imperative utterance could be used to make a request or to issue an order or command. It may not even be used to perform an illocutionary act at all. Utterance mood is therefore inadequate as an "illocutionary force-indicating device," contrary to its use by Searle and Vanderveken (1985). However, given a context, utterance mood contributes to the understanding of a speaker's intent. We regard that contribution as a core effect from which many inferences can be drawn. Our concern here is in specifying a logic to support such inferences and in describing the core effects.

4.1 Utterance Mood: The Case of Imperatives

Utterance mood conveys a speaker's mental state. In this connection, consider imperatives. The utterance of an imperative to perform some action conveys the speaker's chosen desire that the hearer carry out the action, provided the speaker is not thought to have been insincere. Typically, the speaker is also trying to get the hearer to commit himself to the action so that, if all goes well, he does it.

Let us begin to formalize this property of imperatives.

> *Imperative Property*
> After speaker spkr's imperative to addressee addr to do action a, if
> addr does not think that spkr was insincere about his wanting
> addr to do a—that is, if addr does not believe that spkr wanted
> addr to believe falsely that spkr wants addr to do a—then addr
> believes that spkr wants addr to do a.[11]

Let us consider what versions of the Imperative Property should hold as we examine different embeddings of what the hearer thinks the speaker believes. If addr happens to believe that spkr did not want addr to do the action and hence that he is insincere, then the conclusion of the Imperative Property does not hold. The next level of complication involves addr's not thinking that spkr thinks he, spkr, is insincere. The statement of the Imperative Property will reduce to the first conclusion provided that addr thinks spkr is never wrong about his own goals. Next, notice that addr might still think that spkr believes his insincerity has not been noticed. Therefore, addr may be in the following state:

$$\text{(BEL addr (BEL spkr [BEL addr (DONE [SINCERE spkr addr}$$
$$\text{(GOAL spkr } \Diamond p)]?;e)]))}.$$

Under these conditions, addr might think that spkr believes addr would cooperate and thus attempt to achieve p. An analogous property holds at each level of embedding of (BEL addr (BEL spkr . . .)).

We claim that each of these levels is generated by an imperative, provided that there is no corresponding belief in the speaker's insincerity. That is, the hearer jumps to the conclusion that the speaker is sincere as long as there is no belief to the contrary.

To summarize, we propose the following: Let e be an event (type) of uttering an imperative sentence, and let $q \stackrel{def}{=}$ (DONE [∼(SINCERE spkr addr (GOAL spkr $\Diamond$p))]?;e); that is, is spkr's having done the utterance event e being insincere to addr about his wanting p to become true.

IF AFTER e	THEN
∼(BEL addr q)	(BEL addr (GOAL spkr $\Diamond$p))
∼(BEL addr (BEL spkr q))	(BEL addr (BEL spkr (GOAL spkr $\Diamond$p)))
∼(BEL addr (BEL spkr (BEL addr q)))	(BEL addr (BEL spkr (BEL addr (GOAL spkr $\Diamond$p))))

and so on.

We can express all of these properties at once by using the concept of alternating belief. Below, we use that concept to develop a notation for characterizing utterance events, which is then used in formulating a precise statement regarding the effects of imperatives.

4.2 Notation for Describing Utterance Events

We will now define a notation that can be used to describe the effects of declaratives, imperatives, and interrogatives (although in this paper we analyze only imperatives). The purpose of the notation is to factor out the conditions on utterance events necessary for any effects to be realized. Analogous to Searle's (1969) "normal input/output conditions," they specify who is speaking (spkr), who is being addressed (addr), and what kind of sentence has been spoken (indicated by Φ).

Definition 5
$$\Phi \Rightarrow \alpha \overset{def}{=} \forall spkr, addr, e, s, n$$

(ABEL n addr spkr [DONE spkr ((ATTEND addr spkr) ∧
        (UTTER addr s e) ∧ (Φ s))?;e]) ∧

~(ABEL n addr spkr [DONE spkr ~(SINCERE spkr addr α)?;e]) ⊃
(ABEL n addr spkr (DONE spkr e; α?)).

That is, Φ ⇒ α is an abbreviation for a quantified implication roughly to the effect that if a hearer addr believes that e was just done, where e is the uttering by a speaker spkr to addr of a sentence s in syntactic mood Φ, and that addr does not believe that e was done insincerely regarding certain "core attitudes" α associated with utterances of that type, then addr believes that condition α holds. Because we are dealing with utterance events, the contextual preconditions include the "normal input/output conditions," as well as conditions that depend on specific utterance forms. At any level of alternating belief, the conditions include (1) spkr was the agent of e, addr was attending to spkr, e is an event of spkr's uttering sentence s to addr, and predicate Φ held of sentence s, and (2) *after* e, it is not the case (at that level of alternating belief) that the speaker is thought to have been insincere about α in his performing that event e—that is, it is thought after the act that the speaker was insincere before the act. The abbreviation then states that at each level of alternating belief for which (1) and (2) hold, α also holds for the given values of the quantified variables. The utility of the notation is to suppress any mention of condition (1) because it is fixed for all kinds of utterance events. However, α depends on the kind of utterance used, as characterized by Φ.[12]

It should be noted that we do not supply *propositions* as arguments to primitive utterance events, as is done in Allen 1979, Cohen 1979, Perrault and Allen 1980, and chapter 9 of this volume, because doing so requires one to characterize semantically how events can operate on functions from possible worlds to truth-values (or whatever is one's semantic analysis of propositions). We do not know how to do this. By talking explicitly about sentences, we have a hope of integrating a semantic theory with a theory of utterance effects.

4.3 Characterizing Imperatives

Given this notation, the following domain axiom is used to characterize an imperative utterance:

Domain Axiom 1 Imperatives

$$\models \text{IMPERATIVE} \Rightarrow (\text{GOAL spkr} \lozenge [\exists e' \text{ (DONE addr } e') \wedge \\ (\text{FULFILL-CONDS s } e')]).$$

That is, if an imperative is uttered in circumstances where a hearer does not suspect (at some level of alternating belief) that the speaker is insincere in his desire to get an addressed person to believe that he has a certain goal, then the hearer will believe (at that level) that the speaker really has that goal. The goal in question here is that the addressed person should perform something that fulfills the condition expressed by the imperative sentence. So, for example, under normal circumstances, if addr thinks that spkr has just said "Wash the floor" to him, and addr has no reason to doubt the sincerity of spkr, then addr will think that spkr wants him to wash the floor.

The complications regarding ABEL in this axiom handle the situation where some of the conditions are not mutually believed to hold. Note that the level-counting variable n is quantified across both sides of the implication.[13] It therefore picks out each of the above levels of alternating belief. At level $n = 1$ of this axiom, if after the utterance of an imperative, addr thinks that spkr was insincere about his goal that addr do something, then addr need not believe that spkr wants addr to do it. However, at level $n = 3$, addr could believe that spkr thinks that addr believes spkr was sincere, so after uttering the imperative addr could think that spkr believes that addr will believe that spkr wants addr to act.

The same argument can be made for any other levels of embedding of spkr believes that addr believes, and so on. Hence, any level of alternating belief that the speaker is insincere about wanting addr to do the specified action will nullify the conclusion *at that level* of alternating belief, but not at any others. The ability of ABEL to characterize arbitrary depths of alternating beliefs (regarding insincerity and the speaker's goals) in this case allows *one* axiom schema to capture ironic and insincere imperatives as well as the usual case.

Since $\forall w \ (P(w) \supset Q(w))$ implies $\forall w P(w) \supset \forall w Q(w)$, as we quantify over the positive integers indicating levels of alternating belief, we can derive the conclusion that under certain circumstances addr thinks it is mutually believed (in our notation, BMB'ed) that the speaker spkr wants addr to achieve p. Illocutionary acts will be defined to require that the speaker intend to produce such beliefs about mutual beliefs, but it is important to notice that utterance events will not lead to mutual beliefs if performed in circumstances in which the speaker is suspected (at some level) of insincerity. Those cases in which there is a suspicion of insincerity will constitute a "defect" in the performance of an illocutionary act. Although an illocutionary act defective in this way can still have interesting effects, one might not want to classify the utterances in question as a full-blooded illocutionary act. The hearer's deciding to cooperate and attempting to execute the action depends only on what the hearer actually thinks the speaker wants and intends.

With this understanding of the effects of imperatives, we can proceed to the first part of our method for characterizing illocutionary acts: infer from utterance form to illocutionary point. The first step is to derive some of the effects of an imperative and then characterize an attempt to achieve something. We then define an illocutionary act as an attempt to achieve certain effects.

4.4 The Effects of Imperatives

Given no insincerity, the uttering of an imperative by speaker spkr to addressee addr to do action a results in addr's thinking it is mutually believed that spkr wants addr to do a. As a consequence of Assumption 1, if addr does not mind doing the action and is helpfully disposed toward spkr, then we can conclude that addr intends to do the act relative to spkr's desire. From Theorem 1 in chapter 3, we can identify the conditions guaranteeing that an intention to act will in fact be achieved. Let us call those conditions world-right. Then

$$(\text{INTEND}_1 \text{ addr a q}) \land \text{world-right} \supset \Diamond(\text{DONE addr a}).$$

Thus, given an expression of the speaker's desire that the hearer act, the hearer's helpfulness and lack of objections to doing the act, and the appropriateness of the world, we can conclude that the act happens. This is the usual and desired reason for planning to issue an imperative utterance (as a directive), as it shows how the utterance event leads to the achievement of some desirable action and thus behaves like any other step in a plan.

Now, not only do speakers want this chain of effects to take hold when they make public their desires about the initial parts of the chain, under certain circumstances they make public their desires for the rest. To see this, we point out that the following holds:

Proposition 3
> (BMB y x (GOAL x $\Diamond$(DONE y a))) $\land$
> (BMB y x (GOAL x (HELPFUL y x))) $\land$
>
> (BMB y x (GOAL x $\sim$(GOAL y $\Box$ $\sim$(DONE y a)))) $\supset$
>
> (BMB y x [GOAL x (INTEND$_1$ y a [(GOAL x $\Diamond$(DONE y a)) $\land$
> (HELPFUL y x)])])).

This follows from Propositions 1 and 2, along with Assumption 1 and consequential closure of BMB and GOAL. So, if a speaker makes the hearer think it is mutually believed he wants the hearer to do something, and the hearer thinks it is mutually believed that he, the speaker, wants the hearer to be helpful,[14] then the speaker has made the hearer think it is mutually believed that the speaker wants him to intend to do the action relative to the speaker's (chosen) desire.

Similarly, one can extend the line of inference to show that if the hearer thinks it is mutually believed that the speaker wants the "world to be right," then the hearer thinks it is mutually believed that the speaker wants the act to be done eventually. That is, we have embedded the earlier line of inference within (BMB addr spkr (GOAL spkr ...)).

5 Requests

Given all the effects emanating from the uttering of an imperative in the right circumstances, what shall we say a speaker characteristically attempts to achieve when issuing a request? To answer this question, we first need to discuss attempts.

5.1 Attempts

A crucially important property of illocutionary acts, not shared by some other actions (for instance, knocking over a glass of water, or simple utterance events), is that they cannot be performed accidentally or unknowingly. To illustrate this, consider the following example.[15] A blindfolded person reaches into a bowl of flashcards, pulls out three cards, and knowingly turns them toward another person. The cards say "Open the door." One would not be inclined to say that a request to open the door took place, in part because the agent was not committed to conveying that specific content. To exclude such cases from being labeled as communicative action, we first want to examine only actions in which the agent is committed to performing the action, and perhaps to achieving certain states of affairs. Actions so performed are not accidental.

As we have seen in chapter 3, there are at least two kinds of states an agent can be in with respect to a chosen desire, say, p. First, and most strongly, the agent can be committed to achieving p; if the agent fails, we would expect him to try again, all else being equal. This is expressed with P-GOAL and INTEND. A second, weaker mental state is to want to achieve p, but not be committed to achieving it. We express this mental state with the conjunction of the agent's believing p is currently false and his wanting it to become true (next). But, in this state, if the agent fails to achieve p, no prediction about a second attempt would be made. Now, attempts can involve either or both of these types of goal states. To specify both the chosen and committed aspects of attempts, we use the following:

Definition 6
{ATTEMPT x e p q} $\overset{def}{=}$

[(BEL x $\sim$p) $\wedge$ (GOAL x (HAPPENS x e;p?)) $\wedge$
(INTEND$_1$ x e;q?)]? ;e.

That is, an attempt is a complex action that agents perform when they do something (e) desiring to bring about some effect (p) but with intent to produce at least some result (q).[16] Typically, p represents some ultimate goal that may or may not be achieved by the attempt, whereas q represents what it takes to make an honest effort. Consider, for example, attempting to sink a game-winning last shot in a basketball game. The event e in question is a certain movement of the agent's body. The agent is committed to shooting (e) and hence to the ball's being launched unimpeded toward the basket (q); the agent wants to achieve the ball's being in the basket (p). Thus, the agent's commitments to doing the action and to q characterize his doing his part, and the rest is up to luck and/or physical and causal laws.

5.2 *Definition of Request*

To characterize a request or, for that matter, any illocutionary action, we must decide on the appropriate formulas to substitute for p and q in the definition of an attempt. Two observations guide our formulation. First, Allen and Perrault's work (Allen and Perrault 1980; Perrault and Allen 1980) shows that the key to a formal analysis of indirect speech acts is to understand that there may be many routes leading to the conclusion that any particular effect (here the effect of an imperative) holds. Thus, an action for uttering an imperative will not be included as part of requesting, but instead some unspecified sequence of events will be used.

Second, we will use the aforementioned effects of an imperative to specify what the speaker was attempting to achieve. Ultimately the question of what effects should be encapsulated in a complex action expression can be settled only on empirical and philosophical grounds. For example, each choice of intended effect entails certain gating conditions that then become part of the speech act definition. Moreover, by stipulating that a certain effect is *intended*, rather than merely chosen, one states that the agent is committed to achieving it; if he does not, we predict that he will try again. Furthermore, the agent believes that the effects he is attempting to achieve are not already true. Thus, the felicity conditions to which the theorist is committed are determined by the theorist's choice of the commitments attributed to speakers in performing instances of various kinds of illocutionary acts. We argue in favor of one choice below, but it should be emphasized that what has been developed here is actually a framework for formulating many theories.

Let us now define a request by incorporating some of the effects of imperatives. The core effect from which we start is

(BMB addr spkr (GOAL spkr $\Diamond$(DONE addr a))).

That is, after spkr utters an imperative to do a, and addr thinks it is mutually believed that spkr was sincere, addr thinks it is mutually believed spkr wants addr to do a. From this, we can (as mentioned above) derive, under the right conditions, the consequences of Assumption 1 and Proposition 3, that is,

(INTEND$_1$ addr a (GOAL spkr $\Diamond$(DONE addr a)) $\wedge$
(HELPFUL addr spkr)),

and hence,

(BMB addr spkr (GOAL spkr [INTEND$_1$ addr a
(GOAL spkr $\Diamond$(DONE addr a)) (HELPFUL addr spkr)])).

We now incorporate these effects into a complex action expression called REQUEST:

Definition 7
{REQUEST spkr addr e a} $\overset{def}{=}$

{ATTEMPT spkr e ϕ (BMB addr spkr (GOAL spkr ϕ))}

where ϕ is

$\Diamond$(DONE addr a) $\wedge$
(INTEND$_1$ addr a [(GOAL spkr $\Diamond$(DONE addr a)) $\wedge$
(HELPFUL addr spkr)]).

That is, a request is an attempt to achieve some condition while being committed to making that goal public. The goal in question has two parts: first, that some action should eventually take place; and second, that the addressed party should intend to do that action relative to the speaker's wanting it done and to the hearer's being helpfully disposed toward the speaker.[17] We now examine these components of a request in detail.

As remarked upon by Winograd and Flores (1986), conversation implies commitment. A minimal commitment for the performance of an illocutionary act is the speaker's commitment to making it mutually believed that the speaker is in a certain mental state with respect to the content of the utterance. For example, if the speaker asks a hearer to open the door and the speaker learns subsequently that his voice was garbled, we can predict that the speaker will try again to make his chosen desires "public" to the hearer.[18] The commitment, in other words, is to being understood. Specifically, we do *not* require the speaker to commit to the goal he wants to achieve with the request, namely, getting the addressee to perform some action intentionally. If the request is not successful in getting the addressee to act, the speaker may or may not decide to try again.

As for the content of the goal itself, the first part involves the addressee's performing some action. We would not want to classify an utterance as a request if the speaker did not want the action done (even if he was committed to being understood and wanted the addressee to intend to do the action). The reason for the second part of the goal is that it would not be a true request if the addressee could comply without intending to do so. In other words, it should not be possible to request that some action be performed accidentally. Moreover, the intention to act should be relative to the speaker's desire. If the speaker later says "Never mind," the hearer can drop the commitment. This helps to explain why, after acceding to a request—say, with "OK"—the addressee has performed a commissive speech act. Finally, the intention to act should be relative to the addressee's being helpfully disposed toward the speaker. That is, the speaker wants helpfulness to be one of the reasons the hearer could consider dropping the intention to act. This is different from a command, for example where helpfulness is not the issue, and the intention should stay in effect as long as the speaker has authority over the hearer. In the case of a request, the hearer may or may not decide to take on the intention just because he is helpfully disposed (and so drop it when that attitude changes). However, what we are stipulating here is that the speaker *wants* the hearer to form the intention in this way, and the speaker need not have any beliefs about the hearer's helpfulness.

It is important to note that the speech act of requesting requires the hearer to regard it as mutually believed, rather than merely believed to a finite level of embedding, that the speaker wants the hearer to do the action. Thus, felicitous requesting will require that the hearer presume the speaker's sincerity at all levels of alternating belief.

Finally, the above definition works for indirect as well as direct requests. It does not specify *how* the hearer arrives at the mutual belief that the speaker wants the hearer to perform an action. With respect to a direct request, this mutual belief may be an immediate consequence of the speaker's uttering an imperative. But it may also be the result of an inference from some other event(s). For example, if a speaker utters "Get the hammer" to a hearer when the speaker is standing on a ladder and is obviously holding a nail in position, the hearer may infer it as mutually believed that not only should the hearer get a hammer (satisfying the direct request) but he should also hand it to the speaker. This latter mutual belief is sufficient to initiate the (intended) inference path that satisfies the indirect-request interpretation.

5.3 The Point

By turning requests into complex action expressions, we can now say when a request has been made, and so we can reason about what would be true if a request were done. However, we have not had to add anything to the formal language. The notion of requesting is entirely metatheoretic, having been described here with definitions. One could view these definitions as expanded "in line" into their components, but this is not necessary. Furthermore, we do not need to say that communication requires illocutionary-act recognition, since hearers can infer the needed effects and respond appropriately without any such explicit recognition. Simply put, a request is not a new type of primitive event; rather, it is an event of some other type (often, but not only, the utterance of an imperative sentence) that happens to occur in the right circumstances.

This can be seen perhaps most clearly by examining some conditions under which an utterance event e would constitute the performance of a request from spkr to addr to fulfill the conditions of an imperative sentence s. For simplicity, we assume that some event e' is the one and only event that fulfills the conditions of an imperative sentence s and that this is mutually believed by spkr and addr. In addition, we assume the following:

1. (GOAL spkr $\Diamond$(DONE addr e'))—spkr wants addr to do e'.

2. (BEL spkr $\sim$(GOAL addr $\Diamond$(DONE addr e')))—spkr believes addr doesn't already want to do e'.

3. (BEL spkr $\sim$(BMB addr spkr $\Diamond$(DONE addr e')))—spkr believes addr does not already think it is mutually believed addr will do e'.

4. (GOAL spkr (HAPPENS e;[(HELPFUL addr spkr) $\wedge$ $\sim$(GOAL addr $\sim$ $\Diamond$(DONE addr e'))]?))—spkr wants it to be case after his uttering an imperative that addr should be helpful to spkr and not want not to do e'.

5. (HAPPENS e;(BEL spkr ψ?) $\wedge$ (BEL spkr (HAPPENS e;ψ?))

where ψ is (BMB addr spkr
        (GOAL spkr [(HELPFUL addr spkr) $\wedge$
              $\sim$(GOAL addr y $\sim$ $\Diamond$(DONE addr e'))]) $\wedge$
        (DONE (ATTEND addr spkr)?;e) $\wedge$
        (DONE (UTTER addr s e)?;e) $\wedge$
        (DONE (IMPERATIVE s)?;e) $\wedge$
        (DONE (SINCERE spkr addr (GOAL spkr
              $\Diamond$(DONE addr e')))?;e))

In other words, spkr knows that: After the uttering of the imperative sentence, addr thinks it is mutually believed that spkr wants addr to be helpful and not to want not to do e', that the utterance was an imperative directed to addr when addr was attending to spkr, and that in uttering that imperative, spkr was sincere about his goal that addr do e'.

We will not present a formal proof that these assumptions lead to a request here, except to sketch some of the main features.

Let ϕ be [$\diamondsuit$(DONE addr e') $\wedge$ (INTEND$_1$ addr e'
[(GOAL spkr $\diamondsuit$(DONE addr e')) $\wedge$ (HELPFUL addr spkr)])].

That is, ϕ represents addr's eventually doing e' and having the intention to do it so long as addr thinks spkr wants him to and so long as addr is helpful.

Under these conditions, we can show the following:

1. (BEL spkr $\sim\phi$) $\wedge$ (GOAL spkr (HAPPEN spkr e;ϕ)).
So, ϕ is an achievement goal for spkr.
2. (INTEND$_1$ spkr e;(BMB addr spkr (GOAL spkr ϕ))).
Moreover, spkr is committed to making public that he wants ϕ. Notice that we have derived that the agent is committed to making his goals public from conditions that did not include such a commitment. This conclusion can be reached whenever agents went the *very next* action to result in some proposition's holding, and their believing that that action will cause them to believe that the proposition holds.
3. Thus, (HAPPENS {ATTEMPT spkr e ϕ (BMB addr spkr
                                              (GOAL spkr ϕ))}).
4. Thus, (HAPPENS {REQUEST spkr addr e e'}).

It thus follows from the above that an utterance of an imperative in a certain context will constitute the performance of a request.

How much of a chain of effects should be incorporated into the definition of an illocutionary action? Just as mathematicians have the leeway to decide which results are useful enough to be named as lemmas or theorems, so too does the language user, linguist, computer system, or speech act theoretician have a great deal of leeway in deciding which complex action expressions to form and name. Grounds for making such decisions range from the existence of illocutionary verbs in a given language to considerations of efficiency. However, complex action expressions are flexible— they allow different languages and agents to carve up the same chains of inference in different ways. For example, we have shown the implications of committing an agent to producing an effect; if the agent does not achieve it, he will try again. Just how much of any given chain should be defined as constituting the speaker's commitments is a matter of subsequent argument. It is not an essential feature of our analysis.

The complex action expression named REQUEST could thus have been named anything at all. We are not making any claims about the existence of a general mapping between such action expressions and English illocutionary verbs. There could be long chains of inference incorporated into action expressions for which a particular natural language contains no illocutionary verb. For example, an action expression labeled "want-request" might capture the inference from someone's saying "I want p" to the hearer's bringing p about. This freedom allows agents to create complex action expressions for "conventionalized" indirect uses of sentences, even though there is no verb in the natural language to describe those uses.

5.4 Illocutionary-Act Recognition

So what does recognition of an illocutionary act amount to? There are two steps. First, it involves recognizing that the speaker was attempting (and hence intending) to get the hearer to draw certain inferences. In a typical case, after receiving an imperative, the intended addressee would first come to believe mutually with the speaker that the latter wants him to do something. Then, the addressee would need to infer that the speaker wants it to be public that he wants the addressee to form the intention to act because the addressee is helpful.

Now, *if* the hearer in fact adopts the commitment because he comes to believe that the speaker intended him to adopt it by virtue of his helpfulness, the hearer is then embarked on the path of recognizing what illocutionary act was performed. The hearer would need to achieve complete recognition of the intended line of inference so as to have enough information to identify what kind of illocutionary act was being performed. Moreover, the hearer would have to recognize which effects the speaker was committed to, which he was trying to achieve, which he has chosen, and which are merely fortuitous. But our point is that the hearer need not perform this entire recognition procedure—he may just be helpful and do the action. In summary, the first step of illocutionary-act recognition is to determine which effects the speaker intended. This may or may not be done by a hearer.

Consider a case in which a speaker utters "Open the door" to an addressee when it is mutually believed not only that the speaker has authority over the addressee but also that the addressee is helpfully disposed toward the speaker. In such circumstances it may not be clear just which reason for adopting the speaker's expressed desire is intended.[19] But so what? There is no requirement being proposed that utterances are defective (and the conversational state should be repaired) if they are illocutionarily indeterminate to the hearer. Given such indeterminacy, one might want to say that the speaker incompletely or defectively performed an illocutionary act of a given type. But nothing of importance follows from that fact in our theory of rational interaction.[20] There is no reason to believe that speakers intend to achieve all and only the effects encapsulated in some illocutionary verb. The heuristic value of illocutionary-act recognition thus remains to be seen. Our main point here is that actual identification adds nothing in principle.

Finally, because it may take a speaker more than one utterance to perform a complete illocutionary act, and because utterances are often completed by other speakers (Clark and Wilkes-Gibbs, chapter 23 of this volume), hearers would have to recognize which illocutionary act was performed after sequences of utterance events. That is, hearers would have to look back arbitrarily far (subject to constraints such as those described by Grosz and Sidner (1986)) to see which illocutionary acts the current utterance was completing. Illocutionary-act recognition thus seems to us unnecessary, unlikely, and uninformative.

5.5 Summary

We have defined requests in the following way. First, a logic of intention was developed (in chapter 3). Next, imperatives were analyzed, since they are the prototypical way in which directive speech acts are performed. The "core" effects of imperatives, the speaker's desire that the hearer should act, are revealed to the hearer provided the hearer does not believe that the speaker was insincere in making his utterance. Then, we derived other important effects, namely, that the hearer thinks it is mutually believed that the speaker wants him to intend to act because he is helpful and because the speaker wants him to act. Another effect is that if the hearer is in fact helpful and does not mind acting, he forms the intention to act relative to the speaker's desire. Finally, we define a request as an attempt to achieve these conditions, which entails certain commitments. In making requesting into a complex action, we abstract away from any primitive utterance event (or sequence of them); instead, the speaker is viewed as having performed a request if he executes any sequence of actions that produces the needed effects.

To show that these principles can provide the basis for an adequate analysis of illocutionary acts, we show how Searle and Vanderveken's (1985) conditions on requesting can be derived from an independently motivated analysis of intentional action, as Searle and Vanderveken recommend.

6 Deriving Searle and Vanderveken's Conditions on Requesting

Searle and Vanderveken's conditions on speech acts are divided into the *normal input/output, propositional content, preparatory, sincerity,* and *illocutionary point* conditions. We explore each of these in turn for requests. Where it is not superseded by Searle and Vanderveken 1985, we also refer to Searle 1969.

6.1 The Normal Input/Output Conditions

The normal input/output conditions include the (1) speaker's and hearer's ability to speak and understand the relevant language and (2) conditions on the utterance itself, such as audibility. Also included herein would be, presumably, other conditions on the modality of communication, such as distinctive features of speaking on the telephone, computer-mediated conferencing, or text. Finally, normal input/output conditions would exclude "parasitic forms of communication," such as telling a joke or acting in a play.

These input/output conditions are supposed to apply to illocutionary acts per se. In our scheme, however, these conditions apply to utterance events themselves, not to illocutionary acts. A request, for example, can be perfomed even if the participants do not speak a shared language or nothing at all is uttered (though *something* had better be observed, say, a printed word or a gesture). Whereas many of the conditions we propose would be preconditions on any utterance event's conveyance of the speaker's mental state, other conditions depend on the kind of utterance used. Thus, the conditions we state are a function—at least in part—of the utterance event's signaling what it does about the speaker's mental state, as well as of the utterance's form and shared beliefs with regard to its meaning.

The illocutionary-act definitions, however, are independent of these conditions. For the speaker to attempt to achieve various effects with an utterance, he must believe that these conditions hold. But the definition of illocutionary acts depends solely on what the speaker is trying to achieve, not on what he thinks must be true for a specific utterance to achieve it. An utterance event can achieve the effects that are necessary for performing an illocutionary act only if that event occurs under the right conditions. For example, no one would claim that a request uttered over a telephone is a different kind of illocutionary act from one uttered face-to-face.

Finally, "parasitic" forms of communication (such as jokes and irony) are handled in the same way as insincere utterances. Whenever the hearer believes (or believes that the speaker thinks he believes) the speaker is insincere, the effects normally produced by utterances of that kind are correspondingly weakened. Ultimately, when everyone knows the speaker is insincere, the usual effects are not produced. We do not say specifically what *is* produced, but that is another matter.

In sum, the normal input and output conditions should apply to the utterance event itself and not be incorporated directly into the definition of illocutionary acts because instances of the same illocutionary-act type can be performed with many kinds of utterances.

6.2 The Propositional Content Condition
Searle's propositional content condition states that a speaker requests a future act to be done by the hearer. This condition appears in our definition

as the speaker's being committed to making public his chosen desire that the hearer eventually do the requested action.

6.3 The Preparatory Conditions

Searle proposes two preparatory conditions, each of which is partially satisfied by our account. First, the hearer should be able to do the requested act. Second, the speaker believes that the hearer can do so. These conditions seem to us to be too strong. We believe that one can make a perfectly good request independently of whether or not the hearer can *in fact* do the requested act. Furthermore, the hearer may not believe he can do it but may believe that the speaker thinks he can. In fact, we think that speakers can make felicitous requests even though the speaker might not be sure that the hearer can in fact do the act. All that appears to be required is that the speaker not believe that the hearer *cannot* do the act. For example, the point of a request could be, among other things, to confirm that the hearer can perform the act.

Our analysis supports this weaker claim about speakers' beliefs in the following way: First, let us recall that a request is defined to be an event that makes the hearer think it mutually believed that the speaker's goal (chosen desire) is that the hearer eventually carry out a specified action. The semantics of GOAL are such that, if one's goal is $\Diamond p$, one does not believe $\Diamond p$ to be false; that is, one does not believe that $\Box \sim p$. Hence, the hearer would think it mutually believed that the speaker does not believe the hearer will never act as requested. Of course, since a request is an attempt to make the speaker's goals public, if the speaker is sincere, he actually has the goal that the hearer so act, and thus, he is required not to believe the hearer cannot act. Moreover, since the speaker is also attempting to get the hearer to form an intention to do the requested action, the speaker thinks that the hearer does not believe he will never do the requested action. Thus, the semantics of GOAL plays the key role in satisfying a more accurate version of Searle's first preparatory condition.

The second preparatory condition is that it should not be obvious to either speaker or hearer that the latter was going to do the act *"in the normal course of events and of his own accord."*[21] In our framework, this amounts to the hearer's already having a persistent goal to accomplish the act, but one that need not be relative to the speaker's desire. To encode its not being obvious that the hearer has such a persistent goal, we could say that the speaker does not believe (or, perhaps, mutually believe) that the hearer already intends to act. But, again, we believe this statement of the nonobviousness condition to be too strong. If the speaker believed the hearer intended to do the act at the time of making the utterance, he could still be attempting to get the hearer to form a persistent goal to act *relative to the speaker's desire*. That is, one purpose of a request is to get the hearer to do something *for* the speaker.

However, if the hearer is *already* committed to an action *for* the speaker, then a second imperative to do that action will constitute, not a felicitous request, but perhaps a form of badgering. This is so because requests are, in part, attempts to commit the hearer to the speaker; our attempt definition involves the agent's wanting to *achieve* certain effects, and that achievement requires that the speaker believe those effects to be false. Consequently, this form of badgering would not be a full-fledged request by our definition.

6.4 The Sincerity Condition

Searle and Vanderveken's sincerity condition for a request is that the speaker should want the act done. Their condition is included in ours, but we require more. As formalized here, requests are by definition sincere because they involve attempts to make it public that the speaker wants Φ to hold, and the speaker in fact wants Φ. Φ includes both the addressee's intending to do the requested act (relative to the speaker's desire and to the addressee's helpfulness) and the act's eventually being done. Hence, one can show that the definition of SINCERE holds for any true request. Notice that there is nothing stopping a theorist from forming a concept for an insincere request by not including Φ in what the speaker hopes to achieve (the first propositional argument to ATTEMPT); the formalism allows one to create arbitrary complex action expressions even if they are not named in a given language.[22] For us, a request can neither be made if it is ultimately insincere, nor if it is recognized as insincere. This is a theoretical position we have taken, but not one that is forced by the formalism.

6.5 The Illocutionary Point

Searle and Vanderveken state that the illocutionary point of request is that the speech act should be *an attempt* to get the hearer to do a certain act. Following them, this is precisely how we have defined REQUEST.[23] However, most of the other nondirective speech acts described in Searle 1969 are not characterized therein as attempts to achieve some illocutionary point. In our opinion, they should be. By defining illocutionary acts as attempts, one can see why only illocutionary verbs can be used as performatives; for these, only the right intentions and beliefs are necessary. This will be shown in a subsequent paper (Cohen and Levesque 1990b).

We have demonstrated the adequacy of our approach by showing how Searle's conditions on requesting could be derived from principles arrived at independently. Next, we will describe briefly how other illocutionary acts can be handled.

7 Other Illocutionary Acts

We have concentrated here on the prototypical directive illocutionary act. The assertive class is analyzed similarly: after a declarative sentence has been uttered, if there was no suspicion of insincerity (at any level of alternating belief), then the hearer thinks it mutually believed that the speaker believes the propositional content (Cohen and Levesque 1990b). The illocutionary act of assertion is defined as an attempt to achieve a mutual belief (BMB) that the speaker believes the content. The illocutionary act of informing is defined as an attempt to get the hearer to believe the content as a consequence of arriving at this mutual belief about the speaker's belief. Of course, a theory of evidence is needed to describe the conditions under which believing that the speaker believes something should cause the hearer to adopt a similar belief.

What do we have to say about the others, namely, Searle's commissives, expressives, and declaratives? First, we have little to say about expressives; one needs to characterize the mental states (such as sorrow, regret) they embody. Then one needs to correlate utterance features with the fact that the speaker is in one of these mental states. For the time being, we will content ourselves with analyzing expressive speech acts as assertives that the speaker is in the requisite state. If sincere, then he is.

Expressives are frequently conveyed through performative utterances (for instance, "I apologize..."). In a subsequent paper (Cohen and Levesque 1990b) we show how performatives can be analyzed without recourse to a separate category of speech act, namely, the declaration (Searle and Vanderveken 1985). In this kind of speech act, the speaker makes something true by saying so. We can show how the assertive kind of speech act (coupled with institutionally based facts) can solve problems of performatives—problems for which Searle and Vanderveken propose the declaration speech act type.

Last of all, let us consider commissives. According to Searle and Vanderveken, uttering a commissive establishes a "commitment." We claim that a necessary condition on the acceptance of an interpersonal commitment is to make it mutually believed with another agent that one has adopted a persistent goal to achieve something relative to that other agent's desires. This relativization of an internal commitment to another's desires shows why a speaker cannot felicitously promise to do something for a hearer that the speaker knows the hearer does not want. Moreover, it shows why an interpersonal commitment has been made in responding positively to a request; the speaker's intention in requesting involves the hearer's taking on just such a relativized commitment.

According to Searle and Vanderveken, certain commissives such as promises "strengthen" this commitment so that it becomes an obligation.

As we do not analyze obligations here, however, our theory is incomplete—but incomplete in the same way as not having an analysis of regret and sorrow. Still, unlike these mental states, there is clearly much in common between a notion of obligation and our analysis of relativized commitment. Whereas the former is institutional and social in nature, the latter is cognitive. However, we contend that it is the ability to adopt such an internal commitment that makes having an obligation possible.

8 Concluding Remarks

This paper has demonstrated that illocutionary acts need not be primitive but rather can be treated as complex actions. Many properties of these actions can be derived from more basic principles of rational action and from an account of the propositional attitudes affected by the uttering of sentences with declarative, interrogative, and imperative moods. This account satisfies a number of criteria for a good theory of illocutionary acts.

- Most elements of the theory of communication are independently motivated. In particular, the theory of rational action is developed independently of any notions of communication.
- The characterization of the result of uttering sentences with certain syntactic moods is justified both by the results we derive for illocutionary acts and by the results we cannot derive (for instance, we cannot derive a request to perform an action unintentionally).
- Complex action expressions need not correspond to illocutionary verbs in a language. Different languages could capture different parts of the same chain of reasoning, and an agent might have formed such an expression for purposes of efficiency, but it need not correspond to that of any other agent.
- The theory provides solutions to problems of performatives.
- The rules for combining illocutionary acts (characterizing, for example, how multiple assertions could constitute the performance of a request) now have been reduced to rules for combining propositional contents and attitudes. Thus, multi-utterance illocutionary acts can be handled by accumulating the speaker's goals expressed in the utterances in question and showing that the combined effects constitute the illocutionary act.
- Multi-act utterances are also a natural outgrowth of this approach. Sentences can be uttered in circumstances that satisfy the conditions of several illocutionary acts.
- The theory is naturally extendable to indirection (to be argued for in another paper), to other illocutionary acts, such as questions, commands, informs, and assertions, and to the act of referring (Cohen 1984).

In summary, we have presented a theory of speech acts and communication grounded in a theory of rational interaction. In so doing, we have sought to demonstrate that there is no need to propose a separate logic for illocutionary acts; the logics of attitudes and action should be entirely satisfactory.

Notes

1. But perhaps they mean illocutionary-force *potential*. They write, "Part of the meaning of an elementary sentence is that its literal utterance in a given context constitutes the performance or attempted performance of an illocutionary act of a particular illocutionary force" (1985, 7). The question at issue here is whether, as a hearer understands an utterance and knows it meaning, he recognizes (or is intended to recognize) that the specific utterance in that specific context was uttered with a specific illocutionary force. The following remark of Searle's leads us to believe the answer is a affirmative: "But, I wish to claim, the intended effect of meaning something is that the hearer should know the illocutionary force and propositional content of the utterance ..." (1971, 8).

2. "What sort of explanation does the hearer seek of the speaker's utterance? ... However, he seeks also to identify the locutionary and illocutionary act performed by the speaker in his utterance, and this involves ascribing intentions to the speaker, in particular, the intention to be performing a certain illocutionary act (by way of performing a certain locutionary act)" (1979, 89).

3. The words "action" and "act" are sometimes used in philosophical writings to make a type/token distinction. We will not adopt this usage, preferring to let context, and ultimately the formalism, disambiguate the intended meaning.

4. Chosen desires are ones that speech act theorists claim to be conveyed by such illocutionary acts as requests.

5. This is not a *social* commitment. It remains to be seen whether social commitments can be constructed from internal ones.

6. Because the definition of sincerity involves making something true, sincerity is "forward-looking" in time (although the event in question can be the empty sequence). The reason for this temporal dimension is that, without it, no performative utterances would be sincere. Briefly, performatives are analyzed as indicative mood utterances about what the speaker has just done. In other words, they are temporally indexical. The analysis of performatives will say that after having uttered such a sentence, the speaker believes he has just done the named illocutionary act. Typically, *prior* to uttering a performative, the speaker has not *just* performed that speech act, and so he would believe his having just done so is false. So, if sincerity involved only what the speaker believed to be true prior to the utterance, no performatives would be sincere. The above definition allows the speaker to sincerely want to do something to get the hearer to believe he has just done the named illocutionary act. For more details, see Cohen and Levesque 1990b.

7. Of course, these chosen desires must obey the usual constraints. So, the agent cannot believe he will definitely fail to induce a false belief in the agent and yet choose to induce that belief.

8. Barwise (1988) has shown that such an infinite conjunction is strictly weaker than a fixed-point definition of mutual belief, namely, $(\text{BMB } x \, y \, p) \stackrel{def}{=} (\text{BEL } x \, p \ \wedge \ (\text{BMB } y \, x \, p))$.

9. Actually, we should be talking about the truth of *statements*, which resolve the indexicals in the corresponding sentence. Any formulation of a substantive theory for determining which statement is conveyed by a sentence is beyond the scope of this paper. The reader should therefore merely assume that the above makes sense.

10. Subsequent conditions will bind the agent of the event to be the same as the addressee of the imperative.

11. We have taken the position that the effects of utterance events should be context-dependent as a result of Ray Perrault's criticism in this volume of the "attitude-independent" analyses of locutionary acts presented by us in Cohen and Levesque 1985. Without his criticism and suggestions for a approach based on default logic, our analysis would be more complex than it is. Although we differ on substantive technical issues, such as the use of default logic, the two approaches now have much in common.

12. The notation we are using only talks about the beliefs of the person addressed by an utterance. In fact, the ABELs apply much more generally to any person observing the utterance. We could change the argument to ATTEND to be this observer, but leave the argument to UTTER and SINCERE as before to be the person addressed. For simplicity, we will not pursue this generalization here.

13. Notice that spkr and addr are free variables in the axiom and are intended to be captured by the definition of ⇒.

14. Just how speakers make that true is an interesting issue, related to politeness, mitigation, uses of "please," tone of voice, and so on, but it is not an issue we can address here.

15. We are indebted to Ray Perrault for this example.

16. A more general version of ATTEMPT would include an extra propositional argument that would be used as a third argument to INTEND to indicate under what condition the commitment to producing q could be dropped.

17. A more general version of REQUEST would include an additional argument specifying other conditions that would allow the hearer to drop his intention to do the requested action.

18. Of course, the formalism also allows the speaker to give up his attempt if he thinks nothing he can do will make the transmission of his desires any more successful.

19. Note that the speaker's intentions would be clear if he said "Open the door, please" or "Open the door, Private."

20. Of course, various social and institutional consequences could follow from the fact that the speaker did not completely perform a given illocutionary act, but that involves additional stipulations about the institutional and social realm of interaction that we are not addressing.

21. Searle 1969, 66. Emphasis is ours. This condition is not present in Searle and Vanderveken 1985.

22. Hence, the sincerity of an illocutionary act is independent of the sincerity of an utterance. So, this analysis predicts that an ironic utterance can be a sincere request. For example, "It *sure* is cold in here" could be a sincere request to open a window, if the speaker in fact wants the window opened, or could be insincere request to do so if the speaker in fact wants the hearer to receive an electrical shock from touching the window.

23. Searle and Vanderveken (1985) claim illocutionary point determines the rest of the dimensions:

> All general propositional content, general preparatory, and general sincerity conditions are determined by its illocutionary point. The sense in which they are determined is simply that one cannot achieve that illocutionary point without presupposing these preparatory conditions, without expressing these sincerity conditions, and without expressing a proposition satisfying those propositional content conditions (p. 50)

We agree, and our work can thus be regarded as a formal theory in support of that claim.

References

Allen, J. F. (1979). *A plan-based approach to speech act recognition.* Technical Report 121, Department of Computer Science, University of Toronto, Toronto, Ont.

Allen, J. F., and C. R. Perrault (1980). Analyzing intention utterances. *Artifical Intelligence* 15, 143–178.

Appelt, D. (1985). *Planning English sentences.* Cambridge: Cambridge University Press.

Austin, J. L. (1962). *How to do things with words.* Oxford: Oxford University Press.

Bach, K., and R. Harnish (1979). *Linguistic communication and speech acts.* Cambridge, MA: MIT Press.

Barwise, J. (1988). Three views of common knowledge. In M. Vardi, ed., *Proceedings of the Second Conference on Reasoning about Knowledge.* Los Altos, CA: Morgan Kaufmann.

Brachman, R., R. Bobrow, P. Cohen, J. Klovstad, B. L. Webber, and W. A. Woods (1979). Research in natural language understanding. Technical Report 4274, Bolt Beranek and Newman, Inc., Cambridge, MA.

Bratman, M. (1984). Two faces of intention. *The Philosophical Review* 93, 375–405.

Bratman, M. (1987). *Intention, plans, and practical reason.* Cambridge, MA: Harvard University Press.

Clark, H. H. and C. R. Marshall (1981). Definite reference and mutual knowledge. In A. K. Joshi, B. Webber, and I. A. Sag, eds., *Elements of discourse understanding.* Cambridge: Cambridge University Press.

Cohen, P. R. (1979). Chapter 5: The pragmatics/discourse component, research in natural language understanding. Technical Report 4274, Bolt Beranek and Newman, Inc., Cambridge, MA.

Cohen, P. R. (1984). The pragmatics of referring and the modality of communication. *Computational Linguistics* 10, 97–146.

Cohen, P. R., and H. J. Levesque (1980). Speech acts and the recognition of shared plans. In *Proceedings of the Third Biennial Conference,* Canadian Society for Computational Studies of Intelligence, Victoria, B.C.

Cohen, P. R., and H. J. Levesque (1985). Speech acts and rationality. In *Proceedings of the Twenty-third Annual Meeting.* Association for Computational Linguistics, Chicago, IL.

Cohen, P. R., and H. J. Levesque (1990a). Intention is choice with commitment. *Artificial Intelligence* 42.3.

Cohen, P. R., and H. J. Levesque (1990b). Performatives in a rationally-based speech act theory. In *Proceedings of the Twenty-eighth Meeting.* Association for Computational Linguistics, Pittsburgh.

Davidson, D. (1968). Actions, reasons, and causes. In A. R. White, ed., *The philosophy of action.* Oxford: Oxford University Press.

Goldman, A. I. (1970). *A theory of human action.* Princeton, NJ: Princeton University Press.

Gordon, D., and G. Lakoff (1971). Conversational postulates. In *Papers from the Seventh Regional Meeting,* Chicago Linguistic Society, Chicago, IL.

Grice, H. P. Meaning. *Philosophical Review* 66, 377–388.

Grice, H. P. (1969). Utterer's meaning and intentions. *The Philosophical Review* 78, 147–177.

Grice, H. P. (1975). Logic and conversation. In P. Cole and J. Morgan, eds., *Syntax and semantics 3: Speech acts.* New York: Academic Press. Also in D. Davidson and G. Harman, eds. (1975). *The logic of grammar.* Encino, CA: Dickenson.

Grosz, B. J., and C. L. Sidner (1985). Discourse structure and the proper treatment of interruptions. In *Proceedings of the Ninth International Joint Conference on Artificial Intelligence,* Los Angeles, CA.

Grosz, B. J., and C. L. Sidner (1986). Attention, intentions, and the structure of discourse. *Computational Linguistics* 12, 175–204.

Perrault, C. R., and J. F. Allen (1980). A plan-based analysis of indirect speech acts. *American Journal of Computational Linguistics* 6, 167–182.

Perrault, C. R., and P. R. Cohen (1981). It's for your own good: A note on inaccurate reference. In A. K. Joshi, B. Webber, and I. A. Sag, eds., *Elements of discourse understanding*. Cambridge: Cambridge University Press. Also appears as Technical Report 4273, Bolt Beranek and Newman, Inc., Cambridge, MA, July, 1981.

Pollack, M. E. (1986). A model of plan inference that distinguishes between the beliefs of actors and observers. In *Proceedings of the Twenty-fourth Annual Meeing*, Association for Computational Linguistics, New York, NY. Reprinted in M. Georgeff and A. Lansky, eds., *Reasoning about actions and plans: Proceedings of the 1986 workshop*. Los Altos, CA: Morgan Kaufmann.

Sadock, J. (1984). *Toward a linguistic theory of speech acts*. New York: Academic Press.

Searle, J. R. (1969). *Speech acts: An essay in the philosophy of language*. Cambridge: Cambridge University Press.

Searle, J. R. (1971). Introduction. In J. R. Searle, ed., *The philosophy of language*. London: Oxford University Press.

Searle, J. R. (1975). Indirect speech acts. In P. Cole and J. Morgan, eds., *Syntax and semantics 3: Speech acts*. New York: Academic Press.

Searle, J. R. (1983). *Intentionality: An essay in the philosophy of mind*. New York: Cambridge University Press.

Searle, J. R., and D. Vanderveken (1985). *Foundations of illocutionary logic*. New York: Cambridge University Press.

Strawson, F. (1964). Intention and convention in speech acts. *The Philosophical Review* 73, 439–460. Reprinted in J. R. Searle, ed. (1971). *The philosophy of language*. London: Oxford University Press.

Winograd, T., and F. Flores (1986). *Understanding computers and cognition: A new foundation for design*. Norwood, NJ: Ablex.

Chapter 13

Comments on Vanderveken and on Cohen and Levesque

Jerrold M. Sadock

---

1 Introduction

Speech act theory is concerned with providing an account of the fact that the use of expressions of natural language in context invariably involves the accomplishment of certain actions beyond the mere uttering (or writing, or telegraphing) itself. The context and the form of the utterance both enter into the equation. Holding the context constant and varying the utterance changes the accomplishments, and likewise holding the utterance constant and varying the context generally has profound effects on the actions that are performed.

The expressions of natural language have meanings and these meanings mediate the connection between utterance and action. The action that we perform in using language clearly depend to a large extent on what we say, not just on how we say it. Therefore, the job of speech act theory is to make explicit the connections in diagram (1),[1] providing a theory of how the form of the utterance is associated with its content and a theory of how it is that the use of a form with a certain content has certain effects in context. The first theory is part of the theory of grammar, the second a part of the general theory of rational behavior, normally called "pragmatics" in the linguistic literature.

$$(1) \quad \text{FORM} \underset{\text{grammar}}{\longleftrightarrow} \text{CONTENT} \underset{\text{pragmatics}}{\longleftrightarrow} \text{EFFECT}$$

Now these two tasks are intimately related. A theory of speech acts must cover the entire space between utterance form and utterance effect. It therefore would seem that the wrong theory of the connection between form and content should make it difficult or impossible to come up with a reasonable theory of the connection between content and effect, and vice versa. Unfortunately for speech act theorists, this fact is not espceially helpful in discriminating between alternative views of how language does what it does because of the fact that most of the things that we can do with words can be done by uttering *any* words, given the right context. The connection between content and form has to be loose enough to allow, in principle, the use of any content to have any effect. (The only exception is that there are certain sorts of ritual actions—like sentencing a defendant to ninety days in Monterey, starting the Indianapolis car race, pronouncing Sam and Janet man and wife, or christening a child Theophilus—whose accomplishment is stipulated by some social authority as requiring the saying of certain words (Strawson 1971; Morgan 1978).)

The truth of this claim was recently proven scientifically at the University of Chicago Linguistics Department's annual holiday called Goodspeed Day. As part of the proceedings, Nancy Dray and William Eilfort conducted the following experiment: A group of approximately twenty subjects were asked to fill out two index cards each. On a colored card they were to write any sentence of English and on a white one they were to indicate an effect of the kind that could be brought about by uttering a sentence of English. The cards were then collected, the colored cards placed in one hat, and the white cards in another. Ms. Dray then picked a colored card at random and read it to the participants, and Mr. Eilfort did the same with a white card. Volunteers were now asked to provide a context in which the uttering of the sentences that Ms. Dray had read could accomplish the act that appeared on the card that Mr. Eilfort had read.

There was only one case where the participants failed to find a context that did the trick, and that was—predictably—one where the intended effect (the christening of a battleship) was of the kind that can only be accomplished by adhering to a prescribed ritual. In every other case it was a fairly trivial matter to think of a context that worked, and in several cases more than one kind of context was easily found. In fact, the task was so easy that, contrary to the expectations of the experimenters, this endeavor was not a lot of fun. The juxtaposition of the utterance and the suggested effect was often amusing, but the quest for a context connecting the two was not challenging enough to be very interesting. By the time the last pair of cards drawn (utterance: "Was it as good for you as it was for me?"; effect: an apology for having removed the gallbladder from the wrong patient) it was obvious that every participant had a private solution, so no volunteers were even called for.

What makes the speech act game so trivial, and speech act theory so open-ended, is the fact that language does not function directly, by convention or by magic. As emphasized by Cohen and Levesque, speakers are rational and are ordinarily assumed to be behaving rationally in their choice of linguistic action. A speaker chooses the form he utters from among the infinitely many that the language provides. A hearer must then decide why the speaker has chosen just this form, and not any of the others, on this particular occasion, and the original speaker knows that the addressee will do this at the time he formulates his utterance. One of the most important considerations in the choice of a form to speak is, to be sure, the conventional content of that form, but that is by no means the only consideration.

The point is nicely illustrated by the following joke told to me by Howard Stein of the Philosophy Department of the University of Chicago:[2]

> Two peddlers meet on the day of the fair.
> "So tell me, are you going to Lvov or to Bialystock?"
> "I'm going to Lvov."
> "You say you're going to Lvov, because you want me to think that you're going to Bialystock. But if you want me to think you're going to Bialystock, then you must be going to Lvov. So why do you lie to me?"

So speech act theory as described above is too easy. The connection between content and achieved effect is just too lax to provide a useful measure of the success of one theory versus another. Regardless of what content one assigns to a particular form, one will always be able to provide a more or less plausible chain of steps that will connect the postulated meaning with the predicated result. We need to bring other considerations to bear in comparing theories that propose to explain how language is used to accomplish what it does.

2 The Meaning of Force

A number of formal features of uttered sentences play a fairly direct role in determining what effects the utterance will bring off. The formal differences between a declarative sentence and its interrogative counterpart clearly play a role in determining what acts a speaker brings off.[3] Likewise, the choice of the verb in a performative formula has a powerful influence on the effect of a contextualized utterance. This much is banal. Where controversy arises is in the theory of how the markers of sentence type, as Zwicky and I (Sadock and Zwicky 1985) have dubbed them, contribute to the effects that utterances can achieve. Here we encounter important differences of opinion in the literature, and in particular between Vanderveken's theory (V) and Cohen and Levesque's (C&L).

3 V's and C&L's Theories Compared

For V, features of the sentence determine the illocutionary force (IF) of the sentence, where IF is a complex, six-dimensional notion, borrowed from Searle 1975. For C&L, the postulated meaning of the sentence form that enters directly into the calculation of the effect of the utterance is much simpler: "Utterance mood conveys a speaker's mental state" (section 4.1).

Now though these two views contrast in many ways, there are a few points on which they agree. First of all, V tell us that IF lies outside of truth-conditional semantics. He constructs an elaborate auxiliary semantics of success-conditions to supplement the old-fashioned variety that deals in truth-conditions. C&L are not very informative on how exactly it is that utterance mood manages to convey mental states, but from the tone of the paper I gather that this is a matter of convention, as in V's paper, and likewise not a matter of ordinary truth-conditional semantics.

Inasmuch as the two theories differ on how much content the indicators of sentence type convey, they appear to be quite different indeed. Much of what is stipulated as part of IF in V's paper is derived by means of reasoning strategies in C&L's. The arrow labeled "grammar" in (1) is longer for V than it is for C&L, but their pragmatic workload is correspondingly greater.

However, things are not as different as they might seem. V recognizes that there is a good deal of redundancy (a dismaying amount, I think) among the six dimensions of meaning into which IFs are dissected. He tells us that one particular dimension, illocutionary point, determines much of the structure of an IF on the other five dimensions. Thus, V implicitly recognizes the existence of unstated axioms that allow us to work out these redundancies and that working out must take the form of a series of inferential steps, just as it does in C&L's paper.

4 Discussion

Neither of these points of agreement is necessarily correct. Some or all of IF could conceivably be a matter of truth-conditions (or derived from it). Alternatively, some or all of IF could be nonconventional. On the first point, it is worth noticing that both papers choose to analyze performative utterances as assertions. You promise, christen, apologize, and so on, by saying you do. Thus, the main illocutionary effect of this kind of utterance is in fact brought off at least partly through the ordinary truth-conditional logic. This would work in the other cases as well. There is no a priori reason why the particular grammatical features that mark interrogative sentences could not be connected with truth-conditional content as is done under the performative hypothesis. Word order is directly connected with truth-conditions in the determination of subject and object in languages like English, so why could word order, verbal mood, and other nonlexical features of an utterance that mark sentence type not be truth-conditional as well?

As to the matter of conventionality, my previous observation concerning the necessary power of a pragmatic theory again becomes relevant. As C&L amply demonstrate (and as Levinson (1983, 241) briefly pointed out), much of the effect of an utterance can be derived from a germ of content, coupled with assumptions of rationality, sincerity, and cooperativeness on the parts of the participants in the utterance scene. Indeed, it is possible to give a plausible account of the effect of at least some sentence types without assigning any special, illocutionarily relevant content to the type. The most likely candidate for such an analysis, is, of course, the declarative sentence, which could be taken as a "pure" proposition, devoid of any special signs of its assertivity.[4]

On this view there would be a rational rather than a conventional explanation for the frequent use of declarative sentences as assertions. It would go something like this:

> S has uttered a sentence whose meaning is just the proposition P. I believe that he is making a relevant contribution to the conversation. Now the truth of P is clearly relevant in the present circumstances. So in uttering a sentence that means P, S must be trying to get me to believe that P is true; otherwise, he would not have made this utterance but instead would have made either some other utterance or none at all.

In this way one could go much farther than even C&L in explaining the acts achieved by uttering forms of language in entirely nonconventional terms, that is, as functions of rational interaction. But the question is not whether we can do this; we already know we can. Rather, the question is whether we should, and here again other considerations must be brought to bear to decide the issue.

5 Fit with Sentence Type

Arnold Zwicky and I (Sadock and Zwicky 1985) studied the distribution of sentence types, and the formal indicators thereof, in a number of different languages. We found that every language in our sample distinguishes at least a declarative type used (among other things) for making statements, an interrogative type used (among other things) for asking yes-no questions, and an imperative type used (again, among other things) for making requests. Many languages also distinguish, in a parallel fashion, other sentence types (for instance, prohibitives, optatives, exclamatives, promissories, precatives (for curses), and so on). But the three basic sentence types are so common that one would hope that a theory of the content of IF would at least be compatible with these linguistic facts, if not suggest an account of them. I don't find either of the two theories under consideration here particularly enlightening on that score.

According to V, there are five primitive illocutionary points, exactly the five proposed in Searle 1975. V also mentions in the introduction to his paper that there are (quite coincidentally) five sentence types that linguists recognize in English and in "most actual natural languages." But there is a

Table 13.1

Illocutionary point	Sentence type
Assertive	declarative
Commissive	?
Directive	imperative
	interrogative
Declarative	?
Expressive	exclamatory
?	optative

Table 13.2

Point	D.O.F.	Sentence type
Assertive	words-to-world	declarative
Commissive	world-to-words	
Directive		imperative
		interrogative
Declarative	double	?
Expressive	empty	exclamatory
	?	optative

disturbing lack of correspondence between the two sets of five (see table 13.1).

Only two of the five illocutionary points stand in a one-to-one relation with the sentence types, and one of these, the exclamatory, is not among the most frequent types. One of the very most frequent types, the interrogative, is lumped together with the imperative, though these are always distinct in natural languages. Two of the primitive illocutionary points, the commissive and the directive, are not recognized in English. I doubt, in fact, that there is any language on earth that has a sentence type corresponding to the directive point, that is, a special syntactic form used only for performative sentences. In languages that have performatives—and not even all do—the performative is always formally indistinguishable from the declarative.

There is another dimension of meaning for IF that V seems to consider very important, namely, "direction of fit."[5] But direction of fit fails to match one-to-one either with the primitive points or with the common sentence types, since there are only four directions of fit (see table 13.2).

I cannot criticize C&L for failing to achieve a match between the atoms of their features of mood and the sentence types that natural languages actually present, because there is no suggested inventory of such atoms in their work. Simply saying that sentence mood (read: sentence type) "conveys a speaker's mental state" leaves open how many such states can be so conveyed, whether such states are all relatively simple ones, such as belief or intention, or whether they can be complex and have internal structure, and so on.

Suffice it to say that neither of these papers provides a classification of illocutions that comes very close to modeling the way natural languages treat them in their grammars.[6]

6 Toward a Linguistically Significant Decomposition

I will suggest a position intermediate between those of V and C&L in terms of the amount of structure that we find in the IFs of natural language. I would like to urge the view that the complete speech act has three separate, simultaneous functions: a representational function, an expressive function, and a social function. Taking these three dimensions as definitional of illocutionary acts gives us a classification that is at once truer to the grammatical facts of natural language and more elegant than what we find in existing decompositions.

I believe that something like this view of the structure of speech acts is foreshadowed in Frege 1892; something close is also found in Hare 1970.[7] What is interesting for present purposes is that it also emerges from an examination of the inconsistencies within and between the views of V and C&L.

6.1 The Representational Function

The illocutionary point of the assertive type, according to V, "consists in representing as actual a state of affairs" (section 1.3). But, following Searle 1975, V also tell us that other illocutionary types are subject to a "propositional content condition." The recognition of propositional content as an aspect of all normal uses of language echoes Austin's notion that every genuine speech act has a locutionary component, not just those that vouch for the truth of the representation. When one asks a yes-no question, one represents the world as one way or another and asks which of those representations is correct. In fact, it is stretching things to say that the point of an assertoric speech act is to represent a state of affairs as "actual," since the state of affairs in question would have to include the possibility of some state of affairs, the falsity of a state of affairs, and so on. The point of an utterance like "Bill might have left" is not, pace V, to represent as actual the possibility of Bill's having left but—more directly—to represent his having left as possible.

6.2 The Expressive Function

C&L propose that the expression of a propositional attitude be taken as the kernel of content of all sentence types. Now one of V's basic illocutionary points, namely, the expressive, "consists in expressing propositional attitudes of the speaker about a state of affairs" (section 1.3). But V also recognizes an expressive aspect to other illocutions in the form of the sincerity conditions that they are subject to, in virtue of which "the speaker ... expresses psychological states ... about the state of affairs represented by the propositional content" (section 1.3). The conveying of a mental state or propositional attitude is thus a part of every IF, according to V. The expressive class of IFs have this as their basic point, but all (other?) IFs do the same thing through their sincerity conditions. So both papers in fact agree, and agree with me, in assuming an expressive dimension to every normal speech act.

6.3 The Social Function

Finally, let us examine the most complex dimension of the illocutionary act, namely, its power to modify social commitments. C&L endorse Winograd and Flores's (1986) observation that conversation implies commitment, hinting that any normal act of speech has a contractual, social aspect. But the making of a commitment is the illocutionary point of only one of V's five basic points, namely, the commissive type, in which the social obligation is the speaker's.

In considering the social aspect of speech acts, it is important to distinguish whether it is the speaker, the addressee, or others upon whom the speech act imposes, or from whom it discharges, societal obligations. In a promise, a speaker obligation is created; in a question or request, a social burden is placed on the shoulders of the addressee; and in the typical formal performative, an onus is placed upon the society at large.

Pursuing this last idea, let us consider V's (and Searle's (1975)) "declarative" point.[8] According to V, the declarative point "consists in performing an action that brings about a state of affairs ... by representing oneself as performing that action" (section 1.3). Now this is a very peculiar "point," since it includes not only a point (bringing about a state of affairs) but also the manner in which that point is accomplished. This latter is the "mode of achievement" dimension for all other illocutionary points that V recognizes. Furthermore, because the declarative point must be accomplished by representing something, it can only be accomplished by a literal act of the assertive kind, that being the only point that represents the world in a certain way. So it is no accident that English does not have a sentence type corresponding to the declarative point: it could not have. All performative sentences in this theory are necessarily doubly indirect; they are literal assertions, which therefore have a declarative point, which therefore do what the verb says. This strikes me as being a little like determining how many cows are in a pasture by counting the legs and dividing by four.[9]

The problem is that V could not have said that the declarative point consists in simply bringing about a state of affairs, for Austin (1962) taught us that all genuine speech acts have an illocutionary aspect, as well as the locutionary aspect mentioned above. They all bring about some state of affairs and are intended to do so. (See also C&L's remark (section 5) that all illocutionary acts be defined as attempts.)[10]

It is possible that in speaking of performatives as bringing about a state of affairs, V had in mind the sort of point that Austin's paradigm performatives have, namely, the bringing about of a state of affairs that places social burdens on nonparticipants in the speech act. When I christen my boat "*Kreplach*," everyone must call it *Kreplach*, not just those present at the christening. But the creation of a socially defined state of affairs is just as much a part of the assertoric, commissive, and directive speech acts as it is of typical performatives. It is just that the obligations in the case of these mundane types are more personal, extending no further than to the participants in the speech situation. It is because of their power to affect others that the more formal types—christening, sentencing, pronouncing man and wife, and so on—generally require special authority. But any speaker in a conversational exchange receives the mandate to ask questions, make promises and requests, and the like, just in virtue of the voluntary participation of his interlocutor(s).

6.4 *The Classification of Illocutionary Acts*

The remarkable result of all of this is to turn the kind of decomposition that we find in V's paper on its ear. V's five illocutionary points, horizontal values on one of six dimensions of the meaning of illocutions, turn out to be found in one form or another in all the illocutionary types and can therefore be viewed as the classificatory dimensions themselves. Where V has an assertive point, we find a representational dimension. Where he has an expressive point, we see an expressive dimension. And where he has commissive, directive, and declarative points, we note a socio-contractual dimension, with subdimensions regarding whether obligations accrue to the speaker, the addressee, or others. A speech act can simultaneously make some representation of the world, establish or discharge social obligations, and express speaker attitudes ("mental states"), and it normally does all of these things at the same time.

Let us take the act of assertion, for example. Such an act involves representing a state of affairs as obtaining in real world—that is, as true. It commits the speaker to behave as if that state of affairs existed, putting him on the conversational record as certifying the proposition. On the expressive level, the standard assertion expresses the speaker's belief in the truth of the proposition.

But statements can express other attitudes than belief. Hearsay reports express uncertainty and eyewitness accounts express knowledge. Indeed, many languages (for instance, the Siouan language Hidatsa) have no single sentence type corresponding to our declarative and covering the same range of illocutionary acts but divide the assertoric speech acts among several types that differ with regard to the speaker's attitude toward the representation of the world that the utterance makes.

Consider next exclamations, a kind of speech act that poses problems for both V and C&L. V says that for exclamations "... there is no question of success or failure of fit' and their propositional content is in general presupposed to be true" (section 1.3). But this is false. A speaker certainly represents the world (his world) as being a certain way when uttering an exclamation. It is not presupposed to be that way in any known sense of that word. To quote Jerry Morgan when I made an almost identical claim some years back: Boy, are you wrong! C&L, flatly contradicting V, take exclamations to be assertoric and thus to represent some state of affairs as actual, but they claim that what is asserted is that the speaker is in a certain mental state. This too seems wrong. If I say "I am delighted that the weather is so nice here," I really do presuppose (in the pragmatic sense of Stalnaker (1977)) that the weather is nice here. It would be odd for me to say this on a long-distance telephone call if it had not already been established that the weather is nice where I am. But there would be nothing wrong with my announcing this fact to you by saying "Is the weather ever nice here!"

Exclamations, then, represent the world as being a certain way[11] and commit the speaker to behave as if that representation is true, just as assertions do. In what way do they then differ from assertions? Obviously in their value on the expressive plane. Exclamations express not merely belief, but also reactions such as pleasure, disgust, or astonishment.

I turn next to questions. These, I claim, represent the world as a set of alternatives, either a state or its contradiction ("Did he leave (or not)?"), as two different states ("Did he leave, or is he just hiding?"), or as an open-ended set of alternatives described by quantification ("Which books by Chomsky has he read?"). On the representational plane, then, questions do not constitute a uniform class, and for this reason most languages distinguish them formally. Most of the languages Zwicky and I studied differentiated yes-no questions from the others via intonation, as does English. Questions are alike, however, in obligating the addressee to respond and in expressing curiosity. Some languages do have a formal feature that is common to all question types, a sentence particle or verbal mood, for example.

By now it should be obvious what the analysis of requests will look like. They present a picture of the world as unrealized (that is, false). They oblige the addressee to make that state of affairs true, and they express the speaker's desire that this should be the case. Prohibitions are distinct from positive requests, according to this scheme. Though resembling ordinary

Table 13.3

Dimension	Act type		
	Assertion	*Question*	*Request*
Represent	T	T or F	F
Oblige			
Speaker	accept p	——	——
Addressee	——*	answer	cause p
Others	——	——	——
Express	belief	curiosity	desire

*Different sorts of assertoric speech acts place different burdens on the addressee. A response to a question in a court of law, for example, simply commits the speaker to the truth of his statement. It places no responsibilities upon the judge or jury to accept its veracity. A confession of guilt, on the other hand, more or less automatically counts as true for all parties concerned.

requests in terms of the representational and expressive levels, they oblige the addressee to refrain from acting, instead of requiring action. More languages than not have a special "vetative" (Sadock and Zwicky 1985) form for issuing prohibitions. It is perhaps the fourth most common sentence type. These results are summarized in table 13.3.

We get from this table a sense of why it is that most languages show a fundamental sentence-type division reflecting at least these three classes.

1. The contrasts that they display on all three dimensions are just about maximal. Like the three cardinal vowels [i], [u], and [a], these three speech act types are as different in all dimensions as they could be.

2. The three classes of speech acts correspond to natural but nonobligatory associations of properties on the three levels. There is a natural association between an expression of curiosity and an obligation for the addressee to supply information that is given by some general principle of helpfulness, such as the one discussed in C&L. But this association is not perfect in either direction. A census taker asks questions but does not (or is not supposed to) express curiosity. When I say to my wife "I wonder what I did with my glasses," I express curiosity but do not obligate her to enlighten me.

Still, the naturalness of the connections among the values of the various dimensions for the three most frequently grammaticized illocutionary types is obvious.

3. The properties of each basic speech act type are simple properties. This is especially striking in the case of the expressive content, where three of the most fundamental propositional attitudes—belief, curiosity, and desire—are found. There is also an impressive straightforwardness on the representational level, where we find all of the simple and binary formulae that are allowed by the Law of the Excluded Middle.

4. None of the basic types deal in nonparticipant obligations and therefore none of them require the speaker-performer to have any special status.

7 Summary and Conclusions

Some inconsistencies and insufficiencies in the papers of V and C&L have led me sketch out a new scheme for understanding the structure of and relationships among illocutionary acts. This scheme is based upon the three fundamental powers that combine in human language: the ability to represent the world, the ability to alter society, and the ability to express emotions. My argument for this new way of looking at things is based largely on its greater ability to give a plausible account of the forms of language than do existing views, but it is also less redundant, more consistent, and much better motivated than its predecessors.

If I have overstepped my authority as commentator in doing something considerably more ambitious than critiquing these two papers, there is only one explanation: the papers were stimulating and challenging enough to demand this sort of response.

Notes

1. The form itself can have a direct effect on the achievements of an utterance act, but I ignore that important fact in what follows.
2. This appears in a slightly different form in Sadock 1986. The joke is significant enough for speech act theory that it bears repeating.
3. The effect may not be what the form directly dicates, but the form will still be instrumental in determining the effect. For example, the interrogative sentence "Is the Pope Catholic?" ordinarily amounts to positive answer to a preceding question, whereas the corresponding assertion in such a context would have a different effect.
4. This is in fact the traditional position that appears explicitly in Katz and Postal 1964. Ross (1970) is responsible for popularizing the Austinian view that all sentences, including declaratives, be analyzed as including grammatical markers of their illocutionary status. Cresswell (1973) argues for the readoption of the traditional view that declaratives have no formal indicator of their assertoric effect.
5. In a confusing section V writes, "Illocutionary point is the principal component of an illocutionary force because it determines the direction of fit of utterances with that force.... One can justify the completeness of this classification ... by noting that these five illocutionary points exhaust the different possible directions of fit between language and the world" (section 1.3). Since any number of illocutionary points equal to or greater than four could exhaust the four directions of fit, this does not seem like much of a justification for these five illocutionary points.
6. A similar point is made by Zaefferer 1983 and in ongoing dissertation research by William Eilfort (see Eilfort 1989 for preliminary results.)
7. Frege distinguishes the subjective (that is, expressive) dimension of a sign as the "idea" of it. He further distinguishes the purely representational aspect of a declarative sentence as the "thought," while using a third word, "judgment," for the admission of the truth of that sign. Thus, he distinguishes, as do I, among an expressive, a prepresentational, and a social aspect of the whole sign. Hare's three-way distinction among the

phrastic, tropic, and neustic features of languages can also be seen as aimed at something like the same division.

8. This is, of course, not to be confused with the assertoric point of declarative sentences.

9. There is a further problem with this theory of performative sentences that is shared with C&L's. If we perform performatives by representing ourselves as doing so, why do both "I am promising to leave" and "I represent myself as promising to leave" both fail as promises, while succeeding admirably as representations of what is being done? This objection might, I realize, be tossed off as a quibble since it deals with mere facts, but I consider it important nonetheless.

10. I am not sure how this point of view squares with C&L's notion that sentence mood expresses mental states. If they are saying that all illocutionary acts both express an attitude and are intended to count as creating a social fact, I agree with them fully.

11. There might also be nonrepresentational exclamations like "Wow!" or "Phew!" that consist of pure expression, without propositional content.

References

Austin, J. L. (1962). *How to do things with words.* Oxford: Oxford University Press.

Cresswell, M. J. (1973). *Logics and languages.* London: Methuen.

Eilfort, William (1989). The illocutionary module. Paper presented at the Workshop on Autolexical Syntax, University of Chicago, Chicago, IL, April 16, 1989.

Frege, Gottlob (1892). Über Sinn und Bedeutung. *Zeitschrift für Philosophie und philosophishce Kritik* 100, 25–50. Translated as On sense and reference. In P. Geach and M. Black, eds. (1952). *Translations from the philosophical writings of Gottlob Frege.* Oxford: Basil Blackwell. Also in D. Davidson and G. Harman, eds. (1975). *The logic of grammar.* Encino, CA: Dickenson.

Hare, R. M. (1970). Meaning and speech acts. *The Philosophical Review* 79, 3–24. Reprinted in R. M. Hare (1971). *Practical inferences.* London: Macmillan.

Katz, Jerrold J., and Paul M. Postal (1964). *An integrated theory of linguistic descriptions.* Cambridge, MA: MIT Press.

Levinson, Stephen C. (1983). *Pragmatics.* Cambridge: Cambridge University Press.

Morgan, J. L. (1978). Two types of convention in indirect speech acts. In Peter Cole, ed., *Syntax and semantics 9: Pragmatics.* New York: Academic Press.

Ross, John Robert (1970). On declarative sentences. In Roderick A. Jacobs and Peter S. Rosenbaum, eds., *Readings in English transformational grammar.* Waltham, MA: Ginn.

Sadock, Jerrold M. (1986). Remarks on the paper by Deirdre Wilson and Dan Sperber. In *Papers from the Twenty-second Regional Meeting, Part 2,* Chicago Linguistic Society, Chicago, IL.

Sadock, Jerrold M., and Arnold M. Zwicky (1985). Speech act distinctions in syntax. In Timothy Shopen, ed., *Language typology and syntactic description I: Clause structure.* Cambridge: Cambridge University Press.

Searle, John R. (1975). A taxonomy of illocutionary acts. In Keith Gunderson, ed., *Language, mind, and knowledge: Minnesota Studies in the Philosophy of Science, Vol. 7.* Minneapolis, MN: University of Minnesota Press. Reprinted in John R. Searle (1979). *Expression and meaning: Studies in the theory of speech acts.* Cambridge: Cambridge University Press.

Stalnaker, Robert (1977). Pragmatic presuppositions. In Andy Rogers, Bob Wall, and John P. Murphy, eds., *Proceedings of the Texas Conference on Performatives, Presuppositions, and Implicatures.* Arlington, VA: Center for Applied Linguistics.

Strawson, P. F. (1971). Intention and convention in speech acts. In J. R. Searle, ed., *The philosophy of language.* London: Oxford University Press. Originally published in *The Philosophical Review* 73 (1964), 439–460.

Winograd, Terry, and Fernando Flores (1986). *Understanding computers and cognition: A new foundation for design*. Norwood, NJ: Ablex.

Zaeferer, Dietmar (1983). The semantics of sentence mood in typologically differing languages. In S. Hattori, ed., *Proceedings of the Thirteenth International Congress of Linguists*. August 29–September 4, 1982, Tokyo.

Chapter 14

The Meaning of Intonational Contours in the Interpretation of Discourse

Janet Pierrehumbert and Julia Hirschberg

1 Introduction

Recent investigations of the contribution that intonation makes to overall utterance and discourse interpretation promise new sources of information for the investigation of long-time concerns in natural-language processing. In Hirschberg and Pierrehumbert 1986 we proposed that intonational features such as *phrasing, accent placement, pitch range,* and *tune* represent important sources of information about the *attentional* and the *intentional* structures of discourse.[1] In this paper we examine the particular contribution of choice of tune, or *intonational contour,* to discourse interpretation. In particular, we propose that a speaker (S) chooses a particular tune to convey a particular relationship between an utterance, currently perceived beliefs of a hearer or hearers (H), and anticipated contributions of subsequent utterances. We claim that these relationships are compositional—composed from the *pitch accents, phrase accents,* and *boundary tones* that make up tunes. We further propose that the different aspects of tune meaning can be associated with different phonological domains. We assume the *intonational phrase* as our primary unit of meaning analysis.

In the following discussion we put forward a first approximation of a compositional theory of tune interpretation, together with the phonological assumptions on which it is based and the evidence from which we have drawn our proposals. We assume Pierrehumbert's (Pierrehumbert 1980; Beckman and Pierrehumbert 1986a) theory of intonational description, which we describe in sections 2–3. In section 4 we present our general approach to intonational meaning. In sections 5–7 we present the data upon which we base this account. In section 8 we explore avenues of further development for the theory and discuss implications for the study of discourse.

2 Dimensions of Intonational Variation

2.1 Preliminaries

In describing intonation patterns, we distinguish *stress, tune, phrasing,* and *pitch range. Stress* refers to the rhythmic pattern or relative prominence of syllables in an utterance. *Tune* is the abstract source of fundamental frequency patterns—the difference between a typical declarative intonation and a question intonation is a tune difference. English has a very rich tune system, as the reader can appreciate by producing a monosyllable with many different intonation patterns. *Phrasing* refers to how a complex utterance is divided up. Each *intonational phrase* provides an opportunity for a new choice of tune, and as we will show, some parts of the tune serve to mark the *phrase boundaries*. Phrase boundaries are also indicated by the *duration* pattern and by pausing. *Pitch range* controls the graph paper on which the tunes are realized. One may increase one's pitch range for many reasons—for example, to project one's voice or to highlight the information in a particular phrase.

2.2 Stress

The *stress pattern* of an utterance is the pattern of relative prominence of the syllables. Word stress is assigned by lexical-phonological rules. Stress within the phrase is affected by considerations of information structure. For example, the following sentence would usually be produced with the main phrasal stress (the *nuclear stress*) on the word *vitamins*:

(1)   Legumes are a good source of VITAMINS.

However, the nuclear stress would fall on *good* in a context where *sources of vitamins* are already under discussion, as in (2):

(2)   A: Legumes are a pretty poor source of vitamins.
       B: No. Legumes are a GOOD source of vitamins.

Stress manifests itself in the duration, amplitude, and spectral characteristics of the speech segments. In general, syllables with greater stress are more fully articulated than syllables with less stress. Stress pattern is independent of tune, in the sense that a given tune can be applied to materials with many different stress patterns and a given stress pattern can be produced with many different tunes. For example, (1) can be produced either with a falling-rising fundamental frequency (f_0) pattern on *vitamins* or with a rising pattern. These two possibilities are illustrated by the f_0 contours in figures 14.1 and 14.2.

Either pattern can also be applied to the same sentence when the nuclear stress is shifted to *good*, as in (2). Figures 14.3 and 14.4 show the two outcomes in this case.

2.3 Tune and Phrasing

In Pierrehumbert's system of intonational description, tunes are described as sequences of *low* (**L**) and *high* (**H**) tones, which determines the shape of the f_0 contour. Some of these tones (the ones participating in pitch accents)

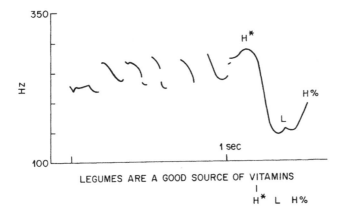

Figure 14.1
Falling-rising pattern on *vitamins*. Reprinted from Pierrehumbert 1980.

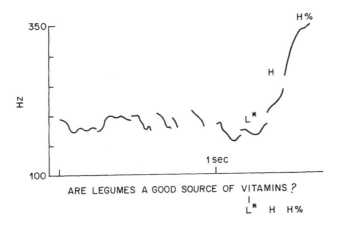

Figure 14.2
Rising pattern on *vitamins*. Reprinted from Pierrehumbert 1980.

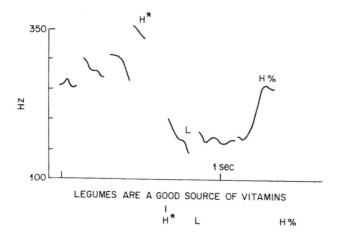

Figure 14.3
Nuclear stress on *good* with a falling-rising pattern. Reprinted from Pierrehumbert 1980.

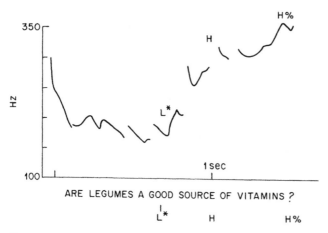

Figure 14.4
A rising pattern with nuclear stress on *good*. Reprinted from Pierrehumbert 1980.

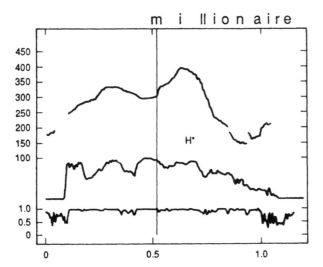

Figure 14.5
A **H*** accent on *millionaire*. Reprinted from Pierrehumbert and Steele, in press.

go with stressed syllables. If the stress pattern for a given sentence is changed, the number and location of pitch accents is changed accordingly. Other tones, the *phrasal tones*, mark the edges of phonological phrases. If the way a sentence is divided into phrases is modified, the number and location of phrasal tones is changed.

Pitch accents mark the lexical item with which they are associated as prominent. There are six different types of pitch accent in English (Beckman and Pierrehumbert 1986a): two simple tones—high and low—and four complex ones. The high tone, the most frequently used accent, comes out as a peak on the accented syllable. It is represented as **H***. The "H" indicates a high tone, and the "*****" that the tone is aligned with a stressed syllable. **L*** accents occur much lower in the pitch range than **H*** and are phonetically realized as local f_0 minima. The other English accents have two tones, of which one is selected to align with the stress. Using the diacritic "*****" to indicate this alignment, these accents can be represented as **L*+H**, **L+H***, **H*+L**, and **H+L***. Accents with two like tones do not exist. Figures 14.5 and 14.6 illustrate the contrast between **H*** and **L+H***. The utterance in both cases is *Only a millionaire*, with the word stress for *millionaire* on the first syllable. The vertical line in the figure indicates the release of the [m] into the vowel. Note that both contours have an f_0 peak on the first syllable of *millionaire*. But there is a pronounced valley before the peak in the case of the **L+H*** accent. Figure 14.7 continues the comparison by illustrating **L*+H** on the same phrase. Now the low f_0

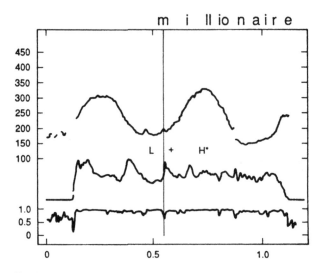

Figure 14.6
A **L + H*** accent on *millionaire*. Reprinted from Pierrehumbert and Steele, in press.

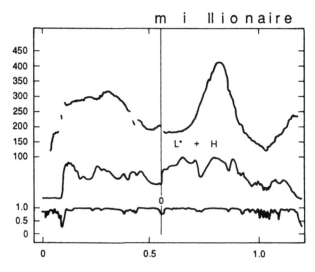

Figure 14.7
A **L* + H** accent on *millionaire*. Reprinted from Pierrehumbert and Steele, in press.

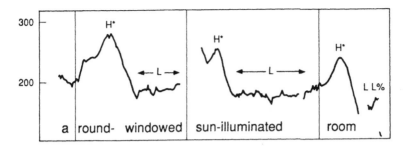

Figure 14.8
An intonational phrase with two intermediate phrases. Reprinted from Beckman and Pierrehumbert 1986a.

value continues past the [m]-release, and the peak occurs in the second syllable.

Beckman and Pierrehumbert 1986a report that two levels of phrasing in English are involved in the specification of tune. These are the *intermediate phrase* and the *intonational phrase*. A well-formed intermediate phrase consists of one or more pitch accents, plus a simple high or low tone (either **H** or **L**), which marks the end of the phrase. Continuing somewhat obsolete terminology from Pierrehumbert 1980, we will refer to this tone as the *phrase accent*. An important phonetic property of the phrase accent is that it controls the f_0 between the last pitch accent of the intermediate phrase and the beginning of the next intermediate phrase—or the end of the utterance. This is illustrated in figure 14.8, where the **L** phrase accent of each of the first two intermediate phrases shows its influence over an extended region. Vertical lines in the figure mark the phrase boundaries, as determined from phonetic segmentation of the utterance.

Intonational phrases are composed of one or more intermediate phrases. The end of an intonational phrase is marked with an additional **H** or **L** tone, which we will refer to as the *boundary tone* and indicate with the diacritic "**%**." This tone falls exactly at the phrase boundary. Since the end of every intonational phrase is also the end of an intermediate phrase, there are altogether four ways that the tune can go after the last pitch accent of an intonational phrase: **L L%, H L%, L H%,** and **H H%**.

A phrase's tune or *melody* is defined by its particular sequence of pitch accent(s), phrase accent(s), and boundary tone. Thus, an ordinary declarative pattern with a final fall is represented as **H* L L%**, a tune with a **H*** pitch accent, a **L** phrase accent, and a **L%** boundary tone. A typical interrogative contour is represented as **L* H H%**. (The contrast between these two melodies was illustrated in figures 14.1–14.4.)

Intermediate and intonational phrases can be identified by pausing and phrase-final syllable lengthening as well as by the extra melodic elements

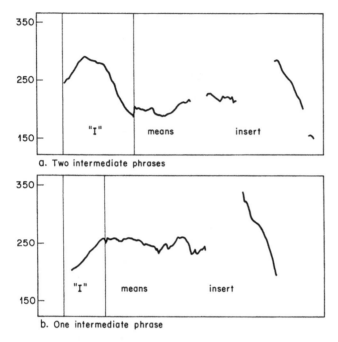

a. Two intermediate phrases

b. One intermediate phrase

Figure 14.9
Alternate phrasings of *"I" means insert*. Reprinted from Beckman and Pierrehumbert 1986a.

of phrase accent and boundary tone present at the end. Figure 14.9 shows a sentence produced in two ways, once with an intermediate phrase boundary after *I* and once as a single intermediate phrase. Note that *I* carries an f_0 fall in (a) and its duration (indicated by the vertical line) is greater than in (b).

2.4 Pitch Range
When S's voice is raised, the overall *pitch range*—the distance between the highest point in the f_0 contour and the *baseline* (the lowest point S realizes over all utterances)—is expanded. Thus, the highest points in the contour become higher and other aspects are affected proportionally. Figure 14.10 shows a simple utterance (the word *Anne*) produced in seven different overall pitch ranges with a **H* L L%** tune. The contours are similar in shape but differ in overall scaling, especially in the peak f_0 value.

In addition to variations in overall pitch range, the intonation system exploits a local time-dependent type of pitch range variation called *final lowering*. In the experiments reported in Liberman and Pierrehumbert 1984 it was found that the pitch range in declaratives is lowered and compressed in anticipation of the end of the utterance. Final lowering begins about

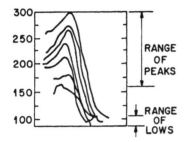

Figure 14.10
Anne produced with seven different pitch ranges. Reprinted from Liberman and Pierrehumbert 1984.

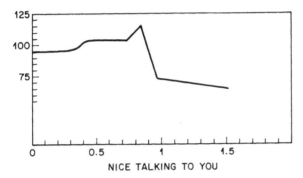

NICE TALKING TO YOU

Figure 14.11
A phrase synthesized with final lowering. Reprinted from Hirschberg and Pierrehumbert 1986.

half a second before the end and gradually increases, reaching its greatest strength right at the end of the utterance.

Both overall pitch range and final lowering enter into intonational interpretation. They are especially important in conveying the hierarchical segmentation of the discourse. Many researchers have observed that the pitch range is expanded at the beginning of a new topic (Schegloff 1979; Brazil, Coulthard, and Johns 1980; Butterworth 1975). In Hirschberg and Pierrehumbert 1986 and Silverman 1987 it was also observed that final lowering reflects the degree of "finality" of an utterance; the more final lowering, the more the sense that an utterance "completes" a topic. Figures 14.11 and 14.12 illustrate this point with contours synthesized by the intonation synthesis program described in Anderson, Pierrehumbert, and Liberman 1984. The first sounds like the usual pronunciation of the sentence *Nice talking to you*, whereas the second creates a sense that S has reservations that are unexpressed for the sake of politeness. Recent experiments

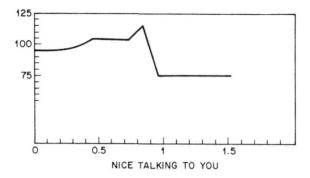

Figure 14.12
A phrase synthesized without final lowering. Reprinted from Hirschberg and Pierrehumbert 1986.

(Silverman 1987) show that pitch range and final lowering can function perceptually to disambiguate texts whose hierarchical structure is unclear.

In addition to its role in signaling overall discourse structure, pitch range interacts with the basic meanings of tunes to give their interpretation in context. For example, if S speaks up, S is likely to sound more assertive. Perceived assertiveness may make some derived interpretations of the tune seem more plausible than others.

3 Tonal Realization

The way that elements of the tune are mapped into f_0 values is discussed in detail in Pierrehumbert 1980 and Liberman and Pierrehumbert 1984. We mention two main effects here in order to help the reader interpret the examples that follow.

Upstep raises the boundary tone after a **H** phrase accent. The sequence **H H%** comes out as a high plateau followed by an additional rise at the very end. The sequence **H L%** comes out as a high plateau without any drop at the end. *Catathesis*, or *downstep*, lowers and compresses the pitch range after any of the two-tone accents. The rule applies iteratively, so that a succession of such accents creates a decending staircase in the f_0 pattern. It is important to note that catathesis affects a **H** phrase accent when one of the two tone accents occurs in nuclear position. The result is a kind of "mid" tone, lower than the preceding **H** tone but still well above the bottom of S's range. The effects of catathesis disappear at an intermediate phrase boundary; for each new intermediate phrase, a fresh selection of overall pitch range is made.

Figures 14.13–14.15 schematize the f_0 contours resulting for different combinations of pitch accent, phrase accent, and boundary tone. The first

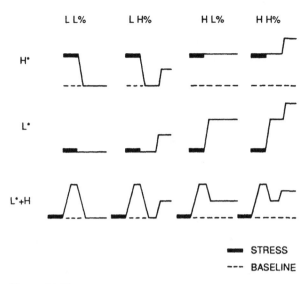

Figure 14.13
Schematic f_0 contours.

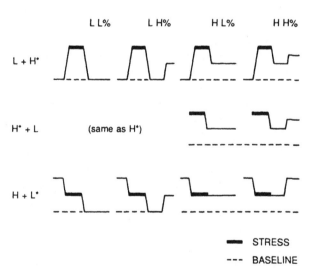

Figure 14.14
Schematic f_0 contours.

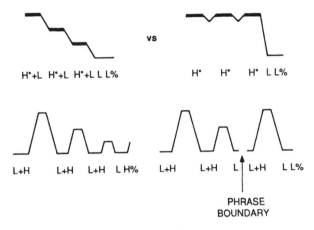

Figure 14.15
Schematic f_0 contours.

two figures provide an inventory of phrase-final configurations, and the third illustrates the operation of catathesis in sentences with several pitch accents.

3.1 Transcription and Theories of Intonational Meaning

The transcription system described here was originally motivated by phonetic and phonological considerations. It aimed at being comprehensive (by affording an analysis for all naturally occurring patterns) while at the same time exhibiting simplicity and symmetry in the abstract representation and the realization rules proposed. Of course, this is not enough. In the segmental domain, linguistic categories are expected to relate both to differences in sounds and articulations and to differences in semantic interpretation. For example, we say that [p] is different from [b] because they are pronounced differently, and because [pit] means something different than [bit] does.

Thus, any theory of transcription must be viewed as provisional unless it is supported by considerations both of sound structure and of interpretation. The transcription theory advances work on interpretation by suggesting what cases count as instances of the same category. Theories differ in the category structure they suggest. An incorrect theory can make it difficult to establish interpretations, by grouping together contours that actually hve disparate meanings or by drawing distinctions that have no meaning.

In view of this situation, we would like to call attention to some ways in which Pierrehumbert's transcription system differs from others in the way contours are cross-classified. First, Pierrehumbert proposes that the inventory of pitch accents is the same in nuclear as in prenuclear position. Nuclear configurations differ from prenuclear ones because of the phrasal tones following the accent. This position contrasts with work in the British school (see, for example, Crystal 1969, O'Connor and Arnold 1961) in which the nuclear configuration is not decomposed, and a fundamental distinction is drawn between the nuclear and prenuclear inventories. If we are persuasive in our account of how pitch accents show stable meanings in different tonal contexts, then the British school work misses important generalizations.

Second, the primitives in the theory are tone levels rather than tone rises or falls. This permits us to describe **H* H H%** and **H* L L%** as involving the same pitch accent. In other approaches, such as those found in Bolinger 1958 and Gussenhoven 1983, these contours are entirely different because one is rising and the other is falling. A very strict dynamic tone theory is unable to differentiate among any of the rising contours (**H* H H%**, **H* H L%**, **L* H H%**, **L* H L%**, **L* L H%**).

Third, the theory has two tones rather than the four proposed in Pike 1945 and Liberman 1975. The reduction to two tones is made possible by using a catathesis rule to describe cases in which the f_0 contour shows a descending staircase of values. Transcription systems lacking a catathesis rule will in general draw excessive distinctions, from the point of view of interpretation.

The particular way the catathesis rule is formulated leads to some important partial similarities. The **H* +L H L%** pattern (which ends with a sustained "mid level tone") is analyzed with the same accent as the "stepping" declarative pattern **H* +L H* +L H* +L L%**. We believe a common meaning can be identified across these two cases, as we will argue below. In other theories, this common meaning is not expected. In particular, in Ladd 1983 catathesis is not triggered by the left-hand context of a tone but is rather an independent feature. Using "!" for this feature, Ladd would give the transcriptions **H* !H** and **H* !H* !H* L**. In these transcriptions the two nuclear pitch accents are different. In Ladd's theory also, the contrast between **H* H L%** and **H* +L H L%** comes out as **H* H** versus **H* !H**. That is, he would be led to look for a difference in the interpretation of the phrase accent, where we would be looking for a pitch accent difference.

4 The Interpretation of Tunes

Past characterizations of the meanings of particular tunes have variously portrayed tune as conveying speaker attitude (O'Connor and Arnold 1961; Liberman 1975), such as politeness, deference, judiciousness, surprise, or seductiveness; emotion, such as hate or anger; speech acts (Sag and Liberman

1975; Liberman and Sag 1974), such as statements, requests, or contradictions; propositional attitudes (Ward and Hirschberg 1985), such as belief, ignorance, or uncertainty; presupposition and focus of attention (Jackendoff 1972; Ladd 1980); as well as less easily characterized meanings such as "up-in-the-airness" and "more to come." However, few of these characterizations have been successful for particular tunes, and none seems appropriate as a general approach to tune meaning.

Though speaker attitude may sometimes be inferred from choice of a particular tune, the many-to-one mapping between attitudes and tune suggests that attitude is better understood as derived from tune meaning interpreted in context than as representing that meaning itself. For example, as Ward and Hirschberg (1985) have shown, speaker uncertainty, incredulity, politeness, and irony can all be derived from the use of the **L*+H L H%** contour in different contexts. Similar problems, as well as experiments that have found pitch range and voice quality to be associated with perceived speaker emotions (Ladd et al. 1985), indicate that emotion is *not* a useful way of characterizing tune. Neither speech acts nor propositional attitudes—at least as standardly understood—appear to provide sufficient characterizations for available tunes in English. For example, the **H* L L%** tune used with simple declaratives is also frequently used with *wh*-questions. It is difficult to see how either a propositional attitude approach or a speech act analysis could produce a meaning for this contour that would accommodate both these common uses. In general, it seems advisable to divorce intonational meaning from speaker beliefs. For example, the **L*+H L H%** contour can be used to convey either that S believes **P** (as in (3)) or that S does not believe **P** (as in (4)):

(3)   A: Who ordered the veal?
      B: I'm having beef
            L*+H L H%

(4)   A: Here's your roast beef, sir.
      B: I'm having beef
            L*+H L H%
      But I'm a vegetarian. There must be some mistake.

A more fruitful approach has been suggested by Gussenhoven (1983). He attempts to characterize the meaning of "nuclear tones" in terms of the status of information with respect to a shared "background," which is developed by speaker and hearer during the course of a conversation. We agree that this sort of information is part of what tunes convey. However, we disagree with the substance of Gussenhoven's description. His interpretations of particular tunes do not appear correct for American English. Also, the transcription system Gussenhoven proposes does not support some of the generalizations we have noted and present below. Empirical counterevidence to some of Gussenhoven's claims appears in Ward and Hirschberg 1985 and Pierrehumbert and Steele 1987. Another account that treats intonational meaning in terms of the information status of accented items with respect to the discourse appears in Brazil, Coulthard, and Johns 1980.

Most analyses of the meaning of intonational contours to date have at least implicitly taken a holistic approach to tune meaning, confining the domain of interpretation to the phrase or utterance (see, for example, Bolinger 1958; O'Connor and Arnold 1961; Ladd 1980). This approach has probably been more a practical matter than a theoretical conviction: it is difficult to identify the "meaning" of parts of a contour until one has some idea of what the "meaning" of the whole might be. However, some of the individual tunes that have been successfully studied suggest that tune meaning is more usefully viewed as compositional. Tunes that share certain tonal features seem intuitively to share some aspects of meaning. For example, tunes such as $L* + H$ L $H\%$, $H*$ L $H\%$, and $L + H*$ L $H\%$ that share a L phrase accent and a H boundary tone share also a sense that the current utterance will be completed by a subsequent utterance (Hirschberg and Pierrehumbert 1986). And various types of question contour, $L*$ H $H\%$ and $H*$ H $H\%$, do share common high phrase accents and boundary tones while differing in the pitch accents used with them. A noncompositional approach fails to capture such generalities. However, the most ambitious attempt to provide a compositional account of intonational meaning (Pike 1945) was hindered by an inadequate representational system.

4.1 A Compositional Approach to Tune Meaning

We propose that speakers use tune to specify a particular relationship between the "propositional content" realized in the intonational phrase over which the tune is employed and the mutual beliefs of participants in the current discourse. Although the interpretation of any token of a tune type may vary along many other dimensions—voice quality, pitch range, as well as nonintonational features—any instance of a given tune will convey the same relationship. So, for example, any $H*$ L $L\%$ tune will have in common with others the conveying of a certain relationship between the proposition realized by the phrase and propositions mutually believed in the discourse—whether that $H*$ L $L\%$ tune is used with a *wh*-question or a syntactic declarative.

Following Clark and Marshall 1981 and Joshi 1982, we understand the *mutual beliefs* of a discourse to be those beliefs that conversational participants come to believe to be shared among them as a direct result of the conversational interaction. In particular, we make use of the notion of *one-sided* mutual belief—A's beliefs about what is mutually believed by A and

B. We will assume that a basic goal of a speaker S is to modify what (S believes) a hearer H believes to be mutually believed. For expository purposes, we will describe S's use of tune in terms of the intention to add to what (S believes) H believes to be mutually believed—or not—or to call attention to certain relationships between propositions realized by an utterance and other propositions that (S believes) H believes to be mutually believed. In this paper we will not specify how these intentions are related to the *intentional structure* of a discourse (Grosz and Sidner 1986). However, it seems clear that aspects of the intentional structure as well as the *attentional structure* of a discourse can be conveyed by choice of tune. For example, S may seek to inform H of some proposition x by communicating that x is to be added to what H believes to be mutually believed between S and H—via the tune S chooses. And S may seek to convey the information status of some item y—say, that y is old information that is to be treated as particularly salient—by the type of accent S uses in realizing y. Note in particular that S's beliefs are *not* specified by choice of tune—the "declarative" contour **H* L L%**, for example, will *not* be translated *S believes x*. But S's belief in x may be inferred from the combined meanings of pitch accents, phrase accents, and boundary tone, as they are used in particular contexts.

Our idea of the compositionality of tune meaning is based upon a hierarchical model of phonological domain, in which the scope of interpretation of tones is the node to which they are attached. So, the components of tune—pitch accents, phrase accents, and boundary tones—are each interpreted with respect to their distinct phonological domains.[2] Pitch accents, phrase accents, and boundary tones each operate on a (progressively higher) domain of interpretation. Not only is each of these types of tone interpreted over a distinct domain, but each contributes a distinct type of information to the overall interpretation of a tune.

Pitch accents convey information about the status of the individual discourse referents, modifiers, predicates, and relationships specified by the lexical items with which the accents are associated. For example, in (5) each **H*** provides information about predicates and arguments that are each denoted by a single lexical item—*train, leaves,* and *seven*—and how S intends these to be interpreted with respect to H's beliefs about their mutual beliefs:

(5)   The train leaves at seven
       H* H*   H* L L%

Accenting or deaccenting of items in general appears associated with S's desire to indicate the relative salience of accented items in the discourse. The type of accent chosen conveys other sorts of information status. For example, accent type can indicate whether accented items or things predicated of them are to be included among items H believes mutually believed or whether they should be excluded, whether something predicated of these items should be inferable from beliefs H already holds, or whether relationships in which S believes the items participate should be identified by H.

Phrase accents convey information at the level of the intermediate phrase. In (5) there is but a single intermediate phrase, with a **L** phrase accent. In (6), however, there are two:

(6)   The train leaves at seven   or nine twenty-five
        H* H*   H*   H   H*   H* L L%

Here, the **H** phrase accent after *seven* has scope over the phrase *the train leaves at seven*, and the **L** phrase accent after *five* has scope over *or nine twenty-five*. We propose that S chooses phrase accent type to convey the degree of relatedness of one such phrase to preceding and succeeding intermediate phrases. Where a phrase like *the train leaves at seven* has a **H** phrase accent, for example, it is more likely to be interpreted as a unit with a phrase that follows.

The boundary tones contribute information about the intonational phrase as a whole. Whereas the domain of phrase accent and boundary tone is the same in (5), they differ in (6), where the **L%** contributes to the interpretation of the whole phrase *the train leaves at seven or nine twenty-five*. And whereas both (5) and (6) consist of single intonational phrases, the exchange in (7) has two:

(7)   a.   The train leaves at seven
             H* H*   H* L H%

        b.   It'll be on track four
             H*   H* L L%

We believe that boundary tones convey information about relationships among intonational phrases—in particular, about whether the current phrase is to be interpreted with particular respect to a succeeding phrase or not. This directionality may be further refined. It seems possible, for example, that the hierarchical and satisfaction-precedence reltionships that Grosz and Sidner (1986) propose as the bases of their intentional structure may be signaled by particular boundary tones.[3] So, in (7) S can indicate by a **H** boundary tone in (7a) that (7a) is to be interpreted with particular respect to a succeeding phrase (7b). In Grosz and Sidner's terms, it seems plausible to postulate a dominance relationship existing between (7a) and (7b)—the satisfaction of the purpose S has in uttering (7b) contributes to the satisfaction of S's purpose in uttering (7a) by further elaboration. So, in (7) the "forward reference" signaled by the boundary tone might be interpreted as indicative of a hierarchical relationship. Certainly with a **L** boundary tone in (7a), the relationship is less clearly marked. Consider the more ambiguous exchange in (8):

(8)   a.   The train leaves at seven
       H* H*   H* L H%
       b.   There's a full moon tonight
       H* H*   H* L L%

With a H boundary tone in (8a), H will be much more likely to try to infer some relatinship between the state of the moon and the departure time of the train than if a L boundary tone is substituted.

So, we propose that tune meaning is composed of the meanings of three types of tone—pitch accents, phrase accents, and boundary tones—which have scope over three different domains of interpretation. Together, these intonational features can convey how S intends that H interpret an intonational phrase with respect to (1) what H already believes to be mutually believed and (2) what S intends to make mutually believed as a result of subsequent utterances. We believe that other characterizations of tune interpretation can in many cases be described in terms of the more general meanings we propose. For example, the conveyance of speaker attitudes like uncertainty or politeness or surprise, the conveyance of performatives like contradiction or declaration, and even turn-taking phenomena can be explained in terms of S's conveyance of various types of information status and propositional relationships—especially when combined with meanings conveyed by other intonational and nonintonational features.

The major support for our compositional approach to intonational meaning comes from an examination of how the different pitch accents are interpreted. In the following section we concentrate on examples in which the same pitch accent is used throughout the phrase and consider the contributions of accent, phrase accent, and boundary tone to the intonational meaning. Any success in identifying the meaning of different accents across different choices of phrase accent and boundary tone tends to support the idea that intonational meanings are compositional. Similarly, success in identifying the meaning of phrase accents when pitch accents and boundary tones are varied or identifying the meaning of boundary tones over the same comparisons also supports a compositional approach. Any success in deriving the varied meanings heretofore associated with particular melodies in different contexts tends to support our ideas about what the basic meanings of melodies can be like.

5   The Interpretation of Pitch Accents

All pitch accents render salient the material with which they are associated.[4] This is true regardless of the type of accent in question. In the phonological descriptions given in Liberman 1975 and Pierrehumbert 1980 this generalization arises because accents may be associated only with the most stressed material in the phrase; in Selkirk 1984 accents are taken to be prior, and accented material becomes stressed. Either way, salience goes with accent location and not with accent type. Accented material is salient not only phonologically but also from an informational standpoint. And items that are deaccented, by extension, do not undergo this salience marking—although they may already be salient or become salient by other means.

For purposes of illustration, we will view the logical form corresponding to an intonational phrase as an open expression in which accented items are replaced by variables.[5] What accentuation means, operationally, in this schema is that each variable has associated with it some indication of S's communication of the variable's information status with respect to what H believes to be mutually believed. This variable may or may not be instantiated with a representation of the accented item, depending upon the accent type employed. By this method, the utterance of (9) might be represented as shown in (10):

(9)   George likes pie
      H*   **H* L L%**

(10) x likes y

       x (**H***)
       y (**H***)

       x = George
       y = pie

The open expression is x *likes* y. The instantiation of x is *George*, a pointer to an individual. The instantiation of y is *pie*, a pointer to a class. Both the individual and the class in question are marked as salient by the mere fact that the lexical items pointing to them are uttered with an accent. The further elaboration of the information status of both *George* and *pie* is indicated by the accent type employed—here, **H***—as we discuss below. In general, we believe that all accent types can be used to convey information to H about how the propositional content of the (perhaps partially) instantiated expression corresponding to the utterance is to be used to modify what H believes to be mutually believed.

5.1 The **H*** Accent

The **H*** accents above and in utterances in general convey that the items made salient by the **H*** are to be treated as "new" in the discourse. More generally, intonational phrases whose accents are all **H*** appear to signal to H that the open expression is to be instantiated by the accented items and the instantiated proposition realized by the phrase is to be added to H's mutual belief space. When combined with a L phrase accent and a L or a H boundary tone, this is the pitch accent of "neutral declarative intonation." That is, it is appropriate when S's goal is to convey information. This contour may also be employed when S believes that H is already aware of the information, if S wishes to convey that it is mutually believed. For example:

> (11)   You turkey
>   H* L L%
>   You deliberately deleted my files
>   H*   H*   H* L L%

The H* accent can also combine with a H phrase accent and either a H or a L boundary tone. The first yields the so-called *high-rise question*. This pattern (H* H H%) may be used in preference to the standard *yes-no question contour* (L* H H%) when the questioned phrase simultaneously conveys information. Pierrehumbert (1980) notes the following examples. In the first example, due to Mark Liberman, he approaches a receptionist with a view to finding out if he is in the right place for his appointment and says,

> (12)   My name is Mark Liberman
>   H* H* H H%

In this case it seems that the entire phrase is intended to convey 'My name is Mark Liberman, and are you expecting me, or, am I in the right place?' That is, the H* accents convey that information is to be added to H's mutual beliefs, and the H phrase accent and boundary tone "question" the relevance of that information. In the second (naturally occurring) example a young woman was asked after a movie whether she liked the picture and replied,

> (13)   I thought it was good
>   H*   H* H H%

This utterance might be glossed 'I thought it was good, but do you agree with me?' Again, S is providing information while asking for a comment on its appropriateness. In either of these cases it seems that a L* H H% contour would be infelicitous—and would probably convey that S was suffering from amnesia!

On syntactic yes-no questions, the contrast between the use of H* and the use of L* is somewhat less striking. However, H* H H% seems more often used when S believes that the answer to a question is yes—a confirmation question. For example, the authors of this paper were hard at work on it, when one wished to confer with the other and uttered,

(14)   May I interrupt you
        H* H H%

With this indirect speech act, it was clear that S thought it likely that an interruption would be permitted. **L* H H%**, on the other hand, conveys more of a sense that S is sincerely in doubt about the nature of the response. This is consistent with the view that S uses **H*** to try to add information to H's mutual belief space.

The comparison of **H* L L%** and **H* H H%** contours provides support for viewing intonational meaning in terms of attempted modifications of H's mutual beliefs. In both cases S attempts to establish that some particular information is shared. So, approaching tune meaning in terms of H's mutual beliefs permits a generalization of the **H*** meaning across both declarative and interrogative contexts.

The last case of the **H*** accent is in the *plateau contour*, currently being investigated by Hirschberg and Ward. This contour, **H* H L%**, has a peak on the accent syllable and then continues at the same high level. It is used to elaborate upon some previous statement—as to provide support or detail—as in (15):

(15)   Wally: Mostly they just sat around and knocked stuff. You
                  know.
                  The school
                      H* H L%
                  Other people
                      H* H L%

Here again instantiated expressions are to be added to H's mutual beliefs, although phrase accent and boundary tone indicate that the relationship of these expressions to other expressions realized in the discourse will differ from **H* L L%** and **H* H H%**.

The comparison of **H* L L%** and **H* H L%** with **H* H H%** provides support for viewing intonational meaning in terms of attempted modifications of H's mutual beliefs. In all cases S attempts to establish that some particular information is shared—by supplying that information for H or by attempting to elicit it. So, approaching tune meaning in terms of H's mutual beliefs permits a generalization of the **H*** meaning across both declarative and interrogative contexts.

5.2 The L* Accent

The **L*** accent marks items that S intends to be salient but not to form part of what S is predicating in the utterance. Schematically, one might say that S conveys that these items are not to be instantiated in the open expression that is to be added to H's mutual beliefs.

L* accents commonly appear in canonical yes-no questions—**L* H H%** —as we noted above. In questions like (16), for example, both *prunes* and *feet* are marked as salient by their **L*** accents:

(16)   Do prunes have feet
        L*   **L* H H%**

However, S predicates nothing of these entities. In fact, S's motivation for marking these items as salient is the desire that H make such a predication. So, one common interpretation of the exclusion of salient items from the predication of an utterance is that S is not able to include them in some predication.

The **L* H H%** contour may also be used to convey incredulity. In such cases the **L*** accent's "salience-without-predication" may be interpreted as signaling that S believes the current instantiation of the open expression to be incorrect. An old Russian émigré joke relies on this usage. A staunch old Bolshevik is forced to confess publicly and reads as follows:

(17)   I was wrong
        L*   **H L* H H%**
        And Stalin was right
              L*   **H L* H H%**
        I should apologize
        L*   **H L* H H%**

S may also employ **L*** accents when the instantiated expression is believed already part of H's mutual beliefs. For example, if S is asked to supply a list of things he wants for his birthday, when his desire for a Pavoni espresso machine is already mutually believed, he may begin,

(18)   Well, I'd like a Pavoni ...
        L*   **L***   **L* L H%**

In this way, S conveys that his desire for this gift is already mutually believed by H. Such utterances may be made for the sake of completeness in listing, as a reminder, or to reassure H that he still wants a present that she has already purchased.

Of course, S may employ **L*** accents to convey this sense of existing mutual belief even when in fact S actually does not believe that this mutual belief exists. Such situations arise when S instructs, reprimands, or contradicts H, conveying that information should already be mutually believed even if it is not. For example, in (19) the use of the **L* L H%** pattern has a rather insulting effect, by suggesting that H should have had in mind something that she clearly did not.

(19)   A: Let's order the Chateaubriand for two.

      B: I don't eat beef
         L*   **L* L H%**

Exchanges like this led Liberman and Sag (1974) to label the **L* L H%** melody *contradiction contour*. However, this description is both too narrow and too broad. As Carlson (personal communication) points out, the melody cannot be used for just any sort of contradiction. It is only appropriate when S intends to convey that H should already be aware of what S is saying. It is not appropriate, for instance, in (20):

(20)   A: My chances? The election isn't over till the last ballot has
         been counted.

      B: #But CBS has just declared you the next president
            L*   **L***   **L***   **L*** **L* L H%**

In addition, the melody is used in many cases (such as (18)) where S is not in any sense contradicting H.

Additional evidence for our account of the meaning of the **L*** accent comes from the common use of this accent with lexical items that have, for independent reasons, been treated as extrapropositional, such as greetings, vocatives, and so-called cue phrases. For example, greetings such as (21) are commonly produced with **L*** accents:

(21)   Good morning
      L*   **L* L H%**

In such cases it would be a mistake to account for the **L*** accent as associated with the conventionality of the statement. Conventional statements that are actually intended to convey information would not be likely to have **L*** accents. Consider the implausibility of continued employment for a switchboard operator who answered callers with (22):

(22)   You have reached AT&T Bell Laboratories
       L*   **L***   **L* L***   **L**   **H%**

Both preposed and postposed vocatives are frequently produced with **L***, especially if S already has H's attention (see Beckman and Pierrehumbert 1986a for a discussion of the phonological analysis of these cases). Consider (23) and (24):

(23)   Anna   your lunch is ready
      L*   **H H***   **H* L H%**

(24)   Your lunch is ready   Anna
      H*   **H* L L* L H%**

A **H*** accent is possible on the preposed vocative if S does not already have H's attention, as in (25):

(25) Anna   your lunch is ready
      H* **L**   **H***   **H* L H%**

It is virtually impossible to use **H*** on the postposed vocative; presumably it makes little sense for S to try to attract H's attention *after* making a point rather than before. If a **H*** is used on a postposed vocative, it has the flavor of a repair.

As a final example, work by Hirschberg and Litman (1987) on *cue phrases* lends support to our account of **L*** accent as excluding items from the predication of an utterance. Cue phrases are expressions such as *okay, but, now, anyway, by the way, in any case, that reminds me* that function to indicate discourse structure explicitly (Reichman 1985; Cohen 1984). Hirschberg and Litman analyzed the intonation of 100 instances of the word *now* in a corpus of recorded naturally occurring dialogues.[6] When *now* was used to signal (discourse) structural—rather than temporal—information, it often received a **L*** accent. In particular, in cases where *now* formed part of a larger intonational phrase, structural uses were either deaccented or accented with **L***. However, when deictic *now* formed part of a larger phrase, it received a **H*** or complex accent—never **L***. So, the communication of structural information correlates with the use of **L***, whereas the communication of temporal "content" correlates with the use of nonaccents. Of course, deictic *now* can have a **L*** accent in some cases that did not appear in the corpus—for example, if it is being questioned.

So, **L*** accents are used by S to exclude the accented item from the predication S intends to be added to H's mutual beliefs. There may be various reasons for and interpretations of this exclusion, including the use of **L*** in yes-no questions (where S requests H to make some predication), or to convey S's denial of some part of a previous predication, or to convey that the accented item already figures in what H currently believes to be mutually believed. Finally, **L*** is often used with items that have been independently analyzed as outside the predication of an utterance, such as greetings, vocatives, and cue phrases.

5.3 The **L + H** Accents

L + H accents are employed by S to convey the salience of some *scale* (defined here following Ward and Hirschberg 1985 as a partial ordering) linking the accented item to other items salient in H's mutual beliefs.

5.3.1 The **L* + H** Accent

The interpretation of the **L* + H** pitch accent in the context of a **L** phrase accent and **H** boundary tone (**L* + H L H%**) has been intensively investigated by Ward and Hirschberg (1985, 1986). In the

1985 paper Ward and Hirschberg account for a large class of naturally occurring tokens in which this contour expresses uncertainty. They point out that, in all of their data, the contour is being used to convey uncertainty about a scale evoked in the discourse. For example, in (26) B expresses uncertainty about whether being a good badminton player provides relevant information about degree of clumsiness:

(26) A: Alan's such a klutz.
      B: He's a good badminton player
          L*+H   L   H%

And in (27) B conveys uncertainty about whether there are "degrees" of "taking out the garbage"—or whether it is an all-or-nothing phenomenon:

(27) A: Did you take out the garbage?
      B: Sort of
          L*+H L H%

In the 1986 paper Ward and Hirschberg address a second class of L*+H L H% uses, the "incredulous" readings. In (27), for instance, A might reply with (28) to convey that the proposed gradedness of garbage removal is unacceptable:

(28) A: Sort of
          L*+H L H%

Ward and Hirschberg unify the "incredulous" and "uncertain" readings of L*+H L H% under the notion of "lack of speaker commitment" to the proposed scale (which they define as a partial ordering) or scalar value. A pilot phonetic study suggests that the difference between the two readings is conveyed by differences in pitch range and tempo.

We suspect that the contour interpretation that Ward and Hirschberg identify for L*+H L H% is more properly associated with the L*+H pitch accent rather than the entire contour. At least the "uncertainty" interpretation is still available when a H phrase accent is substituted for a L phrase accent, as in (29), in which a pet owner calls a missing and somewhat recalcitrant pet:

(29) Leo
      L*+H H L%

And in the hypothetical (30), L*+H is paired with a H phrase accent and H boundary tone—with the same conveyance of uncertainty:

(30) A: We don't have any native speakers of German here. So
          let's work on Chinese.
      B: Jurgen's from Germany
          L*+H   H   H%

We believe that this account of the **L* + H** pitch accent can be recast in the present framework. We propose that S chooses a **L* + H** pitch accent to convey lack of predication and to evoke a scale. Together these can convey the impression of lack of speaker commitment described in Ward and Hirschberg 1986.

*5.3.2 The **L + H*** Accent*   The meaning of the **L + H*** pitch accent is closely related to that of **L* + H**. Use of this accent also evokes a salient scale. However, S employs the **L + H*** accent to convey that the accented item— and not some alternative related item—should be mutually believed. The evocation of a salient scale plus predication can convey the effect of speaker commitment to the instantiation of the open expression with the accented item.

The most common use of **L + H*** in the data we have collected is to mark a correction or contrast. In such cases S substitutes a new scalar value for one previously proposed by S or by H—or for some alternative value available in the context. (31) occurred on a trip to Boston in December:

(31)   A: It's awfully warm for January.

B: It's even warm for December

L + H* L H%

In (32) A and B were looking at the label of a Sambuca Romana bottle, which shows a man kissing the hand of a woman wearing a rather daring evening dress:

(32)   A: I wonder if they're supposed to be married.

B: No, I don't think they're married.

If they were married, he wouldn't be kissing her hand

L + H* L H%

A class of cases discussed in Jackendoff 1972 is closely related. Jackendoff notes that the "background" information in dialogues like (33) has a distinctive intonation pattern:

(33)   A: What about the beans? Who ate them?

B: Fred   ate the beans

H* L   L + H* L H%

The meaning assigned to this exchange is also "contrastive"—something like 'As for the beans, Fred ate them. As for the other food, other people may have eaten it'. Here, B's answer is felicitously produced in two phrases, *Fred* and *ate the beans*; the second, representing the background information, has a fall-rise pattern on *beans*. The phonological analysis of the pattern on *beans* is obscure from Jackendoff's description, but recent unpublished experiments by Liberman and Pierrehumbert strongly suggest that it is $L + H^*$ L H%. Again, the "contrastive" interpretation can be accounted for in our framework as S's commitment to a particular instantiation of an open expression with an item chosen from a salient scale—here, a set of salient foods.

Example (34)—uttered while B was unpacking a new desk lamp—is less obviously interpreted as "contrastive." However, it is easily accommodated by our definition of the meaning of $L + H^*$.

(34)   A: But how does it {the desk lamp} stand up?

    B: Feel that base.
        It weighs a ton
        $L + H^*$ $L + H^*$ L H%

Here, its base "weighing a ton" is one of many possible means by which the lamp might stand up. B commits herself to this from the set of such means. In another example of $L + H^*$ a daughter calls her parents to invite them for dinner. Her mother consults with her father in (35):

(35)   Mother: It's Raymond and Janet on the phone.
                They want to know if we can come for dinner
                $L + H^*$ L H%

Here, an invitation to dinner is implicitly related to a space of possible invitations, possible ways to spend the evening, or perhaps simply possible queries. The mother's use of $L + H^*$ conveys a strong sense of commitment to this accented item—which was interpreted by the daughter as indicating to her father that he should accept the invitation.

5.4 The $H + L$ Accents

The $H + L$ accents, like the $L + H$ accents, are used by S to evoke a particular relationship between the accented items and H's mutual beliefs. $L + H$ accents evoke a salient scale for the accented item. We propose that S uses $H + L$ accents to indicate that support for the open expression's instantiation with the accented items should be inferable by H, from H's representation of the mutual beliefs. The inference can be direct or indirect, and it can be (and indeed usually is) pragmatic rather than logical in character. When using a $H^* + L$ accent, S appears to be making a predication in the same sense as when using H^*. $H^* + L$ thus differs from H^* in conveying that H should locate an inference path supporting the predication. Items accented with H^* might in principle be supported in the same way, but the support is not explicitly evoked by the tune.

We have collected only a few examples of the $H + L^*$ accent, and so we are less confident of its interpretation. In the examples we have, S seems to employ it to convey that the desired instantiation of an open expression is itself among H's mutual beliefs. We conjecture that the basic meaning is the same as that for **H*+L**, except that **H+L*** does not make a predication. One reason for evoking support for an instantiation without making a predication would be (the claim) that the predication is already mutually believed. If this is correct, we should expect to find other contexts of use for this accent.

*5.4.1 The **H*+L** Accent* In some uses of **H*+L**, the inference path S wishes to evoke is so short that the accented items may alternatively be deaccented. In (36a) (due to Gregory Ward) S conveys both that the instantiation of 'I'm looking for someone with x' is particularly salient and that H should infer it from H's mutual beliefs. Perhaps, here, the relevant beliefs include the facts that S has mentioned H's credentials and an interview is in progress.

(36)   I know you have great credentials
    H*   **H***   **H* L H%**
    a. I'm looking for someone with just   such credentials
       H*   **H*+L H*+L H*+L L L%**
    b. I'm looking for someone with just such credentials
       H*   **L**   **L%**

In (36b), however, S does not impart additional salience to H's credentials —which have already been made salient by S's **H*** accent in the previous utterance. Nor does S convey that H should look for an inference path between 'I'm looking for someone with x' and other of H's mutual beliefs.

However, the inference path may not always be so simple. In some cases **H*+L** accents can even be used discourse-initially. In the following (naturally occurring) exchange, C was a linguist whom colleagues A and B found particularly troublesome. A walked into B's office, where B was reading a circular advertising a linguistics position in Tasmania. B looked up and said,

(37)   Let's   nominate C for the Tasmanian   job
    H*+L H*+L H*+L   **H*+L H*+L L L%**

Here, B invites A to consider not only the proposed nomination but also the path—C is obnoxious, obnoxious people should be got rid of, Tasmania is far away—by which it can be inferred.

The **H*+L** accent often has a pedagogical flavor. This is not surprising, since teaching involves pointing the student to inference relationships between old and new information. In assigning appropriate intonation to the synthesized speech for a computer-aided instruction system that teaches beginners how to use a screen editor (*TNT*), we found numerous cases where this accent was useful. In one case *TNT* introduces a "hint" key, which provides learners with suggestions. Subsequent instructions to practice using this key were felicitously accented with H^*+L:

(38) Hint gives you hints if you need help.
      Hit the hint key
      H^*+L H^*+L L L%

However, if the student were instructed to hit this key, say, without prior introduction to its function, H^*+L accents would sound distinctly odd. A plain H^* accent would be more appropriate.

The H^*+L accent can also be used when reading instructions. For example, consider the series of H^*+L accents in (39):

(39) Let's   see
     H^*+L H^*+L L L%
     Put   tab   A   into slot   A
     H^*+L H^*+L H^*+L H^*+L H^*+L L L%
     Turn the model   over
     H^*+L H^*+L H^*+L L L%
     Put   tab   B   into slot   B
     H^*+L H^*+L H^*+L H^*+L H^*+L L L%

Here, S is emphasizing the connections between each instruction and what S has already read or done.

Sometimes S uses H^*+L accents when the inference path to be made salient is quite obscure to H—or even when S has no real belief that H will be able to discover it. In such cases H^*+L sounds pretentious and annoying, as H is told it should be possible to infer something there is no obvious means of inferring.

In the examples given so far, a series of H^*+L accents has been followed by a L phrase accent. When followed by a H phrase accent, the same pitch accent gives rise to a very distinctive pattern in which the voice trails out at a middle level, as in (40):

(40) Jimmy
      H^*+L H L%
      Dinner
      H^*+L H L%

This pattern is often almost chanted and makes its first appearance in the literature as "calling" contour (Pike 1945).

Ladd (1978) points out that it is not really correct to call such contours vocative. He proposes instead that the pattern has a core meaning of "stylization" or shared convention. The contour is suitable even if the convention is a private one between individuals, as in (41), used to convey that H has forgotten his lunch yet again:

(41)   Jacob
        H*+L H L%
        Your lunch
        H*+L H L%

Finally, Ladd points out that this pattern is *in*appropriate for calling out in a real emergency, as in (42):

(42)   #Fire
        H*+L H L%

Our general interpretation of H*+L appears to account for Ladd's examples. (40) is most appropriate when Jimmy is expecting his dinner call, and (41) conveys that Jacob should be able to infer the reason that lunch is being brought to his attention. In addition, we cover some cases that Ladd misses by confining himself to "chanting" utterances. For instance, when one of us was pulled over by the police, the policeman said:

(43)   Ma'am, your car inspection is overdue
        H*+L   H   H%
        I'll have to give you a summons.

In this case there is no past history of overdue car inspections. Rather, S is alluding to mutual beliefs established by the sticker on the windshield and the fact that H was pulled over.

5.4.2 H+L*

There is some difficulty in separating the meaning of H+L* from that of H*+L, because in many cases the phonological analysis in unclear. Both the H*+L and the H+L* accents create downstepping patterns (see section 3); they differ in whether there is an f_0 fall onto or after the accented syllable. If the accented syllables are very close together, the phonetic effect is much the same. However, the difference between the two is conspicuous if the accents are well separated or if the accent precedes a H phrase accent.

In the examples we have collected, H+L* is used to convey that the instantiation of the open expression is already present among H's mutual beliefs. Consider (44), in which S questions H's travel plans:

(44)   It's inconceivable that we'll make that connection
              H*   H+L* L L%

H interpreted this utterance as conveying that H should already know this fact. In another instance one of us had a discussion with her mother-in-law in which they disagreed about why the baby had awakened in the middle of the night. In this discussion the mother-in-law advanced a mutually known fact as the correct explanation:

(45)   She's   teething
       H* H+L* H L%

Though H+L* cannot be used in Ladd's "calling" sense, it is sometimes used with conventionalized expressions, as in (46):

(46)   A: Janet, you've crashed Sweet again.
       B: Oh darn it
          H+L* H L%

The use of H+L* with this and other expletives has a sort of "redundant" effect—during part of its life, Sweet crashed very often. S does not use this accent with expletives when the situation occasioning the expletive is completely new. So, exchanges like (47) seem odd:

(47)   A: I just heard we're not getting a pay raise this year. I don't
          understand—the company's doing so well!
       B: #Oh darn it
          H+L* H L%

In felicitous uses of H+L* with expletives, we might say that S is confirming a reaction previously recognized by H.

5.5 The Compositionality of Accent Meanings

In the description just proposed, the meanings of the starred tones are shared among the different accent types. When the starred tone is L (L*, L*+H, and H+L*), S does not convey that the instantiation of the open expression by the accented item should be added to H's mutual beliefs. For one of a variety of reasons—it may already be there, S may not be certain of its appropriateness, S may not wish or be able to predicate the open expression of the accented item—S does not intend to contribute this instantiation to H's mutual beliefs. However, when the starred tone is H (H*, L+H*, H*+L), S does intend to instantiate the open expression in H's mutual belief space. In addition, we note that items differing only in the location of the star have closely related meanings. L*+H and L+H* both evoke a salient scale. H*+L and H+L* both convey that H should be in a position to infer support for the instantiated expression—whether because it is already represented among H's mutual beliefs about S or because there is an inference path based on the mutual beliefs that supports the instantiation. These observations suggest that the meaning of each particular pitch accent may be derivable from the meanings of its constituent tones, plus some generalization about the interpretation of the star.

However, beyond the observations just made, we are not able to present such a decomposition as yet. The meanings of the two-tone accents all involve identifying a particular relationship between the (propositional content of the) current utterance and H's mutual belief space; for the single-tone accents, no similar relationship is discernible. We have as yet no explanation of why complex tones should convey this additional meaning. Nor can we explain the difference between the $L + H$ interpretation (identify a relevant scale) and the $H + L$ interpretation (identify an inference path) in terms of composition from simple tones. This analysis we leave to further research. We also postpone the question of how phrases with mixed accent types are to be interpreted. Though we might propose a simple solution for mixed H^* and L^* accents—the former contributes to the predication, whereas the latter does not—combining, say, $L + H^*$ and $H^* + L$ in a single phrase will be more difficult to analyze.

6 The Interpretation of Phrasal Tones

Phrase accents have scope over entire intermediate phrases and may consist of either a high (H) or a low (L) tone (see section 2.3). These tones appear to indicate the presence or absence of an interpretive as well as a phonological boundary. A H phrase accent, for example, indicates that the current phrase is to be taken as forming part of a larger composite interpretive unit with the following phrase. A L phrasal tone emphasizes the separation of the current phrase from a subsequent phrase. Most of the support for this analysis comes from cases in which an intonational phrase is composed of several intermediate phrases—without intervening boundary tones. In the case of simpler intonational phrases—with but a single intermediate phrase—it is more difficult to separate the meaning of the phrase accent from the meaning of the boundary tone.

The use of a H phrase accent in listings appears to convey that the resulting list is intended to be exhaustive. For example, compare the use of the H tone in (48)–(49) with (50), in which a L phrase accent is used with the first item of the list:

(48) Do you want apple juice   or orange juice
         H^* H H^* L $L\%$

(49) Do you want apple juice   or orange juice
         L^* H H^* L $L\%$

(50) Do you want apple juice   or orange juice
         H^* L H^* L $L\%$

We interpret this distinction in the following way. By using a H phrase accent in (48), S emphasizes that *apple juice* and *orange juice* form an entity, namely, the set of available juices; by using a L tone in (50), S emphasizes the separate status of each type of juice and thus does not evoke a larger interpretive entity.

Examples (48) and (49) appear to be virtually indistinguishable in meaning. We would suggest that the **L*** in (49) is marking a nonpredication because the predication is being deferred until the items in the list have been specified. From a functional point of view, then, the **L*** is reinforcing an interpretation that is independently conveyed by the phrase accent. Thus, **H*** and **L*** do not differ very much in their interpretation in exhaustive disjunctions.

Note that in both (48) and (50) an intermediate phrase boundary separates the disjuncts; thus, the distinction noted seems clearly due to the type of phrase accent and not to the presence or absence of a phrase break. It may be that failure to produce an intermediate phrase boundary between conjuncts simply leaves their interpretation as an exhaustive or partial set open to H's interpretation. However, the intuition that failure to produce a phrase boundary between the conjuncts might also lead to their interpretation as a single unit raises the question of how an utterance like (51) might differ from (48):

(51)   Do you want apple juice or orange juice
            L*   **H***   **L**   **L%**

To examine this question, we first note that (51) is somewhat unnatural, giving rise to the sense that the first mention of *juice* is somewhat unnecessary. That is, it is a reduced disjunction, *apple or orange juice*, that is actually desired. Since the distinction between disjunctions produced with or without internal phrase boundaries is clearest when scope ambiguities are possible, we might propose a more complex set of comparisons to tease apart the meaning of disjunctions with **H** phrasal tones from the meaning of disjunctions with no internal phrase boundaries. Compare (52) with (53) and (54):

(52)   Do you want an apple or banana cake
            L*   **H*** **L** **L%**

(53)   Do you want an apple   or banana cake
            H*   **H**   **H*** **L** **L%**

(54)   Do you want an apple   or banana cake
            H*   **L**   **H*** **L** **L%**

Without an intermediate phrase boundary, as in (52), the disjunction is most plausibly interpreted as a modifier disjunction, *apple or banana*, modifying *cake*. However, with phrase boundaries, as in (53) and (54), it is most likely that both *an apple* and *banana cake* are being offered. In (53) these items are *all* that is being offered, whereas in (54) other foods may be available as well. So, we suggest that the presence or absence of a phrase boundary can influence the interpretation of the scope of disjunctions (and conjunctions as well, as we discuss below). However, it is the type of phrase accent that conveys whether or not the resulting disjunction will be interpreted as exhaustive.

Choice of phrase accent can also influence the interpretation of relationships between conjoined clauses. It has long been noted (Schmerling 1976) that *and* is asymmetric. In some cases it can convey temporal, causal, or enablement relationships between conjoined clauses. We propose that choice of phrase accent can influence whether or not such an interpretation is conveyed. A **H** phrase accent can favor such an additional meaning; a **L** phrase accent does not. In (55), for example, a **H** tone favors the interpretation that George's ingestion of chicken soup caused his illness:

> (55)   George ate chicken soup   and got sick
>   **H* H* H***   **H**   **H* H* L L%**

In (56) the causal link—though still inferable—is not intonationally reinforced:

> (56)   George ate chicken soup   and got sick
>   **H* H* H***   **L**   **H* H* L L%**

In the more plausibly ambiguous (57) the role of the **H** tone in suggesting a causal link is more easily seen:

> (57)   I opened the door   and the rain poured down
>   **H***   **H* H**   **H* H*   L   L%**

In this example one seems clearly presented with a causal connection between S's action and a natural phenomenon, however implausible that might otherwise be. H is led to extended interpretations of the second conjunct—for example, it might be taken to mean 'the rain poured down on me'.

Similarly, the "implicit conditional" reading of conjunction is favored by **H** phrase accents, as in (58):

> (58)   Eat another cookie   and I'll kill you
>   **H***   **H**   **H* L L%**

7 The Interpretation of Boundary Tones

Boundary tones may also be **H** or **L** but have scope over the entire intonational phrase. As such, they appear to play a considerable role in the conveyance and perception of discourse segmentation. It is a common simplification in studies of discourse coherence to model discourses as sequences of declarative utterances in which the coherence of each new utterance is assessed with respect to those that precede it. Our findings tend to support this model but suggest an additional simplifying generalization. As a first approximation, we propose that choice of boundary tone conveys whether the current intonational phrase is "forward-looking" or not—that is, whether it is to be interpreted with respect to some succeeding phrase or whether the direction of interpretation is unspecified. We propose that a **H** boundary tone indicates that S wishes H to interpret an utterance with particular attention to subsequent utterances. A **L** boundary tone does not convey such directionality.

Note that this proposal differs from the notion that **H** boundary tones signal "other-directed" utterances—those particularly designed to elicit a response. This claim derives particularly from the common occurrence of **H%** in yes-no questions. Though such questions may indeed be described as "other-directed" they are surely no more so than *wh*-questions, which typically are uttered with **L%**. And the "other-directed" generalization does *not* apply to other uses of **H%**.

Consider, for example, utterances bearing *continuation rise*—with a **L** phrase accent and **H** boundary tone—which need not be "other-directed." In a sequence like (59), for example, the **H** boundary tone on (59b) conveys that (59b) is to be interpreted with respect to a succeeding phrase, (59c)— not that (59b) itself is particularly intended to elicit a response:

(59) a. My new car manual is almost unreadable
                                              L L%

  b. It's quite annoying
        L H%

  c. I spent two hours figuring out how to use the jack
                                              L L%

Now contrast (59) with (60). Use of the **H** boundary tone on (60a) tends to convey that (60a) is to be interpreted with respect to (60b):

(60) a. My new car manual is almost unreadable
                                              L H%

  b. It's quite annoying
        L L%

  c. I spent two hours figuring out how to use the jack
                                              L L%

A consequence of these differences is that, whereas the referent of *it* in (60) is likely to be interpreted as *my new car manual*, the referent in (59) is likely to be understood to be 'my spending two hours figuring out how to use the jack'.

In these examples the "forward reference" signaled by a **H** boundary tone can be interpreted as 'this utterance will be completed by a subsequent utterance'. Sequences of similar utterances can produce a similar effect, as in (61):

> (61)   a. George likes cake
> **L   H%**
> b. He adores pie
> **L   H%**
> c. He'll eat anything that's sweet and calorific
> **L   L%**

Both (61a) and (61b) are to be interpreted with respect to a succeeding utterance, (61c); in this case the sense that the first two utterances "are completed by" a third may be interpreted in Grosz and Sidner's (1986) terms as 'the intention underlying (61c) dominates those underlying both (61a) and (61b)', or in the terms of Cohen (1981), Mann and Thompson 1986, or Hobbs (1979) as '(61a) and (61b) provide evidence for (61c)'.

The **H** boundary tones used in yes-no question contours also convey "forward reference." Typically, this reference is cross-speaker. Any yes-no question-answer pair illustrates this phenomenon. For example, (62a)'s **H** boundary tone might also be glossed as '(62a) is to be completed by a subsequent phrase'—here, (62b):

> (62)   a. Does it snow a lot in New Jersey
> **H   H%**
> b. It does this year
> **L   L%**

If the intentions underlying yes-no questions are something like 'make the status of some queried proposition P mutually believed among S and H'—and if a simple or cooperative response has a similar underlying intention as in (62)—then in Grosz and Sidner's (1986) terms, the satisfaction of the intention underlying (62b) contributes to the satisfaction of the intention underlying (62a). Thus, (62a) dominates (62b).

Note that, although **H** boundary tones contribute to the interpretation of intentional structure by signaling the existence of hierarchical relationships, the direction of the dominance relationship is not specified. In (59) and (61) the phrase ending with **H%** is to be dominated by a subsequent utterance. In (60) and (62), on the other hand, the **H%** phrase is to dominate a subsequent utterance. **H%** can also signal that Grosz and Sidner's (1986) satisfaction-precedence relationships hold between siblings, as in (63):

> (63)   a. Attach the jumper cables to the car that's running
> **L   H%**
> b. Attach them to the car you want to start
> **L   H%**

    c. Try the ignition
        L H%
    d. If you're lucky
        L H%
    e. you've started your car
        L L%

The intentions underlying (63a–d) are dominated by that underlying (63e), and, in addition, each of the intentions (63a–c) satisfaction-precedes the next.

So, **H%** can be interpreted as signaling a hierarchical relationship between intentions underlying the current utterance and a subsequent one, although the former may either dominate or be dominated by the latter. In addition, **H%** may signal satisfaction-precedence relationships among intentions underlying sequences of utterances.

S uses a **L** boundary tone to convey that the current utterance may be interpreted without respect to subsequent utterances. Use of this tone throughout a discourse gives the impression that each intonational phrase has separate and equal status in the discourse. Use of **L%** in combination with other phrases ending with **H%** signals the hierarchical and satisfaction-precedence relations described above: in (59) and (60) phrases ending in **L%** "complete" phrases ending in **H%**; in our investigations to date, it does not appear that phrases ending in **H%** can signal this function. **L%** phrases can also represent siblings to phrases ending in **H%**, as the final element in lists. In a variation of (61), (intentions underlying) phrases (64a–c) are siblings dominated by (64d):

  (64) a. George likes cake
           L H%
        b. He adores pie
           L H%
        c. He kills for chocolate mousse
           L L%
        d. He'll eat anything that's sweet and calorific
                       L L%

Another consequence of our account of the meaning conveyed by choice of boundary tone is that phrases with **H** boundary tones do not felicitously end discourse segments. In fact, violations of this generalization, such as (65), clearly convey that there is more that could or should be said:

  (65) So, I guess there's just nothing more to say
                                 L H%

In contrast, the L boundary tone, which does not convey such direction-ality of interpretation, can felicitously be used to begin discourse segments.

8 Discussion

In this paper we have presented the beginning of a compositional theory of the meaning of intonational contours. We propose that S chooses an into-national contour to convey relationships between (the propositional con-tent of) the current utterance and previous and subsequent utterances—and between (the propositional content of) the current utterance and beliefs H believes to be mutually held. These relationships are conveyed compo-sitionally via selection of pitch accent, phrase accent, and boundary tone. Pitch accents convey information about the status of discourse referents, modifiers, predicates, and relationships specified by accented lexical items. Phrase accents convey information about the relatedness of intermediate phrases—in particular, whether (the propositional content of) one inter-mediate phrase is to form part of a larger interpretive unit with another. Boundary tones convey information about the directionality of interpreta-tion for the current intonational phrase—whether it is "forward-looking" or not. So, not only do different features of an intonational phrase convey different aspects of its meaning, but the meaning conveyed by each feature has scope over a different phonological domain. Together, pitch ccents, phrase accents, and boundary tones convey how H should interpret the current utterance structurally—with respect to previous and subsequent utterances—and with respect to what H believes to be mutually believed in the discourse.

Notes

1. We employ the distinction between attentional and intentional structure proposed in Grosz and Sidner 1986.
2. This correspondence between phonological and semantico-pragmatic domain of inter-pretation is suggested by work on Japanese phonology (Pierrehumbert and Beckman, 1988).
3. Grosz and Sidner propose a tripartite view of discourse structure: a *linguistic structure*, which is the text/speech itself; an *attentional structure*, which includes information about the relative salience of objects, properties, relations, and intentions at any point in the discourse; and an *intentional structure*, which relates *discourse segment purposes* (DSPs)—whose recognition is essential to a segment's achieving its intended effect—to one another. Each DSP contributes to the overall *discourse purpose* (DP) of the discourse. DPs and DSPs are intentions whose satisfaction represents the main purpose of a discourse or segment, for instance, "Intend that an agent believe some fact" or "Intend that an agent believe that one fact supports another." Although all DSPs by definition must contribute to the DP, DSPs are also related to one another in two ways. First, DSP1 is said to *contribute to* DSP2 when DSP1 provides part of the satisfaction of DSP2; in this case DSP2 is said to *dominate* DSP1. Second, DSP1 is said to *satisfaction-precede* DSP2 when—

ever DSP1 must be satisfied before DSP2. These relations thus impose two partial orderings on DSPs in a discourse: a dominance hierarchy and a satisfaction-precedence ordering.

4. The question of how an accent becomes associated with certain material is not yet well understood. For example, the general association of accent with components of NPs seems fairly clear: For example, stressing *DRESS* in *the girl in the red DRESS* may serve to focus the whole phrase, the PP, the smaller NP, or simply the N, *DRESS*—whereas stressing *RED* instead in the same phrase, *the girl in the RED dress*, can focus only the adjective. But it is not clear that the various focus possibilities in the first case are all realized identically—that the accented *DRESS* will in each case have the same prominence, for example. And similar constraints on the accenting of parts of a VP are even less well understood.

5. We are not yet prepared to propose a particular representation for intonational meaning, and so this depiction should be understood as metaphorical only. In particular, we do not intend that these open expressions represent the presupposition of an utterance, as previously suggested by Jackendoff (1972) and Wilson and Sperber (1979).

6. This corpus was recorded by Hirschberg and Pollack in 1982 from a Philadelphia radio call-in program, Harry Gross's "Speaking of Your Money" (Pollack, Hirschberg, and Webber 1982).

References

Anderson, M. D., J. B. Pierrehumbert, and M. Y. Liberman (1984). Synthesis by rule of English intonation patterns. In *Proceedings of the International Conference on Acoustics, Speech, and Signal Processing*, San Diego, CA. Vol. 1.

Beckman, M., and J. Pierrehumbert (1986a). Intonational structure in Japanese and English. *Phonology Yearbook 3*, 15—70.

Beckman, M., and J. Pierrehumbert (1986b). Japanese prosodic phrasing and intonation synthesis. In *Proceedings of the Twenty-fourth Annual Meeting*, Association for Computational Linguistics, New York, NY.

Bolinger, D. (1958). A theory of pitch accent in English. *Word 14*, 109—149.

Brazil, D., M. Coulthard, and C. Johns (1980). *Discourse intonation and language teaching*. London: Longman.

Butterworth, B. (1975). Hesitation and semantic planning in speech. *Journal of Psycholinguistic Research 4*, 75—87.

Clark, H. H., and C. R. Marhsll (1981). Definite reference and mutual knowledge. In A. K. Joshi, B. Webber, and I. A. Sag, eds., *Elements of discourse understanding*. Cambridge: Cambridge University Press.

Cohen, R. (1981). Investigation of processing strategies for the structural analysis of arguments. In *Proceedings of the Nineteenth Annual Meeting*, Association for Computational Linguistic. Stanford. CA.

Cohen, R. (1984). A computational theory of the function of clue words in argument understanding. In *Proceedings of the Tenth International Conference on Computational Linguistics*, Stanford, CA.

Crystal, D. (1969). *Prosodic systems and intonation in English*. Cambridge: Cambridge University Press.

Grosz, B., and C. Sidner (1986). Attention, intentions, and the structure of discourse. *Computational Linguistics 12*, 175—204.

Gussenhoven, C. (1983). On the grammar and semantics of sentence accents. Dordrecht, Holland: Foris.

Hirschberg, J., and D. Litman (1987). Now let's talk about 'now': Identifying cue phrases intonationally. In *Proceedings of the Twenty-fifth Annual Meeting*, Association for Computational Linguistics, Stanford, CA.

Hirschberg, J., and J. Pierrehumbert (1986). The intonational structuring of discourse. In *Proceedings of the Twenty-fourth Annual Meeting*, Association for Computational Linguistics, New York, NY.

Hobbs, J. (1979). Coherence and coreference. *Cognitive Science 3*, 67–90.

Jackendoff, R. S. (1972). *Semantic interpretation in generative grammar*. Cambridge, MA: MIT Press.

Joshi, A. K. (1982). The role of mutual beliefs in question-answer systems. In N. Smith, ed., *Mutual knowledge*. New York: Academic Press.

Ladd, D. R. (1978). Stylized intonation. *Language 54*, 517–540.

Ladd, D. R. (1980). *The structure of intonational meaning*. Bloomington, IN: Indiana University Press.

Ladd, D. R. (1983). Phonological features of intonational peaks. *Language 59*, 721–759.

Ladd, D. R., K. Silverman, F. Tolkmitt, G. Bergmann, and K. Scherer (1985). Evidence for the independent function of intonation contour type, voice quality, and F0 range in signaling speaker affect. *Journal of the Acoustical Society of America 78*, 435–444.

Liberman, M. (1975). The intonational system of English. Doctoral dissertation, Massachusetts Institute of Technology, Cambridge, MA. Published by Garland Press, New York, 1979.

Liberman, M., and J. Pierrehumbert (1984). Intonational invariants under changes in pitch range and length. In M. Aronoff and R. Oehrle, eds., *Language sound structure*. Cambridge, MA: MIT Press.

Liberman, M., and I. A. Sag (1974). Prosodic form and discourse function. In *Papers from the Tenth Regional Meeting*, Chicago Linguistic Society, Chicago, IL.

Mann, W. C., and S. A. Thompson (1986). Relational propositions in discourse. *Discourse Processes 9*, 57–90.

O'Connor, J. D., and G. F. Arnold (1961). Intonation of colloquial English. London: Longmans.

Pierrehumbert, J. B. (1980). The phonology and phonetics of English intonation. Doctoral dissertation, Massachusetts Institute of Technology, Cambridge, MA.

Pierrehumbert, J. B., and M. Beckman (1988). *Japanese tone structure*. Cambridge, MA: MIT Press.

Pierrehumbert, J. B., and S. Steele (1987). How many rise-fall-rise contours? In *Proceedings of the Eleventh Meeting*, International Congress of Phonetic Sciences, Tallinn.

Pierrehumbert, J. B., and S. Steele (in press). Categories of tonal alignment in English. *Phonetica*.

Pike, K. (1945). The intonation of American English. Ann Arbor, MI: University of Michigan Press.

Pollack, M. E., J. Hirschberg, and B. Webber (1982). User participation in the reasoning processes of expert systems. MS-CIS-82-9. University of Pennsylvania Philadelphia, PA. A shorter version appears in the *Proceedings of the National Conference*, Association for Artificial Intelligence, Pittsburgh, PA.

Reichman, R. (1985). *Getting computers to talk like you and me: Discourse context, focus, and semantics*. Cambridge, MA: MIT Press.

Sag, I. A., and M. Liberman (1975). The intonational disambiguation of indirect speech acts. In *Papers from the Eleventh Regional Meeting*, Chicago Linguistic Society, Chicago, IL.

Schegloff, E. A. (1979). The relevance of repair to syntax-for-conversation. In T. Givon, ed., *Syntax and semantics 12: Discourse and syntax*. New York: Academic Press.

Schmerling, S. (1976). *Aspects of English sentence stress*. Austin, TX: University of Texas Press.

Selkirk, E. O. (1984). *Phonology and syntax*. Cambridge, MA: MIT Press.

Silverman, K. (1987). Natural prosody for synthetic speech. Doctoral dissertation, Cambridge University, Cambridge.

Ward, G., and J. Hirschberg (1985). Implicating uncertainty: The pragmatics of fall-rise intonation. *Language* 61, 747–776.

Ward, G., and J. Hirschberg (1986). Reconciling uncertainty with incredulity: A unified account of the $L^*+H\,L\,H\%$ intonational contour. Paper presented at the Linguistic Society of America Annual Meeting.

Wilson, D., and D. Sperber (1979). Ordered entailments: An alternative to presuppositional theories. In C.-K. Oh and D. A. Dinneen, eds., *Syntax and semantics 11: Presupposition*. New York: Academic Press.

Chapter 15

The Pierrehumbert-Hirschberg Theory of Intonational Meaning Made Simple: Comments on Pierrehumbert and Hirschberg

Jerry R. Hobbs

Everything I know about intonation I learned from reading Pierrehumbert and Hirschberg's very fine paper. Therefore, for me to write a critique of their paper would be to climb far out on a very long and fragile limb. Nevertheless, I will do just that. The general outline of what I propose here is the same as Pierrehumbert and Hirschberg's—a compositional semantics for tunes in terms of what is mutually believed. But it seemed to me while reading their work that, by tidying up one's theoretical assumptions a bit and by modifying the compositional semantics of complex tones, one could give a somewhat more elegant version of their characterization of intonational meaning.

We will need three background principles. The first is this: Every morpheme in an utterance conveys a proposition. In the sentence

George likes pie.

the information conveyed can be represented

$$(\exists e, x, y) Present(e) \land like'(e, x, y) \land George(x) \land pie(y).$$

The word "George" conveys $George(x)$. The word "likes" conveys $like'(e, x, y) \land Present(e)$. The word "pie" conveys $pie(y)$ for some possible or nonspecific entity y. This principle may seem strange at first blush. What about a word like "the"? But the word "the" conveys a relation between two entities, a linguistic object (namely, the description expressed by the rest of the noun phrase) and an entity in the world, and it says about that entity that it is the most salient mutually known entity of that description. In fact, when we emphasize "the," it is just such a proposition that we are putting forth. Similar stories can be told about other morphemes that are not usually thought of as conveying propositions.

The second background principle concerns what discourse is all about. Imagine the space of all propositions. The speaker and hearer in the dis-

I have profited from discussions with Janet Pierrehumbert and Julia Hirschberg about this work. The research was funded by a gift from the System Development Foundation.

course each have subsets of this space as their own private beliefs. But in addition there is a large overlapping set of mutual beliefs. (There is also a penumbra around mutual beliefs, consisting of those propositions the speaker and hearer both believe but that the speaker doesn't believe the hearer believes, and propositions that the speaker believes both believe but that the hearer really doesn't believe, and so on, but these marginal cases will not concern us in these remarks.) In addition, there are all those propositions that are believed by neither the speaker nor the hearer, many of them because they are false. The prototypical utterance is a bid to turn some of the speaker's private beliefs into mutual beliefs. The utterance is anchored referentially in mutual belief and reaches out into the speaker's private beliefs. An utterance thus contains the given propositions that anchor it referentially and the new propositions that the speaker is informing the hearer of. Much of intonational meaning is concerned with keeping these different partitions of the space of propositions distinguished. For convenience, I will refer to the speaker's private beliefs that are expressed in an utterance as "new," to the relevant mutual beliefs as "given," and, with some violence to the complexity of the matter, to those things the speaker does not believe as "false."

The third background principle concerns discourse structure and will be discussed later.

Now we are in a position to look at a very simple characterization of Pierrehumbert and Hirschberg's theory of intonational meaning. A pitch accent on a morpheme means that the proposition conveyed by the morpheme is important for the correct interpretation of the utterance. When the pitch accent is realized by a H^* tone, the proposition is new. When it is realized by a L^* tone, it is *not* new. Note that I did not say "given"; it may also be not new because it is not believed at all. Thus, L^* is used in Pierrehumbert and Hirschberg's example (3) because the information should already be mutually believed, whereas in (4) it is used because it is false.

A simple tone can be given a prefix, resulting in a complex pitch accent of the form $X + Y^*$ where $X \neq Y$. This conveys a kind of correction or accommodation of what the speaker believes the hearer might incorrectly believe the status of the information to be. Thus, $L + H^*$ says something like, "you might think this information is not new, but it really is new," and $H + L^*$ says, "You might think this information is new, but it really is not new."

The simple tone can also be given a suffix, resulting in the complex pitch accents $L^* + H$ and $H^* + L$. In addition, intermediate phrases and intonational phrases can be given H or L suffixes. A H suffix signals incompleteness or open-endedness. A L suffix *does not* signal incompleteness or open-endedness. Note the scope of the negation here. It is not the case that a L suffix signals completeness; it merely fails to signal incompleteness. "Open-ended" means something like, "What I've just conveyed by that morpheme or phrase requires further discussion before it is entered into mutual belief, or before its status with respect to mutual belief is agreed upon." I discuss below some of the ways this general characterization is instantiated in specific examples.

This is the whole theory.

Thus, I was completely convinced by Pierrehumbert and Hirschberg's account of the meaning of the **H*** pitch accent. It seemed to me that their account of the meaning of the **L*** pitch accent was also right, but could be made a bit cleaner. They say it means "salience without predication" and list a number of ways items can fail to predicate. In my account, there are just two ways something can fail to predicate, that is, fail to be proposed as new. It can be proposed as given or as false. The "given" accounts for their example (18):

(18)   Well, I'd like a Pavoni ...
    L*   **L***   **L* L H%**

The "false" accounts for their example (17):

(17) I   was wrong
   L* H   **L* H H%**

Pierrehumbert and Hirschberg note as a special case that cue phrases generally take a L pitch accent. But we need not see this as a special case. Cue phrases, like all morphemes, convey propositions. They convey propositions about the relations among segments of discourse. But if these relations in fact hold, the segments already stand in that relation, without the cue phrases being used. The cue phrases only help to emphasize relations that are already available in the text because of the information the segments convey. A cue phrase *could* convey a proposition that is either given or new, but usually the proposition will already be given implicitly by the content of the utterances. In fact, to use a **H*** pitch accent would be to suggest that the hearer couldn't figure out the relation from the content and is hence frequently seen as overbearing. A similar story can be told for greetings and vocatives.

The biggest difference between my account and Pierrehumbert and Hirschberg's is in the treatment of complex pitch accents. They decompose them into a **L + H** and a **H + L** pattern, and the placement of the * on either the H or the L. They come up with plausible interpretations for the **L + H** and **H + L** patterns but cannot come up with one for the *-placement or for the compositionality of **L + H** and **H + L**. They say, "... the meaning of each particular pitch accent may be derivable from the meanings of its constituent tones, plus some generalization about the interpretation of the star. However, beyond the observations just made, we are not able to present such a decomposition as yet" (section 5.5). By contrast, my account is completely compositional. There are two basic pitch accents, L^* and H^*, and these can then have a prefix, a suffix, or no affix at all. The meanings of H^* and L^* are exactly the same in simple pitch accents and complex pitch accents; the meanings of the H and L prefixes are related to the meanings of H^* and L^*; and the meanings of the H and L pitch accent suffixes are exactly the same as the meanings of the H and L phrasal and boundary tones. First I will examine some of Pierrehumbert and Hirschberg's examples to reinterpret them in light of my account. I will then present a broader comparison of the two accounts.

According to my account, the $H + L^*$ pitch accent should mean something like, "You might think this is new information, but it's actually not new." One way for it to be not new is for it to be given, so this pitch accent could be used where on the surface the information seems to be new, whereas in fact it is inferable from mutual knowledge and thus given. For instance, in Pierrehumbert and Hirschberg's example (45)

> (45) She's teething
> H^* $H + L^*$ H   L%

the hearer might think the information is new since the utterance is a move in a disagreement, but the speaker is suggesting that the hearer knows or should have known this fact and its relevance.

The other way to be not new is to be false, so my theory predicts another reading for $H + L^*$ that Pierrehumbert and Hirschberg's would not predict. It is difficult to come up with examples of this use of $H + L^*$, because what it would convey is something like "This proposition seems like it would be new, but it is really false," and if it is false, why say it. One way to come up with an example is to find a case where the speaker is denying what the hearer has just said, and in particular, denying the validity of the terms the speaker has used. Thus, suppose someone has just suggested that the analysis I gave of a stretch of discourse was a Freudian account. As it happens, I think Freudian psychology is disreputable and unscientific. I reply,

> It's not a Freudian account
> $H + L^*$

> It's a cognitive account
> H^*

What is conveyed here is not that "Freudian" is not new because it is inferable, as Pierrehumbert and Hirschberg's account would have it, but that it is not new because it is ill-conceived and false.

According to Pierrehumbert and Hirschberg's account, $L + H^*$ conveys a contrast or a correction. According to my account, the H^* indicates that the conveyed proposition is new, whereas the **L** prefix indicates that the hearer may have believed it to be not new. Our two accounts are consistent. There are two ways of being not new. The hearer could have believed the proposition false; this gives rise to the use of **L+H*** for correction. Pierrehumbert and Hirschberg's example (31) illustrates this:

(31)   It's even warm for December
$$\textbf{L+H* L H\%}$$

The hearer seems to believe that it is false that the month is December, and the information that it *is* December is apparently new.

Some examples of contrastive stress can be analyzed similarly. In

John's a lawyer, but he's honest
$$\textbf{L+H*}$$

the hearer may have inferred from "John's a lawyer" is that John is dishonest. But this is false, and the speaker is conveying the true and new information that John is honest.

The second way of being not new is being given. Thus, **L+H*** could say that the speaker might believe the proposition is already mutually known, but it isn't because it contains new information. One way for this to happen is for a set of possible alternatives to be already given and for the proposition to convey the new information about the specific alternative selected. Pierrehumbert and Hirschberg's example (35) is an instance of this:

(35)   They want to know if we can come for dinner
$$\textbf{L+H* L H\%}$$

The hearer knew an invitation for *something* was in the offing. The new information is that it is for dinner.

Let us next examine the suffixes. The **H** suffix on the **L*** pitch accent indicates that the proposition, although conveyed as given or false, is still open. It shouldn't be taken as relevant mutual knowledge until it can be considered further. All of Pierrehumbert and Hirschberg's examples (26) through (30) can be seen to exemplify this pattern.

(26)   He's a good badminton player
$$\textbf{L*+H} \qquad \textbf{L H\%}$$

It is mutually known that he's a good badminton player, but this is open in that the hearer might not have believed it relevant.

(27)   Sort of
$$\textbf{L*+H L H\%}$$

This is given in that the hearer should have known the speaker would carry out the garbage, but open in that it's not really an adequate answer.

(28)   Sort of
        L*+H L H%

This is given in that the hearer had just said it, but open in that it is uninterpretable.

(29)   Leo
        L*+H H L%

This is given in that the recalcitrant pet perhaps already knows it is wanted, but open in that the owner is not quite sure of this.

(30)   Jurgen's from Germany
        L*+H   H H%

Jurgen's existence is given, but the proposition is open because the speaker wonders why the hearer didn't think of it before and hence adds the H suffix to leave the matter open for discussion. To say the sentence with a simple L* pitch accent would be to contradict the hearer without leaving open the possibility that the hearer has an explanation for the oversight. Adding the H suffix mitigates the implied criticism.

My claims that the stressed information in examples (26), (27), and possibly (29) is given do not seem compelling to me. An alternate account might be this. A H suffix cannot be added to a H* pitch accent, for it could not be distinguished from a simple H*. The speaker thus has a choice of conveying the newness of the information or the openness. The openness is chosen, and this forces the pitch accent to be L*. Under this account, we might want to revise the theory to say that the L* does not signal "not new" but rather *fails* to signal "new." The L* pitch accent would then signal one of three things: given, false, or uncommitted.

According to my account, the H*+L pitch accent should say something like, "This is new information, and its truth and status are not open to question." One reason for it not to be open to question is that it is in fact inferable from mutual knowledge. This therefore explains compositionally Pierrehumbert and Hirschberg's observation that it indicates inferability. Thus, the pedantic tone in their (38)

(38)   Hit the hint key
        H*+L H*+L L L%

indicates that the student should already be able to infer this information.

It doesn't seem that inferability should be the only reason an assertion is not open. Authority and expertise are two other possibilities. A sergeant might say to a private,

Dig   that hole
H*+L   H*+L L L%

An obnoxious economist may tell a noneconomist in very positive tones,

Inflation isn't why that happened
$H^* + L$ L L%

Pierrehumbert and Hirschberg argue that $H + L$ means the proposition is inferable. This is the case in my account as well, most of the time, but for two independent reasons. $H + L^*$ usually says that the hearer might think the information is new, but since it is inferable, it is really given. $H^* + L$ says that this is new information and it is beyond dispute because it is inferable from mutual knowledge. However, I came up with examples of uses of each of these complex pitch accents where factors other than inferability justified their use.

According to Pierrehumbert and Hirschberg, $L + H$ evokes a salient scale. Since the set { *false, true* } is a scale, this is too close to vacuous to be compelling. Their association of $L^* + H$ with uncertainty or incredulity can be seen to follow from the openness that the H suffix conveys. Their association of $L + H^*$ with contrast and correction follows from the corrective or accommodative function of the L prefix.

I should say that my account would be a bit stronger if I could argue that a pitch accent is composed of a basic pitch accent H^* or L^* with an optional prefix and an optional suffix. That would mean that there would be pitch accents of the form $L + H^* + L$, conveying something like, "You might think this proposition is not new, but it is new, and that's that," and pitch accents of the form $H + L^* + H$, conveying something like, "You might think this proposition is new, but it's not new, or is it?" But Pierrehumbert and Hirschberg tell me that these do not occur. My account would also be stronger if there were complex tones in which the affix were the same as the basic tone. The complex tone $H^* + H$ would convey, "This is new information, but we can discuss it." Such tones would be hard to distinguish from simple tones, however, so it's easy to see why they'd be of little use in communication.

In my account, suffixes also occur on intermediate phrases and intonational phrases, and there too a H means that the unit—in this case, the phrase—is open. The most common way for a phrase to be open is for it to satisfy Pierrehumbert and Hirschberg's description of the meaning of a H phrase accent: "the current phrase is to be taken as forming part of a larger composite interpretive unit with the following phrase" (section 6). Thus, in their example (55)

(55)   George ate chicken soup   and got sick
       H^* H^* H^* H H^* H^* L L%

the first clause remains open, indicating that there is more to be said about the matter, and the second clause is taken to be strongly linked causally to the first. In (56)

(56)   George ate chicken soup   and got sick
        H*   H* H*   L   H* H* L L%

the causal link is not so strongly implicated. Pierrehumbert and Hirschberg say, "A **L** phrasal tone emphasizes the separation of the current phrase from a subsequent phrase" (section 6). This strikes me as a bit strong. I would say rather that it fails to emphasize the connection.

A **H** boundary tone in an intonational phrase also indicates openness. Pierrehumbert and Hirschberg's analysis of their examples (12) and (13) illustrates two ways for an intonational phrase to be open. In (12)

(12)   My name is Mark Liberman
               H* H*   L H%

the **H** boundary tone sounds strange if we take it to be suggesting that there is more to say about whether the speaker is Mark Liberman. But there is more that needs to be said concerning whether that fact links with the receptionist's expectations. In (13)

(13)   I thought it was good
        H*   H* H H%

the more that the speaker feels needs to be said is some validation of her opinion.

These examples, like yes-no questions, have an other-directed quality, but that is not what the **H** boundary tone signifies directly. Rather, it is derivative on the openness that is conveyed. There is more to be said, and it just happens that the hearer is the one who must say it. (It is an interesting question why ordinary *wh*-questions do not also take **H** boundary tones. One possibility is that incredulous *wh*-questions, which are more open than ordinary *wh*-questions, have preempted the **H** boundary tone.)

Boundary tones in connected discourse constitute just one more instance of the proposed meaning of suffixes. Pierrehumbert and Hirschberg say early in their paper, "An incorrect theory can make it difficult to establish interpretation, by grouping together contours that actually have disparate meanings or by drawing distinctions that have no meaning" (section 3.1). They apply this dictum to the theory of intonational phenomena to good effect, but unfortunately they do not apply it to the theory of discourse. The theory they adopt, that of Grosz and Sidner, is insufficiently rich in structural possibilities. It allows one to notice *some* of the discourse segments here and there and to talk about the obvious inclusion relations among them. But it recognizes only dominance and satisfaction-precedence relations among the intentions associated with the discourse segments. Using a theory this meager in its possibilities for discourse structure, all one can say about the high boundary tone **H%** is that sometimes it means the current segment dominates the next segment, sometimes it means the next segment dominates the current one, and sometimes it means the current one satisfaction-precedes the next one. In other words, it doesn't tell one anything at all.

On the other hand, Pierrehumbert and Hirschberg could have appealed to a theory of discourse structure that focuses on discourse segment *boundaries* in a recursive fashion and asks for each boundary what relation spans that boundary and binds the two segments into parts of a single discourse. There is no shortage of such theories; see, for example, Grimes 1975, Longacre 1976, Hobbs 1978, 1985, Mann and Thompson 1986, or Polanyi 1986. If they had, they would have been in a position to characterize the discourse function of **H** boundary tones in a very elegant fashion.

Thus, the last of the three background principles we must assume is that discourse is typically structured in a hierarchical fashion. Individual utterances, or intonational phrases, are discourse segments, and when some coherence relation links two segments, the two together constitute a composed segment, which can then in turn be a constituent of a larger segment. In such a theory, Pierrehumbert and Hirschberg's example (59)

> (59)　a. My new car manual is almost unreadable
> 　　　　　　　　　　　　**L L%**
>
> 　　　b. It's quite annoying
> 　　　　　　**L H%**
>
> 　　　c. I spent two hours figuring out how to use the jack.

has the structure shown in figure 15.1. Their example (60)

> (60)　a. My new car manual is almost unreadable
> 　　　　　　　　　　　　**L H%**
>
> 　　　b. It's quite annoying
> 　　　　　　**L L%**
>
> 　　　c. I spent two hours figuring out how to use the jack.

has the structure shown in figure 15.2. The differing structures are signaled

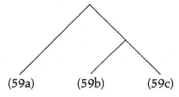

Figure 15.1
Structure of Pierrehumbert and Hirschberg's example (59).

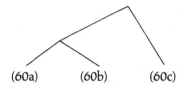

(60a)   (60b)   (60c)

Figure 15.2
Structure of Pierrehumbert and Hirschberg's example (60).

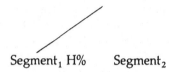

Segment₁ H%   Segment₂

Figure 15.3
The meaning of a **H** boundary tone.

by the boundary tones, and the differing resolutions for the pronoun "it" fall out of these differing structures (Hobbs 1979).

Given this theory of discourse structure, the characterization of the discourse function of boundary tones can be stated quite succinctly and can furthermore be seen as just another example of signaling openness. A **H** boundary tone at the end of an intonational phrase can signal that the intonational phrase ends a segment that is a *nonfinal* subsegment of a larger segment (figure 15.3). A low boundary tone *doesn't* signal this.

As a final illustration, consider Pierrehumbert and Hirschberg's example (7):

(7)   The train leaves at seven
          H*   H*   H* L H%
      It'll be on track four
          H*   H* L L%

The **L** phrase accent after the first sentence says that that bit of information is complete and can be believed as is, while the **H** boundary tone that follows it says that the sentence is not the last segment in the text but will be followed by more, related information.

Again, I feel that Pierrehumbert and Hirschberg's characterization of **L** boundary tones is a bit strong. They say that a **L** boundary tone indicates that the segment is to be interpreted with respect to what has come before, whereas I would say that it simply fails to indicate that the segment is to be interpreted with respect to what is to come. This explains the asymmetry they note at the end of their paper.

In summary, if the modifications I have suggested hold up, we see the English tune system as a simple, elegant structure for communicating the status of the information being conveyed by the utterance. It consists of a mere three elements: a **H*/L*** choice to signal new or not new, a shift from a **L** or **H** to a **H*** or **L*** to indicate a kind of correction or accommodation to what the hearer might have believed the status to be, and a **H** suffix to indicate the status is still an open question. The power and, at the same time, the seeming complexity of the tune system arise from the abstract character of what the intonational elements signify, allowing them to be put to many uses. If all of this is so, then, with the suggested modifications, Pierrehumbert and Hirschberg's theory of intonational meaning is an impressive achievement indeed.

References

Grimes, Joseph (1975). *The thread of discourse*. The Hague: Mouton.

Hobbs, Jerry R. (1978). Why is discourse coherent? Technical Note 176, SRI International, Menlo Park, CA. Also in Fritz Neubauer, ed. (1983). *Coherence in natural-language texts*. Hamburg: Helmut Buske Verlag.

Hobbs, Jerry R. (1979). Coherence and coreference. *Cognitive Science 3*, 67–90.

Hobbs, Jerry R. (1985). On the coherence and structure of discourse. Report No. CSLI-85-37, Center for the Study of Language and Information, Stanford University, Stanford, CA.

Longacre, Robert (1976). *An anatomy of speech notions*. Ghent: Peter de Ridder Press.

Mann, William, and Sandra Thompson (1986). Relational propositions in discourse. *Discourse Processes 9*, 57–90.

Polanyi, Livia (1986). The linguistic discourse model: Towards a formal theory of discourse structure. Technical Report 6409, Bolt Beranek and Newman, Inc., Cambridge, MA.

Chapter 16

Accommodation, Meaning, and Implicature: Interdisciplinary Foundations for Pragmatics

Richmond H. Thomason

1 Introduction

An interest in pragmatics generally arises through concern with the problems of some related field. In my case the related field was semantics. My interest in linguistic meaning originated in philosophical logic; the goal was to develop a logically based semantics in the spirit of Carnap 1947. This methodology was particularly narrow in relation to linguistic evidence. Philosophers in general, and philosophical logicians in particular, tend to concentrate on a few key examples that illustrate deep theoretical issues (though many of these examples seem fairly artificial, from a linguistic standpoint). The philosopher's game is to grapple in the theoretical arena with these few examples. This can lead to deep theories; but considered as theories of language the products of this methodology tend to have a certain artificiality and instability.[1]

Involvement with Montague Grammar acquainted me with semantics as practiced by linguists, and with much more demanding standards of how theories should be related to language. Thinking about examples was not new to me. But the breadth of contact with linguistic evidence, and the goal of putting theories in a systematic relation with this evidence, did seem new.

The tradition that developed out of Montague's work is now a small, but relatively healthy subfield of linguistics, that has generated a considerable literature of its own. Despite the record of progress on specific research topics that made these developments possible, this work hasn't created the sort of secure basis that would enable you, for instance, to write an

Ultimately, this article is a descendent of an unpublished manuscript, called "Semantics, pragmatics, conversation and presupposition," which I presented at the University of Texas in 1973, and circulated privately. Although I revised that paper several times and presented it elsewhere, it remained unpublished because I felt that the theoretical ideas were insufficiently developed. The approach that I take here owes much to the subsequent work of others. I try to acknowledge these debts as they come due in the course of the exposition; in particular, though, I'm indebted to Andrew McCafferty for general conversations on the topic, and for specific comments on drafts of this paper. This version of the paper was written in 1987.

introductory textbook with a sense of confidence in the stability of the material. Moreover, quite basic theoretical issues regarding commonplace linguistic phenomena remain largely unresolved: I am thinking of the interpretation of constructions like the conditional, generic plural, the definite article, and aspect.

In a way, it isn't surprising that attempting to apply these more demanding linguistic standards of evidence to semantic theories wouldn't meet with unqualified success. If this were a straightforward matter, the philosophy of language wouldn't have split earlier in this century into a "logical" school and an "ordinary language" school. During this time there were many clever people thinking about language, and someone would probably have noticed that the division was unnecessary.

Of course, philosophical logicians do recognize the need to relate their theories to evidence having to do with reasoning and language. This accounts for much of the interest in "truth conditions," since one way to refute a theory of validity is to show that some of the inferences it recommends are in fact invalid—that the premisses can be true while the conclusion is false.

But truth conditions are not transparent to observation. Our direct intuitions about the truth and falsity of sentences hold up in circumstances that are too circumscribed to test theories as we would like to test them. When we know all the relevant propositions, and are given enough information about a context, and we are given a sentence that would be appropriate to assert in the context, we can generally agree about whether the sentence is true. But in testing logical theories, the crucial cases are often sentences that would be inappropriate if uttered. And we seem to lack the intuitions that are needed to test validity. Though this has been a major and recurrent difficulty in logic, philosophical logicians have been slow to meet the methodological challenge.

To illustrate the historical point, I'll briefly consider three case studies: Strawson's criticism of Russell's theory of definite descriptions, the motivation of relevance logic, and Grice's causal theory of perception. Readers who are not interested in these details can pass over the next section.

2 Philosophy of Language and Evidence for Truth

2.1 Definite Descriptions

It is difficult to untangle the theoretical issues raised by Strawson (1950). I want to focus only on the methodological issue of what linguistic evidence Strawson is able to present for his conclusion that 'The king of France is wise' is neither true nor false. What this comes down to is an invitation to imagine that, with all appearances of seriousness, someone utters this sentence to you.[2] Strawson performs this experiment, and then makes the following points:

1. You wouldn't respond "That's untrue";
2. If you were asked to say whether you agreed or disagreed with what was said you would say (perhaps with some hesitation) that you didn't do either;
3. You would take someone's assertion of 'The king of France is not wise' to be evidence that he believed that there is a king of France.

Russell, of course, was skeptical about what could be learned about logic from usage. However, in his reply to Strawson he does makes one point bearing on the linguistic evidence.

> ... though I have no wish to support the claim of common usage, I do not think that [Strawson] can claim it either. Suppose, for example, that in some country there was a law that no person could hold public office if he considered it false that the Ruler of the Universe is wise. I think an avowed atheist who took advantage of Mr. Strawson's doctrine to say that he did not hold this proposition false would be regarded as a somewhat shifty character. (Russell 1970, 389)

Neither of the parties in this dispute explicitly confronts the thinness of Strawson's approach to matters of linguistic truth and falsity. The issue of *dissembling* that is raised by Russell's example illustrates the difficulty. Whether or not Russell's atheist is dissembling, we do recognize that dissembling occurs: there are cases in which you can mislead an audience by uttering sentences that nevertheless are true. And once we see this, we can immediately think of many other legitimate ways in which a true utterance can be criticized. Thus, in merely citing our reluctance to assert the sentence, Strawson has made an incomplete case that 'The king of France is not wise' is untrue. He must show that this reluctance is due to the sentence's untruth rather than to some other factor for which we could be criticized in asserting the sentence.

What is needed is some way of testing anomalous utterances for truth and falsity. Direct reflection is obviously of little use, since Russell and Strawson seem to have honestly had opposite intuitions in this case.

At this point, purely philosophical methods seem to have reached an impasse; I myself do not think that the matter can be taken further without an entirely different approach to the evidence.

2.2 Relevance and Conditionals

The theory of the conditional that is developed in Anderson and Belnap 1975 subscribes to the generalization that a conditional is untrue if the antecedent is not relevant to the consequent. The book is largely devoted to technical developments, and like many contributions to philosophical logic does not attempt to give a close examination of the linguistic evidence. But the relevance claim is illustrated by the following example: a mathematician writes a paper in which he makes a conjecture about Banach spaces, and then goes on to write

> In addition to its intrinsic interest, this conjecture has connections with other parts of mathematics that might not occur to the reader. For example, if the conjecture is true, then the first order functional calculus is complete . . . . (Anderson and Belnap 1975, 17)

Anderson and Belnap's point is that the editor would be right in asking the author to remove this claim from the paper; perhaps, as they say, the editor may even remark that the journal requires the antecedent of an asserted conditional to be relevant to its conclusion.

But a moment's thought makes it clear that there are many true mathematical claims that an editor would not allow in a publishable mathematics paper. Trivial claims are certainly among these. A theory of the conditional that makes the author's claim trivial would explain the editor's reaction just as well as one that makes it untrue.

Again, if we directly confront the issue of whether irrelevant conditionals are thereby untrue, we are forced to judge the truth conditions of utterances that in general will be inappropriate. And the issue is just as unclear.

For instance, "monkey's uncle" conditionals provide some evidence that irrelevant conditionals are sometimes treated as true. But as far as I know, there has been no definitive or really systematic study of the evidence on irrelevant conditionals. Relevance logic remains unsupported (and also unrefuted) by the linguistic evidence.

2.3 The Causal Theory of Perception

In Grice 1961, Grice makes methodological points very like the ones that I have made, but in the context of ordinary language philosophy rather than logic. He assumes that linguistic usage is an important test for philosophical theories, and addresses in particular a theory postulating sense-impressions that are caused by material objects in the course of perceptual occurrences. It is crucial to such a theory that statements such as "That looks red to me" are true even in the normal case when, without any suggestion of doubt or dispute, one is face-to-face with an obviously red object. However, statements of this kind are obviously anomalous.

This anomaly was one of the chief weapons invoked by J. L. Austin in his demolition of sense-datum theory.[3] Like Strawson, Austin makes much of the anomaly without directly recognizing truth as an independent issue, and confronting this issue.

For our purposes, the important parts of Grice 1961 are sections 3 and 4 pages 126–146. Grice prefaces these two sections by saying that for a long time he saw no way to use linguistic phenomena to resolve the question of whether these anomalous statements are neither true nor false, or are true but misleading—but that now he believes that this issue can be settled in favor of the latter position. Section 3 consists of a statement of the theory of implicature, including linguistic tests for distinguishing conventional from conversational implicatures. The main point of section 4 is to apply linguistic tests to 'That looks red to me', arguing from the results of these tests that the implicature is conversational.

Here, we have a case in which a philosopher of language does squarely face the issue of truth. And there has been progress; in fact, Grice has proposed his theory of implicature in these sections.[4] But the application of the theory to the philosophical issue is less satisfactory than one would like. In the last analysis, Grice's argument for the truth of statements like "That looks red to me" when 'that' refers to a ripe tomato depends on a highly indirect argument from simplicity; there is a general theory of conversational effects on utterances that predicts that these statements will be anomalous, even if they have the truth conditions that the sense-datum theorist requires. This theory is needed anyway for other purposes, and is explanatory. An alternative theory of truth conditions that invokes truth-value gaps would be more complex than the sense-datum theorist's. Therefore, on the whole, it would be better to say that these statements are true, rather than neither true nor false.

The argument depends on the simplicity and generality of a combination of a two-valued semantic theory with a pragmatic theory of implicature that predicts anomaly. The problem, however, is that simplicity and generality are not the only desirable qualities in a theory; rigor and precision of explanation count for something as well. And though the theory that Grice offers is very plausible, it is too loose-knit to support a good argument from simplicity and generality. Though they are unsatisfactory in many ways, rules for manipulating truth-value gaps can at least be made explicit and precise.[5] The most pleasant solution to this difficulty would be to preserve the generality and plausibility of Grice's aproach, while achieving a more explicit theory, and a much finer texture of explanation. I will urge in this paper that by putting together developments in computer science, linguistics, and philosophy we have some hope of making incremental progress toward this goal.

3 Prospects for Pragmatics

Whether one is a philosopher or a linguist, the process of trying to justice to evidence in cases such as those that I have illustrated quickly convinces one that simple theories of truth and falsity, even if they are made context relative, fail to do justice to the phenomena.[6]

Presupposition is one of the most obvious illustrations of the point. In fact, the use of a nonsemantic strategy of accounting for presupposition goes back about as far as it can, to Frege.

> If one therefore asserts 'Kepler died in misery', there is a presupposition that the name 'Kepler' designates something; but it does not follow that the sense of the sentence 'Kepler died in misery' contains the thought that the name 'Kepler' designates something. If this were the case the negation would have to run not
>
> Kepler did not die in misery
>
> but
>
> Kepler did not die in misery, or the name 'Kepler' has no reference. (Frege 1960, 69)

But if pragmatics rather than semantics is responsible for presupposition, we have to say exactly how it is going to carry out its responsibilities. If linguistic evidence must be confronted by a combined theory that incorporates both semantic and pragmatic elements, we need to have some sense of how explanatory duties will be allocated. Briefly, I have in mind the following picture.[7]

It is semantics that has to do with the interpretation of phrases relative to a context of utterance. Pragmatics should deal with the *use* of interpreted phrases: with what acts a speaker performs by using a phrase in a certain context. Among these acts are things like saying, implicating, insinuating, and presupposing[8]—thus, the message that a speaker *gets across* by saying something in a given context also belongs to pragmatics. And in fact, this is the part of pragmatics that I want to concentrate on here.

If, as Grice feels, the source of such phenomena lies in *principles of rational conversation*, it should be possible to single out certain important types of reasoning mechanisms and data structures that figure in communication among intelligent agents, and that work together to make implicature possible. These features should be independently motivated by linguistic and philosophical considerations, and should be theoretically central. I wish to nominate the following implicature-enablers: *speaker meaning as a sort of coordination-oriented intention, accommodation,* and the notion of *the conversational record*. None of these ideas is new; they have all been introduced by philosophers in the course of foundational projects having to do with pragmatics, and have been found useful by other philosophers, and by linguists.

4 Accommodation as a Stumbling Block

Pointing out the importance of language use, as I have done, is fairly easy. Building a theory of language use is less easy. It is not enough to have a large body of data, and methods for acquiring the data; discourse analysis, for instance, provides this. (See, for instance, Brown and Yule 1983.) And it is not enough to spin out theories. The problem is how to put theories in a productive relation with evidence.

If we take syntax as a model of what we should look for in a theory of pragmatics, we should seek to relate theories to linguistic evidence by way of a robust body of generalizations and tests. Many syntactic generalizations (such as "A tensed verb of an English clause agrees in number with the subject of the sentence") are intuitively appealing, are well supported by grammaticality judgments, and—though they are to a large extent independent of the details of particular theories—can be explained by syntactic theories. These properties enable informally stated generalizations to knit theories to evidence.

In pragmatics, the plausibility of informal rules is diluted by the fact that they are routinely flouted. Because of this, well-motivated generalizations not only will have exceptions, but many of these exceptions will be so flagrant as to seem to undermine their ability to serve as linguistic generalizations. To illustrate the phenomenon, I'll give three examples.

1. *Presuppositions of counterfactuals.* Considering the merits of Stalnaker's claim that when *A* semantically presupposes *B* it will be inappropriate to assert *A* unless *B* is presumed true, Lauri Karttunen says the following.

> For example, consider counterfactual conditionals. It seems clear that a sentence like "If Bill had a dime he would buy you a coke" can be a felicitous utterance even in contexts where the truth of "Bill does not have a dime" is not taken for granted by anybody else but the speaker himself. One can utter a counterfactual conditional "in good faith" with the intent of informing the listener, among other things, that the antecedent clause is false. (Karttunen 1973, 170–171)

Suppose that Karttunen is right about the semantic presuppositions in this case. Even so, does the example provide an argument against Stalnaker? Suppose that in fact there is a primary pragmatic rule that 'If Bill had a dime he would buy you a coke' should not be asserted unless it's presumed that Bill doesn't have a dime. Then the sentence should also be usable to assert that Bill doesn't have a dime; the primary rule can be flouted to achieve this effect.

2. *Factive presuppositions.* To take a similar example, imagine that you see the following sign posted in a hotel elevator.

> We regret that, due to renovations, our swimming pool will be closed to guests during the week of February 3.

The purpose of this sign is to inform guests that the pool will be closed. This would be a violation of Stalnaker's rule, on the assumption that 'regret' is semantically factive. That is, the rule that what is semantically presupposed should already be presumed true is flouted by the sign.

3. *Deictics*. Finally, here is a plausible rule about the use of deictic expressions: Do not use a deictic expression in a context in which the reference is not made clear.[9] As a corollary, you would not expect a conversation to begin with a sentence like 'Three of the others had called her'. But this rule is often flouted in the opening sentences of literary works. The first sentence of Tom Wolfe's *The right stuff* is a particularly striking specimen of the phenomenon. (And, partly because it *is* a violation of the rule, it is an example of good, vivid prose style.)

> Within five minutes or ten minutes, no more than that, three of the others had called her on the telephone to ask her if she had heard that something had happened out there.

The mechanism that figures in this sort of rule violation is *accommodation*, which is described in detail in Lewis 1979. Most generally, accommodation consists in acting to remove obstacles to the achievement of desires or goals that we attribute to others.

I am accommodating you, for instance, if I open the door when I see you approach it with your hands full of packages. We can gain important insights into pragmatics by noticing that accommodations can affect conventions, norms, or data structures, as well as states of nature. A hotel in the Caribbean might accommodate a German tour by accepting German currency, and the U.S. Internal Revenue Service accommodates the public by allowing income figures to be rounded off to the nearest whole number. These examples of accommodation involve temporary or permanent modifications of rules, but accommodation can be spontaneous and ad hoc; discovering that I am a dollar short, a shopkeeper may decide to mark off the price of the item I have bought.

The case in which a shopkeeper regularly marks off his goods for various ad hoc reasons is different from the case in which the goods have no price at all, even though the cash register receipts may be the same for the two cases. In the one case there is a rule established by a marked price, in the other there is not.

There is a natural temptation to say that a linguistic rule can't be a rule if it is regularly flouted. I have come to believe that progress in pragmatics depends on resisting this temptation, and allowing for rules that remain significant even when they are flouted. In his work on implicature, Grice appeals implicitly to such hidden significance; he postulates rules of usage (called maxims), but explains many phenomena by supposing an effect to be achieved by flouting these very rules. Though flouting creates methodological difficulties, I would like to see how far we can get in pragmatics by taking the mechanism behind flouting to be fundamental.

5 Accommodation as a Starting Block

I have been leading up to the point that to accommodate accommodation in pragmatics, we must relax the conception that prevails in syntax of rules or generalizations. If there is such a thing as accommodation, genuine pragmatic rules will be routinely violated, and these violations will not seem anomalous; they will achieve an effect that seems natural and normal. Unfortunately, this relaxation will loosen the connection between theory and evidence. Since rules can regularly be flouted, we can legitimately ignore certain counterexamples to rules; in fact, we can even take instances in which a rule is flouted to provide support for the rule.

In his methodology of science, Aristotle stresses that the accuracy of an inquiry depends on what the subject matter will bear. We should not expect biology to be as accurate as astronomy, or politics to be as accurate as biology. And the best indicator of the accuracy of a science is the extent to which its rules hold for the most part rather than universally. One conclusion that we could draw about pragmatics is that it is less accurate than other cognitive sciences, and in particular that its relation to linguistic evidence is weaker than what prevails in syntax.

Worse still, in pragmatics we can take instances in which a rule is flouted to provide evidence of a sort for the rule. We can argue like this: "There must, in our society, be a rule against hanging up a telephone without closing the conversation, or people would not violate this rule to achieve an effect of snubbing."

Consider the adage "The exception proves the rule." Pedants love to tell you that in this saying 'prove' has its root meaning 'to test', though ignorant people often misconstrue it to have the meaning 'to justify'.[10] No doubt the pedantic point is etymologically correct, and if you are thinking of rules like Ohm's law, it is hard to see how anyone could be wrong-headed enough to subscribe to this proverb. But in the case of social rules, I think we can see some point to the popular misinterpretation of this "linguistic fossil."

I am not recommending that we should declare pragmatics a methodological disaster area in which we encounter rules that have many exceptions, and which in fact are supported by some of these exceptions. I do say that accommodation is a fundamental mechanism in pragmatics, one we simply can't ignore. Unfortunately, it creates methodological problems that we need to work to overcome.

Our best hopes for fostering good interactions between evidence and theory in pragmatics, it seems to me, lie in concentrating on underlying reasoning mechanisms, and on adopting an interdisciplinary approach that spreads the sources of evidence wider than is common in linguistics. If such an approach is successful, perhaps generalizations will nevertheless have some contact with evidence, though this contact may be (even) less direct than what we find in syntax. We might claim, for instance, that the effect of accommodating a rule is always to swap the initial context for one that would have made the utterance appropriate. There is something to this; but the claim remains weak and attenuated unless we can turn this vague "would have made appropriate" into some more well defined operator on contexts. In general, there will be many different ways to adjust the context to make an utterance appropriate; how do we choose the right one?

We also have to look for ways of using indirect evidence, of spreading the evidential support for a pragmatic theory as broadly as possible, and in particular of finding unreflective linguistic processes that relate to pragmatic theory. I think there is little hope that we will find direct tests for distinguishing cases where accommodation is involved from cases in which it isn't: a special tone of voice, for instance, that comes into play when accommodation is invoked. But, for instance, work on intonation such as that described in Pierrehumbert and Hirschberg (chapter 14 of this volume) could be helpful in developing a theory of context. We have to hope that work of this sort will converge to provide the relation to evidence that a successful pragmatics will require.

Another way of constraining theories is by insisting that they be related to experimentation with computer programs. Examining the performance of a program is a powerful way of relating theories to linguistic evidence, and certainly is very different from either the introspective methods that are common in syntax or the more sociological methods that are used in discourse analysis. Moreover, this demand forces theories to be explicit, which is an extremely valuable constraint in pragmatics; and it imposes efficiency requirements as well. Work of the sort reported in this volume shows that theories of language use *can* be implementable. To keep ourselves honest we should now insist, I think, that a pragmatic theory *must* be implementable to be taken seriously.

Concentrating on accommodation means shifting to reconstructed reasoning that underlies utterances. And it suggests that certain reasoning processes, such as intention recognition and cooperation, are central. Successful accommodation requires that we first recognize someone's intention to achieve a goal, and then establish goals of our own that will assist in achieving this goal. These reasoning mechanisms have become prominent in computational thinking about cooperative dialog as well. To a certain extent, this thinking is quite independent from any philosophical or linguistic influence; obviously, for instance, an automatic help system (for, say, the UNIX operating system) will have to guess at the user's purpose when an incorrect command is formulated, and may then even go on to implement the conjectured command. Other computational work, such as that of James Allen, Philip Cohen, and Ray Perrault, not only converges on the reasoning mechanisms that are involved in accommodation, but is influenced by some of the same philosophical work that influenced me. See the bibliography below for references to this work.

6 The Conversational Record

At this point I will begin a more systematic discussion of the components of the pragmatic theory that I am trying to articulate, beginning with the conversational record.

When philosophers discuss rules they think of games, and David Lewis' game is baseball. Although it's hard to find examples of rules of accommodation in baseball,[11] this choice of games helps to make vivid the idea of *scoreboard kinematics*. The baseball scoreboard is a particularly garish way of keeping track of public information about the game at hand.

Similarly, let's imagine a public, evolving representation of the state of a conversation: the *conversational record*. Such representations have been invoked by pragmatic theorists under many names, and for a variety of purposes. The idea can be found in Stalnaker 1972, an early and fundamental contribution to pragmatic theory; and it is developed in Stalnaker's later works (see the bibliography below for references). It also appears in logically inspired theories of temporal reference and anaphora, such as Hans Kamp's discourse representation theory and Irene Heim's file change semantics,[12] and in linguistic work on deixis.[13]

Like the baseball scoreboard, the conversational record will be a bundle consisting of many components, some of which are more stable than others. The baseball scoreboard must record whether there is a runner on first base; it needn't record the batting average of the first baseman. What sort of information is stored on the conversational record?

For one thing, the conversational record should represent information *that is public*, that can be supposed to be available to all the conversational participants. This means that private memories, intentions, and beliefs of participants can't be assumed to be part of the conversational record unless steps have been taken to explicitly enter them. And these steps must conform to procedures that facilitate the publicity of what is entered on the record. I will have more to say about this constraint of publicity in the next section.

Also, just as linguistic evidence is needed to justify a syntactic structure, postulated elements of the conversational record should be supported by evidence from discourse. In general, the form of the argument is that the discourse couldn't develop coherently unless the relevant information were entered on the conversational record. In Stalnaker 1975a, Stalnaker gives as a reason for adding presumptions to the conversational record the fact that utterances like "John has children and all of his children are bald" are acceptable, whereas ones like "All of John's children are bald and he has children" are not. In Heim 1982 and Kamp 1981, broad linguistic support can be found for putting a set of "mentioned items" on the record. Fillmore 1975 gives reasons for adding a "home base" to the record, to account for words like 'go' and 'come'. In Lewis 1979 there is a long list of elements that might well be included in the conversational record, but without any linguistic argumentation for including these elements.

More needs to be done to consolidate this work and to find plausible ways of reasoning about the conversational record—bearing in mind that the evidential situation is complicated by the presence of accommodation and that the conversational record itself is a fairly rarefied theoretical construct, that is not closely connected to linguistic evidence by simple procedures.

The idea of an evolving data structure that influences and is influenced by reasoning processes is familiar from computer science. The intentional structures and focus structures proposed by Grosz and Sidner (in Grosz and Sidner 1986 and in chapter 20 of this volume) are perhaps good examples of structures proposed for computational reasons that would fit naturally on the conversational record. At least, the discourse phenomena that these structures are supposed to underlie—anaphora and topic management—are things that should be public if a conversation is to go well.

I used the word 'perhaps' because Grosz and Sidner's work doesn't make it entirely clear how their structures can be mutually recognized by the participants in a conversation. But the key to clarifying this matter is to discover cues and constraints that can serve to effectively communicate these changing structures to the participants in a discourse. Progress toward implementing their proposals in a relatively general setting would depend on providing such constraints.

The information manipulated by plan-based approaches such as that of Litman and Allen in chapter 17 of this volume and Allen's earlier work is only partially assimilable to the conversational record; the reason for this is that these approaches depend on recognizing intentions and beliefs, and many intentions and beliefs that are recognized by some of the participants in a conversation aren't mutually recognized, and so are not public from a conversational standpoint. Consider the following two cases: (1) Standing by your parked car, you say "I'm out of gas" to me as I pass by; (2) Standing by your parked car, you ask me "Where can I find a phone booth?" We can imagine that in both cases the stage setting is the same: as I approached I heard your engine turning over without starting, and noticed an out-of-state plate. You emerged from the car as I came up. In both cases I can infer that you intend to find a service station; but in the first case the intention is public, in the second it is not.[14]

If (as in the applications that advocates of the plan-based approach have in mind) we will be interested in producing helpful responses, we will in general be interested in using whatever conclusions we can reach about our interlocutors' beliefs and intentions, regardless of whether these are public or not. Intentions and beliefs that are *not* public will be especially important in applications of the sort discussed by Pollack in chapter 5 of this volume, where the task is to identify mistaken beliefs.

Any belief can affect our discourse. (For instance, it may be the topic of conversation.) So a theory of discourse that is continuous with linguistic methodology must limit the data and reasoning processes that are internal to the subject. I am suggesting public data and mutually recognizable processes as a plausible circumscription principle. The main test of this proposal will be its scientific usefulness; but it also has a kind of general plausibility. Mutually believed data, and procedures that contribute to what is mutually believed, are plausible candidates for obtaining a linguistic focus because there are very general considerations connecting mutual belief with convention, and convention with language; see, for instance, Lewis 1969.

There are few intelligent tasks that are merely linguistic, so it isn't surprising that serious applications in artificial intelligence involve both linguistic and extralinguistic reasoning. However, it serves some computational purposes (transportability, in particular), to separate these functions in developing intelligent systems. It remains to be seen whether a separation between domain planning and plan recognition on the one hand, and discourse planning and plan recognition on the other, is appropriate and helpful in artificial intelligence.[15] If it is, the theory that I am advocating here could be seen as the "linguistic" component of a discourse system. Current discourse systems represent the beliefs of the speaker and hearer, but do not attempt also to represent mutual belief. To achieve the separation of components I have in mind, the speaker's and hearer's beliefs would have to be distinguished from the ad hoc collection of mutual presumptions that figures in the conversational record. And some "beliefs" in the earlier work would appear as mutual presumptions. In some cases at least, this adjustment would be in the spirit of the work; what is represented as belief in much of the work is better construed as mutual supposition. Perrault's work in chapter 9 of this volume is a very good example of this.

For my purposes in this paper, the most important component of the conversational record is a structure **P** that determines the *presumptions:* the things that are supposed, or established, at a given stage of the conversation. I'll say that $\mathbf{P} \vdash A$ when **P** yields the conclusion A. These presumptions are perhaps best thought of as a kind of shared memory or common database that the participants construct for the purposes of the conversation.

Of course, presumptions will in general be modified in the course of a conversation. I'll suppose that for each proposition p there is an update operator $\mathscr{A}_p$ on the presumptions that gives the result of updating the presumption structure by adding the proposition p. $\mathscr{A}_p(\mathbf{P}) \vdash p$, and in many cases $\mathscr{A}_p(\mathbf{P}) \vdash q$ if $\mathbf{P} \vdash q$. However, update is a nonmonotonic operation, so that we can have $\mathbf{P} \vdash q$ but $\mathscr{A}_p(\mathbf{P}) \not\vdash q$; also we can have $\mathscr{A}_p(\mathbf{P}) \vdash r$ but $\mathscr{A}_{p \wedge q}(\mathbf{P}) \not\vdash r$, where $\wedge$ is propositional conjunction. Since the conversational record is public, the update operator must be public also. I assume that the reasoning mechanisms that operate here are essentially the same as those that operate in the suppositional or conditional reasoning of a single agent. (This reasoning is not particularly well understood, but fortunately what I will have to say here will not require a detailed theory of it.)

There is a close connection between *assertion* and the update operator; in fact, it is very like the connection between buying something and obtaining it, only perhaps more intimate. The goal of asserting a proposition is updating the conversational record with the proposition; and asserting a proposition is the standard way of updating the conversational record with the proposition.

Assertion as a speech act can't be *identified* with the update operator, because a speaker can effect an update without asserting anything. Though he made an update occur, Herod didn't assert anything when he caused John the Baptist's head to be brought in on a platter. But, just as obtaining is the point of buying, update is the point of assertion.

It is really a methodological issue whether we should expect the conversational record to contain enough information to characterize the goals of all or most speech acts. The goals of insulting and apologizing, for instance, may force additions to the conversational record that could not be supported by linguistic argumentation. But even if our criteria for additions to the conversational record are farily strict, I think we would have the materials for characterizing the goals of many general types of speech acts.

At this point, assertion looks farily simple: the general picture is just this.

Background presumptions		Input proposition		Shifted presumptions
$\mathbf{P}_1$	$+$	p	$\Rightarrow$	$\mathbf{P}_2$

But this simplicity is misleading; it disappears as soon as we talk about the *act* of assertion, rather than just its goal. If we consider how conversants go about achieving updates of the presumptions, things become more complex because of the strategic planning of speech acts. A speaker in a context c in which $\mathbf{P}_1$ is presumed may want to achieve a context in which $\mathbf{P}_2$ is presumed, and so will have the goal of getting p asserted. One way to accomplish this might be to utter a declarative-mood sentence expressing p. But there may be other ways: instead of saying to my wife "I'll need the car this afternoon," I say "I didn't tell you that I'll need the car this afternoon." Strategic speaking of this sort, of course, is one reason why we need a theory of implicature.

7 Public Constructs

The idea of explaining the goals of acts of meaning in terms of the beliefs and intentions of conversants goes back at least to Grice 1957, in which the point of a meaningful assertion is the creation of a belief, and the point of a meaningful imperative the creation of an intention in the hearer. This idea has been reproduced in the computational literature, and in fact can be found in most of the work in which planning is applied to discourse; Allen 1983 is a good example.

According to this picture of things, the participants in a conversation are attempting to work on each other. I have said that I would like to replace this with a slightly different picture, according to which they are working together to build a shared data structure. What I have in mind is like a group of people working on a common project that is in plain view. For instance, the group might be together in a kitchen, making a salad. From time to time, members of the group add something to the salad. But it is assumed at all times that everyone is aware of the current state of the salad, simply because it's there for everyone to see.

Thinking of things in this way is useful philosophically; for instance, see the discussion of speaker meaning in section 9, below. I hope, of course, that it could be useful computationally as well, but at this point the hope is untested.

I grant that in most cases that we'd want to describe as "conversation," there won't be anything like a literally shared memory. Normally, there will be no shared conversational record; each conversant will have its own representation of the record. But it is normal for conversants to assume that the representation is shared, for each conversant to treat its representation of the record *as if* it were a public object. Unless danger signals are perceived, a conversant won't distinguish between its representation of the record and its interlocutors' representation. If we were designing programs for conversing systems along these lines, the aim would be to have things work out so that the representations will start out coordinated, and coordination will be preserved by transformations, so that at all stages the representations of the record will match.[16]

In its simplest form, this would merely be the problem of getting two communicating database programs to exchange information in such a way that if they start out with the same information they will end up with the same information—not a difficult task, if the communication channel is large enough, and is error-free.[17] But the task becomes more complicated if the systems can plan strategic speech acts. To maintain coordination of the record, the two systems must plan these acts so that they will be success-fully decoded; this means that they must plan communication acts in such a way that their plans will be recognized. (A good plan to put something on the conversational record must be a plan for entering the information publicly, in view of the coordination constraint.) This way of looking at the problem could conceivably eliminate some of the logical complexity that finds its way into belief-based computational models of discourse.

To a large extent, the process I indicated would depend on the programs not only employing default reasoning in the recognition of intentions, but on their being able to reflect on this reasoning in planning utterances; that is, these programs must plan their utterances so that their interlocutors will default to the right interpretation. Though, as I say, I can't yet make any claims about the computational advantages of the conversational record, it in fact seems from Perrault's recent work that default reasoning does simplify things considerably. (See chapter 9 of this volume.)

Using presumption rather than belief would help the motivation of Perrault's rules: for instance, by eliminating the need to postulate the principle that hearers believe what speakers say. This is not a plausible principle of either conversation or epistemology. However, it *is* a reason-able principle of conversation that unless someone objects, what a speaker asserts is added to the conversational record.

In saying that assertion does not aim intrinsically at belief, I have driven a wedge between communication and belief. Of course, this also divorces communication from action—and perhaps one motivation of the belief-based approaches was to connect the two. On the view I'm advocating, what is the connection between assertion and belief? Well, the conversa-tional record is like a courtroom record; it is evidence, but we may not choose to believe all of it. What we choose to believe from what we are told is a special case (but a maximally complex special case) of what to make of evidence. Moreover, the very notion of belief is an oversimplifica-tion of the reasoning phenomena. Rather than a single system of beliefs that we maintain and apply in all situations, we are capable of harboring a variety of systems of suppositions, which are activated and which we are more or less willing to act on according to contextual factors. (See Thomason 1987.) Conversational presumption is a case of ad hoc supposi-tion, very like supposition for the sake of argument. However, supposition is usually serious rather than idle, and more often than not is credulous. In such contexts there is no practical difference between presumption and belief.

Consider the case of a congressman interviewing a witness at a hearing. What the congressman has to assume in order to keep track of the conversation and what he believes are two different things. Contrast this with a conversational system that is designed to be a total slave to its interlocutor; here, we can ignore the distinction between presumption and belief, and in other cases we might well ignore the distinction in order to simplify things.[18]

I don't have a very good picture of how the conversational record is initialized in human conversations. Topical or salient mutual beliefs normally go on the record; and so, the better acquainted the conversants, the larger the initial record. If the conversants' models of one another are badly out of phase, we may not be able to reconstruct a record.

The record can be changed in a variety of ways. At the most general level it can be changed either in response to conversational moves of the interlocutors, or by manifest, public occurrences in face-to-face conversations, which add to mutual beliefs. (Remember John the Baptist's head.)

The idea of the conversational record and its kinematics is one place where the research strategies of philosophy, linguistics, and computer science should blend fruitfully and reinforce one another. Philosophers can demonstrate the conceptual need for the idea and reflect on its foundations; linguists can show what things need to be built into the conversational record in order to account for linguistic phenomena; and using devices such as plan recognition, default reasoning, frames, scripts, etc., computer scientists can consider how to represent and augment the conversational record by means of feasible reasoning processes.

8 Plan Recognition

Through a process that is quite different from the methodology of either philosophy or linguistics (since it involves experimentation with the performance of computer programs) computer scientists working on discourse have come to see plan recognition as centrally important. Details on this subject can be found in many of the computational papers in this volume, and in the works cited in these papers.

But philosophical reflections on discourse by themselves can show that plan recognition is central from a general perspective. (Perhaps this point hasn't struck philosophers because plan recognition isn't familiar to philosophers as a category of reasoning.) I am leading up to the point that plan recognition is as important for understanding implicature as deduction is for understanding validity. For now, I want to illustrate the point for two notions that are connected to implicature: *speaker meaning* and *accommodation*.

8.1 Plan Recognition and Speaker Meaning

On a simple version of the account of speaker meaning in Grice 1957, a speaker S means p if S intends the hearer (1) to believe p and (2) to do so partly in virtue of the recognition of intention (1). For some reason, not much has been said in the philosophical literature about the concept that is invoked in (2)—"to come to believe p partly in virtue of recognizing intention i"—even though it is an indispensable part of Grice's analysis, is conceptually complex and philosophically problematic in its own right, and does not appear to be definable in terms of concepts like belief and intention.[19]

It is fair to say that this formula of Grice's is pointing squarely at the mechanism of plan recognition. Plans are wholes constituted of intentions, and we recognize intentions by fitting them into recognized plans.[20] To come to believe p partly in virtue of recognizing intention i is to come to believe p by recognizing a plan that involves i.

This fits in well with the general philosophical strategy of Grice 1957; one of the main goals of the paper is to account for speaker meaning in terms of concepts and capabilities that are not essentially linguistic. And there is nothing inherently linguistic about plan recognition; we are using plan recognition when we infer that someone is going to the airport on seeing them standing with luggage at the limousine stop.

The fundamental notions in Grice's 1957 definition, then, are belief, intention, and plan recognition (though he doesn't make the last of these explicit). Later, I'll suggest that the definition can be improved by substituting the conversational record, planning, and plan recognition for Grice's notions. *Any* good account of speaker meaning, however, should connect acts of meaning to planning and plan recognition, providing ways in which what we know about these reasoning mechanisms can clarify and inform the theory of speaker meaning.

8.2 Accommodation

Acting as if we don't have a flat tire won't repair the flat; acting as if we know the way to our destination won't get us there. Unless we believe in magic, the inanimate world is not accommodating. But *people* can be accommodating, and in fact there are many social situations in which the best way to get what we want is to act as if we already had it. Leadership in an informal group is a good case. Here is an all-too-typical situation: you are at an academic convention, and the time comes for dinner. You find yourself a member of a group of eight people who, like you, have no special plans. No one wants to eat in the hotel, so the group moves out the door and into the street. At this point a group decision has to be made. There is a moment of indecision and then someone takes charge, asks for suggestions about restaurants, decides on one, and asks someone to get two cabs while she calls to make reservations. When no one objected to this arrangement, she became the group leader, and obtained a certain authority. She did this by acting as if she had the authority; and the presence of a rule saying that those without authority should not assume it is shown by the fact that assuming authority involved a certain risk. Someone could have objected, saying "Who do you think you are, deciding where to go for us?" And the objection would have had a certain force.

Another familiar case, involving even more painful risks, is establishing intimacy, as in beginning to use a familiar pronoun to someone in a language like French or German. Here the problem is that there is a rule that forbids us to act intimate unless we are on intimate terms; and yet there are situations in which we want to become intimate, and in which it is vital to do it *spontaneously*, rather than by explicit agreement. If I find myself in such a situation, my only way out is to accept the risk, overcome my shyness, and simply act as if you and I are intimate, in the hope that you will act in the same way. If my hopes are fulfilled, we thereby *will have become* intimate, and it will be as if no social rule has been violated. A process of accommodation will have come to the rescue.

David Lewis elaborates many examples of accommodation—presupposition, permission, definite descriptions, coming and going, vagueness, relative modality, performatives, and planning—most of them having to do with linguistic rules. And he gives the following general scheme for rules of accommodation.

> If at time t something is said that requires component s_n of conversational score to have a value in the range r if what is said is to be true, or otherwise acceptable; and if s_n does not have a value in the range r just before t; and if such-and-such further conditions hold; then at t the score-component takes some value in the range r. (Lewis 1979, 347)

No doubt you could implement rules of accommodation in this form.[21] But I think we can understand the process of accommodation better, and assimilate it more readily to other sorts of resoning, if we think of it in terms of a combination of *plan recognition* and *cooperative goal adoption*.

In fact, I believe that accommodation is a special case of obstacle elimination, a form of reasoning discussed in Allen 1983. Obstacle elimination consists in (1) recognizing the plan of your interlocutor; (2) detecting obstacles to the plan in the form of certain false preconditions of subgoals belonging to the plan; (3) adopting the goal of making these preconditions true; (4) forming a plan to carry this out; and (5) acting on this plan. Step (1) is plan recognition. Step (3) is cooperative goal adoption. The other steps employ forms of reasoning that figure in noncooperative planning by isolated agents.

Opening a door for someone is a form of obstacle elimination. So is adding p to the presumptions when someone says something that presupposes p. The difference between the two has mainly to do with the social nature of the conversational record. In the case of the door, we simply don't have the practical option of acting as if the door were already open. In the case of the conversational record, to act as if the previous state of the record already involved the presumption p is to reset the record. The fact that changes in the conversational record can be made so effortlessly accounts in large part for the extensive role that is played by accommodation in conversation—at least in informal and noncompetitive conversation.

The principle behind accommodation, then, is this:

Adjust the conversational record to eliminate obstacles to the detected plans of your interlocutor.

If the term hadn't already been claimed, this could well have been called the *cooperative principle*.

9 Speaker Meaning

Ordinarily, we mean something by what we say. We can mean things without saying anything, and when we say something the meaning of the words we say need not be the same as what we mean; the literal meaning of our utterances can be displaced. We need an independent account of what it is for a speaker to mean something. Over twenty-five years ago, before he had developed the theory of implicature, Grice published such an account (see Grice 1957).

The paper does not explicitly say where the idea of concentrating on speaker meaning came from; my guess would be that it originated (at least in part) in a critical chain of reflection initiated by J. L. Austin's work on illocutionary acts, and some other philosophers' ill-conceived attempts to characterize meaning in terms of use. The paper presents a definition of what it is for A to mean p by doing x. Grice's account of what he calls "non-natural meaning" is thoroughly familiar to philosophers, but may not be as well known to linguists and computer scientists as his work on implicature. Here is a formuation of the definition that will serve the purposes of this paper:[22]

A means p by x in case A intends an audience to believe p by (in part) recognizing this intention of A's.

For instance, by looking at his watch A means (to B) that it's time to go in case A intends B to believe that it's time to go, and to come to have this belief partly because B recognizes A's action as a sign of A's intention to communicate the belief that it is time to go.

Before suggesting a revision of Grice's definition, I want to return once more to the ingredients of the revision, and to suggest that communicating creatures with the capacity to accommodate each other and the capacity to reflect on this capacity will be able to deal in *strategic meanings:* in speaker meanings that differ from the literal interpretation of the message. That is, creatures with these abilities will implicate.

Part of the capacity to accommodate is the ability to recognize plans, at least in familiar domains in which one is able to plan effectively for oneself. By assumption, communication is such a domain for these creatures. Therefore, these creatures will be able to recognize plans to make p asserted, plans to update the record with p. Since they can accommodate, they can update with p as a result of recognizing such a plan. Since they are able to reflect on their abilities to accommodate, they must in some cases be able to form plans to make things asserted that exploit this communicative mechanism. But an utterance may reveal a plan to make p asserted without using language that literally expresses p.

Most conversational implicatures, I think, are meant;[23] and in fact the response "I didn't mean that" can always be used to renounce an implicature. Take one of Grice's examples: A says "Where does Smith live?" and B replies "Somewhere in the south of France," implicating that B is not able to specify the town where Smith lives. Here, it seems right to say that B *meant* that he didn't know what town Smith lives in.

One effect of the revision I'll propose of Grice's 1957 definition is that strategic assertion will be an instance of meaning. Like Grice, I offer this suggestion in an experimental spirit, though I have in mind a somewhat different arena of experimentation. In this spirit, the proposal is tentative. I hope that at least it is a good beginning.

> To mean p is to intentionally reveal an intention to make p asserted through the hearer's recognition of the status of an intention or plan of the speaker's.

Notice that this is a considerable departure from Grice's 1957 definition; and it makes plan recognition central to meaning. In fact, it is very close to saying that to mean something is to communicate it through plan recognition. It is also much less convoluted than Grice's definition;[24] nevertheless, it gives much the same results as Grice's, over a healthy spread of cases.

It should be clear now that to make p asserted is to add p to the presumptions of the conversational record; perhaps by updating the presumptions only with p, perhaps by updating them with other propositions as well. And when I discuss examples, it will become clear that the intention may have either an "activated" status, or a "frustrated" status.

This is an account of "indefinite meaning"—of what it is for p to be *a* thing that is meant, to be one among many things that are meant. Just as a plan may have multiple goals, we often mean several things by a given utterance. For instance, in Example 3, below, A means by "There's a gas station around the corner" that there is a gas station around the corner and also that the station is open. Just as one goal may dominate a plan with multiple goals, we often identify one meaning as preeminent among the things that are meant on a given occasion; this is *what is meant* on that occasion, or *the meaning*. This "definite" sort of meaning is not easy to characterize, and neither Grice nor I try to define it.

I'll illustrate the definition with some examples, chosen for variety.

Example 1. A says "I'll need the car," meaning that A will need the car. In this case the plan is to add a proposition p to the record by uttering a sentence that expresses p. The intention that is meant to be recognized is the very intention to assert p. I am in effect agreeing with Grice that when p is meant, the assertion may be intended to "take hold" partly because of the recognition of the intention to assert it. That is what happens in this case. I'm not sure, though, that this is so in all cases of meaning p.

Example 1 is a humdrum case, of course, but humdrum cases can be important, and actually these simple cases are problematic for Grice's 1957 definition, because they require the postulation of far-fetched hidden intentions underlying automatic, unreflective actions. Of course, postulating such intentions is a fundamental tactic not only of Grice's methodology, but of much work in cognitive psychology. If we subscribe to this methodology, I think we can say that the speaker intends his plan to make p asserted to be recognized. And in general, a hearer who did not recognize an intention to make p asserted would not update the record with p.[25] My own methodology also depends on ascribing far-fetched plans to conversational agents, plans that these agents might not reflectively acknowledge. So at least, I think I can make the following claim: if this case fits Grice's 1957 definition, then p would not become asserted without the recognition of the intention to assert it.

Example 2. A looks at his watch, meaning that it's getting late. Here A plans to make the proposition that it's getting late asserted. In some cases of this sort, at least, A intends the recognition of his intention to assert p to figure in the assertion mechanism. It is these cases that seem to be the ones that we would intuitively think to be instances of meaning that p. This is exactly what Grice noticed in motivating his 1957 definition. If, for instance, A's plan were rather to make the hearer aware that A thinks it's late and so to offer to leave, we would be less likely to call it a case of meaning anything. The account that I am urging agrees with Grice in claiming that in this second case nothing is meant either. But the reason for this is rather that A would have no practical reason to consider this to be a way of asserting p. I am supposing that the intentions involved in meaning must (like any intentions) be practical; and so A can't mean p unless A has a more or less sensible plan for putting p on the public record. What we have said in this case about A's intentions does not suffice to do this, because it doesn't sustain the creation of a mutual presumption. For instance, A is not, so far as we have described this case, intending that the hearer presume that A presume that the hearer presume p.

Example 3. A says to B "There's a gas station around the corner," meaning that the gas station is open.[26] I am imagining a context in which B plainly needs gas, in which A's discourse plan is to recommend to B a plan for getting gas, and in which B can easily recognize this discourse plan.

Ordinarily in such a case, I'd want to say that A intends the proposition that the station is open to be added to the conversational record. And in general, when a speaker openly recommends a plan, he (equally openly) invites the presumption that it is feasible: that the preconditions of the plan that are not within the agent's control are true (or will be true at the appropriate time). This seems a reasonable principle of conversation, as plausible as the principle of deliberation that in planning from an intended goal to a plan involving subgoals, intention will transfer to the subgoals. So in recommending a plan to get gas at a station, one is openly inviting the presumption that the station is open.

In this case, however, the primary discourse intention is to add to the record the proposition that there is a gas station around the corner; the intention to add the proposition that it is open (if the intention exists) is secondary. (This is what makes the assertion an implicature.) And unfortunately, the notion of what counts as a secondary intention is rather loose. When I buy a state lottery ticket in Pennsylvania, do I intend to contribute to the fund for the elderly that I know it supports? It is hard to say.

But secondary meanings are also hard to pin down; and if my definition is right, this is because they involve secondary intentions. In the gas station case, perhaps the best we can hope for is indicative evidence, such as the fact that in this case it would be natural for B to reply "How long will it be open?" We can also see that it is A's intention to recommend a plan *to get gas* that serves here to create the meaning.[27] Notice, for instance, that if B were on foot and had said to A "I need to make a phone call," then this same verbal response in A's mouth would not mean that the gas station was open—at least in cases where public telephones are often outside of gas stations.

A noteworthy point. We could have stated the proposed definition of meaning like this:

> To mean p is to intentionally reveal an intention i_1 to make p asserted through the hearer's recognition of the status of an intention or plan i_2 of the speaker's.

In the first two examples, $i_1 = i_2$. But in Example 3, i_2 is the intention to propose a plan for getting gas. For Grice (if we equate my "presumption" and his "belief" for the moment), the intention to make p asserted/believed must be part of the reason for the assertion taking hold. I am not sure how to settle this point definitively, but in the gas station case it seems to me that the speaker does mean (in many normal cases) that the gas station is open, and that it is more plausible to say that the assertion is intended to take not because of recognition of the intention to assert that it is open, but rather simply through recognition of the speaker's plan to assist the hearer with his domain problem. Certainly there is a direct chain of reasoning from recognizing this dominant plan to the presumption that the station is open, and there is no need to postulate as figuring in this process the recognition of a separate intention to assert that the station is open.

This is a significant organizational difference between my proposal and Grice's 1957 definition. It may expose me to counterexamples, but so far I haven't discovered any.

Example 4. B says to A: "I need to send a letter to Smith; where is he?" A says "Somewhere in the south of France," meaning (among other things) that A does not know what city Smith lives in. Like the previous example, this is a case in which the speaker's purpose is to assist the hearer with a domain plan. However, the response clearly is inadequate for B's purposes. Again, I have no definitive way of showing that A intends to add to the record the proposition that A doesn't know where Smith lives. It is indicative that B could say "Well, do you know where Jónes lives?" with heavy stress on 'Jones'. Also, in most cases A would want it understood that he is cooperating. I'll assume that A intends the proposition to be added.

In this case, I want to say that A is disclosing two plans: a discourse plan to answer B's question (on which A is acting) and a frustrated domain plan to help B mail the letter. Recognition of the frustrated intention to tell B the address, and identifying A's lack of knowledge as the obstacle to fulfilling the intention, is the reasoning process that is meant to enable the proposition that A does not know what city Smith lives in to be added to the presumptions.

Example 5. A says to Johnny, in the presence of B: "Now Johnny, tell B you dug up his bush." Here A does reveal an intention to make a proposition asserted, but also issues a command that will make the proposition asserted without reference to that intention. In cases such as this, A may or may not intend p to be added to the record (in part) through the recognition of an intention or plan of A's. If A does so intend, then according to the definition A means p; if not, A is trying to get Johnny to mean p, without meaning p himself. This result seems right to me. In cases where the alternative presumption-recording process is particularly vivid, like the head-on-the-platter case, it is more difficult to imagine the speaker meaning anything.

As in Example 2, practicality comes into play here. The reason why the intention is implausible is that an intention to have recognition of the intention to assert p figure in making p asserted would simply not be very realistic in such cases. Except in lapses, like the case in which the Reverend Spooner said "Leave by the town drain," meaning "Leave by the down train," I assume that our discourse intentions are normally practical.

Example 6. A and B are planning to go shopping. They need $50. B says "I have $20." A says "I have $40." A does not mean by this that A has more money than B.

There is no point in making things easy for ourselves by restricting the application of a theory of speaker meaning to positive instances. Negative cases are particularly good ways to discover weaknesses in theories.

This example illustrates a general point about intention-based accounts of speaker meaning; for such accounts to work, the intensionality of meaning has to be supported by an equal intensionality in intention. If there is no difference between intending to make p asserted and intending to make q asserted, then there can be no difference between meaning p and meaning q.

Unfortunately, there is no direct way to test for subtle differences of intentions of this sort. On the one hand, it does seem in this example that A meant he had $40, and didn't mean—even among other things—that he had more money. On the other hand, we'd expect A to say "Yes" if we performed the experiment of asking him "Did you mean to say that you had more money than B?" All this shows, I think, is that 'Did you mean to say' is used to query people about the consequences of what they said, without distinguishing these clearly from what they said. More generally, 'Did you mean to do' does not distinguish between intentions and foreseeable side effects, which is exactly the distinction we need to make here. To achieve some progress in these negative cases, it seems that we will need to say more about the intensionality of intentions in general, and of intentions to assert in particular, and also to find tests that extract more reliable conclusions from the evidence. The philosophical background, of course, suggests that it won't be easy to make progress on these matters.

Though the example points to weaknesses in the account, it is at least not a counterexample. The definition tells us that A didn't mean that he had more money than B if he didn't intentionally reveal an intention to assert that he had more money than B through B's recognition of an intention or plan of A's. And this seems plausible to me. If we change it to a case in which A does intentionally reveal such an intention (say, A and B have been arguing about who has more money), we change whether A means that he has more money.

On very crude grounds—simply asking oneself whether it would be natural to acknowledge an intention to assert something—I think that the judgments I have made here about whether p is intended to be asserted are plausible. But we badly need to be able to say much more about the reasoning mechanism, to show how intentions to assert are recognized. (It follows from what I said before that there must be coordination between the cases in which practical intentions of this sort exist and cases in which their recognition will occur.) In effect, what is needed is an account of discourse plans and how they are recognized. I hope that work such as that of Litman and Allen will help to fill in these details (see chapter 17 of this volume).

The major strategic difference between this revision and Grice's approach is the substitution of the presumption dimension of the conversational record for belief. As I indicated, this eliminates a class of glaring counterexamples to Grice's 1957 definition: answers to examination questions, where the hearer already believes the answer, or statements by a witness who has no hope that what he is putting on the courtroom record will be believed by the audience. Also, I am hoping that the fact that the conversational record must be public will absorb much of the complexity of Grice's meaning account.

Openly meaning to assert p is very close to meaning p. This is an (intended) consequence of the revised account. It is part of the definition that one must mean to assert p when one means p. Conversely, if A means p, A is intending to have the assertion take hold through recognition of the status of an intention of A's. And ordinarily when one openly intends to assert p (that is, when one intends to assert p in a way that aims at making itself recognized), there is no independent mechanism that will equally well cause p to be asserted. Usually we only intend to do things that need to be done. The main class of counterexamples are cases in which there is a separate mechanism, but the mechanism is not independent: the cases that I can think of are like Example 5. These do happen, but not all that frequently. And besides, most of them are cases in which it is not unnatural to say that the proposition is meant: for instance, it is plausible that I mean that you ate my candy when I say "Come on, admit that you ate my candy."

10 The Update Mechanism

It should be clear that I am aiming for a close relation between meaning and the mechanism for updating the conversational record. In the declarative case, the central mechanism is simply *the recognition of intentions to assert*— that is, the recognition of intentions to perform the update in question— and this is a special case of accommodation.

In fact, I am proposing as a general rule that whenever an intention to assert p is recognized, the record is updated with p. It is this rule, I think, that forms the core of the insight that conversation is in some sense cooperative.

This principle, of course, is a default rule; the update will in general not take hold if some appropriate participant in the conversation objects. Also, the principle is subject to felicity principles similar to those noted in Austin 1962b. For instance, the assertion may not take if the speaker is not authorized to make it: in ritual circumstances, as when someone speaks out of turn in a courtroom, and also in informal cases when someone simply speaks out of turn. And it may not take if the proposition is grossly off the topic.

The picture of update that I painted earlier is complicated by the fact (which shows up clearly in some of the examples that I presented in section 9, above) that speakers often kill many conversational birds with one stone; they intend at once to assert a number of propositions. In such cases, we can assume that the update is achieved by adding the conjunction of the propositions that are meant (though of course there may be differences in salience among the asserted propositions). However, we can expect that the problem of plan recognition in discourse will be complicated by this multiplicity of utterance functionality, since the recognition of multiple plans appears to be a much more difficult problem in general than that of single plans.

As I have said, for the record to remain public, the update process must remain coordinated; there must be a convergence between the things that are meant and the things that are recognized as meant; this will depend on successful modeling of the hearer by the speaker.

11 Conversational Implicature as Based on Accommodation

I have never been convinced that it is very useful to use the term 'conventional implicature' for the phenomena that Grice aggregates under this label.[28] So in what follows I'll simply talk about implicature, meaning something close to what Grice meant by conversational implicature. And I will confine myself, as before, to cases of assertion.

Implicature is chiefly to be classified with straightforward cases of assertion. Roughly, an implicature is something that in general we would agree is said and is meant, but that is meant indirectly, so that the speaker could (perhaps disingenuously) exercise an option to disavow it, saying "I didn't say that."[29]

Consider again the examples of section 9. In Example 1, something (the proposition that it's getting late) is meant, but not implicated. In Example 3, A says and means (but does not implicate) that there is a gas station around the corner; A also means and implicates that the station is open. In Example 4, A says and means (but does not implicate) that Smith lives in the south of France; A also means and implicates that A does not know what city Smith lives in.

Largely because the notion of implicature is negative (roughly, it intersects what is meant with what is *not* said explicitly), I think its main theoretical importance is to call our attention to the fact that many things are meant without being explicity said. Of more importance are the mechanisms that allow meaning to outstrip what is explicitly said: mechanisms like plan recognition, goal sharing, and accommodation. I have tried to write this paper to focus on these underlying mechanisms, and this must have made it seem that I was never going to get to the point. Now I would like to try to apply what I have said to implicature.

Part of what I am claiming is that accommodation is a common underlying *cause* of implicature, a cause that results in an assertion-like transformation of the presumptions.

But this effect can take various forms—in particular, it may involve either an *accommodated revision of the background presumptions*, or an *accommodated revision of the input proposition*. This distinction gives rise to two kinds of conversational implicatures: *background implicatures* and *assertional implicatures*.[30]

An example of a background implicature is the case in which I say "I regret that I can't help you," saying and meaning that I regret that I can't help you, and meaning that I can't help you. (This is a case in which the implicature is both entailed and presupposed by what is said.) Another rather different example, which I'll discuss in more detail later, is "Arnold doesn't know that his shoelace is untied," used to implicate that Arnold's shoelace is untied. In both of these cases, I think, something is said that would be inappropriate if the current presumptions didn't involve the implicated proposition. The actual current presumptions may not involve this proposition, and the speaker makes the utterance with the intention that the hearer will accommodate it by amending the current presumptions, as well as adding the proposition that is directly asserted.

In a way, the term 'background implicature' is misleading; a background implicature, as the above examples show, may be the most important and newsworthy proposition that is conveyed by an utterance. In general, matters having to do with things like newsworthiness are orthogonal to matters having to do with mode of conversational presentation.

A case of an assertional implicature (one that I'll soon discuss in more detail) is the example in which I say "I didn't tell you I'll need the car" to my wife, implicating that I'll need the car. Here, the proposition that is literally asserted can't be used for update; it is already presumed. Rather, it is the implicature that is asserted. And if Grice is right about irony, some uses of this turn of speech will be assertional implicatures: for instance,

"Television is doing wonderful things for the ability of the American college freshman to write."

12 An Example

Let's consider again the case in which I say to my wife "I didn't tell you I'll need the car this afternoon." When I say this, of course, the main thing that I want to get across is that I'll need the car; and I do manage to get this across. But what I literally say is that I didn't tell her I would need it.

This is rewarding example to consider. It is a natural case in which to invoke Grice's Maxim of Quantity, and applications of this maxim in general show his theory to best advantage. However, if we look for explanatory detail, the results are far from satisfactory.

Invoking Grice's Maxim of Quantity, you could account for this implicature by imagining my wife asking herself what the point could be of my making this utterance. We both believe (and believe that we believe, and so on) that I haven't told her anything about needing the car this afternoon; it's no news. So the point of what I said must have been to do something else. A search for the point leads to the hypothesis that I mean that I will need the car.

This explanation is really not very satisfactory: (1) it doesn't explain how the interpretive reasoning gets started, and (2) it offers little or no hope of showing how it reached the conclusion that it does.

The problem with (1) has to do with belief. It isn't enough to say that my utterance is trivial when taken literally, since it is not in general true that we look for a hidden meaning when the literal message is trivial. The reason for this is that the contents of the conversational record may not coincide with what is mutually believed. Take Stalnaker's barber shop example, in which the barber offers you the following piece of news: "We've been having nice weather." Both of you *know* that the weather has been nice, and you both know that you know it. But you don't look for a hidden message: the barber means that the weather has been nice, and that is about all that he means. The problem is, why would it be unreasonable for my wife to interpret my remark about the car as like the barber's remark—an attempt to make conversation? Furthermore, there are many cases other than ones involving trivial assertions in which we do reconstruct implicatures; and we need some general way of explaining why this occurs.

Here it seems to me that computational work on planning provides a much more promising approach. In almost any sort of conversation we always feel compelled to reconstruct the plans of our interlocutors; and we want to see how the message we ascribe to them fits into a model of their purposes. If we can't do this, we are likely to resort to accommodation in order to make it fit. Triviality is one feature that makes it more difficult to achieve this sort of fit; and this is why an assertion that is literally trivial is likely to give rise to implicatures.

As for (2), I'll discuss the Maxims in more detail later, in section 13. But it should be clear that the Maxim of Quantity, and Grice's other maxims, really provide no clues as to how my wife could arrive at the proposition that I need the car. Presumably there are many relevant, informative, true things I could have said at this point in the conversation; and much stronger constraints are needed to limit the search initially and guide it to the one correct target, to the proposition that I'll need the car.

Here too, it seems to me that reconstructed plans are helpful. This conversational implicature seems to me to be induced by the recognition of the following plan. [I am reviewing my plans for the afternoon.] (a) I will need the car this afternoon; but (b) I can't assume that I can use it without my wife's agreement; and (c) the first step in negotiating for her agreement would be to tell her that I will need the car; but (d) I haven't yet told her that. So, since she is within conversational range (let us assume), it is natural for me to establish the immediate practical goal of telling her that I will need the car, with the expectation that this will enable her to recognize my domain plan.

But there are many ways of telling her this, and at this point I need to engage in discourse planning to choose a way of asserting that I'll need the car. The question is this: why is saying "I didn't tell you I'll need the car this afternoon" a feasible way of achieving my discourse goal?

The success of this discourse strategy, I think, depends in part on the fact that the sentence is negative and comes at the beginning of a discourse unit. Such sentences invite the hypothesis that they express a *lack*, and in fact point to an obstacle in a plan (of the speaker's, or perhaps someone else). This means that it is a default rule in interpreting discourse to seek such an interpretation of a negative sentence in such a position. For instance, if I begin a conversational unit by saying "There isn't a doorstop in this room," it would be appropriate for you to say "Why would you want a doorstop?" and it would be disingenous of me to say "I didn't say I wanted a doorstop." Thus, I can suppose that saying "I didn't tell you I'll need the car this afternoon" will launch a search on my wife's part for a plan of mine that would be thwarted by my not telling her that I needed the car. If she has a normal ability to recognize domain plans, this should suffice to meet my discourse goal.

As for why I should choose this way of saying it—rather, say, than "I'll need the car this afternoon"—the more complicated sentence is likely to be salient in cases in which I had intended to speak to her about my plans but had forgotten. Here I have detected an obstacle in my own plans, and that obstacle is foremost in my mind. And it is just in such cases that I am more likely to use a phrasing like "I didn't tell you I'll need the car this afternoon."

To a process of monitoring our interlocutors' plans and asking how a postulated meaning agrees with these plans, I believe we should also add a *mutual plan of the conversation*. In discussing the idea of the conversational record, I alluded to constraints on the way in which this record develops. Discourse must have a structure that enables us to anticipate, reconstruct, and remember the progress of a conversation. Many implicatures are generated by such *discourse expectations*, such as the implicature in the following dialog that Harry is home.[31]

> [Two people, A and B, are talking at work about a fellow worker.]
> A: "Where's Harry?"
> B: "He's sick."

This implicature, I think, is set in motion by the discourse expectation that the normal response to a question should help to answer the question.

13 Grice's Account of Implicature

In this section I provide further background concerning Grice's account of conversational implicature, and elaborate on the criticisms I referred to earlier in this paper.[32] This section is self-contained and can be omitted by readers who do not want to hear more about Grice.

Grice finds the source of conversational implicatures in the "cooperative principle." He does not explain this principle in much detail, merely saying that a participant in a conversation can always opt out, saying "My lips are sealed: I will say no more." In accounting for actual cases of conversational implicature, he appeals to four maxims: Quantity, Quality, Relation, and Manner. Grice's explanations of particular implicatures involve reconstructed bits of reasoning, showing how the implicature would be a reasonable thing to guess the speaker to mean, given the circumstances and what was literally said, or "said in the favored sense."

I believe that there is some truth in founding a central class of implicatures on the cooperative principle, and that requirements such as the *mutuality* of the conversational record may point to a deep level at which conversation must be cooperative in order to be possible at all. And accommodation, with its component process of goal sharing, is obviously cooperative. Nevertheless, not all conversational implicatures seem to be based on cooperation in any realistic sense; certainly, implicatures are possible in situations that can only be described as hostile and uncooperative. To apply the cooperative principle to such examples, you would have to appeal to shared goals that are relatively trivial, such as the goal of speaking in English. These don't seem very promising as explanations of pragmatic phenomena.[33]

I believe that it helps us to get a better grip on the relevant sort of cooperation if we think not so much of shared *domain goals* as of a shared sense of where the conversation has been and of where it is heading: the common plan of the conversation. Sharing a plan of the conversation may involve shared goals, but these have to do with discourse rather than with the subject at hand, and such goals, along with a common sense of the conversational record, can be shared even though the participants have few domain goals in common. Of course, many conversations also involve shared goals having to do with the task at hand, and these can enter into implicatures as well.

It isn't clear how Grice's maxims derive from the cooperative principle. But the internal looseness of Grice's theory is less important than the explanatory looseness of the maxims, their shapelessness when confronted with the phenomena.

Quantity, for instance, raises as many problems as it settles. This maxim tells us to say as much as is required. But that is a bit like asking a friend what you should wear to a party and being told to dress appropriately.

We obviously can't say all that we know. In a real, interactive conversation we can't even say all that we feel is relevant and helpful; we have to make a selection (either a reasoned or a random selection), and to hope that things will get sorted out satisfactorily as the conversation progresses. For example, when I tell you that Otto lives in Cambridge, I may be in a position to tell you that his mother knows that he lives there. The latter is more informative. It may even be pertinent. But I may still not choose to say it. And when I simply say that Otto lives in Cambridge, I do not implicate that his mother doesn't know that he lives there.

The moral is that we can never appeal *merely* to Quantity in explaining why, for instance, 'I tried to cash your check' implicates 'I didn't cash your check'.

The maxim of Relevance is even worse. Just about any implicature can be explained by invoking relevance. But such explanations are idle without some way of separating what is relevant at a given stage of a conversation from what is not.

My suggestion, then, is that we should replace the maxims with a general theory of group planning of public data structures, with special application to conversational planning. This theory should then yield many principles, more specific than the maxims, and deriving from the idea that what a speaker means should fit in and cohere with the conversational plan, and with the reconstructed plans of our conversational partners. The example of 'I didn't tell you I'll need the car' was supposed to illustrate the advantages of this approach in a specific case. (Given what I've said about speaker meaning, this is really just a theory of how implicatures are meant.) A general advantage of such an approach is that, just as plans have a complex structure (containing, among other things, subplans, with habits or automatic routines at the lowest level), we should expect to find a variety of explanatory principles, of varying particularity, that serve to regulate conversational planning.

14 A Bit beyond Foundations: The Case of Not Knowing

We test foundations by trying to put something on them. What needs to be put on these foundations is a broad spectrum of studies showing how to give detailed explanations of why implicatures are generated in some cases, and why they are not in others. Since these matters are very sensitive to context, it is really necessary to simultaneously develop a theory of the context, including representations of the features that affect implicature, as well as an account of how implicature is dependent on context. This is a special case—but a very complex special case—of developing a theory of data structures and of the reasoning procedures that interact with these data structures.

The present paper doesn't show enough detail to show that the foundation I have argued for will support the weight of implicature. However, McCafferty 1987 provides an extended study that goes much farther in this direction. And I would like to conclude by discussing one more example: the implicature that accompanies denials that someone knows something. This is a difficult case, one that has concerned me for a long time. I'm still not certain that I have gotten to the bottom of it.

Ordinarily, in saying that Arnold doesn't know that his shoelace is untied, I implicate that his shoelace is untied. The implicature appears to be conversational. For one thing, the implicature disappears in contexts in which it would be natural to stress the word 'know' (and in other contexts as well).[34] For another, 'know' is one of a class of predicates taking 'that' complements that carry an implicature of this sort: some of these, like 'aware', 'realize', and 'see', are synonyms or near-synonyms of 'know'. Others, like 'discover', 'find out', and 'remember', are more distant.[35]

I have changed my mind often about this implicature. One explanation that has survived many of these changes appeals to two things. (1) Often, whoever is speaking about a topic is liable to be given "expert" status. The expert is presumed to know the answers to the range of questions associated with the topic. Of course, this presumption is defeasible. But it has a certain prima facie force. Probably all of us who have unguardedly introduced a topic, only to be pressed with embarrassing questions, have suffered from this rule. (The worst case is to read an academic paper.) In a relatively nonstructured situation, the role of expert can shift: it usually falls on the last person who has made an undefended assertion about a topic.

This has the consequence that in the absence of anything suggesting the contrary, there will be a presumption that the speaker who says "Arnold doesn't know that his shoelace is untied" will be presumed to know whether Arnold's shoelace is untied. (An added factor in this case is that the speaker doesn't choose to use the version with 'whether' rather than the version with 'that'. Because of the semantic differences between 'whether' and 'that', this would have the effect of hedging.)

(2) Denying that someone knows something will have a *point*. The question of whether someone knows something doesn't ordinarily arise unless we are conerned to praise or blame him, or to explain or predict some action, opinion, or the like. But, on the supposition that a proposition is false, denying that someone knows the proposition can serve neither of these purposes. It is no defect to be ignorant of what is false. And if something is false, the connections are undercut between the hypothesis that someone doesn't know it and his actions. (This is why, when a proposition is in doubt at a stage of a conversation,[36] and we are interested in someone's actions or opinions, we speak of whether he *believes* the proposition, or *knows whether* it is true, not of whether he knows it.)

Of course, there is another explanation, like the one that I invoked in a previous example: negative sentences like this one suggest obstacles to plans. That would have to be relaxed a bit, since in this case it is more an obstacle to Arnold's general welfare that is at stake. The explanation depends on the fact that Arnold's not knowing p couldn't be an obstacle to anything unless p were true. This explanation works over a wide range of examples, but I suspect that it would be hard to make it do justice to the full range of cases.

The explanation would have to be filled in with a number of rather particular, perhaps even listlike, principles about conversation and reasoning. And the trouble with lists is that it is very hard to tell when we should call them complete. But perhaps cognitive psychology could provide some help in organizing the lists. Also, the reasoning I have been describing is highly defeasible. To make sense of it, we need a theory of default reasoning. But we badly need such a theory anyway: in logic, cognitive psychology, and artificial intelligence. My hope is that these disciplines can be made to work together in accounting for conversational implicatures.

I'll conclude with a brief and very incomplete attempt to explain why stressing the word 'know' cancels the implicature in 'Arnold doesn't knów that his shoelace is untied'.

I favor a pragmatic account of contrastive stress: I believe that stress conventionally implicates that a list of alternatives of a certain form is open at a certain stage of the conversational record. I think of such a list as a pair

$\langle \lambda x A, Y \rangle$, where Y is a (possibly empty) set of values of the variable 'x'. For instance, the alternative list $\langle \lambda x (Arnold\ kissed\ x), \{Betty, Sue\} \rangle$ might be a reasonable background for 'Arnold kissed Súe', with heavy stress on 'Sue'. We must think of sets of alternatives as part of the conversational record. (It clearly would not do to identify the sort of *active* opening of options that goes along with a set of alternatives with a mere absence of suppositions. More is conveyed by contrastive stress of 'Sue' in 'Arnold kissed Súe' than absence of the supposition that Arnold didn't kiss someone else.)

It follows from what we have said about rules of conversation that contrastive stress can be used as a way of *implicating* that certain alternatives are open. Which alternative list is called up by such an implicature is heavily dependent on the context.

Second, stressed negatives are usually used, when they are used assertively, to exclude certain members of a list of alternatives and to force the remaining alternatives. The following case is typical. "She's in her office or at home. But she isn't in her office. So she must be at home." (There also often is implicature, which seems to be conversational, to the effect that the excluded alternative was the favored one, so that it is somewhat surprising that it is excluded.)

Third, if an alternative is presented to knowledge, we expect it to be belief. In fact, the alternative set $\{know, believe\}$ is so natural that it is hard to force a different alternative set involving knowledge.

From these things, we can infer that 'Arnold doesn't know that his shoelace is untied' will ordinarily be used to say that Arnold believes that Arnold's shoelace is untied, though he does not know it. Ever since Plato, philosophers have known that knowledge is not the same thing as true belief. Even so, it remains true that we do not ordinarily claim that someone believes something without knowing it unless we want to cast some doubt on the belief: to open the alternative that it is false. Thus, any implicature that the belief is true will be cancelled in this case.

One useful moral of this case study is that we should not think of the conversational record merely as an accumulation of the suppositions that are in force at a stage of the conversation. It is a much richer and more diverse structure than this; and it contains, among other things, representations of the alternatives that are conceived as open. It is instructive, too, that this is just what is needed in order to represent interrogative speech acts.

It is perhaps a more important moral that considering evidence having to do with contrastive stress led us to a small, closed list of notions: the list consisting of knowledge and belief. And earlier, we were led to the thought that in order to obtain satisfactory explanations of implicature we would need to invoke such lists, and that it would be nice to have tests for their completeness.

One fruitful source of evidence bearing on these lists, I would like to suggest, is contrastive stress.

Notes

1. A good example is Russell's theory of descriptions, according to which 'the' generates both an existential claim and a uniqueness claim. An enormous philosophical literature developed over the existential claim and relatively little attention was paid to uniqueness, though there are obvious counterexamples, and the theoretical consequences of doing justice to them are probably more far-reaching. See McCawley 1985.
2. The paper has been reprinted so often that it is not very useful to cite page numbers. The passage I refer to begins with the fourth paragraph of part III.
3. Austin 1962a. This book consists of manuscript notes for lectures given regularly at Oxford since 1947, and revised after Austin's death by G. Warnock.
4. See Grice 1975 and Grice 1978 for published excerpts of the theory. The most extensive presentation of the theory is in Grice's William James Lectures, which have been widely circulated in unpublished form.
5. I myself advocated a semantic rather than a pragmatic approach to category mistakes in Thomason 1972. I have never been entirely happy with semantic theories of discourse anomaly even in this simple case, but I remain sympathetic to anyone who prefers these theories to pragmatic approaches because of their rigor, and for lack of anything better to take their place.
6. See, for instance, Kempson 1975, which makes points very similar to those I am summarizing here, with supporting evidence and many references to the literature.
7. This is pretty much the same as Stalnaker's proposal in Stalnaker 1972.
8. I would also include speaker meaning, for example, meaning that it's getting late, or meaning for someone to open the window, as a kind of act-scheme, if not an act.
9. The closest thing I have been able to find in the literature to a formulation of this rule is in Heim 1983: "For every definite, update an old card." This presupposes that a reference must already be established for every definite noun phrase; in effect, Heim's rule is the special application of our general rule to deictic uses of the definite article.
10. Here is what one pedant (Burman (1975, 79)) has to say: "This is one of the most fatuous of proverbs, as usually applied. Quite clearly the exception cannot prove a rule; quite the opposite; it *disproves* it."
11. Where there is competition and conflict, there is less likely to be accommodation; so in institutions like games, where bickering is undesirable, we are likely to regiment away the need for accommodation by codifying a more or less elaborate body of explicit rules.
12. See Kamp 1981, Heim 1982, and Heim 1983.
13. See Fillmore 1975.
14. For instance, in Case (1) you believe that I believe that you intend to find a service station; in Case (2) you probably don't believe this.
15. Work such as that of Litman and Allen seems to be moving in this direction; see chapter 17 of this volume.
16. Or match well enough. In many realistic situations an approximation of coordination will suffice, especially if there is a mechanism for detecting and correcting miscoordinations. (Such mechanisms clearly exist in human communication; much of the redundancy in conversation serves to check coordination. For instance, this seems to be why it is natural not only to ask a question but to explain the point of the question, as in an example cited by Pollack in chapter 5: "I want to talk to Kathy, so I need to find out the phone number of St. Eligius.")

17. The job is impossible if these assumptions are relaxed; see Halpern and Moses 1984.

18. But obviously, the distinction is needed in some computational applications: cases in which a variety of users can access a database, and need to be allowed different privileges in updating the database. If we had a system of this sort that also had sophisticated discourse capabilities, we might well want to separate presumption from belief in order to have effective conversational capabilities as well as integrity of data. Such a system, like a human being, would have to capable of harboring multiple systems of suppositions.

19. McCafferty 1987 is an exception.

20. In a way, this point is trivial, since single intentions can count as (degenerate) plans. In fact, however, we hardly ever recognize such simple plans in isolation.

21. This would require a distinction between "first-order requirements"—what is required by conversational rules other than the rules of accommodation—and the other rules. Also, the "such-and-such" clause would have to be either replaced with explicit conditions, or eliminated by invoking default reasoning.

22. Like the version of the definition that I presented in section 8.1, this is the declarative case only of the definition. But this version involves a self-referential intention, rather than two intentions, one of which refers to the other. I prefer this second version of the definition, though I think it would be very difficult to argue on the basis of linguistic evidence for one version or the other.

23. At least on an indefinite construal of speaker meaning; and this construal is clearly the target of Grice's analysis. (I realize that this remark is obscure; I'll clarify it soon.)

24. I am not denying that the reflections and convolutions of Grice's definition are part of the subject matter; but the idea is to locate them elsewhere. In particular, on the approach that I am trying to develop they are concealed in the mutuality of the conversational record.

25. This is plausible at least for human hearers. It would not apply, of course, to natural-language understanding systems that depended only on parsing.

26. Of course, this is a secondary meaning. The primary meaning—*what* A meant by saying "There's a gas station around the corner"—is that there's a gas station around the corner.

27. Or at least, it creates the meaning that A doesn't suspect that the gas station may be closed. If we add the presumption that A is a local expert, we get the proposition that the station is open.

28. It is clear enough from Grice's tests for distinguishing types of implicature that conventional implicatures will have something to do with linguistic convention. It is not so clear that they are always implicatures. Suppose that you say "Billie likes ice cream" and I say "Susie likes ice cream too." According to Grice's terminology, I "conventionally implicate" that someone else likes ice cream. But do I *implicate* it in this case?

29. There are, I think, some implicatures that can't be disavowed this way; in particular, implicatures that are entailed or presupposed by what is said.

30. New foundations for pragmatics should provide a theory-based classification of implicatures. I hope that this is at least a first step toward such a classification.

31. I'm referring to an implicature that, like most implicatures, involves a certain amount of stage setting—more than I've provided in this case. Accommodate me.

32. Though I use the word 'criticisms', I don't mean to suggest that I think of myself as a party to any significant philosophical dispute with Grice. I have the impression that Grice was tentative in the William James Lectures about his account of conversational implicatures, and may not have been entirely satisfied with its ability to generate detailed explanations of a wide range of cases. On the whole, I believe that linguists and computer scientists have taken the details of Grice's theory more seriously than they

perhaps should have. It is important to remember that Grice's William James Lectures were never prepared for publication. Since I haven't corresponded with Grice about the ideas in this paper, I don't know how seriously he takes the tactics of his theory, or what the actual points of agreement and disagreement are between our current views.

33. Of course, the cooperative principle is useful (though at a general level that needs to be supplemented with more specific rules) in explaining some things that are related to conversational implicature, such as the inference that the speaker doesn't know whether the coffee beans are in the cupboard or the refrigerator if he says that the coffee beans are in the cupboard or in the refrigerator. But at this point, the inferences that are made seem to be shading off into natural meaning, and I am not sure that I want to call them implicatures; compare the inference that the speaker believes what he asserts.

34. This is an application of Grice's cancellability test; it assumes that contrastive stress does not affect literal meaning, an assumption that I believe can be justified.

35. In this paragraph, I have applied Grice's cancellability and nondetachability tests for conversational implicature.

36. I hope it is clear that I am invoking two sorts of plans in accounting for implicatures: a common plan of the conversation, and plans of the participants. (The latter plans may be reconstructed by other participants in the conversation.)

References

Allen, J. (1983). Recognizing intentions from natural language utterances. In M. Brady and R. Berwick, eds., *Computational models of discourse*, pp. 107–166. Cambridge, MA: MIT Press.

Allen, J., and C. R. Perrault (1980). Analyzing intention in dialogues. *Artificial Intelligence* 15, 143–178.

Anderson, A., and N. Belnap, Jr. (1975). *Entailment*, vol. 1. Princeton, NJ: Princeton University Press.

Austin, J. (1962a). *Sense and sensibilia*. Oxford: Oxford University Press.

Austin, J. (1962b). *How to do things with words*. Oxford: Oxford Univeristy Press.

Brown, G., and G. Yule (1983). *Discourse analysis*. Cambridge: Cambridge University Press.

Burman, T. (1975). *The dictionary of misinformation*. New York: Thomas Y. Crowell Co.

Carnap, R. (1947). *Meaning and necessity*. Chicago: University of Chicago Press.

Cohen, P., and H. Levesque (1980). Speech acts and the recognition of shared plans. In *Proceedings of the Third Biennial Conference, Canadian Society for Computational Studies of Intelligence*, pp. 263–271. Victoria, British Columbia: Canadian Society for Computational Studies of Intelligence.

Cohen, P., and H. Levesque (1990a). Persistence, intention, and commitment. This volume.

Cohen, P., and H. Levesque (1990b). Rational interaction as the basis for communication. This volume.

Fillmore, C. (1975). *Santa Cruz lectures on deixis*. Bloomington, IN: Indiana University Linguistics Club.

Frege, G. (1960). On sense and reference. In P. T. Geach and M. Black, eds., *Translations from the philosophical writings of Gottlob Frege*, pp. 56–78. Oxford: Basil Blackwell.

Grice, H. P. (1957). Meaning. *The Philosophical Review* 66, 377–388.

Grice, H. P. (1961). The causal theory of perception. *Proceedings of the Aristotelian Society*, supplementary vol. 35, 121–152.

Grice, H. P. (1975). Logic and conversation. In P. Cole and J. Morgan, eds., *Syntax and semantics 3: Speech acts*, pp. 41–58. New York: Academic Press. Also in D. Davidson and G. Harman, eds., (1975). *The logic of grammar*, pp. 64–75. Encino, CA: Dickenson Publishing Co.

Grice, H. P. (1978). Further notes on logic and conversation. In P. Cole, ed., *Syntax and semantics 9: Pragmatics*, pp. 113–128. New York: Academic Press.

Grosz, B., and C. Sidner (1986). Attention, intentions, and the structure of discourse. *Computational Linguistics* 12, 175–204.

Grosz, B., and C. Sidner (1990). Plans for discourse. This volume.

Halpern, J., and Y. Moses (1984). *Knowledge and common knowledge in a distributed environment*. Technical Report, IBM.

Heim, I. (1982). *The semantics of definite and indefinite noun phrases*. Amherst, MA: Graduate Linguistics Student Association, University of Massachusetts.

Heim, I. (1983). File change semantics and the familiarity theory of definiteness. In R. Bäuerle et al., eds., *Meaning, use, and the interpretation of language*, pp. 164–189. Berlin: Walter de Gruyter.

Kamp, J. A. W. (1981). A theory of truth and semantic representation. In J. Groenendijk, T. Janssen, and M. Stokhof, eds., *Formal methods in the study of language*, pp. 277–322. Amsterdam: Mathematical Center.

Karttunen, L. (1973). Presuppositions of compound sentences. *Linguistic Inquiry* 4, 169–271.

Kautz, H. (1990). A circumscriptive theory of plan recognition. This volume.

Kempson, R. (1975). *Presupposition and the delimitation of semantics*. Cambridge: Cambridge University Press.

Lewis, D. (1969). *Convention*. Cambridge, MA: Harvard University Press.

Lewis, D. (1979). Scorekeeping in a language game. *Journal of Philosophical Logic* 8, 339–359.

Litman, D., and J. Allen (1990). Discourse processing and commonsense plans. This volume.

McCafferty, A. (1987). *Reasoning about implicature*. Doctoral dissertation, University of Pittsburgh, Pittsburgh, PA.

McCawley, J. (1985). Actions and events despite Bertrand Russell. In E. LePore and B. McLaughlin, eds., *Actions and events: Perspectives on the philosophy of Donald Davidson*, pp. 177–192. Oxford: Basil Blackwell.

Perrault, C. R. (1990). An application of default logic to speech act theory. This volume.

Perrault, C. R., and P. Cohen (1980). A plan-based analysis of indirect speech acts. *American Journal of Computational Linguistics* 6, 167–182.

Pierrehumbert, J., and J. Hirschberg (1990). The meaning of intonational contours in the interpretation of discourse. This volume.

Pollack, M. (1990). Plans as complex mental attitudes. This volume.

Russell, B. (1970). Mr. Strawson on referring. *Mind* 66, 385–395.

Stalnaker, R. (1972). Pragmatics. In D. Davidson and G. Harman eds., *Semantics of natural language*, pp. 380–397. Dordrecht: D. Reidel.

Stalnaker, R. (1973). Presuppositions. *Journal of Philosophical Logic* 2, 447–457.

Stalnaker, R. (1975a). Pragmatic presuppositions. In M. Munitz and P. Unger, eds., *Semantics and philosophy*, pp. 197–213. New York: Academic Press.

Stalnaker, R. (1975b). Indicative conditionals. *Philosophia* 5, 269–286.

Stalnaker, R. (1978). Assertion. In P. Cole, ed., *Syntax and semantics 9: pragmatics*, pp. 315–332. New York: Academic Press.

Strawson, P. (1950). On referring. *Mind* 59, 320–344.

Thomason, R. (1972). A semantic theory of sortal incorrectness. *Journal of Philosophical Logic* 2, 209–258.

Thomason, R. (1987). The multiplicity of belief and desire. In M. Georgeff and A. Lansky, eds., *Reasoning about actions and plans: Proceedings of the 1986 workshop*, pp. 341–360. Los Altos, CA: Morgan Kaufmann.

Chapter 17

Discourse Processing and Commonsense Plans

Diane J. Litman and James F. Allen

1 Introduction

Work on discourse understanding in artificial intelligence has produced a wide range of seemingly incomparable techniques, each addressing a slightly different problem. A recent paper by Grosz and Sidner (1986) is a first attempt at synthesizing and extending the different approaches into a coherent theory of discourse. Key to their framework is the incorporation of two distinct nonlinguistic components—the attentional (related to focus of attention) and the intentional (related to plans and goals)—into a theory of discourse structure. However, in *task-oriented dialogues*[1] an important distinction must also be made between discourse intentions and another nonlinguistic notion relevant to discourse theory: *commonsense*[2] task knowledge. This distinction is needed to account for subdialogues that do not directly correspond to commonsense tasks, for example, clarification and correction subdialogues. In this paper we present a plan recognition model for task-oriented dialogue understanding that explicitly separates what one explicitly says in a discourse about a task from commonsense knowledge about a task itself. We define a set of commonsense *discourse plans*, plans that can be dynamically generated from execution or discussion of commonsense task plans, and distinguish these discourse plans from the task plans. Furthermore, we distinguish discourse intentions from both task and discourse plans, that is, from commonsense plans to which discourse intentions refer. By incorporating knowledge about discourse plans into a commonsense framework, we can account for a wide variety of subdialogues in a discourse while maintaining the computational advantages of the plan-based approach.

Consider Dialogue Fragments 1–3, portions of a task-oriented cooking dialogue collected at AT&T Bell Laboratories:

Dialogue Fragment 1: Subtask Subdialogues
Teacher: Anyway um, and blend that for about twenty seconds. OK?

This research was supported in part by the Office of Naval Research under contract number N00014-80-C-0197 and in part by NSF grant IST-8504726.

Student: Uh huh.
Teacher: And now add, uh three quarters of a cup of heavy cream.
Student: OK.
Teacher: OK and you are to blend that for at least thirty seconds.

Dialogue Fragment 2: A Clarification Subdialogue
Teacher: OK the next thing you do is add one egg to the blender, to the shrimp in the blender.
Student: *The whole egg?*
Teacher: *Yeah, the whole egg. Not the shells.*
Student: Gotcha. Done.

Dialogue Fragment 3: A Correction Subdialogue
Teacher: OK, and now, um just wash off the parsley and um, put it on a paper towel to drain, and then we'll set up the plates. Are you hungry?
Student: Of course.
            Now there looks like there's mud in with this stuff.
Teacher: *Really?*
Student: *Really.*
Teacher: *Oh good, great, well, there's mud in the parsley?*
            We'll skip the parsley.
Student: *Sure looks like it to me.*
Teacher: *Oh goodness. OK, so*
Student: *I don't do have that much experience.*
Teacher: *OK.*
Student: *With parsley.*
Teacher: OK, take out five plates, 'cause I'm afraid the fish is going to start to get cold.

Fragment 1 illustrates subdialogues that directly correspond to cooking subtasks, and Fragments 2–3 illustrate subdialogues that do not correspond to such subtasks. For the purposes of this paper, we will call task-oriented subdialogues that do not correspond to execution or description of domain tasks *generated* subdialogues. For example, the clarification in Fragment 2 is generated by an underspecified description of a subtask, and the correction of Fragment 3 is generated by a problem encountered during the execution of a subtask. Although previous plan-based approaches (Allen and Perrault 1980; Carberry 1985; Grosz 1977; Sidner 1985) work well for subtask subdialogues (as in Fragment 1), they encounter difficulty in accounting for generated subdialogues such as clarifications and corrections. One reason for this difficulty is that previous plan-based models have not clearly distinguished between what one says in a discourse about a task and the actual knowledge about the domain task itself. For example, previous theories have only allowed discourses to describe steps in task plans (for instance, Grosz 1977) or to be steps in task plans (for instance, Allen and Perrault 1980). As Fragments 2 and 3 illustrate, there are also many ways that discourses can indirectly refer to task plans, for example, via clarifications and corrections. Although work in discourse structure (Grosz and Sidner 1986; Reichman-Adar 1984) has been more careful about maintaining a distinction between discourse intentions and commonsense task plans, such models have not been concerned with the recognition of task plans. Furthermore, they too have neglected the class of "interrupting" discourse intentions corresponding to generated task-related subdialogues.

In this paper we present a plan recognition model for task-oriented dialogue understanding that explicitly separates discourse intentions from commonsense plans that are the objects of such intentions. We define two types of commonsense plans: (1) *domain plans*, plans used to model the tasks, and (2) *discourse plans*, domain-independent plans that can be generated from execution or discussion of domain plans. Our discourse plans represent a new source of commonsense knowledge, mediating between task plans and an important class of discourse intentions. Our approach has several important advantages. First, the incorporation of discourse plans into a theory of task plan recognition allows us to account for a wider variety of task-oriented dialogues (for instance, dialogues with dynamically generated subdialogues such as clarifications and corrections) than previously considered. Second, the discourse plan formulation provides a clean computational model. Plans are a well-defined method of representation, but more importantly, the techniques of plan recognition can be adapted to identify appropriate discourse plans from utterances. Also, plans that usually are considered discourse plans may themselves become the topic of conversation and thus temporarily be viewed as domain plans. For example, clarifications may themselves become the objects of other clarifications. Since both the task and the generated discourse interaction are represented as plans, we can use the same techniques to handle clarifications to an arbitrary depth of nesting (in principle).

The next sections detail our new model of plan recognition. First, we elaborate on the distinction between domain plans, discourse plans, and discourse intentions. We then outline a simple theory of plans that is adequate for the purposes of this paper and show how discourse intentions, discourse plans, and domain plans are defined in this framework. Finally, we present a plan recognition technique for recognizing and relating commonsense structures of discourse and domain plans and illustrate our model with a detailed example.

2 Domain Plans, Discourse Plans, and Discourse Intentions

In this section we present examples illustrating the distinctions between discourse intentions and commonsense plans, and between commonsense domain plans and commonsense discourse plans. As discussed above, such distinctions are necessary to adequately account for subdialogues that are generated during execution and discussion of commonsense tasks.

Consider Dialogue 4 and figure 17.1, a simple task-oriented dialogue fragment and the commonsense task plan underlying it:

Dialogue 4
(1)   Person: I'd like to buy a ticket to New York.

(2)   Here's five dollars.

(3)   Clerk: The next train leaves in five minutes—better hurry.
              (handing Person a ticket)

(4)   Person: OK, thanks.

Figure 17.1 shows the recursive decomposition of a plan into its subplans, with an implicit temporal ordering from left to right. Thus, TAKE-TRIP consists of a BUY-TICKET plan (which itself consists of three subplans), followed by a GOTO-TRAIN plan, followed by a GETON-TRAIN plan. To simplify the current discussion, we will assume that this TAKE-TRIP plan is prebuilt. Formal definitions of plans, and their construction from observed actions, will be discussed later in the paper.

Let us examine why discourse intentions should not be conflated with commonsense plans. First, discourse intentions are not identical to commonsense plans. The discourse intentions underlying the beginning of Dialogue 4 are roughly (1) that Person intends Clerk to believe that Person would like to buy a ticket to New York (and maybe that Person intends Clerk to believe that (1) was a request for a ticket), and (2) that Person intends Clerk to believe that Person is giving Clerk five dollars to buy the ticket. In contrast, the commonsense knowledge underlying Dialogue 4 corresponds to the task plans to which these discourse intentions refer,

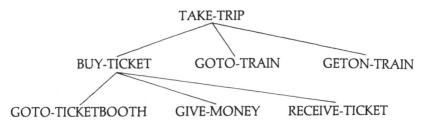

Figure 17.1
Sketch of a commonsense task plan to take a trip.

such as BUY-TICKET and GIVE-MONEY. In other words, commonsense plans are purely abstract structures, whereas discourse intentions are states of mind describable in terms of these structures.[3]

Second, there is no one-to-one correspondence between discourse intentions and steps in the associated commonsense plan. For example, discourse intentions may have only indirect relevance to commonsense plans (for instance, "Thanks" of utterance (4)). Furthermore, besides containing plans referred to in the dialogue (BUY-TICKET and GIVE-MONEY), the task plan contains plans that are inferred using commonsense knowledge, such as TAKE-TRIP, GETON-TRAIN. Although such plans are not explicitly mentioned, their recognition is necessary to provide cooperative behavior such as helpful responses (Allen and Perrault 1980). The helpful response (3) depends on Clerk's inference that BUY-TICKET is a subplan of a larger plan to take a trip. Inferred plans are also needed to account for actions that are never mentioned (Grosz and Sidner 1986), such as Clerk handing Person a ticket (RECEIVE-TICKET).

Third, the structure of discourse intentions does not necessarily follow the structure of the underlying commonsense task plan. Consider Dialogue 5, taken from a corpus of transcripts recorded at an information booth in the Toronto train station (Horrigan 1977) (Dialogue 6 will also be from this corpus):

Dialogue 5
   (5)   Clerk: Yes.
   (6)   Person: Can you tell me where to catch the GO trains?
   (7)   Clerk: Just go down to the bottom of the stairs here.
   (8)   Person: Do you get tickets down there too?
   (9)   Clerk: Yes.
  (10)   Person: Thanks.

Although the discourse intentions involve steps in the task plan of figure 17.1—namely, GOTO-TRAIN and BUY-TICKET—the discourse intentions are presented in a different order than the steps would be executed. This situation is often true of the "information-seeking" form of task dialogues (Carberry 1985).

To summarize, then, discourse intentions (1) are a different sort of entity than commonsense plans; (2) do not necessarily refer to any or every step in the associated commonsense plan; and (3) do not necessarily mirror the execution structure of associated commonsense task plans.

Now let us turn to the claim that in addition to commonsense domain plans, we need to introduce a set of commonsense plans called discourse plans. First, note that discourse intentions may refer to plans generated by, but not explicitly in, the domain plan (for instance, clarifications and corrections; see Litman and Allen 1987). That is, "in addition to the intentions arising from steps in the plan, the intentional structure typically contains ... intentions generated by the particular execution of the task and the dialogue" (Grosz and Sidner 1986, 187). Recall Fragments 2 and 3, in which the underlying cooking plan was at times referred to only indirectly, via plans to clarify and correct it. A more complicated example involving the generation of plans from domain as well as from other generated plans is illustrated in Dialogue 6:

Dialogue 6
(11) Person: Where do I get the CAN-AM train?
(12) Clerk: It's not until six.
(13)   They're meeting at cubicle C.
(14) Person: Where's that?
(15) Clerk: Just go down here.
(16)   It's on the right-hand side.
(17) Person: OK, thank you.

The discourse intention of (11), that Person intends that Clerk intends that Clerk clarify Person's plan to take a trip, is generated when Person realizes that GOTO-TRAIN (again using figure 17.1) cannot be executed, since the location of the train is unknown. The discourse intention of (14) is generated when Clerk's response (13) still does not provide enough information to execute the plan. In other words, these discourse intentions refer to a discourse plan clarifying the domain task and to a discourse plan clarifying this clarification, respectively. Thus, in the case of generated subdialogues, a set of discourse plans such as clarifications and corrections is needed to mediate between the discourse intentions and the domain plans.

Second, discourse plans should be considered part of commonsense knowledge for two reasons. First, discourse plans adhere to the three discourse intention/commonsense plan distinctions discussed above. That is, discourse plans are abstract structures that may be referred to by discourse intentions (as in utterance (11)), that may account for actions that are never mentioned[4] (imagine replacing the linguistic clarifications of utterances (12)–(13) with a nonlinguistic clarification such as handing the person a schedule), and so on. Second, by treating discourse plans and domain plans uniformly, discourse plans may themselves temporarily be viewed as domain plans (as in utterance (14), where a clarification is the domain plan of another clarification), to an arbitrary depth of nesting.

In the next section we present a much fuller discussion of discourse plans. We characterize the set needed, show how to integrate the representation of discourse plans into a domain planning framework, then specify the interaction between domain plan, discourse plan, and discourse intention recognition.

3 Identifying and Representing Plans

3.1 Representing Domain Plans

Domain plans represent typical tasks that might be performed in a given domain and correspond to the topics of task-oriented dialogues. Such commonsense knowledge has been the mainstay of previous plan-based works. Domain plans are represented as actions and states connected by causality and subpart relationships. Every plan has a *header*, a parameterized action description that names the plan. The *parameters of a plan* are the parameters in the header. As in other planning models (such as STRIPS (Fikes and Nilsson 1971) and NOAH (Sacerdoti 1977)), plans may contain *prerequisites, effects,* and a *decomposition.* Prerequisites are conditions that need to hold (or be made to hold) before the plan can actually be applied. Effects are statements that hold after the plan has been successfully executed. We will ignore most prerequisites and effects throughout this paper, except when needed in examples. Decompositions enable hierarchical planning. Although a plan may be usefully thought of as a single action at the level of description of the header, the plan may be decomposed into primitive (that is, executable) actions and other abstract action descriptions (that is, other plans). Such decompositions may be sequences of actions, sequences of subgoals to be achieved, or a mixture of both. For the purposes of this paper we are ignoring all temporal complexities in plans; plans are simply a linear sequence of actions.

Also associated with each plan is a set of applicability conditions called *constraints.* These are similar to prerequisites, except that the planner never attempts to achieve a constraint if it is false. Thus, any action whose constraints are not satisfied in some context will not be applicable in that context.

A library of *plan schemas* will be used to represent knowledge about typical speaker tasks. *Plan instantiations* are formed from such general schemas by giving values to the schema parameters. We will use the term *plan* to refer to both plan schemas and instantiations (the intended meaning should always be clear from the context). A plan recognizer will use the plan schemas to recognize the plan instantiation that produced an executed action. In particular, the recognizer will be concerned with recognizing plans from linguistic actions executed as part of a dialogue. The plan recognizer can build up structures of such instantiations, such as the structure sketched in figure 17.1. Before the process of plan recognition, such a structure is only implicit (and one of many possibilities) in the knowledge base.

Figure 17.2 presents some examples of plan schemas. The first plan indicates a primitive action, GOTO, and its effect, and the second through fourth plans indicate nonprimitive actions. For example, the third

| HEADER: | GOTO(agent, location, time) |
| EFFECT: | AT(agent, location, time) |

- -

| HEADER: | MEET(agent, arriveTrain) |
| DECOMPOSITION: | GOTO(agent, gate(arriveTrain), time(arriveTrain)) |

- -

HEADER:	BOARD(agent, departTrain)
DECOMPOSITION:	GOTO(agent, gate(departTrain), time(departTrain))
	GETON(agent, departTrain)

- -

HEADER:	TAKE-TRAIN-TRIP(agent, departTrain, destination)
DECOMPOSITION:	SELECT-TRAIN(agent, departTrain, departTrainSet)
	BUY-TICKET(agent, clerk, ticket)
	BOARD(agent, departTrain)
CONSTRAINTS:	EQUAL(destination, station(departTrain))
	EQUAL(destination, station(departTrainSet))
	EQUAL(departTrain, object(ticket))

Figure 17.2
Some plan schemas for the train domain.

plan summarizes a simple plan schema with header "BOARD (agent, departTrain)," with parameters "agent" and "departTrain," and with a decomposition consisting of the two steps indicated. The prerequisites, effects, and constraints are not shown. Other plans needed in this domain include plans to select trains, plans to buy tickets, and so on. To process dialogues in other domains (such as cooking, as in Fragments 1–3), a different set of domain plans would be relevant.

Throughout this paper we assume that formulas are expressed in a typed logic that will be reflected in the naming of variables. Thus, in the above formulas, *agent* is restricted to entities capable of agency, *departTrain* is restricted to trains, and so on. These types are organized into type hierarchies as commonly found in semantic network formalisms.

3.2 Discourse Plans

In addition to domain-dependent task plans, we introduce into the plan-based framework a small set of plans called *discourse plans*. Discourse plans are domain-independent plans that can be generated by other plans in the course of any task-oriented dialogue. For example, discourse plans can be generated from problems with the execution of a particular task (as in a task correction) as well as from problems with the discourse itself (as in a clarification). Discourse plans allow the recognition of an important class of subdialogues. Like domain plans, discourse plans can be the object of discourse intentions. However, whenever a discourse plan is recognized, recognition of the generating discourse and/or domain plan will also be generated by this recognition.

Our set of discourse plans can be abstractly characterized as the set of ways in which a single plan structure can be manipulated. For the purposes of plan recognition, it is useful to roughly divide the set into three classes: the plans that effectively continue a plan as expected; the plans that involve clarification and correction of a plan; and the plans that introduce new plans. These classes of plans are summarized informally below, via examples:

The Continue Class

TRACK-PLAN: In cases where an executing task action is nonlinguistic, a discourse plan can be generated that involves talking about the execution of this action. An example of this is utterance (2), which describes the handing of the money to Clerk.

The Clarification Class

IDENTIFY-PARAMETER: This discourse plan is generated when a task cannot be executed due to lack of information. In particular, IDENTIFY-PARAMETER provides a suitable description for a term instantiating a parameter of an action such that the hearer is then able to execute the action. For example, to execute the action GIVE-MONEY (P, AMT), P must know some description of AMT stated in terms of dollars, say VALUE-IN-DOLLARS (AMT, 5). Examples of requests for this discourse act include utterances (6), (8), (11), and (14). Examples of the discourse act itself include utterances (7), (9), (12), (13), (15), and (16).

CORRECT-PLAN: This involves specifying correction of a plan in order to ensure its success after unexpected events at runtime. There is no instance of this in the train dialogues, but an example might be to replace utterance (3) with "The fares just went up—you'll have to give me a ten." Fragment 3 also provides an example.

The Topic Shift Class

INTRODUCE-PLAN: This introduces a new plan for discussion that is not part of the previous topic of conversation. Utterance (1) (taken literally) is an example. Usually, however, plan introduction is performed implicitly. For example, utterance (1) only introduces beliefs about a plan into a conversation; it does not reflect speaker or hearer intentions about the plan's execution. In contrast, consider an utterance such as "Give me a ticket to New York." Here, introduction of the plan as a topic is implicit in the request for its execution.

MODIFY-PLAN: This introduces a new plan by performing some modification on a previous plan. There is no instance of this in the dialogues presented above, but an example might be to replace utterances (8)–(9) with "How about the buses?"

Though other discourse plans in each of these classes could be developed, the small set shown is sufficient to understand an interesting class of subdialogues in several domains (Litman and Allen 1987).

Except for the fact that discourse plans have other plans as parameters (and are thus technically *metaplans*),[5] our representation of discourse plans is identical to that for domain plans. In order to define them fully, however, let us introduce some language for referring to other plans. Developing a fully adequate formal theory of this is a large research effort in its own right and cannot be addressed here. Our approach so far is meant to be suggestive of what is needed and is specific enough for our preliminary implementation.

To talk about the structure of plans, we extend our ontology to include plans as objects. We then introduce several predicates that concern plans:

PARAMETER (P, plan): asserts that the term P is a parameter of the action description in the header of the specified plan. More formally, P is an instantiation of one of the parameters of the plan schema that *plan* itself is an instantiation of. Given the definition of BOARD in figure 17.2, PARAMETER (S, BOARD (S,TR1)) and PARAMETER (TR1, BOARD (S, TR1)) are true.

STEP (subplan, plan): asserts that *subplan* is part of the decomposition of *plan*. More formally, *subplan* is an instantiation of one part of the decomposition of the plan schema that *plan* itself is an instantiation of. Give the definition of BOARD in figure 17.2 STEP (GOTO (S, gate (TR1), time (TR1)), BOARD (S, TR1)) and STEP (GETON (S, TR1), BOARD (S, TR1)) are true.

Plans are not the only objects whose structure we need to examine. In addition, we will need to refer to parameters of actions and propositions. Thus, we will be working in a logic admitting plans, actions, and propositions as objects. The PARAMETER predicate will be used to make assertions about the structure of all these types of objects.

Figure 17.3 presents the formal representation of two example discourse plans, namely, IDENTIFY-PARAMETER from the clarification class and INTRODUCE-PLAN from the topic switch class. Unlike domain plans, such discourse plan schemas remain constant across all domains.

IDENTIFY-PARAMETER provides a suitable description of a parameter that enables the hearer to then execute an action in the clarified plan.[6] It is

HEADER:	IDENTIFY-PARAMETER(speaker, hearer, parameter, action, plan)
DECOMPOSITION:	INFORMREF(speaker, hearer, parameter, proposition)
EFFECT:	KNOW-PARAMETER(hearer, parameter, action, plan)
CONSTRAINTS:	PARAMETER(parameter, action) STEP(action, plan) PARAMETER(parameter, proposition)

. . . .

HEADER:	INTRODUCE-PLAN(speaker, hearer, action, plan)
DECOMPOSITION:	INFORM(speaker, hearer, WANT(speaker, action))
EFFECT:	BEL(hearer, WANT(speaker, plan))
CONSTRAINT:	STEP(action, plan)

Figure 17.3
Some discourse plan schemas.

performed by describing the parameter via some proposition. (INFORM-REF will be further explained in the section on speech acts.) There are several constraints on the relationship between the discourse plan and *plan* (the plan generating the discourse plan), namely, that *parameter* must be a parameter of an *action* that must be in the *plan*, and that the describing *proposition* involves *parameter*. The description should be sufficient to allow the hearer to execute the action, all other things being equal. This effect on the hearer is summarized by the assertion

KNOW-PARAMETER (hearer, parameter, action, plan).

For example, if agent P knows how many dollars a certain ticket sells for, then

KNOW-PARAMETER (P, AMT,
GIVE-MONEY (P, AMT), BUY-TICKET (P, C, TKT))

is true. In other words, the agent P knows a description of AMT sufficient to be able to perform the GIVE-MONEY act in the BUY-TICKET plan. Though the axiomatization of KNOW-PARAMETER is problematic, we will be using it only in simple cases where its use is straightforward.

INTRODUCE-PLAN introduces a plan into a conversation. In particular, it allows a discourse intention to just refer to a plan (rather than refer to a plan by executing it, clarifying it, and so on). INTRODUCE-PLAN is performed by stating a particular goal of the speaker (the decomposition), where the goal is a subgoal of *plan* (the constraint). The effect is that the hearer is then aware of the speaker's plan.

3.3 Discourse Intentions

Discourse intentions are purposes of the speaker, expressed in terms of both the task plans of the speaker (the domain plans) and the plans recursively generated by these plans (the discourse plans). We will limit ourselves to two types of discourse intentions: those in which agents intend to do these plans, and those in which agents intend other agents to intend to do these plans. We will use the speech act REQUEST to represent the latter case.[7]

Though the recognition of a *structure* of discourse intentions (Grosz and Sidner 1986) plays an important role in the recognition of discourse structure, this problem is not considered here. As discussed above, we are concerned with the recognition of structures of commonsense plans, to which individual discourse intentions refer.

3.4 Speech Act Definitions

To model speech acts (Searle 1969), we are assuming plan-based definitions as in Allen and Perrault 1980. In particular, figure 17.4 shows the formulation of the speech acts REQUEST, INFORM, and INFORMREF (a variation needed to handle "wh"-questions). INFORMIF, needed to handle yes-no questions, will not be needed for later examples and is thus not shown. We are also omitting our treatment (Litman and Allen 1987) of indirect speech acts (Searle 1975).

Unlike Allen and Perrault, we have explicitly added an effect that the hearer then believes the preconditions held if the act is done successfully. This could be inferred from first principles, but adding it to the definition allows us to use a simple plan recognition algorithm throughout the paper.

The only other difference from Allen and Perrault 1980 is that we have added an extra parameter to the INFORMREF action and the KNOWREF assertion. The assertion KNOWREF (A, t, p) means that A knows a description of term t, which satisfies proposition p and is informative enough to execute a plan.

This is simply a notational variant that is closer to the actual implementation. Thus, rather than stating the goal to know when train TR1 leaves as

KNOWREF (A, the x: depart-time (TR1, x)),

as in Allen and Perrault 1980, we write

KNOWREF (A, ?time, EQUAL (depart-time (TR1), ?time)).

Not all such assertions involve the equality predicate. For example, the

HEADER:	REQUEST(speaker, hearer, action)
PREREQUISITE:	WANT(speaker, action)
DECOMPOSITION:	SURFACE-REQUEST(speaker, hearer, action)
EFFECTS:	WANT(hearer, action)
	KNOW(hearer, WANT(speaker, action))
CONSTRAINT:	AGENT(action, hearer)

. . . .

HEADER:	INFORM(speaker, hearer, proposition)
PREREQUISITE:	KNOW(speaker, proposition)
DECOMPOSITION:	SURFACE-INFORM(speaker, hearer, proposition)
EFFECTS:	KNOW(hearer, proposition)
	KNOW(hearer, KNOW(speaker, proposition))

. . . .

HEADER:	INFORMREF(speaker, hearer, term, proposition)
PREREQUISITE:	KNOWREF(speaker, term, proposition)
DECOMPOSITION:	achieve KNOW(hearer, proposition)
EFFECT:	KNOWREF(hearer, term, proposition)
CONSTRAINT:	PARAMETER(term, proposition)

Figure 17.4
Speech act definitions.

representation of the goal behind the utterance "What do you want me to do?" would be

> KNOWREF (speaker, ?speaker-action, WANT (hearer, ?speaker-action)).

We can define this operator formally within a possible-worlds semantics of the BELIEF operator by using "quantifying in" as done in Allen and Perrault 1980. Although this analysis is not fully satisfactory, it is adequate for our present purposes.

3.5 An Example
To illustrate the relationships between discourse intentions, domain plans, and discourse plans generated from domain plans, consider again the first few utterances of Dialogue 6, repeated below for convenience:

> (1) Person: Where do I get the CAN-AM train?

(2)   Clerk: It's not until six.

(3)   They're meeting at cubicle C.

(4)   Person: Where's that?

Using the plan schemas defined above, we can represent the discourse intentions behind these utterances informally as follows:

(1)   Person intends that Clerk intends that
            Clerk identify the location parameter
            of the GOTO step of a BOARD CAN-AM train plan.

(2)   Clerk intends that
            Clerk identify the time parameter
            of the GOTO step of a BOARD CAN-AM train plan.

(3)   Clerk intends that
            Clerk identify the location parameter
            of the GOTO step of a BOARD CAN-AM train plan.

(4)   Person intends that Clerk intends that
            Clerk identify a parameter
            of the identify-parameter of (3) above.

Note that each discourse intention refers to a discourse plan,[8] which itself refers to its generating domain (as in (1), (2), (3)) or discourse (as in (4)) plan (and so on recursively, for discourse plans). In other words, each discourse intention ultimately points to a portion of a commonsense domain plan instantiation structure.

More formally, let us reconsider the intention behind utterance (1). We will show later that this intention refers to the discourse plan

IDENTIFY-PARAMETER(Clerk, Person, location(CAN-AM train),
        GOTO(Person, location(CAN-AM train), time(CAN-AM
        train)),
        TAKE-TRAIN-TRIP(Person, CAN-AM train, destination
        (CAN-AM train))),

which itself refers to the GOTO subplan,

GOTO(Person, location(CAN-AM train), time(CAN-AM train)),

of the (BOARD subplan of the) domain plan

TAKE-TRAIN-TRIP(Person, CAN-AM train, destination
        (CAN-AM train)).

Figure 17.5 sketches this situation. In the next section we discuss how to recognize such commonsense plan structures.

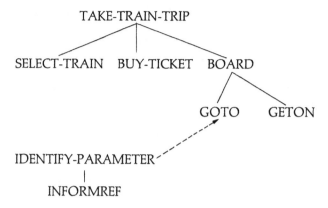

COMMONSENSE KNOWLEDGE

DISCOURSE INTENTION

Person intends that Clerk intends
   IDENTIFY-PARAMETER referring to GOTO

Figure 17.5
Example analysis: Where do I get the CAN-AM train?

4 Domain and Discourse Plan Recognition

4.1 Overview

The task of the plan recognizer is to recognize a domain plan structure, and any discourse plans generated by this structure, to which the discourse intentions of an input utterance refer. That is, the plan recognizer's task is not only to infer a domain plan (as in previous systems) but also to infer any plans generated by this domain plan that are relevant to the discourse intentions. The plan recognizer has at its disposal a library of domain plan schemas varying with the domain and a library of discourse and speech act plan schemas (as in figures 17.2–17.4), as well as the representation of the parse of the input utterance. The plan recognizer will use this information to associate each utterance with an intention referring to a domain plan, either directly or through a series of generated discourse plans. If the interpretation is ambiguous, a discourse intention and set of commonsense plans are created for each interpretation.

4.2 Plan Chaining and Constraint Satisfaction

The plan recognizer builds a domain plan by finding a sequence of instantiations of domain plan schemas, each one containing the previous one in its decomposition,[9] beginning with a plan schema connected to the surface speech analysis produced by the parser. In the simplest case, the speech act matches the decomposition of a domain plan or is a request for an act that matches the decomposition of a domain plan. In more complicated cases, the speech act is connected to a domain plan by a sequence of discourse plans related to the domain plan. Here, the speech act matches the decomposition of a discourse plan or is a request for an act that matches the decomposition of a discourse plan.

Since every discourse plan takes another plan as an argument, when any discourse plan is recognized from a speech act, an associated domain plan will implicitly be introduced. Furthermore, the constraints relating the discourse plan to this domain plan add information about the domain plan enabling further plan recognition. For instance, utterance (1) in Dialogue 4—"I'd like to buy a ticket to New York"—could be identified as a part of discourse plan to introduce a plan, with constraints that specify that buying a ticket is a step of the plan being introduced. To constrain the plan being introduced in this way, we can invoke the plan recognizer recursively, starting with buying a ticket as the observed action. For example, this act could be a step in a plan to take a train trip. Since taking a trip is a domain plan, no other plans are introduced and recursive plan recognition halts.

Once a set of discourse and domain plans is recognized, each is expanded top down by adding the definitions of all steps and substeps (based on the plan libraries), until there are no unique expansions for any of the remaining substeps. For example, once TAKE-TRAIN-TRIP is recognized from BUY-TICKET, it is expanded to include SELECT-TRAIN and BOARD as well (recall figure 17.2).

Though plan chaining is a simple tree search and thus theorectially terminates, if unconstrained it can be both costly and unable to yield a unique plan interpretation. The search process needs to be controlled with various heuristics and limited by dividing it into incremental stages.

4.3 Coherence Heuristics

The search process described above does not take into account the influence of the active discourse context.[10] One coherence heuristic controls the plan recognition process by preferring the recognition of plans that are related to currently active plans, rather than to plans constructed from first principles. That is, portions of the plans referred to by a current discourse intention may have already been recognized as objects of previous discourse intentions.

Furthermore, when several discourse and domain plans can be related to currently active plans, other coherence heuristics place a further preference ordering on the recognition process. (When there are no active plans, as at the beginning of a dialogue, the plan recognizer applies the heuristics to the library of domain plan schemas instead.) In particular:

1. The recognition of steps in domain plans or in continuation discourse plans is attempted first. If the utterance can be viewed as intending (or requesting that another intend) a linguistic step in an already intended plan, or in a continuation discourse plan, then it is classified as such without further consideration. The speaker is believed to be doing exactly what is expected in the given situation.
2. Clarification plans are attempted next. If the utterance cannot be viewed as a continuation but can be viewed as a clarification discourse plan generated by an intended plan, then it is classified as such without further consideration.

Thus, the plan recognizer prefers an utterance interpretation that directly continues rather than clarifies (that is, indirectly refers to) a plan.

Although these heuristics and their ordering have not been validated with psychological experimentation, they have intuitive appeal. For example, preferring current plans over plans constructed from first principles, and continuations of these plans over clarifications, allows the preferred discourse behavior to default to the earlier plan-based systems in which a dialogue contains no topic changes or unexpected subdialogues. The heuristics also follow the principle of Occam's razor, since they are ordered so as to introduce as few new plans as possible.

4.4 Linguistic Clues

In many models of discourse (Grosz 1977; Reichman-Adar 1984; Cohen 1983; Grosz and Sidner 1986) rules of conversational coherence have been shown to govern the use of surface linguistic phenomena such as cue phrases and choice of reference. Thus, in addition to coherence heuristics, the plan recognizer can also use surface linguistic phenomena to control its search. In particular, the information conveyed by such phenomena takes precedence over the coherence heuristics used by the plan recognizer in the linguistically unmarked case.

For example, consider recognizing a clarification that is not prefaced by a cue phrase. Using the coherence preferences, the plan recognizer first tries to interpret the utterance as a continuation, and only when these efforts fail, as a clarification. This is because a clarification is less expected in the unmarked case. However, if a clarification class discourse plan is prefaced with a cue phrase such as "no," a continuation is not tried first. This is because a signal for a plan such as a correction is explicitly present. (As in other models of discourse, we are assuming that cue uses of lexical items can be distinguished from other uses, for example by intonation (Hirschberg and Litman 1987).) Cues thus ease the recognition of relationships that would otherwise be difficult to understand.

4.5 Plan-Based Heuristics

Although the plan recognizer may suggest a plan as a linguistically coherent interpretation, the plan may still be eliminated from further consideration by a set of heuristics based on rational planning behavior as in Allen and Perrault 1980. For example, plans that are postulated whose effects are already true are eliminated, as are plans whose constraints cannot be satisfied.

4.6 Incremental Search

When the heuristics and linguistic constraints cannot eliminate all but one postulated plan, the chaining stops, even when a solution path has not yet been found. In other words, search terminates after branch points. For example, since BOARD and MEET plans can be recognized from a GOTO (recall figure 17.2), chaining would halt with two branches if both plans were plausible. Such premature termination is typical in dialogue processing (see, for example, Carberry 1985), since later utterances in a dialogue often eliminate many of the branches. Cohen, Perrault, and Allen (1982) also argue that rational speakers would not have intended inferences in branches since such inferences could not have been drawn unambiguously. Thus, the plan recognition process halts either when we have uniquely incorporated the utterance into our expectation structure as defined by our heuristics or when the search space becomes too large. In the latter case the plan remains ambiguous.

5 An Example

This section uses the framework developed in the previous sections to illustrate the recognition of the commonsense domain and discourse plans underlying a dialogue.[11] Although the behavior to be described is fully specified by the theory, our implementation corresponds only to the model of plan recognition from first principles. Simulated computational processes have been implemented elsewhere, however. For example, the current system assumes that a highly specialized semantic grammar (Brown and Burton 1977) has parsed the utterances in the train domain. This allows the avoidance of some difficult parsing issues and concentration on the plan recognition model. Though such a grammar has been implemented, it is currently not hooked up to the plan recognition system. Litman 1985 contains a full discussion of the implementation and associated issues of knowledge representation. Also, the theory at present does not concern itself with the planning or generation of natural-language responses. The examples will describe what the system should do (using the actual response in the dialogue as a guide).

As our example, let us return again to the initial utterances of Dialogue 6:

Person: Where do I get the CAN-AM train?
Clerk: It's not until six.
          They're meeting at cubicle C.
Person: Where's that?

The initial state of the plan recognition system consists of a library of speech acts, discourse plans, and domain plans regarding trains (that is, plans such as those found in figures 17.2–17.4). Upon hearing the initial utterance, the following simulated parse is also input to the system:

SURFACE-REQUEST(Person1, Clerk1,
    I1:INFORMREF(Clerk1, Person1, ?term, EQUAL
    (?term, loc(dtrain1)))).

A SURFACE-REQUEST for an INFORMREF is recognized from the inter-rogative mood of the utterance, as in Allen and Perrault 1980. The type of *dtrain1*, the train referred to by "the CAN-AM train," is restricted to a departing train using the verb "get." The INFORMREF action will be referred to using the name "I1."

Since we are at the beginning of a dialogue, the plan recognizer uses its general plan schemas rather than previously recognized plan instantiations to construct its analysis. According to coherence preference (1), the plan recognizer first checks to see whether the SURFACE-REQUEST matches (or is a request for an action that matches) the decomposition of a domain plan schema, or matches a continuation discourse plan referring to a do-main plan. These attempts fail, however.

According to coherence preference (2), the plan recognizer then checks to see whether the SURFACE-REQUEST can be related instead to a clarifi-cation discourse plan schema. This time there is a successful match: Person is requesting Clerk to perform an action, I1, that matches the decomposi-tion of the IDENTIFY-PARAMETER clarification discourse plan.

Before pursuing the candidate IDENTIFY-PARAMETER plan any fur-ther, the plan recognizer checks on the plan's reasonableness using the plan-based heuristics. In satisfying the constraints on IDENTIFY-PARAMETER (Clerk1, Person1, ?parameter, ?action, ?plan), that is,

1. PARAMETER(?parameter, ?action)
2. STEP(?action, ?plan)
3. PARAMETER(?parameter, EQUAL(?parameter, loc(dtrain1))),

a second plan is introduced (?plan) that must have a step ?action that contains the location of a train, described via the equality of the INFORMREF. The only eligible plan for ?action is GOTO. A new plan is

COMMONSENSE KNOWLEDGE

PLAN1

   IDENTIFY-PARAMETER(Clerk1, Person1, loc(dtrain1), GO1, PLAN2)

                    |

   I1:INFORMREF(Clerk1, Person1, ?term, EQUAL(?term, loc(dtrain1)))

PLAN2

   GO1:GOTO(?agent, loc(dtrain1), ?time)

Figure 17.6
Chaining and constraint satisfaction produce intermediate plan structures.

thus created containing GOTO and arbitrarily called PLAN2. This state of affairs is shown in figure 17.6, where the name of a plan structure appears at the top left-hand corner. The plan recognizer also verifies that the effects of the recognized plans are not already satisfied.

The plan recognition algorithm is now recursively called on this GOTO. Decomposition chaining yields both the BOARD and MEET plans. The MEET plan is eliminated due to typing constraint violation; dtrain1 is already known to be a departing train from the parse. Since the expected agent of the BOARD plan is the speaker, ?agent is heuristically set equal to Person1. Finally, chaining proceeds from BOARD to TAKE-TRAIN-TRIP, and since TAKE-TRAIN-TRIP is a domain plan (that is, no more plans are introduced), plan recognition ends. The plans are expanded top down to include the rest of their steps, with the final structures shown in figure 17.7. (The dotted lines indicate the information inferred from the top-down chaining.)

Note that the plan recognizer has constructed a domain plan structure and a discourse plan generated by this structure, to which the discourse intention of the utterance (Person's REQUEST) refers. Loosely, this discourse intention is that Person intends that Clerk intends to clarify a part of Person's domain plan. (Although we have now abstracted discourse structure (as opposed to commonsense plan) processing out of our model, this discourse intention could then be manipulated by attentional and intentional processing, as in previous formulations of our work (Litman and Allen 1987) or as in Grosz and Sidner 1986.) Note too that the domain plan structure contains more domain information than explicitly referred to by the discourse intention. The necessity for this "extra" domain plan recognition was discussed earlier in the paper.

COMMONSENSE KNOWLEDGE

PLAN1

    IDENTIFY-PARAMETER(Clerk1, Person1, loc(dtrain1), GO1, PLAN2)

              |

    I1:INFORMREF(Clerk1, Person1, ?term, EQUAL(?term, loc(dtrain1)))

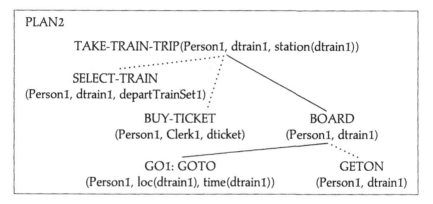

Figure 17.7
Plans recognized after the first utterance.

Clerk's planning of the response is not specified in this theory. What the system should do will be sketched here. The system, examining the commonsense plans and discourse information, responds with both a helpful response ("It's not until six") and the expected clarification ("They're meeting at cubicle C"). These utterances execute a new clarification discourse plan IDENTIFY-PARAMETER (Clerk1, Person1, time(dtrain1), GO1, PLAN2), which we will call PLAN3, and the existing discourse plan, PLAN1. Thus, at the stage just before Person1 speaks again, the commonsense knowledge base would contain PLAN1, PLAN2, PLAN3.

Person then asks "Where's that?", which would be parsed into the linguistic action as follows:

    SURFACE-REQUEST(Person1, Clerk1
        INFORMREF(Clerk1, Person1, ?term1,
        EQUAL(?term1, loc(CubicleC))))).

This analysis assumes the appropriate resolution of "that" to CubicleC by an immediate focus mechanism such as Sidner's (1983). This makes the example simpler. In this case the plan recognition would work even if the "that" were not resolved and left as an unknown constant, as discussed below.

Although Clerk thought the utterance executing PLAN1 achieved the desired Person KNOW-PARAMETER, in actuality it did not provide a description enabling Person to execute the GOTO of PLAN2. Instead we have another request for clarification. The plan recognizer attempts to relate this utterance to the active commonsense plans based on the coherence heuristics. The first preference fails since the SURFACE-REQUEST does not execute or continue any of the steps in TAKE-TRAIN-TRIP (which should have been resumed if the previous clarifications were understood), or in plans 1 and 3 (since they are completed). The second preference succeeds, and the utterance is recognized as requesting a new clarification, IDENTIFY-PARAMETER (Clerk1, Person1, loc(Cubicle C), S-I, PLAN1), where S-I is the SURFACE-INFORM representing the clerk's realization "They're meeting at cubicle C," of I1. This process is basically analogous to the process discussed in detail above, except that PLAN1 to which the IDENTIFY-PARAMETER refers is found rather than constructed. Note, too, that the plan to which the IDENTIFY-PARAMETER refers is now a discourse plan rather than a domain plan.

As mentioned above, if in the input "that" was originally unresolved (that is, CubicleC is unknown), "that" will be correctly resolved later as a side effect of the plan recognition. In particular, the appropriate binding will be made during the constraint propagation process connecting the current IDENTIFY-PARAMETER to PLAN1.

6 Summary

We have presented a model for recognizing domain task plans underlying task-oriented dialogues, as well as discourse tasks generated by these domain tasks, to which a discourse can also refer. Our model accounts for subdialogues generated by a task, such as clarifications and corrections, yet maintains the computational advantages of the plan-based approach.

Commonsense knowledge about generated discourse interactions was incorporated into a planning framework using the same plan-based formalism previously used for representing domain knowledge. Such knowledge was needed to mediate between task plans and many discourse intentions. This new knowledge was formalized using a set of discourse plans, plans explicitly encoding indirect relationships between discourse intentions and domain plans. This formulation allowed us to easily recognize discourse plans of domain plans, as well as discourse plans generated by other discourse plans to an arbitrary level of nesting.

Domain and discourse plans were recognized and related by a context-dependent, heuristic plan recognition algorithm. First, a discourse or domain plan was recognized from every utterance. The recognition of this plan was constrained by preferring continuations of expected plans over clarifications, and already existing plans over plans constructed from first principles. If the recognized plan was a discourse plan, the formal constraints specifying the discourse and domain plan relationships were then used to recursively generate recognition of the domain plan from recognition of the discourse plan. These constraints provided the link between what one indirectly said in a discourse about a task and the commonsense knowledge about the task itself.

Notes

1. Task-oriented dialogues occur when the topic of a dialogue is related to a particular domain task (for instance, take a train trip). As such, our task-oriented dialogues are a generalization of the "task-oriented" dialogues of Grosz (1977) (dialogues in which two people work cooperatively on a task that is performed during the dialogue) and the "information-seeking" dialogues of Carberry (1985) (dialogues in which an agent seeks information with respect to a task that is not executed during the dialogue).
2. Commonsense knowledge refers to the intuitive beliefs and theories about the world used by many artificial intelligence systems.
3. Although we have taken a "data-structure view of plans" (Pollack 1986), even if one takes a "mental phenomenon view of plans" (Pollack 1986), discourse intentions are still not identical to plans (Grosz and Sidner 1986).
4. Because "discourse" plans may in theory account for nonlinguistic actions, as well as for reasons discussed below, we originally called such plans "metaplans" (Litman 1985). We changed terminology, however, since "metaplan" has various other uses in the literature (see, for example, Wilensky 1983), and to date we have only been concerned with linguistically realized metaplans.
5. Wilensky (1983) has also discussed the role of metaplans in plan-based natural-language understanding systems. However, there are several important differences between Wilensky's work and the work reported here. First, Wilensky's metaplans are concerned with interactions between multiple plans and are used to handle issues of concurrent goal interaction. The metaplans of this work are concerned with manipulations of single plans and are used to handle issues of discourse. Moreover, Wilensky does not specify representation or recognition details (for example, the mechanisms relating metaplan and nonmetaplan recognition), issues that we explicitly address in this paper.
6. This formulation of IDENTIFY-PARAMETER is a simplification of the version found in Litman and Allen 1987. It is sufficient for the examples covered in this paper.
7. In previous formulations of our work (Litman and Allen 1987) INTRODUCE-PLAN was also used to represent this latter type of discourse intention. By making explicit the separation between discourse intentions and commonsense plans, the two situations can now be clearly distinguished.
8. It is important to remember that although in this dialogue all discourse intentions refer to the domain plans indirectly, direct reference is also possible. An example would be the intention behind the utterance "Person: Sell me a ticket to New York"—that is, Person intends that Clerk intends that Person BUY-TICKET to New York.
9. Plan chaining can also be done via effects and preconditions. Pollack (1986) even allows recognition of nonexistent library plans. To keep the examples simple, all plan schemas have been expressed so that chaining via decomposition is sufficient.
10. In this paper we assume the existence of a separate attentional component of discourse structure (Grosz and Sidner 1986). Such a component abstracts the focus of attention of

the discourse participants. See Litman and Allen 1987 for a previous formulation of our work that directly incorporated such a component in the form of a plan stack.

11. For the purposes of this paper, we limit ourselves to discourse intentions recognized from single utterances. Litman and Allen 1987 illustrates the treatment of a restricted class of multiple utterances.

References

Allen, J. F., and C. R. Perrault (1980). Analyzing intention in utterances. *Artificial Intelligence* 15, 143–178.

Brown, J., and R. Burton (1977). Semantic grammar: A technique for constructing natural language interfaces to instructional systems. Technical Report 3587, Bolt Beranek and Newman, Inc., Cambridge, MA.

Carberry, M. S. (1985). Pragmatic modeling in information system interfaces. Doctoral dissertation and Technical Report 86-07 (1986), Department of Computer and Information Sciences, University of Delaware, Newark, DE.

Cohen, P. R., C. R. Perrault, and J. F. Allen (1982). Beyond question answering. In W. Lehnert and M. Ringle, eds., *Strategies for natural language processing*. Hillsdale, NJ: L. Erlbaum Associates.

Cohen, R. (1983). A computational model for the analysis of arguments. Technical Report CSRG-151 and Doctoral dissertation, University of Toronto, Toronto, Ont.

Fikes, R. E., and N. J. Nilsson (1971). STRIPS: A new approach to the application of theorem proving to problem solving. *Artificial Intelligence* 2, 189–208.

Grosz, B. J. (1977). The representation and use of focus in dialogue understanding. Technical Note 151, Artificial Intelligence Center, SRI International, Menlo Park, CA.

Grosz, B. J., and C. L. Sidner (1986). Attention, intentions, and the structure of discourse. *Computational Linguistics* 12, 175–204.

Hirschberg, J., and D. Litman (1987). Now let's talk about 'now': Identifying cue phrases intonationally. In *Proceedings of the Twenty-fifth Annual Meeting*, Association for Computational Linguistics, Stanford, CA.

Horrigan, M. K. (1977). Modelling simple dialogs. Master's thesis and Technical Report 108, University of Toronto, Toronto, Ont.

Litman, D. J. (1985). Plan recognition and discourse analysis: An integrated approach for understanding dialogues. Doctoral dissertation and Technical Report 170, University of Rochester, Rochester, NY.

Litman, D. J., and J. F. Allen (1987). A plan recognition model for subdialogues in conversation. *Cognitive Science* 11, 163–200.

Pollack, M. E. (1986). A model of plan inference that distinguishes between the beliefs of actors and observers. In *Proceedings of the Twenty-fourth Annual Meeting*, Association for Computational Linguistics, New York, NY.

Reichman-Adar, R. (1984). Extended person-machine interfaces. *Artificial Intelligence* 22, 157–218.

Sacerdoti, E. D. (1977). *A structure for plans and behavior*. New York: American Elsevier.

Searle, J. R. (1969). *Speech acts: An essay in the philosophy of language*. New York: Cambridge University Press.

Searle, J. R. (1975). Indirect speech acts. In P. Cole and J. Morgan, eds., *Syntax and semantics 3: Speech acts*. New York: Academic Press.

Sidner, C. L. (1983). Focusing in the comprehension of definite anaphora. In M. Brady and R. C. Berwick, eds., *Computational models of discourse*. Cambridge, MA: MIT Press.

Sidner, C. L. (1985). Plan parsing for intended response recognition in discourse. *Computational Intelligence* 1, 1–10.

Wilensky, R. (1983). *Planning and understanding*. Reading, MA: Addison-Wesley.

Chapter 18

Communicative Intentions, Plan Recognition, and Pragmatics: Comments on Thomason and on Litman and Allen

Kent Bach

Like others concerned with discourse and plan recognition, both Thomason and Litman and Allen appreciate the importance of the audience's recognition of the speaker's intentions and plans. Yet they ovelook certain important concepts and distinctions from recent work in the theory of speech acts. I am not suggesting that this oversight leaves their approaches with insoluble problems; rather, I am suggesting that their approaches can benefit by taking these notions into account. After all, plans are systems of intentions, and speech act theory is concerned with speaker's intentions and their recognition. However, there are many faces to a speaker's intentions, and the role and even the relevance of the audience's recognition of an intention depends on the kind of intention it is. In order to show this, I will sketch a theoretical framework within which to comment on the target papers.

1 Theoretical Framework

In general, a person's behavior counts as an action (or at least an attempted action) of a certain sort in virtue of his intention. Generally it makes no difference whether any witnesses happen to identify this intention, much less whether the agent intends them to do so. For example, your bodily movements count as practicing break dancing no matter what an observer thinks, or what you intend him to think, you are doing. However, in the case of an utterance, where there is a presumption of audience-directed communication, the audience has reason to think that the speaker intends him to recognize this intention, that is, to identify what he is doing in making the utterance. Moreover, the intention for him to recognize this intention is not a distinct intention; rather, it is the very intention that he is to recognize. This is the intention that constitutes the utterance as an act of communication, as an *illocutionary* act with a certain force and content. As such, it succeeds just in case the hearer recognizes that intention.

However, in saying something, a speaker is likely to have intentions of several different sorts. One hardly ever intends merely to communicate:

being understood is intended to produce some effect on one's audience, perhaps to further some larger plan. For example, suppose my wife asks me, "Where did you go after the meeting last night?" Her *communicative* intention consists in expressing the desire that I tell her where I went after the meeting (that is, the one that we mutually believe I attended). But she might be feigning interest and not really want to know. If she does want to know, her *perlocutionary* intention is that I tell her. She may have the further intention, depending on my answer, to ask further questions. Depending on the nature of these questions, she may or may not intend me to know her ulterior purposes.

The point of distinguishing these intentions is that the role and even the relevance of the audience's recognition of an intention depends on the sort of intention it is. Audience recognition is essential to the fulfillment of communicative intentions, important to the fulfillment of certain other intentions, incidental to the fulfillment of other intentions, and incompatible with the fulfillment of still others. Some are not only intended to be recognized, their fulfillment *depends on* their recognition. However, with a communicative intention, its fulfillment actually *consists in* its recognition, for that is simply the intention that one's utterance be understood. In the above example, I may or not may give my wife an answer (I might say, "I left," thereby implying that what I did was none of her business). I will give her an answer only if I recognize her intention that I do so, but even then I might not. Either way, her communicative intention would have been fulfilled, inasmuch I would have understood her question. I may or may not have recognized her intention to find out what happened at the Philosophers' Club (our neighborhood bar), but, let's suppose, I am *not* to recognize her surreptitious intention to find out if our neighbor was there (he attended the meeting with me, and *his* wife wants to know where *he* went but does not want me to realize that and hopes I will volunteer this information to my wife).

Neither Litman and Allen's model (or, so far as I know, other current work in artificial intelligence) nor Thomason's conjectures take into account the differences among intentions as to how their recognition relates to their fulfillment. In defense of Litman and Allen, it might be argued that because they restrict their attention to task-oriented dialogues (indeed, to ones in which there is full cooperation among the participants), these differences are inconsequential. Everything is aboveboard: there are no hidden or ulterior intentions, and in each case the speaker possesses the attitude he is expressing. However, to the extent that these simplifying assumptions are made, the scope of Litman and Allen's model is limited. Moreover, presumably it is meant to model human interlocutors and not merely application-specific question-and-answer systems, as in database management, decision support, and project management systems. But then the question arises of how a given dialogue is identified as task-oriented (and cooperative) in the first place. In other words, on what basis does a person to whom a question is ostensibly directed (I say ostensibly, because he must infer that it is directed to him) determine that the questioner is indeed carrying out some plan to which an answer to the question is relevant? The model does not include a plan for determining when the model applies. Yet in real life we commonly have to determine that a speaker is engaging us in some plan of his, and we do this by relying partly on what he says, partly on what he appears to be doing, and partly on mutual knowledge (either "common sense" or more intimate information). As for Thomason, who does not limit himself to task-oriented dialogues, he realizes that conversations need not be as cooperative as Grice seems to have suggested. He senses the importance of the difference between communicative and other purposes and rightly observes that cooperation is, as far as discourse is concerned, essential only for communication. Even so, he does not take into account the various sorts of intentions mentioned above, whose distinction, I maintain, is crucial for an adequate theory of discourse.

It was Grice who first saw the distinctively reflexive character of communicative intentions ("speaker meaning"). He originally suggested that a speaker means something by his utterance iff he intends his utterance "to produce some effect in an audience by means of the recognition of this intention" (1957, 385). However, this formulation has had its problems. One problem is precisely how to spell out the structure of this intention (is it iterative rather than reflexive?), and various modifications of the original definition have been proposed,by such philosophers as Strawson (1964), Searle (1969), Schiffer (1972), Recanati (1986), and Grice himself (1969). Another problem, evident from the phrase "produce some effect" (Grice later replaced it), is that the intention specified in the original definition is to produce a perlocutionary effect, such as a belief or even an action, rather than the illocutionary effect of understanding (Searle 1969, 47).

Despite the difficulties with Grice's original formulation, I do not quarrel with his fundamental insight that speaker meaning is a matter of reflexive intention (see Bach 1987b for a defense of this against Recanati's 1986 objections). The point is not merely that communicative intentions refer to themselves (Harman has argued (1986, 85–88) that all intentions refer to themselves) but rather that the audience identifies the speaker's intention partly on the basis that he is to identify it. That is why Grice's original formulation contained the phrase "by means of the recognition of this intention." However, precisely what is the content of a communicative intention, such that it can specify the means for its own fulfillment, that is, such that the audience is to recognize it partly on the basis that he is to take himself as intended to do so?

Observing that Grice described a reflexive intention as the intention to produce an effect by means of recognition of this intention but that he did not impose any restriction on the intended effect, Harnish and I ask "what sorts of illocutionary [that is, communicative] effects—effects consisting in recognition of reflexive intentions, can there be? In other words, what can be the content of a communicative intention?" (1979, 15). Then we offer our definition of communicating, which we construe not as meaning something but, for greater generality, as expressing a propositional attitude:

> EXP
> For S to express an attitude to H is for S reflexively to intend H to take S's utterance as reason to think S has that attitude.

H understands S's utterance if H identifies the attitude in question—for example, a belief in the case of a statement or a desire in the case of a request. It is another question whether H takes S actually to possess that attitude, much less forms a corresponding attitude, such as a belief or an intention. If H thinks S possesses the attitude he is expressing, in effect H is taking S to be sincere in what he is communicating. However, there is no question about S being sincere in his communicative intention itself—in that regard there is only the question of what he is communicating, that is, of what attitude he is expressing. This intention must be identified before the question of his sincerity (in respect of that attitude) can even arise.

According to EXP, to perform an act of communication—that is, to make an utterance with a communicative intention—is to express an attitude. S may or may not actually possess it, but that question is irrelevant to the purely communicative aspect of his utterance. Harnish and I give an extensive taxonomy of communicative (illocutionary) acts in terms of expressed attitudes (Bach and Harnish 1979, chap. 3). In each case, the speaker's communicative intention is to express both a primary propositional attitude and a correlative intention regarding the hearer's attitude in response. Here are some typical cases:

Illocutionary act	Primary attitude expressed	Intention expressed regarding H's attitude
statement	belief that p	belief that p
request	desire for H to D	intention to D
apology	regret for D-ing	forgiveness of S for D-ing
promise	intention to D	belief that S is obligated to H to D

If the speaker actually possesses the intention he is expressing regarding the hearer, this intention is his primary *perlocutionary* intention. That, in turn, may be part of some larger plan that the utterance is helping to further.

What is involved in recognizing speakers' communicative intentions, as in conversational implicature? Thomason correctly remarks that Grice's maxims of conversation do not provide sufficient information for detailed explanations or implementations (Sperber and Wilson (1986, 31–38) have made the same observation). However, Grice had no such ambition for his theory of implicature, inasmuch as the same utterance in different contexts can imply different things. He was well aware that specific features of a conversational situation provide the input for the generation of implicatures. For example, what counts as the relevant sort of information and the right amount of it obviously depends on the situation. That is why Harnish and I, in proposing the Speech Act Schema (figure 18.1) as a model of communicative intention and inference, acknowledge that the SAS does not give the precise details needed to explain how one identifies a particular communicative intent. "It gives no indication how certain mutual beliefs are activated or otherwise picked out as relevant, much less how the correct identification is made" (1979, 93). We also observe that "an inference in the pattern of the SAS is not deductive but is what might be called an inference to a plausible explanation, namely of the speaker's utterance" (p. 92)—the hearer is satisfied with the first good explanation that comes to mind. We have no account of how particular explanations come to mind or of what makes a certain one seem good. The SAS is meant only to provide the ingredients for a model of the defeasible reasoning involved in understanding (see Bach 1984 for a more general discussion of default reasoning). It cites several presumptions or defeasible mutual beliefs (these are propositions people take for granted unless there is reason to the contrary). They include the linguistic presumption (LP), that the participants are speaking the same language, the presumption of literality (PL), and the communicative presumption (CP), that a given utterance is being made with an identifiable intention. Also, we recast Grice's conversational maxims (and a few others) as presumptions (Bach and Harnish 1979, 62–65). Of special importance is the CP, which for us replaces Grice's Cooperative Principle. The CP drives the hearer's inference to the speaker's intention (it implies that there is an inference to be made) but, of course, it does not give the directions. As a whole, the SAS merely schematizes hearers' inferences.

2 Thomason

In view of the fact that so little is known about the psychology of such inferences I seriously doubt that anything more than than this can be done at present. For this reason, among others, I think it is unrealistic to expect Thomason's goal of a formal pragmatics to be fulfilled in the foreseeable

The SAS covers nonliteral and indirect, as well as literal and direct illocutionary acts. S is F-ing that P if in the presence of some H, S utters a sentence e (in some langusge L) in mood * intending, and expecting (pursuant
to the LP, the CP, and the PL) H to recognize that he intends, H to infer
(from the fact that S means ... by e and the fact that S is thereby saying that
*(...p...)) that S is F-ing that P. On occasion S may be also F'-ing that Q.
That is, S intends, and expects H to recognize that S intends, H to reason
thus:

		Basis
L1.	S is uttering e.	hearing S utter e
L2.	S means ... by e.	L1, LP, MCBs
L3.	S is saying that *(...p...).	L2, LP, MCBs
L4.	S, if speaking literally, is F^*-ing that p.	L3, CP, MCBs

Either (direct literal)

L5.	S could be F^*-ing that p.	L4, MCBs
L6.	S is F^*-ing that p.	L5, PL

And possibly (literally based indirect),

L7.	S could not be merely F^*-ing that p.	L6, MCBs
L8.	There is some F-ing that P connected in a way identifiable under the circumstances to F^*-ing that p, such that in F^*-ing that p, S could also be F-ing that P.	L7, CP
L9.	S is F^*-ing that p and thereby F-ing that P.	L8, MCBs

Or (direct nonliteral)

L5'.	S could not (under the circumstances) be F^*-ing that p.	L4, MCBs
L6'.	Under the circumstances there is a certain recognizable relation between saying that p and some F-ing that P, such that S could be F-ing that P.	L3, L5', CP
L7'.	S is F-ing that P.	L6', MCBs

And possibly (nonliterally based indirect).

L8'.	S could not merely be F-ing that P.	L7', MCBs
L9'.	There is some F'-ing that Q connected in a way identifiable under the circumstances to F-ing that P, such that in F-ing that P, S could also be F'-ing that Q.	L8', CP
L10.	S is F-ing that P and thereby F'-ing that Q.	L9', MCBs

Figure 18.1
The speech act schema. LP = linguistic presumption; MCB = mutual contextual belief;
CP = communicative presumption; PL = presumption of literality. From Bach and Harnish
1979, chap. 4.

future (unless its domain is artificially simplified and its data artificially limited). That's assuming there is a theoretical motivation for a formal pragmatics.

Incidentally, Thomason alludes to a conception of semantics that is common to most varieties of formal semantics today, be it truth-theoretic, model-theoretic, or possible-worlds semantics. Thomason says that "semantics . . . has to do with the interpretation of phrases relative to a context of utterance" (section 3). My question is whether this is not semantics but pragmatics. If it is to be semantics, then there must be some well-defined function such that reference is determined by meaning as a function of context. The trouble is that there is no such function, as I argue in chapter 4 of Bach 1987a. I can't go into detail here, but the general idea is that the speaker's intention plays an essential role in determining reference and this intention cannot be construed as an element of context. I argue also that if speaker intention is included in context, context is too ill defined for reference to be a function of it.

Thomason does not say why we should "take syntax as a model of what we should look for in a theory of pragmatics" (section 4). There is nothing clearly analogous to the notion of a well-formed sentence. We might say that an utterance is "well formed" if the communicative intention behind it is recognizable by the audience, but no rules comparable to syntactic rules are needed (or could be devised) to explain that. Rather, what is needed is a theory of rational cooperative behavior, applicable specifically to speaker intentions and audience inferences. The SAS specifies the sorts of presumptions and considerations that might go into such a theory, but being merely a model of what goes into successful communication, it does not explain when communication succeeds and when it doesn't.

Thomason describes a hearer's task at a given stage of a discourse as reconstructing the speaker's plan, often as part of a mutual plan of the conversation. I think he exaggerates the extent to which there is a *plan* of conversation, at least if that implies more than merely a shared direction of conversation—conversations often go neither according to plan nor contrary to plan, namely, when there is no plan. What Thomason calls reconstructing a speaker's plan is, for Grice and for Harnish and me, a matter of identifying the speaker's communicative intention, which may or may not be made explicit. Thomason brings up Grice's (1957) account of speaker meaning but does not address the issues that, as noted earlier, have led to various reformulations. Instead, he simply suggests amending Grice's account to say that part of the speaker's aim is to put something on the conversational record. I would agree with his suggestion if what he means is roughly the same as what Harnish and I have in mind when we define an act of communication as the act of expressing an attitude (a belief, a desire, a feeling), defined earlier by EXP. For surely a speaker intends not only that a given utterance be understood but also that its content (or at least the "gist" of it) be remembered. Also, recall that EXP takes into account the fact that a speaker can express an attitude even if he does not possess it. So as people express attitudes to one another, they jointly build a cumulative record of these attitudes. Since they need not be sincere, and even if they are sincere may not agree with one another, the notion of conversational record that belongs to an account of ongoing communication should not involve a shared representation of how things are in the world. However, Thomason speaks not of putting propositional attitudes but of putting propositions themselves on the record. Accordingly, it is not clear how he would take the possibility of insincerity and disagreement into account. I would suggest enforcing the distinction between communicative and other aspects of a speaker's intention.

It seems to me that several to Thomason's key notions, unless I have misunderstood them, are implicit in the model schematized by the SAS. For example, what Thomason calls *background implicatures* are special cases of indirect speech acts, and what he calls *assertional implicatures* are special cases of nonliteral speech acts. As the bottom of the SAS indicates, they can occur together, just as Thomason points out. And, as Harnish and I have argued (1979, 165–172), various other phenomena that Grice has discussed under the heading of implicature can also be subsumed under the SAS.

As far as I can tell, the notion of *accommodation* is implicit in the SAS. For example, there are various points (L7, L5', and L8') in the SAS at which the audience can be intended to think that under the circumstances the speaker could not be, or could not merely be, performing the illocutionary act that has come to mind at that point. When that happens, at the next point (L8, L6', or L9') the audience is intended in effect to accommodate the speaker in the manner indicated. Also, although Thomason refers to "rules of accom-modation," it is not clear that they are needed in a model of successful communication. Given the overarching CP, which licenses a search for an identifiable communicative intention, the audience can rely on relevant mutual contextual beliefs. For example, if a speaker appears to be using a certain word in a puzzling way, the audience should try to make an appropriate adjustment (perhaps the speaker is using "flaunt" for "flout") and make an exception to the LP rather than waive the CP.

Finally, as indicated above, what Thomason calls the *conversational record* amounts to a subset of what Harnish and I call *mutual contextual beliefs*, which play a major role in guiding communicative intentions and infer-ences. For once the speaker has succeeded in communicating an attitude, this very fact itself normally becomes a matter of mutual belief. We gener-ally take for granted the communicative success of prior utterances and repeat ourselves only when not understood or when intent on producing a special effect.

3 Litman and Allen

Recent work in artificial intelligence, as exemplified by Litman and Allen's work, has made substantial progress at modeling discourse understanding as plan recognition. From the standpoint of speech act theory the idea of modeling discourse understanding as plan recognition is certainly a reasonable approach, for utterances are fundamentally communicative. What makes them communicative is that they are made with an intention whose fulfillment consists in its recognition—you succeed at communicating, regardless of what else you may be trying to do, if your utterance enables your audience to recognize the intention with which you are making that very utterance. Moreover, communicative (illocutionary) intentions generally are accompanied by perlocutionary intentions, and individual utterances are usually parts of larger plans. So it is plausible to suppose that identifying a speaker's perlocutionary intentions and broader plans is often relevant to identifying his communicative intention.

I agree, then, that the plan recognition approach is quite appropriate for modeling discourse understanding. Nevertheless, I must register some skepticism about the plausibility of heuristic plan recognition algorithms, even Litman and Allen's, notwithstanding their elegant features. I am well aware that constructing an algorithm requires making simplifying assumptions, but simplifying assumptions must be independently motivated. They cannot have as their sole basis the requirement that one's model needs them. Otherwise, cases used in theoretical idealization become special cases or even degenerate cases, losing some or all of their theoretically important features. For example, Litman and Allen implicitly make the simplifying assumption that everything is aboveboard in a discourse, that is, that communicative and perlocutionary intentions coincide. Having pointed out the danger in this assumption early on, I won't dwell on it here and will instead focus on a more specific simplifying assumption that Litman and Allen make.

They assume that a definite and unique plan schema is connected to the surface speech analysis produced by the parser, as in an utterance of

Where do I get the CAN-AM (train)?

But compare that utterance with each of the following:

Where do you get the CAN-AM?
Where do I receive the CAN-AM?
Where do I get on the CAN-AM?
Where do I get off the CAN-AM?
Where do I find the CAN-AM?
Where is the CAN-AM?

Where do I get the connection to Hamilton?
Where do I get the train that I won?
Where do I get the best service?
Where do I get the best view?

Could you tell me where I might get the CAN-AM?
I wonder if you could tell me where I might get the CAN-AM.
It would be nice if you could tell me where I might get the CAN-AM.
I would like to know where I might get the CAN-AM.
I wish I knew where I might get the CAN-AM.
I can't find the CAN-AM.
I want to go to Tornoto.

I will leave it as an exercise to work through each of these examples to see how well Litman and Allen's model works for it and to what extent that model must be extended. For instance, consider the different sorts of linguistic and commonsense knowledge that must be cited to account for the diverse roles of the word "get" in the various examples in the first and second groups. And when no such verb occurs, as in "Where is the CAN-AM?", how is the domain plan to be identified? What about the various indirect requests in the third group? Perrault and Allen's (1980) account of certain indirect speech acts may work for some of these cases but not for all of them. At any rate, the explanatory value of Litman and Allen's model depends on how broadly it can be extended to a broader range of cases and, if it is limited in its ultimate scope, on whether some other model doesn't work as well but on a wider range of cases.

Similarly, consider that TAKE-TRAIN-TRIP is but one of many plans of which GOTO might be a step. There are also such plans as SEE-OFF-DEPARTING-FRIEND, PEDDLE-SANDWICHES, and SEARCH-FOR-CONTRABAND. Notice, further, that being able to recognize the intention behind an utterance such as "Where is the CAN-AM train?" does not require identifying the larger plan. Thus, it is not always true, as Litman and Allen contend, that the discourse intention makes reference to the plan of which it is a part. To identify the plan, the recognizer may require information from sources other than the utterance or even the immediate context. On the other hand, as I suggested earlier, in some cases identifying the plan may be necessary to identifying the discourse intention. For instance, the speaker may have won a train in a contest and, supposing this fact to be known to the recognizer, is asking where he goes to receive his title to the train.

Finally, it is important to emphasize the fact, as discovered by Grice, that in understanding an utterance, an addressee, unlike a recognition system, relies on the supposition that he is intended to identify the intention with which the utterance is being made. This fact makes an important difference, just as the analogous fact makes an important difference in activities like playing in an orchestra, driving in Rome (where they don't seem to have the concept of a lane), and playing charades. Consider the following examples, adapted from the work the economist and game theorist Thomas Schelling (1960) did around the time that Grice's original article appeared. Suppose I tell you I have in mind a certain U.S. president and I want you to think of the one I am thinking of. . . . . Did you think of Bush? Suppose I tell you I have in mind a certain letter of the alphabet and I want you to think of the one I am thinking of. . . . . Did you think of the letter "A"? Let's assume that you thought of the "right" one in each case, that is, the one that I was thinking of. In each case we both thought of what might be called the *salient* choice, the one that possessed a certain distinctive feature that each of us could count on the other to be thinking of, partly by supposing that we could somehow match each other's reasoning. But how did we do this? What made a certain choice the salient one was different in each case. Salience is not an intrinsic property, but something highly context-dependent. What is salience? I don't know, but I do know that whatever it is, it has a lot to do with communication and understanding.

4 Conclusion: Methodological Observations

I have tried to put Thomason's and Litman and Allen's papers into the broader perspective of speech act theory. In conclusion, it will be worthwhile to make some general methodological remarks concerning theorizing, in this case about communication and discourse.

First of all, we should distinguish the different roles played by different approaches, including philosophical analyses, computational models, psychological models, and logics. Computational models give samples of how information might be represented and processed but do not, in general, purport to be faithful to the psychological facts. Psychological models obviously do, but to that extent they are hard to come by. Philosophical analyses attempt to spell out the essential ingredients, to provide a "conceptual topography" of a phenomenon or process. Logical approaches, such as those of Jones (chapter 8 of this volume) and of Vanderveken (chapter 11), may seek to formalize any of the other approaches. We might say that the aims of these approaches, respectively, are explicitness, fidelity, conceptual precision, and formal precision. Needless to say, they are not mutually exclusive; but they are not mutually inclusive either.

Second, regardless of the kind of approach being taken, it is important to distinguish proper from improper simplification. In particular, although idealization is necessary for model building and for other sorts of theorizing, not just any sort of simplification will do—there must be a good rationale for which features of the theoretical domain under consideration are built into and which are locked out of the theory/model. In other words, you can't stipulate that the phenomena in a domain have just those features that your theory/model happens to be equipped to deal with. Moreover, you can't assume that what appears to be a good theory/model of a subdomain is automatically a good subtheory/partial model of the domain—essential features of the domain may have been excluded and the scope of the data may have been arbitrarily restricted. Improper simplification often occurs in semantics, for example, whenever a semantics for a "fragment" of English is given without any regard to whether it can coherently be extended to constructions not under consideration.

Any model of people's communicative behavior must cover people's ability to produce utterances with recognizable communicative intentions as well as their ability to recognize the communicative intentions behind other people's utterances. In my view there has been a tension in the ongoing effort to produce such a model: the guiding principles are too broad while the detailed implementations are too narrow. I agree with Thomason that general rules like Grice's maxims don't yield determinate predictions about concrete cases and, unless supplemented with much more detail, seem good for little more than ad hoc explanations. A model must be general enough to apply to a wide, indeed open-ended range of cases if it is to have any explanatory value, but, like Litman and Allen's, it must be detailed enough to make explicit the flow of information in the system being modeled. The dilemma is how to devise models that are neither too vague or otherwise uninformative nor too constrained or otherwise too specific.

References

Bach, K. (1984). Default reasoning: Jumping to conclusions and knowing when to think twice. *Pacific Philosophical Quarterly* 65, 37–58.

Bach, K. (1987a). *Thought and reference*. Oxford: Oxford University Press.

Bach, K. (1987b). On communicative intentions: A reply to Recanati. *Mind and Language* 2, 141–154.

Bach, K., and R. Harnish (1979). *Linguistic communication and speech acts*. Cambridge, MA: MIT Press.

Grice, H. P. (1957). Meaning. *The Philosophical Review* 66, 377–388.

Grice, H. P. (1969). Utterer's meaning and intentions. *The Philosophical Review* 78, 147–177.

Harman, G. (1986). *Change in view*. Cambridge, MA: MIT Press.

Perrault, C. R., and J. F. Allen (1980). A plan-based analysis of indirect speech acts. *American Journal of Computational Linguistics* 6, 167–182.

Recanati, F. (1986). On defining communicative intentions. *Mind and Language* 1, 213–242.

Schelling, T. (1960). *The strategy of conflict*. Cambridge, MA: Harvard University Press.

Schiffer, S. (1972). *Meaning*. Oxford: Oxford University Press.

Searle, J. (1969). *Speech acts: An essay in the philosophy of language*. Cambridge: Cambridge University Press.

Sperber, D., and D. Wilson (1986). *Relevance*. Cambridge, MA: Harvard University Press.

Strawson, P. F. (1964). Intention and convention in speech acts. *The Philosophical Review* 73, 439–460.

Chapter 19

Collective Intentions and Actions

John R. Searle

This paper begins with an intuition, a notation, and a presupposition. The intuition is: Collective intentional behavior is a primitive phenomenon that cannot be analyzed as just the summation of individual intentional behavior; and collective intentions expressed in the form "we intend to do such-and-such" or "we are doing such-and-such" are also primitive phenomena and cannot be analyzed in terms of individual intentions expressed in the form "I intend to do such-and-such" or "I am doing such-and-such." The notation is: S (p). The "S" stands for the type of psychological state; the "p" stands for the propositional content, the content that determines the conditions of satisfaction. Like all such notations, it isn't neutral; it embodies a theory. The presupposition is: All intentionality, whether collective or individual, requires a preintentional Background of mental capacities that are not themselves representational. In this case that implies that the functioning of the phenomena represented by the notation requires a set of phenomena that cannot be represented by that notation.

The questions the paper addresses are: Is the intuition right? (It is denied by most of the authors I have read on the subject.) And if it is right, can it be made to fit the notation? How, if at all, can we capture the structure of collective intentions within that notation? And what role does the Background play in enabling us to function in social collectives? These questions are not innocent. The larger question they form a part of is: How far can the theory of intentional action in *Intentionality* (Searle 1983) be extended to become a general theory?

1 The Intuition

Let's start with the intuition. The first half of the intuition could hardly be wrong. It seems obvious that there really is collective intentional behavior as distinct from individual intentional behavior. You can see this by watching a football team execute a pass play or hear it by listening to an orchestra. Better still, you can experience it by actually engaging in some group activity in which your own actions are a part of the group action.

The problem is with the second half of the intuition, the idea that the collective behavior is somehow not analyzable in terms of individual behavior and that the collective intention is somehow not reducible to a conjunction of singular intentions. How, one wants to ask, could there be any group behavior that wasn't just the behavior of the members of the group? After all, there isn't anyone left to behave once all the members of the group have been accounted for. And how could there be any group mental phenomenon except what is in the brains of the members of the group? How could there be a "we intend" that wasn't entirely constituted by a series of "I intend"s? There clearly aren't any bodily movements that are not movements of the members of the group. You can see that if you imagine an orchestra, a corps de ballet, or a football team. So if there is anything special about collective behavior, it must lie in some special feature of the mental component, in the form of the intentionality.

I want to build up to a characterization of the special form of collective intentionality by fist trying to justify the first part of the original intuition.

Thesis 1
There really is such a thing as collective intentional behavior that is not the same as the summation of individual intentional behavior.

I said this seems obvious, but it is important to see how pervasive collective behavior is. It is by no means confined to human beings but rather seems to be a biologically primitive form of animal life. Studies of animal behavior are filled with accounts of cooperative behavior, but it does not take a specialist's knowledge to recognize. Consider two birds building a nest together, or puppies playing on a lawn, or groups of primates foraging for food, or even a man going for a walk with his dog. In humans, collective behavior typically involves language, but even for humans it does not invariably require language or even conventional ways of behaving. For example, I see a man pushing a car in the street in an effort to get it started; and I simply start pushing with him. No words are exchanged and there is no convention according to which I push his car. But it is a case of collective behavior. In such a case *I* am pushing only as part of *our* pushing.

Perhaps the simplest way to see that collective behavior is not the same as the summation of individual behavior is to see that the same type of bodily movements could on one occasion be a set of individual acts and could on another occasion constitute a collective action. Consider the following sort of example: Imagine that a group of people are sitting on the grass in various places in a park. Imagine that it suddenly starts to rain and they all get up and run to a common, centrally located shelter. Each person has the intention expressed by the sentence "I am running to the shelter."

But for each person, we may suppose that his or her intention is entirely independent of the intentions and behavior of others. In this case there is no collective behavior; there is just a sequence of individual acts that happen to converge on a common goal. Now imagine a case where a group of people in a park converge on a common point as a piece of collective behavior. Imagine that they are part of an outdoor ballet where the choreography calls for the entire corps de ballet to converge on a common point. We can even imagine that the external bodily movements are indistinguishable in the two cases; the people running for shelter make the same types of bodily movements as the ballet dancers. Externally observed, the two cases are inditinguishable, but they are clearly different internally. What exactly is the difference? Well, part of the difference is that the form of the intentionality in the first case is that each person has an intention that he could express without reference to the others, even in a case where each has mutual knowledge of the intentions of the others. But in the second case the individual "I intend"s are in a way we will need to explain, derivative from the "we intend"s. That is, in the first case, even if each person knows that the other people intend to run to the shelter and knows that the other people know that he intends to run to the shelter, we still do not have collective behavior. In this case at least, it seems no set of "intend"s, even supplemented with beliefs about other "I intend"s, is sufficient to get to the "we intend." Intuitively, in the collective case the individual intentionality, expressed by "I am doing act A," is derivative from the collective intentionality, "We are doing act A."

Another clue that collective intentions are different from a mere summation of individual intentions is that often the derived form of an individual intention will have a different content from the collective intention from which it is derived. We can see this in the following sort of example. Suppose we are on a football team and we are trying to execute a pass play. That is, the team intention, we suppose, is in part expressed by "We are executing a pass play." But now notice: no individual member of the team has this as the entire content of his intention, for no one can execute a pass play by himself. Each player must make a specific contribution to the overall goal. If I am an offensive lineman, my intention might be expressed by "I am blocking the defensive end." Each member of the team will share in the collective intention but will have an individual assignment that is derived from the collective but has a different content from the collective. Where the collective's is "We are doing A," the individual's will be "I am doing B," "I am doing C," and so on.

But supposing we got the characterization of the "I intend"s just right, couldn't we show how they add up to a "we intend"? I think not, and this leads to our second thesis:

Thesis 2

We-intentions cannot be analyzed into sets of I-intentions, even I-intentions supplemented with beliefs, including mutual beliefs, about the intentions of other members of a group.

I think most philosophers would agree that collective behavior is a genuine phenomenon; the disagreement comes in how to analyze it. One tradition is willing to talk about group minds, the collective unconscious, and so on. I find this talk at best mysterious and at worst incoherent. Most empirically minded philosophers think that such phenomena must reduce to individual intentionality; specifically, they think that collective intentions can be reduced to sets of individual intentions together with sets of beliefs and especially mutual beliefs. I have never seen any such analysis that wasn't subject to obvious counterexamples, but let us try it out to see why it won't work. To have an actual sample analysis to work with, let us try that of Tuomela and Miller (1988), which is the best I have seen.

Leaving out various technical details, we can summarize their account as follows. An agent A who is a member of a group "we-intends" to do X if

1. A intends to do his part of X.
2. A believes that the preconditions of success obtain; especially, he believes that the other members of the group will (or at least probably will) do their parts of X.
3. A believes that there is a mutual belief among the members of the group to the effect that the preconditions of success mentioned in point 2 obtain.

This account is typical in that it attempts to reduce collective intentions to individual intentions plus beliefs. I, on the contrary, am proposing that no such reduction will work, that "we-intentions" are primitive. And I think it is easy to see what is wrong with the Tuomela-Miller account: a member of a group can satisfy these conditions and still not have a we-intention.

Consider the following situation. Suppose a group of businessmen are all educated at a business school where they learn Adam Smith's theory of the hidden hand. Each comes to believe that he can best help humanity by pursuing his own selfish interest, and they each form a separate intention to this effect; that is, each has an intention he would express as "I intend to do my part toward helping humanity by pursuing my own selfish interest and not cooperating with anybody." Let us also suppose that the members of the group have a mutual belief to the effect that each intends to help humanity by pursuing his own selfish interests and that these intentions will probably be carried out with success. That is, we may suppose that each is so well indoctrinated by the business school that each believes that his selfish efforts will be successful in helping humanity.

Now consider any given member A of the business school graduating class.

> 1. A intends to pursue his own selfish interests without reference to anybody else, and thus, he intends to do his part toward helping humanity.
>
> 2. A believes that the preconditions of success obtain. In particular, he believes that other members of his graduating class will also pursue their own selfish interests and thus help humanity.
>
> 3. Since A knows that his classmates were educated in the same selfish ideology that he was, he believes that there is a mutual belief among the members of his group that each will pursue his own selfish interests and that this will benefit humanity.

Thus, A satisfies the Tuomela-Miller conditions, but all the same, he has no collective intentionality. There is no we-intention. There is even an ideology, which he and the others accept, to the effect that there should not be a we-intention.

This case has to be distinguished from the case where the business school graduates all get together on graduation day and from a pact to the effect that they will all go out together and help humanity by way of each pursuing his own selfish interests. The latter case is a case of collective intentionality; the former case is not. Cooperative collective goals may be pursued by individualistic means, as is also shown by the following example. Suppose one of the members of a softball team loses his wallet at the game. Suppose the members reason that the chances of finding it are best if they each act separately; and each searches for the wallet in his own way, ignoring the others. They then set about in a coordinated and cooperative way to search for the wallet by acting with complete lack of coordination and cooperation. Unlike the original counterexample, these are genuine cases of collective behavior.

Could we avoid such counterexamples by construing the notion of "doing his part" in such a way as to block them? I think not. We are tempted to construe "doing his part" to mean doing his part toward achieving the *collective* goal. But if we adopt that move, then we have included the notion of a collective intention in the notion of "doing his part." We are thus faced with a dilemma: if we include the notion of collective intention in the notion of "doing his part," the analysis fails because of circularity; we would now be defining we-intentions in terms of we-intentions. If we don't so construe "doing his part," then the analysis fails because of inadequacy. Unless the we-intention is built into the notion of "doing his part," we will be able to produce counterexamples of the sort I have outlined above.

The reason that we-intentions cannot be reduced to I-intentions, even I-intentions supplemented with beliefs and beliefs about mutual beliefs, can be stated quite generally. The notion of a we-intention, of collective intentionality, implies the notion of *cooperation*. But the mere presence of I-intentions to achieve a goal that happens to be believed to be the same goal as that of other members of a group does not entail the presence of an intention to cooperate to achieve that goal. One can have a goal in the knowledge that others also have the same goal, and one can have beliefs and even mutual beliefs about the goal that is shared by the members of a group, without there being necessarily any cooperation among the members or any intention to cooperate among the members.

I have not demonstrated that no such analysis could ever succeed. I am not attempting to prove a universal negative. But the fact that the attempts that I have seen to provide a reductive analysis of collective intentionality fail for similar reasons—namely, they do not provide sufficient conditions for cooperation; one can satisfy the conditions in the analysis without having collective intentionality—does suggest that our intuition is right: we-intentions are a primitive phenomenon.

However, my claim that there is a form of collective intentionality that is not the product of some mysterious group mind and at the same time is not reducible to individual intentions has plenty of problems of its own, and we must now set about solving some of them. The most difficult problem we can put in the form: What exactly is the structure of we-intentions? We will not be in a position to answer that question until we answer a prior question about how we can reconcile the existence of collective intentionality with the fact that society consists entirely of individuals and no facts about any individual mental contents guarantee the existence of any other individuals. I believe it is facts such as these that have led people to believe that there must be a reduction of we-intentions to I-intentions.

Anything we say about collective intentionality must meet the following conditions of adequacy:

Constraint 1
It must be consistent with the fact that society consists of nothing but individuals. Since society consists entirely of individuals, there cannot be a group mind or group consciousness. All consciousness is in individual minds, in individual brains.

Constraint 2
It must be consistent with the fact that the structure of any individual's intentionality has to be independent of the fact of whether or not he is getting things right, whether or not he is radically mistaken about what is actually occurring. And this constraint applies as much to collective intentionality as it does to individual intentionality. One way to put this constraint is to say that the account must be consis-

tent with the fact that all intentionality, whether collective or individual, could be had by a brain in a vat or by a set of brains in vats.

These two constraints amount to the requirement that any account we give of collective intentionality, and therefore of collective behavior, must be consistent with our overall ontology and metaphysics of the world, an ontology and metaphysics based on the existence of individual human beings as the repositories of all intentionality, whether individual or collective.[1]

Thesis 3

The thesis that we-intentions are a primitive form of intentionality, not reducible to I-intentions plus mutual beliefs, is consistent with these two constraints.

Actually, I think it is rather simple to satisfy these constraints. We simply have to recognize that there are intentions whose form is: We intend that we perform act A; and such an intention can exist in the mind of each individual agent who is acting as part of the collective. In cases like that of the football team each individual will have further intentional content, which in ordinary English he might express in the form "I am doing act B as part of our doing act A." For example, "I am blocking the defensive end as part of our executing a pass play." We need only note that all the intentionality needed for collective behavior can be possessed by individual agents even though the intentionality in question makes reference to the collective.

In the cases described above, if I am pushing only as part of our pushing, or if I am blocking the defensive end as part of our executing a pass play, the intentionality, both plural and singular, is in my head. Of course, I take it in such cases that my collective intentionality is in fact shared; I take it in such cases that I am not simply acting alone. But I could have all the intentionality I do have even if I am radically mistaken, even if the apparent presence and cooperation of other people is an illusion, even if I am suffering a total hallucination, even if I am a brain in a vat. Collective intentionality in my head can make a purported reference to other members of a collective independently of the question whether or not there actually are such members.

Since this claim is consistent with the brain in the vat fantasy, it is a fortiori consistent with each of our constraints. It is consistent with Constraint 2, because the brain in the vat formulation is just the most extreme form of stating this constraint; it is consistent with Constraint 1, because we are not required to suppose that there is any element in society other than individuals—that is, the supposition is entirely consistent with the fact that society is made up entirely of individuals. It is consistent with the fact that there is no such thing as a group mind or group consciousness, because it only requires us to postulate that mental states can make reference to collectives where the reference to the collective lies outside the bracket that specifies the propositional content of the intentional state. The thought in the agent's mind is simply of the form "We are doing so and so."

Perhaps an uncomfortable feature of the analysis is that it allows for a form of mistake that is not simply a failure to achieve the conditions of satisfaction of an intentional state and is not a simply a breakdown in the Background. It allows for the fact that I may be mistaken in taking it that the "we" in the "we intend" actually refers to a we; that is, it allows for the fact that my presupposition that my intentionality is collective may be mistaken in ways that go beyond the fact that I have a mistaken belief. I do indeed have a mistaken belief if I have a collective intention that is not in fact shared, but on the proposed analysis, something further has gone wrong. Now, this does violate a very deep Cartesian assumption that we feel inclined to make. The assumption is that if I am mistaken, it can only be because one of my beliefs is false. But on my account, it turns out that I can not only be mistaken about how the world is but am even mistaken about what I am in fact doing. If I am having a hallucination in supposing that someone else is helping me push the car, that I am only pushing as part of our pushing, then I am mistaken not only in my belief that there is somebody else there pushing as well but also about what it is that I am doing. I thought I was pushing as part of our pushing, but that is not in fact what I was doing.

2 The Notation

I now turn to the notation. What exactly is the formal structure of collective intentionality? In order to state the structure of collective cases, we need to remind ourselves of the structure of intentionality for singular actions. An action of, say, raising one's arm has two components: a "mental" component and a "physical" component. The mental component both represents and causes the physical component, and because the form of causation is intentional causation, the mental causes the physical of way of representing it. In ordinary English we can say: when I succeed, my trying to do something casues an effect of a certain type, because that is what I was trying to achieve. In the notation that I have found useful and perspicuous we can represent these facts, when the action is one of raising one's arm, as follows:

i.a. (this i.a. causes: my arm goes up) CAUSES: MY ARM GOES UP.

The expressions in lowercase letters represent the mental component. The type of intentional state is specified outside the bracket; in this case "i.a." stands for intention-in-action; and the expressions inside the bracket represent the conditions of satisfaction, what must be the case if the state is to be satisfied. Where intentions are concerned, these conditions are causally self-referential; that is, it is part of the conditions of satisfaction that the state itself must cause an event of the type represented in the rest of the conditions of satisfaction. The expressions in capital letters on the right represent actual physical events in the world. If the i.a. is successful, then the action will consist of two components, a "mental" and a "physical" component, and the condition of satisfaction of the mental is that it should cause a physical event of a certain type. Since we are supposing it is successful, the above notation represents the fact that it does cause an event of that type. All of these facts are summarized in the above abbreviation.

I want the notation to seem absolutely clear, so I will write out a paraphrase in ordinary English, treating the whole expression as if it were a sentence instead of a diagram of the structure of an intention:

> There is an intention-in-action that has as its conditions of satisfaction that that very intention-in-action causes it to be the case that my arm goes up; and all of that mental stuff really does cause it to be the case in the physical world that my arm goes up.

Now let us remind ourselves of how it works for a slightly more complex case involving a by-means-of relation. Suppose a man fires a gun by means of pulling the trigger. He has an intention-in-action whose content is that that very intention-in-action should cause the pulling of the trigger, which in turn should cause the firing of the gun. If the intention is satisfied, the whole complex event looks like this:

> i.a. (this i.a. causes: trigger pulls, causes: gun fires) CAUSES: TRIGGER PULLS, CAUSES: GUN FIRES.

Once again, the expressions in lowercase letters represent the contents of the mind, and the expressions in capital letters represent what happens in the real world. Since we are assuming that the contents of the mind are satisfied in subsequent formulations, we can simply leave out the reference to the real world. If satisfied, the contents of the mind can be read off directly onto the world. Previously we introduced the colon, which is read (with appropriate adjustments) as "it to be the case that ..." and enables us to convert the sentence or other expressions that follow into singular terms. Here we introduce the comma, which is read as "which" and converts the subsequent expressions into a relative clause. Thus, the stuff inside the parentheses in this example is to be read in English as follows:

> This intention-in-action causes it to be the case that the trigger pulls, which causes it to be the case that the gun fires.

Now, let us apply these lessons to the study of collective behavior. To that end, let us look at another case.

Suppose Jones and Smith are engaged in a piece of cooperative behavior. Suppose they are preparing a hollandaise sauce. Jones is stirring while Smith slowly pours in the ingredients. They have to coordinate their efforts because if Jones stops stirring or Smith stops pouring, the sauce will be ruined. Each has a form of collective intentionality that he could express as "We are preparing hollandaise sauce." This is a collective intention-in-action and it has the following form:

i.a. (this i.a. causes: sauce is mixed).

Now the puzzle is, how does this collective intention cause anything? After all, there aren't any agents except individual human beings, and somehow intentional causation has to work through them and only through them. I believe one of the keys to understanding collective intentionality is to see that in general the by and by-means-of relations for achieving the collective goal have to end in individual actions. Thus, we might ask the cooks, "How are you preparing the dinner?" "Well," they might answer, "first by making the sauce; then by cooking the meat." But at some point somebody has to be in a position to say, for example, "I am stirring." In such cases the individual component of the collective actions plays the role of means to ends. Jones's stirring is the means to making the sauce in the same sense that pulling the trigger is the means to firing the gun. Jones has an intentional content that we could express in English as:

We are making the sauce by means of me stirring.

And Smith has the intentional content:

We are making the sauce by means of me pouring.

From the point of view of each agent there are not two actions with two intentions that he is performing. Rather, just as in the gun case there is only one intention and one action—to fire the gun by means of pulling the trigger—so in the collective case each agent has only one intention that represents his contribution to the single collective action:

Jones: i.a. (this i.a. causes: ingredients are stirred).
Smith: i.a. (this i.a. causes: ingredients are poured).

But we still haven't solved our problem. In the case of the individual action there is a single intention that encompasses the by-means-of relations. I intend to fire the gun by means of pulling the trigger. One intention, one action. The relation of the means-intention to the overall intention is simply part-whole: the whole intention represents both the means and the ends, and it does that by representing the by-means-of relation according to which one achieves the end by means of the means.

But how exactly does it work where the means is individual and the goal is collective? The answer to that question is not at all obvious. Let us try some possibilities. It is tempting to think that such intentions might contain collective intentionality right down to the ground, that there might simply by a special class of collective intentions and that is all that is needed. On this account, from Jones's point of view the intentionality is this:

> collective i.a. (this collective i.a. causes: ingredients are stirred, causes: sauce is mixed).

But this "collectivist" or "socialist" solution can't be right because it leaves out the fact that Jones is making an individual contribution to a collective goal. If I am Jones, this account leaves it as mysterious how the collective intentionality can move my body. Surely one feels like saying, I personally have to intend to do something if the sauce is ever going to get mixed.

But the opposite view, according to which it is all individual intentionality, a "capitalist" or "individualist" solution, fares no better:

> singular i.a. (this singular i.a. causes: stirred, causes: mixed).

This is unsatisfactory because it is consistent with there being no collective intentionality at all. I might stir in the knowledge that you were doing something that together with my stirring would produce the desired result without any collective intentionality. In short, this formulation is consistent with the claim that there is no such thing as collective intentionality, it is just an accumulation of individual intentionality; and that view we have already rejected.

Well, suppose we try to capture both the collective and individual components in the following way. Suppose we treat the collective intention as causing the singular intention:

> collective i.a. (this collective i.a. causes: singular i.a., causes: stirred, causes: mixed).

The feature of this analysis that makes me think it must be false is the fact that a separate i.a. is in the scope of the collective i.a. This would imply that the collective intention isn't satisfied unless it causes me to have a singular i.a. And that can't be right, because my collective intention isn't an intention to make it be the case that I have a singular intention; it is the intention to achieve some collective goal for which my singular intention stands as means to end. A clue that this must be wrong is provided by the fact that it is quite unlike the case of ordinary singular action where my intention to fire the gun by means by pulling the trigger consists in only one complex intention, not two intentions where one causes the other as part of its conditions of satisfaction. Of course, in the singular cases an intention can cause me to have a subsidiary intention, by practical reasoning. But even in such cases it doesn't necessarily have to cause the subsidiary intention in order to be satisfied. In the singular case there is just one intention in the agent's head: to fire the gun by means by pulling the trigger. Now why should there be two intentions in each agent's head in the collective case?

Well, let's try a new start. Let's ask intuitively what is going on. Intuitively, we are intentionally making the sauce and if I am Jones, my share is that I am intentionally stirring the ingredients. But what exactly is the relation between the collective and the individual intention? It seems to me it is exactly like the relation of the intention to pull the trigger and the intention to fire the gun: just as I fire the gun by means of my pulling the trigger, so We make the sauce by means of Me stirring and You pouring. As far as my part is concerned, We intend to make the sauce by means of Me stirring. But don't those have to be two separate intentions, one singular i.a. and one collective i.a.? No, no more than there have to be two separate intentions when I fire the gun by means of pulling the trigger. The real distinction between the singular and the collective case is in the type of intention involved, not in the way that the elements in the conditions of satisfaction relate to each other. The form of the intention in the singular case is to achieve goal B by way of doing means A. That is, it isn't just any old type of i.a., it is an achieve-B-by-means-of-A type of i.a. So we might think of the notation that represents this type of i.a. as containing two free variables, "A" and "B"; and these variables are then bound by clauses inside the brackets that function as nouns. What we are trying to say is that I have an achieve-B-by-means-of-A sort of intention whose content is that that-the-trigger-pulls-as-A casues it to be the case that-the-gun-fires-as-B. And we can represent this as follows:

i.a. B by means of A (this i.a. causes: A trigger pulls, causes: B gun fires).

Similarly, in the structure of collective action, there is only one (complex) i.a., and it isn't just any old type of i.a.; it is an achieve-collective-B-by-means-of-singular-A type of i.a. And when it comes to the notation, we bind those free variables in the representation of the type of intention by clauses functioning as singular noun phrases inside the brackets:

i.a. collective B by means of singular A (this i.a. causes: A stirred, causes: B mixed).

I am not sure this is the right analysis, but it does seem to be better than the three others we considered. It allows for both the collective and the individual component in the agent's intentions. And it does so in a way that avoids making the paradoxical claim that the collective act causes the individual act. Rather, the individual act is part of the collective act. The intention to stir is part of the intention to mix by means of stirring in the same way that in the gun case the intention to pull is part of the intention to fire by means of pulling.

3 The Presupposition

But now the next question arises, what sort of beings are we that we have the capacity to form such intentions? Ultimately the answer to that has to be biological, but there is a more restricted sense of the question that we can still address: What general Background capacities and phenomena are presupposed by the sketch of collective intentionality I have just given? The manifestation of any particular form of collective intentionality will require particular Background skills, the ability to stir or play football, for example. But are there any features of the Background that are general or pervasive (even if perhaps not universal) for collective behavior? I think there are, but they are not easy to characterize. They are the sorts of things that old-time philosophers were driving at when they said things like "Man is a social animal" or "Man is a political animal." In addition to the biological capacity to recognize other people as importantly like us, in a way that waterfalls, trees, and stones are not like us, it seems to me that the capacity to engage in collective behavior requires something like a preintentional sense of "the other" as an actual or potential agent like oneself in cooperative activities. The football team has the sense of "us against them" and it has that sense against the sense of the larger us of "teams playing the game"; the orchestra has the sense of "us playing in front of them" and it has that sense as part of the larger us of "participants in the concert." "But," one might object, "surely this sense of others as cooperative agents is constituted by the collective intentionality." I don't think so. The collective behavior certainly augments the sense of others as cooperative agents, but that sense can exist without any collective intentionality, and what is more interesting, collective intentionality seems to presuppose some level of sense of community before it can ever function.

It is worth noticing in passing that most forms of competitive and aggressive behavior are forms of higher-level cooperation. Two men engaged in a prizefight are engaged in a form of competition, but it is a form of aggressive competition that exists only within a higher-level form of cooperation. Each prizefighter has the intention to hurt the other, but they have these intentions only within the frame of the higher-order intention to cooperate with each other in engaging in a prizefight. This is the distinction between a prizefight and a case of one man simply assaulting another man in a dark alley. And what goes for the prizefight also goes for football games, business competitions, courtroom trials, and in many cases even armed warfare. For human beings, most social forms of aggressive behavior require higher-level cooperation. For one person even to insult another at a cocktail party requires an extremely sophisticated higher level of cooperation among the participants in the insult.

Not all social groups are engaged in goal-directed behavior all the time. Some of the time they are just, for instance, sitting around in living rooms, hanging out in bars, or riding on the train. Now the form of collectivity that exists in such cases isn't constituted by goal-directed intentionality, because there isn't any. Such groups are, so to speak, ready for action but they are not yet engaged in any actions (they have no collective intentions-in-action) nor are they planning any (they have no collective prior intentions). Nonetheless, they have the type of communal awareness that is the general pecondition of collective intentionality.

On the basis of such preliminary reflections I want to advance the following thesis:

> *Thesis 4*
> Collective intentionality presupposes a Background sense of the other as a candidate for cooperative agency; that is, it presupposes a sense of others as more than mere conscious agents, indeed as actual or potential members of a cooperative activity.

Now, what is the argument for this thesis? I don't know of anything like a conclusive argument; nonetheless, the considerations that incline me to this view are something like the following. Ask yourself what you must take for granted in order that you can ever have or act on collective intentions. What you must suppose is that the others are agents like yourself, that they have a similar awarecess of you as an agent like themselves, and that these awarenesses coalesce into a sense of *us* as possible or actual collective agents. And these conditions hold even for total strangers. When I go out of my door into the street to help push the stranger's car, part of the Background is that each of us regards the other as an agent and as a candidate to form part of a collective agent. But these are not in the normal case "beliefs." Just as my stance toward the objects around me and the ground underneath me is that of their being solid, without my needing or having a special belief that they are solid; and just as my stance toward others is that of their being conscious agents, without my needing or having a special belief that they are conscious; so my stance toward others with whom I am engaged in collective behavior is that of their being conscious agents in a cooperative activity, without my needing or having a special belief to that effect.

I believe that if we could fully understand the Background sense of others as possible agents, we would see that certain attempts to understand the character of society must be wrong. It is tempting to think that collective behavior presupposes communication, that speech acts in conversation are the "foundation" of social behavior and hence of society. It is perhaps equally tempting to suppose that conversation presupposes collective behavior, that social behavior is the foundation of conversation and hence of any society in which communication plays an essential role. There is obviously something to be said for each of these views. But I am here suggesting that we cannot explain society in terms of either conversation in particular or collective behavior in general, since each of these presupposes a form of society before they can function at all. The biologically primitive sense of the other person as a cnadidate for shared intentionality is a necessary condition of all collective behavior and hence of all conversation.

We can now conclude with:

Thesis 5

The notation, and hence the theory, of *Intentionality* together with a certain conception of the role of the Background can accommodate collective intentions and actions.

Note

1. Readers will recognize that these two constraints are close to "methodological individualism" and "methodological solipsism" as traditionally construed. I am anxious if possible to avoid sinking into the morass of the traditional disputes, so I am trying to present a version of these in which they can be construed as just commonsensical, pretheoretical requirements.

References

Searle, John R. (1983). *Intentionality: An essay in the philosophy of mind.* New York: Cambridge University Press.

Tuomela, Raimo, and Kaarlo Miller (1988). We-intentions. *Philosophical Studies* 53, 367–389.

Chapter 20

Plans for Discourse

Barbara J. Grosz and Candace L. Sidner

---

1 Intentions and Actions in Discourse Structures Theory

In Grosz and Sidner 1986 we proposed a theory of discourse structure comprising three components: a linguistic structure, an intentional structure, and an attentional state. These three constituents of discourse structure deal with different aspects of the utterances in a discourse. Utterances—the actual saying or writing of particular sequences of phrases and clauses—are the linguistic structure's basic elements. Intentions and the relations of *domination* and *satisfaction precedence* provide the basic elements of the intentional structure. Attentional state contains information about the objects, properties, relations, and discourse intentions that are most salient at any given point. It is an abstraction of the focus of attention of the discourse participants; it serves to summarize information from previous utterances crucial for processing subsequent ones, thus obviating the need for keeping a complete history of the discourse.

In our earlier paper we argued that the natural segmentation of a discourse reflects intentional behavior; each segment is engaged in for the purpose of satisfying a particular intention. That intention is designated as the discourse segment purpose (DSP), that is, the basic reason for engaging in that segment of the discourse. DSPs are intended to be recognized. The utterances in a discourse provide information necessary for a hearer or reader to determine what the speaker or writer's DSPs are. We raised a number of questions about the recognition of intentions that play this key role in the discourse and that are present in the intentional structure (not all

The authors wish to thank Martha Pollack for her comments on this paper, and the System Development Foundation for the workshop at which it was first presented.

The research reported in this paper was made possible in part by a gift from the System Development Foundation to SRI International. Funds for the second author were provided by the Defense Advanced Research Projects Agency and were monitored by the Office of Naval Research under contract number N00014-85-C-0079. The views and conclusions contained in this document are those of the authors and should not be interpreted as necessarily representing the official policies, either expressed or implied, of the Defense Advanced Research Projects Agency or of the United States government.

of the intentions expressed in utterances of the discourse appear in the intentional structure).

Our basic view is that a conversational participant needs to recognize the DSPs and the dominance relationships between them in order to process subsequent utterances of the discourse; the intentional structure is part of the context of the discourse. Although in our previous paper we pointed out a number of kinds of information that would play a role in processing —specific linguistic markers, utterance-level intentions, and general knowledge about actions and objects in the domain of discourse—we did not propose an actual processing model. A computational theory of the recognition of DSPs depends on underlying theories of intention, action, and plans. These theories must be appropriate for discourse actions and intentions.

Previous work on planning and plan recognition for natural language might seem to provide the basis for such theories. However, as we examined that work, we realized that various assumptions it made about plans, actions, and agents were inappropriate for the general discourse situation and precluded any simple type of generalization. In particular, it did not provide the right basis for explaining collaborative behavior. Discourses are fundamentally examples of collaborative behavior. The participants in a discourse work together to satisfy various of their individual and joint needs. Thus, to be sufficient to underlie discourse theory, a theory of actions, plans, and plan recognition must deal adequately and appropriately with collaboration.

Discourses may exhibit two types of collaborative behavior: collaboration in the domain of discouse (for example, working together to write a paper) and collaboration with respect to the discourse itself. Although we cannot yet define (either intensionally or extensionally) "collaboration with respect to a discourse," it includes not only surface collaborations (such as coordinating turns in a dialogue) or use of appropriate referring expressions (Grosz 1978; chapter 23 of this volume) but also collaborations related to the discourse purpose. For example, the participants collaborate to ensure that the utterances of the discourse itself provide sufficient information to make possible the satisfaction of the discourse purpose. We have examined, and will discuss in this paper, the sorts of plans and intentions involved in what we called the "action" case—roughly, the recognition of DSPs that embed in some way intentions to perform actions. We will thus focus in this paper on collaboration in the domain. In chapter 19 of this volume Searle addresses similar issues concerning appropriate theories for explaining how two (or more) people work together to accomplish goals; although his detailed proposals are different, they appear to be similar in spirit.

In this paper we first examine the characteristics of the discourse situation and the ways in which they affect plan recognition. We then briefly review and critique previous work on plans and plan recognition for natural language. We address two particular concerns: an imbalance in the typical characterization of the speaker and hearer roles, and the need to coordinate intentions of different agents. Finally, we propose a new type of plan, one that more naturally underlies the type of collaborative effort that dialogues typically comprise. We discuss briefly how this type of plan can be used to constrain the recognition process.

2 The Character of Plans Underlying Discourse

At any point in a discourse, a participant may form and undertake a number of different plans. Of all such plans, we will be interested only in those that are intended to be recognized by the other discourse participant; this is much like Grice's depiction of the class of intentions underlying an utterance that are intended to be recognized. As we discussed in our previous paper, there is no simple mapping between linguistic expressions and the intentions and plans underlying a discourse. No distinguished type of (linguistic) expression is used to convey information about plans intended to be recognized.

For example, definite descriptions may convey intended-plan information or may be designed for entirely different purposes. In designing a definite description, a speaker may plan to add information that aids a hearer in identifying an object (see Appelt 1985); this plan is not intended to be recognized. In contrast, descriptions that are conversationally relevant (Kronfeld 1986) are realizations of plans that are intended to be recognized. Likewise, there are plans for sequences of utterances only some of which are intended to be recognized. For instance, a speaker may plan to convey the information in a discourse segment in a certain sequence (conventionally used to convey such information) without intending that the hearer recognize this plan (see McKeown 1985). Finally, in some discourses a speaker may intend that his plan not be recognized, because its recognition would foil his goals (see, for instance, the socially oriented plans discussed by Hobbs and Evans (1980)).

Plan recognition is the process of inferring an actor's plan on the basis of partial information about a portion of it. Plan recognition for discourse concerns the recognition of plans that are intended to be recognized. This simple definition, when put into practice, is colored by a multitude of issues. Some of these are foundational questions about the nature of a plan. Is a plan a collection of actions that an actor is about to undertake? Is it a collection of an actor's intentions and beliefs to act in some way? Can a plan include actions performed by other agents or refer to beliefs held by another agent? Other questions concern the conditions under which a particular plan is inferred. What is the relation between the actor of a plan and an inferring agent (that is, the agent who is inferring the actor's plan)?

Does the actor know that he is being observed? Is there any attempt on the part of the actor to ensure that the inferring agent has all the information needed to infer the plan? How do the actor and inferring agent share information about the plan?

The communicative situation exerts strong constraints on the plan recognition problem for natural-language processing. Each discourse participant undertakes plans to accomplish his own desires and collaborates in plans to achieve the desires of other participants. Discourse participants are thus both actors and inferring agents involved in the recognition of each other's plans. As we will show later, collaborative plans play a prominent role in discourse; their construction and use require that participants make clear to one another how their actions will coordinate and contribute to the satisfaction of the discourse purpose. Thus, speakers must provide in their utterances sufficient information about their beliefs and intentions for their hearers to be able to determine how these contribute to the (collaborative) plan, and hearers must be attuned to those cues of language as well as to properties of the discourse situation that constrain their inference of the plan.

Various linguistic devices provide explicit information about intentions; of these, the most extensively considered have been cue phrases (Grosz and Sidner 1986; Polanyi and Scha 1983; Reichman-Adar 1984) and intonation (Hirschberg and Pierrehumbert 1986; Hirschberg and Litman 1987). For example, speakers can use such devices to tell their hearers when they complete a discourse segment (reflecting a belief that they have said all that needs to be said to satisfy its DSP) and are moving onto another DSP and segment. They also may use them to signal the temporary interruption of one segment (and the attempt to satisfy its DSP) so that they may pursue another unrelated (but momentarily more important) DSP.

Furthermore, although discourse participants may hold a wide range of mutual beliefs, each has private beliefs. None has either complete or perfect information, and in general their beliefs may differ. In particular, the knowledge that discourse participants bring to the discourse about the plans of others is incomplete, and their beliefs about how actions can be combined to achieve desired states is often different. Typically the information needed to infer the plan of another discourse participant is conveyed not in a single utterance but in a sequence of utterances. Thus, the plan recognition process for discourse entails incremental recognition on the basis of partial information, accommodation of uncertainty (for instance, treating disjunctive possibilities), and strategies for resolving inconsistencies in beliefs among participants (Pollack 1986).

Finally, two types of actions may be performed by participants in a discourse: domain actions and communicative actions. Domain actions are those actions that change the world directly. Communicative actions, ac-

complished by utterances, directly affect the beliefs of the discourse participants (and may through this lead to domain actions that affect the outside
world). They may also affect the state of the discourse—for example,
change the attentional state by pushing or popping focus spaces or by
introducing new entities into a space.

3 Plans and Plan Recognition Algorithms Thus Far

Some of the assumptions underlying prior work on plan recognition for
natural-language processing have differed from the characterization of discourse we have just sketched. Typically, it has been assumed that one agent
(*the* speaker) had desires and produced utterances and the other agent (*the*
hearer) attempted to infer from these utterances the speaker's goals and
plans; we will dub this the *master-slave assumption*. In addition, it has been
assumed that the inferring agent's knowledge of actions and how they are
related constitutes a correct and complete description of what agents can
do. Furthermore, the predominant representation of plans has been one
originally developed for planning by a single agent who is situated in a
world that only changes as a result of her own actions. In this section we
briefly review the main constructs used in prior work, critique their use as
the basis for plan recognition in discourse, and discuss which representations and processes can be adapted to support the kind of communicative
situation that we have in mind.

In the past fifteen years a number of AI researchers have explored issues
concerned with the representation of plans and actions, and algorithms for
inferring one particular plan on the basis of partial information (Bruce 1975;
Bruce and Newman 1978; Schmidt, Sridharan, and Goodson 1978; Allen
1979; Allen and Perrault 1980; Sidner 1983, 1985; Kautz and Allen 1986).
In the natural-language processing work on plan recognition, a speaker
(filling the actor role) engages a hearer (the inferring agent) in discussion
about actions and conditions that the speaker desires. The speaker may
want the hearer to do some specific act (for example, to flip the living room
light switch to turn on the living room lights) or to do whatever act will
produce a specific effect (say, make it light in the living room). The speaker's
utterances serve the purpose of telling the hearer the particular act or effect,
and possibly some other information. The hearer (as inferring agent) is
assumed to be ready to carry out the specific act or produce the effect once
it is clear what it is. This research has also assumed that the actor (speaker)
was aware of the inferring agent (hearer) and intended for the inferring
agent to draw certain conclusions about the actor's plan (called the *intended
recognition assumption* (Cohen 1981)).

Almost all of the work on plan recognition algorithms has been based on
the same representational formalism, namely, that developed for STRIPS

(Fikes and Nilsson 1981) and its descendents (such as NOAH (Sacerdoti 1977)). In this formalism operators are used to model actions, where an operator comprises three parts: a description of an action in terms of subactions (the body),[1] a precondition needed to be true to carry out the action, and an effect that holds once the action is accomplished. Because the body of an operator could contain subactions, the operators could in principle express decompositions of actions into other actions. A plan was an assembly of operators that described how to get from an initial state to a final state (called the *goal*). In both STRIPS and NOAH, operators were actually schemata for a class of actions; for example, the operator Pickup(a x) described the class of actions that included such instances as Pickup(Johnnie redtruck) and Pickup(Robot1 screw2). The operators were not in subsumption hierarchies: no mechanism existed to express the relations among operator classes (for instance, that the operator for transfer of objects by agents subsumes the operators for giving, taking, stealing, dropping off, and so on).

The STRIPS formalism was developed for planning purposes; it had to be adapted in several ways before it could be used for plan recognition. To reconstruct the plan of another agent, recognition processes used heuristic rules that indicated how an agent's desires could be linked to preconditions, bodies, or effects of actions. Allen's system used operator definitions, the bodies of which contained at most single actions. Sidner and Kautz each augmented the formalism to include subsumption hierarchies over both the operators as a whole and the decompositions of actions within the body of an operator. In addition, their operator bodies typically include sequences of multiple subactions.

Plan recognition work for language processing has proposed various explanations for why hearers need to infer a speaker's plan and how they do so. In their pioneering work on speech acts and plan recognition, Allen and Perrault (1980) assumed that both the speaker's goal and his plan for satisfying that goal were unknown to the hearer. They defined a recognition process for inferring a speaker's goal and plan; it used information from a single utterance combined with (presumed shared) knowledge of possible plans. The inferred plan comprised a combination of communicative actions and domain actions. It reflected the hearer's reasoning about how the speech act was related to the speaker's desire. Allen and Perrault also showed how the plan provided the context in which to determine an appropriate response. In particular, after inferring the speaker's goal and his plan for achieving that goal, a cooperative hearer would provide information that was missing in the plan and needed in order for it to be carried out by the speaker.

In Sidner's work the goal and plan also were inferred, but incrementally over successive utterances of the conversation. Sidner augmened Allen's original framework by concentrating on the recognition of complex descriptions of actions and on the multi-utterance nature of discourse. According to her theory, a hearer was to accomplish whatever specific actions a speaker had conveyed as desired. Each utterance was viewed as providing partial information about the speaker's plan. Thus, after each utterance the hearer was considered to have a partial description (which we will call the hearer's *action description*) of the speaker's plan; information in subsequent utterances enabled the hearer to refine the action description. Since actions were modeled in an abstraction (subsumption) hierarchy, plan recognition was taken to be a process of recognizing a more specific goal by deriving more specific action descriptions from the abstraction hierarchy. The specific action description inferred at the end of the discourse (segment) was considered to be the speaker's plan.

To illustrate how to use the refined action description, we will consider the following simple example. Someone says, "I'm going on a date tonight. Can you pick up something at the florist for me?" In this example recognition is simplified because the speaker makes explicit the (domain) desire (to go on a date) that leads to his secondary desire that the hearer do a specific action (get something from the florist) that will aid in the satisfaction of his primary desire. The speaker intended that the hearer would recognize that the florist visit is in aid of the speaker's plan for meeting the date-desire; thus, the action of visiting the florist is to obtain flowers for the date. Furthermore, the hearer is intended to use this information to choose flowers appropriate to the occasion (red roses rather than a potted plant).

Plan recognition can be much more complex, when it requires refinement over several utterances of a discourse without a direct statement of what the speaker was up to. If a speaker asked a hearer to get his good suit from the cleaners, and then a while later asked for something from the florist, and that the car be washed and filled with gas, the hearer could again infer that the speaker was about to go on a date. However, in this case an incremental search of the action abstraction hierarchy would be undertaken. The first utterance provides a piece of information to infer that the speaker may be getting dressed up to go somewhere; the later utterances provide the additional information needed to conclude that the more specific plan is to go on a date.

Kautz's general theory of plan recognition redefined the plan recognition process as deduction based on a set of observations, an action taxonomy, and one or more simplicity conditions (Kautz and Allen 1986, 123). The general criteria underlying his algorithm include that two or more actions may be interleaved and that an action can simultaneously be part of more than one action description. His theory makes no specific assumptions about communication between a speaker and a hearer. Thus, the recognition algorithm takes the view of observing actions without the actor of the plan having awareness of the inferring agent's presence (called *keyhole recognition* (Cohen 1981)). Kautz's model takes a more general view of plan recognition than previously done.

However, Kautz's model includes some more restrictive assumptions as well. It assumes that recognition is undertaken with a complete list of observed actions.[2] The model also incorporates three important limiting assumptions about the representation of actions:

1. The specialization hierarchy encodes a complete and mutually exclusive set of specializations.
2. The decomposition hierarchy is complete.
3. If two observed actions might be part of one plan, they are taken to be part of the same plan.

(Assumption 3 is called the *simplicity condition.*)

Assumptions 1 and 2 were also made, explicitly or implicitly, in all work prior to Kautz's. These assumptions are problematic for plan recognition applied to discourse because the participants operate with incomplete knowledge of one another. Pollack (1986) argues this case quite clearly in considering appropriate responses to questions.

Assumption 3 has been made as a means of limiting the observer's incremental search for the most general plan the observed agent is pursuing.[3] This assumption limits search by constraining the number of possible plans. It thus helps in those cases in which actions *do* fit together. However, it offers no special help in those cases in which two (sequentially observed) actions are not part of the same plan.

The fact that communication in natural language rests in part on an assumption of intended recognition allows for a modified form of Assumption 3, which aids communication in both action cases: a speaker must mark those cases where two actions are not part of the same plan. By marking such shifts, a speaker provides the information needed to reduce the incremental search when two actions do not fit; combined with the assumption of intended recognition, it justifies a hearer's assuming in the absence of such markings that two actions are intended to fit. Thus, plan recognition for natural language is more constrained than the general (keyhole) recognition case considered by Kautz.[4]

In addition to the problems just discussed, previous plan recognition work has had two major problems (pointed out by Pollack (1986)). First, the view of plans as being composed solely of collections of actions (and their associated preconditions and effects) is insufficient. The definition of a plan must account for the ways in which the intentions of the agent who is (about) to perform the actions and his beliefs about those actions affect the appropriateness and success of the plan.

The current state of plan recognition research derives in part from the nature of the tasks addressed by STRIPS-type systems (namely, those involving robots) and in part from a particular set of natural-language domain tasks (namely, ones that reflected the master-slave assumption). In such settings it might, at first glance, seem possible to ignore the intentions of the planning agent and the ways in which the beliefs of the planning and inferring agents may differ. However, for natural language more than a single agent may be involved in carrying out a plan and more than one agent must have access to knowledge about the plan. Thus, any model (or theory) of the communicative situation must distinguish among beliefs and intentions of different agents.

A second problem with prior plan recognition (and, as it turns out, planning) models is the underlying model of actions on which they rest. As Pollack (1986) has shown, the notions of precondition, body, and effect have been used to encode a variety of different types of relationships in different ways on different occasions. They are not well defined either theoretically or in practice. For example, in the STRIPS-type formalisms, opening a door can be described by an action operator with header (Open (agent, door)), precondition (Not-Open(door)), effect (Open(door)), and body [Put(agent, Hand-On-Knob(door)), Turn-Knob(agent, door), Pull-Knob(agent, door)]. This description fails to encode information such as which actions enable other actions, which actions must stand in a sequence, which actions actually accomplish the end action and which are supplementary, and what relation preconditions and effects bear to the subactions of the action operator. As Allen (1984) has remarked, the formalisms do not provide a natural description of simultaneous action or treat goals of maintenance (that is, desires that certain properties of the current state of the world be maintained, such as the desire to stay healthy). The STRIPS formalism has no calculus of these aspects of actions; prior plan recognition research has not provided it.

Pollack redefined plans in order to explain a type of language behavior involving errors in speaker's plans. She defined plans as mental states of agents, that is, as a particular set of their intentions and beliefs. An agent's (speaker or hearer) simple plan was defined in terms of a set of beliefs and intentions: beliefs about the relations among various intended actions and about the executability of those actions, and intentions (of the agent) regarding those actions.[5]

To infer the speaker's plan, Pollack pursued a special case of plan recognition for her natural-language examples. Given a stated speaker desire and a stated action that was to generate additional (unspecified) actions to achieve the desire, the plan recognizer found a path between the desire and stated action by filling in the unspecified generated actions. This kind of plan recognition algorithm was not a departure from the earlier work, but it made use of a very different formalism for a plan.

Pollack's plan formalism allowed her to make a new distinction: the actor's plan to achieve some P and the inferring agent's own (and possibly different) description of how to achieve P. Once the actor's plan was inferred, the inferring agent could inspect it to determine which of the (actor's) beliefs in the plan differed from her own beliefs about domain actions. These differences could form the basis of a response that suggested to the actor a more appropriate set of actions for achieving her goal.[6]

Pollack's definitions of intentions and of the simple plan of an agent provide a much richer and cleaner model an agent's plan to achieve some desire on the basis of a simple action or sequence of actions. The richness originates with the addition of intentions and of beliefs about execution and generation among actions. Her model clearly distinguishes among believing that actions fit together in certain regular ways, believing that one can execute those actions, and actually intending to act.

Pollack's definition of plans has turned out to be most useful to us for discourse theory because it rests on a detailed treatment of the relations among actions (relations of generation and enablement) and because it distinguishes the intentions and beliefs of an agent about those actions. Since her plan model is the simple plan of a single agent, we need to extend the model to plans of two or more collaborative agents. Extension to plans involving enabling as well as generating actions will await another paper.

4 Shared Plans

Shared plans are a notion intended to remedy several problems we mentioned above: the tendency of existing work to make the master-slave assumption, the embedding of intended actions in the context "speaker intends hearer to intend" in describing the speaker plans that are to be inferred, and the frequent failure to distinguish between building an agent that does plan recognition and providing a description of the state in which recognition occurs.

In our previous paper we pointed out that discourse segment purposes (DSPs) are a natural extension of Gricean intentions at the utterance level. In extending Grice's definitions to the discourse level for the action case, we argued that DSPs were of the form Intend(ICP, Intend(OCP, Do(A)) ...), where ICP is the discourse participant who initiates the segment, OCP is the other participant,[7] and the ellipsis includes subordinate intentions, not crucial for the point at hand. This definition was a natural extension of work on utterance-level intention recognition that linked a speaker's desires with a hearer's action or intention to act (for instance, Allen's Nested-

Planning Rule includes expressions of the form Want(Speaker, Want(Hearer P))).

Although the definition of DSPs seems approximately right, tying it to plan recognition and plan recognition algorithms requires a definition of what it would mean for one agent (ICP) to intend that another agent (OCP) do (or intend to do) something. The usual notion of intention cannot be extended naturally to cover this case. Although previous work on plan recognition (at the utterance level) uses such a notion, it presumes, rather than provides, a definition. Furthermore, there have been strong philosophical arguments that intention is a first-person attitude, that is, that the objects of intention are actions of the intending agent (see, for example, Bratman 1983; Davis 1979).

Second, serious consideration of dialogue makes it clear that the master-slave assumption is the wrong basis on which to build a theory of discourse. This assumption encourages theories that are unduly oriented toward there being one controlling agent and one reactive agent. Only one agent has any control over the formation of the plan; the reactive agent is involved only in execution of the plan (though to do so he must first figure out what that plan is). We conjecture that the focus of speech act and plan recognition work on single exchanges underlies its (implicit) adoption of the master-slave assumption. To account for extended sequences of utterances, it is necessary to realize that two agents may develop a plan together rather than merely execute the existing plan of one of them. That is, language use is more accurately characterized as a collaborative behavior of multiple active participants.

Finally, language use is not the only form of cooperative behavior that requires a notion of shared plans. A variety of nonlinguistic actions and plans cannot be explained solely in terms of the private plans of individual agents (see Searle's argument in chapter 19 of this volume). For example, consider the situation portrayed in figure 20.1. Two children each have a pile of blocks; one child's blocks are blue, the other's green. The children decide to build together a tower of blue and green blocks. It is not the case that their plan to build this tower is any combination of the first child's plan to build a tower of blue blocks with some empty spaces (in just the right places to match the other child's plan) and the second child's plan to build a tower of green blocks with some empty spaces (again in just the right places). Rather, they have some sort of joint plan that includes actions by each of them (the first child adding blue blocks, the second green ones).[8] In a more practical vein, the concept of shared plans provides a foundation for theories of collaborative behavior that could provide for more flexible and fluent interactions between computer systems and users undertaking joint problem-solving activities (for example, systems for diagnosis).

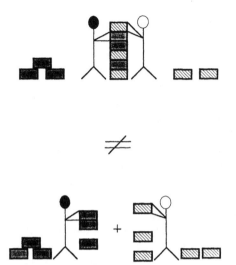

Figure 20.1
A collaborative block-building example.

5 *Shared Plans in Discourse*

To account for the collaborative behavior we believe is manifest in discourse, we will define a new construct, that of two agents' having a shared plan. The definition is based on Pollack's definition of a single agent's having a simple plan.[9] Like Pollack, we will adopt Allen's interval-based temporal logic as the basic formalism for representing actions. We will use Pollack's modification of the predicate representing the occurrence of an action, OCCURS: the predication OCCURS(α, G, t) is true if and only if an action of act-type α is performed by G during time interval t.

Pollack defined the SimplePlan of the single agent as follows:

SimplePlan(G, α_n, [$\alpha_1, \ldots, \alpha_{n-1}$], t2, t1) $\Leftrightarrow$

1. BEL(G, EXEC(α_i, G, t2), t1) for i = 1, ..., n−1 &

2. BEL(G, GEN(α_i, α_{i+1}, G, t2), t1) for i = 1, ..., n−1 &

3. INT(G, α_i, t2, t1) for i = 1, ..., n−1 &

4. INT(G, BY(α_i, α_{i+1}), t2, t1) for i = 1, ..., n−1.

Thus, the four main clauses in Pollack's schema concern (1) an agent's beliefs about executability of his actions, (2) an agent's beliefs about generation relationships between actions,[10] (3) intentions of the agent to do actions, and (4) intentions for the actions being done to play a role in the plan itself. In general, for shared plans we modify her schema as follows:[11]

SharedPlan(G1, G2, A) ⇔

1. $MB(G1, G2, EXEC(\alpha_j, G_{\alpha_j}))$

2. $MB(.......)$

3. $MB(G1, G2, INT(G_{\alpha_j}, \alpha_j)))$

4. $MB(G1, G2, INT(G_{\alpha_j}, BY(\alpha_j, A)))$

5. $INT(G_{\alpha_j}, \alpha_j)$

6. $INT(G_{\alpha_j}, BY(\alpha_j, A))$.

The index j ranges over all of the acts involved in doing A; for each α_j one of the agents, G1 or G2, is the agent of that action. We use G_{α_j} to denote that agent. That is, the action consisting of the act-type α_j, done by agent G_{α_j} (G1 or G2 as appropriate), at time t contributes to G1 and G2's plan to accomplish A. Like Pollack, we use the constructor function Achieve to turn properties (that is, states of affairs) into act-types. If G1 and G2 construct a SharedPlan to have a clean room, we will say there is a SharedPlan(G1, G2, Achieve(Clean-room)).

The content of Clause 2 depends on the types of actions being done. We will consider four key classes of SharedPlans here: those involving simultaneous actions by two agents, conjoined actions by two agents, sequence of actions by two agents, and actions by only one agent.

This definition differs from Pollack's in two ways: the beliefs about relations among actions are mutual beliefs, and different agents may perform different of the actions. Because different agents may be involved in acting, it becomes necessary to add that there is mutual belief among all participants about one another's intentions and about the way in which those intentions support the achievement of the overall goal. Notice that this means that a SharedPlan is not simply the mutual belief of one (or two) SimplePlans.

It may seem that mutual belief is too strong a demand on the discourse because not all of the intentions and actions in the SharedPlan are (necessarily) made public by the utterances in the discourse. The very fact that both participants know they are constructing a SharedPlan obviates this difficulty. It allows a discourse participant to infer those mutual beliefs needed for the SharedPlan but not mentioned (provided he does not have information to the contrary) and to assume that other participants will do the same.

The SharedPlan thus provides a key piece of the puzzle of defining relevance in a discourse. One of its functions is to distinguish from among all those mutual beliefs not explicitly mentioned in the discourse the ones that are relevant to the discourse; they are those that play a role in the SharedPlan. The SharedPlan is constructed from a combination of those beliefs and intentions explicitly mentioned and those prior mutual beliefs selected on the basis of the need to construct the SharedPlan. Any belief needed for there to be a plan, but not mentioned, is a relevant prior belief. Any belief that cannot be inferred on the basis of what has been made explicit and on prior beliefs must be made explicit or inferable.

It has been argued (for example, in Sperber and Wilson 1986) that mutual belief is not the appropriate relation for communication. A central part of this argument is, roughly, that the participants do not need to have identical beliefs, and furthermore there is no reason to believe that people actually do have identical beliefs. However, in the case of a SharedPlan mutual belief is crucial to action; multiple agents cannot act with any assurance unless there is such mutual belief (Halpern and Moses 1984).

We are still, however, left with the question of how the participants come to agree to construct a SharedPlan. We believe this depends on a conversational rule similar to Grice's conversational principles. The rule operates in the absence of evidence to the contrary; that is, it is a default rule. One of the conditions under which this rule will not apply is if it is mutually believed that agent G1 can achieve P on her own. The rule stipulates only that there will be mutual belief of a desire to achieve a SharedPlan;[12] to move from this to working on the SharedPlan requires that other participants assent (either implicitly or explicitly). A first approximation to this rule is that if the participants believe that one of them—say, G1—has a particular desire—say, to achieve a state in which P holds—and they are cooperative (in general, and with respect to achieving states like P in particular), and if they are communicating about the desire to achieve P, then they mutually believe that G1 has a desire for them to construct a SharedPlan to achieve P. The following is a shorthand version of this rule:

Conversational Default Rule 1 (CDR1)
$MB(G1, G2, Desire(G1, P)$ &
$\qquad Cooperative(G1, G2, P)$ &
$\qquad Communicating(G1, G2, Desire(G1, P))) \Rightarrow$
$MB(G1, G2, Desire(G1, Achieve(SharedPlan(G1, G2, Achieve(P)))))$.

Likewise, if agent G1 desires that some action be performed that requires G2 to do some (sub)actions, and G1 and G2 are cooperative (in general, and with respect to doing actions like A in particular), and if they are communicating about the desire to do A, then they mutually believe that G1 has a desire for them to construct a SharedPlan to A. We will refer to this version of CDR1, with A replacing P and Achieve(P) as appropriate, as CDR1'.[13]

CDR1 (and CDR1') establishes the mutual belief of G1's desire for a SharedPlan. Before it can be said that G1 and G2 have a SharedPlan or even are working on achieving a SharedPlan, it also must be the case that MB(G1, G2, Desire(G2, Achieve(SharedPlan(G1, G2, Achieve(P))))). To establish this mutual belief, G2 has to assent either explicitly or implicitly.

When G1 and G2 each have (and know the other has) the desire to achieve a SharedPlan but have not yet achieved the SharedPlan, they can be considered to have a partial SharedPlan. This partial plan plays an important role in discourse interpretation. We will use the notation SharedPlan*(G1, G2, Achieve(P)) to indicate that G1 and G2 have agreed to work toward having a SharedPlan but have not yet achieved one. A partial SharedPlan*, like a SharedPlan, is a collection of beliefs and intentions. It may be partial in either of two ways. First, it may contain only some of the full collection of beliefs and intentions of its associated full SharedPlan. Second, some of the beliefs included in it may be only partially specified, as subsequent examples will illustrate.

The existence of a SharedPlan* provides a crucial element of the background against which to interpret utterances. In particular, it provides the basis for linking the desire on the part of one agent for another agent to act to the intentions of the second agent to act. Again, this connection is not a hard rule but rather reflects a default assumption of the discourse situation. In particular, if there is a partial SharedPlan* and a desire on the part of one agent—say, G1—for another—say, G2—to do some action, and G2 believes he can perform that action and that by performing the action he will be contributing to the achievement of P, then G2 will (in the absence of reasons to the contrary) adopt an intention to do the action. Again in shorthand, we have

> *Conversational Default Rule 2 (CDR2)*
> [SharedPlan*(G1, G2, Achieve(P)) &
> MB(Desire(G1, Do(G2, Action)) &
> MB(G1, G2, Exec(G2, Action)) &
> MB(G1, G2, *Contribute*(Action, Achieve(P)))]
> ⇒ Intend(G2, Action) & MB(G1, G2, Intend(G2, Action)).

This rule is a schematic. *Contribute* is a place holder for any relation (such as GEN, ENABLE) that can hold between actions when one can be said to contribute (for example, by generating or enabling) to the performance of the other.

We are now in a position to look at some particular examples of Shared-Plans to see both how the second clause of the definition is fleshed out and how the SharedPlan can be used to explain certain properties of discourse. In the discussion, we will refer to various utterances that provide information for clauses of some SharedPlan or SharedPlan*. It is important not to confuse such references with any notion of filling in a frame for a Shared-Plan. A SharedPlan is not a data structure (or any mental construct analogous to one) but rather is a way for us to attribute a certain collection of beliefs and intentions to discourse participants. The participants in a discourse mutually believe they are working toward establishing the beliefs and intentions that are necessary for one to say that they have a Shared-Plan. They also share knowledge (at least implicitly) of which beliefs and intentions are necessary for them to be in the mental state corresponding to having a SharedPlan. They use the discourse in part to establish mutual belief of the appropriate beliefs and intentions.

5.1 Simultaneous Actions

The first type of SharedPlan to consider is one in which two agents must act simultaneously to achieve the desired state of affairs. We will refer to such plans as SharedPlan1 (G1, G2, Achieve(Simultaneous-result)). As an example of simultaneous actions by different agents, we will consider the case of two agents, G1 and G2, lifting a piano together. In SharedPlans of this type, Clause 2 is of the form

$$MB(G1, G2, [OCCURS(\alpha_i, G1, T1) \Leftrightarrow GEN(\beta_j, \gamma, G2, T1) \,\&$$
$$OCCURS(\beta_j, G2, T1) \Leftrightarrow GEN(\alpha_i, \gamma, G1, T1)], T0)$$

or, more succinctly,

$$MB(G1, G2, GEN\text{-}Simultaneous[\alpha_i \,\&\, \beta_j]), \gamma, G1\&G2, T1], T0).$$

For simultaneous actions, it must be mutually believed that each agent's own actions will have the proper generation relationship with the desired action (γ) if, and only if, the other agent performs her actions at the same time. Simultaneous actions are distinguished by the need for the time of performance of both actions to be the same.[14]

We begin with a very simple discourse example. Although the example involves simultaneous action (itself complicated), the discourse includes explicit mention of relevant intentions and explicit assent on the parts of both participants to undertaking various actions.

Discourse 1
1. S1: I want to lift the piano.
2. S2: OK.
3.   I will pick up this [deictic to keyboard] end.
4. S1: OK.
5.   I will pick up this [deictic to foot] end.
6. S2: OK.
7.   Ready?
8. S1: Ready.

We will assume an analysis like Perrault's (see chapter 9 of this volume) using defaults for determining the immediate consequences of each utterance. Hence, from utterances 1, 3, and 5, respectively, the participants can infer

1'. MB(S1, S2, Desire(S1, lift(piano)))

3'. MB(S1, S2, INT(S2, lift(keyboard-end)))

5'. MB(S1, S2, INT(S1, lift(foot-end))).

From Clause 1' and CDR1' and appropriate assumptions about the agents' cooperativeness, they can infer that

MB(S1, S2, Desire(S1, Achieve(SharedPlan1(S1, S2, lift(piano))))).

Hence, following Utterance 1, G2 could (coherently) respond in any one of the following ways:

- explicitly dissent from accepting the SharedPlan ("I can't help now"),
- implicitly dissent ("I hurt my back"),
- explicitly assent to construct a SharedPlan (above example),
- implicitly assent to construct a SharedPlan ("Which end should I get? Do you have a handtruck?").

In Utterance 2, S2 explicitly assents to work on achieving the Shared-Plan for lifting the piano. Utterance 3, by providing the information in Clause 3', provides information needed for the SharedPlan. It expresses the intentions exhibited in Clauses 3 and 4 of the SharedPlan and implicitly expresses S2's belief that S2 can execute the intended action. S1's assent to this proposed action in Utterance 4 allows derivation of mutual belief of executability as well as the relevance of this act to achieving the desired goal (that is, a portion of the belief exhibited in Clause 4). Analogously to Utterance 3, Utterance 5 expresses intentions (now additional ones) exhibited in Clauses 3 and 4, as well as a new individual belief about executability. Utterance 6 allows derivation of mutual belief of executability.

This discourse does not include any explicit mention of the generation relationship exhibited in Clause 2. From the context in which Utterances 3 and 5 are uttered, the participants can infer that the mentioned actions are seen to participate in a generation relationship with the desired action. That these actions together are sufficient is implicit in Utterances 7 and 8. S1 and S2 can now infer that the generation relation exhibited in Clause 2 holds. Therefore, the SharedPlan comprises the following mutual beliefs and intentions:

SharedPlan1(S1, S2, lift[piano])

1. MB(S1, S2, EXEC(lift(foot-end), S1)) & MB(S1, S2, EXEC(lift (keyboard-end), S2))

2. MB(S1, S2, GEN-Simultaneous[lift(foot-end) & lift (keyboard-end), lift(piano), S1 & S2])

3. MB(S1, S2, INT(S2, lift(keyboard-end))) & MB(S1, S2, INT(S1, lift(foot-end)))

4, MB(S1, S2, INT(S2, BY(lift(keyboard-end), lift(piano)))) & MB (S1, S2, INT(S1, BY(lift(foot-end), lift(piano))))

5. INT(S2, lift(keyboard-end)) & INT(S1, lift(foot-end))

6. INT(S2, BY(lift(keyboard-end), lift(piano))) & INT(S1, BY(lift (foot-end), lift(piano))).

This use of the concept of a SharedPlan eliminates the need for any notion of one agent's intending for another agent to intend some action; that is, we have no need for clauses of the form Intend(G1, Intend(G2, Do (Action))). Rather (as exhibited in Clause 2), the participants must have mutual belief of the ways in which actions by each agent done simultaneously generate a single (joint) action (namely, lift(piano)). As stated in Clause 6, S2 intends to lift the piano by lifting the keyboard-end (alone); she can do this only because she believes (there is a mutual belief) that S1 will simultaneously lift the foot-end.

In addition, one can attribute to S2 the intention to lift the piano by lifting the keyboard-end as exhibited in Clause 6. Rather than rely on a notion of "we-intentions" as does Searle in Chapter 19 of this volume, we postulate individual intentions embedded in a plan for joint action. Plans for joint action include (mutual) beliefs of the ways in which the actions of individual agents contribute to the performance of a desired (joint) action of which they are a part.

The desire to provide an appropriate account of imperative utterances (that is, one that did not depend on the notion of one agent's intending for another agent to intend to do some action) was a primary motivation for SharedPlans. Hence, we turn next to a variant of the preceding discourse that is differentiated by the use of an imperative, in Utterance 4. Notice that essentially the same information about how to lift the piano, and about intentions to do various actions, is conveyed in this variant.

Discourse 2
1. S1: I want to lift the piano.

2. S2: OK.

3. S1: I will pick up this [deictic to foot] end.

4.   You get that [deictic to keyboard] end.

5. S2: OK.

6. S1: Ready?

7. S2: Ready.

In this discourse, just as in Discourse 1, Utterances 1 through 3 establish that SharedPlan*(S1, S2, lift(piano)) and that S1 intends to lift the foot-end as part of the SharedPlan. The imperative in Utterance 4 conveys that Desire (S1, Do(S2, lift(keyboard-end))). Given the SharedPlan*, CDR2 would apply if Believe(S2, EXEC(lift(keyboard-end), S2)) and there were some α for which Believe(S2, GEN-Simultaneous[lift(keyboard-end) & α, lift (piano)]). In this case there is such an α, namely, (lift(foot-end), S1). S2's assent in Utterance 5 conveys these two beliefs, and hence we can conclude in addition that INT(S2, lift(keyboard-end)) and INT(S2, BY(lift(keyboard-end)), lift(piano)). The remainder of this discourse and the derivation of SharedPlan1 goes as in the first discourse.

As a final variant of the first discourse, we consider an example in which information conveyed in multiple utterances in Discourse 1 and Discourse 2, is conveyed in the utterances of a single turn by one participant. This single-speaker sequence achieves the same purposes as the longer sequence involving both participants did in the previous dialogues.

Discourse 3

1. S1: I want to lift the piano. You get that end;
   I'll get this end.

2. S2: OK.

3. S1: OK. Ready, lift.

In Utterance 1, S1 expresses not only a desire but also a proposed way of satisfying that desire; in combination with CDR1, this gives a proposal for a shared plan and also some details about the beliefs and intentions involved. In particular, Utterance 1 conveys S1's beliefs about executability, his intentions to perform certain actions, and his beliefs about the role of these actions in satisfying the desire to have the piano lifted. In Utterance 2, S2 assents to participating in the SharedPlan, to the appropriate mutual beliefs (that is, those in Clauses 1 through 4) holding, and to her having the necessary intentions for Clauses 5 and 6. The major difference between this discourse and the previous ones is that S2 does not get a chance to assent to a SharedPlan until most of the details of the plan are formulated and proposed by S1. Thus, S2's "OK" in Utterance 2 is assent to far more than in the previous examples. An indication of S2's implicit assent to the construction of a SharedPlan comes from her not interrupting S1; had S2 not wanted to participate in a SharedPlan, it would be most natural for her to say so immediately.

5.2 Conjoined Actions

A similar type of SharedPlan may be constructed when the actions of two agents taken together, but not necessarily simultaneously, achieve a desired result. For example, a table may be set by two people each of whom performs some of the necessary actions (for instance, one putting on the silverware, the other the plates and glasses). In such cases there is a simple conjunction of actions, rather than a need for simultaneity. That is, although the actions must all be performed within some time interval—say, T_E—they need not be performed at exactly the same time. For this case, SharedPlan2(G1, G2, Achieve(Conjoined-result)), Clause 2 is of the form

$$MB(G1, G2, [\bigwedge_{i=1}^{n} OCCURS(\alpha_i, G_{\alpha_i}, T_{\alpha_i}) \Leftrightarrow$$
$$OCCURS(\gamma, G1\&G2, T_E)], T0)$$
$$\text{where } DURING(T_i, T_E)$$
$$\text{and } \neg (\exists \alpha_j, \alpha_k ENABLE[(OCCURS(\alpha_j, G_{\alpha_j}, T_{\alpha_j})),$$
$$(OCCURS(\alpha_k, G_{\alpha_k}, T_{\alpha_k}))]).$$

Whereas the time intervals T_i must all be within the interval T_E, they may or may not overlap or be disjoint. In addition, the conjoined actions cannot serve to enable one another.

Again, more briefly,

$$MB(G1, G2, GEN\text{-}Conjoined[\alpha_i, \gamma, G1\&G2, T_E], T0).$$

A discourse or dialogue for this variant is similar to that of the simultaneous action; the main difference is in exact times at which the actions are done.

5.3 Sequences of Actions

A somewhat more complicated variant of SharedPlan is one in which a sequence of actions together generate the desired action. For example, turning a doorknob followed by pulling on the doorknob together (under appropriate conditions—say, the door being unlocked) generate opening the door.

For SharedPlan3(G1, G2, Achieve(Sequence-result)), Clause 2 is of the form

$$MB(G1, G2, [\bigwedge_{i=1}^{n} OCCURS(\alpha_i, G_{\alpha_i}, T_{\alpha_i}) \Leftrightarrow$$
$$OCCURS(\gamma, G1\&G2, T_E)], T0)$$
$$\text{where } START(T_1, T_E) \text{ and } FINISH(T_n, T_E) \text{ and } MEETS(T_i, T_{i+1})$$
$$\text{and } \neg (\exists \alpha_j, \alpha_k ENABLE[(OCCURS(\alpha_j, G_{\alpha_j}, T_{\alpha_j})),$$
$$(OCCURS(\alpha_k, G_{\alpha_k}, T_{\alpha_k}))]).$$

The interval T_i meets the next interval in the sequence and the intervals fully span the interval T_E of γ.

Or, more briefly,

MB(G1, G2, GEN-Sequence[α_i, γ, G1&G2, T_E], T0).

The case of a sequence of actions generating a desired action is not the same as an action enabling another action. Both α and β must be done to achieve γ, and α must be done before β, but α does not enable β. In the doorknob example, turning the knob does not enable pulling on it; this can be seen quite simply by noting that one can also pull and then turn. The two actions together generate opening the door.

The discourses for this variant may again be similar to that of the preceding cases; however, the sequencing of actions must be made explicit or already be mutually believed.

5.4 SharedPlans with a Single Actor

The final cases we will consider are SharedPlans in which only one agent actually performs any actions. One such SharedPlan is analogous to Pollack's SimplePlans; the others are analogous to the three cases (simultaneous, conjoined, sequential actions) discussed previously. We will give the definition for the first case. The others differ only in Clause 2; the appropriate change can be determined straightforwardly from the multi-agent cases.

A single-agent SharedPlan differs from Pollack's SimplePlan in that the initial desire that leads to the plan is one agent's (say, G1) whereas another agent (say, G2) acts. For this case, the definition is

SharedPlan4 (G1, G2, α_n, T1, T0)

1. MB[G1, G2, EXEC(α_i, G2, T1), T0] i $= 1, \ldots, n-1$

2. MB[G1, G2, GEN(α_i, α_{i+1}), G2, T1), T0] i $= 1, \ldots, n-1$

3. MB[G1, G2, INT(G2, α_i, T1, T0), T0] i $= 1, \ldots, n-1$

4. MB[G1, G2, INT(G2, BY(α_i, α_{i+1}), T1, T0), T0] i $= 1, \ldots, n-1$

5. INT[G2, α_i, T1, T0]

6. INT[G2, BY(α_i, α_{i+1}), T1, T0]

SharedPlan4 appears equivalent to a SimplePlan (as Pollack has defined it) embedded in a mutual belief context, combined with G2's in fact having this SimplePlan, that is, SimplePlan(G2, α_n, α_i, T1, T0) [i $= 1, \ldots, n-1$] and MB[G1, G2, SimplePlan(G2, α_n, α_i, T1, T0)] [i $= 1, \ldots, n-1$]. However, this formulation does not provide a basis for explaining how to derive MB(G1, G2, INT(G2, Achieve(P))) from MB(G1, G2, Desire(G1, P)), nor how to infer subsequently that G2 has a SimplePlan for achieving P and that G1 and G2 mutually believe G2 has this SimplePlan. The first of these inferences is most difficult, because it requires explaining how the desire on the part of one agent leads to intentions on the part of the other agent. The combination of SharedPlans and the CDRs (along with rules about what agents must assent to) provides the needed link.

We will illustrate the role of SharedPlan4 and the two CDRs in explaining the following dialogue from a corpus collected by Mann (we present it as cited in Litman 1986):

Discourse 4
1. User: Could you mount a magtape for me?
2.   It's tape1.
3.   No ring please.
4.   Can you do it in five minutes?
5. System: We are not allowed to mount that magtape.
6.   You'll have to talk to operator about it.
7.   After nine A.M. Monday through Friday.
8. User: How about tape2?

Rather than viewing the User's first turn, Utterances 1 through 4, as describing a plan the User alone has for achieving certain goals, we will view it as initiating a dialogue to construct a SharedPlan in which the System and User collaborate to satisfy the User's desire to have a particular tape mounted in a particular way. Because in this example only the System will perform any physical actions, it is a case of SharedPlan4.

We discuss only the User's first turn. As in the final piano example, each of Utterances 1 through 4 provides partial information about the Shared-Plan. Again, the System's implicit concurrence (for instance, it doesn't interrupt) allows the User to continue providing additional information. Utterance 1 proposes a SharedPlan* and subsequent utterances provide continual refinement of it. More particularly, Utterance 1 results in

MB(User, System, Desire(User, tape-mounted(tapeX))) for some tape, tapeX.

From CDR1 (and the System's implicit cooperativeness for this specific request) we can infer that

MB(User, System, Desire(User, Achieve(SharedPlan
(User, System, tape-mounted(tapeX))))).

From the lack of an interruption by the System, the User can infer that SharedPlan*(User, System, Achieve[tape-mounted(tapeX)], Now, t2). To get from this state to one in which there is actually a SharedPlan requires, among other things, that a mutual belief of the form

MB[User, System, INT(System, mount-tape(tapeX), t2, NOW), NOW].

However, as written this intention is not well formed because of the use of the variable tapeX. For the System to have an intention to mount any tape, it must know the identity of the tape to be mounted. The variable tapeX does not specify an individual tape. The User's second utterance, Utterance 2, thus contributes to constructing a SharedPlan by establishing the identity of the tape to be mounted.[15] It is from this utterance that the System can infer tapeX = tape1. (We say more about how this happens in section 6.) Utterance 3 modifies information presented so far by stating that the desired action is a specialization of the tape-mounting operation, a mounting with no ring. Finally, Utterance 4 sets constraints on the time of execution of the action (NOW + fewer than 5 minutes).

If the System had responded, "Yes, I will," to Utterances 1 through 4, then the User and System would have succeeded in constructing a Shared-Plan comprising the following beliefs and intentions (where tape-mounted-NR is true if the tape is mounted with no ring). CDR2 is essential to the derivation of Clauses 3 through 6 of this SharedPlan.

SharedPlan for mounting tape1

1. MB[User, System, EXEC(mount-tape-NR(tape1), System, NOW + 5min), NOW]

2. MB[User, System, GEN(mount-tape-NR(tape1), Achieve(tape-mounted-NR(tape1)), System, NOW + 5min), NOW]

3. MB[User, System, INT(System, mount-tape-NR(tape1), NOW + 5min, NOW), NOW]

4. MB[User, System, INT(System, BY(mount-tape-NR(tape1), Achieve(tape-mounted-NR(tape1))), NOW + 5min, NOW), NOW]

5. INT(System, mount-tape-NR(tape1), NOW + 5min, NOW)

6. INT(System, BY(mount-tape-NR(tape1), Achieve(tape-mounted-NR(tape1))), NOW + 5min, NOW).

To explain the System's actual response, it is necessary to consider the state of the developing SharedPlan just prior to Utterance 5. At this point the User has made public a set of beliefs she holds about tape-mounting actions, about relations among them, and about intentions that she desires the System to have; the System is aware of these beliefs. With Utterance 5, the System establishes that the User's proposed SharedPlan cannot be constructed. In particular, the System makes it clear that NOT[EXEC(mount-tape-NR(tape1), System, NOW + 5min)]. Subsequent utterances provide an alternative proposal for satisfying the User's original desire.

6 Feedforward and Backward

The previous section describes how Utterance 2 contributes to constructing the SharedPlan. However, it is also the case that the SharedPlan provides a context in which to interpret Utterance 2. The ways in which information flows both forward and backward in this discourse can best be seen by adopting an action-oriented stance toward utterances. In particular, an utterance itself is an action that can generate and enable other actions. From this perspective Utterances 1 through 4 may be seen to have among their effects the establishment of the SharedPlan. We want to look briefly at the more local utterance-to-utterance effects and their interactions. By uttering, "Could you mount a magtape for me?" the User generates[16]

> Achieve(MB, User, System,
>   [Desire(User, Informif(System, User,
>   EXEC(System, mount-tape(tapeX))
>   for some tapeX s.t. magtape(tapeX)))]),

which in turn generates

> Achieve(MB, User, System,
>   [Exists(tapeX, magtape(tapeX) &
>   Desire(User, tape-mounted(tapeX)))]).

Another effect of Utterance 1 is to create a discourse entity, in this case tapeX. Under the condition that there is some discourse entity that is a tape —say, tapeZ—any utterance of "It's tape1" conditionally generates (as defined by Goldman (1970) and Pollack (1986)) Achieve (MB, User, System, tapeZ = tape1). In this discourse the User's first utterance provides the discourse entity that satisfies this condition, namely, tapeX. Thus, Utterance 1 enables Utterance 2 to generate Achieve(MB, User, System, tapeX = tape1). Thus, we see Utterance 1 as feeding forward a discourse entity and Utterance 2 as feeding back (to the partial SharedPlan) information to flesh out the plan.

Finally, we might note that this treatment of action descriptions parallels previous observations about object descriptions. The way in which Utterances 1 through 4 of Discourse 4 provide increasingly more information about the particular tape-mounting action the User wishes the System to undertake is similar to the use of multiple utterances to provide additional information about some object. For example, someone might describe a particular book to you as, "The book is on the coffee table. It's Percy's *The Message in the Bottle*. Bright orange cover and silver letters."

7 Further Work

The notion of SharedPlan was developed both to help explain the collaborative type of plans that seem to underlie discourse and to provide the basis for recognition of intention at the discourse (as opposed to utterance) level. Further exploration of this notion requires fundamental research in two areas: (1) specification of relations between actions that are more complex than generation (such as enabling relations) and their role in SharedPlans of various sorts; (2) examination of the details of the recognition process (such as recognition algorithms for beliefs and intentions that must be shared for there to be a SharedPlan).

As Pollack has pointed out, the enabling relationship and the way it enters a plan introduces a number of complexities into the plan formalization and recognition process. Although a detailed treatment of enabling relationships awaits further research, we can use a simple example to illustrate how enabling relations would fit with SharedPlans.

Consider the utterance "Please pass the butter" in a context where the speaker is eating dinner with the hearer and the dinner includes corn on the cob (and nothing else that can be buttered). Figure 20.2 shows the action decomposition relevant to this utterance and the buttering of a cob of corn. In place of the generation relation that is used in plan definitions for Pollack's SimplePlan and the SharedPlans presented in this paper, the plan sketched in this figure requires more complex action relationships. A portion of this decomposition will form the core of the beliefs of a SharedPlan

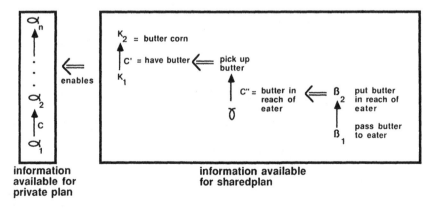

Figure 20.2
Private and SharedPlans for passing butter to butter corn.

that results in satisfying a condition on a private SimplePlan. The Shared-EnablePlan(S, H, Achieve(Have-Butter)) satisfies the condition (Have-Butter) needed for S's SimplePlan of SimplePlan(... Achieve(buttered-corn)).

Prior work on plan formalisms and plan recognition used a notion of subactions or step decomposition to capture some of the relationships we have portrayed here. However, as the example about door-opening in section 5.3 illustrates, step decomposition is used ambiguously to refer to generation relations, enabling relations, and sequencing relations among actions.

The recognition process for SharedPlans as sketched in this paper proceeds essentially as follows: the initial utterances put on the table a proposal that there be a shared plan developed and carried out to satisfy the initiating conversational participant's desire; the subsequent utterance must somehow address this proposal, either accepting or denying it; assuming the proposal is accepted, subsequent utterances can provide information about any of the beliefs or intentions embedded in the definition of a SharedPlan. This process differs significantly from prior work on recognition in that it does not presume a fixed plan on the part of one participant, the form and content of which must be inferred by the other(s). Instead, collaborative planning entails a negotiation in which information about actions, action relationships, desires, and intentions is made sufficiently clear for all participants to know how actions will be used to satisfy desires. Plan recognition is then the determination of these beliefs and intentions.

Notes

1. STRIPS itself had only preconditions and effects; NOAH added bodies to the formalism.
2. Kautz has considered incremental algorithms, but it is unclear just how these differ from the basic algorithm, that is, when the complete list of actions is available.
3. It has been made in all work that attempted to treat the possibility of multiple plans being pursued simultaneously.
4. Cohen (1983) proposes a similar role for cue phrases in limiting search for deriving the structure of arguments. Sidner (1985) and Litman (1986) make similar claims for plan recognition.
5. A simple plan relates actions only by the relation of generation (Goldman 1970); enabling relations among actions remain to be examined in future work.
6. Pollack's work, like all previous work, assumes that the inferring agent has complete and accurate knowledge of domain actions.
7. We introduced these terms because either participant can be a speaker of other utterances in the segment and hence the usual (master-slave assumption) use of *speaker* and *hearer* to differentiate roles will not work.
8. This example provides an extremely productive analogy for modeling dialogue. Each utterance or segment is like a block, placed by the participant (builder) on the existing structure (discourse or tower) to extend it in ways that help achieve the original purpose. A major difference, however, is that the tower is an end in itself whereas the discourse is a means to achieve the discourse purpose.

9. This means for the moment we will only consider actions related by generation; we will discuss the extension to enabling relationships later.
10. In an extended model of plans and actions, other types of relationships between actions (such as enabling relationships) would be included here.
11. We are leaving out the time parameters for the moment but will include them below in those cases where certain of their properties are important.
12. Agents will be said to have achieved a SharedPlan if they reach a state in which they have the beliefs and intentions required for them to have a SharedPlan.
13. In the remaining rule and plan specifications, we will use Achieve(P) as the desired action and will not include the generalization to A that is straightforward to derive.
14. A precise definition of the appropriate grainsize for measuring such sameness is beyond the scope of this paper.
15. We presume the indirect interpretation of Utterance 1. The direct interpretation of this utterance—that is, querying whether EXEC(mount-tape(tapeX), System, t2)—would lead to another SharedPlan. One might argue that it is only with Utterance 2 that we are sure about the indirection.
16. We are sketchy about the indirectness here because that is not our main point.

References

Allen, J. F. (1979). A plan-based approach to speech act recognition. Technical Report 121, Department of Computer Science, University of Toronto, Toronto, Ont.

Allen, J. F. (1984). Towards a general theory of action and time. *Artificial Intelligence* 23, 123–154.

Allen, J. F., and C. R. Perrault (1980). Analyzing intention in utterances. *Artificial Intelligence* 15, 143–178.

Appelt, D. (1985). Planning English referring expressions. *Artificial Intelligence* 26, 1–33.

Bratman, M. (1983). *Castañeda's theory of thought and action.* In J. Tomberlin, ed., *Agent, language, and the structure of the world: Essays presented to Hector-Neri Castañeda with his replies.* Indianapolis, IN: Hackett.

Bruce, B. C. (1975). Belief systems and language understanding. Technical Report 2973, Bolt Beranek and Newman, Inc., Cambridge, MA.

Bruce, B. C., and D. Newman (1978). Interacting plans. *Cognitive Science* 2, 195–233.

Cohen, P. R. (1981). The need for identification as a planned action. In *Proceedings of the Seventh International Joint Conference on Artificial Intelligence*, Vancouver, B.C.

Cohen, R. (1983). A computational model for the analysis of arguments. Technical Report CSRG-151, Computer Systems Research Group, University of Toronto, Toronto, Ont.

Davis, R. (1979). Interactive transfer of expertise. *Artificial Intelligence* 12, 121–157.

Fikes, R. and N. J. Nilsson (1971). STRIPS: A new approach to the application of theorem proving to problem solving. *Artificial Intelligence* 2, 189–208.

Goldman, A. I. (1970). *A theory of human action.* Princeton, NJ. Princeton University Press.

Grosz, B. J. (1978). Discourse analysis. In D. Walker, ed., *Understanding spoken language.* New York: Elsevier North-Holland.

Grosz, B. J., and C. L. Sidner (1986). Attention, intentions, and the structure of discourse. *Computational Linguistics* 12, 175–204.

Halpern, J., and Y. Moses (1984). Knowledge and common knowledge in a distributed environment. In *Proceedings of the Third ACM Conference on the Principles of Distributed Computing*, ACM, Vancouver, B.C.

Hirschberg, J., and D. Litman (1987). Now let's talk about 'now': Identifying cue phrases intonationally. In *Proceedings of the Twenty-fifth Annual Meeting*, Association for Computational Linguistics, Stanford, CA.

Hirschberg, J., and J. Pierrehumbert (1986). The intonational structuring of discourse. In *Proceedings of the Twenty-fourth Annual Meeting*, Association for Computational Linguistics, New York, NY.

Hobbs, J., and D. Evans (1980). Conversation as planned behavior. *Cognitive Science* 4, 349–377.

Kautz, H. A., and J. F. Allen (1986). Generalized plan recognition. In *Proceedings of the National Conference*, American Association for Artificial Intelligence, Philadelphia, PA.

Kronfeld, A. (1986). Donnellan's distinction and a computational model of reference. In *Proceedings of the Twenty-fourth Annual Meeting*, Association for Computational Linguistics, New York, NY.

Litman, D. J. (1986). Linguistic coherence: A plan-based alternative. In *Proceedings of the Twenty-fourth Annual Meeting*, Association for Computational Linguistics, New York, NY.

McKeown, K. R. (1985). *Text generation*. New York: Cambridge University Press.

Polanyi, L., and R. Scha (1983). On the recursive structure of discourse. In *Connectedness in sentence, discourse and text*. Tilburg University.

Pollack, M. E. (1986). A model of plan inference that distinguishes between the beliefs of actors and observers. In *Proceedings of the Twenty-fourth Annual Meeting*, Association for Computational Linguistics, New York, NY.

Reichman-Adar, R. (1984). Extended person-machine interface. *Artificial Intelligence* 22, 157–218.

Sacerdoti, E. D. (1977). *A structure for plans and behavior*. New York. American Elsevier.

Schmidt, C. F., N. S. Sridharan, and J. L. Goodson (1978). The plan recognition problem: An intersection of psychology and artificial intelligence. *Artificial Intelligence* 11, 45–83.

Sidner, C. L. (1983). What the speaker means: The recognition of speaker's plans in discourse. *International Journal of Computers and Mathematics* 9, 71–82.

Sidner, C. L. (1985). Plan parsing for intended response recognition in discourse. *Computational Intelligence* 1, 1–10.

Sperber, D., and D. Wilson (1986). *Relevance*. Cambridge, MA: Harvard University Press.

Chapter 21

Artificial Intelligence and Collective Intentionality: Comments on Searle and on Grosz and Sidner

Jerry R. Hobbs

1 Comments on Searle

I'm a hard-core, unreconstructed AI researcher, and so I naturally read Searle's paper from a hard-core AI point of view. That point of view forces one to recast his argument into other terms, but once the recasting is done, one's reaction is, "Of course, who would ever have thought otherwise?"[1] This point of view, however, leads one to see collective intentionality in a larger framework and also leads one, for independent reasons, to disagree with his final conclusion.

First, let me outline the hard-core AI point of view, as I see it. An *agent* (a person or a successful AI program of the future) is a planning mechanism. The agent has *beliefs* and *goals* and uses its beliefs, especially beliefs about what kinds of things cause or enable what other kinds of things, to construct *plans* for achieving those goals. To eliminate spurious mysteries like the mystery of where goals come from, we can think of an agent as going through the world continually modifying, in light of the new beliefs it acquires through perception and reasoning, a plan to achieve the single goal "I thrive."[2]

A goal is simply a proposition, or rather a logical expression representing a proposition, that the agent tries to make true. The proposition can be anything, not just actions on the part of the agent; there are no restrictions on its predicates or arguments. Just as pick-up(I, BLOCK3, NOW) is a possible goal, so are push({JOHN, I}, CAR5, NOW) and win(S.F.GIANTS, World-Series, 1996). The goals can represent events in which I myself am the agent and am able to perform directly, events I can bring about in concert with others, and events I have little control over. The goals can be immediate, like the first two, or they can be long-term, like write(I, Great-American-Novel, Before 2002).[3]

The agent's beliefs are likewise logical expressions that are manipulated in complex ways by the planning mechanism and other processing of the agent's. The agent's beliefs accord with perception, and he or she or it acts as though the beliefs were true. Of particular interest are the agent's beliefs about what causes or enables what else, since they are the material out of which plans are built.

A plan consists of a top-level goal, such as "I thrive," and decompositions of this goal into subgoals and these subgoals into further subgoals, and so on. (For convenience, I'll usually refer to the subgoals simply as goals.) The events described in the subgoals of a goal must be believed in aggregate to cause or enable the event described in the goal. High-level, long-term goals can and usually do have lower-level, more immediate goals, so write(I, Great-American-Novel, Before 2002) might ultimately spawn the subgoal buy(I, PENCIL, NOW). A plan is thus a representation of believed causal relations among events. This is not all, however. To be a plan, it must terminate in actions the agent is capable of executing directly at the appropriate time, such as move(I, ARM1, NOW), or in conditions that will be true at the appropriate time anyway, such as coast-down(CAR5, HILL2, NOW).

An agent moves through the world continually elaborating, modifying, and executing a plan for achieving the goal "I thrive." The agent at any given time may execute an action, discover from the environment's response that it was unsuccessful, replan, perhaps even abandoning some high-level subgoals of "I thrive," execute another action, be satisfied of its success, take some time to develop its long-term plan, and so on.[4]

Many of the notions of folk psychology can be recast into the terms of this framework. Routine or habitual behavior can be viewed as the execution of precompiled plans. Intentions can be viewed as goals, providing we don't take our intuitions about the use of the English word "intend" too seriously. Future-directed intentions (see Bratman, chapter 2 of this volume) are high-level goals expressing conditions in the future. Intentions-in-action are low-level goals to be executed now. Desires can be viewed as beliefs about the efficacy of one event or condition causing another, where both are tied ultimately to the goal of "I thrive." Admittedly, desires don't *feel* like other beliefs, but they can be modeled formally as such, and doing so has the advantage of placing them in a framework that allows them to be analyzed, as most if not all of our desires can be. For example, I have a desire around two o'clock every afternoon to eat a candy bar. But this is not undecomposable; it is directly related to giving me pleasure, which is related in some complex way with my thriving, but it also gives me a burst of energy that makes me more productive in the afternoon and is thus related to other, high-level goals. Reactions to events in the environment, even intense and immediate reactions like jumping into a river to save one's child, can be viewed formally as examples of rapid replanning in light of new information from the environment, even though, again, they don't *feel* like replanning.[5]

That's the whole story.

Well, almost. There is one more piece to the puzzle. Among people's and other agent's beliefs about causal forces in the world are their folk theories of human action based on the notion of "intention." If we are hiking up the side of a mountain and we suddenly see a bunch of one-ton boulders hurtling down, we panic. If we are walking on the sidewalk of El Camino and see a bunch of one-ton automobiles hurtling past, not ten feet away, we don't worry. The difference between these two situations is intention. We believe the drivers of the automobiles intend to keep off the sidewalk. We have theories about what kinds of action people will intend in various circumstances, and we believe that people usually do what they intend to do. These theories, or belief systems, allow us to predict a great many events with significant reliability. It is important to keep distinct the two roles of intention I have introduced. The terminology of "goal," "belief," and "plan" is the metalanguage with which the cognitive life of agents is described. The folk theory of human action involving the predicate intend is one particular set of beliefs among others, that is, one particular set of logical expressions, that the agent has.

Now, from the hard-core AI point of view, Searle's statement that we have collective intentions translates into a statement that an agent can have as goals in its plan, logical formulas whose predicates describe actions that collectives engage in and whose agent argument is such a collective. Thus, an agent, me for example, can form a plan with the goal that you and I push the car ("We push car") that decomposes into the subgoals "I push car" and "You push car," with the proper temporal relations between these actions. "I push car" is a goal that can be executed directly (let's say, although it could be further decomposed into individual bodily movements). The goal "You push car" might be achieved by a variety of means. It may be that, as in Searle's example, it's already true. It may be that I have to ask you, or it may be that you do it simply out of your "sense of community," a notion I discuss below. In addition, for me to believe I'm engaging in collective action, I have to have the belief that it is mutually believed by both of us that we have the same plan. This mutual belief is what gives me the belief that the events you are responsible for will happen at the appropriate time.

An agent's collective intention is then a plan with such a collective goal, and the corresponding belief in the mutual belief in the plan. The role of the mutual belief is to assure each agent in the collective that the other agents have the right intentions and will thus perform the right actions at the right times.

Now let's look at the MBA examples. In the noncollaborative case I have a plan of pursuing my own selfish interests as a way of achieving the goal "I help humanity." Moreover, I believe it is mutually believed among all MBAs that if x is an MBA, then x will have plan of pursuing x's own interests as a way for x to help humanity. Let $P_1(x)$ be the plan

x helps humanity.
|
x pursues self-interest.

Then my plan $P_1(I)$ is

I help humanity.
|
I pursue self-interest.

In addition, I have the belief

$mb(MBAs, (\forall x \in MBAs) has\text{-}plan(x, P_1(x)))$.

In the collaborative case I have a plan P_2 whose goal is "All of us MBAs help humanity," one of whose subgoals is "I pursue my own selfish interests" and whose other subgoals are "x pursues x's own selfish interests" for every other MBA x:

We help humanity.
_____|_____   . . .
I pursue self-interest.   A pursues self-interest.   B pursues self-interest.

Moreover, I have the belief that it is mutually believed among all of us MBAs that every MBA has this plan:

$mb(MBAs, (\forall x \in MBAs) has\text{-}plan(x, P_2))$.

Thus, collective intention, when properly recast into a language of beliefs, goals, and plans, understood in their technical senses, is straightforward to characterize in the standard AI planning formalism. Moreover, we can now see collective intentionality as one part of a much larger picture. Nearly everything we do is intricately intertwined with events beyond our direct control happening in the environment. We depend on the universe behaving in certain ways. When I run my pen across the page, I depend on the physical properties of the pen to leave a trace of ink behind it. Our actions are often no more than mere nudges that enable these processes. I might push my car on a slight decline to overcome static friction, so that gravity can accelerate it to the desired speed. When I flip a light switch to turn on a light, I am only performing the last small required action in an enormous chain of events and conditions that society and physics have prepared for me.

Collective actions are a special case of this mesh of the agent with the world at large. The agent has as a goal that the team execute a pass play, for example. A subgoal of this is that he block the defensive end; he can take care of this on his own. Another subgoal is that the quarterback throw the ball at the proper time and in the proper way; belief in mutual belief in a common plan assures our agent that this will happen at the appropriate time. Another event in the plan, yes, as a subgoal if the plan is carried out to that level of detail, is that the ball follow the right sort of parabolic arc; the agent's beliefs about physics, naive or otherwise, assure him of that.

All of this has been so easy it makes one suspect there are really some deeper issues involved here. And indeed there are. The events and conditions represented in the agent's beliefs, goals, and hence plans, have to be framed out of concepts made available by the agent's implicit or explicit folk theories, or systems of belief, about various classes of phenomena. To analyze collective action, therefore, we need better explications and formalizations of people's folk theories of social entities and social action, including some concepts which Searle in this and other writings has made significant contributions to our understanding of, such as commitment, which creates mutual belief in a collective plan among agents, and responsibility, which holds each agent to his or her part.

This point, in fact, is relevant to an argument Searle makes against "talk about group minds, the collective unconscious, and so on." It seems to me the criterion for the acceptability of this vocabulary is the same as it is for any other vocabulary: What work does it do for us? Although I personally don't expect things to turn out that way, the vocabulary would be perfectly acceptable if description in its terms yields a successful theory of social action, say, as successful as our theories of personal action couched in terms like "belief," "goal," "plan," and perhaps "intention." It would be especially acceptable if we were able to articulate its terms with the terms of a successful theory of personal action.

Searle closes section 1 of his paper with an argument that collective intentionality introduces a new and perhaps disturbing fact—"that I can not only be mistaken about how the world is but am even mistaken about what I am in fact doing." But this is not a feature of collective intentionality per se. Rather, it is a feature of the larger framework of hierarchical planning in which I have tried to embed collective intentionality. If while driving I take my foot off the accelerator and I think I'm coasting down a slight hill in my car, whereas in fact I'm on a slight upgrade being carried along by inertia, I'm mistaken about what I am doing. In both this case and Searle's, I have a high-level goal involving in its implementation agencies other than myself. I believe correctly that I am doing my part to achieve this goal. I believe mistakenly that the other agencies are doing their parts.

By embedding collective intentionality in the larger framework of our interactions with causal forces in the world in general, I don't mean to imply that there are no distinctions to be made between people and other natural entities, like rivers and stones. Of course people are very complex, and we interact with other people in very complex ways that we don't experience with rivers and stones. But rivers are also very complex, and we interact with them in complex ways that we don't experience with people and stones.

Section 2 of Searle's paper is a valiant struggle toward an adequate hierarchical planning formalism, without benefit of the relevant literature. In fact, his treatment of hierarchical planning, as well as his emphasis on the importance of notation and his adherence to materialism and methodological solipsism, are so much in tune with the prevailing views and concerns in AI that one wonders why in other papers he has attempted to cast himself as a critic of AI.

In any case, there is one issue he is concerned with in section 2 that is not captured, at least explicitly, in the hard-core AI planning framework. He wants to preserve in his notation for collective intention the self-referential character of intention that his notation for individual intention makes explicit. When one intends to perform an action, one moreover intends that this very intention will cause that action. My favorite illustration of this aspect of intention is from Theodore Dreiser's *An American Tragedy*. The hero, Clyde Griffiths, stands up in a rowboat with the oar, intending to knock his pregnant girl friend into the water and drown her. He slips, the oar hits her and knocks her into the water, and she drowns. He intended to knock her into the water, he knocked her into the water, but the intention didn't cause the knocking.[6]

This self-referentiality has certainly not been made explicit in any planning formalism. But is it implicit? I think one can argue that it is. In an AI framework the self-referentiality means that an agent's goal that an event e occur itself plays a causal role in the occurrence of e. But this is the case. Because the agent is a planning mechanism, once a goal is formed it persists, unless the plan is modified. The goal is decomposed into executable actions, and when the appropriate time for these actions arrives, they are executed. This is simply the way the planning mechanism works. Thus, the goal does play a causal role in its own achievement. Clyde Griffiths modified his plan at the last instant, so his prior goal to kill his girl friend was not the direct cause of the oar hitting her.

Moreover, agents are aware of this self-referentiality. When an agent plans, he knows the plan has to bottom out in events that will happen at the appropriate time. One of the principal ways events can happen at the appropriate time is by being actions the agent is capable of executing directly. One does not normally plan to have lucky accidents at the appropriate times; it is too undependable; too many such plans fail.[7] The agent knows, in the form of some folk theory or other, that he is a planning mechanism, so he knows that if he decomposes his goals to executable actions and as long as he does not modify his plan, his goals will play a causal role in their own achievement. Of course, the agent must be able to know when the goal to perform a directly executable action has caused that action. This happens because of feedback from effectors. Via this feedback the agent can distinguish between when the effectors are moved and when they do the moving, even though the trajectory is the same, and the agent has become or has always been aware of the correlations between this feedback and the process of planning. When the feedback is absent, as it sometimes is in injury or under medication, our sense of the intention causing the action falters.[8] In Clyde Griffiths' case, he would have known either that his arms that were carrying the oar toward his girl friend were being moved rather than doing the moving, or that if they were doing the moving, it was as part of a suddenly new plan to brace himself rather than as part of his just abandoned or postponed plan to kill her.

In section 3 Searle raises the very interesting issue of the "sense of community" we can feel and its relation to collective action. From a hard-core AI point of view, a first attempt at a characterization of what it means for an agent to have a sense of community would be this (and here I try to stick closely to what Searle has said). I have a sense of community with a set of other agents if I believe it is mutually believed by me and the members of that set that we are all "actual or potential members of a cooperative activity," and moreover I have a long-term goal of maintenance that this remain true. This may not explain the warm feeling often associated with some of my senses of community;[9] AI and cognitive science generally have little to say about warm feelings. Nevertheless, I would bet that this or something like it explains the ways a sense of community is manifested in action.

It might be objected that to characterize a sense of community in terms of mutual belief has things the wrong way around. Social animals must have a sense of community and they surely don't have mutual beliefs. I don't want to get deeply into biology. But there is a range of experiences we people have that shows the correspondence between complexity of beliefs and the depth of the sense of community they engender. At the bottom of the scale is the situation in which I'm rushing toward a shelter and, unbeknownst to me, so are many other people. One level above is the situation that transpires after it has gradually dawned on all of us that everyone else has the same goal. This already constitutes a weak sense of community. At a higher level is the situation in which some of the people use their knowledge of the common goal to determine their own actions, as when a pickpocket plans where he will place himself in the coming crush. More complex social behavior is possible when everybody in a crowd behaves in a dependable way in order that others may depend on their behavior; waiting one's turn to get through the entrance to the shelter, assuming others will be fair, could be explained in this manner. Finally, there is fullblown collective action, with its mutual belief in a common plan, of the sort exemplified by a previously choreographed convergence on the shelter. At the lower end of this scale, people can act on the basis of how they believe others will act. But human behavior is complex and these beliefs are often wrong. At the higher end of the scale, mutual belief, commitment, and a sense of responsibility make the behavior of others more reliable, allowing each agent to risk and hence achieve more individually, and allowing the collective as a whole to accomplish more. When we participate in a dance, we put ourselves at risk. When a ballerina executes a grand jeté, she needs to know her partner will be there to catch her.[10]

A sense of community is thus not part of a mysterious or unanalyzable "Background." Rather, it consists of certain beliefs and goals, certainly in the technical senses of the terms, and, I think, even in the ordinary senses of the terms, although my ordinary English may have become hopelessly tainted by my work in AI. Searle says that "these are not in the normal case 'beliefs'," likening them to "my stance toward the objects around me and the ground underneath me ... being solid, without my needing or having a special belief that they are solid." Such an appeal to intuition won't work on a hard-core AI researcher like me. My intuition is that it is obvious that I have a belief that the ground is solid, again not only in the technical sense of "belief" but in the ordinary sense as well. When someone out of a background sense of community spontaneously offers to help me push my car, I think there *is* a rule that can be stated explicitly that he or she is acting in accordance with. In fact, it has a name. It's called the Golden Rule.[11]

How do we acquire a sense of community? The same ways we acquire other beliefs and goals. We learn from experience and by being told that particular groups have the potential for cooperative activity, and we adopt in the ongoing plan with which we approach daily life the goal of maintaining this situation, because we have determined that it helps us thrive. People are certainly predisposed to acquire senses of community with those with whom they are or might be engaged in cooperative activity, just as people are predisposed to acquire beliefs about up and down and the solidity of physical objects. There might even be an abstract sense of community hard-wired in, just waiting to be instantiated with various convenient specific communities. But none of this changes the basic outlines of the AI account. It is no more significant than the hardware-software distinction in computer science. It is still just beliefs and goals.

Searle argues against the position, presumably that of Habermas, "that collective behavior presupposes communication, that speech acts in conversation are the 'foundation' of social behavior and hence of society." He wants to argue that there must be a prior sense of community for either collective behavior or communication to occur. This is a chicken-and-egg problem, and the solution is same as in the chicken-and-egg problem. A sense of community, collective behavior, and communication evolve together, both in the evolution of the species and in the development of the individual. We are born knowing how to suckle and desiring to cuddle. Engaging in this collective behavior establishes a small-scale sense of community, which makes possible further collective behavior and communication. Language is learned, enabling us to learn the rules and conventions of quite complex social activities. And so on, until we arrive at the complex creatures we are.

2 Comments on Grosz and Sidner

In all work in AI there is a powerful vision that informs the research and can be used as a vocabulary for analysis, and there are the rather simpler and weaker procedures that are actually implemented. The latter are scaled-down versions of the former that one resorts to just because of the difficulties of implementation that every AI programmer is aware of. Grosz and Sidner have chosen to begin their paper with a review of the implemented versions of previous work, rather than of the grander visions. From this perspective, they are quite right in saying the previous work has not dealt with collaborative planning. Previous researchers have dealt with complex collaborative and even more complex conflictual planning on an informal level (for instance, Bruce and Newman 1978; Hobbs and Evans 1980; Wilensky 1978), but previous *implementations* have made the simplifying assumption that only a single agent is doing the planning and acting. Though Grosz and Sidner do not offer an implementation, they do propose a formalism, and if it were successful, it would represent an advance in the study of planning. Unfortunately, it is not successful, and Searle's paper and my critique of Searle's paper are relevant to the question of why it fails. The crucial issue turns out to be the issue of whether a goal is an action or an event.

In single-agent planning this question does not matter very much. Suppose the goal is for the agent A to move BLOCK1. We can express this by a wff representing an event:

move(A, BLOCK1).

We can express it by a wff representing a state that is the end state of the event:

moved(A, BLOCK1).

Or we can express it by a lambda-expression representing the action whose performance by the agent would constitute the event,

λx [move(x, BLOCK1)],

or, as it is more commonly written,

move(BLOCK1).

In single-agent planning translation from any one of these forms to any of the others is trivial. Unfortunately, in multi-agent planning this is no longer the case. Since actions can be performed by more than one agent, we need to be explicit about who is doing what. It is no longer possible for goals to be actions (or at least actions that leave the agent unspecified).

In much of the previous work Grosz and Sidner cite, the agent was made explicit in goals and in operators for effecting goals. In her very fine work, Pollack, dealing only with single agents, was able, as a simplification, to use actions as goals. Grosz and Sidner have tried to carry this simplification over to multi-agent planning, with unfortunate consequences. This apparently was not mere negligence on their part, but a conscious decision. They say, "The desire to provide an appropriate account of imperative utterances (that is, one that did not depend on the notion of agent's intending for another agent to intend to do some action) was a primary motivation for SharedPlans" (section 5.1). I take it that the key intuition here is that one can intend only one's *own* actions. This illustrates one of the pitfalls of taking the ordinary English word "intention" too seriously, especially in the context of a philsophical tradition that has emphasized intentions-in-action over future-directed intentions.

As a consequence of this decision, Grosz and Sidner's formalism is less than perspicuous. We find, for example, expressions of the following sort:

GEN-Simultaneous[lift(foot-end) & lift(keyboard-end), lift(piano), S1&S2].

S1 and S2 are agents. The first problem is whether we are to take the symbol & to mean conjunction, as it usually does, and if so, what the conjunction of S1 and S2 means. Is it, for example, the same as the conjunction of S2 and S1, or is there some significance to the order of the "conjuncts" in the first and third arguments of GEN-Simultaneous? Does the order mean that necessarily S1 is lifting the foot-end and S2 the keyboard-end? It is just not clear who is doing what. If we do a string match of this expression with its definition, we may surmise that the authors use ampersands where they should have commas. Otherwise, the expression has no compositional semantics and is very misleading.

Similarly, and crucially, in the expression

INT(S2, BY(lift(keyboard-end), lift(piano))),

who is lifting the piano? Surely not S2. And S1 is mentioned only in the next conjunct. And what does BY mean? Lifting the keyboard-end does not by itself effect the lifting of the piano. Does BY mean something like "contribute to"? We are just not told.

This may seem a mere notational quibble, but notational difficulties often signal underlying ontological difficulties, and that is the case here.

The use of a notation like lift(foot-end), rather than lift(S1, foot-end), must have come from a desire to preserve actions on the part of a single agent as the only possible object of an intention, and as Searle shows in his paper, this simply won't do. In fact, under the most reasonable interpretation of the unclear portions of Grosz and Sidner's formalism, the definition they give of a SharedPlan is an axiomatization of Tuomela and Miller's attempt to reduce collective intention to individual intention-in-action. As such, it falls prey to Searle's MBA counterexample.

Let us demonstrate this in detail. Suppose S1 and S2 are two of the MBAs who intend to help humanity by serving their own interests. We will show that they have a SharedPlan to help humanity by showing that they satisfy Grosz and Sidner's definition of a SharedPlan at the beginning of section 5. Satisfying Clause 1, they mutually believe that S1 is going to serve his own interests and that S2 is going to serve her own interests. Satisfying the most reasonable reading of Clause 2, they mutually believe that simultaneously serving their own interests will generate helping humanity. Satisfying Clause 3, they mutually believe they each intend to serve their own interests. Satisfying Clause 4, they mutually believe that S2 intends to help humanity by serving her own interests, and similarly for S1. Satisfying Clause 5, they each intend to serve their own interests. Satisfying Clause 6, S2 intends that by serving her own interests, she will—accomplish? contribute to?—the helping of humanity, and similarly for S1. They therefore satisfy Grosz and Sidner's definition of SharedPlan, but as Searle has pointed out, they are not engaging in collective behavior.

Precisely what is missing in this account is what Searle has tried to captured in his notion of we-intentions, and what I have argued is simply a matter of having as a goal an action whose agent is a collective. There is no intention that *we* do something. Moreover, this is a possibility that Grosz and Sidner explicitly reject in their belief that agents can only intend their own actions.

The differences among the four accounts can be summarized succinctly as follows. Tuomela and Miller attempt, by defining collective intention, to reduce it to individual intention-in-action and mutual belief. Grosz and Sidner posit a special operator for collective intention, which they call SharedPlan, but by defining it they also attempt to reduce it to individual intention-in-action. Searle simply stipulates the existence of we-intentions and says they must be, not *defined*, but *implemented* in terms of individual intentions-in-action. I argue that Searle's we-intentions are simply "intentions that we ..." and as such are particular examples of the manifold ways in which agents plan their intricately meshed interactions with the world in general.

The difficulties with Grosz and Sidner's action notation have another unfortunate effect. They are forced to invent what in this paper is only a few, but must eventually be a myriad, new GEN relations—one for when the actions are done simultaneously, one for when the times overlap a bit, one for when they are sequential, and so on. It is easy to see where this leads. If the collective action is something involving many agents and precise timing, such as Searle's example of a pass play, we would end up with predicates like GEN-49ers-pass-play-1987-36A. A more reasonable notation would have agents and times as explicit arguments. For example, suppose aggr is an operator that takes two wffs representing events and returns the aggregate event, and AGGR maps two individuals into the aggregate of the two. Then one could, say, with much more clarity,

GEN(aggr(lift(S1, keyboard-end, t1), lift(S2, foot-end, t1)),
    lift(AGGR(S1, S2), piano, t1)).

Here it is clear who is doing what and when. No GEN-Simultaneous operator would be needed, and no further GEN operators would be needed for other temporal relations among the actions. The relations would be captured by relations among the time arguments of the predications representing the events. The more explicit and perspicuous notation would force them to abandon their intuition that agents cannot have as goals actions on the part of other agents, but so much the better, for one would then see shared plans as one example of how agents plan their actions to mesh with the larger fabric of what will happen in the rest of the world.

Instead of this elaboration on the interaction of collaborative action and time, it would have been interesting to see an examination of collaborative planning where the actions are discursive in nature, and not primarily physical events in the world such as lifting pianos. I have in mind the sort of behavior that occurs often in a conversation when the participants are so much in synch that one feels they are carrying out a single shared discourse plan. This is especially notable in Falk's (1980) examples of dueting and in Wilkes-Gibbs's (1986) examples of completions. Similar behavior is exhibited in Clark and Wilkes-Gibbs's negotiations of referential expressions (see chapter 23 of this volume).

Two more points are worth commenting on. First, Grosz and Sidner were eager to eliminate the "master-slave" assumption underlying their previous work. This is the your-wish-is-my-command rule that says the hearer adopts the speaker's goals. But they have not replaced it with anything else that can do a similar job. There is rule CDR1 that says that generally a statement of a desire is a request for help, and there is rule CDR2 that says that generally agents try to achieve the shared goals in ways their coparticipants desire.[12] But there is no rule that allows us to go from G1's desire for a shared plan to G2's adoption of that plan. In their analyses of the simple dialogues, they are silent about how that move is made. From Utterance 1 of Dialogue 1 we can infer that S1 wants them both to lift the piano, and from Utterance 2 of Dialogue 1 we can infer that S2 has accepted the shared plan. But *why* S2 accepted it is left a mystery. This is certainly safe, and perhaps even appropriate if we are only eaves-dropping on the conversation and want to know what shared plan of action has finally been arrived at. But if we are modeling S2's behavior, then we would definitely have to say something about why S2 chose to adopt the shared plan. Even if we are modeling S1's behavior, we need some way of explaining why S1 thought expressing his desires would lead to S2's adopting them for her own. Of course, the real story here is *much* more complicated than a "master-slave" assumption. We go through all sorts of maneuvers to get others to adopt our desires as their own. It would have been interesting to see an explication of how some of this happens. In its absence, this account no longer explains why a speaker would bother to express his or her desires at all.

Incidentally, Grosz and Sidner attribute the prevalence of the master-slave assumption to the fact that most work on planning has involved only single utterances. This is possibly true in part, for in the case of single-utterance interpretation such a stance is justified. We can decompose the problem of responding to an utterance into the problem of the hearer's determining what to do if he or she were to do everything the speaker desired, and the separate problem of deciding whether or not to actually do it. In investigating the first of these problems, one might as well adopt the master-slave assumption. A more likely source for the prevalence of the assumption, however, is in the fact that much of the early work on multi-utterance dialogue focused on expert-apprentice dialogues, where the apprentice was assumed to be willing to do everything the expert desired.[13]

My second point is illustrated in Grosz and Sidner's account of Dialogue 1. They go through a curious bit of analysis. "From the context in which Utterances 3 and 5 are uttered, the participants can infer that the mentioned actions are seen to participate in a generation relationship with the desired action. That these actions together are sufficient is implicit in Utterances 7 and 8. S1 and S2 can now infer that the generation relation exhibited in Clause 2 holds." But this is surely not right. The real, and obvious, story is that they both already know what it takes to lift a piano and they know that it is common knowledge in our culture.[14] The general problem is that Grosz and Sidner, in this work as elsewhere, do not give sufficient emphasis to the importance of background knowledge in the interpretation of discourse.

Notes

1. This is actually a rational reconstruction. The historical facts are this. I read Searle's description of the problem, and I thought, the answer is such and such. Then I turned the page and read that some people thought the answer was such and such, but here was a counterexample. I thought, "Oh." *Then* I was driven to analyze the problem from

a hard-core AI point of view, which led me to say, "Who would ever have thought otherwise?"

2. Which may or may not have "I survive" as a subgoal.

3. This notation, by the way, does not constitute a serious proposal for an adequate knowledge representation language. Serious proposals do exist.

4. Some in AI may object to my calling this *"the* hard-core AI view." I'm sure, however, they would object more strongly if I claimed originality. I believe it is the point of view at least implicit in Sacerdoti 1977. It is the view expressed in Hobbs and Evans 1980. Rosenschein (1981) formalized Sacerdoti's work along rather different lines. He dismissed hierarchical planning in a few sentences and built his model around the temporal sequence of the agent's actions. This seems to me a mistake. By contrast, I have dismissed the temporal sequence of actions in a few sentences and built my account around the hierarchical character of the planning. It is my view that this hierarchicality is fundamental to the ability of finite creatures like us to operate in an information-rich world, whereas time is just one of many things we reason about and negotiate our way through.

5. I have just introduced a technical vocabulary, and there's a real chance for misunderstanding here. Philosophers often view their task as one of probing ordinary English words, like "belief," "goal," "plan," and "intention," to their conceptual roots, taking their intuitions about these words very seriously. By contrast, an AI researcher plunders ordinary English for lexical items to turn into technical terms. In the framework I have presented, "belief," "goal," and "plan" are technical terms, and "intention" is not. These technical terms are defined precisely and henceforth are unrelated to the ordinary English words except etymologically. In particular, beliefs, goals, and plans need not be conscious, and we can have as goals events such as relaxing and chatting that wouldn't be thought of as especially goal-directed in ordinary folk psychology. Explanations are constructed using these technical terms, and the explanation either succeeds or fails to account for the relevant evidence. Actually, this is not quite true. The ordinary English words are used for their suggestive power. One thinks of an intuitively satisfying explanation in ordinary English terminology, based on folk psychology. One then tries to translate this account into technical terminology. But whether the technical version succeeds as an explanation has nothing to do with its intuitive roots. It depends only on whether it accounts for the behavior in question and meshes well with a theory that accounts for much more of the behavior.

6. He was convicted of first-degree murder nevertheless.

7. Many people buy lottery tickets, but not so many people buy a Mercedes on credit *because* they've bought a lottery ticket.

8. I need not point out that today, in the age of the computer, unlike in the age of Descartes, the causal influence of the mental on the physical is no more mysterious than the conversion of electromagnetic energy into mechanical energy.

9. For example—and this is true—I am sometimes moved to tears reading the *California Driver's Handbook*.

10. It would be interesting to know what various social animals are willing to risk where they must depend on the behavior of others. My sense is that dogs, for example, rarely enter into situations they can't bail out of in fairly short order if their support fails. It's not easy to train a dog to ride a seesaw.

11. A typical sort of argument Searle and others have made elsewhere against the possibility of explicating this background as a set of formal rules operated on by complex inferential processes goes like this: Suppose you went into a restaurant and ordered a hamburger, and the waitress brought you a purple felt pillow six feet in diameter in the shape of a hamburger. How could a formal system be able to deduce this was inappro-

priate? It could never have anticipated such a situation, and so it could not have had a rule like, "Waitresses don't bring customers purple felt pillows six feet in diameter in the shape of a hamburger when they order hamburgers." All of the examples I have heard in arguments like this have been derivable, at least informally, in a fairly straightforward manner from ordinary facts that it is quite reasonable to suppose people have and find useful every day—facts about what kinds of things are edible, the normal colors, shapes, sizes, and material constitutions of common objects, how much food constitutes a reasonable meal, and so on. There are of course problems in how to state and reason about this knowledge, problems that are being addressed vigorously by a large number of researchers. Another argument rests on the necessarily context-dependent nature of interpretation, but this is an argument against only the most naive attempts at formalization. It has been the major thrust of AI work in natural-language processing to discover precisely how context, represented as a structured knowledge base, contributes to the determination of interpretations.

12. This is still pretty slavish behavior. It is more common in equal partnerships to negotiate the means as much as the ends are negotiated.

13. A better way to look at the expert-apprentice dialogues is in terms of who possesses what knowledge. The expert is in possession of the general principles, while the apprentice possesses knowledge of the specific situation. This is true in doctor-patient interviews and in service encounters in general. It is curious that general knowledge usually confers power.

14. Actually, anybody I could lift a piano with could probably lift it alone.

References

Bruce, Bertram C., and Dennis Newman 1978. Interacting plans. *Cognitive Science* 2, 195–233.

Falk, Jane (1980). The conversational duet. In *Proceedings of the Sixth Annual Meeting, Berkeley Linguistics Society, Berkeley, CA.*

Hobbs, Jerry R., and David Andreoff Evans (1980). Conversation as planned behavior. *Cognitive Science* 4, 349–377.

Rosenschein, Stanley J. (1981). Plan synthesis: A logical perspective. In *Proceedings of the Seventh International Joint Conference on Artificial Intelligence*, Vancouver, B.C.

Sacerdoti, Earl (1977). *A structure for plans and behavior.* New York: American Elsevier.

Wilensky, Robert (1978). Understanding goal-based stories. Research Report 140, Department of Computer Science, Yale University, New Haven, CT.

Wilkes-Gibbs, Deanna (1986). Collaborative processes of language use in conversation. Doctoral dissertation, Department of Psychology, Stanford University, Stanford, CA.

Chapter 22

A Reply to Hobbs

Barbara J. Grosz and Candace L. Sidner

In the introduction to his commentary on our paper, Hobbs contrasts "powerful visions" with "rather simpler and weaker procedures that are actually implemented" and then suggests that our review of previous work is merely about implementations, not visions. He is wrong on two counts, one quite serious in a volume of interdisciplinary work intended for audiences with different disciplinary training and inclinations. Before commenting briefly on several technical points, we must address the flawed premise in his commentary.

Since the mid-1970s it has been well accepted within the AI research community that one must distinguish one's theory from one's implementation and that before an implementation is useful as a tool of scientific inquiry,[1] one must have a theory on which it is based. It is also commonplace that visions, no matter how grand, are not theories. We will assume that the contrast between grand vision and theory is quite clear (one cannot, for example, test a vision as one can a theory) and not dwell on it further here.

Because Hobbs seems to have missed the determinative distinction between theory and implementation, it is worth exploring some for those who might conclude from his comments that AI is still confusing the two. Computational theories are concerned with *what* is being computed; implementations are concerned with the details of *how* the computation is carried out. The reader interested in an extensive exposition of this distinction may consult Marr's book on vision (Marr 1982). As Marr argues quite convincingly, the failure to distinguish between theory and implementation was a critical impediment to progress in the field through the mid-1970s.

Hobbs errs not only in missing this crucial theoretical level but also in claiming that our review addresses only implementations. The review is concerned with the theories investigated in alternative approaches, not implementations. Our paper presents an initial theory that is significantly different from previous work. This theory—whether or not it turns out to be correct—is the contribution of the paper.

The one substantive technical issue Hobbs raises concerns the meaning of the act-type constructor function BY.[2] Given Pollack's definitions in chapter 5 of this volume, the use of BY must be restricted to actions that are related by the generation relation. For other types of actions, Clauses 4 and 6 of SharedPlan require instead a "Contributes" relation with the following semantics: the relation "Contributes" holds between actions α and β just in case the performance of α (in a suitable time interval) contributes to the performance of β; α must be a member of a set of actions α_i for which $R(\alpha_i, \beta, G_i, T)$, where R is one of the specified action relations (for instance, generation, enabling, simultaneous-generation).

For example, take α to be the action of typing a "u"; α is then a member of the set of actions, α_i, forming the action sequence type "u";type "n";type "i";type "t". It stands in a Contributes relation to the action β of typing the word "unit" since GEN-Sequence$[\alpha_i, \beta, G, T]$. Analogously to BY as defined by Pollack, the Contributes relation provides a way of stating how one action fits into a larger action; however, by using a relation rather than a function, we are able to consider relationships among actions with different agents. For example, we can use the relation to say that *my* writing a paragraph contributes to *our* writing a paper.

Finally, one of the main claims of our paper is that the joint activity modeled by SharedPlans cannot be decomposed into some function of the individual plans of individual agents. Hobbs's reply presumes this is the case without acknowledging that it is a significant departure from previous theories. It appears we have convinced him of a most important point.

Notes

1. People built useful bridges long before there was any theory to explain how the bridges stayed up. Likewise, an implementation may be useful for what it does, even if there is no underlying theory to support or explain how it does so.
2. His principal conerns about GEN-Simultaneous are addressed in our paper, in which GEN-Simultaneous is used merely as a shorthand for the longer expression that does make explicit times and agents.

References

Marr, David (1982). *Vision*. San Francisco: W. H. Freeman.

Chapter 23
Referring as a Collaborative Process
Herbert H. Clark and Deanna Wilkes-Gibbs

Conversation is the fundamental site of language use. For many people, even for whole societies, it is the only site, and it is the primary one for children acquiring language. From this perspective other arenas of language use—novels, newspapers, lectures, street signs, rituals—are derivative or secondary. How, then, do speaking and understanding work in conversation? For psychologists this ought to be a central question, but surprisingly, it has not been. The main attempts to answer it have come instead from philosophy and sociology.

Among philosophers the study of conversation grew out of an analysis of what speakers mean and what listeners understand them to mean. The idea was that, when speakers utter sentences, they do so with certain intentions toward their addressees. They assert, request, promise, and perform other illocutionary acts, and their interlocutors are expected to recognize these intentions (Austin 1962; Grice 1957, 1968; Schiffer 1972; Searle 1969). In 1967 Grice argued that, for this scheme to work, people in conversation must be cooperative. Speakers must try to "make their contribution such as is required, at the stage at which it occurs, by the accepted purpose or direction of the talk exchange in which [they] are engaged" (Grice 1975, 45). Only then can their partners go beyond what is "said" to infer what is conversationally "implicated" (Grice 1975, 1978).

Among sociologists the issue has been how people direct the course of conversation and repair its inherent troubles. As this work has shown, people in conversation manage who is to talk at which times through an intricate system of turn taking (Sacks, Schegloff, and Jefferson 1974). Further, when one person speaks, the others not only listen but let the speaker know they are understanding—with head nods, *yes's*, *uh huh's*, and other so-called back-channel responses (Duncan 1973; Goodwin 1981; Schegloff

We thank A. V. Belyaeva, E. V. Clark, E. P. Francik, R. J. Gerrig, W. J. M. Levelt, D. Morrow, G. L. Murphy, G. Redeker, and H. Stark for valuable counsel on this work. The project was supported by grant MH-20021 from the National Institute of Mental Health, grant BNS 83-20284 from the National Science Foundation, the Nederlandse Organisatie voor Zuiver-Wetenschappelijk Onderzoek, and the Center for the Study of Language and Information.

1981; Yngve 1970). When listeners don't understand, or when other troubles arise, they can interrupt for correction or clarification (Schegloff, Jefferson, and Sacks 1977). The participants also have techniques for initiating, guiding, and terminating conversations and the topics within them (Schegloff 1968; Schegloff and Sacks 1973).

In both traditions a central issue is coordination: How do the participants in a conversation coordinate on the content and timing of what is meant and understood? The issue, however, cannot be resolved within either tradition alone. In the first tradition conversation is idealized as a succession of illocutionary acts—assertions, questions, promises—each uttered and understood clearly and completely (Gazdar 1979; Kamp 1981; Stalnaker 1978). Yet from the second tradition we know that many utterances remain incomplete and only partly understood until corrected or amplified in further exchanges. How are these two views to be reconciled?

In this paper we propose a resolution for an essential use of language: how people in conversation coordinate in the making of a definite reference. Our concern is not with semantic reference, but with speaker's reference—not, for example, with what the phrase *the clown with the red nose* means, but with what the speaker does in referring, say, to a clown as part of an assertion that the clown is funny (Donnellan 1978; Kripke 1977; Searle 1969). Our premise is that making such a reference is a collaborative process requiring actions by both speakers and interlocutors. To some it may appear self-evident that the process is collaborative, but it is one thing to assume it is and quite another to understand why it is and how it works. The goal here is important, since, if conversation is fundamental, its processes are likely to underlie or shape those in other uses of language as well.

In the first section of this paper, then, we offer evidence for the premise itself and outline what we will call a collaborative model for the process of reference. In the second and third sections we describe an experiment on referring and use it to corroborate and fill in details of the model. In the final section we return to the general issue of coordination and note problems still to be resolved.

1 Referring in Conversation

Traditionally, philosophers, linguists, and psychologists have presupposed what might be called a *literary model* of definite reference. Speakers refer as if they were writing to distant readers. When Elizabeth selects the noun phrase *the clown with a red nose* in talking to Sam, the assumption is that she intends it to enable him to identify the clown uniquely. She satisfies her intentions by issuing the noun phrase. Her act of referring is cotemporal with that noun phrase, beginning with *the* and ending with *nose*. Further, she retains complete responsibility and control over the course of this process. Sam hears the definite description as if he were reading it and, if successful, infers the identity of the referent. But his actions have no bearing on hers in this reference.

The literary model makes these tacit idealizations. (1) The reference is expressed linguistically with one of three standard types of noun phrase— a proper noun (for instance, *Napoleon, King George*), a definite description (*this year, the man with the moustache*), or a pronoun (*he, this, they*). (2) The speaker uses the noun phrase intending the addressee to be able to identify the referent uniquely against their common ground. (3) The speaker satisfies her intention simply by the issuing of that noun phrase. And (4) the course of the process is controlled by the speaker alone.

A conversational model of the process, however, ought to look quite different for three reasons. First, in conversation unlike writing, speakers have limited time for planning and revision. They need to overcome this limitation, and in doing so they may exploit techniques possible only in conversational settings. Second, speech is evanescent. The listener has to attend to, hear, and try to understand an utterance at virtually the same time it is being issued. That requires a type of process synchronization not found in reading. And third, listeners in conversations aren't mute or invisible during an utterance. Speakers may alter what they say midcourse based on what addressees say and do.

Indeed, once we look at actual conversations, we find that the four idealizations of the literary model are very wide of the mark. To see this, let us turn to eight types of examples that fail on one or more of these assumptions.

1.1 Eight Problems

1. *Self-corrected noun phrases.* Consider this attested utterance: *She was giving me all the people that were gone this year I mean this quarter y'know* (from Schegloff, Jefferson, and Sacks 1977, 364, in simplified notation). The speaker began the referential process by uttering *all the people that were gone this year,* but corrected the last two words to *this quarter* in what Schegloff, Jefferson, and Sacks (1977) called a *self-initiated repair.* The referential process, clearly, isn't cotemporal with one particular noun phrase, since two noun phrases were uttered in succession. It is more naturally described as a process in which the speaker decided midcourse to repair the initial noun phrase, indicated here change with *I mean,* and then uttered *this quarter* (see Levelt 1983). The process began with *all the people* and was completed with *y'know.*

2. *Expanded noun phrases.* Although the first noun phrase a speaker utters may be technically correct, the speaker may still judge it insufficient and change course, as here (from Cohen 1985):

> S: Take the spout—the little one that looks like the end of an oil can—
>
> J: Okay.
>
> S: —and put that on the opening in the other large tube. With the round top.

S began with *the spout*. But when he saw that it was insufficient for J to pick out the referent, he expanded on it with the parenthetical noun phrase. Ordinarily, parenthetical phrases are nonrestrictive—not needed for identifying the referent. Here, the parenthetical phrase *was* deemed necessary, and S changed course midutterance to add it.

3. *Episodic noun phrases.* For similar reasons, once S completed *the other large tube*, he judged that to be insufficient as well and added the restrictive phrase *with the round top* under a separate intonation contour, as part of a new tone group. He produced a single noun phrase, but intonationally, he divided in into two information units. We will call this an *episodic noun phrase*, and it is another nonstandard type.

4. *Other-corrected noun phrases.* The process becomes more complicated when the addressee makes the repair, as with A's reference to Monday in this example (from Schegloff, Jefferson, and Sacks 1977, 369):

> B: How long y'gonna be here?
>
> A: Uh- not too long. Uh just til uh Monday.
>
> B: Til- oh yih mean like a week f'm *tomorrow.*
>
> A: Yah.
>
> B: [Continues]

A initiated the referential process by uttering *Monday*. Uncertain of the intended referent, B offered a correction, which A accepted, all before B proceeded. The process took place over several turns and was participated in by both A and B.

In the four cases so far, then, the speakers changed the course of their reference after uttering an initial noun phrase. They did so in reaction to both their own and their addressee's judgments of inadequacy or error. But speakers are not merely reactive. At other times they bring addressees into the referential process by the very design of their utterance. Consider the next four classes of examples.

5. *Trial noun phrases.* Some noun phrases are uttered with a rising intonation, or *try marker* (Sacks and Schegloff 1979), imposed on them, as in this example (from Cohen 1985):

> S: Okay now, the small blue cap we talked about before?
>
> J: Yeah.

S: Put that over the hole on the side of that tube—
J: Yeah.
S: —that is nearest to the top, or nearest to the red handle.

With *the small blue cap we talked about before?* S asks J to say whether or not he has understood S's reference. The process begins when S utters this phrase and ends only with J's *Yeah*. If J hadn't understood, the process would have continued as here (from Sacks and Schegloff 1979):

A: ... well I was the only one other than than the uhm tch *Fords?*,
   Uh Mrs, Holmes Ford? You know uh =
   ⌈ = the the cellist?
B: ⌊ Oh yes. She's she's the cellist.
A: Yes. Well she and her husband were there.

When A received no reply to *Fords?*, she offered the expanded noun phrase *Mrs. Holmes Ford?* and then went to *the cellist?* before B implicated that she had identified the referent. The referential process was continued until A said *Yes*, confirming that B's display of understanding was correct.

6. *Installment noun phrases.* Speakers can also utter noun phrases in *installments*, as we will call them, and invite addresses to affirm their understanding of each installment. In the earlier example, S began *the hole on the side of that tube*, paused for confirmation from J, and then completed the noun phrase with *that is nearest to the top, or nearest to the red handle*. As with his trial noun phrase, S made the course of his reference contingent on the addressee's midcourse response.

7. *Dummy noun phrases.* Speakers sometimes initiate the referential process with terms like *what's-his-name, whatchamacallit, whatzit,* or *thingamabob*, which we will call *dummy* nouns or noun phrases. Consider: *If he puts it into the diplomatic bag, as um—what's-his-name, Micky Cohn, did, then it's not so bad* (from Svartvik and Quirk 1980, 35). The speaker recognized from the start that *what's-his-name* was inadequate as a definite description. Yet, pressed for time, he used it to initiate the referential process until he could replace it with an adequate noun phrase, *Micky Cohn*. Dummy noun phrases are *not* standard, and when speakers use them, they do *not* intend them to enable their addresses to identify the referent uniquely. Dummy noun phrases are uttered only as part of a more extended process.

8. *Proxy noun phrases.* In some circumstances, the speaker makes it clear that a noun phrase is to come next, but the addressee actually utters it. Here is one many spontaneous examples recorded by Wilkes-Gibbs (unpublished):

A: That tree has, uh, uh ...
B: Tentworms.

A: Yeah.

B: Yeah.

A initiated the referential process by halting at a place where he needed a noun phrase and uttering two *uh*'s. B helped out by offering a proxy, or stand-in, noun phrase she thought appropriate. A confirmed the proxy with *Yeah*, and then B responded to A's full assertion. B took part in the process from the very beginning.

As all eight examples make plain, a conversational model of the referential process must be quite different from the literary model. First, many noun phrases are distinctly nonliterary in form or nonstandard in intonation. These include trial, episodic, installment, dummy, and proxy noun phrases. Second, the process takes a very different course in conversation than in literature. In all eight examples, speakers went beyond the issuing of standard noun phrases; in three examples they deliberately drew the addressees into the process; and in three they began by knowingly issuing a questionable or inadequate noun phrase. What characterizes these examples is that the speaker and addressee put in extra effort, generally together, to make sure the reference has been understood. To understand the process of referring, we need to know how this works.

1.2 Establishing Understanding

Suppose A, a man, is speaking to B, a woman, and refers to a dog. In making the reference, according to most theories, A intends the identity of the dog to become part of A's and B's mutual knowledge or beliefs (see Clark and Marshall 1981). Establishing such mutual knowledge or belief is a stringent requirement. To meet it, A must convince himself that the identity of the dog is truly going to become part of their common ground. If at any moment in making the reference he thinks it won't, he should change or expand on what he has done so far. The same requirement applies to B, since she is trying to understand A's reference. To meet it, she should find ways of letting A know, as she listens, whether or not she is understanding him. Indeed, A should suppose that she is cooperating in precisely this way.

For each reference, then, A and B should have procedures for establishing the mutual belief, at some level of confidence, that B has identified A's reference. We have already seen evidence in our examples that they do. These procedures, we will argue, are inherently collaborative.

The evidence is clearest when B believes she may *not* have identified A's referent and attempts to repair the problem, as in our earlier example:

B: Til- oh yih mean like a week f'm tomorrow.

A: Yah.

These turns constitute a *side sequence*, a block of exchanges embedded within or between anticipated contributions to the conversation (Jefferson 1972; Schegloff 1972). So although the side sequence was initiated by B, it was completed by A before the conversation was allowed to proceed. That was needed for them to *mutually* believe that B has now understood A's reference correctly.

More often, A and B have to establish that B *has* understood the reference, and for this, B can use a simple expedient: allowing the next contribution to continue. Suppose the conversation had continued this way:

B: How long y'gonna be here?

A: Uh- not too long. Uh just til uh Monday.

B: Oh that's too bad.

By asserting *Oh that's too bad*, B would be passing up the opportunity to correct a possible misunderstanding and would thereby be implicating that she understood A's reference. "Regularly, then," as Sacks, Schegloff, and Jefferson (1974, 728) put it, "a turn's talk will display its speaker's understanding of a prior turn's talk, and whatever other talk it marks itself as directed to" (see also Goffman 1976). Note that going on wouldn't necessarily mean B had truly understood. She might not recognize her misunderstanding, or she might want to claim she had understood when she hadn't. But in either case, going on is a signal that B believes she has understood. In the first case she is making a mistake; in the second she is using the signal to deceive.

The same mutual belief can be established more directly by what Schegloff (1981) has called *continuers*, as in his example from a radio call-in show (p. 80):

A: Now, I wanna ask you something, I wrote a letter. (pause)

B: Mh hm,

A: T'the governor

B: Mh hm::,

A: -telling 'im what I thought about i(hh)m!

B: (Sh:::!)

A: Will I get an answer d'you think.

B: Yes.

By inserting the continuers *mh hm* and *sh:::* while A's turn was still underway, according to Schegloff, B was showing, first, that she was paying attention and realized that A was in the middle of an extended unit of talk. At the same time, she was explicitly signaling that she was passing up the opportunity to initiate a repair on the turn so far and, by implication, that she understood the turn so far. With the second *Mh hm::*, for example, she was claiming to understand the phrase *t'the governor* and, therefore, the definite reference it contained. The same holds for the other definite references.

B may even be intended to interrupt A as soon as she believes she has identified the referent, as in this example (from Sacks, quoted in Jefferson 1973, 59):

> A: I heard you were at the beach yesterday. What's her name, oh you know, the tall redhead that lives across the street from Larry? The one who drove him to work the day his car // was-
>
> B: Oh *Gina!*
>
> A: Yeah Gina. She said she saw you at the beach yesterday.

A indicated he would go on until B identified the referent. Indeed, he stopped at B's interruption and completed the process by confirming B's identification with *Yeah Gina*.

Taken together, this evidence suggests that A and B accept mutual responsibility for each definite reference. Roughly speaking, they try to establish the mutual belief that B has understood A's reference before they go on. So far we have only informal examples of how they do this. The challenge is to characterize the system and the logic behind it.

1.3 Mutual Acceptance

The idea behind the view of reference we are taking is this: A and B must *mutually accept* that B has understood A's references before they let the conversation go on. Conversations proceed in an orderly way only if the common ground of the participants accumulates in an orderly way (see Clark 1985; Clark and Carlson 1981; Gazdar 1979; Stalnaker 1978). A and B must therefore establish the mutual belief that B has understood, or appears to have understood, A's current utterance before they go on to the next contribution to the conversation. They establish that belief, we argue, through an acceptance process.

The two basic elements in this process are (1) a presentation and (2) an acceptance. Suppose A wants to refer to a mutually identifiable dog. To do so, he *presents*, as we will put it, the standard noun phrase *the dog that just barked*. With this presentation A presupposes a number of things. First, he believes B is now paying attention, is able to hear and identify the words, and understands English. Second, he believes B can view the referent as fitting the description "dog that just barked." That is, he believes that referent r can be viewed under description d. And third, he believes B will be able to pick out r uniquely with this description d along with the rest of their common ground.

Once A has made this presentation, B must accept it, and A and B must mutually recognize that acceptance. We propose that B has two main methods of accepting it. First, she can *presuppose acceptance*, as illustrated earlier, by continuing on to the next contribution or by allowing A to continue. Letting the next contribution begin is mutually recognized as an acceptance of the last presentation. Second, she can *assert acceptance*, as with continuers, *yes, right, I see*, and head nods. These, too, are mutually recognized as acceptances of the last contribution.

But B may have reasons for *not* accepting A's presentation. She may not have heard it fully; if so, she might respond, *What?* or *The dog that just what?* She may not accept *d* as a description of *r*; then she might respond, *That's a toy not a dog*. Or she may not accept that *d* is sufficient with their common ground to pick out *r* uniquely; then she might respond, *Which one?* When B doesn't accept the presentation, A must deal with B's implicit or explicit questions until B does accept it. That may take several exchanges.

As our examples show, however, A's presentation can take more complicated forms. It can be a trial or installment noun phrase, which B can accept only by assertion. It can be a dummy noun phrase, which B isn't intended to accept until amended. It can be a self-corrected or expanded noun phrase, which B is to accept only as amended. It can even be a proxy noun phrase made by B, which A is then intended to accept.

These informal examples, though suggestive, still do not specify precisely how the acceptance process works. For that we need more systematic evidence.

2 References in an Experimental Task

In search of such evidence we turned to a communication task originally devised by Krauss and Glucksberg (Krauss and Weinheimer 1964, 1966, 1967; Krauss and Glucksberg 1969, 1977; Glucksberg, Krauss, and Higgins 1975; see also Asher 1979). In our version two students were seated at tables separated by an opaque screen. In front of each student were 12 cards, each showing one of the so-called Tangram figures in figure 23.1. For the person we will call the *director*, the cards were already arranged in a target sequence of two rows of six, and for the person we will call the *matcher*, the same figures lay in an identical matrix but in a random sequence. (For ease of exposition, we will talk as if the director were male and the matcher female, even though both sexes took both roles in our task.) The director's job was to get the matcher quickly and accurately to rearrange her figures to match the target ordering. They could talk back and forth as much as they needed, but the director was to go through the positions in the array sequentially (numbered 1 to 6 on the top row and 7 to 12 on the bottom). After they had matched their arrangements, the

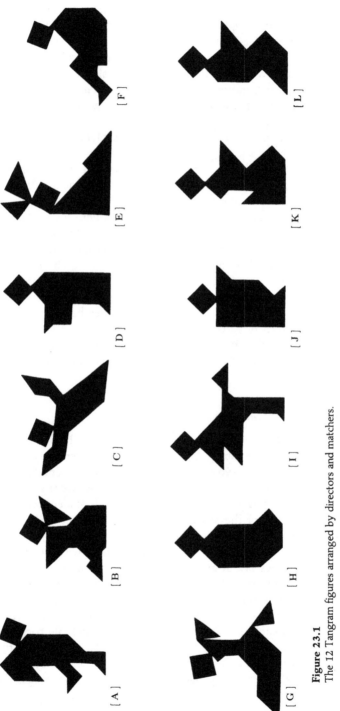

Figure 23.1
The 12 Tangram figures arranged by directors and matchers.

director's and matcher's figures were placed in two new random orders, the director's new sequence became the new target, and the procedure was repeated. They carried out the task six times, for six trials.

The collaborative view of reference makes several global predictions about this task. First, it should take the two partners many words to reach acceptance the first time they encounter a figure since they will often need nonstandard techniques such as episodic, installment, or expanded noun phrases. Later references to the same figure should be shorter since they can appeal to prior acceptance of a related description and succeed more often with standard noun phrases, which are typically shorter. This reasoning would account in part for Krauss and Weinheimer's (1964) original finding that, as people referred repeatedly to the same figure, they tended to shorten their noun phrases, although only if their listeners could speak in return. The collaborative view also predicts that, since the later references are more likely to be standard noun phrases, they should require fewer turns. For this prediction there is no evidence. We will defer more detailed predictions about the acceptance process itself.

2.1 Method

Eight pairs of partners each arranged 12 figures on each of six trials. The 12 figures, each formed from different arrangements of seven elementary shapes, were selected from a book with 4000 such figures collected by Elffers (1976) from the ancient Chinese game of Tangram. These 12 were chosen because their varying abstraction and similarity seemed to provide a good range of difficulty. Two copies of each figure were cut out of black construction paper and pasted individually on white 15 cm by 20 cm cards. The identifying letters in figure 23.1 did not appear on the stimuli.

The two students in each session drew lots for director and matcher roles. They were told they had identical figures and would play the game six times while timed and tape-recorded. A timer was started on each trial when both students were ready, and stopped when they were satisfied they had finished. After each trial the two orderings were checked and the students were told of the positions of any mismatches. The error rate was only 2%. The six trials took about 25 minutes. The students, seven men and nine women, were Stanford University undergraduates fulfilling a course requirement.

One of us transcribed the conversations, including changes of speaker, back-channel responses, parenthetical remarks, interruptions, hesitations, false starts, and basic intonational features; the other checked the transcripts, especially for intonation. The transcripts contained 9792 words, reflecting the positioning of 576 figures (12 figures on six trials by eight pairs of students).

2.2 General Patterns

For a broad picture of what occurred, consider this very simple series of utterances by one director for figure I on trials 1 through 6:

1. All right, the next one looks like a person who's ice skating, except they're stricking two arms out in front.
2. Um, the next one's the person ice skating that has two arms?
3. The fourth one is the person ice skating, with two arms.
4. The next one's the ice skater.
5. The fourth one's the ice skater.
6. The ice skater.

As this series illustrates, directors generally referred to the location (e.g., *the fourth one*) and then asserted something about the Tangram figure to be placed in that location. On trial 1 directors always *described* the figure, generally with an indefinite reference (e.g., *a person who's* ...). On trials 2 through 6, in contrast, they *referred* to the figure with a definite description (e.g., *the ice skater*). Directors tended to use nonstandard noun phrases in the early trials (e.g., this director's trial and episodic noun phrases in trials 2 and 3) and standard noun phrases later (e.g., *the ice skater*).

Partly because of these features, this director took many more words to secure acceptance of his presentation on trial 1 than on trial 6. As predicted, this pattern held in general. Figure 23.2 shows that directors used an average of 41 words per figure in trial 1 but only 8 words per figure in trial

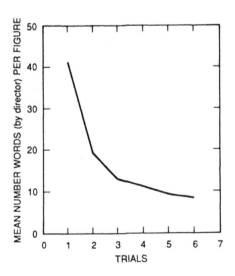

Figure 23.2
Average number of speaking turns per figure taken by directors on each trial.

6. This decline is highly significant, $F(1,35) = 44.31$, $p < .001$. The decline was steepest from trial 1 to trial 2 and had almost disappeared by trial 6.

The example we have cited, however, is atypical in that the director took only one turn on each trial for this figure; it is also incomplete in that we have omitted the matcher's single turns. More often, the two partners took many turns for a single placement, and as predicted, the number of turns they needed declined from trial 1 to trial 6. Figure 23.3 shows that the director averaged 3.7 turns per figure on trial 1 but only about one per figure by trial 6. This trend was also highly significant, $F(1,35) = 79.59$, $p < .001$. So figure 23.2 includes the director's words not just from his first turn on each figure but from *all* of his turns on that figure.

The director and matcher became more efficient not only from one trial to the next but also from the beginning to the end of each trial. Figure 23.4 plots the number of words per figure over the 12 spatial positions in the arrangements for trials 1, 2, and 6. Since the figures were randomly assigned to the positions on each trial, there is some confounding of figures with positions, but the pattern is still clear. On trial 1, there was a steep decline in word count (4.6 words per position) as the two partners worked from position 1 to position 12 ($F(1,77) = 40.01$, $p < .001$). On trials 2 and 6, there were successively smaller declines (1.0 and .4 words per position), both also significant ($F(1,77) = 5.83$, 7.16, $p < .05$). Number of turns per figure shows a similar pattern.

The general decline in number of words used from position 1 to position 12 is predicted by the collaborative view but also by others. By any

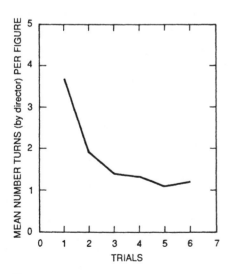

Figure 23.3
Average number of speaking turns per figure taken by directors on each trial.

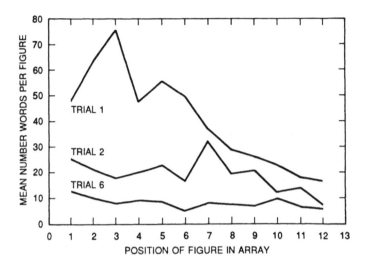

Figure 23.4
Average number of words per figure used by directors on trials 1, 2, and 6 plotted by position of the figure in the array.

reasonable theory of information or reference (for example Olson 1970), the fewer figures there are in the array, the less information it should take to distinguish the target from the remainder. In the limit, the figure in position 12 needs only a minimal description since it is the only one left—for example, *Number 12 is the last one.* Indeed, sometimes it wasn't even mentioned. The number of turns should decrease by the same reasoning, as it did.

The decline from position 1 to position 12, however, got smaller from trial 1 to trial 6, and that is predicted by the collaborative view but not by general theories of information. By the collaborative view, as we will justify later, the two partners come to rely on descriptions mutually accepted on previous trials, forming shorter noun phrases accepted in fewer turns until they arrive at optimal descriptions. This is nicely illustrated in the example cited. But as the descriptions become optimal, they should be less influenced by the physical context. The decline from position 1 to position 12 should be largest on trial 1, when reaching acceptance takes many words, and smallest on trial 6, by which time the two partners have perferred descriptions. This is precisely what occurred. The difference in slopes between trials 1, 2, and 6 was significant ($F(2,284) = 15.49$, $p < .001$). By information theory, in contrast, going from one position to the next should reduce the array size as much on trial 6 as on trial 1; hence, the slopes should remain the same. This prediction is disconfirmed.

Finally, the 12 figures also varied in difficulty, $F(11,77) = 5.94$, $p <$ 0.001. Figure B, the most difficult one, averaged 26.5 words per trial, eliciting 39.6 words on trial 1. Figure C, the easiest, averaged only 9.7 words per trial, with 24 words on trial 1.

Having sketched the global performance in this task, we now turn to details of the referential process itself.

3 Collaborating on References

Our primary goal here is a process model of how speakers and addressees collaborate in the making of a definite reference. The collaborative model, as we will call it, must do more than list the devices used—trial noun phrases, interruptions, continuers, and the like. It must spell out how the process of mutual acceptance gets initiated, carried through, and completed. The process usually begins with the speaker issuing a noun phrase. But these noun phrases come in many types, as already noted, and do no more than initiate the process. The model must show how these noun phrases are organized as a system and how they enter in a uniform way into the referential process as a whole. We must resist the temptation, engendered by the literary model of reference, to treat standard noun phrases as genuine and all others as aberrations, for that doesn't explain the role of any of the noun phrases in the process.

Definite references to the Tangram figures, as noted earlier, occurred only on trials 2 through 6. In the simplest pattern, the director would refer to a position (for example, *Number 4*) and assert which figure appeared there (*is the guy leaning against the tree*), and the matcher would signal she had placed it with *okay, all right, got it*, or *right*, as in this exchange:

A: Number 4's the guy leaning against the tree.

B: Okay.

Sometimes the matcher responded with two moves, as in *Okay, I've got it,* or with a brief confirmation of the description plus an okay, as in *Dancer, okay.* The director would then go to the next position. These all constitute what we will call the *basic exchange*.

Our main interest is in the director's use of the noun phrase for the figure as a whole, here the *the guy leaning against the tree*. By the collaborative view, he presents it as a means for the matcher to identify the intended figure, and she is expected to accept it. In the basic exchange, indeed, the matcher uses her *okay* to assert (1) that she believes she has identified the figure correctly, and (2) that she has placed the figure in the right location. In doing so, she presupposes (3) that she accepts the director's presentation, including his perspective on the referent. Sometimes the matcher handled these components separately. One matcher signaled her identification (1) and acceptance (3) but signaled trouble with (2), finding and placing the figure: *Okay, um. Wait, just a sec, just a sec. I can't find it again. God ... Okay, okay.* So in the basic exchange, the acceptance process is canonical: the director presents a noun phrase, and the matcher presupposes her acceptance.

The basic exchange should only be possible when the matcher can accept the director's initial presentation without refashioning it. If so, basic exchanges should have occurred seldom on early trials, but often on later trials, where they could be based on prior mutually accepted descriptions. The percentages of basic exchanges on trials 1 through 6 were 18, 55, 75, 80, 88, and 84. This trend is highly significant, $F(1,55) = 84.19$, $p < .001$. Since the basic exchange requires fewer words and turns than most other exchanges, this accounts for much of the decrease in word count and turns in figure 23.2 and 23.3.

Within the structure of the basic exchange, we can now examine the three processes by which the two partners reached mutual acceptance of each reference—initiating, refashioning, and evaluating presentations.

3.1 Initiating a Reference

Suppose the director has just uttered *Number 4 is ...*, intending the next noun phrase to pick out a particular figure. It is at this moment that the referential process gets initiated. We will call the first full noun phrase uttered at the point the *initial* presentation. These noun phrases fall into at least six distinct types.

1. *Elementary noun phrase.* The director utters this type of noun phrase in a single tone group, such as *the guy leaning against the tree*. Presumably, he believes the matcher can accept it canonically. This is the type of noun phrase that usually occurred in basic exchanges.

2. *Episodic noun phrase.* The director utters this type of noun phrase in two or more easily distinguished episodes or tone groups, as in *Number 7's the goofy guy that's falling over, with his leg kicked up*. The first episode ends with *over* and is immediately followed with more of the same noun phrase in a second episode.

3. *Installment noun phrase.* The director utters this type of noun phrase in episodes too, but gets explicit acceptance of each installment before going on, as in this exchange:

A: And the next one is the one with the triangle to the right ...
B: Okay.
A: With the square connected to it.

The director doesn't end the first installment with a try marker but does indicate by his intonation that he intends to go on. His pause is effective in getting the matcher to respond.

4. *Provisional noun phrase*. Often, the director presents a noun phrase he comes to realize is inadequate—a provisional noun phrase—and immediately expands on it without prompting, as in *And the next one is also the one that doesn't look like anything. It's kind of like the tree?* Note that the expansion is *not* part of the initial noun phrase, but comes in a new clause.

5. *Dummy noun phrase*. A speaker usually utters this type of noun phrase, such as *the whatchamacallit*, as a stand-in until he or his partner can produce a more complete noun phrase. We found no dummy noun phrases in our transcripts, though, as we noted, they are found elsewhere.

6. *Proxy noun phrase*. If the director pauses long enough, and if the matcher has some confidence she knows what he is about to say, she can present all or the final part of a noun phrase by proxy, as here:

A: And number 12 is, uh, ...

B: Chair.

A: With the chair, right.

B: Got it.

In some cases, speakers actively solicits proxy noun phrases with *what's the word?* or *you know,* or by the way they pause or gesture. We found only five clear initial proxy noun phrases in our transcripts, although elsewhere we have documented their existence in great detail (Wilkes-Gibbs, unpublished).

Any of these six types of noun phrases can end with a try marker, as in *Um, the next one's the person ice skating that has two arms?* With it, one partner asks the other for an explicit verdict on the noun phrase, or installment, before they go on. Note that try markers don't turn assertions into questions; this utterance doesn't mean "Is the next one the person ice skating that has two arms?" The noun phrase is the only element within the scope of the try marker. With it the speaker queries whether the noun phrase is acceptable as it stands.

Try markers should be used for noun phrases the director is less certain will be accepted. In our task, as it happened, it was impossible to distinguish try markers on initial noun phrases, which almost always came at the ends of utterances, from rising intonation for the utterances as wholes. Our directors often used rising intonation to mark utterances as members of a list, with the final member getting a falling intonation. Indeed, as the directors went from trial 2 through trial 6, they used the list intonation to end steadily more of the utterances containing their initial noun phrases, from 41% through 78%.

Each type of noun phrase is generally marked by the speaker for its *status*, which reflects the speaker's confidence in the noun phrase being produced. Episodic, installment, and provisional noun phrases almost always had distinctive intonation patterns in our data; dummy noun phrases

Table 23.1
Rules of projection for next move.

| Type of noun phrase | Projected next more | |
	Unmarked	With try marker
Elementary	Implicated acceptance	Explicit verdict
Episodic	Implicated acceptance	Explicit verdict
Installment	Explicit acceptance	Explicit verdict
Provisional	Self-expansion	Self-expansion
Dummy	Self-expansion	Proxy
Proxy	Explicit acceptance	Explicit verdict

have distinctive lexical content, as with *what's-her-name*; and proxy noun phrases are identifiable by the change in speakers and often by the first speaker's hesitation as well. Each of these noun phrases can be modified by a try marker, by which the speaker implies there is some possibility of a negative verdict. Truly elementary noun phrases are identifiable by their lack of special features.

These status markings, we propose, are used by speakers to project the next move in the acceptance process. For an analogy, consider questions and answers as a type of adjacency pair (Schegloff and Sacks 1973). When A asks B a question, it is "expectable" that B answer it in the next utterance. B's next utterance, of course, need not be an answer, but it is interpreted by its relation to what is expected. The answer is the preferred response. Likewise, an installment of a noun phrase by A projects an explicit acceptance by B; with an added try marker, it projects an explicit verdict: accept or not accept. These projections, however, are unlike true adjacency pairs, in which the first and second parts are always produced by different speakers. A provisional noun phrase by A projects an expansion by A and *not* by B. The moves that we propose are projected by each noun phrase are shown in table 23.1. They are consistent with our data, though they need more support. If confirmed in further work, they become excellent evidence that the two partners tacitly recognize they are engaged in an acceptance process.

In selecting a noun phrase, the director presumably aims at several ideals. He prefers uttering the initial noun phrase himself. He prefers it to be elementary—not an episodic or installment noun phrase; to be adequate, free of errors, and uttered fluently—not in need of refashioning; and to be no more prolix than necessary (Grice 1975). Elementary noun phrases should therefore be the most preferred, and proxy noun phrases the least. Our data are consistent with this ordering though hardly definitive. Table 23.2 lists the percentages of initial references on trials 2 through 6 that belonged to each category; the descriptions listed are those utterances in which a figure was described rather than identified, for example, *Okay, number 7 is*

Table 23.2
Percentages of six types of initial noun phrases for trials 2 through 6.

Type of noun phrase	Trial				
	2	3	4	5	6
Elementary	52	68	69	80	72
Episodic	11	10	8	6	5
Installment	0	0	0	0	1
Provisional	17	14	8	2	6
Dummy	0	0	0	0	0
Proxy	0	1	2	1	1
Description	17	7	12	9	14
Unclassified	3	0	1	2	1

$N = 96$ per column.

like she's dancing. The head is tilted. As the table shows, there were too few installment, dummy, and proxy noun phrases to test. But, as predicted, episodic and provisional noun phrases, which were used only when necessary, declined and by trial 6 had mostly disappeared (linear trend, $F(1,28) = 9.02$, $p < .01$) What remained were the preferred elementary noun phrases, which increased significantly over trials, $F(1,28) = 17.02$, $p < .01$.

3.2 Refashioning a Noun Phrase

An initial noun phrase that isn't acceptable must be refashioned. This is accomplished in three main ways.

1. *Repair.* In planning and uttering each noun phrase, speakers monitor what they are doing and, on detecting a problem, set about repairing it (Laver 1973; Levelt 1983; Schegloff, Jefferson, and Sacks 1977). These self-repairs were legion in our transcripts, as in *Um, next one is the guy, the person with his head to the right but his legs are, his one leg is kicked up to the left.* There were also many of what Levelt (1983) has called *covert* repairs, as in *Okay, number, uh, 4 is the, is the kind of fat one with the legs to the left—er, I mean, to the right.* In repeating *is the,* the director might well have been repairing something he was about to say even if we have no way of determining what. The numbers of self-repairs on trials 1 through 6 were 85, 30, 20, 8, 7, and 6; the instances of repeated words were 47, 14, 10, 4, 7, and 1. These declines contribute to the decrease in word count in figure 23.2.

Repairs could also be initiated by the addressee, but all of these in our data could be classified in one of the next two categories.

2. *Expansion.* Once the director has completed a noun phrase, he or the matcher may judge it to be inadequate for the purposes at hand and in need of a phrase, clause, or sentence of expansion. If the initial noun phrase is provisional, the director will expand on it without prompting, as in these two examples:

Okay, number 1 is the just kind of block-like figure with the jagged right-hand side. *The left side looks like a square.*

Okay, number 6 is the guy, uh, sitting down with his legs to the left, *and he's kind of leaning his head over.*

Note that the clauses in italics are *not* part of the initial noun phrases, but expansions added to improve on them. If we call the description in the initial noun phrase x and that in its expansion y, then what the director and matcher end up mutually accepting is the compound description $x + y$.

Self-expansions like these should be needed less often the more clearly the director can formulate his initial noun phrases, and they were. The percentages of figure placements with self-expansions, under a strict criterion, were 25, 17, 11, 6, and 10 on trials 2 through 6. This decline also helps account for the decrease in word count in figure 23.2.

When the matcher didn't find the director's initial noun phrase x clear enough, she could signal the need for an expansion y, as in this example:

A: Okay, the next one is the rabbit.

B: Uh—

A: That's asleep, you know, it looks like it's got ears and a head pointing down?

B: Okay.

In the side sequence here, the matcher used *Uh*—with an extended, level intonation to signal that she needed more description, and the director complied. Requests for expansion like this took many forms, often occurring more than once on a single figure. Many times the matcher signaled uncertainty with a tentatively voiced *um*, *uh huh*, or *yes?* as if saying, "I'm still uncertain, so please expand on your noun phrase." Other times she displayed silence where a reply could have been expected—such as at a pause after a completed utterance. Still other times she repeated the main part of the director's description with a rising intonation, as in this example:

A: Uh, person putting a shoe on.

B: Putting a shoe on?

A: Uh huh. Facing left. Looks like he's sitting down.

B: Okay.

Prompts of this latter type occurred on 15, 3, 3, 2, 1, and 1% of the figure placements on trials 1 through 6.

Overall, matchers should have had less need to request expansions if they had previously found a mutually acceptable description for a figure. On trial 1, 36% of the figure placements included at least one request for expansion (counting prompts as a subtype); on trials 2 through 6, the percentages decreased to 12, 8, 3, 1, and 3. So requests for expansions also contribute to the decrease in word count and turns in figures 23.2 and 23.3.

The matcher herself often expanded on the director's noun phrase, almost always in the form of a request for confirmation, as in this example:

> A: Um, third one is the guy reading with, holding his book to the left.
>
> B: Okay, kind of standing up?
>
> A: Yeah.
>
> B: Okay.

The matcher initiated a side sequence by accepting what the director had said so far (x) with *Okay*—a *postponement*, as we will call it—but by asking him to confirm her expansion y. Once he accepted it, the side sequence was complete, and with her next *Okay*, the matcher presupposed acceptance of the amended noun phrase $x + y$. Requests for confirmation, like the other forms of expansion, also declined over trials, occurring in 37, 12, 8, 6, 1, and 2% of the figure placements on trials through 6.

Logically, at least some episodic noun phrases might be considered initiating noun phrases plus self-expansions. In this view the director presents an elementary noun phrase *the goofy guy that's falling over*, immediately judges it inadequate, and then adds the restrictive phrase *with his leg kicked up* in a new tone group, all before allowing the matcher to respond. So he adds an expansion just as he does to a provisional noun phrase, but here the expansion is still part of the initial noun phrase and not a new clause. Consistent with this view, the number of episodic noun phrases declined over trials—11, 10, 8, 6, and 5 in trials 2 through 6 (table 23.2)—just as other forms of expansion did.

3. *Replacement.* Once the director had finished his noun phrase, the matcher could reject it and present a noun phrase of her own, which we will call a *replacement*. The following is one example:

> A: Okay, and the next one is the person that looks like they're carrying something and it's sticking out to the left. It looks like a hat that's upside down.
>
> B: The guy that's pointing to the left again?
>
> A: Yeah, pointing to the left, that's it! (laughs)
>
> B: Okay.

Since the director's noun phrase x was still unacceptable, the matcher presented a description z from an alternative perspective, which the director then accepted. Indeed, the director took up her replacement on the next trial when he said, *And the next one's the guy pointing to the left*. Replacements are different from expansions. In presenting z, the matcher was rejecting x

and replacing it with z, expressing a different description and not merely an additional one. What the two of them accepted in the end wasn't $x + z$, but simply z.

Most replacements in our transcripts included try markers, as in this example. With the demands of the task, it was rare for a matcher to have a strong enough hypothesis to make a replacement. Also, then, replacements by the matcher shouldn't be that prevalent. They occurred on only, 10, 5, 0, 2, 2, and 0% of the figure placements in trials 1 through 6.

3.3 Passing Judgment on Presentations

A presentation, expansion, or replacement that is put forward needs to be judged acceptable or unacceptable. That can be accomplished by three methods.

1. *Acceptance.* Once one person has presented a noun phrase, the partner can *presuppose acceptance* by continuing on to the next contribution, as when the matcher completes the basic exchange with *Okay.* Or the partner can *assert acceptance*, as in the last example, when the director replied *Yeah* to the matcher's trial replacement. Both types occurred in our transcripts.

2. *Rejection.* A partner can reject a noun phrase either directly or by implication. The clearest rejections are asserted, as in *Oh, the ice skater?* followed by *Y—er, no.* Implicated rejections can also be clear, as when the matcher made the replacement *The guy that's pointing to the left again?* Face to face, a partner can offer other signals, like quizzical looks, which should also be effective.

3. *Postponement.* The partner can also signal that she accepts the presentation so far but is postponing final judgment until it is expanded, as with a tentatively voiced *Okay.*

The matcher can also render verdicts by interrupting the director, but then she is generally signaling more than mere acceptance or rejection. Here is one example:

A: Okay, our kneeling person with the hook on the—
B: ⌈Okay.
A: ⌊—left side.

Although the matcher may simply have suffered from mistiming, she was more likely signaling that she didn't need such an extensive description or any further qualifications (see Jefferson 1973, 59).

3.4 The Acceptance Process

As these results demonstrate, the acceptance process is played out in conversation, as in other human affairs, as a series of steps. It takes at least two such steps—a presentation and its acceptance—but it may take more.

Table 23.3
Mutual acceptance as a recursive process.

Initiating a reference	
To initiate a reference,	present x_1 or
	invite x_1
If an x_1 is invited,	present x_1
Refashioning a noun phrase	
If x_i is inadequate,	present revision x_i' or
	expansion y_i or
	replacement z_i or
	request x_i', y_i, or z_i
If an x_i', y_i, or z_i is requested,	present x_i', y_i, or z_i
If x_i', y_i, or z_i is presented,	let $x_{i+1} = x_i'$, $x_i + y_i$, or z_i
Concluding a reference	
If x_i is adequate,	accept x_i
If x_i is adequate and accepted,	conclude mutual acceptance

With the devices summarized in table 23.3, the possibilities are, indeed, unlimited.

The basic process, which might be called the *acceptance cycle*, consists of a presentation plus its verdict. Let x, y, and z stand for noun phrases or their emendations. A present x and then B evaluates it. If the verdict is not positive, then A or B must refashion that presentation. That person can offer a repair x', an expansion y, or a replacement z. The refashioned presentation, whether x', $x + y$, or z, is evaluated, and so on. Acceptance cycles apply iteratively, with one repair, expansion, or replacement after another, until a noun phrase is mutually accepted. With that, A and B take the process to be complete.

A positive verdict from B alone, however, may not bring the process immediately to completion, since A may not be satisfied that B has understood A's reference. This leads to what we will call *follow-ups*, turns initiated immediately after one partner has accepted the noun phrase, as here:

A: The first one's the one I said looked like a rabbit last time.

B: Okay.

A: You've got that one, right?

B: Yeah.

Sometimes follows-ups seemed to have been initiated because the director couldn't tell whether the matcher's *Okay* meant "I understand you so far" or "I have identified the figure and have placed it in my array." Other times they came on the heels of an error or confusion in the previous trial; the director had good reason for seeking reassurance. Still other times they were initiated because the director didn't seem satisfied with his description, even though the matcher had accepted it, as here:

> A: Okay, the next one looks, is the one with the person standing on one leg with the tail.
>
> B: Okay.
>
> A: Looks like an ice skater.
>
> B: Yeah, okay.

On all later trials, this director referred to the figure as an ice skater.

Follow-up sequences may be a good indicator of the director's confidence in the accuracy of their mutual beliefs about the referent. As this would suggest, the number of follow-ups decreased with successive acceptances for each figure. The percentages of figure placements with follow-ups on trials 1 through 6 were 35, 12, 6, 6, 1, and 5.

A mutual acceptance, once reached, can also later be reconsidered. Recall that the goal of the acceptance process is to establish the mutual belief that the listener has understood what the speaker meant. Once a mutual acceptance has been arrived at, many things can shake those beliefs. The mutual acceptance might have been premature or mistaken, and all it takes to revoke it is some reason for thinking it was in error. Mutual acceptances were reconsidered in several cases in our task.

3.5 Minimizing Collaborative Effort

In classical theories of least effort (for instance, Brown 1958; Brown and Lenneberg 1954; Krauss and Glucksberg 1977; Olson 1970; Zipf 1935), speakers try to utter the shortest noun phrases that will enable their addressees to pick out the referent in context. These theories tacitly assume that speakers work alone, again a literary model of reference with all its problems for conversation. Still there seems to be minimization of effort in conversation. Our proposal is that speakers and addressees try to minimize collaborative effort, the work both speakers and addressees do from the initiation of the referential process to its completion. The principle of least collaborative effort, as we will call it, is needed to account for many features of the acceptance process.

In the collaborative model there is a trade-off in effort between initiating the noun phrase and refashioning it. The more effort a speaker puts into the initial noun phrase, in general, the less refashioning it is likely to need. Why don't speakers always put in enough effort to avoid refashioning? There are three main reasons.

1. *Time pressure.* Speakers may realize they cannot design the ideal noun phrase in the time allowed. So (1) they may be forced to invite or accept a proxy noun phrase rather than have addressees wait for them to plan their own. Or (2) they may have to use a dummy or provisional noun phrase to

give themselves time to plan a better description, which they offer in an immediate expansion. Or (3) they may utter a noun phrase and, finding it inadequate so far, amend it in a second episode.

2. *Complexity.* Speakers may realize that the noun phrase they are designing is too complex to be easily understood, so they present it in installments.

3. *Ignorance.* Speakers may realize that they don't know enough to decide what addressees would accept anyway, so they are forced into trial and error. They try out a description and leave it to the addressees to refashion if it isn't acceptable. This is one origin of try markers.

The six types of initial noun phrases, each modifiable by a try marker, are therefore devices that enable speakers to deal with these three constraints and yet minimize collaborative effort.

The devices used in refashioning are also designed to minimize collaborative effort. Take repair. As Schegloff, Jefferson, and Sacks (1977) noted, repairs are subject to two strong preferences: speakers prefer to repair their own utterances rather than let interlocutors do it; and speakers prefer to initiate their own repairs rather than let interlocutors prompt them to do it. These preferences have several consequences. One is that speakers repair their own utterances as soon as they detect problems (Levelt 1983). This way they minimize the time a potential misunderstanding is on the floor. Speakers also avert potential exchanges as the interlocutor tries to correct the misunderstanding. That minimizes the number of exchanges needed before mutual acceptance. Together, the two preferences help minimize collaborative effort.

Or take expansion and replacement. As with repairs, speakers prefer to make their own expansions unprompted, as in provisional noun phrases and continuations of episodic noun phrases. As for the addressees, they could in principle respond to every noun phrase they didn't understand with *What?*, but that wouldn't be very informative. For collaborative efficiency they try to pinpoint their problem. When possible, they prompt specific expansions (for instance, *Putting a shoe on?*), offer their own expansions (*Kind of standing up?*), or offer replacements (*The guy that's pointing to the left again?*). They also answer speakers' queries. So addressees minimize collaborative effort by indicating quickly and informatively what is needed for mutual acceptance.

The canonical reference is also predicted by least collaborative effort. In it speakers present an elementary noun phrase and addressees presuppose their acceptance. That is, it consists of a minimal noun phrase (not complex enough to warrant installments) and no extra exchanges. So the canonical reference is preferred because it minimizes effort by both parties.

The principles of least effort and of least collaborative effort, therefore, make very different predictions. Least effort predicts that every reference is made with (1) a standard (literary) noun phrase that (2) is as short as possible and yet (3) specifies the referent uniquely in that context. Least collaborative effort predicts that references can be made with (1) nonstandard, nonliterary noun phrases, (2) with ones the speaker believes are *not* adequate in context, and (3) with devices that draw addressees into the process. In particular, it predicts trade-offs between effort in initial noun phrases and effort in refashioning. It predicts preferences for self-repair and self-initiated repair. It predicts expansions and replacements, and informative requests for expansion. And it predicts a preference for canonical references. On all these counts the evidence favors least collaborative effort.

4 Speaking Generally

Participants in conversation, we have demonstrated, work together even in such a basic process as the making of a definite reference. Our proposal, more generally, is that they take for granted this principle:

Principle of mutual responsibility
The participants in a conversation try to establish, roughly by the initiation of each new contribution, the mutual belief that the listeners have understood what the speaker meant in the last utterance to a criterion sufficient for current purposes.

With definite reference their attempts take the form of an acceptance process. The speaker initiates the process by presenting one of at least five types of noun phrases or by inviting a sixth. Both speaker and addressees may repair, expand on, or replace this noun phrase in iterative fashion until they arrive at a version they mutually accept. In this process they try to minimize collaborative effort, presenting and refashioning these noun phrases as efficiently as possible. One result is that the preferred form of reference is the one in which the speaker presents an elementary noun phrase and the addresses presuppose their acceptance of it without taking an extra turn.

The principle of mutual responsibility, however, places two important caveats on this process. The mutual belief is to be established "roughly by the initiation of each new contribution" and "to a criterion sufficient for current purposes." Although our findings don't bear directly on these caveats, we think they are crucial.

4.1 The Criterion Problem

In our proposal the participants aren't trying to ensure perfect understanding of each utterance but only understanding "to a criterion sufficient for current purposes." What are these purposes, and how much is sufficient?

Some conversational purposes are broad and dictate a generally high or low criterion for understanding. Suppose A is telling B where he lives. If B's purpose is to be able to get to his house, she will set her criterion high. If it is merely to break the ice at a party, she will set it low. We have all endured, at a low criterion, people who have talked about each of six children and their families, none of whom we care a whit about. The speaker and addressee may even set discrepant criteria, as when a parent talks to a child. In our task the two partners presumably both set their criteria high, since they were trying to get each figure placed without error before going on. That is one reason they were so diligent in reaching acceptances, often explicit ones.

Even in situations of low or discrepant criteria, however, the ground rules of mutual responsibility are still in force. The participants mutually accept each contribution, at least tacitly, before going on to the next. Granted, they may often be play-acting their parts. Yet even in these conversations we should find coordinating signals such as back-channel responses and try markers (though perhaps distributed more unevenly), however insincere they may be. And speakers should feel they are being understood well enough even when they are not.

Many purposes in conversation, however, change moment by moment as the two people tolerate more or less uncertainty about the listener's understanding of the speaker's references. The heavier burden usually falls on the listener, since she is in the best position to assess her own comprehension. When the speaker utters *I just found the keys*, marking the noun phrase as an elementary (rather than a provisional or trial) presentation, the listener is under strong pressure to accept it. After all, the speaker marked it as elementary, so he must believe it to be adequate for current purposes. If she rejects it, she risks offending him by indicating that it wasn't adequate. She also risks revealing her own incompetence if indeed it should have been adequate. Finally, like the speaker, the listener wants to minimize collaborative effort—to avoid extra steps in the acceptance process—and that, too, puts pressure on her to accept. All this encourages her to tolerate a certain lack of understanding, even to feign understanding when it is not justified. She may do this trusting that the holes will be filled in later, or that they won't have serious consequences.

The listener must tolerate uncertainty anyway. Although the two parties might like to mutually accept each element second by second as they proceed. this ideal is impractical. Certain definite references, for example, cannot be understood until the speaker has completed his utterance. In *Although he doesn't know it yet, we are buying a new bicycle for Harry*, the referents for *he* and *it* cannot be identified until *Harry* has been uttered. It would be premature of the addressee to ask, *Who doesn't know what?* after the first clause. The natural place to ask such questions is immediately after the utterance is complete.

In this view the two partners assume a unit of conversation we have called the *contribution*. It consists, minimally, of the utterance of one sentence on the topic of conversation, where the sentence can be full or elliptical, or even a quasi-sentence like *Coffee, please*. But to become a contribution, the utterance has to be mutually accepted before the initiation of the next contribution, and that process may require repairs, expansions, and replacements of all or part of the initial presentation. Indeed, as Schegloff, Jefferson, and Sacks (1977) have shown, speakers are usually allowed to present utterances without being interrupted. The place their partners initiate most repairs and expansions and offer most replacements is immediately after the presentation and before the next contribution is initiated. It is for this reason that allowing a new contribution to proceed is tantamount to a mutual acceptance of the old one.

4.2 Modes of Language Use

Conversation, though fundamental, isn't the only site of language use. There are novels, newspapers, and letters—literary uses—as well as radio and television broadcasts, sermons, tape-recorded messages, large lectures, and many others. In these circumstances the participants may not have full access to one another and hence cannot adhere to the principle of mutual responsibility as it has evolved for conversation. The principle may get weakened or modified in various ways. Precisely how it is weakened or modified defines a family of *language modes*. In this paper we have described on such mode, the collaborative mode, but there are many others. We will mention just a few.

In many circumstances, as in literary forms, lectures, and radio broadcasts, writers and speakers are distant from their addressees in place, time, or both. They might be assumed to adhere to a weakened version of mutual responsibility:

> *Principle of distant responsibility*
> The speaker or writer tries to make sure, roughly by the initiation of each new contribution, that the addressees should have been able to understand his meaning in the last utterance to a criterion sufficient for current purposes.

How people adhere to the principle should depend on whether they are speaking or writing, and whether the product is extemporaneous or planned.

In spontaneous speech without concurrent listeners, speakers still monitor what they say (Levelt 1983) and can therefore change course in the process of making a reference. If so, they should still (1) initiate the process with elementary, episodic, provisional, and dummy noun phrases and (2) repair, expand, and even replace their initial noun phrases. It is just that they do all this without feedback from listeners. In a study by Levelt (1983), people were asked to describe complex spatial networks into a tape recorder. As expected, they produced large numbers of what we have called repairs, expansions, and replacements. This is typical of such monologues (see also Goffman 1981; Maclay and Osgood 1959). On the other hand, people don't shorten their repeated references as much when speaking into a tape recorder (Krauss and Weinheimer 1966).

Writers with time to plan, edit, and rewrite, however, should satisfy their responsibilities to readers by eliminating everything but elementary proposals, and many writers do. Others retain a sprinkling of provisional noun phrases, repairs, expansions, and replacements apparently to affect a spontaneous style or for other rhetorical effects. So here are two noncollaborative modes, one spontaneous and one planned, both the result of adhering to the principle of distant responsibility.

There may be several collaborative modes. In a study by Cohen (1985), pairs of people were recorded as they (1) spoke over a telephone hookup or (2) typed messages that were stimultaneously displayed on both their own and their partner's computer terminals. The task was for one partner to instruct the other in how to assemble a water pump. In both environments the two partners used methods we have argued are part of the acceptance process. But, as Cohen demonstrated, the partners with spoken access used much finer-grained methods than those in the keyboard condition. Instructors on the telephone, for example, were more likely to ask their partners explicitly to identify a referent before they went on. On the keyboard, the two partners couldn't go as quickly, use nuances of intonation, or interrupt each other with such precise timing, so they apparently adapted their collaborative techniques to fit the limitations. How people adapt to such constraints in general is an open question.

Social factors also govern the collaborative mode. An army private being dressed down by a commanding officer is simply not allowed to interrupt or offer the feedback usually found among equals. Yet the officer can interrupt the private, request confirmations, offer replacements, and do much else. In a study by Ragan (1983), interviewers of job applicants initiated many side sequences, whereas the applicants never did. Further, applicants were much more likely than interviewers to qualify statements, revealing uncertainty about the adequacy of their presentations, and to seek acceptance with *you know*. So the form that collaboration takes is also adapted to certain social constraints. How the participants make these adaptations has yet to be established.

Participants in a conversation, we have argued, are mutually responsible for establishing what the speaker meant. Definite reference is only one part of that process. They must collaborate, in one way or another, on most or perhaps all other parts of speaker's meaning as well. Collaboration may take one form for word denotation, another for demonstrative reference, a third for assertions, and so on, yet there should be commonalities. The techniques documented for definite reference are likely useful for other parts of the speaker's meaning too.

References

Asher, S. R. (1979). Referential communication. In G. J. Whitehurst and B. J. Zimmerman, eds., *The functions of language and cognition*. New York: Academic Press.

Austin, J. L. (1962). *How to do things with words*. Oxford: Oxford University Press.

Brown, R. (1958). How shall a thing be called? *Psychological Review* 65, 14–21.

Brown, R., and E. H. Lenneberg (1954). A study in language and cognition. *Journal of Abnormal and Social Psychology* 49, 454–462.

Clark, H. H. (1985). Language use and language users. In G. Lindzey and E. Aronson, eds., *The handbook of social psychology*, vol. 2. 3rd ed. New York: Harper and Row.

Clark, H. H., and T. B. Carlson (1981). Context for comprehension. In J. Long and A. Baddeley, eds., *Attention and performance IX*. Hillsdale, NJ: L. Erlbaum Associates.

Clark, H. H., and C. R. Marshall (1981). Definite reference and mutual knowledge. In A. K. Joshi, B. Webber, and I. A. Sag, eds., *Elements of discourse understanding*. Cambridge: Cambridge University Press.

Cohen, P. R. (1985). The pragmatics of referring and the modality of communication. *Computational Linguistics* 10, 97–146.

Donnellan, K. S. (1978). Speaker reference, descriptions and anaphora. In P. Cole, ed., *Syntax and semantics 9: Pragmatics*. New York: Academic Press.

Duncan, S. D. (1973). Toward a grammer for dyadic conversation. *Semiotica* 9, 29–47.

Elffers, J. (1976). *Tangram: The ancient Chinese shapes game*. New York: McGraw-Hill.

Gazdar, G. (1979). *Pragmatics: Implicature, presupposition, and logical form*. New York: Academic Press.

Glucksberg, S., R. M. Krauss, and E. T. Higgins (1975). The development of referential communication skills. In F. E. Horowitz, ed., *Review of child development research*, vol. 4. Chicago: University of Chicago Press.

Goffman, E. (1976). Replies and responses. *Language in Society* 5, 257–313.

Goffman, E. (1981). *Forms of talk*. Philadelphia, PA: University of Pennsylvania Press.

Goodwin, C. (1981). *Conversational organization: Interaction between speakers and hearers*. New York: Academic Press.

Grice, H. P. (1957). Meaning. *The Philosophical Review* 66, 377–388.

Grice, H. P. (1968). Utterer's meaning, sentence-meaning, and word-meaning. *Foundations of Language* 4, 1–18.

Grice, H. P. (1975). Logic and conversation. In P. Cole and J. L. Morgan, eds., *Syntax and semantics 3: Speech acts*. New York: Academic Press. Also in D. Davidson and G. Harman, eds. (1975). *The logic of grammar*. Encino, CA: Dickenson.

Grice, H. P. (1978). Further notes on logic and conversation. In P. Cole, ed., *Syntax and semantics 9: Pragmatics*. New York: Academic Press.

Jefferson, G. (1972). Side sequences. In D. Sudnow, ed., *Studies in social interaction*. New York: Free Press.

Jefferson, G. (1973). A case of precision timing in ordinary conversation. *Semiotica* 9, 47–96.

Kamp, J. A. W. (1981). A theory of truth and semantic representation. In J. Groenendijk, T. Janssen, and M. Stokhof, eds., *Formal methods in the study of language*, part 1. Amsterdam: Mathematical Centre Tracts.

Krauss, R. M., and S. Glucksberg (1969). The development of communication: Competence as a function of age. *Child Development* 40, 255–256.

Krauss, R. M., and S. Glucksberg (1977). Social and nonsocial speech. *Scientific American* 236, 100–105.

Krauss, R. M., and S. Weinheimer (1964). Changes in reference phrases as a function of frequency of usage in social interaction: A preliminary study. *Psychonomic Science* 1, 113–114.

Krauss, R. M., and S. Weinheimer (1966). Concurrent feedback, confirmation, and the encoding of referents in verbal communication. *Journal of Personality and Social Psychology* 4, 343–346.

Krauss, R. M., and S. Weinheimer (1967). Effect of referent similarity and communication mode on verbal encoding. *Journal of Verbal Learning and Verbal Behavior* 6, 359–363.

Kripke, S. (1977). Speaker's reference and semantic reference. In P. A. French, T. E. Uehling, Jr., and H. K. Wettstein, eds., *Contemporary perspectives in the philosophy of language*. Minneapolis, MN: University of Minnesota Press.

Laver, J. D. M. (1973). The detection and correction of slips of the tongue. In V. A. Fromkin, ed., *Speech errors as linguistic evidence*. The Hague: Mouton.

Levelt, W. J. M. (1983). Monitoring and self-repair in speech. *Cognition* 14, 41–104.

Maclay, H., and C. E. Osgood (1959). Hesitation phenomena in spontaneous English speech. *Word* 15, 19–44.

Olson, D. R. (1970). Language and thought: Aspects of a cognitive theory of semantics. *Psychological Review* 77, 257–273.

Ragan, S. L. (1983). Alignment and conversational coherence. In R. T. Craig and K. Tracy, eds., *Conversational coherence: Form, structure, and strategy*. Beverly Hills, CA: Sage Publications.

Sacks, H., and E. A. Schegloff (1979). Two preferences in the organization of reference to persons in conversation and their interaction. In G. Psathas, ed., *Everyday language: Studies in ethnomethodology*. New York: Irvington Publishers.

Sacks, H., E. A. Schegloff, and G. Jefferson (1974). A simplest systematics for the organization of turn-taking in conversation. *Language* 50, 696–735.

Schegloff, E. A. (1968). Sequencing in conversational openings. *American Anthropologist* 70, 1075–1095.

Schegloff, E. A. (1972). Notes on a conversational practice: Formulating place. In D. Sudnow, ed., *Studies in social interaction*. New York: Free Press.

Schegloff, E. A. (1981). Discourse as an interactional achievement: Some uses of un-huh and other things that come between sentences. In D. Tannen, ed., *Analyzing discourse: Text and talk*. Georgetown University Roundtable on Languages and Linguistics 1981. Washington, DC: Georgetown University Press.

Schegloff, E. A., G. Jefferson, and H. Sacks (1977). The preference for self-correction in the organizations of repair in conversation. *Language* 53, 361–382.

Schegloff, E. A., and H. Sacks (1973). Opening up closings. *Semiotica* 8, 289–327.

Schiffer, S. (1972). *Meaning*. Oxford: Clarendon Press.

Searle, J. R. (1969). *Speech acts: An essay in the philosophy of language*. Cambridge: Cambridge University Press.

Stalnaker, R. C. (1978). Assertion. In P. Cole, ed., *Syntax and semantics 9: Pragmatics*. New York: Academic Press.

Svartvik, J., and R. Quirk (1980). *A corpus of English conversation*. Lund, Sweden: Gleerup.

Yngve, V. H. (1970). On getting a word in edgewise. In *Papers from the Sixth Regional Meeting*, Chicago Linguistic Society, Chicago, IL.

Zipf, G. K. (1935). *The psychology of language*. Boston: Houghton-Mifflin.

Index

1) get more series about understanding Austin: illocutionary/perlocutionary.

Ground act perlocutionary acts in terms of others behaviors.

2. We characterize speech acts in terms of effects they have on the listeners subsequent behavior.

↳ "A simple model of decision-making, rather than a full planning model."

Extensions to SB could consider a full mDP allowing for planning.

↳ major distinction is between planning and decision making

illocutionary = the "meaning" of a sentence — the communicative content of the act.

perlocutionary = the "results" of a sentence — the effects of the communicative act on someone's mental state.